PREFACE

This is the third annual edition of the *NBC News/Rand McNally World Atlas & Almanac*. Our premiere edition in 1990 and second edition in 1991 have been a great success. NBC News and Rand McNally have built on that success with our updated 1992 edition featuring *Countries in the News, World Maps*, a *World News Briefs* section, a *World Themes* section, and a *Gazetteer of Nations*.

As I stated in our previous editions, the mission of this exciting publication is to contribute to worldwide news and geographical literacy in the home and in our nation's schools. We live in an international environment, and the *World Atlas & Almanac* will aid in understanding the world news reported by NBC News and others.

The first section, *World News Briefs*, is a chronology of the major news events and developments worldwide, including late-breaking news not covered in other sections–for example, latest developments in organizing Middle East peace conferences, the London economic summit, civil strife in Yugoslavia, and the coup attempt in the Soviet Union.

This year's *World Themes* section, which features major issues of worldwide significance, includes the Gulf War, 500th Anniversary of Columbus's voyage to the New World, United Nations, 1991 Election, People Who Make a Difference, and Sports.

The *Countries in the News* section features eight world regions and more than 30 countries with new and updated information.

Just as the *World Atlas & Almanac* continues to be an annual undertaking of NBC News and Rand McNally, it should continue to serve as a handy reference tool, providing that added piece of information to enhance your perspectives on world news.

Tom Brokaw
NBC Nightly News Anchor

WORLD NEWS BRIEFS

SEPTEMBER 1990

9 President George Bush and President Mikhail Gorbachev of Soviet Union meet at Helsinki and declare support for sanctions against Iraq.

23 South African President F.W. de Klerk is received by President Bush at White House, in first visit by a South African chief of state in 45 years.

24 Soviet parliament grants Gorbachev emergency powers.

OCTOBER 1990

1 President Bush addresses United Nations General Assembly, promising to liberate Kuwait.

3 Germany is united as one nation for first time since end of World War II. U.S. and U.S.S.R. reach agreement on conventional forces in Europe.

8 Israeli police kill 19 Palestinians in riot on Temple Mount in Jerusalem's Old City.

NOVEMBER 1990

19-21 Conference on Security and Cooperation in Europe convenes in Paris to formally end cold war and sign treaty reducing Warsaw Pact and NATO conventional forces.

22 Margaret Thatcher resigns as prime minister of United Kingdom. President Bush spends Thanksgiving with G.I.'s in Saudi Arabia.

29 U.N. Security Council sets January 15 deadline for Iraqi withdrawal from Kuwait.

DECEMBER 1990

9 Lech Walesa is elected president of Poland.

20 Soviet Foreign Minister Eduard Shevardnadze resigns, warns that hard-liners are plotting new dictatorship.

JANUARY 1991

1 Crisis hits credit unions and small banks in Rhode Island. Gov. Bruce Sundlun orders 45 privately insured institutions temporarily closed.

10 U.S. Congress authorizes use of force against Iraq.

13 Soviet troops crack down on pro-independence movement in Lithuania, killing 15 people.

17 U.S.-led international coalition begins air war against Iraq.

18 Eastern Airlines ceases operations.

23 Iraq purposely causes huge oil spill in Persian Gulf. Census Bureau releases 1990 census data for American cities. Big-city mayors criticize "undercount."

26 Tens of thousands of protesters march in Washington against war in Persian Gulf.

27 New York Giants defeat Buffalo Bills in Super Bowl, 20-19.

29 Bush outlines war aims in State of the Union Message.

31 Tensions mount in Yugoslavia between Croatian nationalists and Yugoslavian central government.

FEBRUARY 1991

4 Bush Administration presents $1.45 trillion budget proposal to Congress. Pete Rose is declared ineligible for Hall of Fame.

5 U.S., Mexico and Canada open talks on Free Trade Agreement.

15 Government reports that U.S. trade deficit has reached seven-year low.

24 Allies initiate ground war to liberate Kuwait.

28 President Bush orders cease-fire as Kuwait is liberated.

MARCH 1991

2 Kurdish and Shiite rebellions begin in Iraq against Saddam Hussein's regime.

3 Beating of black motorist by Los Angeles police prompts calls for resignation of Commissioner Daryl Gates.

16 Saddam claims victory over rebels.

APRIL 1991

3 Kurdish resistance to Saddam is crushed; massive refugee exodus begins.

5 U.S. unemployment hits 6.8 percent, highest since 1986.

11 U.N. declares formal cease-fire in Iraq.

18 President Bush unveils new education program, calling for national student testing and creation of model schools in each Congressional district. One-day rail strike is ended by special legislation in Congress.

19 Evander Holyfield defeats George Foreman to retain heavyweight boxing title.

23 Lockheed wins $80 billion contract for new advanced fighter jet. President Bush welcomes Gen. Norman Schwarzkopf home from Persian Gulf.

28 Former Sen. Paul Tsongas becomes first Democrat to announce as Presidential candidate.

29 Devastating cyclone hits Bangladesh.

MAY 1991

3 President Bush publicly denies reports that he made deal with Iranian officials during 1980 Presidential campaign to delay release of American hostages in Teheran until after election.

21 Former Indian Prime Minister Rajiv Gandhi assassinated at election rally. In Ethiopia, dictator Lieut. Col. Mengistu Haile Mariam resigns and flees to exile in Zimbabwe, as civil war in Ethiopia continues.

GANDHI ASSASSINATED

Rajiv Gandhi, a former prime minister of India and leader of the Congress Party, was assassinated on May 21 during an election campaign appearance in a small town near Madras. A bomb exploded while Gandhi was walking from his automobile to a platform erected for a rally. Fourteen other people

were killed by the blast. Election officials postponed scheduled elections for three weeks. Gandhi's mother, Prime Minister Indira Gandhi, also met her death by assassination when she was slain by her Sikh bodyguards in 1984.

23   U.S. Supreme Court upholds controversial Bush Administration regulations prohibiting physicians in Federally funded birth control centers from mentioning abortion option to patients.
28   Rebel troops take Ethiopian capital of Addis Ababa, as civil war comes to end.

JUNE 1991
25   Croatia and Slovenia declare independence from Yugoslavia.

CIVIL WAR ERUPTS IN YUGOSLAVIA
The Republics of Slovenia and Croatia declared independence from Yugoslavia on June 25, 1991, quickly triggering an outbreak of civil war. The federal army moved quickly to crack down on the breakaway republics with infantry, artillery and air attacks that left hundreds dead. Initially the European Community and the United States were leery of the secessionist movements and supported efforts to keep Yugoslavia intact. But the brutality of the military repression, and the fact that the military was largely commanded by Serbian Communists and seemed to have escaped civilian government control, alarmed Western governments. The European Community threatened to cut off aid to Yugoslavia and sent a diplomatic team to negotiate a cease-fire and help search for a peaceful solution. An EC-arranged truce collapsed on July 2 when renewed fighting broke out. Further EC peace efforts also ended in fail-

ure. The Yugoslavs themselves hammered out a new truce August 7, but reports of ethnic fighting kept trickling in. The situation remained volatile. In September bloody fighting erupted again in Croatia.

26   Yugoslav federal troops move on Croatia and Slovenia.
28   European Community sends peace mediators to Yugoslavia.
29   EC-brokered truce calls for Yugoslav federal troops to return to barracks and secessionist republics to suspend declarations of independence.

JULY 1991
2   In Yugoslavia, EC truce collapses as renewed fighting breaks out.
9   International Olympic Committee lifts ban against South Africa's participation in Olympic competition.
10   President Bush lifts economic sanctions against South Africa, citing progress made in overturning apartheid.
15-17   Leaders of industrialized democracies meet in London. Soviet President Gorbachev discusses aid to Soviet Union with Western leaders on final day of summit.

ECONOMIC SUMMIT HEARS PLEA FOR AID FROM GORBACHEV
The 17th annual Economic Summit of the leaders of the seven major industrial democracies convened in London this year. The leaders of Germany, Japan, the U.S., the United

Kingdom, France, Italy and Canada left many issues unresolved and disagreed on how best to help stabilize the crisis-ridden Soviet economy. The French and Germans favored massive assistance to the U.S.S.R., but the U.S. and Britain favored a more cautious approach. In an unprecedented development, Soviet President Mikhail Gorbachev arrived in London to meet with Western leaders on the final day of the conference, but all he came away with was a promise of technical assistance, not economic aid.

In private meetings, Gorbachev and President Bush ironed out the remaining details of an arms-control treaty for long-range nuclear weapons.

18   Syria accepts U.S. proposals for Middle East peace conference.

MIDDLE EAST PEACE TALKS
Secretary of State James Baker's shuttle diplomacy in the Middle East finally seemed to pay off in July 1991, when five Arab states (Jordan, Saudi Arabia, Lebanon, Syria and Egypt) reversed their previous positions and endorsed a U.S. proposal for a Middle East peace conference, to be jointly sponsored by the U.S. and the Soviet Union. Most important was the decision of Syria's President Hafez al-Assad to abandon his hard-line stance and agree to a number of conditions designed to meet Israeli objections to a peace conference. On August 1, Israeli Prime Minister Yitzhak Shamir agreed to participate in the conference as well, though he was adamant that Israel would not surrender any occupied territory, including the Golan Heights, which Syria desperately wants back. Shamir also refused to negotiate with any Palestinians from East Jerusalem (which Israel annexed) or anyone linked to the Palestine Liberation Organization (P.L.O.). No date has yet been set for the conference, and the issue of Palestinian participation must still be resolved.

30-31   Presidents Bush and Gorbachev meet in Moscow summit, sign strategic arms treaty.

WORLD NEWS BRIEFS

U.S. AND SOVIETS SIGN NUCLEAR TREATY

Presidents George Bush and Mikhail Gorbachev signed an historic agreement in Moscow July 31 that will cut back long-range nuclear weapons by more than 30 percent over the next seven years. Though the two nations will continue to have large nuclear arsenals trained at each other (approximately equivalent to the levels of 1982), experts agree that the threat of a superpower nuclear conflict no longer hangs over humanity.

31 National Association for the Advancement of Colored People (NAACP) and American Federation of Labor–Congress of Industrial Organizations (AFL-CIO) announce opposition to nomination of Clarence Thomas to Supreme Court.

AUGUST 1991

8 British hostage John McCarthy is released in Lebanon.

11 American hostage Edward A. Tracy is released in Lebanon.

16 Reformer Aleksandr Yakovlev, former top aide to Gorbachev, resigns from Communist Party, warning that hard-liner coup is imminent.

19 Communist hard-liners stage coup. Gorbachev is detained at vacation home in Crimea. Eight-member emergency committee takes power, with vice president Gennady Yanayev taking over as president. Yanayev tells reporters that Gorbachev is ill. Coup leaders order troops into Moscow and Baltic republics. Boris Yeltsin, democratically elected president of Russian republic, leads resistance to coup, calls for general strike. Protesters gather at Russian republic's parliament building, called "White House." Elite troops throw support to Yeltsin.

20 More troops mobilized in Moscow and Baltics, taking over broadcast facilities. Independent newspapers shut down. In Moscow, three civilians die in clashes with armored vehicles moving on "White House." First signs appear that coup is unraveling as two members of emergency committee resign, citing poor health. Massive protests occur in Leningrad, Moscow and Moldavia. Thousands of miners strike, but general strike does not materialize. Estonia declares independence.

21 Coup collapses. Yeltsin reports coup leaders are fleeing Moscow. Military units begin withdrawal from Moscow. Latvia opts for independence.

23 Gorbachev returns to Moscow, denounces coup leaders and criticizes Communist Party leaders for supporting or not resisting coup.

24 Gorbachev resigns as general secretary of Communist Party, ending 74 years of Communist rule. Ukraine joins list of republics breaking from U.S.S.R.

25 Byelorussia issues independence declaration.

27 Moldavia declares independence, announces plans to work for eventual unification with Romania.

29 Soviet Parliament suspends Communist Party operations, pending investigation of its role in coup attempt.

30 Azerbaijan comes out for independence.

31 Uzbekistan and Kirghizia become first Asian republics to seek independence from Moscow.

SEPTEMBER 1991

1 U.S. recognizes independence of Baltic republics. In Moscow, Gorbachev and Yeltsin push new proposal for Union treaty.

THE SOVIET UNION: CONSEQUENCES OF A FAILED COUP

For three days in August the world was shaken by events in Moscow. On the eve of the signing of a new Union treaty that would have changed the nature of the U.S.S.R. forever, Communist Party hard-liners, their heads buried in the past, staged a coup and tried to stem the tide of history. The Union treaty would have given increased powers to the nine republics choosing to remain in the U.S.S.R. and laid the groundwork for departure of six republics that had already declared their desire to secede eventually. For the hard-liners this treaty was treason, and so they acted.

In the end, the plotters totally miscalculated. They didn't appreciate the decline of Communist Party authority or the strength of the new-found democratic spirit in the Soviet Union. Key segments of the military and the K.G.B. secret police refused to carry out their orders. Boris Yeltsin, the maverick president of the Russian republic, led the resistance to the coup. Hundreds of thousands of common citizens took to the streets. In three days the coup failed. All but one of the plotters were arrested. The other, Boris Pugo, Minister of the Interior, committed suicide.

The failure of the coup only accelerated the very process the hard-liners had tried to block. Communist Party activities in the factories, in the Army and in the K.G.B. were banned. In Moscow, Communist Party headquarters was shut down and sealed off. Mikhail Gorbachev ordered all his cabinet members to resign, replaced them with men committed to reform, and then resigned as leader of the Party. Yeltsin's political influence was now in ascendance. The coup managed to block the signing of the Union treaty, but only because now the republics were demanding even more autonomy than before. By September 1, ten republics had declared independence (eight did so in the days during and after the coup, and two, Lithuania and Georgia, had done so previously). Armenia had scheduled a referendum on independence for September. Meanwhile Gorbachev

and Yeltsin worked feverishly to come up with a formula for some new type of Soviet Union for the future, concentrating foreign and defense policy in the hands of a central government with all other powers reserved for the republics.

What kind of Soviet Union will exist in the future will be determined by the course of the political convulsions shaking the world's second greatest military power.

NEW SOVIET WHO'S WHO

In the aftermath of the failed hard-line Soviet coup, changes in Soviet leadership have come fast and furious. Boris Yeltsin, president of the Russian republic, has emerged as the most important leader in the country, and many of his supporters have been named to key government positions. Mikhail Gorbachev remains as president, but his authority is greatly eroded as Soviet republics have declared their independence from Moscow. Gorbachev continues to struggle to keep some form of union alive and promises direct elections for the Soviet presidency in

1992. Here is a quick rundown on some of the new players in Soviet politics.

Boris Pankin: Foreign Minister ... born 1931 ... only ambassador to oppose coup.
Ivan Silayev: Head of committee on economic reform ... favors privatization.
Yevgeny Shaposhnikov: Defense Minister ... born 1942 ... air force general ... opposed coup.
Anatoly Sobchak: Mayor of Leningrad ... born 1937 ... popular reform leader ... led massive demonstrations against coup ... widely expected to run for president of Soviet Union against Gorbachev next year.
Vadim Bakatin: K.G.B. chief ... born 1938 ... considered liberal ... wants to "liquidate" K.G.B. interference in Soviet life.

DEATHS 1991

Lee Atwater, Republican Party leader, March 29.
Enrique Bermudez, Nicaraguan Contra leader, February 16.
Frank Capra, movie director, September 3.
Bert Convy, performer, July 15.
Colleen Dewhurst, actress, August 22.

Hamilton Fish, former Congressman, January 18.
Eugene Fodor, travel writer, February 18.
James Franciscus, actor, July 8.
Rajiv Gandhi, former Indian prime minister, May 21.
Martha Graham, dancer and choreographer, April 1.
Graham Greene, author, April 3.
John Heinz, U.S. Senator from Pennsylvania, April 4.
Douglas Kiker, television journalist, August 14.
Jerzy Kosinski, author, May 3.
Michael Landon, actor, July 1.
Harry Reasoner, television journalist, August 6.
Frank Rizzo, former mayor of Philadelphia, July 16.
Earl Robinson, composer, July 20.
Isaac Bashevis Singer, author, July 25.
Danny Thomas, performer, February 6.
John G. Tower, former Senator from Texas, April 5.
Robert F. Wagner, former mayor of New York City, February 12.

TABLE OF CONTENTS

18

30

NBC News/Rand McNally World Atlas & Almanac
Copyright © 1992 by Rand McNally and Company.
Pages 1-64 copyright © 1992 by NBC News International, Inc.
Pages 65-192 copyright © 1992 by Rand McNally and Company from maps
and data published in the *Quick Reference Atlas*, copyright © 1992; and *World
Facts and Maps*, copyright © 1992; and from flags copyright © 1992 by Rand
McNally and Company.

43

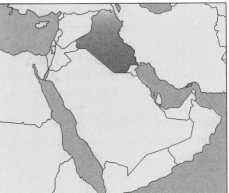

55

65

Library of Congress Cataloging-in-Publication Data
NBC News/Rand McNally world atlas & almanac.
   p. cm.
   Focuses on events in 1991 placed in the context of past events and forseen issues.
   Includes index to maps and gazetteer.
   ISBN 0-528-83457-6
   1. Atlases.   2. World politics—20th century.   3. History, Modern—20th century—Chronology.   4. Almanacs. I. NBC News.   II. Rand McNally and Company.
G1021.N435 1991 <G&M>   91-31782
912—dc20   CIP
                                               MAP

GULF WAR

The vague outlines of the post-cold war era were just beginning to emerge when Iraq invaded Kuwait on August 2, 1990, and gave the new world order a severe test. Saddam Hussein apparently believed that the world would simply stand by and watch as his army, the fourth largest in the world, arbitrarily settled a border dispute by overrunning the oil-rich sheikdom of Kuwait. It was probably the worst political miscalculation in recent memory.

Led by the United States, with United Nations authorization, a 28-nation coalition gathered a force of more than a million soldiers and sailors to isolate the aggressor, block further aggression against Saudi Arabia and eventually expel Iraq from Kuwait. For six months the world lived through a daily drama of confrontation and brinksmanship. Western hostages were taken by the Iraqis and released, Western embassies in Kuwait fell under siege, international diplomats searched fervently for a peaceful last-minute solution, and the American people and Congress considered whether America should go to war. In January the United Nations deadline came and went, and the allies initiat-

ed a merciless air war, bombing Iraq back into a "pre-industrial" state, as a U.N. fact-finding team would later report after a post-war inspection. After more than five weeks of bombardment, ground forces were unleashed, quickly overrunning Iraqi positions. Tens of thousands of Iraqi troops surrendered immediately or deserted and started running for home.

American public opinion opposed Saddam's invasion from the very beginning. But most Americans wanted to give U.N. sanctions a chance to work. Even after the U.N. Security Council gave Saddam a January 15 deadline and authorized the use of force, a plurality of Americans were opposed to taking offensive action. Amid predictions that as many as 10,000 Americans might die and 35,000 might be wounded in a war against Iraq, a majority of Democrats in the House and Senate voted against going to war just hours before President George Bush ordered Operation Desert Storm to begin. But once Congress gave its approval, the nation united behind the war effort. Proving that nothing succeeds like success, by the end of the war President Bush was basking in unprecedent-

ed popularity.

After the war, Kurds and Shiite Moslems rebelled against Saddam's rule. But President Bush refused to support the rebels, who were intent on dismantling Iraq. U.S. policy-makers wanted to get rid of Saddam while keeping the country intact. Saddam's troops quickly crushed the rebels, and the world watched in dismay as a new tragedy began to unfold. Two million Kurdish refugees fled the vengeful wrath of Saddam's troops and streamed into the mountainous regions bordering Turkey and Iran. As many as a thousand per day were dying from the cold, starvation and disease. A new Operation Provide Comfort began as allied forces went into northern Iraq to set up camps for the refugees and provide protection against Saddam's troops. By July the allied troops withdrew to installations just across the Turkish border and security was taken over by U.N. police.

U.N. officials now faced the difficult task of enforcing the stringent cease-fire provisions, which included a dismantling of Iraq's nonconventional war capability, maintaining a neutral buffer zone between Iraq and Kuwait, and Iraqi reparations to Kuwait totaling $8 billion. Iraqi officials were less than cooperative with U.N. inspectors who attempted to verify the destruction of Iraq's chemical and biological weaponry, nuclear material, and ballistic missiles with a range of more than 93 miles. In one instance, Iraqi soldiers fired warning shots over the heads of U.N. inspectors looking for material that could be used in manufacturing a nuclear weapon. Under pressure from Western powers who accused Iraq of lying and warned of dire consequences (President Bush would not rule out surgical air strikes), Iraq repeatedly updated its list of proscribed materials.

Meanwhile Saddam remains in power and the U.S. still wants to get rid of him, by means of ongoing economic and political pressure. At the London Economic Summit in July 1991 the leaders of the seven major industrial democracies agreed to keep the sanctions in place.

General Norman Schwarzkopf briefs journalists on aerial war.

CHRONOLOGY OF THE GULF CRISIS

1990

July 17: Iraqi government accuses Kuwait of constructing military posts on Iraqi territory and stealing $2.4 billion dollars' worth of Iraqi oil.

July 25: Iraq demands $2.4 billion in compensation from Kuwait. Saddam Hussein discusses border dispute with U.S. Ambassador April Glaspie, who gives Saddam mixed signals, saying U.S. does not take positions in border disputes between Arab brothers.

July 31: Iraqi and Kuwaiti officials meet in Jiddah, Saudi Arabia, in effort to resolve dispute.

August 1: Talks collapse.

August 2: Iraq invades Kuwait. Kuwait appeals to other Arab nations for help. Emir flees to safety in Saudi Arabia.

August 3: President George Bush announces U.S. naval units being sent to Gulf region. United Nations Security Council condemns invasion by 14 to 0, demanding an "immediate and unconditional withdrawal from Kuwait." Yemen is the only Security Council member to abstain. U.S. Secretary of State James Baker and Soviet Foreign Minister Eduard Shevardnadze issue unprecedented joint statement denouncing invasion. Iraq moves troops toward Saudi border.

August 6: Security Council votes to impose economic sanctions against Iraq, with Yemen and Cuba abstaining.

August 7: U.S. fears for safety of nearly 3,000 Americans trapped in Kuwait and 500 in Iraq. Americans are confined to hotels in Baghdad. More than 120,000 Iraqi troops reported in Kuwait. Turkey shuts down Iraqi oil pipeline running through Turkey.

August 8: Iraq announces annexation of Kuwait.

August 9: First American ground troops and combat aircraft arrive in Saudi Arabia in beginning of Operation Desert Shield, defensive move to protect Saudi territory from possible Iraqi invasion. Iraq seals its borders, stranding thousands of foreign nationals. U.N. Security Council declares annexation of Kuwait "null and void."

August 10: Saddam Hussein calls for Holy War to "rescue" Moslem shrines in Saudi Arabia and drive Western forces out of Middle East. Leaders of 12 Arab nations agree to join multinational force to defend Saudi Arabia.

August 15: Iraq offers Iran formal settlement to Iraq-Iran War, which ended in 1988 with U.N.-brokered cease-fire. Iraq grants virtually all of Iran's war goals.

August 16: Iraq begins to round up stranded Americans in Kuwait and Iraq. Multinational force reaches 125,000-troop level.

August 17: U.S. Navy begins de facto blockade of Iraq.

August 18: Security Council authorizes use of force to back up sanctions.

August 22: U.S. calls up military reservists.

August 23: Saddam appears on Iraqi television in carefully staged meeting with Western detainees.

August 24: Iraqi troops surround U.S. Embassy in Kuwait after Americans refuse to vacate premises. American reservists and National Guardsmen begin reporting for duty.

August 25: U.N. Security Council authorizes naval action to stop shipping if necessary to enforce sanctions.

August 26: Iraq cuts off electricity and water

U.S. STRATEGY OUTWITS THE IRAQI MILITARY

American strategy in the Persian Gulf War relied upon an elaborate ruse to outwit Iraqi forces. Map 1—International coalition troops initially massed at the Kuwaiti border, causing the Iraqis to prepare elaborate defenses against a massive frontal assault. At the same time, naval exercises in the Persian Gulf gave the impression that an amphibious attack was also planned. Map 2— After allied air attacks wiped out Iraqi radar and reconnaissance capabilities, General Schwarzkopf ordered key allied forces and logistics bases to shift secretly to the west, outflanking the Iraqi forces. Map 3— When the ground war began on February 23, American and Saudi forces feigned a massive attack from the south, while the main attack took the Iraqis by surprise as allied forces swooped down on them from the west and cut off lines of retreat.

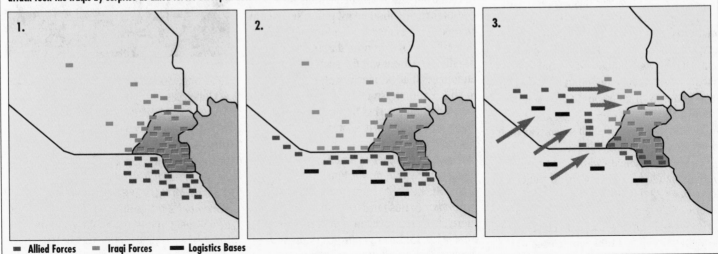

■ Allied Forces   ■ Iraqi Forces   ■ Logistics Bases

GULF WAR

supplies for Western diplomats in Kuwait who continue to defy orders to evacuate embassies. Pentagon announces that Gen. Norman Schwarzkopf has established command headquarters in Saudi Arabia.

August 27: U.S. sailors search Iraqi tanker in Red Sea, in first boarding since blockade began.

August 29: Saddam offers to withdraw from Kuwait, but only if sanctions are lifted and Iraq gets guaranteed access to Persian Gulf and control of Rumailah oil field that juts into Kuwait.

August 30: First U.S. combat troops based in Europe dispatched to Gulf.

September 4: American diplomats seek pledges of financial support from U.S. allies to defray costs of Gulf mobilization.

September 5: Saddam calls on Arab masses to overthrow leaders of Egypt and Saudi Arabia.

September 6: Bush accepts Baghdad's offer to speak to people of Iraq via videotaped message.

September 7: First U.S.-arranged airlift flight brings 171 American women and children out of Kuwait.

September 9: Presidents Bush and Mikhail Gorbachev of Soviet Union meet at Helsinki Summit and issue joint declaration of support for sanctions against Iraq.

September 11: President delivers televised address outlining U.S. goals in Persian Gulf.

September 14: U.S. ground troops in Saudi Arabia now number 100,000.

September 16: President Bush's message to Iraqi people, assuring them that U.S.'s quarrel is not with them but with their leaders, is broadcast in Baghdad. Security Council adopts resolution condemning Iraqi raids on diplomatic compounds in Kuwait.

September 18: Iraqi troops in Kuwait now number 360,000.

September 20: Oil prices hit seven-year high of nearly $35 dollars per barrel.

September 21: Saddam warns his people of coming "mother and father" of all battles.

September 22: Last U.S.-chartered airlift of American citizens fleeing Iraq and Kuwait leaves for U.S., ending evacuation that brought more than 2,000 people back to U.S.

September 23: Saddam threatens to blow up oil fields.

September 25: Security Council extends economic embargo to include air traffic. Baghdad releases videotaped message from Saddam Hussein to American people, a rambling speech of more than one hour.

September 27: Price of crude oil reaches all-time high of just over $40 per barrel.

September 29: State Department warns of possible Iraqi-sponsored terrorism.

September 30: Saddam tries to link withdrawal from Kuwait to negotiations on comprehensive Middle East peace settlement.

October 1: President Bush addresses U.N. General Assembly, vowing that Iraq's annexation of Kuwait will not stand. Israel announces that gas masks will be distributed to all 4.5 million Israelis.

October 8: Since crisis began, average price of gas at U.S. pumps has jumped 26.5 cents per gallon.

October 23: Number of American hostages being held by Iraq now estimated at more than 700.

November 6: Bush orders up to 240,000 more troops deployed in Gulf region.

November 15: Bush's approval rating in *Los Angeles Times* poll drops to 49 percent, reflecting widespread unease about handling of Gulf crisis.

November 20: While attending European security conference in Paris, President pressures Soviets to support U.N. resolution authorizing use of force to expel Iraq from Kuwait.

November 22: Bush shares Thanksgiving dinner with G.I.'s in Saudi Arabia.

November 23: Despite accusations of Syrian involvement in international terrorism, Bush meets with Syrian President Hafez al-Assad in Geneva, declaring willingness

to "work with any nation willing to oppose Iraqi aggression."

November 29: Security Council authorizes use of military action if Iraq does not pull out of Kuwait by January 15.

November 30: In apparent strategy shift, U.S. offers diplomatic exchange on ministerial level to seek peaceful solution to crisis.

December 10: Saddam Hussein begins release of U.S. hostages.

December 14: New York Times poll finds only 45 percent of Americans favor military attack if Iraq fails to meet withdrawal deadline; 48 percent oppose.

December 21: Iraq threatens use of chemical weapons if war erupts.

December 24: Saddam says Israel will be first target if war comes.

1991

January 2: North Atlantic Treaty Organization (NATO) agrees to send 40 jet fighters to bolster Turkish defenses at Iraq's northern border.

January 6: Saddam declares Iraq ready for "the mother of all battles."

January 7: Pentagon releases guidelines for media coverage in event of war, including controversial provisions for review of all stories by military officials.

January 9: Noncombat death toll in Persian Gulf operations reaches 96.

January 10: Congress authorizes use of force against Iraq; majority of Democrats in both Houses vote no.

January 15: U.N. deadline for withdrawal is reached.

January 17: Multinational forces begin massive air assault against Iraqi targets. President Bush addresses American public on television—drawing biggest TV audience in history.

January 18: Iraq fires first Scud missiles at Israel.

January 25: Iraq begins pumping oil into Persian Gulf, creating worst oil slick in history.

January 26: Twenty-four Iraqi jets land in Iran, seeking safe haven.

February 12: Soviet envoy arrives in Baghdad seeking to negotiate quick end to hostilities.

February 13: Allied bombers hit Baghdad shelter, killing 300 civilians. Allies insist shelter was military command post.

February 21: Soviet diplomatic efforts to end war collapse.

February 24: Ground war begins as allies attack.

February 25: Iraqi Scud missile kills 28 Americans in Saudi Arabia.

February 26: Saddam offers to withdraw, renounces annexation of Kuwait. U.S. troops cut off Iraqi retreat.

February 27: Iraq agrees to comply with U.N.

resolutions.

February 28: U.S. orders allied cease-fire. Baghdad orders troops to stop fighting.

March 1: Bush calls on Iraqi people to overthrow Saddam.

March 2: Anti-Saddam rebellion begins among Shiite Moslems in southern Iraq and Kurdish minority in northern provinces. U.N. Security Council sets tough terms for permanent cease-fire.

March 14: Emir of Kuwait returns to Kuwait City.

March 16: Saddam claims victory over Shiite rebels, vows to crush Kurdish uprising.

March 22: U.N. Security Council relaxes blockade of food shipments to Iraq after reports of impending catastrophe for civilians.

April 3: Iraq crushes last Kurdish resistance. Nearly two million refugees stream into Turkish and Iranian border areas.

April 7: U.S. planes bring relief supplies to Kurdish refugees.

April 11: U.N. declares formal cease-fire.

April 16: President Bush orders allied troops to establish security zone for Kurds in northern Iraq so refugees can return home.

THE KURDS
The Kurds are a nationality without a country. There are perhaps 20 million Kurds living in the mountainous region of southwest Asia, which covers parts of Turkey, the Soviet Union, Syria, Iran and Iraq. The Kurds speak a language similar to Persian. They are a predominantly rural people, earning their living by farming and herding sheep and goats. Kurdistan has never existed as an independent nation, but the people have yearned for freedom and independence. Their struggle for political and cultural freedom brought them into conflict with the Turks during World War I, with Iraq in the 1970's, with Iran after Ayatollah Khomeini took power in 1979 and again with Iraq in 1991.

COLLAPSE OF THE EASTERN BLOC

A West Berliner swings a sledgehammer trying to destroy the Berlin Wall near Potsdamar Platz.

The fallout from the collapse of Communism continued to spread during the past year. The cold war is over. Germany is now one united nation. In November 1990, NATO (the North Atlantic Treaty Organization) and the Warsaw Pact officially declared that they no longer consider each other enemies. A few months later the Warsaw Pact was formally dismantled and COMECOM, the Soviet bloc's trade alliance, disintegrated. Then, spectacularly, a hardline coup against Soviet President Mikhail Gorbachev ended in failure, and Communist Party rule in the Soviet Union itself collapsed. The fate of the Soviet Union remains very much in doubt. The other former Soviet satellites are gripped by terrible recession and economic misery. Each wants to join the European Community and cash in on the prosperity of the Common Market. Long-suppressed nationalism and ethnic hatreds threaten to consume the Soviet Union, Romania, and Czechoslovakia, and have already plunged Yugoslavia into civil war.

For 45 years the clash between East and West dominated the international scene. The two generations of foreign policy experts trained in cold war strategies are still trying to figure out what comes next.

COLD WAR CHRONOLOGY

1945 *February:* Yalta Summit Conference grants Soviets dominance in Eastern Europe.
May: Nazi Germany surrenders.
June: Defeated Germany divided into four zones of occupation.

1946 *March:* Winston Churchill coins phrase "Iron Curtain."

1948 *April:* U.S. announces Marshall Plan to rebuild Europe.
June: Communists blockade Berlin. Berlin Airlift begins.

1949 *May:* North Atlantic Treaty Organization (NATO) is formed. Soviets lift blockade.
September: West Germany founded.
October: Mao leads Communists to power in China. East Germany is founded.

1950 *June:* Korean War breaks out.

1953 *June:* Workers' rebellion in East Germany crushed by Russian forces.

1955 *May:* Warsaw Pact organized.

1956 *October:* Hungarian Revolution crushed by Soviet tanks.

1958 *November:* Nikita Khrushchev demands Western powers pull out of Berlin.

1959 *January:* Fidel Castro triumphs in Cuba.

1960 *May:* Summit conference collapses in dispute over downing of American U-2 spy plane over Soviet Union.

1961 *April:* Bay of Pigs invasion by C.I.A.-backed Cuban exiles ends in disaster.
August: Communists put up Berlin Wall to stop refugee exodus to West.

1962 *October:* Cuban Missile Crisis.

1965 *May:* American ground forces sent to Vietnam.

1968 *August:* Warsaw Pact troops from Soviet Union, Poland, East Germany, Hungary and Bulgaria invade Czechoslovakia to crush reform movement. Romania refuses to participate in invasion. Albania withdraws from alliance.

1972 *May:* Era of East/West detente begins.

1979 *December:* Soviets invade Afghanistan. Detente ends.

1980 *September:* Solidarity formed in Poland, first free trade union in Communist bloc.

1981 *January:* President Ronald Reagan begins massive military buildup and supports anti-Communist rebels in third world.

1983 *March:* Reagan terms Soviet Union "evil empire."
Reagan announces Strategic Defense Initiative (Star Wars).

1985 *March:* Mikhail Gorbachev assumes leadership in Soviet Union.
Perestroika and *glasnost* reforms begin.
November: Geneva Summit—Gorbachev and Reagan talk face-to-face for first time.

1987 *December:* Gorbachev and Reagan sign Intermediate-Range Nuclear Forces (I.N.F.) Treaty in Washington.

1989 *June:* Solidarity candidates win first partly free election in Communist bloc countries.
July: Warsaw Pact summit meeting asserts right of each member to pursue its own course.
November: Berlin Wall is opened, and Stalinist regimes in Soviet satellite countries collapse.

1990 *February and March:* Moscow reaches agreement with Hungary and Czechoslovakia on withdrawal of Soviet troops by mid-1991.
June: Warsaw Pact summit agrees to transform alliance into association of "sovereign and equal states ... built upon democratic principles," but by end of month, Hungarian parliament votes to quit Pact.
September: East Germany withdraws from Warsaw Pact just days before unification with West Germany. Soviets agree to pull out 370,000 troops by 1994.
November: Cold war officially ends: At European Security Conference in Paris, NATO and Warsaw Pact leaders sign Conventional Forces in Europe agreement and declare they are no longer enemies.

1991 *January:* Czechoslovakia calls for abolition of Warsaw Pact.
February: Soviet Union announces decision to dismantle Pact by April 1.

The United Nations has been experiencing a resurgence in power and prestige over the past year. During the four and a half decades of East-West confrontation, the U.N. often found itself powerless to intervene in major international disputes. But now, as world leaders shape the "new world order" of the post-cold war period, the U.N. may yet fulfill the role it was intended to play, as was seen in the Security Council's decisive actions against Iraq after its invasion of Kuwait. U.N. Secretary General Javier Perez de Cuellar will retire soon, and a search is underway to find a replacement who will be able to guide the organization in the crucial period ahead.

Members of the U.N. Security Council voted demanding Iraq destroy its weapons of mass destruction in exchange for a permanent cease-fire in the Gulf War. *From left:* Iraqi Ambassador Abdul Amir al-Anbari sits as Soviet Ambassador Yuli Vorontsov, British Ambassador Sir David Hannay and U.S. Ambassador Thomas Pickering vote for the resolution.

ORGANIZATION OF THE U.N.

Members: There are 159 member nations in the U.N.

General Assembly: All member nations are represented in the General Assembly, with one vote each. The General Assembly controls the U.N. budget, levies dues, helps select members of other U.N. organs, and debates key world issues.

Security Council: The 15-member Security Council is responsible for maintaining world peace. There are five permanent members, each of whom has veto power over council decisions: the United States, China, the United Kingdom, France and the Soviet Union. Other members are elected to two-year terms by the General Assembly.

Secretariat: The Secretariat is the administrative arm of the U.N., responsible for the day-to-day functioning of U.N. programs throughout the world. The Secretariat is headed by the Secretary General, who also serves as adviser to the Security Council.

Economic and Social Council: The Economic and Social Council focuses on questions pertaining to living standards, health, education, culture and human rights.

International Court of Justice: Headquartered in The Hague, the Netherlands, the International Court of Justice is the judicial branch of the U.N., resolving international legal disputes.

Trusteeship Council: This council was formed to help a number of non-self-governing territories gain political independence after World War II. All but one (Palau Islands, administered by the U.S.) have achieved independence.

Major Specialized Agencies: Food and Agriculture Organization (FAO); International Labor Organization (ILO); International Monetary Fund (IMF); UNESCO (U.N. Educational, Scientific and Cultural Organization); World Bank; World Health Organization (WHO).

CHRONOLOGY

1945 U.N. Charter signed at San Francisco Conference.

1946 Decision made to establish headquarters in New York City.

1948 Universal Declaration of Human Rights adopted.

1950 U.N. Security Council decides to send troops to block Communist invasion of South Korea.

1953 North Korea and U.N. sign truce ending Korean War.

1956 U.N arranges cease-fire in Suez crisis.

1960 Security Council sends peacekeeping forces to the Congo (now Zaire).

1964 Security Council sends forces to Cyprus.

1966 Security Council imposes sanctions on white regime in Rhodesia (now Zimbabwe).

1967 Security Council arranges cease-fire to end Six-Day War between Arab countries and Israel.

1971 General Assembly expels Nationalist China and admits Communist China to U.N.

1973 U.N. officials help arrange partial cease-fire to end Yom Kippur War in Middle East.

1988 U.N. helps arrange Soviet pullout from Afghanistan and cease-fire in Iran-Iraq War.

1989 Security Council approves peace-keeping force for Namibia.

1990- Security Council opposes Iraqi
1991 invasion of Kuwait and authorizes use of force by allied coalition to restore Kuwaiti independence.

THINGS TO WATCH

Who will be the next Secretary General of the United Nations?
What role will the U.N. play in establishing the post-cold war world order?

WORLD ECONOMY

Alan Greenspan

Workers cluster around a phone bank as stocks tumble on the opening morning following rejection by the House of President Bush's budget reduction plan. The rejection deflated investors' hopes for an early reduction in interest rates.

The world economy was a mess in 1991. The words "sluggishness" and "standstill" were heard often from leading economists. Recession hit hard in the United States, Canada and the United Kingdom, and other Western industrial nations experienced declining growth rates and rising unemployment. In Eastern Europe, the economic costs of the transition from Communism to free-market economies exceeded even the gloomiest worst-case scenarios. All of the former Communist bloc countries suffered economic contraction, including the Soviet Union itself. The United Nations reported that world economic growth dropped to 1 percent in 1990 and predicted zero growth for 1991. Since world population growth is projected at 1.8 percent, all this translates into a declining standard of living, especially for the 4.5 billion people living in the impoverished third world and Eastern Europe. The potential social and political discontent arising from such misery can be very dangerous. Such a grim outlook contradicts the hopes for a world of peace and prosperity evoked by the end of the cold war.

With the collapse of the East-West confrontation that dominated the international scene since the end of World War II, there has been a rise in nationalism and regionalism that threatens to undermine further the world economy. GATT (General Agreement on Tariffs and Trade) negotiations collapsed last year over disagreements about subsidies to farmers in the countries of the European Community. While the EC bureaucracy subsequently offered to scale back on subsidies and opened up the possibility of reviving the talks, the proposal still has to be approved by the EC's 12 member countries. This may not be easy, as there has been a growing trend for member nations to oppose proposals of the EC bureaucracy. At the London Economic Summit in July, the leaders of the major European industrial countries failed to endorse U.S. proposals to cut agricultural subsidies. In the spring of 1991, the U.S. called upon its allies to cut interest rates in an effort to revive the world economy, but Germany, desperately trying to attract foreign capital to help finance unification with East Germany, refused to go along.

The model of Europe 1992 and its promise of a single, common market is being emulated around the globe. The U.S., Canada and Mexico are in the process of ironing out a treaty to create a free trade zone. Japan is improving trade relations with its neighbors, and the governments of Argentina, Brazil, Paraguay and Uruguay are committed to creating a common market that will stretch from the Equator to the Antarctic. Whether this new economic regionalism will help or harm the world economy depends upon the attitude these free trade zones take toward countries outside the region—whether they facilitate world trade or throw up new barriers.

In June, Alan Greenspan, chairman of the Federal Reserve Board, told Congress that the U.S. economy had hit bottom but that there were as yet no signs of recovery. A month later, he announced that the recovery had begun. Other economists were less optimistic. A sizable portion of this year's crop of college graduates found it impossible to land decent jobs. Major companies were still cutting back, laying off thousands of employees. Thirty states and 50 major cities were in financial crisis, forced to lay off thousands of workers, cut services and raise taxes. Economic revival in the Western industrial powerhouses is the key to improving economic conditions around the world, and much depends on what happens in the year to come.

THINGS TO WATCH

Will the recession in the major Western countries end?

Will solutions be found for the ailing Eastern European economies?

Will economic regionalism lead to a global commercial war or increased international cooperation?

DISASTERS & REFUGEES

The plight of the world's refugees was a top news story in 1991. As soon as the U.S.-led international coalition had defeated the Iraqi military and driven it out of Kuwait, anti-Saddam Hussein rebellions began among the Kurdish minority in northern Iraq and pro-Iranian Shiite Moslems in the south. However, troops loyal to Saddam Hussein's government quickly quelled the uprisings, and an estimated two million refugees began fleeing to safety in Turkey, Iran and United Nations-occupied territory in southern Iraq. Death from starvation, disease and exposure threatened to take a heavy toll. Relief agencies and Western governments quickly delivered food and supplies to the region on an emergency basis, and American troops began to set up refugee camps in protected enclaves within Iraq. In all, experts report that the crisis in the Persian Gulf triggered one of the most massive short-term migrations in human history – involving an estimated 5 million people, including workers from throughout the Middle East, Asia and Africa who fled the war zone and returned to their home countries.

Despite all the talk of a "new world order" and the resolution of several longstanding East-West confrontations around the globe, the world refugee problem is getting worse, much worse. Over the past six years the number of refugees has nearly doubled – jumping from 9.5 million to nearly 18 million– due to the combined impact of disasters, man-made and natural, from wars to floods.

In Sudan, a country plagued by years of civil war and drought, there are nearly 750,000 refugees and 4.5 million displaced persons, and half the country's population of 24 million risks death by famine. In fact, famine threatens a massive death toll throughout the Horn of Africa – in Ethiopia, Somalia and Djibouti, as well as Sudan. Elsewhere in Africa, civil war has left 1.2 million displaced persons in Liberia and 8.6 million facing famine in Mozambique. In Malawi there are more than 900,000 refugees from the the civil war in neighboring Mozambique.

In Asia, 3.7 million Afghans continue to bide their time in refugee camps in Pakistan,

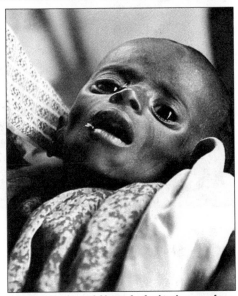

An Ethiopian refugee child cries for food in the arms of his mother at the Kelato refugee camp on the Somali-Ethiopian border.

326,000 Cambodians live in camps in Thailand, and another 50,000 refugees are housed in Hong Kong. More than 100,000 fled an erupting volcano in the Philippines. In Bangladesh, 150,000 people were killed during a cyclone and subsquent floods and nearly 4 million displaced from their homes. In Peru, more than 130,000 were hit by a cholera epidemic and more than 200,000 displaced from their homes.

The scope of the human tragedy of the refugee crisis is indescribable. What's worse, it's often avoidable. Shortsighted agricultural policies, emphasizing cash crops and disrupting traditional forms of farming, often create a situation where a local agricultural population produces for export, is no longer able to feed itself, and contributes to the creation of deserts out of once-fertile lands. The massive over-cutting in lumber operations on the mountainsides of Nepal makes its low-lying neighbor Bangladesh vulnerable to devastating floods. While millions face starvation in the third world, Western governments still pursue agricultural policies encouraging farmers to take acreage out of cultivation as a means of bolstering market prices. The problem will not go away by itself and will not be easy to solve.

WORLD'S REFUGEES

	DISPLACED	REFUGEES	THREATENED BY FAMINE	CHOLERA PATIENTS
Middle East	2.4 million			
Iran		3.8 million		
Turkey		500,000		
ASIA				
Philippines	70,000			
Hong Kong		50,000		
Cambodia	150,000			
Thailand		454,000		
Pakistan		3.7 million		
AFRICA				
Somalia	400,000	360,000		
Ethiopia		800,000		
Djibouti		78,000		
Sudan	4.5 million	750,000	12 million	
Mozambique			8.6 million	
Malawi		910,000		
Liberia	1.2 million			
SOUTH AMERICA				
Peru	200,000			130,000

Refugees are defined as people who have been forced to flee their country.
Displaced persons are those who have been forced out of their homes but remain in their own country.

First row L to R: German Chancellor Helmut Kohl, French President Francois Mitterrand, Italian Premier Giulio Andreotti, Danish Premier Poul Schleuter and formerBritish Prime Minister Margaret Thatcher. *Second row L to R:* are Foreign Ministers: Greece's Antoni Samaras, Belgium's Marc Eyskens, EC's M.F. Andriessen, Denmark's Uffe Elleman-Jensen, Germany's Hans Dietrich Genscher, Italy's Gianni De Michelis and France's Roland Dumas.

GOVERNING BODIES OF THE EC

The Commission of the European Communities: Executive branch ... based in Brussels, Belgium.

Council of Ministers: Legislative branch ... meets monthly ... presidency of the council rotates every six months ... European Summits are held every six months.

European Parliament: Subsidiary part of legislative branch ... acts primarily as public forum for debate of proposed legislation.

Court of Justice: Judicial branch.

CHRONOLOGY

1952 European Coal and Steel Community created by Belgium, France, Italy, Luxembourg, the Netherlands and West Germany.

1958 Rome Treaties signed, establishing European Atomic Energy Community (Euroatom) and European Economic Community (EEC).

1973 Britain, Denmark, Ireland join EC.

1981 Greece joins EC.

1985 White Paper on creating one European market adopted.

1986 Spain and Portugal join EC.

1988 Dispute breaks out with U.S. over shipments of hormone-treated beef to EC countries.

1989 Economic Summit of leading industrial democracies mandates EC to coordinate aid to evolving democracies in Eastern Europe.

1990 France and West Germany issue call for political as well as economic unification of EC members.

1991 New non-Communist regimes in Eastern Europe apply for membership in EC. Hesitations grow among EC members on single monetary system.

Western Europe is moving swiftly toward economic integration in 1992. A whole series of reforms are scheduled to be implemented by December 31, 1992, among the 12 member nations of the European Community (EC), and these will change the way the countries of Western Europe and their citizens interact — financially, legally and socially. Nationalistic trade barriers on the Continent will topple, and one single market of more than 320 million people and economic production of $2.4 trillion per year will be created.

As the deadline draws near, a number of last-minute problems have arisen. Former British Prime Minister Margaret Thatcher had been the EC's main opponent to the establishment of a unitary European currency. When she resigned in early 1991 and was replaced by John Major, many observers believed monetary union would proceed without a hitch. But recently, Denmark, Luxembourg, Germany and others have begun to express hesitations about a single monetary system. Some member states have criticized the EC bureaucracy's policies. The deepening recession in Europe has caused a number of governments to rethink the EC's anti-subsidy orientation. A flood of membership applications from new democratic regimes in Eastern Europe has triggered uneasiness in some of the EC's poorer countries, like Portugal, Spain and Greece, which fear that EC funds would be diverted to the even-weaker economies in the East.

WHAT IS THE EUROPEAN COMMUNITY?

There are 12 nations in the European Community (EC) today: Belgium, Britain, Denmark, France, Greece, Ireland, Italy, Luxembourg, the Netherlands, Portugal, Spain and Germany. The EC's origins go back to treaties that set up the European Coal and Steel Community in 1952, and the Rome Treaties of 1958 that set up the European Economic Community (EEC) and the European Atomic Energy Community. The EC is often referred to as the EEC or Common Market.

The EC was the brainchild of French statesman Jean Monnet. His plan was to transform Europe into a federation, a kind of United States of Europe, and he saw economic integration as a means to achieve political integration. But the dream has been a long time becoming reality. Economic reforms came slowly, member nations were reluctant to give up their sovereignty to EC bureaucracies, and new forms of trade barriers sprang up every time an old one was dismantled.

Economic difficulties in the 1970s put everything on hold. But in the mid-1980s, EC leaders realized that they had to prevent Europe from falling too far behind Japan and the U.S. A 1985 White Paper drafted under the leadership of Britain's Lord Cockfield set up a master plan for creating one internal market in Europe by the end of 1992, and that plan is well underway.

The 1992 Presidential campaign got off to a slow start. President George Bush looked invulnerable, and Democrats were reluctant to plunge into the fray. The President came out of the Gulf War with an unprecedented 90 percent popularity rating, and even as the summer of 1991 began he was still running at over 80 percent in the polls. More and more Americans have switched party allegiance to the Republicans over the past decade, and Campaign '92 will not be easy for the Democrats.

Four years ago in the summer of 1987, Democratic hopefuls were already wending their way through Iowa, the first state to hold a Presidential caucus, delivering their message to anyone who would listen. But by the summer of 1991, Paul Tsongas, the Massachusetts liberal who resigned from the U.S. Senate in 1984 after he was diagnosed with cancer (the disease is now in full remission), was the only candidate to declare openly for the Presidency. Virginia Gov. C. Douglas Wilder, the first black to be elected governor since Reconstruction, stopped short of announcing his candidacy but created a committee to explore possibilities and begin fundraising.

Meanwhile the Democratic National Committee has been busy hunting for a strategy that could topple Bush and give the Democrats another crack at the White House. The Democrats are considering writing off states where they don't stand a chance, and concentrating instead on pivotal states where an all-out campaign could give them a victory in the Electoral College.

While the President is basking in his successes in foreign affairs, he is considered vulnerable on domestic issues. He is open to attack on education, energy, the environment, health, the war on drugs, the burgeoning budget deficit, gun control, the economic recession and even abortion (a majority of Americans favor legalized abortion). On taxes, Bush broke the "read-my-lips-no-new-taxes" promise he made in the 1988 campaign. Many Americans are still worried about the wisdom of Bush's choice of Dan

TENTATIVE 1992 DEMOCRATIC PRIMARY SCHEDULE

February 17:	Iowa (caucus)		Oklahoma	April 28:	Pennsylvania
February 23:	Maine (caucus)		Rhode Island	May 5:	Indiana
February 25:	New Hampshire		Tennessee		Ohio
	South Dakota		Texas	May 12:	Nebraska
March 3:	Colorado	March 17:	Illinois		West Virginia
	Maryland		Michigan	May 19:	Oregon
March 7:	Wyoming (caucus)	March 24:	Connecticut	May 26:	Arkansas
March 10:	Super Tuesday	April 7:	Kansas		Kentucky
	Florida		Minnesota		Washington
	Georgia		New York	June 2:	Alabama
	Louisiana		Wisconsin		California
	Massachusetts	April 11 & 13:	Virginia (caucus)		New Jersey
	Mississippi	April 19:	Alaska (caucus)	June 9:	North Dakota
	North Carolina				

Quayle as Vice President.

Unless something unforeseen happens, and the President decides to step down after only one term, Bush will run on his record of achievement in foreign affairs, hoping that the economy will revive enough to keep the Democrats from making significant inroads on his popularity. Republicans will be sure to chide Democrats for their vote against military action in the Persian Gulf (a majority of Democrats in the House and the Senate voted against authorizing military action in January 1991).

Here is a brief rundown on possible Democratic candidates:

Sen. Lloyd Bentsen, Texas: As a Vice Presidential candidate in 1988, Bentsen seemed more Presidential to many voters than running mate Michael Dukakis.

Sen. Bill Bradley, New Jersey: Bradley has earned a reputation as a tax reformer and has lately been attacking the Bush Administration's civil rights record.

Gov. Bill Clinton, Arkansas: A leader of the new conservative wing of southern Democratic leaders who seek to wean the party from its traditional liberal platform to more moderate, mainstream policies.

Gov. Mario Cuomo, New York: With his fiery keynote address at the 1984 convention, Cuomo stole the show from party standard-bearer Walter Mondale and earned a reputation as champion of the downtrodden. He has run into trouble in New York recently as the recession and declining state revenues have

forced him to make unpopular budget cuts.

Rep. Richard Gephardt, Missouri: An early front-runner in 1988, Gephardt faded fast. Currently majority leader in the House, he has been popular with organized labor.

Sen. Albert Gore, Tennessee: A Senate moderate considered capable of challenging Bush for mainstream support.

Jesse Jackson, Washington D.C.: Currently serving as Washington's symbolic "shadow senator," Jackson is considering a third bid for the Presidency. As a representative of the party's far left, Jackson fared well in 1988 among blacks and labor voters in industrial states.

Sen. Jay Rockefeller, West Virginia: As a popular liberal in his home state and with Rockefeller family wealth, he may be able to do well in an abbreviated race in which access to expensive television advertising time will be crucial.

Gov. C. Douglas Wilder, Virginia: The nation's first black governor since Reconstruction, Wilder combines a reputation as a fiscal conservative with a commitment to maintaining needed human services.

Paul Tsongas, Massachusetts: A one-term senator from Massachusetts who gave up his seat in 1984 to fight cancer, Tsongas is considered a long shot. He calls for a new form of probusiness, liberal politics, emphasizing state intervention in the economy to support research and development and tax policies to encourage long-term investment, similar to policies prevailing in Japan and Germany.

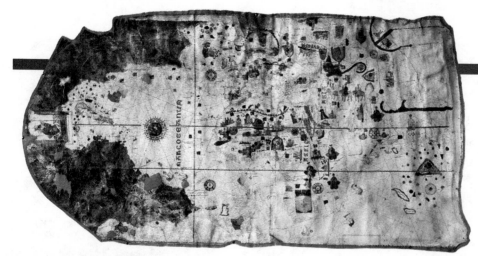

Juan de La Cosa, who sailed with Columbus, drew this map on ox hide in 1500. It is the earliest surviving cartographic record of the voyages of Columbus.

In 1992 the world marks the 500th anniversary of Christopher Columbus's historic voyage to America. Historians no longer believe many of the myths we learned as children about Columbus's "discovery of America." First of all, Columbus didn't "discover" America; native Americans had been living here for thousands of years before his arrival, and there is considerable evidence that Norse explorers landed on the North American continent hundreds of years before Columbus. Columbus didn't really set out to prove the world was round; most educated people in his day already believed that. (His aim was to find a direct shipping route to the Orient.) His crew members were by and large honest men, not the dregs of Spanish prisons.

Nonetheless, Columbus's voyage to the New World changed the course of history, for it opened up permanent contact between Europe and the Western Hemisphere. Columbus didn't live long enough to understand the real nature of his accomplishment. He thought the Earth was much smaller than it actually is and believed that China and Japan were just a few weeks' sail west of Europe. He called the native people he encountered when he landed in the Bahamas "Indians" because he believed he had reached India. In Cuba, he sent a landing party ashore with a letter from King Ferdinand and Queen Isabella of Spain in search of the Emperor of China. On his fourth voyage, Columbus looked for a passage to the Indian Ocean because he believed that South America was a short distance southeast of China.

The Columbus Quincentenary is not without its controversies. Some groups claim that the great seaman was not an Italian from Genoa named Cristofer Colombo, but a man named Cristofer Colon, a Jew of Norwegian-Spanish descent. Others, especially native American groups, are not interested in celebrating an event that they see as the beginning of genocide and destruction of native American cultures.

A yearlong celebration is planned in Spain, throughout Latin America and in the U.S. Replicas of the Nina, the Pinta and the Santa Maria will embark from Spain on a re-creation of Columbus's original voyage and will visit major American cities.

COLUMBUS'S FIRST VOYAGE

August 3, 1492: Columbus's fleet of three ships, the Santa Maria, the Nina and the Pinta, sail from Palos, Spain.
August 12: Columbus reaches San Sebastian in Canary Islands. Ships take on supplies, repairs are made.
September 6: Ships depart, sailing westward.
September 9: Crew members lose sight of land as they continue sailing westward.
September 16: Patches of floating seaweed observed by crew members.
September 24: Sailors mistakenly believe land has been sighted.
September 30: Fleet completes three weeks of sailing without sight of land, a navigational record.
October 7: Another mistaken report of land sighting causes considerable discontent among crew members.
October 10: Angry sailors threaten mutiny. Columbus agrees to turn around if land is not sighted within three days.
October 12: Land sighted at 2 A.M. At noon Columbus leads landing party ashore at San Salvador in Bahamas.
October 28: Columbus explores coast of Cuba.
December 25: Santa Maria wrecked at Cap-Haitien in Haiti.
January 16, 1493: Nina and Pinta begin return voyage. Columbus sails on Nina.
February 13-14: During severe storm, Nina and Pinta become separated.
February 15: Nina arrives in Azores, waits for 10 days, then resumes homeward voyage without Pinta.
March 3: Nina arrives in Lisbon, Portugal, remaining there 10 days.
March 15: Nina returns to home port of Palos, Spain. Pinta arrives a few hours later.

COLUMBUS'S FOUR VOYAGES TO AMERICA

First Voyage
August 3, 1492–March 15, 1493:
Columbus commanded fleet of three ships and 90 men ... landed at San Salvador in Bahamas ... explored coasts of Cuba, Hispaniola.

Second Voyage
September 25, 1493–June 1496:
Commanded fleet of 17 ships with more than 1,000 crew and colonists ... explored West Indies ... established first European colony in New World, on northern coast of Hispaniola, under command of his brother, Diego ... explored coast of Cuba.

Third Voyage
May 30, 1498–1500:
Commanded three ships ... explored Trinidad and coast of Central and South America ... after encountering discontent among colonists at Hispaniola, was arrested and returned to Spain in chains ... later released by royal command.

Fourth Voyage
May 9, 1502–November 7, 1504:
Commanded four ships ... explored Central American coast looking for passage to what he believed was Indian Ocean ... traded with Indians of Costa Rica and Panama.

SPORTS

Bo Jackson

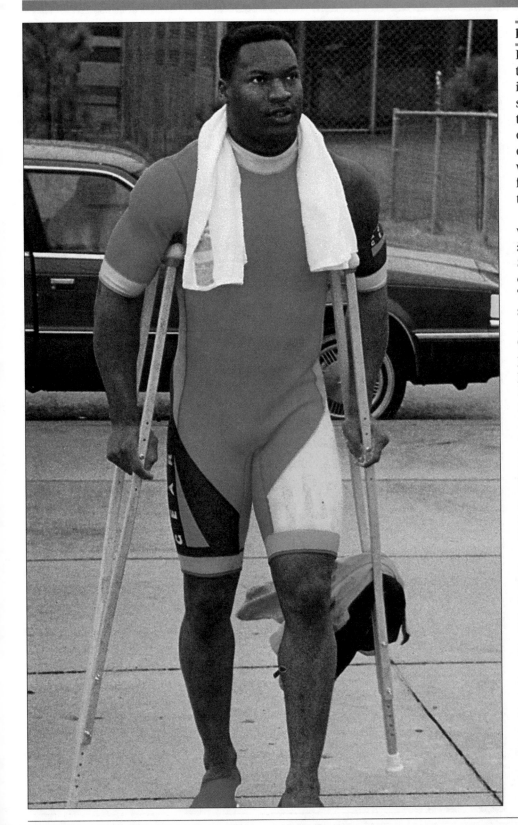

BASEBALL

In a surprise upset, the Cincinnati Reds beat the Oakland Athletics in four straight games in the 1990 World Series. Finishing regular-season play with 103 victories, and winning the American League pennant for the third consecutive season, the defending world champion Athletics were heavily favored to whip Cincinnati, but the A's were no match for the Reds, who outscored them 22-8 in the series.

Runaway player salaries were a big story when the 1991 baseball season opened. The average player salary hit an incredible $890,000 a year, 53 percent higher than opening day 1990. According to the New York Times, 223 of the 708 major leaguers were slated to earn more that $1 million, including 32 with salaries of more than $3 million. The Oakland Athletics topped all teams with a payroll of $36.43 million ($1.35 million per player). In the National League, the New York Mets had the highest payroll at $32.59 million ($1.25 million per player).

Texas Rangers pitcher Nolan Ryan, at age 44, continued to amaze baseball fans in 1991, hurling his seventh career no-hitter on May 1. On the same day, Oakland's Rickey Henderson broke Lou Brock's major league record of 938 stolen bases. Brock took 19 seasons to set his record; Henderson is only in his 13th year in the big leagues.

Major League Baseball owners approved new National League franchises for Miami and Denver, to begin competing in the 1993 season. Former Cincinnati star Pete Rose was ruled ineligible for Hall of Fame honors because he was banned from baseball for his gambling involvement.

The future career of Bo Jackson, who stars in both professional football and baseball, was still in question, following a serious hip injury during the football season.

BASKETBALL

Michael Jordan led the Chicago Bulls to their first-ever National Basketball Association championship, as the Bulls defeated the Los

SPORTS

Angeles Lakers four games to one. The victory was especially sweet for Jordan, who finally put to rest criticism that he was too much of an individualistic player to help his team to a title. In college basketball, coach Jerry Tarkanian was unable to guide the Running Rebels of the University of Nevada —Las Vegas to a second consecutive national title. The Duke University Blue Devils avenged their 103-73 rout by U.N.L.V. in the1990 finals by eking out a 79-77 victory over U.N.L.V. in the semifinals and then going on to beat Kansas, 72-65, in the finals.

FOOTBALL

In the closest title game ever, the New York Giants defeated the Buffalo Bills, 20-19, in Super Bowl XXV on January 27, 1991, in Tampa. The Giants' strategy to keep the ball out of the hands of Buffalo's explosive offense worked perfectly. New York managed to hold onto the ball for a Super Bowl record 40:33 minutes. It was the Giants' second title under head coach Bill Parcells, who later announced his retirement to pursue a career as a football broadcaster for NBC Sports.

HOCKEY

The Pittsburgh Penguins took their first National Hockey League Stanely Cup championship by defeating the Minnesota North Stars, four games to two.

BOXING

In October 1990, Evander Holyfield took the undisputed world heavyweight title from James (Buster) Douglas with a knockout in the third round. Holyfield successfully defended his title against former champion George Foreman, who had engineered a comeback at age 42. A 3-1 underdog going into the fight, Foreman won the hearts of the crowd as he managed to hang on for the full 12 rounds without being knocked down, before losing the decision to Holyfield. Meanwhile, former champion Mike Tyson, who lost his title in a surprise upset to Douglas in February 1990, continued his own comeback by stopping Donovan (Razor) Ruddock with a seventh-round T.K.O. on March 18.

GOLF

In April, Welshman Ian Woosnam won the 55th Masters golf tournament on the final hole. It was his first victory in a major tournament. In June, Payne Stewart took the 91st U.S. Open golf tournament. The tournament was marked by tragedy when a spectator was killed by lightning during a storm.

TENNIS

Major tournament winners in 1991 were Boris Becker and Monica Seles at the Australian Open, Jim Courier and Seles at the French Open, and Michael Stich and Steffi Graf at Wimbledon. In a surprise development, Seles, who had won the first two legs of the 1991 Grand Slam, withdrew from Wimbledon competition at the last minute. Seles, a 17-year old Yugoslavian, blamed minor injuries suffered in an accident.

OLYMPICS

The 1992 Winter Olympics open February 8 in Albertville, France, the Summer Olympics July 25 in Barcelona, Spain. The Olympics are supposed to be for athletes, a sports festival where the world's best compete against each other, but politics are never far away. The Olympics were interrupted by world war twice in this century. In 1936 Adolf Hitler tried to use the Berlin Games to show off Aryan superiority. The 1972 Summer Games in Munich were marred by a Palestinian terrorist attack that left 11 Israeli Olympians dead. When the Soviet Union invaded Afghanistan in December 1979, the U.S. led a boycott of the Moscow Games in protest. In 1984, the Soviets orchestrated a less effective retaliatory boycott against the Los Angeles Games.

Politics lurks behind the scenes at the 1992 Games, as well—but this time the theme is unity and inclusion, not boycotts. Reunited Germany is fielding one team this year,

heavily made up of athletes from the former East German sports machine, now under the tutelage of coaches from West Germany. In the 1950's and early 60's, East and West Germany sent a single, combined team to the Olympics. But by the mid-1960's East German Communism had focused on international athletic competition as a source of national prestige. In the totalitarian East German society, talented children as young as 6 years old were taken from their families and put into intensive training programs. While the East German sports machine is largely defunct today, this Olympiad will be the last hurrah for the products of that machine, and perhaps Germany's last chance for winning big at the Games.

Another big political story is the return of South Africa to the Games after a 31-year exile. South Africa was expelled from the International Olympic Committee in 1976 because of its apartheid policies, but it had actually not sent a team to compete since 1960 because of threatened boycotts by Communist and African countries. Now that the legal apparatus of apartheid is largely dismantled and sanctions have been lifted by the European Community and the U.S., South Africa is being brought back into the world athletic community. An integrated South African team is expected to do particularly well in track-and-field events.

For the U.S., hopes are riding on welterweight sensation Oscar De La Hoya to win a gold medal in boxing. De La Hoya has won more than 200 amateur fights and is un-

defeated since 1987. He wants to win the gold to fulfill a deathbed promise he made to his mother, who died of cancer.

In track, Carl Lewis is expected to do well in the 100-meter dash, in which he took home the gold in 1988 after the original winner, Canadian Ben Johnson, was disqualified for using steroids. Lewis is also out to set a new record in the long jump, sporting an incredible winning streak of 66 consecutive competitions as of the summer of 1991. Another man to watch is the Soviet Union's Sergei Bubka, an electrifying pole-vaulter who has already broken the 20-foot barrier in indoor competition and is working on clearing that mark in outdoor competition as well.

The U.S. Olympic basketball squad will be stronger than ever this year, because for the first time professional players will be permitted to compete.

At the Winter Games, the U.S. hockey team will face stiff competition from the Soviet Union, Sweden, Finland, Czechoslovakia and Canada. In downhill skiing, A.J. Kitt and Tommy Moe have the best chances of winning medals. The American ladies' figure-skating team will be especially strong, with five world medalists (Kristi Yamaguchi, Tonya Harding, Nancy Kerrigan, Jill Trenary and Holly Cook) vying for the three slots on the Olympic team. In men's skating, Todd Eldredge and Christopher Bowman are expected to be strong competitors. In pair skating, Natasha Kuchiki and Todd Sand are expected to lead the American team in challenging Soviet domination in the sport.

SCHEDULE

The Winter Olympics
Albertville, France
February 8 - 23

The Summer Olympics
Barcelona, Spain
July 25 - August 9

PEOPLE WHO MAKE A DIFFERENCE

JAVIER PEREZ DE CUELLAR

Peruvian diplomat Javier Perez de Cuellar retires this year after two terms as Secretary-General of the United Nations. Selected as a compromise candidate to succeed Kurt Waldheim in 1982 (some observers characterized him as "everyone's last choice"), de Cuellar has grown in stature over the past decade. With the collapse of Communism in 1989 and the end of the cold war, the influence and prestige of the U.N. enjoyed a resurgence, and for the first time it seemed that the U.N. could play the role of international peacekeeper that it was originally intended to fulfill. De Cuellar played a crucial role in guiding the cumbersome U.N. apparatus into the new era in international relations.

The first Latin American (and only the second non-European) to head the U.N., the 72-year-old de Cuellar has had a long career as a Peruvian diplomat and U.N. official. In 1976, as a U.N. emissary, he played a pivotal role in bringing an end to ethnic violence between Turks and Greeks on Cyprus. During his tenure as Secretary-General, de Cuellar boosted morale and reduced red tape in the U.N. bureaucracy, broke ground by appointing women to high-ranking posts and coordinated U.N. efforts against Iraq's invasion of Kuwait.

GEN. NORMAN SCHWARZKOPF

Affectionately known as "the Bear" or "Stormin' Norman," Gen. Norman Schwarzkopf is America's first genuine military hero since the Korean War, thanks to his stunning success in the Persian Gulf. Schwarzkopf is likened by many to Dwight D. Eisenhower, the supreme commander of U.S. forces in World War II who parlayed his popularity into a successful bid for the Presidency in 1952, and there is plenty of speculation that Schwarzkopf, too, will enter politics following his retirement after 35 years in the military. Though Republicans believe the 57-year-old general is a kindred spirit, Schwarzkopf insists he's a political independent, with strong views on education, the war against drugs and environmental issues.

He graduated from West Point in 1956 and served two combat infantry tours in Vietnam, where he was wounded twice. Before commanding multinational forces against Iraq in the Persian Gulf War, he commanded U.S. ground forces in the 1983 invasion of Grenada.

EDUARD SHEVARDNADZE

As foreign minister of the Soviet Union during the first five years of the Gorbachev era, Eduard Shevardnadze helped engineer momentous changes in Soviet foreign policy that have altered the course of history. A strong supporter of Mikhail Gorbachev's reform program, the former Communist Party leader of the Georgian Republic worked quietly behind the scenes with his American counterparts George P. Shultz and James A. Baker to orchestrate crucial breakthroughs in arms control and international relations. During his tenure, the world saw fast-moving and unanticipated changes in the world scene: reduced East-West tension, the first international treaty to eliminate an entire class of nuclear weapons, the end of Soviet domination in Eastern Europe and the end of the cold war. A new era in Soviet-U.S. cooperation was ushered in when Shevardnadze and Baker issued a joint declaration denouncing the Iraqi invasion of Kuwait in August 1990.

Demonstrating that his primary loyalty was not to Gorbachev, the man, but to the reform program, Shevardnadze dramatically resigned as foreign minister in December 1990 and warned that Gorbachev's sudden accommodation with Communist hard-liners threatened to lead to a new dictatorship. He then went on to set up Russia's first independent think tank, the Foreign Policy Association, and subsequently resigned from the Communist Party to co-found a new reform opposition party.

THURGOOD MARSHALL

Thurgood Marshall's decision to retire from the Supreme Court at age 83 and his probable replacement by a much more conservative justice will have profound implications for American society for decades to come. A member of the Court for 24 years, Marshall voted with the majority on important decisions of the Warren Court, including Roe v. Wade, which legalized abortion. As the Court's center of gravity shifted to the right over the years, as conservatives were named to the bench by Presidents Ronald Reagan and George Bush, Marshall became the voice of dissent. The last Supreme Court liberal appointed by a Democratic President, Marshall was a strong advocate of civil liberties and civil rights and an opponent of the death penalty. He was blunt and outspoken, both in debates within the Court and in the public arena. While most judges maintain an aloofness from the political questions of the day, Marshall openly criticized the civil rights records of the Reagan and Bush Administrations and decried what he called the erosion of past gains made by minorities in America.

Thurgood Marshall first made his reputation as a pioneering lawyer for the National Association for the Advancement of Colored People and spearheaded the N.A.A.C.P. effort in the landmark Brown v. Topeka Board of Education case, which overturned school desegregation in 1954. President Lyndon B. Johnson appointed him as the first black to serve on the Supreme Court in 1967. In 1990, Marshall told reporters that he had a lifetime appointment and had every intention of serving it. He said he expected to die at the age of 110. But deteriorating health and growing disenchantment with his philosophical isolation led to his decision to retire.

FANG LIZHI

Fang Lizhi, China's pre-eminent astrophysicist, has been called "the Andrei Sakharov of China," but unlike the Soviet physicist who for years personified the human rights movement in the Soviet Union and was rehabilitated before his death in 1989, Lizhi is still officially an outcast in Chinese society. Since 1986, Lizhi had used his position as a world-renowned scientist to call for democratization in China as the only way to achieve a transition to a modern society. Though he played no public role during the prodemocracy demonstrations that were brutally suppressed by government troops in June 1989, the Communists blamed him for inspiring what they called an attempted counter-revolution, and Lizhi was forced to seek refuge in the American Embassy in Beijing.

Lizhi and his wife, Li Shuxian, also an astrophysicist, remained at the American Embassy until June 1990, when they were allowed to leave for Great Britain. The 55-year-old scientist continues to speak out against political oppression in China.

PEGGY SAY

There were ticker-tape parades to welcome home the American soldiers and sailors who spent up to seven months in the Middle East to combat Saddam Hussein's aggression. But for Peggy Say there is still nothing to celebrate. Say is the sister of Terry Anderson, the chief Middle East correspondent for the Associated Press and America's longest-held hostage in Lebanon. Anderson was captured March 16, 1985, by members of Hizbullah, the Shiite Moslem fundamentalist group with close ties to Iran. As spokesperson for the families of other Americans being held hostage in Lebanon, she has pressured the U.S. Government to step up its efforts to gain the hostages' release. She has gone to Damascus and lobbied prominent Syrians and Palestinians to help locate her brother, and she has endured those excruciating moments when optimism that release was near was suddenly dashed. In June 1985, when the Reagan Administration won the release of American hostages on TWA Flight 847, there was a momentary hope that the other hostages would be freed. Likewise, when the war in the Gulf in 1991 brought with it an end to civil war in Lebanon, improved U.S. relations with Syria (which controls Beirut) and with Iran (which influences Hizbullah), and plans for a Middle East peace conference, release of the remaining Western hostages in Beirut seemed imminent. Meanwhile, Say, who has written a book about her efforts to win freedom for her brother, refuses to let the American people forget about the Americans still held in captivity.

UNITED STATES

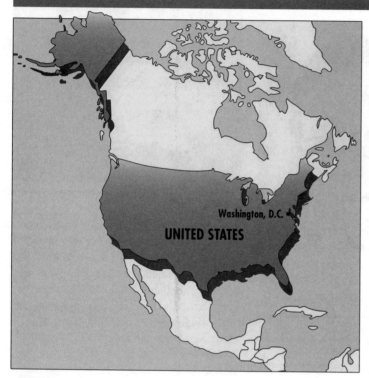

Washington, D.C.

UNITED STATES

George Bush's leadership during the Persian Gulf crisis finally silenced all talk about his alleged "indecisiveness" and the "wimp factor" that had dogged his first three years in office. Bush's image as a steely-nerved, decisive international leader is now firmly established.

Bush emerged from the war with a record-high 91 percent approval rating and looked like a shoo-in for re-election. Many observers were openly wondering who the Democrats would be able to find to run as a sacrificial lamb in the 1992 campaign. However, the President still finds himself vulnerable on domestic issues. There is a widespread perception that he is enthusiastic only about international affairs and neglects crucial domestic problems. Critics attack him for lack of leadership on education, energy, environmental policies, health, drugs, the budget deficit, gun control and the recession. In May, the President developed an irregular heartbeat, and the nation grew uneasy at the prospect that Vice President Dan Quayle, who had never overcome the image of a political lightweight, might take over the Oval Office. The wisdom of Bush's choice of Quayle loomed again as a possible campaign issue. However, the most critical obstacle to Bush's re-election will be whether the economy can manage to rebound out of the recession before voters go to the polls November 3, 1992.

KEY DATES IN THE BUSH ADMINISTRATION

1989

January 20: George Bush inaugurated.
February 6: Bush outlines plan to bail out savings and loan industry.
February 10: President makes first trip outside U.S., visiting Canada to promise action on acid rain.
February 19: Bush departs for Far East, attending Japanese Emperor Hirohito's funeral and visiting China and South Korea.
March 4: President refuses to intervene in Eastern Airlines labor dispute.
March 9: Senate rejects nomination of John Tower for Secretary of Defense.
March 13: Bush imposes temporary ban on importation of Chilean fruit after Customs officials discover two cyanide-contaminated grapes.
March 14: Bush restricts importation of semiautomatic weapons.
March 24: Exxon Valdez spills 10.1 million gallons of crude oil in Prince William Sound in Alaska. Bush criticized for slow Government response.
April 5: Bush outlines $441 million education plan.
May 13: Bush urges overthrow of Panamanian dictator Manuel Noriega.
May 29: At NATO summit, Bush proposes to expedite negotiations to cut conventional forces in Europe.
June 6: Bush denounces massacre at Tiananmen Square in Beijing and cuts arms shipments to Chinese government.
July 9-13: President visits Poland and Hungary.
July 13: Bush attends Economic Summit and bicentennial of French Revolution in Paris.
September 5: Administration outlines war on drugs.
September 29: Bush signs aid package for victims of Hurricane Hugo.
October 3: Coup attempt against Noriega fails in Panama. Administration criticized for not supporting rebels.
October 18: President declares earthquake disaster in northern California.
December 2-3: Bush meets Soviet President Mikhail Gorbachev at Malta Summit.
December 11: President defends Administration against criticism of secret contacts with Chinese government, which appear to violate sanctions imposed after repression of pro-democracy movement.
December 20: Bush orders invasion of Panama to oust and arrest Noriega.

1990

January 31: President delivers State of the Union message.
February 15: Bush travels to Cartenga, Colombia, for antidrug summit with presidents of Bolivia, Colombia and Peru.
February 25: Administration hails Nicaraguan electoral victory of Violeta Chamorro and defeat of Sandinistas.
March 1: President supports compromise on Clean Air Act, which environmentalists charge weakens efforts to clean up pollution.
March 8: Bush unveils national transportation policy, which places cost burden for rehabilitation of infrastructure on state and local governments.
March 29: Bush addresses AIDS conference, vows compassion for victims.
April 17: President prompts criticism from environmentalists by insisting more research is necessary to determine whether greenhouse effect really exists, rather than out-

President George Bush poses with soldiers during a stop at an air base in Dhahran, Saudi Arabia.

lining plan of action to combat the problem.

May 9: President hints he might agree to raise taxes to meet Gramm-Rudman budget-deficit guidelines.

May 31-June 3: Bush holds second summit with Mikhail Gorbachev in Washington, D.C.

July 9-10: Bush hosts Economic Summit in Houston.

August 2: Iraq invades Kuwait. U.S. freezes Iraqi and Kuwaiti assets.

August 3: U.S. orders naval forces to Persian Gulf.

August 7: Bush orders air and ground forces to Saudi Arabia.

August 9: First American troops arrive in Saudi Arabia.

August 18: President Bush wins U.N. Security Council approval for economic blockade against Iraq.

August 22: Bush orders call-up of military reservists.

September 9: Bush and Gorbachev meet at Helsinki Summit, jointly urge Iraq to pull out of Kuwait.

November 6: Additional troops are ordered to Persian Gulf theater.

November 19: President attends Paris Conference on Security in Europe, at which cold war between East and West is officially ended.

November 22: Bush spends Thanksgiving with troops in Saudi Arabia.

November 23: President holds controversial meeting with Syrian President Hafez al-Assad.

November 29: U.N. Security Council sets January 15 deadline for Iraq to withdraw from Kuwait and authorizes military action if necessary.

November 30: Bush offers Iraq diplomatic exchange of visits on foreign minister level in effort to avoid military confrontation.

1991

January 3: Brady handgun-control bill introduced in Congress.

January 9: Geneva meeting between Secretary of State James Baker and Iraqi Foreign Minister Tariq Aziz produces no breakthroughs.

January 12: Congress authorizes use of force in Persian Gulf after January 15 deadline.

January 16: War to liberate Kuwait begins with allied air strikes against Iraqi positions. President delivers television address to the nation.

January 29: President delivers State of the Union message.

February 20: Bush unveils new national energy plan.

February 23: Ground war against Iraq begins.

February 27: U.S. announces victory against Iraq.

March 6: President addresses the nation, outlines postwar goals.

March 11: Administration proposes new anticrime legislation.

March 20: Bush announces 70 percent debt reduction for Poland.

April 5: Administration orders relief aid for Kurdish refugees.

April 7: Bush announces support for free trade treaty with Mexico.

April 18: President signs legislation to end one-day railroad strike.

April 23: Gen. Norman Schwarzkopf visits President at White House.

April 25: Congress passes $1.46 trillion budget.

April 28: Major industrial nations reject U.S. proposal to drop interest rates.

May 3: President Bush denies published reports that he met with Iranian officials in1980 to delay Iranian hostage release until after 1980 Presidential election.

May 4: President admitted to Bethesda Naval Hospital with irregular heartbeat.

May 7: Last U.S. troops exit Iraq.

May 22: Supreme Court issues 5-4 decision upholding controversial Government guidelines restricting family-planning clinics receiving Federal funds from even mentioning abortion option to patients.

June 4: Bush calls for extension of China's Most Favored Nation trading status, despite continued human rights violations in China.

June 10: Millions laud Desert Storm forces in New York City ticker-tape parade.

June 18: Federal Reserve Board chairman, Alan Greenspan, testifies before Congress that economy has hit bottom but recovery has not yet arrived.

KEY PEOPLE IN THE BUSH ADMINISTRATION

J. Danforth Quayle: Vice President ... born 1947 ... member of House of Representatives from Indiana 1977-81 ... member of Senate 1981-88.

James A. Baker III: Secretary of State ... born 1930 ... White House Chief of Staff and Secretary of Treasury under Reagan ... Bush's top campaign strategist.

Nicholas F. Brady: Treasury Secretary ... born 1930 ... headed commission that studied 1987 stock market collapse.

Richard Cheney: Secretary of Defense ... born 1941 ... White House Chief of Staff under Ford ... member of House of Representatives from Wyoming 1978-89.

Richard Thornburgh: Attorney General ... born 1932 ... former Governor of Pennsylvania.

Manuel Lujan: Secretary of the Interior ... born 1928 ... member of House of Representatives from New Mexico 1968-88.

Edward Madigan: Secretary of Agriculture ... born 1936 ... member of House of Representatives from Illinois 1972-91.

Robert Mosbacher Sr.: Secretary of Commerce ... born 1927 ... prominent businessman.

Lynn Martin: Secretary of Labor ... born 1939 ... member of House of Representatives from Illinois 1981-91.

Dr. Louis Sullivan: Secretary of Health and Human Services ... born 1933 ... former president of Morehouse School of Medicine.

Jack Kemp: Secretary of Housing and Urban Development ... born 1935 ... member of House of Representatives from New York 1971-88.

Samuel Skinner: Secretary of Transportation ... born 1938 ... headed Regional Transportation Authority of Illinois.

James D. Watkins: Secretary of Energy ... born 1927 ... long naval career, member Joint Chiefs of Staff ... chairman of Presidential Commission on AIDS under Reagan.

Lamar Alexander: Secretary of Education ... born 1940 ... governor of Tennessee 1979-87 ... pioneered programs to improve education in Tennessee.

Edward J. Derwinski: Veterans Affairs Secretary ... born 1926 ... member of House of Representatives from Illinois 1959-83.

John Sununu: White House Chief of Staff ... born 1939 ... former governor of New Hampshire.

Richard Darman: Director, Office of Management and Budget ... Deputy Chief of Staff 1981-85 ... Deputy Treasury Secretary 1985-87.

Thomas Pickering: Ambassador to the United Nations ... born 1931 ... Foreign Service veteran.

Carla Hills: U.S. Trade Representative ... born 1934 ... former Secretary of Housing and Urban Development in Ford Administration.

Michael J. Boskin: Chairman of Council of Economic Advisers ... born 1945 ... former director of National Bureau of Economic Research.

Bob Martinez: Director of Office of National Drug Control Policy ... born 1934 ... governor of Florida 1987-91.

THINGS TO WATCH

Will President Bush be re-elected?
Will the U.S. pull out of the recession?

CENSUS

Whether there are 248.7 million or 253.8 million people living in the United States, the final 1990 census total will probably be decided in court. The Census Bureau acknowledges that they missed about 5.1 million people in 1990–mostly poor and minority-group members in large cities around the country. Secretary of Commerce Robert A. Mosbacher, who oversees the Census Bureau, decided, however, to reject recommendations to revise population figures, and that has big-city mayors around the country hopping mad. Since the census is used as the basis for allocating billions of dollars in Federal aid and in reapportioning political representation in Congress and at the state and local levels, the political ramifications of Mosbacher's decision are tremendous.

Complaints about the accuracy of the census are nothing new. Even back in 1790 President George Washington complained that the nation's first census failed to count everyone. The difference today is that advances in computer technology open up the possibility of compensating for human error to arrive at a more accurate figure. Some critics charge that Mosbacher's decision to stick with the original data is politically motivated, a way of minimizing the influence of big cities, which tend to vote Democratic. However, the Secretary insisted that his decision was based on a strict interpretation of the Constitution, which calls for an enumeration of the population, not a computer projection, and a fear that the use of computer projections might introduce still other errors into the data. Lawsuits have been filed, and the courts will make the final decision in due course.

No matter which numbers ultimately become official, the 1990 census reflects a dramatic growth in minority and immigrant populations in the U.S. The percentage of Asians in America almost doubled in the last decade, fueled by the entry of 3.8 million Asians and Pacific Islanders, many of them fleeing political unrest in Southeast Asia. Filipinos, Vietnamese, Koreans and Asian Indians more than doubled their numbers since 1980. The Latino population increased by 40 percent. The most ethnically diverse state in the nation is California: 69 percent white, 9.6 percent Asian, 7.4 percent black, 0.8 percent American Indian and 13.2 percent other ethnicities.

ETHNIC DIVERSITY IN THE U.S.

GROUP	1980	1990	CHANGE
White	83.1%	80.3%	-3.4%
Black	11.7%	12.1%	+3.4%
Latino	6.4%	9.0%	+40%
American Indian	0.6%	0.8 %	+33%
Asian	1.5%	2.9%	+93%
Other	3.0%	3.9%	+30%

AMERICA'S LARGEST CITIES

New York

1990 Census	7,322,564
Adjusted (+3.0%)	7,552,000

Los Angeles

1990 Census	3,485,398
Adjusted (+5.1%)	3,671,000

Chicago

1990 Census	2,783,726
Adjusted (+2.6%)	2,857,000

Houston

1990 Census	1,630,553
Adjusted (+5.0%)	1,716,000

CANADA

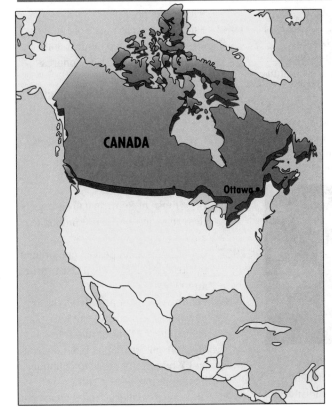

Prime Minister Brian Mulroney with President Bush in Washington, D.C.

Canadian Prime Minister Brian Mulroney faces a serious political challenge in keeping Canada together. Nationalism and separatism in the French-speaking Quebec province have been a dominant feature of Canadian politics for 30 years. The Quebecois fear that assimilation into English-speaking North America will destroy their culture and language. Efforts to placate Quebec's fears through a package of constitutional amendments, known as the Meech Lake Accords, collapsed in 1990 when the provincial premiers of Manitoba and New Brunswick refused to ratify the amendments.

Following rejection, separatist sentiment in Quebec gained momentum. Quebec's ruling Liberal Party, led by Robert Bourassa, issued an ultimatum threatening to hold a referendum on secession by the fall of 1992 if greater autonomy for Quebec is not granted.

Meanwhile, Prime Minister Mulroney is desperately trying to hammer out some kind of compromise. But his efforts are running into serious problems. Many English-speaking Canadians resent Quebec's nationalist demands and are in no mood for compromise. The economy is in terrible shape and Mulroney is taking the blame. A highly touted free-trade agreement with the U.S. in 1988 hasn't brought the promised economic benefits. Instead, factories have been shut down, unemployment has grown and the federal deficit seems stuck at $30 billion. An unpopular sales tax imposed last December and high interest rates also contribute to Mulroney's troubles. Polls show that his popular support has dwindled to less than 20 percent, which makes it very difficult for him to exert the necessary leadership to keep Canada intact.

WHO'S WHO

Brian Mulroney: Prime Minister...born 1939 ...leader of Progressive Conservative Party.

CHRONOLOGY

1960 Movement for French-Canadian rights begins in Quebec province.

1963 Front for the Liberation of Quebec (F.L.Q.) begins terrorist attacks.

1967 French President Charles de Gaulle visits Quebec and stirs separatist sentiment when he says, "Long live free Quebec!"

1968 Liberal Pierre Elliot Trudeau elected Prime Minister. The separatist Parti Quebecois (P.Q.) organized.

1969 Trudeau pushes through legislation making Canada officially bilingual.

1970 F.L.Q. terrorists kidnap two hostages and murder one of them. Trudeau invokes War Measures Act.

1976 The P.Q.'s Rene Levesque becomes provincial premier in Quebec.

1979 Liberals lose national elections. Trudeau is replaced by Conservative Joseph Clark.

1980 Trudeau returns as prime minister. Quebec voters reject separatism in special referendum.

1982 Trudeau implements a new federal constitution over objections of Quebec.

1984 Trudeau retires. Conservative Brian Mulroney takes power.

1987 Mulroney summons provincial premiers to conference at Meech Lake resort to discuss constitutional revisions that would decentralize powers and satisfy concerns of French Quebec. Agreement on constitutional amendments dubbed "Meech Lake Accords." Ratification by all provinces required by June 1990.

1988 Mulroney and President Ronald Reagan negotiate free-trade agreement.

1989 Mulroney re-elected. Separatist sentiment is rekindled in Quebec.

1990 Prime ministers of provinces of Manitoba and New Brunswick refuse to endorse Meech Lake Accords. Separatist sentiment in Quebec grows. Constitutional crisis looms.

1991 Separatist sentiment continues to grow. Quebec's ruling Liberal Party endorses ultimatum calling for Canada to grant greater autonomy to Quebec, or referendum on secession will be held. Mulroney's popularity plummets.

THINGS TO WATCH

Will Canada be torn by constitutional crisis? Will Quebec secede?

NICARAGUA

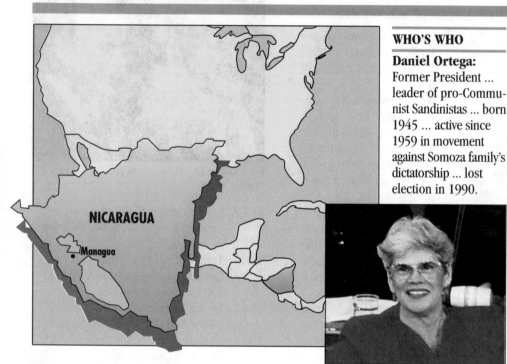

NICARAGUA

Managua

WHO'S WHO

Daniel Ortega:
Former President ... leader of pro-Communist Sandinistas ... born 1945 ... active since 1959 in movement against Somoza family's dictatorship ... lost election in 1990.

Violeta Chamorro: President ... born 1929 ... leader of U.N.O. (National Opposition Union), coalition of 14 parties ... publisher of *La Prensa*, Nicaragua's leading nongovernment newspaper ... widow of Pedro Joaquin Chamorro, liberal opponent of Somoza, assassinated in 1978.

CHRONOLOGY

1927-1933	Augusto Cesar Sandino leads unsuccessful peasant uprising.
1934	Sandino assassinated.
1936	Anastasio Somoza Garcia seizes power.
1956	Anastasio Somoza Garcia assassinated.
1961	Luis Somoza takes over. Sandinista National Liberation Front formed.
1966	Anastasio Somoza Debayle becomes dictator.
1979	Somoza overthrown. Sandinistas take power, ally with Cuba and Soviet Union.
1980	U.S. warns Nicaragua not to aid rebels in El Salvador. Somoza assassinated while in exile in Paraguay.
1981	Daniel Ortega emerges as top Nicaraguan leader. President Ronald Reagan decides to supply Contras with weapons.
1982	Sandinistas declare state of emergency. First battle between Contras and Sandinistas occurs. U.S. Congress restricts aid to Contras.
1983	Congress votes $24 million Contra-aid package.
1984	C.I.A. role in mining Nicaraguan harbors revealed. Congress rejects aid to Contras.
1985	Congress votes $27 million in non-military aid to Contras.
1986	U.S. House of Representatives rejects Reagan request for $100 million to aid Contras.
1987	Central American peace plan, drafted by Costa Rican President Oscar Arias, announced.
1989	Central American presidents reach new peace agreement, call for disbanding of Contras and free elections in Nicaragua. U.S. Congress and White House agree to continue humanitarian aid to Contras.
1990	Opposition candidate Violeta Chamorro wins surprise landslide election victory over Sandinista candidate Ortega. Ortega abides by election results but pledges to defend revolution's gains. After much discussion, Contras disarm. Sandinista-led unions stage strikes, demanding large wage increases to offset inflation and impeding Chamorro's efforts to return nationalized property to previous owners.
1991	Chamorro continues to move cautiously to privatize economy. Sandinista strikes continue and Party congress is planned to revamp leadership. Former Contra leader Enrique Bermudez is murdered in Managua.

THINGS TO WATCH

Will Chamorro hold her coalition together? Will the Sandinistas impede Chamorro's policies?

President Violeta Chamorro's first year in power has not been easy. The pro-Communist Sandinistas who ruled Nicaragua for 11 years are still the largest single political party in the country and are determined to block any efforts to undo agrarian reforms or health and social programs instituted while they held power. Chamorro's own National Opposition Union (U.N.O.) coalition comprises 14 ideologically disparate parties, ranging from far right to far left, and she's having difficulty keeping them together.

Chamorro's greatest achievement has been defusing the military situation. She got the Contras to lay down their arms and cut the Popular Army, still controlled by the Sandinistas, from 80,000 to 28,000 troops. But the nation's economic situation is still a disaster. Estimates of unemployment range from 25 to 50 percent, inflation is more than 3000 percent per year, and economic assistance from the U.S. has been delayed. Chamorro is desperately seeking international support to keep Nicaragua's experiment in democracy afloat.

EL SALVADOR

Advancing government troops, one with an M-60 machine gun, in position against F.M.L.N. rebels.

EL SALVADOR
• San Salvador

Civil war has ravaged this tiny country for more than 11 years. Nearly 75,000 people have died and half a million have been displaced by the war. Since 1980, the U.S. has pumped in more than $3.3 billion in aid to defeat the rebels trying to overthrow the Salvadoran government. United Nations-sponsored negotiations during the past year seem to have made progress. Now that the cold war is over, rebel leaders have renounced Marxism and the government has taken steps to revamp the military. A tentative peace agreement was reached in April 1991, and there is hope that this seemingly endless war will soon stop.

WHO'S WHO

Roberto d'Aubuisson: Right-wing political leader ... born 1943 ... spent 20 years in Salvadoran military ... founder of Alianza Republicana Nacionalista (ARENA) ... widely considered to be real power behind President Alfredo Cristiani.

Alfredo Cristiani: President ... born 1947 ... former champion athlete ... successful businessman ... elected 1989 as candidate of right-wing ARENA party.

POLITICAL ORGANIZATIONS

Alianza Republicana Nacionalista (ARENA): Rightist party ... founded and led behind the scenes by Roberto d'Aubuisson.
Christian Democrats: Moderate party ... backed by U.S ... held power 1984-89 ... lost election in 1989.
Democratic Convergence: Socialist coalition.
Farabundo Marti National Liberation Front(F.M.L.N.): Coalition of five Marxist guerrilla groups.

CHRONOLOGY

1932 Peasant leader Farabundo Marti organizes unsuccessful revolt against wealthy landowners.
1933-1972 Army and wealthy families rule the country.
El Salvador becomes prosperous coffee exporter, but peasants remain in poverty.
1972 Jose Napoleon Duarte elected president, but military prevents him from taking office.
1973-1978 Duarte flees into exile. Opposition to military regime mounts.
1979 Military coup staged by reformist army officers. Moderate military-civilian junta set up with U.S. backing.
1980 Most civilian junta members resign after army blocks reforms. Leftist guerrillas unite to form Farabundo Marti National Liberation Front (F.M.L.N.). Duarte joins new junta, which pushes for land reform. Right-wing death squads attack critics of regime. Archbishop Oscar Romero assassinated. Four American women missionaries murdered by death squads.
1981 F.M.L.N. receives aid from Cuba and Nicaragua and launches major offensive. U.S. aid to government increases sharply. Roberto d'Aubuisson founds rightist Republican Nationalist Alliance (ARENA).
1982 Right-wing ARENA party wins elections, controls National Assembly and suspends land reform.
1984 Moderate Jose Napoleon Duarte elected president.
1989 Negotiations with guerrillas collapse. ARENA candidate Alfredo Cristiani wins presidential election. Rebels launch massive offensive in November. Right-wing death squads murder six Jesuit priests.
1990 Former President Duarte dies. Government and rebels agree to negotiate. U.S. military assistance is slashed after government moves slowly in bringing murderers of Jesuits to justice. Rebels launch new offensive.
1991 President George Bush resumes military aid to El Salvador after rebels shoot down U.S. helicopter and murder captured crew members. U.N.-sponsored negotiations continue amid high hopes of achieving cease-fire. ARENA party wins March elections but loses parliamentary majority. Leftist politicians gain 12 percent of the vote and take seats in parliament for first time since civil war began. Rebels and government negotiators announce tentative peace agreement.

THINGS TO WATCH

Will negotiations succeed in ending the war? Will hard-line military officers resist a negotiated settlement?

CUBA PANAMA

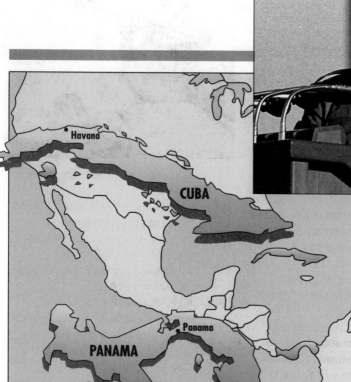

Cuban President Fidel Castro addresses a crowd in Havana on the 37th anniversary of the start of his revolution.

Time seems to be running out for Castro's revolution. Rejecting Mikhail Gorbachev's *glasnost* and *perestroika*, Castro adopted the defiant slogan of "Socialism or Death." But the collapse of Communism in Eastern Europe and the upheavals in the Soviet Union have caused a sharp decline in trade and subsidies. In late 1990, Castro declared a "special period in time of peace" — a devastating austerity program, that has sent Cuba into a headlong retreat from the 20th century. Horse-drawn carts and oxen are replacing automobiles and tractors. Seven hundred thousand bicycles are being imported to replace motor vehicles.

Castro talks of "perfecting Communism." Parliamentary democracy is ruled out, but internal party practices may be liberalized and official atheism relaxed. But as hardships and disillusionment grow, it will take more than such window dressing to keep the regime afloat.

WHO'S WHO

Fidel Castro: President and party leader ... born 1927 ... overthrew Batista dictatorship in 1959 ... tried to export guerrilla-style revolutionary movements to other Latin countries.

CHRONOLOGY

1953 Fidel Castro leads unsuccessful revolt against dictatorship of Fulgencio Batista.
1956 Castro begins new revolt.
1959 Batista overthrown; Castro takes power.
1961 Bay of Pigs invasion by U.S.-backed anti-Castro exiles ends in defeat.
1962 Cuban missile crisis: Soviets withdraw missiles from Cuban installations.
1967 Cuban hero Ernesto "Che" Guevara killed while leading guerrilla forces in Bolivia.
1975 Cuban forces sent to aid revolutionary regime in Angola.
1980 Thousands of refugees flee Cuba during Mariel boatlift.
1988 Cuba agrees to withdraw from Angola.
1989 Withdrawal from Angola begins.
1990 Castro cracks down on human-rights activists, imposes draconian austerity.
1991 Party members prepare for special Party Congress to map new course for Cuban Communism.

More than a year after the U.S. invasion, Panama is still plagued by serious problems. The new regime was shaken by a December 1990 coup attempt by former troops of Manuel Noriega. The loyalty of the national police force to the democratic regime headed by President Guillermo Endara is in doubt. Economic reconstruction has progressed at a snail's pace, and the Panama Canal is falling into disrepair. President Endara's popularity has shriveled to 14 percent. U.S. aid is sorely needed to keep the fragile Panamanian democracy afloat.

WHO'S WHO

Guillermo Endara: President ... born 1936 ... leader of Democratic Alliance of Civic Opposition (A.D.O.C.).
Manuel Noriega: Deposed dictator ... born 1934 ... captured by U.S. military forces during 1989 invasion ... currently facing drug charges in Florida.

CHRONOLOGY

1903 Panama, backed by U.S., revolts against Colombia; gives U.S. permission to build Panama Canal.
1914 Panama Canal opens.
1968 Brig. Gen. Omar Torrijos takes power.
1977 U.S. and Panama sign treaty to end American control of canal by 1999.
1979 Panama Canal Zone transferred to Panama.
1981 Torrijos dies in airplane crash.
1983 Manuel Noriega emerges as de facto ruler of Panama.
1988 Noriega indicted on drug trafficking charges in U.S. Reagan Administration imposes economic sanctions in effort to force Noriega from office.
1989 *May:* Fraud and violence mar presidential election.
December: U.S. troops invade Panama, capture Noriega and disperse Noriega's forces. Guillermo Endara and other rightful victors in May election take power.
1990 U.S. court proceedings against Noriega continue. Endara asks U.S. help in putting down coup attempt by pro-Noriega military men.
1991 Economic and political difficulties continue as Endara's popularity plummets.

HAITI

CENTRAL AMERICA & THE CARIBBEAN

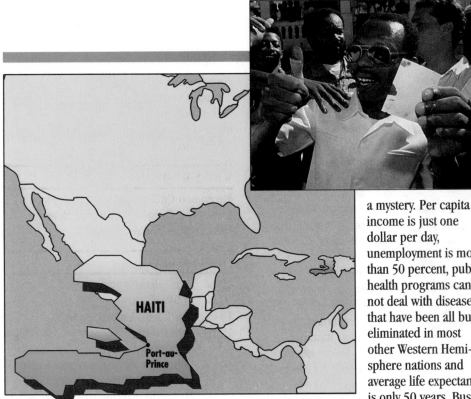

This desperately poor, tiny nation is still struggling to overcome the horrible legacy of the corrupt Duvalier family dictatorship, which controlled the country for nearly 30 years until it was overthrown in 1986. The Rev. Jean-Bertrand Aristide, a Roman Catholic priest who had been expelled from his Church order for his leftist views, was overwhelmingly elected president in December 1990 in the only truly democratic election in Haiti's history. In January Roger Lafontant, former leader of the dreaded Tonton Macoutes, Duvalier's secret police, led a coup attempt to block Aristide from taking office and "save" Haiti from Communism. Thousands of Aristide's supporters poured out of the slums of Port-au-Prince and marched on the presidential palace to defend Haiti's newborn democracy. Soon thereafter, loyalist troops intervened to crush the coup.

Aristide promised to bring the Tonton Macoutes to justice and promptly purged the army of high-ranking military officers whose loyalties to democracy were suspect. Aristide's plans for dealing with the grueling economic poverty in Haiti, however, remain

a mystery. Per capita income is just one dollar per day, unemployment is more than 50 percent, public health programs cannot deal with diseases that have been all but eliminated in most other Western Hemisphere nations and average life expectancy is only 50 years. Businessmen are uneasy about Aristide's radicalism and strong Marxist support. The poor are filled with high expectations for a better future. Haiti's experiment with democracy will have tough going in the days ahead.

WHO'S WHO

Rev. Jean-Bertrand Aristide: President ... born 1953 ... leftist Roman Catholic priest ... expelled from Church order because of his "class struggle" beliefs.

CHRONOLOGY

1957 Francois "Papa Doc" Duvalier becomes president.

1964 Duvalier declares himself "president for life."

1971 Duvalier dies, succeeded by his son, 19-year-old Jean-Claude "Baby Doc" Duvalier.

1971- Baby Doc maintains dictatorial rule,
1986 backed up by Tonton Macoutes. Haiti remains one of most impoverished nations in Latin America.

1986 *January:* Anti-government unrest erupts.
February: Duvalier flees to exile in

France. Three-man junta, led by Lieut. Gen. Henri Namphy, takes control.
October: First national election in 30 years chooses Constituent Assembly to draft new constitution. Voter turnout is light.

1987 *March:* Voters approve new constitution.
June: Namphy's troops try to control election. Rioting breaks out, 30 people killed.
November: Government-backed thugs disrupt elections, attack voters with guns and machetes, killing 34. U.S. suspends aid to junta.

1988 *January:* New election boycotted by most opposition parties. Leslie Manigat elected president.
June: Military coup overthrows Manigat, returns Namphy to power.
September: Coup deposes Namphy. Lieut. Gen. Prosper Avril, former aide to the Duvaliers, takes over.

1989 *April:* General Avril survives attempted coup.

1990 *January:* Avril imposes state of siege.
March: Anti-Avril demonstrations erupt. Avril resigns, goes into exile in U.S. Maj. Gen. Herard Abraham takes over, promising transition to civilian government. Supreme Court Justice Ertha Pascal-Trouillot becomes provisional president.
December: Rev. Jean-Bertrand Aristide, left-wing priest, wins presidency.

1991 *January:* Roger Lafontant, former leader of Tonton Macoutes, leads coup attempt. Thousands of Aristide's supporters take to streets. Loyalist military forces led by General Abraham quash coup.
February: Aristide inaugurated, promising to bring Tonton Macoute thugs to justice.

THINGS TO WATCH

Will Aristide hold power?
Will relations between Haiti and U.S. improve?

BRAZIL

BRAZIL

• Brasilia

When President Fernando Collor de Mello took office in March 1990 as Brazil's first democratically elected president since 1960, he promised to lick the nation's serious economic problems within a year and lift the country into the ranks of the rich industrialized nations. Collor staffed his economics ministry with university professors espousing novel, quick-fix tactics for Brazil's runaway inflation (over 1,000 percent a year). On his second day in office, Collor froze more than $100 billion in Brazilian bank accounts. The experimental policies were a dismal failure. Not only did inflation persist, but the Brazilian economy plunged into its worst recession in history. Industrial output fell by 8.6 percent, and the gross domestic product declined by 4.6 percent —

the worst since official recordkeeping began. Brazil's foreign debt has risen to $122 billion — the largest among developing nations. In early 1991, the government imposed wage and price controls in a desperate effort to rein in inflation, but these measures were largely ignored and prices rose by 80 percent anyhow in a single month.

More and more people have to choose between paying rent and buying food. In Brazil's largest city, Sao Paulo, impoverished families live in makeshift shelters under bridges and viaducts so that they can spend what little money they have on food for their children rather than rent.

Big-city crime and poverty, already at crisis proportions when the new administration took office, have become even worse. Thousands of street children, turned loose by their families, are forced into lives of crime and violence. Some businessmen, fearful that rampant crime will ruin business, have recruited "death squads" to drive the criminals away. These squads terrorize, beat and even kill young street kids, all in the name of law and order.

After his first year in power, Collor fired his economic advisers and appointed more conservative, conventional economists to restore confidence in the Brazilian economy. He also joined with the presidents of Argentina, Paraguay and Uruguay in taking the first steps to set up a South American

common market that would stretch from the Equator to the Antarctic. Whether or not Collor can turn things around will have important implications for the future of Brazil's fledgling democracy.

WHO'S WHO

Fernando Collor de Mello: President ... born 1949 ... leader of National Renewal Party ... moderate socialist.

CHRONOLOGY

1942 Brazil declares war against Germany in World War II.

1945 Brazil joins United Nations.

1960 National capital is relocated from Rio de Janeiro to newly constructed city of Brasilia, deep in Amazon region.

1964 Military overthrows democratically elected leftist regime of Joao Goulart.

1985 Generals transfer power to civilians. Electoral college selects Tancredo Neves as president to preside over four-year transition period to full democracy. Neves dies before taking office; vice president Jose Sarney becomes president.

1988 Brazil faces worldwide criticism for policies deemed likely to destroy Amazon rain forest.

1989 Economic situation worsens. Brazil holds first democratic presidential election since 1960.

1990 Fernando Collor de Mello inaugurated as president, promising swift action to end Brazil's disastrous four-digit inflation rate.

1991 Collor's economic shock treatments fail to cure inflation problems. Economy plunges into worst-ever recession. Collor replaces key economic officials to restore faith in government, promises more conventional approach.

THINGS TO WATCH

Will Brazil's economic situation improve?

ARGENTINA

Buenos Aires

The regime of President Carlos S. Menem continues to face grave difficulties in Argentina. Menem managed to rein in partially the hyperinflation that was threatening to destroy the Argentine economy when he took power in June 1989. But in January 1991 another round of hyperinflation threatened when the Argentine currency, the austral, suddenly lost more than 27 percent of its value against the U.S. dollar in just four days. Menem reshuffled his cabinet, replacing his economics minister and promising to "dollarize" the economy by printing new australs in the future only if U.S. dollar reserves held by Argentina's central bank increase by a corresponding amount.

In December 1990 dissident military units staged a bloody coup attempt, briefly seizing army headquarters in Buenos Aires. In an effort to mollify the military, Menem pardoned six high-ranking officers who had been imprisoned for human rights crimes committed during the "dirty war" against leftists and other critics of the military dictatorship that ruled the country in the 1970's. Meanwhile, the Menem regime has been shaken by corruption charges. Two of the president's closest aides and several close relatives have been accused of soliciting bribes. His son, Carlos Jr., has been linked to a suspected drug and money-laundering kingpin. Menem declared a "moral emergency" and promised an all-out campaign to root out corruption.

WHO'S WHO

Carlos Saul Menem: President ... born 1931 ... leader of Justicialist Party (Peronist) ... son of Syrian immigrants ... born a Moslem, converted to Roman Catholicism ... imprisoned for five years during military dictatorship.

CHRONOLOGY

1943 Military dictatorship takes power. Juan Domingo Peron holds posts of vice president, minister of war and secretary of labor and social welfare. U.S. and Britain refuse to recognize new regime, branding it antidemocratic and pro-Fascist.

1945 Argentina declares war on Germany and is promptly recognized by U.S.

1946 Peron becomes president.

1952 Peron re-elected.

1955 Peron ousted, goes into exile.

1973 Peron returns as president.

1974 Peron dies; his wife, Maria Estela (Isabel) Peron, becomes president.

1976 Mrs. Peron ousted by military.

1976- Military dictatorship rules with iron
1983 hand, waging "dirty war" against opponents. Nine thousand people disappear.

1982 Argentina suffers humiliating defeat by British Navy in Falklands War.

1983 Military transfers power to civilian government. Political prisoners freed. Raul Alfonsin elected president.

1987 Army officers mutiny over imprisonment of military men for human rights crimes committed during "dirty war."

1988 Similar mutinies break out in January and December.

1989 Economic situation deteriorates. Peronist candidate, Carlos Saul Menem, elected president. Country prepares for first peaceful transfer of power between elected civilian presidents from rival political parties in 60 years. Inflation surges out of control and food riots erupt. Menem pardons "dirty war" human rights criminals.

1990 Economic problems continue to worsen and social unrest grows. Austerity measures introduced. Menem's authority weakens and military officers attempt coup in December.

1991 Corruption scandals grow, including accusations against members of Menem's own family. Menem pardons and releases imprisoned military leaders convicted of human rights violations during "dirty war."

THINGS TO WATCH

Will Argentine economic and social problems be solved?
Will Menem stay in power?
Will military leaders interfere with civilian rule?

UNITED KINGDOM

London

Margaret Thatcher dominated British politics for more than a decade. Her abrasive style and austere policy decisions severely eroded her popularity in the late 1980's. By April 1990 her popularity had sunk to the lowest level ever recorded for a British prime minister. By November 1990 Thatcher had lost the support of her own Conservative Party and was forced to step down.

Thatcher was known as the "Iron Lady" because of her unwavering determination. Eventually this determination proved her undoing. In foreign affairs, she isolated her government by taking a go-slow attitude on key aspects of the European Community's market-integration plan for 1992 (especially the idea of setting up a single European currency) and on German reunification after the fall of the Berlin Wall.

But it was the poll tax at home that really got her into trouble. She pushed through a controversial tax change to finance local governments, replacing local property taxes with an extremely regressive per capita tax on each adult living in a household. It touched off some of the angriest rioting in Britain in modern times. Then the economy slipped into a serious recession, inflation rose sharply and unemployment grew. Conservative politicians decided that only a fresh face could revive party fortunes. Thatcher was ousted, and John Major, a low-key party stalwart who had been in charge of public spending under Thatcher, was chosen as the new prime minister. Major continued to oppose any precipitous moves toward a single EC currency, but instead of going it alone he began lining up support from other countries. He announced plans to repeal the hated poll tax, though the plan he introduced still retained certain key poll tax features.

Major's strong stand against Iraqi aggression in Kuwait, his working-class background and affable nature quickly won him widespread public support, but as the economy continued its plunge into recession this popularity quickly evaporated. With a new election expected sometime in 1992, Major dropped interest rates in an effort to revive the economy. Whether the economy pulls out of the doldrums quickly will have a big impact on the Conservatives' chances of remaining in power.

WHO'S WHO

John Major: Prime Minister ... born 1943 ... Conservative Party leader ... working-class background ... has only secondary-school education, no university training ... youngest prime minister in nearly 100 years.
Margaret Thatcher: Former Prime Minister ... born 1925 ... pursued conservative economic policies ... led the country 1979-1990.

CHRONOLOGY

1979 Margaret Thatcher becomes first woman to head a modern European government.

1980- Thatcher's popularity drops during
1981 recession. Squabbles break out in her Cabinet. Polls show her most unpopular prime minister in British history.

1982 Falklands War breaks out with Argentina. Thatcher rallies nation and popularity soars.

1983 Thatcher wins re-election.

1984 I.R.A. bomb explodes at Grand Hotel during Conservative conference. Thatcher and Cabinet members escape, but four others are killed.

1984- Thatcher takes tough stance against
1985 coal miners' strike.

1986 Striking printers are defeated at Wapping printing plant owned by Rupert Murdoch, due to Thatcher's anti-picketing legislation.

1987 Thatcher elected for third time; becomes longest-serving British prime minister in 20th century.

1989 Thatcher celebrates 10th anniversary in office; takes cautious attitude on German reunification following collapse of Berlin Wall.

1990 Thatcher's popularity plunges during controversy over newly imposed poll tax; anti-tax riots erupt around the country. Economy drifts into recession. Britain becomes strongest supporter of United States-led efforts to drive Iraq out of Kuwait.

1991 Recession deepens. Thatcher resigns. John Major becomes prime minister, pledges to repeal poll tax.

THINGS TO WATCH

Will the economy turn around?
Will Conservatives remain in power?

FRANCE

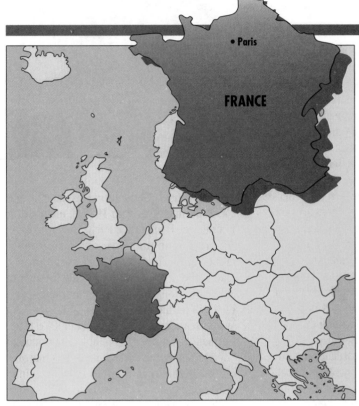

A fter 10 years in power, France's President Francois Mitterrand is the West's senior statesman. In France, some hail Mitterrand for restoring the nation as a world power. Others denounce him for abandoning Socialist ideals to remain in office. Mitterrand will retire at the end of his current term in 1995, or perhaps sooner, and younger Socialist leaders are already jockeying for position to succeed him. The Socialists originally came to power in 1981 on a program of economic and social reforms, which they were forced to abandon by the mid-1980's. In many respects Socialist austerity policies in France today are hardly discernible from those that might have been introduced by conservative parties.

After the fall of Communism in Eastern Europe in 1989, France seemed politically adrift, without a clear policy orientation. But Mitterrand quickly adapted, reinforcing ties with Germany, bolstering France's leadership role in the European Community, improving relations with the Soviet Union, making a bid for influence among emerging democracies in Eastern Europe — especially Rumania —

and taking a tough stance against Iraqi aggression in the Middle East.

At home the Socialists face an uncertain future as the nation is beset by high unemployment, corruption scandals, urban decline and growing racism against North African immigrants. In May 1991 Mitterrand replaced Prime Minister Michel Rocard, a moderate Socialist with presidential ambitions, with Edith Cresson, a Mitterrand loyalist and the first woman in French history to hold such a high post. Whether the Socialists can cling to power after Mitterrand steps aside remains to be seen.

WHO'S WHO

Francois Mitterrand: President ... born 1916 ... elder statesman of Socialist Party ... elected president in 1981 and 1988.
Edith Cresson: Prime Minister ... born 1934 ... Mitterrand loyalist ... first woman prime minister.
Michel Rocard: Former Prime Minister ... born 1930 ... moderate member of Socialist Party ... possible candidate for president.
Jacques Chirac: Former Prime Minister 1986-88, 1974-76 ... born 1932 ... leader of conservative Rassemblement pour la Republic ... currently mayor of Paris.

CHRONOLOGY

1944	Allied forces liberate France from Nazi occupation.
1946-1954	French troops fight Communist insurgency in Indochina.
1949	France joins NATO.
1954	France loses war against Communist rebels in Indochina.
1957	France joins European Common Market.
1958	Charles de Gaulle becomes president.
1962	Algeria wins independence from France.
1968	Student demonstrations and massive workers' strikes erupt.
1969	De Gaulle resigns as president; succeeded by Georges Pompidou.
1974	Pompidou dies; Gaullist Party splits into rival groups. Valery Giscard d'Estaing of Independent Republican Party takes presidency.
1981	Socialist Party wins elections. Francois Mitterrand inaugurated as president.
1986	Socialists lose control of parliament. Conservative Jacques Chirac becomes prime minister. Mitterrand continues as president.
1988	Mitterrand re-elected president. Socialists win plurality in parliament, but not majority. Chirac resigns as prime minister, replaced by moderate Socialist Michel Rocard. Labor unrest breaks out among public-sector employees.
1989	France celebrates bicentennial of French Revolution. Extreme right-wing party makes inroads among working-class voters with appeals to anti-immigrant sentiments.
1990	French leaders try to adjust to change in political situation in Europe following collapse of Communism in Eastern Europe.
1991	France supports United Nations mobilization in Persian Gulf. Mitterrand names Edith Cresson as France's first woman prime minister, replacing Michel Rocard.

THINGS TO WATCH

Who will succeed Mitterrand?
Will the Socialists retain power?
What role will France play in the post-cold war world order?

GERMANY

Chancellor Helmut Kohl

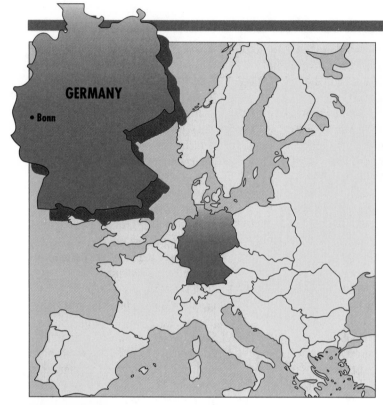

The euphoria that erupted when the Berlin Wall crumbled, carrying the people of East and West Germany toward national reunification with bewildering speed, is now long gone. Chancellor Helmut Kohl led his Christian Democratic Union (C.D.U.) coalition to an overwhelming victory in the first all-German elections in December 1990 with visions of a new prosperity for everyone and a promise that taxes would not be raised to pay for reunification. But cold reality soon set in; there would be no economic miracles for Germany. The costs of reunification had been seriously underestimated (the figure may reach one trillion dollars over the next decade). Kohl was forced to break his campaign pledge, and new taxes to finance reunification went into effect in June, causing tax protesters to besiege the chancellor with chants of "liar, liar." An angry electorate threw the Christian Democrats out of power in Kohl's home state for the first time in 44 years.

Instead of prosperity, the former East Germany has plunged into economic depression. Some experts predict unemployment might reach 50 percent in eastern Germany,

and already crime, suicide and political discontent have begun to increase. More people are fleeing from the east to the west in search of jobs than before the Wall crumbled. Tensions between easterners and westerners are also growing, and commentators are beginning to talk about a "wall in the head" that still divides the country. Opposition to relocating the capital to Berlin, in accordance with the treaty of reunification, has presented a political embarrassment and upset easterners. Kohl's popularity in eastern Germany is now so low that he avoids public appearances in that part of the country.

Meanwhile, the popularity of Bjoern Engholm, the new leader of the opposition Social Democratic Party (S.P.D.), is soaring, and S.P.D. leaders are predicting victory in the next national elections in 1994. The S.P.D. now has a majority in the upper house of parliament and can veto government legislative proposals, forcing the C.D.U. to seek compromise solutions to political problems.

In Europe, Kohl's economic difficulties have lessened fears that Germany would dominate the European Community after the elimination of trade barriers in 1992. German hesitations to send combat troops to help liberate Kuwait have also undercut Germany's clout in the international arena.

WHO'S WHO

Helmut Kohl: Federal Chancellor (West Germany) ... born 1930 ... leader of Christian Democratic Union ... chancellor since 1982.

Hans-Dietrich Genscher: Foreign Minister (West Germany) ... born 1927 ... member of liberal Free Democratic Party.

Bjoern Engholm: Leader of Social Democratic Party ... born 1939 ... elected party leader May 1991 ... serves as state premier of Schleswig-Holstein and is member of upper house of parliament.

Willy Brandt: Former Chancellor (West Germany) ... born 1913 ... elder statesman of Social Democratic Party ... served as mayor of West Berlin when Berlin Wall went up in 1961.

Lothar De Maiziere: Former Prime Minister (East Germany) ... born 1940 ... leader of Christian Democrats ... allied with Helmut Kohl's Christian Democratic Union in West Germany ... after reunification, entered cabinet as minister without portfolio.

Wolfgang Schaeuble: Interior Minister ... born 1942 ... member of Christian Democratic Union ... being groomed as C.D.U. successor to Kohl.

CHRONOLOGY

1945 Nazi Germany surrenders to Allies. Britain, France, Soviet Union and U.S. occupy Germany, take joint control of Berlin.

1948 Soviet Union imposes Berlin Blockade, refusing passage to Berlin through Russian-occupied eastern Germany.

1949 Berlin Blockade lifted. East and West Germany established as separate countries.

1953 Soviet forces suppress revolt in East Germany.

1955 West Germany joins NATO; East Germany joins Warsaw Pact.

1958 Russia demands West withdraw from Berlin.

1961 Communists build Berlin Wall.

1969 Social Democrat Willy Brandt becomes chancellor of West Germany.

1971 Russia, Britain, France and U.S. sign agreement stabilizing status of West Berlin.

1973 East and West Germany sign agreement calling for closer ties.

1974 Brandt resigns as chancellor after revelations that close aide was spy for East Germany. Social Democrat Helmut Schmidt becomes chancellor.

1982 Schmidt and Social Democrats lose vote of confidence. Helmut Kohl of Christian Democratic Union heads new right-center coalition government.

1985 President Ronald Reagan provokes controversy by visiting Bitburg cemetery, where Nazi storm troopers are buried.

1987 Christian Democratic Union/Free Democratic Union coalition wins elections in West Germany. East German leader, Erich Honecker, rejects Mikhail Gorbachev's reform program.

1989 *July:* Hundreds of East Germans seek refuge at West Germany's embassy in Hungary.
September: Hungary allows thousands of East German refugees to depart for West Germany. New Forum, East German dissident group, holds founding conference.
October: Freedom trains, carrying East German refugees from West German embassies in Prague and Warsaw, permitted to pass through East Germany to West. East Germany celebrates its 40th anniversary. Prodemocracy demonstrations break out in Leipzig, East Germany, spread throughout country. Honecker resigns under pressure.
November 9: Berlin Wall falls.
December: Communist Party loses monopoly on power in East Germany.

1990 *March 18:* East Germany's first free elections bring right-center party to power, set stage for speedier German reunification.
May 5: "Four-plus-two" negotiations, involving the four occupying powers (Britain, France, Soviet Union and U.S.) plus the two German states, begin on future of united Germany.
May 31: Presidents George Bush and Mikhail Gorbachev meet at Washington summit, disagree strongly on whether unified Germany should be neutral or part of NATO. (Issue later resolved in favor of NATO membership for Germany.)
July 2: East and West German economies unified.
October 3: Germany becomes united nation for first time since end of World War II.
December 2: Promising prosperity for reunited Germany and no new taxes, Chancellor Helmut Kohl leads Christian Democratic Union coalition to overwhelming victory in first all-German elections.

1991 Kohl's popularity plunges as economic situation worsens. Germany balks at sending combat troops to join U.S.-led coalition in Persian Gulf; pledges financial support instead.

THINGS TO WATCH

Will the Christian Democrats remain in power?
Will the economic situation in eastern Germany improve?

Young demonstrators criticize the chancellor in Leipzig.

SOVIET UNION

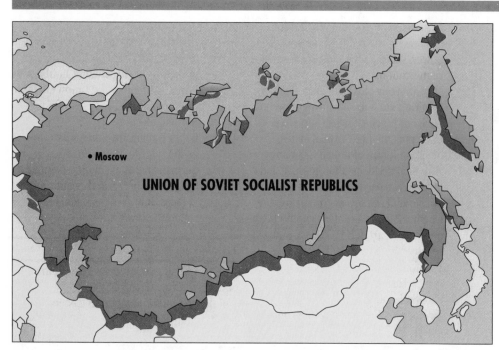

• Moscow

UNION OF SOVIET SOCIALIST REPUBLICS

E vents have moved fast and furious in the Soviet Union in the past year. Mikhail Gorbachev continued his desperate effort to block the centrifugal forces that seem to be pulling the Soviet Union apart. Gorbachev lunged from crisis to crisis, improvising political solutions without a master plan. At one point he moved to the right and made a deal with hard-liners, which prompted Foreign Minister Eduard Shevardnadze to resign in protest in December 1990 and warn of the possibility of a new dictatorship. Later Gorbachev moved to the left, reaching agreement with presidents of nine of the 15 Soviet republics (including Boris Yeltsin, the maverick ex-Communist president of the Russian republic) on a new Union treaty that would guarantee greater autonomy to local governments. But all this political maneuvering didn't lead to a stable political situation or improve Gorbachev's political control. On the eve of the signing of the new Union treaty in August 1991, Communist Party hard-liners staged a coup in Moscow to block the treaty and turn back the clock on the reforms introduced under Gorbachev's *perestroika* and *glasnost* policies. But the coup quickly collapsed as Yeltsin mobilized popular

resistance and rank-and-file members of the military and the K.G.B. refused to follow the orders of the coup leaders. When it was all over, Gorbachev was restored to power, but in a diminished capacity. Yeltsin's political influence was on the rise, and the Communist Party was relegated to the dustbin of history. Dramatic changes are still to come in the U.S.S.R. Another new Union treaty is being negotiated, which will grant even more autonomy to the republics. The Soviet economy remains a nightmare, and there are fears of hunger riots during the coming winter. The future is very much in doubt.

WHO'S WHO

Mikhail Gorbachev: President of Soviet Union ... born 1931 ... introduced *perestroika* and *glasnost* ... gave approval for satellite countries to democratize, shed Communist Party governments ... detained by hard-liners during 1991 coup attempt.
Eduard Shevardnadze: Former Foreign Minister ... born 1928 ... supports *glasnost* and *perestroika*.
Boris Yeltsin: President of Russian Federation ... born 1931 ... advocates accelerated

economic and political reforms ... leader of popular resistance to hard-line coup attempt.

KEY EVENTS IN THE GORBACHEV YEARS

1985
March 11: Gorbachev elected Communist Party General Secretary.
November: Geneva Summit. Gorbachev and President Ronald Reagan talk face to face for first time.

1986
April: World learns of accident at Chernobyl nuclear power plant.
October 11-12: Reykjavik Summit. Historic arms-control breakthrough collapses when Gorbachev demands end to S.D.I. (Star Wars) development and strict adherence to 1972 A.B.M. (Anti-Ballistic Missile) Treaty.
December: Prominent dissident Andrei Sakharov released from internal exile.

1987
June: Supreme Soviet passes legislation putting economic restructuring in place.
December 7-10: Washington Summit. Reagan and Gorbachev sign historic Intermediate-Range Nuclear Forces (I.N.F.) Treaty.

1988
February 11-26: Violent demonstrations erupt in Armenia. Demonstrators demand reunification with Nagorno-Karabakh Autonomous Region in neighboring Azerbaijan.
February 17: Radical reformer Boris Yeltsin removed from Politburo.
February 28: Thirty-two people die in ethnic clashes in Azerbaijan.
May 29-June 2: Moscow Summit. Reagan and Gorbachev exchange copies of ratified I.N.F. Treaty.
June 28-30: Gorbachev consolidates power at Communist Party conference.
September 30: Gorbachev further consolidates power in Kremlin shake-up. Gorbachev assumes presidency.
December 7: Gorbachev addresses United Nations General Assembly, announces unilateral Soviet cuts in conventional forces; returns abruptly to Moscow because of devastating earthquake in Soviet Armenia.

Thousands of jubilant Muscovites march to Red Square carrying a giant Russian tricolor flag, celebrating the failure of the three-day hard-line coup attempt.

1989

February 15: Soviet troops withdraw from Afghanistan.

March 26: Free elections held for Supreme Soviet seats.

April 3-5: Gorbachev visits Cuba, fails to convince Castro to accept liberalization policies.

April 25: Gorbachev forces mass resignation of 74 opponents at Central Committee meeting.

May 25: Gorbachev elected president.

July: Half-million coal miners strike over pay and living conditions.

August: Solidarity comes to power in Poland.

October: Hungarian Communists renounce Leninism.

November: Berlin Wall falls. Prodemocracy movement spreads to Bulgaria and Czechoslovakia.

December 7: Lithuania adopts multiparty system.

December 14: Andrei Sakharov dies.

December 22: Romanian dictator Ceaucescu overthrown.

1990

January 16: Virtual civil war breaks out between Azerbaijanis and Armenians; troops sent to restore order.

February 11: Ethnic violence flares in Tadzhikistan; troops rushed to Baku.

March 11: Lithuania declares independence.

March 13: Congress of People's Deputies approves plan to create stronger presidency and to end Communist monopoly on power.

March 14: Gorbachev elected president for five-year term.

March 31: Gorbachev begins crackdown on Lithuania.

May 31-June 3: Presidents Bush and Gorbachev hold summit in Washington, D.C.

June 29: Lithuania freezes independence legislation.

July 12: Following 28th Communist Party Congress, Yeltsin and other reformers resign party membership.

July 20: Government proposes 500-day economic reform program.

August 3: U.S.S.R. and U.S. issue joint denunciation of Iraqi invasion of Kuwait.

August 31: Gorbachev pulls back from radical reform proposals.

September 9: At Helsinki Summit Bush and Gorbachev reaffirm unity against Iraq.

September 21: Rumors of possible coup attempt against Gorbachev reported.

September 24: Gorbachev given emergency powers.

October 15: Gorbachev wins Nobel Peace Prize.

November 23: Agreement on new Union treaty reached with nine of fifteen Soviet republics.

December 2: Hard-liners appointed to key posts in Interior Ministry.

December 20: Foreign Minister Eduard Shevardnadze resigns, warns of coming dictatorship.

1991

January 2: Soviet troops crack down in Lithuania.

January 16: Last-minute Soviet diplomatic efforts to avoid war in Persian Gulf fail.

February 9: Ninety percent of Lithuania voters back secession.

March 1: Coal miners' strike begins.

March 3: Referendums in Latvia and Estonia back independence from Moscow.

May 5: Coal miners' strike ends; Kremlin agrees to surrender control of mines to Russian republic.

June 12: Yeltsin elected president of Russian republic in popular balloting.

August 19: Hard-liners stage coup. Yeltsin mobilizes popular resistance to coup.

August 21: Coup collapses.

August 22: Gorbachev returns to Moscow.

(See World News Briefs, pages 2-5, for complete coverage of the Soviet coup and aftermath.)

HISTORICAL CHRONOLOGY

1917	Russian Revolution is led by Vladimir Lenin.
1924	Lenin dies; Stalin takes over.
1938	Stalin purges old-line Bolshevik leaders.
1953	Stalin dies.
1955	Nikita Khrushchev reveals Stalin's crimes.
1956	Soviet troops crush rebellion in Hungary.
1962	U.S. and U.S.S.R. confront each other in Cuban Missile Crisis.
1964	Khrushchev removed; replaced by Leonid Brezhnev.
1968	Soviet troops suppress liberalization in Czechoslovakia.
1982	Brezhnev dies; succeeded by Yuri Andropov.
1984	Andropov dies; succeeded by Konstantin Chernenko.
1985	Chernenko dies; succeeded by Gorbachev.

THINGS TO WATCH

Will the Soviet Union stay as one country?
Will Gorbachev remain President?
Will the West bolster the Soviet Union with financial aid?

POLAND

Poland was the first East European nation to overthrow Communism, but its transition to democracy and a market economy has been no smoother than any other. The Solidarity government, led by Prime Minister Tadeusz Mazowiecki, imposed an economic shock-treatment program that caused falling real wages, a sharp decline in the standard of living and a drastic drop in industrial production. Solidarity leader Lech Walesa criticized Mazowiecki for proceeding too slowly with privatization of industry and for policies that hurt working people. After Gen. Wojciech Jaruzelski, a Communist-era holdover, resigned Poland's presidency, Walesa won an acrimonious presidential campaign, which split Solidarity and caused some of his old union colleagues to brand him a potential dictator. They are particularly concerned about Walesa's promises to "accelerate" economic reform by presidential decrees — a power not granted in the Polish constitution.

Walesa successfully secured a 50 percent reduction in Poland's debt to Western nations, and U.S. President George Bush granted Poland a 70 percent reduction in debt to the U.S. This gave Walesa some breathing room, but Poland still faces serious problems. Parliament, still controlled by former Communists and their supporters, has dissolved itself, with new elections set for fall 1991. Rival plans for economic reconstruction will be debated in the months ahead. The Polish people are getting restless with the slow process and discomforts of the transition to a market economy.

WHO'S WHO

Lech Walesa: President and Solidarity leader ... born 1943 ... trained as electrician ... founded Solidarity in 1980 ... arrested in 1981 ... received Nobel Peace Prize in 1983.

Gen. Wojciech Jaruzelski: Former President and former Communist Party leader ... born 1923 ... long military career ... took Party leadership following outbreak of labor unrest in early 1980s ... resigned Party membership in 1989.

Tadeusz Mazowiecki: Former Prime Minister ... born 1927 ... first non-Communist prime minister in 40 years ... prominent Roman Catholic intellectual and newspaper editor ... close adviser to Solidarity ... imprisoned during martial law imposed in December 1981.

CHRONOLOGY

1939 Germany and Soviets invade Poland; World War II breaks out.

1944 Soviets "liberate" Poland from Germany.

1949 Communists take power.

1956 Workers riot over wages and food prices.

1970 Workers riot over food-price increases; 45 killed.

1976 Workers strike against 60 percent food-price increases.

1980 One hundred percent increases in meat prices trigger massive strike wave. Workers led by Lech Walesa occupy Lenin Shipyard in Gdansk and demand free trade unions and political reform. Solidarity founded.

1981 Government imposes martial law, arresting thousands of Solidarity activists, including Walesa.

1982 Walesa released from prison.

1983 Government lifts martial law. Walesa wins Nobel Peace Prize.

1988 New strike wave erupts.

1989 Round-table discussions between Solidarity and Communist officials begin. Solidarity re-legalized, wins landslide election victory. Solidarity's Tadeusz Mazowiecki becomes prime minister. Jaruzelski resigns from Communist Party, remains president of Poland.

1990 Solidarity government institutes drastic economic reform program. Communist Party dissolves. Jaruzelski resigns presidency, succeeded by Lech Walesa. Solidarity splits during fractious presidential campaign.

1991 Poland seeks membership in European Community. New stock exchange opens in Warsaw. Poland wins debt reduction from Western powers.

THINGS TO WATCH

Will the Walesa government succeed in economic reform?
Will social unrest grow?

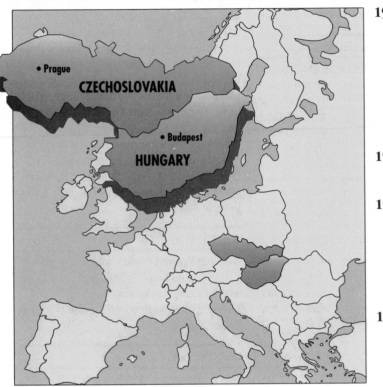

The post-Communist-era transition period has not been easy for Czechoslovakia. Following the fall of the Communist regime, disagreements soon broke out within the new government about how to proceed with privatization of the economy. By March 1991, Civic Forum, the reform organization that led the revolution, had split into two separate organizations: free marketers and social democrats. Ethnic tensions between Slovaks and Czechs surfaced, and a Slovakian separatist movement gained strength. President Vaclav Havel is trying to get the economy back on its feet and hopes to gain entrance to the European Community by the year 2000.

WHO'S WHO

Vaclav Havel: President ... born 1936 ... playwright and dissident leader.

CHRONOLOGY

1938 Nazi Germany seizes Czechoslovakia.
1945 Czechoslovakia regains independence.
1948 Communists take over.

1968 Liberal reforms begin in "Prague Spring." Soviet troops and forces from other Warsaw Pact countries invade.
1977 Charter 77, human rights group, forms.
1987 Miklos Jakes becomes new Communist Party leader. Charter 77 marks 10th anniversary.
1988 Charter 77 demonstrations mark 20th anniversary of Prague Spring. Anti-reformists control party.
1989 *February 21:* Vaclav Havel imprisoned for dissident activity.
May 17: Havel released.
November: Prodemocracy demonstrations spread. Top party leaders resign.
December: Communists abandon monopoly on power. Havel becomes president.
1990 New power-sharing plan gives Communists minority role in cabinet. Soviet troops begin withdrawal.
1991 Slovakian separatists gain strength as tensions between Slovaks and Czechs grow. Disagreements over privatization of economy leads to split in Civic Forum.

Hungary is also going through a difficult transition to a market economy. The collapse of the Soviet bloc's Comecom market has caused serious problems for industry in eastern Hungary. By contrast, firms located in western Hungary are experiencing a boom in trade with the West. The inflation rate is running at more than 30 percent annually, and many workers fear they will lose their jobs as more and more inefficient state enterprises are privatized. Prime Minister Jozsef Antall, leader of the conservative Hungarian Democratic Forum, has recovered from a bout with cancer and is trying to get Hungary into the European Community.

WHO'S WHO

Jozsef Antall: First freely elected prime minister in four decades ... born 1932 ... leader of Democratic Forum, center-right party.

CHRONOLOGY

1919 Communist revolution lasts for a few months before regime loses power.
1941 Hungary enters World War II as ally of Nazi Germany.
1944 Germany occupies Hungary.
1945 Hungary and Allies sign truce.
1946- Communists gain control of
1949 government.
1956 Hungarian Revolution: Russian tanks crush rebellion.
1968 Government adopts New Economic Mechanism, lifting trade restrictions, introducing productivity incentives and legalizing private services.
1982 Hungary joins International Monetary Fund.
1988 Reformers gain at Communist Party conference.
1989 Conservative hard-liners ousted from Central Committee; constitutional reforms and plans for multiparty parliament drafted; Communist Party renounces Leninism; hard-liners split to form orthodox Stalinist Party.
1990 First democratic elections since 1945 bring right-of-center coalition to power.
1991 Hungary asks to join European Community. Collapse of Eastern Europe's Comecon market causes serious economic problems. Inflation reaches 33 percent.

The revolutionary euphoria that engulfed this East European nation after the overthrow of the brutal regime of Nicolae Ceausescu has been supplanted by an atmosphere of crisis and confusion. Ethnic tensions erupt into violence in the streets. Pro-Fascist ideologies, dormant since World War II, have reappeared. There is growing mistrust of the ruling National Salvation Front, which includes many former Communists in its ranks and relies on heavyhanded tactics to keep control. Three factions compete for control within the military. Members of the Securitate, Ceausescu's dreaded secret police, still function openly in the state bureaucracy. The economic situation is even worse than it was in the final days of Ceausescu. Romanians have little historical experience with democracy, and the transition to a new post-Communist social order will not be smooth.

WHO'S WHO

Ion Iliescu: President ... born 1921 ... leader of National Salvation Front ... longtime friend of Mikhail Gorbachev.

CHRONOLOGY

1944 Soviet troops occupy country, overthrow pro-German government. Romania joins Allies.

1947 Romania becomes Communist country.

1962 Romanian Communists insist on independence from Moscow.

1965 Nicolae Ceausescu takes power, opens trade relations with West.

1987 Ceausescu introduces drastic austerity program.

1989 *November:* Ceausescu denounces prodemocracy movement.
December: Ceaucescu overthrown, flees capital, captured, tried and executed. National Salvation Front (N.S.F.) takes power. Civil war rages for several days.

1990 Communist Party dissolves. Opposition parties form to prepare for free elections. N.S.F. wins May elections.

1991 As political discontent grows, N.S.F. leaders convene special party conference to improve image and adopt social democratic program.

Bulgaria faces its worst economic crisis in history. In 1990 the Communist Party renamed itself "Socialist" and managed to win big in the May parliamentary elections. But the ex-Communists were unable to lead the country in a smooth transition to democracy, and the government was forced to resign in December 1990. A multiparty coalition government replaced it, led by Dimiter Popov, a lawyer without political affiliation who was trusted by all parties. New elections are planned, but meanwhile the economy is a mess. The crisis in the Persian Gulf made a bad situation worse. Iraq owed Bulgaria $1.2 billion, which it had agreed to pay off in oil exports. U.N. sanctions against Iraq cut off the shipments and cost Bulgaria dearly. The patience of the Bulgarian people is beginning to wear thin.

WHO'S WHO

Dimiter Popov: Prime Minister ... born 1927 ... lawyer with no party affiliation ... appointed interim prime minister.
Todor Zhivkov: Deposed hard-line Stalinist leader ... born 1911.

CHRONOLOGY

1939 Bulgaria enters World War II as ally of Nazi Germany.

1944 Soviet Army invades Bulgaria; coalition led by Bulgarian Communists overthrows pro-German government.

1946 Monarchy abolished; Communist leader Georgi Dimitrov becomes head of state.

1949 Dimitrov dies; succeeded by Vulko Chervenkov.

1952 Todor Zhivkov becomes Communist Party chief.

1989 Zhivkov forced from power by reform-minded Communist Politburo members.

1990 Communist Party changes its name to Bulgarian Socialist Party; wins parliamentary elections but is unable to rule effectively. Government resigns in December, and new multiparty cabinet takes over.

1991 Bulgarian economic situation worsens. Deposed dictator Zhivkov becomes first old-line Stalinist leader in Eastern Europe to face criminal charges since collapse of Communism in 1989.

YUGOSLAVIA

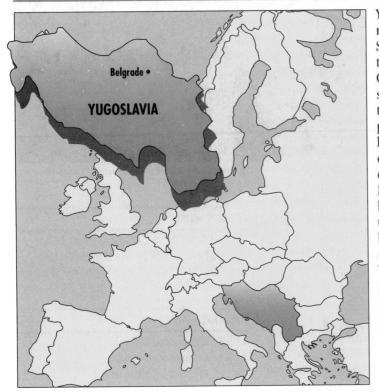

Yugoslavia today totters on the brink of civil war. Nationalist and ethnic unrest threatens to destroy a fragile national unity, which was never very strong under the best of conditions. Yugoslavia has always been an amalgam of diverse and sometimes antagonistic ethnic groups. Until his death in 1980, Marshal Josip Tito, Yugoslavia's national hero and longtime Communist leader, kept the ethnically divided nation united with his blueprint for decentralized political decision-making. He organized the country into six republics (Serbia, Croatia, Slovenia, Bosnia-Hercegovina, Montenegro and Macedonia) and two autonomous provinces located within Serbia (Vojvodina, an ethnic Hungarian enclave in the north, and Kosovo, an Albanian area in the south). But that political system has essentially fallen apart.

Non-Communist governments elected in the more prosperous republics of Croatia and Slovenia threaten to secede if they are not granted greater autonomy. They bristle at continued attempts by Slobodan Milosevic, a hard-line Stalinist who rules in Serbia,

Yugoslavia's largest republic, to impose Serbian hegemony on the other republics. If Croatia and Slovenia secede, Milosevic threatens to annex parts of those republics that have large concentrations of ethnic Serbians. In March, Milosevic brought the country to the brink of civil war by recalling Serbia's representatives in Yugoslavia's collective presidency and paralyzing its efforts to deal with secessionist threats. It was all part of an effort to goad the military, whose officer corps is 70 percent Serbian and Communist, into overthrowing the national government and suppressing the secessionist movements. But military leaders were afraid that their conscript army would disintegrate along ethnic lines and decided not to intervene, forcing the politicians to seek some kind of compromise to avert open civil war for the moment.

Prime Minister Ante Markovic is the only major political leader trying to maintain national unity, and his efforts have earned support from the Bush Administration. But Markovic's efforts to revive Yugoslavia's collapsed economy and to bring down the incredible 600 percent inflation rate have been hampered by the continuing civil strife.

CHRONOLOGY

1941 Military overthrows pro-German government; Nazi forces invade; Tito organizes resistance army called the Partisans.

1945 Yugoslavia emerges from World War II under Communist rule, with Tito as leader.

1948 Yugoslavia and Soviet Union sever relations because of ideological divergences.

1980 Tito dies.

1987 Wage controls provoke worker unrest.

1988 Austerity measures imposed. Prices soar. Workers protest, storm parliament. Serbian nationalism grows. Serbian protesters demand annexation of Kosovo, an Albanian ethnic area. Prime minister and cabinet resign amid economic chaos.

1989 Markovic named new premier of national government. Ethnic Albanians in Kosovo protest curbs on autonomy.

1990 Strikes and rioting break out in Kosovo. National Communist Party congress ends in disarray. Secession sentiment grows in Slovenia.

1991 Secession sentiment strengthens in Slovenia, spreads to Croatia. Economy collapses as civil war threatens. Political chaos continues.

WHO'S WHO

Slobodan Milosevic: Controversial leader of Serbia's Communist Party, renamed Social Democratic Party ... born 1941 ... appeals to Serbian nationalism ... seeks to dominate Yugoslavia.

Ante Markovic: Prime Minister ... born 1925 ... Croatian ... guerrilla fighter during German and Italian occupation in World War II ... favors liberalization ... only key political figure trying to stem tide toward dissolution of Yugoslavia.

Milan Kucan: Slovene Communist leader ... President of Slovenian republic ... born 1941 ... favors independence for Slovenia.

Franjo Tudjman: President of Croatia ... born 1922 ... favors independence for Croatia.

THINGS TO WATCH

Will ethnic and nationalist tensions lead to the unraveling of Yugoslavia?
Can civil war be averted?

ALBANIA

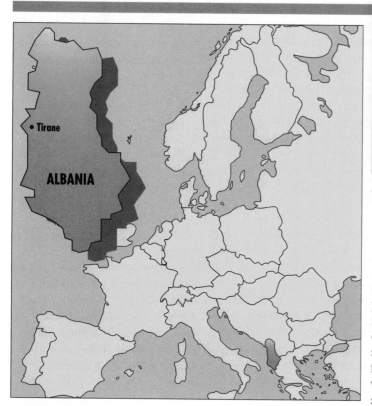

Supporters of the Democratic Party during a rally in front of the Democratic headquarters in Tirana, one day after the first free election in 46 years.

Albania is the last hard-line Stalinist stronghold in Europe. A comparatively backward Communist nation, with repressed ethnic and religious minorities, Albania has the poorest economy in Europe. For 40 years Albania was ruled by Enver Hoxha, a fervent Stalinist who died in 1985. Anyone who opposed his hard-line policies was eliminated, and the country was largely sealed off from the rest of the world.

Officially, President Ramiz Alia, Hoxha's handpicked successor, termed the collapse of Communism in Eastern Europe a "terrible tragedy" and vowed to maintain the Stalinist legacy of Enver Hoxha. But the tide of history proved stronger than Stalinist decrees. In the last weeks of 1989, student protests gave warning that the prodemocracy movement was headed Albania's way. Eager to avoid the fate of other hard-liners in Eastern Europe, Alia introduced a program of moderate reforms in January 1990. But social unrest continued to mount among students, intellectuals and workers, and Alia was forced to

propose even more sweeping reforms, including the promise of a mixed market economy and multi-party elections. In the meantime, thousands of young dissidents sought refuge in foreign embassies and were eventually allowed to leave the country for the West.

In foreign affairs, the government moved away from an almost paranoid isolationism and opened up to the outside world. Alia understood that the only hope for retaining control in Europe's poorest and most backward nation was to secure help from the West. He soon learned that without democratic elections in Albania, Western aid would not be forthcoming. For the first time, the government allowed the organization of an opposition party, the Democratic Party, led by intellectuals, many of whom used to be Communists. The first multiparty parliamentary elections were held in April 1991, with the Communists winning an overwhelming majority, based largely on rural support. With support waning in the cities and among workers, Alia realized he had to form a coalition government in order to bring political calm to the nation and institute the painful austerity measures necessary to turn the country around. So far the Democratic Party refuses to cooperate with the Communists, and the political future of Albania is still very much in doubt.

WHO'S WHO

Ramiz Alia: President and leader of Communist Party ... born 1925 ... handpicked successor to longtime dictator Enver Hoxha ... favors moderate reform.

CHRONOLOGY

1939 Conquered by Italian Fascist forces.
1944 Communists, led by Enver Hoxha, take over after liberation from Axis control.
1948 Hoxha breaks with Yugoslavia, remains close ally of Moscow.
1961 Hoxha severs ties with Moscow, allies with China.
1967 Religion officially outlawed.
1978 Albania breaks with China, pursues isolationist policy.
1985 Hoxha dies, succeeded by Ramiz Alia.
1989 Alia decries collapse of Communism in Eastern Europe; student demonstrations break out.
1990 Alia begins tentative steps toward liberalization.
1991 Political and economic crisis deepens. Police suppress anti-Communist protests. Communist Party wins two-thirds majority in parliament in first multiparty elections since World War II.

THINGS TO WATCH

Will pro-democracy forces grow stronger?
Will the Communist Party retain control?

JAPAN

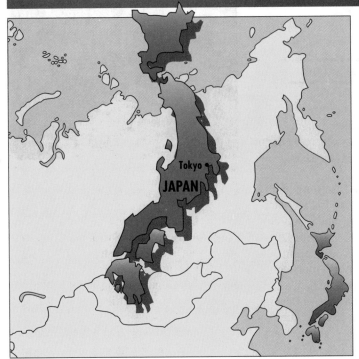

Prime Minister Toshiki Kaifu came to power in 1989 as an interim leader. At the time, the Liberal-Democratic Party (L.D.P.), the conservative party that has ruled Japan without interruption for 36 years, found itself in terrible trouble. High-ranking party leaders were tainted by corruption and sex scandals. A disgusted electorate had given the L.D.P. a big scare in elections for the upper house of parliament. Party leaders who preside over the factions that control the L.D.P. chose Kaifu as prime minister because he was clean. Kaifu turned out to be a stronger choice than anticipated, leading the L.D.P. to a decisive parliamentary victory in February 1990.

Meanwhile economic tensions between the United States and Japan, the world's two largest economies — which produce 40 percent of the world's wealth — increased. Despite previous Japanese concessions to open its markets to American goods, the Japanese trade surplus with the U.S. remains at more than $50 billion per year, prompting continued American pressure. For instance, the U.S. wants Japan to lift import restrictions on foreign rice. There was a brief flare-up in

1991 over Japanese objections to the display of a 10-pound bag of American rice at a U.S. trade show in Tokyo.

Kaifu's popularity took a nosedive when he pledged $9 billion to support the deployment of U.S.-led coalition forces against Iraq's invasion of Kuwait. Opponents charged the pledge violated Japan's constitutional ban on foreign military involvement. His failure to negotiate a deal with Soviet President Mikhail Gorbachev in April for the return of four Japanese islands seized by the Soviets in the closing moments of World War II was also a blow to his prestige. Kaifu's term expires in October 1991 and already his rivals are maneuvering for position. The L.D.P. is expected to retain power easily. The next prime minister will be determined by a narrow circle of party leaders.

WHO'S WHO

Emperor Akihito: Born 1933 ... ascended to throne January 1989 ... broke with many traditional Imperial customs ... received secular education ... married a commoner ... traveled extensively abroad.

Toshiki Kaifu: Prime Minister ... born 1931 ... elected Liberal-Democratic Party leader August 1989 ... untainted by L.D.P. scandals.

CHRONOLOGY

1945 Japan surrenders in World War II. Hirohito allowed to continue as Emperor but forced to renounce claims to divinity. Allied forces occupy Japan.
1947 Japan adopts democratic constitution.

1948 Socialist Party rules briefly.
1951 Japan signs peace treaty with U.S.
1952 Allied occupation ends.
1955 Rival conservative groups merge to form Liberal-Democratic Party (L.D.P.), which has ruled Japan ever since.
1956 Japan admitted to United Nations.
1950- Japanese economy undergoes
1980's unparalleled growth.
1980's Western trading partners begin to pressure Japan about restrictive trading practices.
1988 Ruling Liberal-Democratic Party hit by influence-peddling scandal.
1989 Emperor Hirohito dies. L.D.P. bribery scandal grows. Prime Minister Takeshita implicated in scandal and resigns, replaced by Sosuke Uno. U.S. accuses Japan of unfair trade practices. Prime Minister Uno named in sex scandal. L.D.P. loses badly in elections for control of less important upper house of parliament. Uno resigns, succeeded by Toshiki Kaifu.
1990 Parliament dissolved. L.D.P. wins elections. Tough round of trade negotiations pits U.S. against Japan. Japanese stock market collapses, yen's value declines sharply. Japan reluctantly agrees to open more of its market to American goods. Prime Minister Kaifu's popularity declines after he pledges $9 billion to support U.S.-led multinational force in Persian Gulf.
1991 Trade difficulties continue between Japan and U.S. Negotiations with Soviet President Mikhail Gorbachev for return of four Japanese islands seized by Red Army in World War II fail.

THINGS TO WATCH

Will Kaifu remain in power?
Will trade relations between the U.S. and Japan improve?
Will negotiations with the Soviet Union be successful?

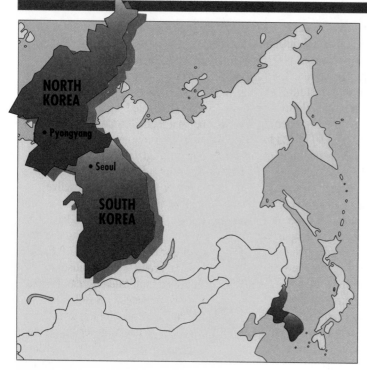

South Korean delegate, right, and North Korean delegate, left, exchange handshakes prior to the first round of Inter-Korean Premiers talks in Seoul.

developing its own nuclear weapons.

WHO'S WHO

SOUTH KOREA
Roh Tae Woo: President ... born 1932 ... currently co-leader of Democratic Liberal Party.
Kim Dae Jung: Prominent opposition leader (Peace and Democracy Party) ... born 1924.
Kim Young Sam: Formerly prominent opposition leader (Reunification Democratic Party) ... now co-leader of ruling Democratic Liberal Party ... born 1927.

NORTH KOREA
Kim Il Sung: President ... born 1912 ... built up cult of personality around his leadership.

CHRONOLOGY

1948 Republic of Korea (South Korea) created. Syngman Rhee elected president.
1950 Korean War begins.
1953 Armistice ends Korean War.
1960 Riots break out after fraudulent South Korean presidential election. Rhee resigns and civilian government takes over.
1961 Civilian government overthrown in coup led by Gen. Park Chung Hee.
1968 North Korean Navy seizes U.S.S. Pueblo, American intelligence ship cruising off North Korean coast. North Korean commandos try to assassinate President Park.
1972 Park declares martial law and enacts new constitution eliminating popular election of president.
1979 Park assassinated by head of Korean Central Intelligence Agency. Gen.

Chun Doo Hwan leads new coup.
1980 More than 200 South Korean students die as troops crush prodemocracy uprising in Kwangju.
1983 Soviet Union shoots down Korean airliner over Soviet airspace, killing 269 passengers. North Korean agents accused of planting bomb that killed 17 South Korean officials during visit to Rangoon, Burma.
1985 Opposition leader Kim Dae Jung returns from exile in U.S.
1987 Student demonstrations and labor strikes break out demanding democratization and economic reform. Chun restores direct presidential elections. Chun's chosen successor, former general Roh Tae Woo, wins election.
1988 Summer Olympic Games hosted by Seoul.
1990 President Roh and Kim Young Sam merge their political parties to form Democratic Liberal Party, with strong majority in parliament. Reunification discussions continue.
1991 South Korea improves relations with U.S.S.R. Roh regime's plan for separate U.N. memberships for North and South Korea prompts massive student protests. Labor unrest grows.

THINGS TO WATCH

Will progress be made toward reunification?
What will happen if North Korea gets nuclear weapons?
How long can Roh Tae Woo resist pressure to fulfill his many promises of reform?

Korea is the last bastion of the cold war, the only country still divided into two separate states because of East-West conflict. Both North Korea and South Korea have tried to adapt to the changing world. North Korea is looking for Western trading partners to replace its former Communist bloc customers and has rekindled relations with its old adversary, Japan. South Korea has improved ties with China and the Soviet Union. Soviet leader Mikhail Gorbachev even stopped off for a brief visit to discuss South Korea's offer of $3 billion in trade assistance to the Soviet Union.

Reunification talks between North and South Korea seem stalled over South Korea's proposal that the two Koreas apply for separate seats in the United Nations. The North wants a loose confederation between the two Koreas, with each keeping its current economic and social system but sharing a single U.N. seat. Student demonstrations in South Korea opposed the two-seat plan as an obstacle to national unity. Pressure grows on President Roh Tae Woo to continue democratic reforms. Recently, Western intelligence reports bring the news that North Korea may be close to

CHINA

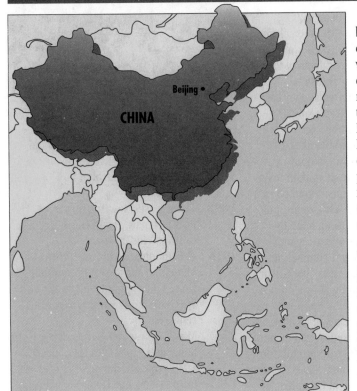

China continues to be ruled by die-hard octogenarian Stalinists who favor a certain degree of economic reform but insist on maintaining tight Communist Party control of society. But they can't live forever, and before long pressure may again grow for political change to correspond to economic change.

WHO'S WHO

Deng Xiaoping: Senior leader ... born 1904 ... officially retired from politics, but still dominant figure in Communist Party ... ordered crackdown against prodemocracy movement.

Zhao Ziyang: Deposed Communist Party Chairman ... born 1919 ... considered sympathetic to students' demands for democratic reform ... lost internal struggle with hard-liners for control of party and government.

Li Peng: Prime Minister ... born 1928 ... stepson of Chou Enlai (first premier of Communist China) ... a hard-liner.

Wuer Kaixi: Prodemocracy student leader ... born 1968 ... escaped to exile in West.

Wang Dan: Prodemocracy student leader ... born 1969 ... reportedly arrested by Chinese police.

Fang Lizhi: Astrophysicist and prominent dissident ... born 1936 ... considered the "Chinese Sakharov" ... sought and received asylum at U.S. Embassy in Beijing following crackdown at Tiananmen Square ... allowed to emigrate to England in June 1990.

More than two years after the massacre at Tiananmen Square, the political trials of prodemocracy activists continue in China. Requests from the European Community and Amnesty International that foreign observers be allowed to attend the trials were rebuffed by the Communist government. Despite the profound changes in other Communist nations, China has relied on state terror to maintain Communist Party rule.

In 1991, human rights advocates once again urged President George Bush to rescind China's Most Favored Nation (M.F.N.) status as a trading partner unless the government agreed to liberalize. But for the second consecutive year, the Bush Administration decided to renew M.F.N. status for China anyhow. The President cited the necessity to keep China from becoming diplomatically isolated and to reward it for its cooperation in the struggle against Iraqi aggression during the Persian Gulf crisis. Congressional Democrats vowed to fight the M.F.N. decision.

CHRONOLOGY

1949 Communist Revolution triumphs; new regime takes power October 1.

1950 China enters Korean War against U.N. forces.

1958 Mao adopts Great Leap Forward policy.

1966 Mao calls for Cultural Revolution.

1972 President Richard Nixon visits China.

1976 Cultural Revolution ends; Mao dies.

1979 U.S. and China normalize relations.

1986 Student demonstrations call for democratization.

1987 Hu Yaobang, reformist Communist Party chairman, removed following prodemocracy outbursts.

1989 Prodemocracy demonstrations begin. Soviet leader Mikhail Gorbachev visits Beijing as demonstrators demand "glasnost" in China. Hundreds of thousands of demonstrators occupy Tiananmen Square. Martial law declared. Hard-liners and moderates dispute what to do about demonstrations. Hard-liners win and military crackdown begins.

1990 Chinese government lifts state of emergency in Tibet and releases 211 political prisoners in bid to mollify foreign critics. President Bush announces decision to renew China's Most Favored Nation trading status despite repression in China. Students in Beijing mark anniversary of Tiananmen Square massacre with violent demonstrations. Chinese exiles hold memorial ceremonies in many countries.

1991 China opposes Iraq's invasion of Kuwait in key U.N. Security Council votes. Despite continued crackdown on prodemocracy advocates, Chinese leaders improve relations with Western powers and Soviet Union. President Bush's decision to once again extend China's M.F.N. status despite dismal human rights record triggers Congressional fight in Washington.

THINGS TO WATCH

Will China democratize?

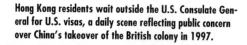

Hong Kong residents wait outside the U.S. Consulate General for U.S. visas, a daily scene reflecting public concern over China's takeover of the British colony in 1997.

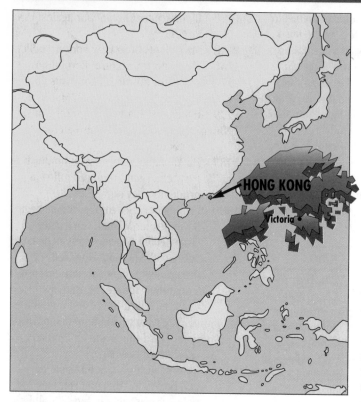

more than 56,000. Great Britain is offering to give 50,000 middle-class residents of the colony British passports, so they can leave Hong Kong if conditions get unbearable after 1997.

Now a colony of nearly six million inhabitants crammed into a tiny, 410-square-mile area, Hong Kong became a thriving industrial and commercial center after World War II. Hong Kong's 38,000 factories export vast quantities of textiles, electronics, and metal and plastic products to the United States, West Germany, Great Britain and Japan. China plans to use Hong Kong as a major conduit for trade with the West, but no one really knows how much life will change under Communism.

WHO'S WHO

Sir David Wilson: Governor ... born 1935 ... long career in foreign service and training as China scholar, speaks Mandarin Chinese fluently ... key figure in negotiating agreement to transfer control of Hong Kong to China in 1997.
Jiatun Xu: Hong Kong Director, Xinhua (New China News Agency) ... born 1916 ... highest-ranking Chinese official in Hong Kong ... oversees Beijing's political and economic interests in the British colony.

CHRONOLOGY

1839 Opium War breaks out between Great Britain and China in dispute over Chinese efforts to block British smuggling of opium into China.

1842 After winning Opium War, British

gain control of Hong Kong Island, population 5,000.

1860 Britain gains control of Kowloon Peninsula.

1898 China leases New Territories, northern part of current Hong Kong, to British for 99 years.

1911 Revolution in China overthrows Manchu dynasty, sets up republic. Hong Kong's population swells to 500,000 by 1915 with influx of refugees.

1937 More Chinese refugees arrive in Hong Kong after Japan invades China. By 1939 population reaches 1,600,000.

1941-1945 Japanese occupy Hong Kong during World War II. Population declines to 600,000.

1949 Refugees fleeing Communist revolution in mainland China increase number of residents to two million.

1950's Hong Kong becomes important industrial center.

1962 Food shortages in China send more immigrants to Hong Kong. Population rises to 3 million.

1970's China begins to invest heavily in Hong Kong.

1984 China and Great Britain agree to transfer control of Hong Kong to China in 1997 when Britain's lease of New Territories expires. Agreement specifies that Hong Kong can keep its capitalist economy for 50 years, but many Hong Kong professionals and business people begin to emigrate to Europe, the U.S., Canada and Australia.

THINGS TO WATCH

Will wave of emigration from Hong Kong continue?
How will Hong Kong adjust to Communist rule?

The clock is ticking for Hong Kong. In 1984, Great Britain and China reached agreement on returning the British dependency to Chinese authority in 1997. The agreement stipulates that Hong Kong will become an autonomous district within China, with self-rule in all matters except foreign and military affairs, and will be allowed to keep its capitalist, free-enterprise economy for at least 50 years. Worries about what the future really holds for Hong Kong were heightened after Beijing cracked down on prodemocracy demonstrators in the massacre at Tiananmen Square in 1989. Chinese proposals for local government after 1997 call for only 50 percent of the legislature to be chosen by direct election.

Uneasy about the future, a lot of people have been leaving the colony, worsening an already acute labor shortage. The exodus of skilled workers, professionals and businessmen emigrating to the United States, Britain, Canada and Australia has been growing every year. In 1989, 42,000 emigrated; in 1990,

PHILIPPINES

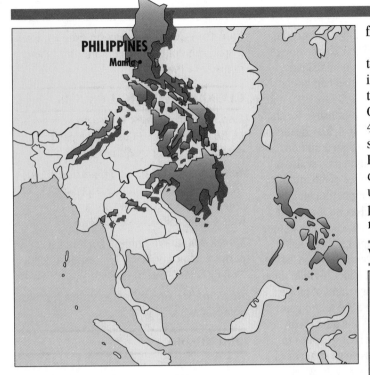

The stage is set for powerful political drama in the Philippines this year. The difficult negotiations for a renewal of the American lease on Clark Air Force Base — the largest U.S. base outside the States — is at a critical juncture. At the same time, the country is gearing up for a presidential election. President Corazon Aquino, who rose to power in the People Power revolution that overthrew the late dictator Ferdinand Marcos in 1986, has promised not to seek re-election. Ten potential candidates are vying for support to win party nominations for the presidency.

Aquino's six years in power have been tumultuous. Her promises of reform have gone largely unfulfilled. The gap between rich and poor is still huge, and terrible poverty still afflicts most of the population. There are shortages of electrical power, rice, water and transportation. There have been six military coup attempts against her administration, and she has failed to put down a Communist guerrilla insurgency. The government has been stymied in its efforts to reclaim the estimated $5 billion looted by the Marcos family from the national treasury when they

fled the country in 1986.

Leading contenders to replace Aquino include Defense Secretary Fidel V. Ramos and Oscar Orbos, Aquino's 40-year-old executive secretary. How the Philippines' fledgling democracy will bear up under the heat of the presidential campaign remains to be seen.

WHO'S WHO

Corazon Aquino: President ... born 1933 ... educated in New York ... lived in exile in U.S. 1980-83 with her husband, Benigno Aquino ... member of United Nationalist Democratic Organization (UNIDO).
Salvador Laurel: Vice President ... born 1928 ... leader of UNIDO.

CHRONOLOGY

1965 Ferdinand Marcos elected president.
1969 Marcos re-elected in fraud-tainted election.
1972 Marcos imposes martial law as unrest grows.
1981 Martial law ends, but Marcos retains broad powers under new security legislation.
1983 Opposition leader Benigno Aquino assassinated by government soldiers at Manila airport as he returns from exile.
1985 As pressure for democratization grows, Marcos announces presidential election for February 1986.

Opposition parties unite behind Corazon Aquino, widow of Benigno Aquino, as candidate for president, and Salvador Laurel, leader of UNIDO, as vice presidential candidate.
1986 Election marred by charges of widespread fraud. Marcos claims victory, but Aquino calls for campaign of civil disobedience. Defense Minister Juan Ponce Enrile and Lieut. Gen. Fidel V. Ramos break with Marcos, denounce election fraud and throw support to Aquino. Hundreds of thousands of civilians block troops from attacking dissident military leaders. Marcos flees to exile in Hawaii, and Aquino takes power.
1988 Marcos and wife, Imelda, indicted in New York on charges of stealing public funds from Philippines and defrauding American banks.
1989 Ferdinand Marcos dies in exile; Aquino bars burial for Marcos in Philippines. Coup attempted by right-wing officers in December; 113 die.
1990 Imelda Marcos goes on trial in New York and wins acquittal. Opposition Senator Enrile arrested for alleged role in December 1989 rebellion. Supreme Court orders Enrile released on token bail. Fighting breaks out in Luzon province when government forces try to arrest suspended Gov. Rodolfo Augilnaldo for his role in December coup attempt.
1991 Difficult negotiations between U.S. and Philippines on renewing lease for American military bases begin to make progress. Aquino's popularity continues to decline. Ten presidential hopefuls jockey for position in 1992 election.

THINGS TO WATCH

What will be the future of U.S. bases in the Philippines?
Will the elections proceed peacefully?

CAMBODIA

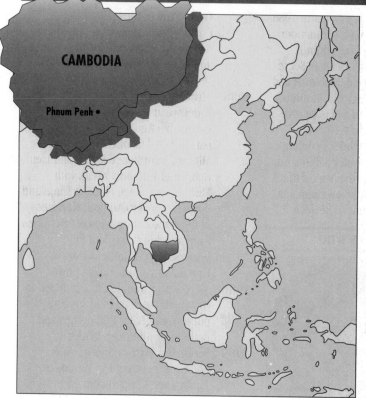

CAMBODIA

Phnum Penh •

Efforts to end 12 years of civil war in Cambodia are at a crucial stage. The Vietnamese-backed Communist government in Phnum Penh and the three rebel groups allied behind Prince Sihanouk's government in exile accepted a U.N.-proposed peace plan in September 1990, but a cease-fire was delayed by squabbling over implementation of the plan. Under the plan, the U.N. would temporarily administer the country until free elections were held.

In the meantime, each faction has been busy trying to boost its own vote-getting potential. The U.S. has given $20 million in humanitarian aid to the two non-Communist groups in Sihanouk's coalition, which control a small enclave inhabited by 500,000 people, in an effort to win the "hearts and minds" of Cambodian peasants. The U.S. has run into considerable criticism from official U.N. relief agencies who argue that aid distribution should not be politically motivated and that assistance is desperately needed for the eight million Cambodians living in near-starvation in the rest of the country. The dreaded Khmer Rouge, the Communist party that ruled Cambodia from 1975 to 1979 and was responsible for the "killing fields" deaths of more than a million Cambodians, is also a member of Sihanouk's coalition, though it receives no direct aid from the U.S. The Khmer Rouge has been using its control over valuable gem mines to build up a reserve fund of more than $100 million and stockpile a two-year supply of weapons to improve its chances of taking power. Whether the U.N. plan can soon be implemented and whether the Khmer Rouge will be kept out of the new government remain to be seen.

WHO'S WHO

Prince Norodom Sihanouk: Former King of Cambodia, now head of state of Government of Democratic Kampuchea in exile (recognized by United Nations)...born 1922...ruled Cambodia for nearly 30 years until overthrown by right-wing coup in 1970...figurehead chief of state under Khmer Rouge rule, 1975-79... organized national resistance movement against Vietnamese occupation.

Pol Pot: Military leader of Khmer Rouge (Cambodian Communists)...born 1929... prime minister, 1975-79...overthrown by Vietnamese invasion in 1979.

Hun Sen: Prime Minister of Vietnamese-backed regime (not recognized by U.N.)... born 1951...world's youngest prime minister ...split with Pol Pot in 1977...became prime minister in 1985.

CAMBODIAN POLITICAL GROUPS

Kampuchean People's Revolutionary Party (K.P.R.P.): Pro-Soviet Communist party currently in power in Phnum Penh.

Khmer People's National Liberation Front (K.P.N.L.F.): Non-Communist opposition group led by Son Sann...works in coalition with Sihanoukists and Khmer Rouge.

Khmer Rouge: Pro-Chinese Communist party...held power 1975-79...responsible for "killing fields"...led by Pol Pot.

Sihanoukists: Group loyal to Prince Norodom Sihanouk.

CHRONOLOGY

1953 Cambodia gains independence from France.
1965 Prince Sihanouk breaks ties with U.S.
1970 Lon Nol overthrows Sihanouk.
1975 Pol Pot leads Khmer Rouge in overthrow of Lon Nol government. Period of the killing fields begins.
1979 Vietnamese invade and install new government.
1982 Anti-Vietnamese factions form united front.
1987 Sihanouk holds peace talks with Vietnamese-installed prime minister.
1988 Vietnamese troops begin withdrawal.
1989 Vietnamese troops complete withdrawal.
1990 Peace negotiations break down, then resume. U.S. steps up humanitarian aid to non-Communist rebel factions. U.N.-sponsored peace plan wins agreement but bogs down in disagreements about implementation.
1991 Negotiations resume in effort to revive U.N. plan and end 12-year-old civil war.

THINGS TO WATCH

Will the U.N. peace plan succeed?
What role will the Khmer Rouge play?

THAILAND

Temple of the Golden Buddha in Bangkok

was Chatichai's attempt to subordinate the armed forces to civilian leadership.

The new junta dissolved parliament, abolished the constitution and imposed martial law. A new law banned the old trade unions, permitting them to reorganize only as social or charitable organizations. Political gatherings by more than five people were also banned. Junta leaders appointed Anand Panyarachun as interim prime minister and promised new elections by April 30, 1992.

Thailand, once known as Siam, is the only Southeast Asian nation that was never colonized by Western powers. Until 1932, the nation was ruled by an absolute monarchy, but a revolution led by Thais educated in France forced a transition to a constitutional monarchy. While the king continued as head of state (and has traditionally exercised considerable influence over the military, parliament and the general population), the monarchy no longer ruled. The military quickly gained the upper hand in Thai society, and even when civilians were allowed to run the country, they did so at the sufferance of the generals. Since 1932 there have been 17 coups or attempted coups in Thailand.

The most recent coup toppled the government of Chatichai Choonhavan, himself a former general, in February 1991. Chatichai's government was the first democratically elected regime in 13 years, and many people believed that coups had become a thing of the past. But military leaders charged that the government was riddled with corruption and that Chatichai was trying to split the military. While the charges of corruption were largely true, what probably upset the generals most

WHO'S WHO

King Bhumibol Adulyadej: Head of state ... born 1927 ... constitutional monarch ... does not exercise direct power, but widely revered in Thailand ... his support sought by all factions.

Anand Panyarachun: Interim Prime Minister ... born 1933 ... former Ambassador to United States ... political moderate ... promises to restore democratic government.

CHRONOLOGY

1932 Revolution overturns absolute monarchy. Constitutional monarchy instituted.

1941 Thailand surrenders to Japanese invaders after resisting for several hours, then signs alliance treaty with Japan.

1942 After Japanese attack on Pearl Harbor in December 1941, Thailand declares war on U.S. and Great Britain. Free Thai Movement begins working with Allies to oust Japanese.

1957 Field Marshal Sarit Thanarat overthrows government of Field

Marshal Pibul Songgram, who had served as prime minister during Japanese occupation and led Thailand after World War II. Sarit institutes pro-U.S. policies.

1963 Sarit dies; succeeded by Field Marshal Thanom Kittikachorn. Thanom permits U.S. to build air bases in Thailand, which are later used during Vietnam War for air strikes against Communist forces in Vietnam.

1967 Thailand, Indonesia, Malaysia, the Philippines and Singapore organize Association of Southeast Asian Nations (ASEAN) to promote cultural, social and economic cooperation.

1973 Students revolt against military rule. Rule by democratically elected government instituted.

1976 Military leaders oust elected government, arrest thousands of dissidents.

1979 Civilian government restored.

1981 Coup attempt fails.

1985 Another coup attempt quashed.

1988 Former general Chatichai Choonhavan becomes first democratically elected prime minister in 13 years. (Other civilian rulers held appointive seats in parliament.) Under Chatichai, economy thrives.

1991 Military junta overthrows elected government, outlaws trade unions. Anand Panyarachun appointed interim prime minister.

THINGS TO WATCH

Will democratic government be restored in Thailand?

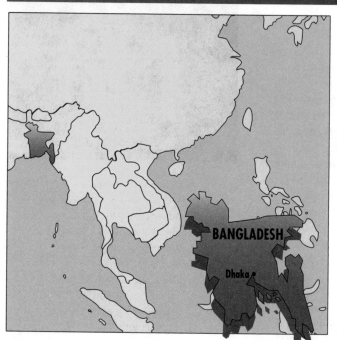

BANGLADESH

Dhaka

Bangladesh is one of the poorest nations in the world, with a per capita income of less than $170 a year. For years the country has been ruled by corrupt politicians. As much as two-thirds of the $2 billion per year in foreign aid poured into Bangladesh by wealthier nations may have been siphoned off over the years. Squalor, disease and suffering are rife in Bangladesh. In November 1990 massive protest demonstrations forced President Mohammad Ershad, a general who seized power in a 1982 coup, to resign from office and pave the way for a return to democratic rule. Plans call for a switch from a presidential system in which the presidency is considered the seat of all power, to a parliamentary democracy in which the prime minister would be the chief executive and the president would be a largely ceremonial head of state.

Democratic elections were held in February 1991, but no party emerged with the necessary two-thirds majority to form a new government, and it took a few weeks of bickering for a ruling coalition to take form between the Bangladesh Nationalist Party, which had 164 seats in parliament but was

12 short of the necessary two-thirds, and an Islamic fundamentalist party with 18 seats.

A massive cyclone hit the low-lying Bangladesh coastline on April 29, 1991, killing more than 150,000 people. Government relief efforts were paralyzed, and aid had to be brought in from India and other countries. Prime Minister Khaleda Zia requested the help of a special U.S. military task force to bring in food and medical supplies before the death toll escalated even further. Bangladesh's vulnerability to flooding is exacerbated by over-cutting of lumber on mountainsides in neighboring Nepal, causing heavy rains to rush down mountain slopes into Bangladesh's coastal regions. The country is so poor and so overpopulated that almost immediately after one devastating storm has passed, hundreds of thousands of people move right back into the same dangerous, flood-prone areas even before the debris has been cleared. They have nowhere else to go.

Bangladesh's newborn democracy will face difficult going in the months ahead as the government seeks to fight corruption and lift the nation out of grinding poverty.

WHO'S WHO

Khaleda Zia: Prime Minister ... born 1945 ... widow of assassinated president Ziaur Rahman ... leads Bangladesh Nationalist Party ... country's first woman prime minister ... promises to restore democracy.

CHRONOLOGY

1947   Britain grants independence to India and creates state of Pakistan, comprising West Pakistan and East Pakistan (now Bangladesh).

1960's   Tensions between East and West Pakistan grow.

1970   Cyclone and tidal wave hit East Pakistan, killing 266,000 people. East Pakistanis accuse West Pakistani-dominated government of delaying relief shipments.

1971   Civil war breaks out; East Pakistanis declare independence as Bangladesh. Government forces enter India in pursuit of rebel guerrillas. India joins forces with rebels and defeats government.

1972   Rebel leader Sheik Mujibur Rahman becomes prime minister.

1975   Mujibur becomes president under new consitution, outlaws opposition parties. Military officers assassinate Mujibur. Ziaur Rahman (known as Zia) takes power.

1981   Zia assassinated; Vice President Abdus Sattar becomes president.

1982   Gen. H. M. Ershad seizes power in bloodless coup, takes over presidency.

1983   Khaleda Zia, Zia's widow, becomes leader of Bangladesh Nationalist Party.

1987   Opposition parties unite behind Khaleda's leadership and begin campaign to restore democracy.

1988   Worst monsoon floods in history put 75 percent of Bangladesh underwater, leave 25 million homeless.

1990   Ershad resigns following massive protest demonstrations, paves the way for transition to democratic rule.

1991   Khaleda becomes first woman prime minister, vows to restore full parliamentary democracy. Cyclone hits Bangladesh, causing massive flooding and 150,000 deaths.

THINGS TO WATCH

Will Bangladesh continue on the road to democracy?
Will economic conditions improve?

AFGHANISTAN

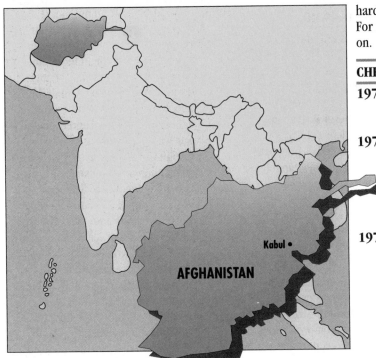

Four young boys stand before the wrecked remains of their bombed village in eastern Afghanistan. The 11-year-old boy, second from right, already knows how to use the AK-47 assault rifle he is holding.

The war in Afghanistan continues to drag on, with no end in sight. When the Soviets pulled their troops out in 1989, hopes were high in the West that the Soviet-backed government would collapse quickly. But the U.S.-backed Islamic rebels have been unable to pull off any significant military victories. The government has successfully defended the cities and has once again been taking the war to the countryside.

So far more than 1.5 million Afghans have died. More than half of Afghanistan's prewar population of 16 million have fled their homes, with more than three million taking refuge in Pakistan, two million in Iran and the rest displaced within Afghanistan.

Agreement has been reached between U.S. and Soviet negotiators on a simultaneous cutoff of arms shipments to both sides in the conflict, but the Soviets want the agreement linked to an overall political settlement and to include third-party countries like Saudi Arabia and Pakistan. Further progress may be hampered by the resignation of Soviet Foreign Minister Eduard Shevardnadze in December 1990 and the growing influence of hard-liners in Moscow. For now, the war goes on.

CHRONOLOGY

1973 King Zahir Shah overthrown and exiled.

1978 Soviet-trained military officers stage coup. Rebellion breaks out in the provinces.

1979 *September:* Communist factional dispute ends in palace coup.
December: Soviet Union invades.

1980 President Jimmy Carter imposes trade embargo on U.S.S.R. and calls for boycott of Moscow Olympics. Refugees flee to Pakistan at rate of 80,000 per month. U.S. begins covert support of anti-government rebels.

1981 President Ronald Reagan lifts embargo on U.S. grain exports to Soviet Union.

1982 2.5 million Afghan refugees reported in Pakistan.

1984 Soviet troop level reaches 115,000. Soviets launch saturation-bombing raids against rebel positions.

1985 Soviet casualties reach 20,000. Desertions and draft evasion decimate ranks of Afghan army. Seven major guerrilla groups form coalition in Pakistan. U.N. sponsors secret talks between Pakistan and Afghanistan in Geneva.

1986 New Communist leader, Najibullah, proposes national reconciliation and unilateral cease-fire. U.S. supplies rebels with Stinger missiles.

1987 Guerrillas reject reconciliation. Fighting continues.

1988 *March:* U.N. mediators sponsor new round of negotiations in Geneva.
April: Agreement reached on Soviet pullout.

1989 *February:* Soviet withdrawal completed. Najibullah vows to fight on. Rebel factions quarrel but finally name provisional government in exile. Rebels prove unable to win major victory over government forces. Factional differences in Communist regime in Kabul lead to two unsuccessful coup attempts led by Defense Minister Shahnawaz Tanai.

1990 Tanai leads still another unsuccessful coup attempt in March and is forced into exile. Fighting continues.

1991 U.S.-Soviet talks on ending war in Afghanistan progress. Factional disputes among rebel groups continue as Najibullah regime clings to power.

THE MUJAHADEEN

The Afghan rebels call themselves Mujahadeen, or Holy Warriors. In 1989 the seven main rebel factions agreed to establish a government in exile but remained sharply divided by internal bickering between Islamic fundamentalists, who want a revolutionary Islamic state, and traditionalists, who favor a return to rule by tribal or village leaders. The exile government has been recognized by Malaysia, Sudan, Saudi Arabia and Bahrain and by the Islamic Conference Organization.

THINGS TO WATCH

Will the U.S. and Soviet Union scale down military supplies to warring factions?
Will the war continue, or will there be peace?

IRAN

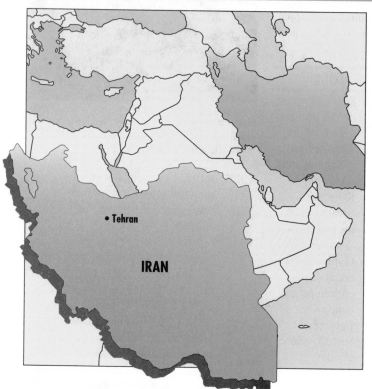

• Tehran

IRAN

Iran's moderate leadership finally seems to have gained the upper hand in its dispute with hard-line fundamentalists who want to continue the extremist polices of the late Ayatollah Ruhollah Khomeini. President Hashemi Rafsanjani easily pushed aside extremist demands that Iran support Iraq's Saddam Hussein against the "Great Satan" United States. Instead, Rafsanjani criticized the invasion, declared Iran neutral and offered to facilitate negotiations. After the war, Iran offered asylum to nearly two million Kurdish and Shiite Moslem refugees who fled Iraq after rebellions against Saddam's regime were ruthlessly crushed by the Iraqi military.

Rafsanjani understands that Iran needs to repair its relations with the West and its Arab neighbors in the Persian Gulf in order to revive its war-torn economy. Western governments have responded favorably to Iran's attempts to reintegrate itself into the international community but are waiting for Iran to use its influence to gain the release of Western hostages still held by pro-Iranian terrorists in Lebanon.

WHO'S WHO

Ali Khamenei: Supreme religious leader of Iran ... born 1940 ... elected president of Iran in 1981 and 1985.

Hashemi Rafsanjani: President ... born 1934 ... regarded as pragmatic moderate, but capable of quickly switching to hard-line position when politically expedient.

CHRONOLOGY

1963 Ayatollah Khomeini forced into exile.

1978 Anti-Shah demonstrations erupt. Ayatollah Khomeini and aides coordinate struggle from exile in France.

1979 Shah leaves Iran. Ayatollah Khomeini returns to hero's welcome in Iran and takes power. Islamic students seize U.S. Embassy and take 54 American hostages.

1980 Hostage crisis continues. Abolhasan Bani-Sadr elected president. U.S. rescue mission fails. Border clashes between Iran and Iraq break out. Iraq invades Iran.

1981 American hostages released on President Ronald Reagan's Inauguration Day. Bani-Sadr dismissed as president, flees to exile.

1985 U.S. officials engage in secret arms deals with so-called Iranian moderates.

1986 Iran-Contra scandal breaks in U.S.

1987 U.S. provides protection to civilian shipping in Persian Gulf as Iraq-Iran War continues. Iraqi missiles hit U.S.S. Stark, killing 37 American sailors. Iranian pilgrims riot in Mecca; 400 killed.

1988 Teheran hit by Iraqi missiles. U.S. warships destroy Iranian offshore oil rigs. Khomeini appoints Hashemi Rafsanjani as commander in chief of military. U.S.S. Vincennes shoots down civilian Iranian airliner, killing 290. Khomeini concedes to moderates in regime and agrees to end war with Iraq on basis of U.N. resolution. Hundreds of regime's political opponents executed.

1989 Khomeini denounces Salman Rushdie's novel *The Satanic Verses* as blasphemous and offers reward for Rushdie's murder. Khomeini dies after cancer surgery. Ayatollah Khamenei succeeds Khomeini as supreme religious leader. Rafsanjani becomes president.

1990 Rafsanjani attempts to moderate Iran's hard-line policies and end Iran's international isolation. Iran intervenes with Shiite extremists in Lebanon to secure release of two American hostages, in bid to repair relations with West. To avoid two-front war, Iraq's Saddam Hussein settles Iraq-Iran War, granting all Iranian demands. Hard-liners want Iran to back Iraq against U.S., but Rafsanjani declares neutrality.

1991 Iran remains neutral when war breaks out in Persian Gulf. Iraqi jet fighters escape war zone and land in Iran. Iran seizes planes, interns crews and refuses to release them until war ends. When postwar Kurdish and Shiite rebellions fail, two million refugees flee to safety in Iran. Rafsanjani and moderates gain upper hand in dispute with hard-line Islamic fundamentalists and seek improved relations with Western powers.

THINGS TO WATCH

Will moderates remain in control?
Will relations improve with the West?

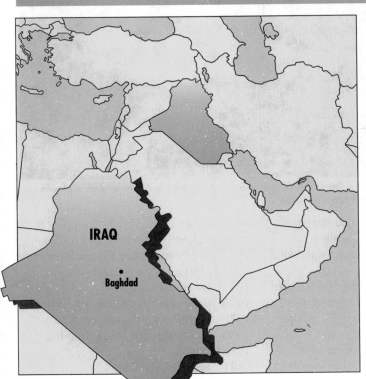

IRAQ

Baghdad

Saddam Hussein still clings to power in Baghdad. Somehow the Iraqi despot has managed to survive a humiliating military defeat in Kuwait, popular revolts by the Kurdish minorities in the north and Shiite Moslem rebels in the south of Iraq, and the continued enforcement of United Nations economic sanctions. He has been forced by circumstance to promise democratization and limited autonomy to the Kurds, but at the same time he has moved to appoint family members and loyalists to key government positions to bolster his dictatorial rule.

The Security Council voted to permit Iraq to import food and medical supplies, but since the sanctions still prohibit Iraq from earning revenues from the export of petroleum products, there is little money available to make food and medical purchases. The economic sanctions will continue until Iraq dismantles its biological, chemical and nuclear weapons capabilities and agrees to a U.N. formula for paying war reparations to Kuwait. So far, Saddam has been resisting demands that he hand over 30 percent of Iraq's future oil revenues to Kuwait.

Meanwhile, the ones who suffer most in Iraq are the poor and the young. Some Western officials are still hoping that members of the ruling Baathist Party will eventually overthrow Saddam and constitute a more cooperative government.

WHO'S WHO

Saddam Hussein: President ... born 1937 ... leader of left-wing Baathist Party.

CHRONOLOGY

1943 British forces defeat pro-Nazi Iraqi military leaders, and Iraq enters World War II with Allies.

1945 Iraq helps establish Arab League.

1948 Iraq joins Arab war against newly created state of Israel.

1950's Foreign companies begin petroleum production in Iraq. Government shares profits.

1958 Military overthrows and kills King Faisal. Gen. Abdul Karim Qasim becomes premier. Qasim shifts Iraq from pro-West orientation and accepts assistance from Communist bloc.

1961 Ethnic Kurds living in northern provinces rebel against central government.

1963 Military officers allied with Baathist Party overthrow and assassinate Qasim, then squabble among themselves. Abdul Salam Arif emerges as ruler.

1966 Arif dies, succeeded by brother Abdul Rahman Arif.

1968 Ahmed Hasan al-Bakr overthrows Arif, establishes military regime controlled by Baathist Party.

1970 Agreement granting self-rule to Kurds ends Kurdish rebellion.

1973 Government takes over foreign oil companies.

1974 Renewed fighting erupts between government forces and Kurds.

1979 Al-Bakr resigns, succeeded by Saddam Hussein.

1980 War breaks out between Iraq and Iran.

1981 Israeli jets bomb nuclear reactor under construction in Iraq.

1984 Iraq resumes diplomatic relations with U.S. after 17-year interruption. Iraq begins missile attacks on Iranian oil tankers in Persian Gulf, prompting Iranian counterattacks.

1987 Kuwait asks major-power intervention to guarantee freedom of navigation in Persian Gulf. U.S. and other Western powers send Navy vessels to Persian Gulf. Iraqi missile mistakenly fired at U.S.S. Stark, killing 37 U.S. servicemen. U.N. Security Council calls for end to war.

1988 United Nations cease-fire ends Iraq-Iran War. Iraq reportedly uses chemical weapons against Kurdish rebels.

1990 Iraq invades Kuwait and masses troops at Saudi border. U.N. Security Council denounces invasion, imposes economic sanctions against Iraq and authorizes deployment of international military force. Security Council sets January 15, 1991 deadline for Iraqi pullout from Kuwait.

1991 Coalition forces launch massive air attacks against Iraqi positions. After nearly six weeks of aerial bombardment, allies unleash ground war and rout Iraqi forces in four days. Kurds and Shiite Moslems begin unsuccessful rebellions against Saddam Hussein. Nearly two million refugees flee to Turkey, Iran and coalition-occupied southern Iraq.

(For a complete rundown on the Persian Gulf War see pages 8-11.)

THINGS TO WATCH

Will Saddam Hussein be overthrown?
Will economic sanctions be lifted?

KUWAIT

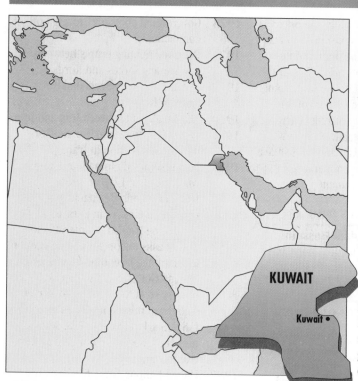

Geysers of flame and thick, toxic smoke spew from just a few of the hundreds of oil wells set afire by fleeing Iraqi troops.

Even before Iraq invaded this tiny desert kingdom on August 2, 1990, Kuwait had many serious problems. Though the country was rich because of its vast oil reserves, the economy was weakened by a decade of declining oil prices, poor management and corruption. Political and religious dissent were suppressed. Women and immigrants were denied basic political rights. Parliament had been disbanded by royal decree in 1986, and all power was concentrated in the hands of the al-Sabah family, which had ruled the country for more than 200 years.

The war only aggravated these problems. The royal family has been slow to move to rebuild the country. More than 500 oil-well fires, set by retreating Iraqi forces in the final moments of the war, continue to blaze, and the oil reservoir may have suffered permanent damage, which will make Kuwait oil much more expensive to extract in the future.

Kuwaitis who remained at home and resisted the Iraqi occupation are critical of government leaders who fled to safety in exile, and have been clamoring for democratization. Military leaders have demanded that royal family members who ordered the withdrawal of Kuwaiti tanks from the border be excluded from the government. Human rights groups and Western governments have criticized widespread vigilantism, killings, beatings, torture and lack of due process for Palestinians in Kuwait accused of collaborating with the Iraqis.

WHO'S WHO

Sheikh Jaber al-Ahmed al-Sabah: Emir ... born 1928 ... 13th ruler in the al-Sabah dynasty.

Sheikh Saad al-Abdulla al-Sabah: Crown Prince and Prime Minister ... born 1928 ... heir apparent to throne ... cousin to emir ... handles domestic matters primarily.

CHRONOLOGY

1762	Al-Sabah family become hereditary rulers of Kuwait.
1899	Great Britain takes over control of Kuwait's defense.
1934	Kuwait Oil Co. receives oil concession.
1936	Oil drilling begins.
1961	Kuwait gains independence from Great Britain.
1963	Kuwait joins United Nations.
1973	Kuwait sends troops to participate in Yom Kippur War against Israel.

Government cuts off oil supplies to U.S. and Netherlands and curtails shipments to other Western supporters of Israel as part of Arab oil embargo.

1974	Oil embargo lifted.
1975	Government nationalizes Kuwait Oil Co.
1976	Kuwait's emir dissolves parliament.
1980-1988	Kuwait supports Iraq in Iraq-Iran War.
1981	New parliament elected.
1983	Seventeen Islamic fundamentalists imprisoned for series of bombings.
1985	Terrorists linked to Islamic Jihad, pro-Iranian group based in Lebanon, attempt car-bomb assassination of emir and demand release of imprisoned terrorists.
1986	Emir dissolves parliament again. Because of Kuwait's financial support of Iraqi war effort, Iran begins attacks on Kuwaiti oil fleet. U.S. reregisters Kuwaiti tankers as American vessels and sends U.S. warships to provide escort.
1990	Negotiations to settle border dispute with Iraq collapse. Iraq invades. Royal family flees to Saudi Arabia. U.N. Security Council dispatches multinational force to Persian Gulf area.
1991	U.N. force liberates Kuwait. Al-Sabah family returns from exile, declares martial law. Demands for democratization grow.

THINGS TO WATCH

Will democratization come to Kuwait?
Will oil-well fires be brought under control?

SAUDI ARABIA

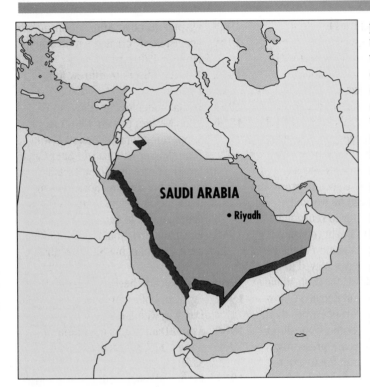

SAUDI ARABIA

• Riyadh

R uled for six decades by the royal family of Ibn Saud, who founded modern Saudi Arabia in 1932, this desert kingdom is the world's largest oil exporter and the cradle of Islamic civilization. Staunch allies of the U.S., the Saudis have performed a delicate balancing act between loyalties to Washington and responsibilities to the Islamic world. A moderate in the hectic world of Arab politics, Saudi Arabia had long provided financial support to the Palestinian Liberation Organization.

When Iraq invaded Kuwait and threatened to destroy Middle East equilibrium, the Saudis invited the U.S. to lead an international military coalition to protect its own oil fields from Iraqi aggression and to liberate Kuwait, and offered to put up billions of dollars to help underwrite the operation. Saudi financial aid to the P.L.O. was cut off when Yassir Arafat supported Saddam Hussein's invasion of Kuwait.

Experts believe it will take the Saudis at least three years to overcome the negative impact of the Gulf War on its economy. Demands for social reform, freedom of the press and public participation in government were largely put on hold during the war. The only exception was a demonstration by wealthy Saudi women demanding repeal of legal prohibitions against women driving automobiles. The long-simmering debate on the liberalization of Saudi society will surely intensify in the period ahead, though the outcome is still in doubt.

WHO'S WHO

King Fahd: Head of State ... born 1922 ... Fahd is the fourth of modern Saudi Arabia founder Ibn Saud's 45 sons (by 22 wives) to serve as king ... has little formal education ... as young man was considered a playboy ... as king has presided over modernization of Saudi economy while maintaining Moslem customs.

King Fahd at the Royal Palace in Jeddah

CHRONOLOGY

1891 Saud family loses control of Saudi territory, which is divided among various tribal groups and Ottoman Empire. Saud family leaders flee to exile in Kuwait.

1906 Abd al-Aziz Ibn Saud begins 25-year military struggle to reunite Saudi territory under Saud family control.

1932 Ibn Saud proclaims Kingdom of Saudi Arabia.

1936 Oil exploration begins.

1938 First major oil deposit discovered, but large-scale production, dominated by foreign oil companies, begins only after end of World War II in 1945.

1945 Saudi Arabia becomes charter member of United Nations.

1953 Ibn Saud dies, succeeded by his son Saud.

1964 Saud gives up throne, succeeded by his brother Faisal.

1967 Saudi Arabia supports Egypt, Syria and Jordan in Six Day War with Israel.

1973 Saudi government takes partial control of Arab American Oil Co. (Aramco). Following Arab defeat in Yom Kippur War, Saudi Arabia embargoes oil shipments to nations that supported Israel, triggering international oil crisis.

1974 Saudi officials begin negotiations for complete takeover of Aramco by 1980.

1975 King Faisal assassinated, succeeded by his half-brother Khalid.

1982 Khalid dies, succeeded by his half-brother Fahd.

1990 King Fahd opposes Iraqi invasion of Kuwait, invites international forces, led by United States, to send troops to Saudi Arabia to block further Iraqi aggression and undertake liberation of Kuwait.

THINGS TO WATCH

Will ruling Saud family permit democratization? What position will Saudis take toward Yassir Arafat and the P.L.O.?

EGYPT

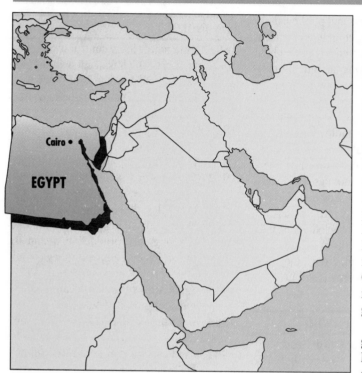

Egyptian President Hosni Mubarak doesn't have the charisma of a Gamal Abdel Nasser or the statesmanlike stature of an Anwar el-Sadat, his predecessors as president of Egypt. His low-profile style has caused some people to call him a dull, plodding leader. But after 10 years in power Mubarak has accomplished a lot. Not only has he overcome Egypt's ostracism by other Arab states after Sadat's peace treaty with Israel in 1978, but he's also restored Egypt to a leadership role in the Arab world. During the Iraq-Iran War, Egypt backed Iraq, but when tensions rose between Iraq and tiny Kuwait in the summer of 1990, Mubarak intervened to avoid a confrontation and secured a pledge from Iraqi President Saddam Hussein not to invade Kuwait. When Saddam broke his promise and invaded on August 2, Mubarak condemned the aggression, led the fight against Saddam in the Arab League and dispatched troops to join the international forces deployed in Saudi Arabia.

Mubarak has also been outspoken on Third World debt problems and has criticized Western efforts to force poor countries to adopt drastic austerity programs. He rejected U.S. and International Monetary Fund (I.M.F) pressure to cut government subsidies on food and energy because he feared sudden price hikes would trigger massive social unrest. Instead he worked patiently to renegotiate Egypt's debt repayment. In recognition of the key role Egypt played in the Gulf War, the Bush Administration decided to forgive part of Egypt's debt.

At home, opposition groups are pressuring Mubarak not to extend emergency political measures put in place when Sadat was assassinated in 1981 and to restore full democracy in the Arab world's largest nation.

WHO'S WHO

Hosni Mubarak: President ... born 1928 ... became president after assassination of Anwar el-Sadat in 1981 ... characterized by low-profile style ... restored Egypt's participation in Arab League without reneging on Camp David Accords with Israel.

CHRONOLOGY

1869	Suez Canal completed.
1914	Great Britain establishes protectorate over Egypt.
1922	Egypt gains nominal independence from Britain.
1940-1942	British forces confront Axis powers, Germany and Italy, in major battles on Egyptian soil during World War II.
1948-1949	Egypt joins other Arab nations in war against newly created Jewish state of Israel in Palestine.
1952	Military officers overthrow King Farouk.
1954	Gamal Abdel Nasser takes power.
1956	After Western powers withdraw support for construction of Aswan Dam, Nasser nationalizes Suez Canal. Israel, France and Great Britain invade, but U.S. and Soviet Union denounce invasion. United Nations arranges end to fighting.
1958	Egypt and Syria join to form United Arab Republic, but Syria withdraws in 1961.
1960	Construction begins on Aswan Dam.
1967	Egypt and other Arab nations lose Six Day War with Israel.
1968	Aswan Dam begins operation.
1970	Nasser dies, succeeded by Anwar el-Sadat.
1973	Egypt and other Arab countries lose Yom Kippur War against Israel.
1976	Egypt breaks with Soviet Union.
1978	Egypt and Israel sign Camp David Accords to end 30 years of conflict. Other Arab countries ostracize Egypt for reaching separate peace with Israel.
1981	Islamic fundamentalists assassinate Sadat. Hosni Mubarak becomes president. Emergency laws restricting political opponents of regime are invoked. Mubarak reaffirms peace treaty with Israel but begins efforts to mend relations with Arab governments.
1990	Mubarak takes strong action in Arab League to oppose Iraq's invasion of Kuwait and sends troops to join coalition of multinational military forces in Saudi Arabia.
1991	Domestic pressure grows for Mubarak to relax emergency laws and restore full democracy.

THINGS TO WATCH

Will full democracy be restored in Egypt? Will Egypt overcome its economic difficulties?

SYRIA

President George Bush and Syrian President Hafez al-Assad meet in Geneva to discuss the Gulf crisis.

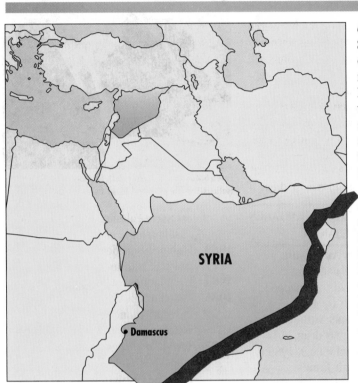

SYRIA

• Damascus

Syria is one of the big beneficiaries of the Persian Gulf War. Before the war, Syria was extremely isolated in the international community, and even within the Arab world itself. Western powers considered Syria a "terrorist state," with links to numerous terrorist attacks in Europe. Arab countries were furious with Syria's President Hafez al-Assad, a longtime adversary of Iraq's Saddam Hussein, for his support of Iran during the Iraq-Iran War. With Russia's virtual pullout from the Middle East, Syria lost its major international support.

When Saddam Hussein invaded Kuwait, Assad backed United Nations efforts to defend Saudi Arabia from further Iraqi aggression and sent 20,000 troops to join the international coalition. With a reputation as a radical Arab state, Syria bolstered the coalition's credibility in the Arab world and quickly benefited from its newfound respectability. Assad was given a free hand to settle the civil war in neighboring Lebanon, where Syria has vital interests. Diplomatic relations between Britain and Syria were restored, and President George Bush held a private summit with Assad in Geneva,

despite the fact that Syria is still officially classified as a terrorist nation by the State Department. After the war, Damascus became a regular stop in U.S. shuttle diplomacy efforts to resolve the Arab-Israeli dispute.

Human rights activists have expressed alarm about Assad's sudden international acceptance. Syria is charged with killing as many as 10,000 of its own people and Palestinians in Lebanon. The 1982 massacre in the city of Hama, where more than 5,000 rebel guerrillas and civilians alike were slaughtered, is testimony to Assad's ruthlessness. Thousands have been imprisoned without trial, and public hangings of his political opponents contribute to the terror. Whether increased contact with the West will lead to liberalization remains to be seen.

WHO'S WHO

Hafez al-Assad: President ... born 1930 ... leader of Baath Socialist Party ... seized power in 1970 ... longtime opponent of Iraq's Saddam Hussein.

CHRONOLOGY

1914-1918 Syria revolts against Turkish Ottoman Empire during World War I.

1920 Following WW I, League of Nations divides Syrian territory into four states — Syria, Lebanon, Palestine and Transjordan — and gives France mandate to manage Syrian affairs.

1946 France grants Syria full independence.

1948 Syria participates in Arab war against newly created state of Israel.

1958 Syria joins with Egypt to form United Arab Republic (U.A.R.).

1961 Syria withdraws from U.A.R.

1960's Baathist Party takes power, nationalizes industry and monopolizes foreign trade.

1967 Arab forces, including Syrian troops, are defeated by Israel in Six Day War. Israel occupies Golan Heights in southwest Syria.

1971 Hafez al-Assad becomes president.

1973 Syrian forces again fail to defeat Israel in Yom Kippur War.

1976 Syrian troops intervene in Lebanese civil war.

1980 Assad supports Iran in Iraq-Iran War.

1982 More than 5,000 rebels massacred in city of Hama.

1983 Syrian troops stationed in Lebanon confront American troops sent there as part of international peacekeeping force. Syrians shoot down two American jet fighters, killing one pilot and capturing another, Lt. Robert O. Goodman Jr. Goodman's release is arranged by Rev. Jesse Jackson in January 1984.

1986 British accuse Syria of links to terrorist plot to blow up Israeli jet in Britain.

1990 Syria opposes Iraqi invasion of Kuwait; sends troops to join international coalition in Saudi Arabia. President Bush holds controversial meeting with Assad in Geneva.

1991 Syria balks at attending Middle East peace conference.

THINGS TO WATCH

What role will Syria play in Middle East peace talks?

Will Syria improve its human rights record?

LEBANON

Freed Briton John McCarthy, left, is embraced by United Nations Secretary-General Javier Perez de Cuellar.

LEBANON

• Beirut

The civil war that ripped Lebanon apart is over after 16 years. An estimated 150,000 lives were lost. There was $16 billion in damage, almost 800,000 people (25 percent of the population) fled the country, and "Lebanonization" became a synonym for chaos. Most of Lebanon's warring factions accepted an Arab League peace plan at a meeting in Taif, Saudi Arabia, in 1989. The only holdout was Gen. Michel Aoun, the Christian leader of the Lebanese Army, who rejected the pact and waged a fruitless "war of liberation" for almost two years. Finally, President Elias Hrawi asked the Syrian military to intervene. Within two days it was all over, and Aoun fled to the French Embassy for asylum.

Beirut is still a shambles, but optimism has returned to the capital. Thousands of refugees are coming back, businesses are opening and reconstruction has begun.

Many problems remain, and the situation is still fragile. The Hrawi government signed a new treaty of cooperation with Damascus, guaranteeing Syrian dominance over

Lebanon, which angered Christians and alarmed Israel, whose troops still patrol a nine-mile-deep security zone in the southern part of Lebanon. Shiite factions, loyal to Iran, still hold 10 Western hostages — five of them Americans — and refuse to release them.

AMERICAN HOSTAGES IN LEBANON

Terry Anderson: Associated Press journalist, kidnapped March 16, 1985.
Thomas Sutherland: University dean, kidnapped June 9, 1985.
Joseph James Cicippio: University official, kidnapped September 12, 1986.
Jesse Turner: Professor, kidnapped January 24, 1987.
Alann Steen: Kidnapped January 24, 1987.

WHO'S WHO

Elias Hrawi: Maronite Christian ... born 1926 ... President of new government elected under Arab League peace plan.

CHRONOLOGY

1975 Fighting erupts in Beirut.
1982 *June:* Israel invades Lebanon.
August: P.L.O. evacuated from Lebanon under supervision of multinational force.
September 10: Multinational force withdraws.
September 14: President Bashir Gemayel assassinated, succeeded by brother Amin Gemayel.
September 15: Israeli troops enter West Beirut.
September 16-17: Phalangist militiamen, under Israeli control,

massacre Palestinians at Sabra and Shatila refugee camps.
1983 Hizballah suicide terrorist attack kills 241 U.S. Marines in Beirut.
1984 U.S. Marines withdraw.
1985 Israeli troops withdraw, remain only in security zone in southern Lebanon.
1987 Terry Waite, Anglican Church envoy, kidnapped while negotiating for release of Western hostages.
1988 Gemayel leaves office. Moslems and Christians set up rival regimes.
1989 Renewed fighting breaks out between rival Moslem factions. Lieut. Col. William R. Higgins, American officer assigned to U.N. observer forces, murdered by kidnappers. Gen. Michel Aoun resists Taif peace formula. Rene Muawad, first president elected under Arab League plan, assassinated, replaced by Elias Hrawi.
1990 Fighting breaks out between rival Christian factions. Hostages Frank Herbert Reed and Robert Polhill freed by pro-Iranian captors. Syrian forces crush Aoun's rebellion.
1991 With Syrian support, central government consolidates its authority.
August 8: British hostage John McCarthy is released.
August 11: American hostage Edward A. Tracy is released.

THINGS TO WATCH

Will remaining hostages be freed?
Will the peace settlement hold?

JORDAN

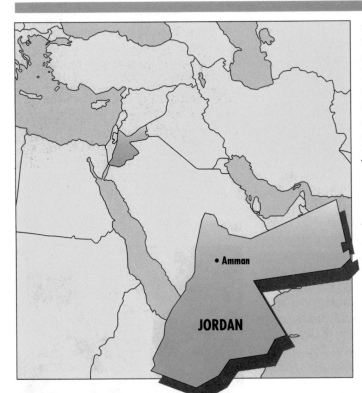

King Hussein of Jordan found himself in a very difficult political situation during the Persian Gulf crisis. He had long been considered a staunchly pro-Western moderate in the Arab world, but Iraqi leader Saddam Hussein's militant anti-Western rhetoric hit a responsive chord among the Palestinians who make up 40 percent of the Jordanian population, and Jordan, moreover, was economically dependent on trade with Iraq. Mass demonstrations in the streets were supportive of the Iraqi cause, and Jordanian shopkeepers displayed Saddam's portrait in shop windows. Some 80,000 Jordanians volunteered to fight for Iraq , if needed. King Hussein tried to find a middle ground. On the one hand, he formally denounced Iraq's invasion of Kuwait, but on the other hand he opposed the use of outside military forces in the Middle East and called for a peaceful Arab solution to the crisis instead. Such neutrality was interpreted as sympathy for Iraq, and angry Saudis cut off oil supplies and other trade.

Jordan wound up losing its foreign trade markets in Saudi Arabia, Kuwait and Iraq — affecting about one-third of its annual exports. The Saudis and Kuwaitis are still bitter, and U.N. economic sanctions are still in effect against Iraq. Shipping to Iraq through Jordan's port of Aqaba, a major transshipment point for Iraq-bound goods, is down sharply. Jordan's gross national product has dropped 10 percent, and the economy has lost $2 billion in revenues. Unemployment jumped from 15 percent before the war to an estimated 30 percent.

After the war, King Hussein tried to repair relations with the U.S. and other Arab states and promised more democratic reforms. But growing economic hardships may fuel social unrest.

WHO'S WHO

King Hussein: Head of state ... born 1935 ... Arab world's longest-serving ruler ... officially neutral during Persian Gulf crisis in 1990-91.

CHRONOLOGY

1921 British establish Transjordan (now Jordan), carved out of territory seized from Ottoman Empire during World War I, and install King Abdullah on throne.

1950 Jordan annexes West Bank region.

1951 King Abdullah assassinated in Jerusalem by Palestinians.

1952 Hussein becomes king at age 16.

1967 In Six Day War, Israel seizes West Bank and East Jerusalem. More than 300,000 Palestinian refugees flee to Jordan, causing severe political dislocation. Martial law imposed.

1970 Tensions between Jordanian authorities and P.L.O. reach breaking point. Jordanian troops attack and defeat P.L.O. forces.

1974 Arab leaders declare P.L.O. only legitimate representative of Palestinian people. However, Jordan continues to administer and fund West Bank public services.

1978 Hussein marries American-born Lisa Halaby, daughter of former head of Pan American Airways.

1985 Hussein signs treaty with P.L.O. leader Yassir Arafat, pledging joint work for peace in Middle East and establishment of confederation between Jordan and future Palestinian state.

1986 Hussein suspends treaty with P.L.O. because of Arafat's refusal to accept U.N. Security Council Resolutions 242 and 338, which recognize Israel's right to exist.

1987 Palestinian *intifada* (uprising) erupts on West Bank and in Gaza.

1988 King Hussein renounces claims on West Bank and urges P.L.O. to assume legal and administrative responsibility.

1989 Government relaxes political restrictions in effect since martial law declared in 1967 and permits parliamentary elections.

1990 Jordan maintains official neutrality during Persian Gulf crisis, but Jordanian public opinion supports Iraq. Saudi Arabia cuts off trade relations with Jordan, and Gulf states interrupt financial aid.

1991 King Hussein tries to repair ties to U.S. and other Arab states. Further democratic reforms planned.

THINGS TO WATCH

Will social unrest grow as economic difficulties continue?
Will Jordan overcome its international isolation?

ISRAEL WEST BANK

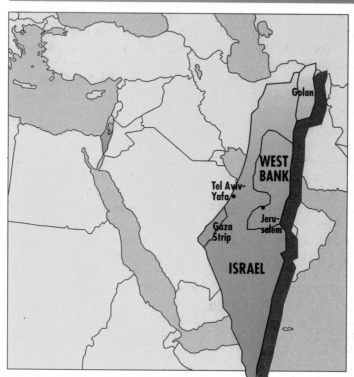

When the Gulf War ended, hopes were high that there was a "window of opportunity" to hammer out a comprehensive Middle East peace plan — that somehow the conflict between Israel and its Arab neighbors could finally be resolved. Iraqi attempts to break Arab adherence to the U.S.-led international coalition by linking resolution of the Gulf crisis to the Palestinian question had failed completely. Israel's compliance with U.S. requests to keep out of the Gulf War even after Iraqi-launched SCUD missiles hit Israeli cities also contributed to the optimism.

U.S. Secretary of State James A. Baker began a campaign of shuttle diplomacy to arrange an international conference, making four trips to the Middle East between March and early June. By June it began to look like the "window" had been missed, and the peace process began to unravel. Arab countries wanted the U.N. to sponsor a series of ongoing conferences. Israel, miffed by a U.N. resolution branding Zionism as racism, refused to consider U.N. participation on any level but was willing to attend a one-time-only conference sponsored by the U.S. and the Soviet Union; after that it wanted to negotiate one-on-one with the Arab states. Then Saudi Arabia decided it wasn't interested in participating in any conference whatsoever. Syria wanted Israel to give back the Golan Heights, which it has occupied since 1967. Israeli Prime Minister Yitzhak Shamir intransigently defied U.S. pressure to cede occupied territory for peace and bristled at American criticism of Israel's accelerated program of Jewish settlement on the West Bank. Shamir insisted that the West Bank is part of Biblical Israel and vital to Israeli national security. He vowed never to give an inch of land.

Meanwhile in Israel, the Palestinian *intifada* (uprising), which began in December 1987, continues, and conditions for Palestinians on the West Bank and in Gaza worsen. By June 1991, Palestinian activists had killed 318 Arabs suspected of being Israeli collaborators, Israeli troops and civilians had killed 781 Palestinians, and 69 Jews had lost their lives. During the Persian Gulf War, Israeli authorities closed down crossing points from the occupied territories into Israel, and many Palestinians could not get to their jobs. After the war, many found their jobs had been taken by the Russian Jewish immigrants who have been flooding into the country. Despite U.N. condemnation, Israel continued to expel suspected activists from the territories. Because the Palestine Liberation Organization (P.L.O.) lost credibility and support in the Arab world for backing Iraq in the Persian Gulf crisis, the debate over who should represent the Palestinians in peace negotiations was reopened.

WHO'S WHO

Yassir Arafat: P.L.O. Chairman ... born 1929 ... founder and leader of Al Fatah organization.
Shimon Peres: Leader of Labor Party ... born 1923 ... considered moderate ... favors negotiations with Palestinians.
Yitzhak Shamir: Prime Minister ... born 1915 ... Leader of Likud Party ... a hard-liner ... opposed to U.S. plan for peace talks with Palestinians.

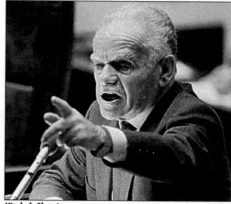

Yitzhak Shamir

PALESTINIAN GROUPS

Palestine Liberation Organization: Umbrella organization for several Palestinian factions. Generally recognized as representative of Palestinian people.

Component groups of P.L.O.:
Al Fatah: Founded 1959. Led by Yassir Arafat. Considered moderate, centrist. Largest Palestinian militia. Based in Tunisia.

Palestine Communist Party: Founded 1920. Led by Suleiman Ennadjab. No militia.

Salka: Founded 1967. Pro-Syrian. Led by Issam Kadi and Samini Attari. Small militia. Based in Syria.

Arab Liberation Front: Founded 1969. Led by Abdul-Rahmin Ahmed. Tiny militia. Based in Iraq.

Popular Front for the Liberation of Palestine (P.F.L.P.): Founded 1967. Led by Dr. George

Habash. Hard-line Marxist. Second-largest militia. Based in Syria.

Palestinian National Council: Political arm of P.L.O. Functions as parliament in exile.

Palestinian splinter groups:
Revolutionary Council of Fatah: Split from Arafat in 1970's. Led by Abu Nidal. Terrorist group. Based in Libya.

Fatah Uprising: Split from Arafat in 1982. Led by Abu Moussa. Small militia. Based in Syria.

Democratic Front for the Liberation of Palestine: Split from Habash in 1969. Led by Nayef Hawatmeh. Third-largest militia. Based in Syria.

P.F.L.P.-General Command: Split from Habash's P.F.L.P. in 1967. Led by Ahmed Jibril. Based in Syria.

Palestine Liberation Front: Split from PFLP-GC in 1976. Led by Abu Abbas. Tiny militia. Based in Iraq.

CHRONOLOGY

1948 Israeli War for Independence.
1956 Suez War.
1967 *June:* Six-Day War. Jewish settlement of occupied West Bank begins.
November: U.N. Security Council adopts Resolution 242, calling for Israeli withdrawal from West Bank and recognition of right to exist for all states in region.
1973 Yom Kippur War. U.N. Security Council adopts Resolution 338, calling for peace settlement in Middle East.
1974 P.L.O. gets permanent-observer status at U.N.
1977 *June:* Menachem Begin elected Israeli prime minister.
November: Egyptian President Anwar el-Sadat becomes first Arab leader to visit Israel.
1978 Camp David peace talks take place among Sadat, Begin and President Jimmy Carter.
1979 Sadat and Begin sign peace treaty at White House.

1981 Sadat assassinated.
1982 Israel invades Lebanon.
1983 Yitzhak Shamir succeeds Begin as prime minister.
1984 Israeli Unity Coalition government formed. Labor Party leader Shimon Peres and Likud's Shamir alternate as prime minister.
1985 Israel completes withdrawal from Lebanon.
1987 *December:* Palestinian uprising begins.
1988 *July:* Jordan's King Hussein renounces all claim to sovereignty over West Bank territories.
November: Likud and Labor form new coalition government. Likud gets prime minister and foreign minister posts. Palestinian National Council declares formation of independent Palestinian state.
December: In address to U.N. General Assembly meeting in Geneva, Arafat renounces terrorism, recognizes Israel's right to exist and accepts U.N. Resolutions 242 and 338. U.S. opens dialogue with P.L.O.
1989 Palestinian uprising continues. Talks between U.S. and P.L.O. proceed slowly.
1990 Palestinian uprising continues. Political crisis erupts in Israel over American proposal for direct peace talks with Palestinians. Government falls. Labor attempts but fails to constitute ruling coalition, and governmental crisis continues.

Two Israeli soldiers worked all night in the rubble of houses heavily damaged in an Iraqi SCUD missile attack in the Tel Aviv area.

Deranged Israeli murders seven Palestinian laborers, sparking violent riots in Gaza, West Bank and Arab neighborhoods within Israel itself. Likud forms new right-wing coalition government.
1991 In compliance with U.S. request, Israel does not retaliate against SCUD missile attacks launched from Iraq during Persian Gulf War. U.S. deploys and sends crews to operate Patriot antimissile batteries to protect Israel against SCUD attacks. Secretary of State James Baker fails in bid to get Israeli government to consider withdrawal from occupied West Bank territories as concession in Middle East peace process.

THINGS TO WATCH

Will the *intifada* continue?
Will the Middle East peace process be revived?

SOUTH AFRICA

Winnie and Nelson Mandela

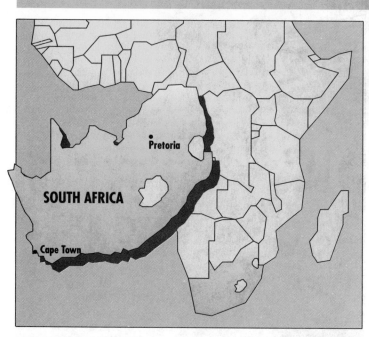

South Africa continues on its tortuous path toward democracy and racial justice. President Frederik Willem de Klerk has issued a call for an end to all apartheid laws, prompting the European Community to lift economic sanctions against South Africa. Right-wing efforts to block de Klerk's liberalization drive have fallen flat. The biggest obstacle is the persistence of factional violence in the black community, often pitting followers of Nelson Mandela's African National Congress (A.N.C.) against members of the rival Inkatha Freedom Party, led by Zulu Chief Mangosuthu Buthelezi. In the last four years, more than 5,000 people have died in the black-against-black violence. The A.N.C. accuses pro-apartheid forces of being responsible for the factional violence and insists that the government take action to stop the bloodshed, refusing to participate in negotiations on a new constitution unless the government acts decisively. The A.N.C. wants the government to withdraw legal approval for Inkatha members to carry traditional "cultural" weapons (such as machetes and spears). Face-to-face negotiations between Mandela and Buthelezi failed to end the violence.

WHO'S WHO

Bishop Desmond Tutu: Anti-apartheid leader ... born 1931 ... advocate of non-violence ... Anglican Archbishop of Cape Town ... Nobel Peace Prize winner 1984.

Nelson Mandela: Anti-apartheid leader ... born 1918 ... leader of African National Congress ... sentenced to life imprisonment in 1964 ... released February 1990.

Frederik Willem de Klerk: President of South Africa ... born 1936 ... proponent of liberalization.

Mangosuthu Gatsha Buthelezi: Hereditary Zulu Chief and leader of Inkatha Freedom Party ... born 1928.

CHRONOLOGY

1948 National Party comes to power, imposes apartheid.

1958 Prime Minister Hendrik F. Verwoerd assassinated.

1960 Sharpeville Massacre: Police kill 69 anti-apartheid demonstrators.

1961 South Africa withdraws from British Commonwealth.

1964 Nelson Mandela convicted of treason, imprisoned for life.

1976 Blacks riot in Soweto and other locations; police kill 600 protesters.

1978 Pieter Willem Botha becomes prime minister.

1980's Government relaxes some apartheid restrictions.

1984 Blacks stage demonstrations against apartheid. Bishop Desmond Tutu wins Nobel Peace Prize.

1985 Demonstrations continue.

1986 National state of emergency declared by government. European Community and U.S. impose sanctions.

1987 State of emergency renewed.

1989 Botha replaced by Frederik Willem de Klerk. De Klerk vows to maintain apartheid but also promises liberalization.

1990 De Klerk legalizes 60 banned black African organizations, frees Mandela and offers negotiations. Right-wing white groups denounce de Klerk's concessions, form armed vigilante groups. Violence and demonstrations continue. Negotiations between Mandela and de Klerk begin.

1991 Negotiations between Mandela and Zulu Chief Mangosuthu Buthelezi's Inkatha Freedom Party fail to end black factional violence. De Klerk calls for end to all apartheid laws and visits Washington. European Community lifts economic sanctions against South Africa. Winnie Mandela convicted as accessory in kidnapping and assault case. President George Bush proposes end to U.S. sanctions against South Africa.

THINGS TO WATCH

Will Mandela and de Klerk succeed in negotiations?
Will the U.S. lift sanctions against South Africa?
Will black factional violence end?

WORLD GEOGRAPHICAL INFORMATION

Equatorial diameter of the earth, 7,926.38 miles.
Polar diameter of the earth, 7,899.80 miles.
Mean diameter of the earth, 7,917.52 miles.
Equatorial circumference of the earth, 24,901.46 miles.
Polar circumference of the earth, 24,855.34 miles.
Mean distance from the earth to the sun, 93,020,000 miles.
Mean distance from the earth to the moon, 238,857 miles.
Total area of the earth, 197,000,000 square miles.

Highest elevation on the earth's surface, Mt. Everest, Asia, 29,028 feet.
Lowest elevation on the earth's land surface, shores of the Dead Sea, Asia, 1,312 feet below sea level.
Greatest known depth of the ocean, southwest of Guam, Pacific Ocean, 35,810 feet.
Total land area of the earth (incl. inland water and Antarctica), 57,800,000 square miles.

Area of Africa, 11,700,000 square miles.
Area of Antarctica, 5,400,000 square miles.
Area of Asia, 17,300,000 square miles.
Area of Europe, 3,800,000 square miles.
Area of North America, 9,400,000 square miles.
Area of Oceania (incl. Australia) 3,300,000 square miles.
Area of South America, 6,900,000 square miles.
Population of the earth (est.1/1/91), 5,350,000,000.

Principal Islands and Their Areas

ISLAND	Area (Sq. Mi.)
Baffin I., Can.	195,928
Banks I., Can.	27,038
Borneo (Kalimantan), Asia	287,300
Bougainville, Papua New Guinea	3,600
Cape Breton I., Can.	3,981
Celebes (Sulawesi), Indon.	73,057
Ceram (Seram), Indon.	45,801
Corsica, France	3,352
Crete, Greece	3,189
Cuba, N.A.	42,800
Cyprus, Asia	3,572
Devon I., Can.	21,331
Ellesmere I., Can.	75,767
Flores, Indon.	5,502
Great Britain, U.K.	88,795
Greenland, N.A.	840,000
Guadalcanal, Solomon Is.	2,060
Hainan Dao, China	13,100
Hawaii, U.S.	4,034
Hispaniola, N.A.	29,300
Hokkaidō, Japan	32,245
Honshū, Japan	89,176
Iceland, Europe	39,800
Ireland, Europe	32,600
Jamaica, N.A.	4,200
Java (Jawa), Indon.	51,038
Kodiak I., U.S.	3,670
Kyūshū, Japan	17,129
Leyte, Philippines	2,785
Long Island, U.S.	1,377
Luzon, Philippines	40,420
Madagascar, Africa	227,000
Melville I., Can.	16,274
Mindanao, Philippines	36,537
Mindoro, Philippines	3,759
Negros, Philippines	4,907
New Britain, Papua New Guinea	14,093
New Caledonia, Oceania	6,252
Newfoundland, Can.	42,031
New Guinea, Asia-Oceania	309,000
New Ireland, Papua New Guinea	3,500
North East Land, Norway	6,350
North I., New Zealand	44,274
Novaya Zemlya, Sov. Un.	31,900
Palawan, Philippines	4,550
Panay, Philippines	4,446
Prince of Wales I., Can.	12,872
Puerto Rico, N.A.	3,500
Sakhalin, Sov. Un.	29,500
Samar, Philippines	5,100
Sardinia, Italy	9,301
Shikoku, Japan	7,258
Sicily, Italy	9,926
Somerset I., Can.	9,570
Southampton I., Can.	15,913
South I., New Zealand	57,870
Spitsbergen, Norway	15,260
Sri Lanka, Asia	24,900
Sumatra (Sumatera), Indon.	182,860
Taiwan, Asia	13,900
Tasmania, Austl.	26,200
Tierra del Fuego, S.A.	18,600
Timor, Indon.	5,743
Vancouver I., Can.	12,079
Victoria I., Can.	83,897
Vrangelya (Wrangel), Sov. Un.	2,800

Principal Lakes, Oceans, Seas, and Their Areas

LAKE Country	Area (Sq. Mi.)
Arabian Sea,	1,492,000
Aral'skoye More, (Aral Sea) Sov. Un.	24,700
Arctic Ocean,	5,400,000
Athabasca, L., Can.	3,064
Atlantic Ocean,	31,800,000
Balkhash, Ozero, (L.) Sov. Un.	7,100
Baltic Sea, Eur.	163,000
Baykal, Ozero, (L. Baikal) Sov. Un.	12,200
Bering Sea, Asia-N.A.	876,000
Black Sea, Eur.-Asia	178,000
Caribbean Sea, N.A.-S.A.	1,063,000
Caspian Sea, Iran-Sov. Un.	143,240
Chad, L., Cameroon-Chad-Nig.	6,300
Erie, L., Can.-U.S.	9,910
Eyre, L., Austl.	3,700
Gairdner, L., Austl.	1,700
Great Bear Lake, Can.	12,095
Great Salt Lake, U.S.	1,680
Great Slave Lake, Can.	11,030
Hudson Bay, Can.	475,000
Huron, L., Can.-U.S.	23,000
Indian Ocean,	28,900,000
Japan, Sea of, Asia	389,000
Koko Nor, (Qinghai Hu) China	1,650
Ladozhskoye Ozero, (L. Ladoga) Sov. Un.	683
Manitoba, L., Can.	1,785
Mediterranean Sea, Eur.-Afr.-Asia	967,000
Mexico, Gulf of, N.A.	596,000
Michigan, L., U.S.	22,300
Nicaragua, Lago de, Nic.	3,150
North Sea, Eur.	222,000
Nyasa, L., Malawi-Mozambique-Tanz.	11,150
Onezhskoye Ozero, (L. Onega) Sov. Un.	3,753
Ontario, L., Can.-U.S.	7,540
Pacific Ocean,	63,800,000
Red Sea, Afr.-Asia	169,000
Rudolf, L., Ethiopia-Kenya	2,473
Superior, L., Can.-U.S.	31,700
Tanganyika. L., Afr.	12,350
Titicaca, Lago, Bol.-Peru	3,200
Torrens, L., Austl.	2,300
Vänern, (L.) Swe.	2,156
Van Gölü, (L.) Tur.	1,420
Victoria, L., Ken.-Tan.-Ug.	26,820
Winnipeg, L., Can.	9,416
Winnipegosis, L., Can.	2,075
Yellow Sea, China-Korea	480,000

Principal Mountains and Their Heights

MOUNTAIN Country	Elev. (Ft.)
Aconcagua, Cerro, Argentina	22,831
Annapurna, Nepal	26,504
Antofalla, Volcán, Argentina	20,013
Api, Nepal	23,399
Apo, Mt., Philippines	9,692
Ararat, Turkey	16,804
Ayers Rock, Australia	2,844
Barú, Volcán, Panama	11,410
Belukha, Gol'tsy, Soviet Union	14,783
Bia, Phu, Laos	9,252
Blanc, Mont, France-Italy	15,771
Blanca Pk., Colorado, U.S.	14,317
Bolívar (La Columna), Venezuela	16,411
Borah Pk., Idaho, U.S.	12,662
Cameroon Mtn., Cameroon	13,451
Carrauntoohil, Ireland	3,414
Chimborazo, Ecuador	20,561
Chirripó, Cerro, Costa Rica	12,530
Colima, Nevado de, Mexico	13,993
Cook, Mt., New Zealand	12,349
Cotopaxi, Ecuador	19,347
Cristóbal Colón, Pico, Colombia	19,029
Damāvand, Qolleh-ye, Iran	18,386
Dhaulāgiri, Nepal	26,810
Duarte, Pico, Dominican Rep.	10,417
Dychtau, gora, Soviet Union	17,073
Egmont, Mt., New Zealand	8,260
Elbert, Mt., Colorado, U.S.	14,431
El'brus, Gora, Soviet Union	18,510
Elgon, Mt., Kenya-Uganda	14,178
eNjesuthi, South Africa	11,306
Erciyeş Daği, Turkey	12,848
Etna, Mt., Italy	10,902
Everest, Mt., China-Nepal	29,028
Fairweather, Mt., Alaska-Canada	15,300
Finsteraarhorn, Switzerland	14,022
Foraker, Mt., Alaska, U.S.	17,400
Fuji-san, Japan	12,388
Gannett Pk., Wyoming, U.S.	13,785
Gasherbrum, China-Pakistan	26,470
Gerlachovský Stít, Czechoslovakia	8,710
Giluwe, Mt., Papua New Guinea	14,331
Glittertinden, Norway	8,110
Gongga Shan, China	24,790
Grand Teton Mtn., Wyoming, U.S.	13,766
Grossglockner, Austria	12,461
Gunnbjørn Fjeld, Greenland	12,139
Hadūr Shu'ayb, Yemen	12,336
Haleakala Crater, Hawaii, U.S.	10,025
Haltiatunturi, Finland-Norway	4,357
Hekla, Iceland	4,892
Hkakabo Razi, Burma	19,296
Hood, Mt., Oregon, U.S.	11,239
Huascarán, Nevado, Peru	22,205
Huila, Nevado de, Colombia	18,865
Hvannadalshnúkur, Iceland	6,952
Illampu, Nevado, Bolivia	20,873
Illimani, Nevado, Bolivia	21,151
Iztaccíhuatl, Mexico	17,343
Jaya, Puncak, Indonesia	16,503
Jungfrau, Switzerland	13,642
K2 (Godwin Austen), China-Pakistan	28,250
Kāmet, China-India	25,447
Kānchenjunga, India- Nepal	28,208
Karisimbi, Volcan, Rwanda-Zaire	14,787
Kātrīnā, Jabal, Egypt	8,668
Kebnekaise, Sweden	6,962
Kenya, Mt., Kenya	17,058
Kerinci, Gunung, Indonesia	12,467
Kilimanjaro, Tanzania	19,340
Kinabalu, Gunong, Malaysia	13,455
Klyuchevskaya, Soviet Union	15,584
Kommunizma, Pik, Soviet Union	24,590
Korab, Albania-Yugoslavia	9,026
Kosciusko, Mt., Australia	7,316
Koussi, Emi, Chad	11,204
Kula Kangri, Bhutan	24,784
Lassen Pk., California, U.S.	10,457
Llullaillaco, Volcán, Argentina-Chile	22,057
Logan, Mt., Canada	19,524
Longs Pk., Colorado, U.S.	14,255
Makālu, China-Nepal	27,825
Margherita Pk., Zaire-Uganda	16,763
Markham, Mt., Antarctica	14,272
Maromokotro, Madagascar	9,436
Matterhorn, Italy-Switzerland	14,692
Mauna Kea, Hawaii, U.S.	13,796
Mauna Loa, Hawaii, U.S.	13,680
McKinley, Mt., Alaska, U.S.	20,320
Meru, Mt., Tanzania	14,978
Misti, Volcán, Peru	19,098
Mitchell, Mt., North Carolina, U.S.	6,684
Moldoveanu, Romania	8,343
Mulhacén, Spain (continental)	11,424
Musala, Bulgaria	9,596
Muztag, China	25,338
Muztagata, China	24,757
Namjagbarwa Feng, China	25,446
Nanda Devi, India	25,645
Nānga Parbat, Pakistan	26,650
Narodnaya, Gora, Soviet Union	6,214
Neblina, Pico da, Brazil-Venezuela	9,888
Nevis, Ben, United Kingdom	4,406
Ojos del Salado, Nevado, Argentina-Chile	22,615
Ólimbos, Cyprus	6,401
Ólimbos, Greece	9,570
Orizaba, Pico de, Mexico	18,406
Orohena, Mont, French Polynesia	7,352
Paektu san, North Korea-China	9,003
Paricutín, Mexico	9,213
Parnassós, Greece	8,061
Pelée, Montagne, Martinique	4,800
Pico, Cape Verde	9,281
Pidurutalagala, Sri Lanka	8,281
Pikes Pk., Colorado, U.S.	14,110
Pissis, Monte, Argentina	22,241
Pobedy, pik, China-Soviet Union	24,406
Popocatépetl, Volcán, Mexico	17,887
Pulog, Mt., Philippines	9,606
Rainier, Mt., Washington, U.S.	14,410
Ras Dashen Terara, Ethiopia	15,158
Rinjani, Gunung, Indonesia	12,224
Rosa, Monte, Italy-Switzerland	15,203
Ruapehu, New Zealand	9,175
St. Elias, Mt., Alaska, U.S.-Canada	18,008
Sajama, Nevado, Bolivia	21,463
Sawdā', Qurnat as, Lebanon	10,114
Scafell Pikes, England, U.K.	3,210
Semeru, Gunung, Indonesia	12,060
Shām, Jabal ash, Oman	9,902
Shasta, Mt., California, U.S.	14,162
Snowdon, Wales, U.K.	3,566
Tahat, Algeria	9,541
Tajumulco (Vol.), Guatemala	13,816
Tirich Mīr, Pakistan	25,230
Tomanivi (Victoria), Fiji	4,341
Toubkal, Jebel, Morocco	13,665
Triglav, Yugoslavia	9,393
Trikora, Puncak, Indonesia	15,584
Tupungato, Portezuelo de, Argentina-Chile	22,310
Turquino, Pico de, Cuba	6,496
Vesuvio (Vesuvius), Italy	4,190
Victoria, Mt., Papua New Guinea	13,238
Vinson Massif, Antarctica	16,864
Waddington, Mt., Canada	13,260
Washington, Mt., New Hampshire, U.S.	6,288
Weisshorn, Switzerland	14,783
Whitney, Mt., California, U.S.	14,491
Wilhelm, Mt., Papua New Guinea	14,793
Wrangell, Mt., Alaska, U.S.	14,163
Xixabangma Feng (Gosainthan), China	26,286
Zugspitze, Austria-Germany	9,721

Principal Rivers and Their Lengths

RIVER Continent	Length (Mi.)
Albany, N.A.	610
Aldan, Asia	1,412
Amazonas-Ucayali, S.A.	4,000
Amu Darya, Asia	1,578
Amur, Asia	2,744
Amur-Argun, Asia	2,761
Araguaia, S.A.	1,400
Arkansas, N.A.	1,459
Athabasca, N.A.	765
Brahmaputra, Asia	1,770
Branco, S.A.	580
Brazos, N.A.	900
Canadian, N.A.	906
Churchill, N.A.	1,000
Colorado, N.A. (U.S.-Mex.)	1,450
Columbia, N.A.	1,200
Congo (Zaïre), Africa	2,900
Cumberland, N.A.	720
Danube, Europe	1,776
Darling, Australia	864
Dnepr, (Dnieper) Europe	1,400
Dnestr, (Dniestr) Europe	840
Don, Europe	1,162
Elbe, Europe	720
Euphrates, Asia	1,510
Fraser, N.A.	851
Ganges, Asia	1,560
Gila, N.A.	630
Godāvari, Asia	930
Green, N.A.	730
Huang, (Yellow) Asia	3,395
Indus, Asia	1,800
Irrawaddy, Asia	1,300
Juruá, S.A.	1,250
Kama, Europe	1,122
Kasai, Africa	1,338
Kolyma, Asia	1,323
Lena, Asia	2,700
Limpopo, Africa	1,100
Loire, Europe	625
Mackenzie, N.A.	2,635
Madeira, S.A.	2,013
Magdalena, S.A.	950
Marañón, S.A.	1,000
Mekong, Asia	2,600
Meuse, Europe	575
Mississippi, N.A.	2,348
Mississippi-Missouri, N.A.	3,740
Missouri, N.A.	2,315
Murray, Australia	1,566
Negro, S.A.	1,300
Neman, Europe	582
Niger, Africa	2,600
Nile, Africa	4,145
North Platte, N.A.	618
Ob'-Irtysh, Asia	3,362
Oder, Europe	565
Ohio, N.A.	981
Oka, Europe	900
Orange, Africa	1,300
Orinoco, S.A.	1,600
Ottawa, N.A.	790
Paraguay, S.A.	1,610
Paraná, S.A.	2,800
Parnaíba, S.A.	850
Peace, N.A.	1,195
Pechora, Europe	1,124
Pecos, N.A.	735
Pilcomayo, S.A.	1,550
Plata-Paraná, S.A.	3,030
Purús, S.A.	1,860
Red, N.A.	1,270
Rhine, Europe	820
Rhône, Europe	500
Rio Grande, N.A.	1,885
Roosevelt, S.A.	950
St. Lawrence, N.A.	800
Salado, S.A.	900
Salween, (Nu) Asia	1,750
São Francisco, S.A.	1,988
Saskatchewan-Bow, N.A.	1,205
Sava, Europe	585
Snake, N.A.	1,038
Sungari, (Songhua) Asia	1,140
Syr Dar'ya, Asia	1,370
Tagus, Europe	625
Tarim, Asia	1,328
Tennessee, N.A.	652
Tigris, Asia	1,180
Tisa, Europe	607
Tobol, Asia	989
Tocantins, S.A.	1,640
Ucayali, S.A.	1,220
Ural, Asia	1,509
Uruguay, S.A.	1,025
Verkhnyaya Tunguska, (Angara) Asia	1,105
Vilyuy, Asia	1,647
Volga, Europe	2,194
White, N.A. (Ar.-Mo.)	720
Wisła (Vistula), Europe	630
Xiang, Asia	930
Xingu, S.A.	1,230
Yangtze, (Chang) Asia	3,900
Yellowstone, N.A.	671
Yenisey, Asia	2,543
Yukon, N.A.	1,770
Zambezi, Africa	1,700

MAP SYMBOLS

The map is a unique means of recording and communicating geographic information. By reducing the world to a smaller scale and symbolizing reality, it enables us to see regions of the earth well beyond our ordinary range of vision. Thus, a map represents one of the most convenient, accurate, and effective ways to learn about size, distance, direction, and the geographic features of our planet.

An atlas is a collection of general reference maps and, whether readers are interested in the political boundaries of the Middle East or in the distribution of oil reserves, an atlas is an indispensable aid to understanding the many facets of our complex earth and the general course of world events.

Basic continental and regional coverage of the world's land area is provided by this atlas. The reference maps, preceded by a map of the world, follow a continental arrangement: Europe, Asia, Australia, Africa, North America, and South America.

Many of the symbols used are self-explanatory. A complete legend below provides a key to the symbols on the reference maps in this atlas.

The surface configuration of the earth is represented by hill-shading, which gives the three-dimensional impression of landforms. This terrain representation conveys a realistic and readily visualized impression of the surface.

If the world used one alphabet and one language, no particular difficulty would arise in understanding nonalphabetic languages. However, some of the nations of the world use nonalphabetic languages. Their symbols are transliterated into the Roman alphabet. In this atlas a "local-name" policy generally was used for naming cities and towns and all local topographic and water features. However, for a few major cities the Anglicized name was preferred and the local name given in parentheses, for instance, Moscow (*Moskva*), Vienna (*Wien*), Cologne (*Köln*). In countries where more than one official language is used, a name is in the dominant local language. The generic parts of local names for topographic and water features are self-explanatory in many cases because of the associated map symbols or type styles.

Map Symbols

CULTURAL FEATURES

Political Boundaries

------ International

------ Secondary: State, Provincial, etc.

Cities, Towns and Villages
(Not applicable to maps at 1:20,000,000 or smaller scale or to those with legend in map margin)

PARIS — 1,000,000 and over

Ufa — 500,000 to 1,000,000

Győr — 50,000 to 500,000

Agadir — 25,000 to 50,000

Moreno — 0 to 25,000

TŌKYŌ — National Capitals

Boise — Secondary Capitals

Transportation

——— Railroads

- - - - - Railroad Ferries

· · · · · · Caravan Routes

Other Cultural Features

Dams

+ + + + + Pipelines

▲ Pyramids

∴ Ruins

LAND FEATURES

△ Peaks, Spot Heights

= Passes

WATER FEATURES

Lakes and Reservoirs

Fresh Water

Fresh Water: Intermittent

Salt Water

Salt Water: Intermittent

Other Water Features

Swamps

Glaciers

Rivers

Canals

Aqueduct — Aqueducts

= = = = = = Ship Channels

Falls

Rapids

Springs

△ Water Depths

Sand Bars

Reefs

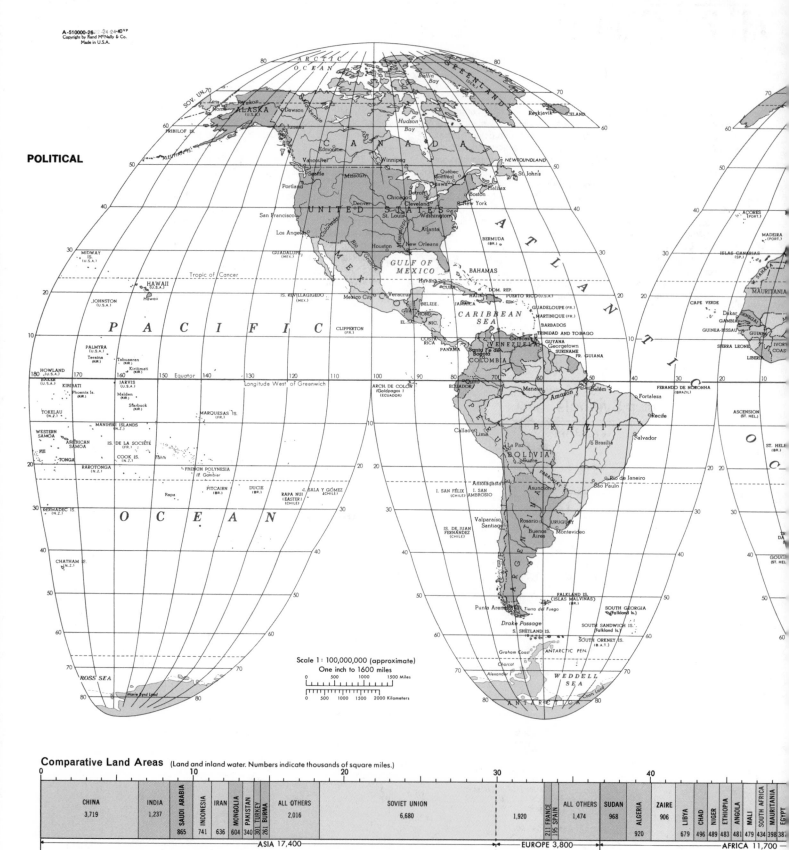

POLITICAL

Scale 1 : 100,000,000 (approximate)
One inch to 1600 miles

0   500   1000   1500 Miles

0   500   1000   1500   2000 Kilometers

Comparative Land Areas (Land and inland water. Numbers indicate thousands of square miles.)

0		10							20		30		40							

| CHINA 3,719 | INDIA 1,237 | SAUDI ARABIA 865 | INDONESIA 741 | IRAN 636 | MONGOLIA 604 | PAKISTAN 340 | TURKEY 301 | BURMA 261 | ALL OTHERS 2,016 | SOVIET UNION 6,680 | 1,920 | FRANCE 211 | SPAIN 195 | ALL OTHERS 1,474 | SUDAN 968 | ALGERIA 920 | ZAIRE 906 | LIBYA 679 | CHAD 496 | NIGER 489 | ETHIOPIA 483 | ANGOLA 481 | MALI 479 | SOUTH AFRICA 434 | MAURITANIA 398 | EGYPT 38. |

←————————— ASIA 17,400 —————————→ ←— EUROPE 3,800 —→ ←———— AFRICA 11,700

Comparative Populations (Numbers indicate millions of people) 1/1/89 estimate

0	10	20	30	40	

| CHINA 1,094.7 | INDIA 825.0 | INDONESIA 185.9 | JAPAN 123.0 | BANGLADESH 111.4 | PAKISTAN 109.0 | VIETNAM 66.0 |

←—————————————————————— ASIA 3,131 —————————————————————→

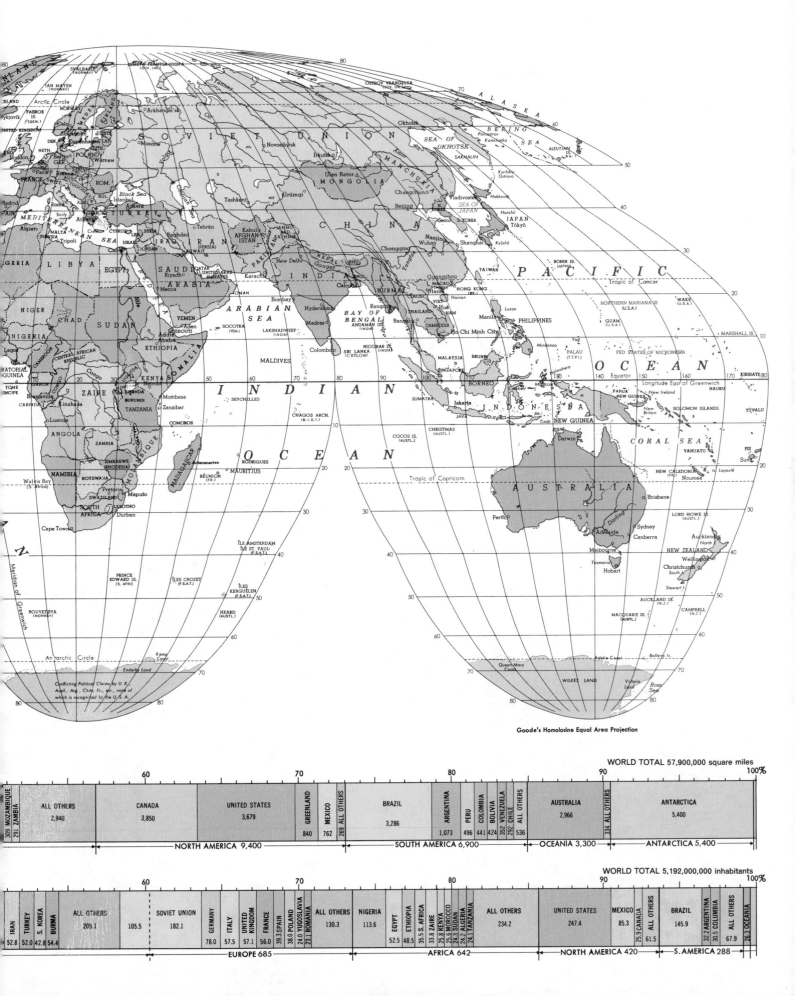

Goode's Homolosine Equal Area Projection

WORLD TOTAL 57,900,000 square miles

MOZAMBIQUE 309	ZAMBIA 291	ALL OTHERS 2,940	CANADA 3,850	UNITED STATES 3,679	GREENLAND 840	MEXICO 762	ALL OTHERS 269	BRAZIL 3,286	ARGENTINA 1,073	PERU 496	COLOMBIA 441	BOLIVIA 424	VENEZUELA 352	CHILE 292	ALL OTHERS 536	AUSTRALIA 2,966	ALL OTHERS 334	ANTARCTICA 5,400

NORTH AMERICA 9,400 — SOUTH AMERICA 6,900 — OCEANIA 3,300 — ANTARCTICA 5,400

WORLD TOTAL 5,192,000,000 inhabitants

IRAN 52.8	TURKEY 52.0	S. KOREA 42.8	BURMA 54.4	ALL OTHERS 205.1	SOVIET UNION 182.1	GERMANY 78.0	ITALY 57.5	UNITED KINGDOM 57.1	FRANCE 56.0	SPAIN 39.3	POLAND 38.0	YUGOSLAVIA 24.0	ROMANIA 23.1	ALL OTHERS 130.3	NIGERIA 113.6	EGYPT 52.5	ETHIOPIA 48.5	S. AFRICA 35.5	ZAIRE 33.8	KENYA 25.8	MOROCCO 24.2	SUDAN 24.2	ALGERIA 24.1	TANZANIA 24.1	ALL OTHERS 234.2	UNITED STATES 247.4	MEXICO 85.3	CANADA 25.9	ALL OTHERS 61.5	BRAZIL 145.9	ARGENTINA 32.2	COLOMBIA 30.5	ALL OTHERS 67.9	OCEANIA 26.3

EUROPE 685 — AFRICA 642 — NORTH AMERICA 420 — S. AMERICA 288

40,000 SQ MI
AREA

0   100   200
Miles

ARCTIC

ICELAND

Reykjavik
Reykjanes
Eskifjördur

ATLANTIC OCEAN

Arctic Circle

FAEROE IS.
(Den.)

SHETLAND IS.
(Br.)

Lerwick

ORKNEY IS.
(Br.)

HEBRIDES

SCOTLAND

GLASGOW
Aberdeen
Dundee
Edinburgh

BRITISH
ISLES

NORTHERN IRELAND
Belfast

IRELAND

Carlisle
NEWCASTLE

UNITED
KINGDOM

Galway
Dublin
(Baile Átha Cliath)

LIVERPOOL
LEEDS
MANCHESTER

Cork
Cobh

CAPE CLEAR

BIRMINGHAM
Leicester
Kingston upon Hull

ISLES OF SCILLY

LANDS END

Southampton
Portsmouth

LONDON

Dover

English Channel

CHANNEL IS.
(Br.)

Cherbourg
Le Havre
Rouen

Brest

Rennes

PARIS

St. Nazaire

Orléans

Nantes
Tours

La Rochelle

FRANCE

Dijon

Bay of Biscay

El Ferrol
La Coruña
C. DE FINISTERRE

Gijón
Oviedo
Santander
S. Sebastián

Bordeaux

Clermont-
Ferrand

Lausanne
Geneva

LYON

Vigo

Porto
(Oporto)

Coimbra

Bilbao
PYRENEES

Bayonne

Toulouse

Nîmes

MARSEILLE

Toulon

Salamanca
Valladolid

ANDORRA

PORTUGAL

LISBON
(Lisboa)

MADRID
SPAIN

Zaragoza

BARCELONA

Tarragona
Tortosa

Valencia

SARDINIA
(It.)

CORSICA
(Fr.)

Ajaccio

SARDINIA
(It.)

Cádiz
Sevilla

SIERRA MORENA

Murcia

Cartagena

ISLAS BALEARES
(Sp.)

MENORCA

MALLORCA
Palma

IBIZA

C. DE LA NAO

Málaga
Almería

SIERRA NEVADA

Tanger
Gibraltar (Br.)
Ceuta (Sp.)

DEL ALBORAN
(Sp.)

Algiers
(El Djazair)

Oran

Rabat
Fès

Casablanca

MOROCCO

ATLAS MOUNTAINS

ALGERIA

Constantine

Bizerte
Tunis

TUNISIA

MEDITERRANEAN

MALTA

Palermo
Messina

SICILY
(It.)

Mt. Etna
10 902

Catania

C. PASSERO

TYRRHENIAN
SEA

Cagliari

C. SPARTIVENTO

NORTH
SEA

Trondheim
(Nidaros)

DOVRE
FJELL
Glittertinden

Bergen

Stavanger

Kristiansand

LINDESNES

NORWAY

Oslo

Karlstad

Göteborg

ÁLborg

DENMARK

COPENHAGEN
(København)

HAMBURG

Kiel
Lübeck

Bremen

Hannover

NETHERLANDS

AMSTERDAM
The Hague
('s-Gravenhage)

ROTTERDAM

ANTWERP

BELGIUM

BRUSSELS

LILLE

Calais

Reims

Strasbourg

ESSEN
COLOGNE
Bonn

GERMANY

Mainz

LUX.
Luxembourg

FRANKFURT a. M.

Nürnberg

STUTTGART

MUNICH

Bodensee

Zürich
Bern

SWITZERLAND

Mont Blanc
15 771

MILAN

TURIN

Genoa

Nice

MONACO

Livorno

La Spezia

Bologna

Florence

SAN
MARINO

ROME
(Roma)

NAPLES
(Napoli)

Vesuvio
4190

Bari

Brindisi

APENNINES

Venice

Trieste

Ancona

IONIAN
SEA

Golfo di
Taranto

Stavanger

SWEDEN

Sundsvall

Umeå

Gävle

Uppsala

Norrköping

STOCKHOLM

GOTLAND
Visby

ÖLAND

BORNHOLM
(Den.)

Malmö

Szczecin

BERLIN

Magdeburg
Leipzig
Dresden

PRAGUE

Plzeň
Brno

CZECHOSLOVAKIA

VIENNA
(Wien)

Bratislava

Graz
Maribor

AUSTRIA

Ljubljana

Zagreb

YUGOSLAVIA

Zadar

Split

Sarajevo

Dubrovnik

Cetinje

Shkodër

ALBANIA

Tirane

Durrës

KÉRKIRA

Hammerfest

Vardø
Varangerfjord

LOFOTEN IS.

Narvik

LAPLAND

Murman
Monchegorsk
Kirovsk
Kandalaksha

Kebnekaise
6426

Luleå
Tornio

Oulu

Vaasa

FINLAND

Turku
Hangö

Helsinki

Gulf of Finland

ST. PETERSBURG
(Leningrad)

Kronshtadt

Tallinn

ESTONIA
Tartu

Pärnu

Novgorod

Pskov

S.S.R.

Velikie

Riga
LATVIA

Liepāja

Daugavpils

Klaipeda

LITHUANIA

Kaliningrad
SOV. UN.

Kaunas
Vilnius

Gdańsk

Grodno

Bialystok

BELORUSSIA

Minsk

Mog

Baranovichi
Bobru

Pripyat

Pinsk

POLAND

Toruń
Poznań

WARSAW

Łódź

Wrocław

Lublin

Brest

KATOWICE
Kraków
Przemyśl

Ostrava

L'vov

Drogobych
Vinnitsa

Ivano-Franko

Chernovtsy

UKRA

Rovno

Zhito

Berdichev
Ternopol

CARPATHIANS

Miskolc

Debrecen

HUNGARY

BUDAPEST

Szeged

Subotica

Novi
Sad

Oradea
Cluj-
Napoca

ROMANIA

CARPATI MERIDIONALI
(TRANSYLVANIAN ALPS)

Belgrade

Niš

Skopje

Bitola

Thessaloníki

GREECE

ATHENS
(Athinai)

Izm

Kalámai

ÁKRA TAÍNARON

CRETE (Gr.)
Khaniá
Irákli

Khaniá

Sofia
(Sofiya)
STARA PLANINA
(BALKAN MTS.)

Plovdiv

RHODOPE MTS.

BULGARIA

Ruse

BUCHAREST

Ploiești

Brăila

Galaţi

Iaşi

Chişi

Constanța

DANUBE

LÉSVOS

Córinth

IONIAN
SEA

Longitude West of Greenwich   Longitude East of Greenwich

Cities,
Towns,
and
Villages

0 to 25,000   100,000 to 250,000   1,000,000 and over

25,000 to 100,000   250,000 to 1,000,000   Major urbanized area

0   50 100   200   300   400   500 Miles

0   100   200   400   600   800 Kilometers

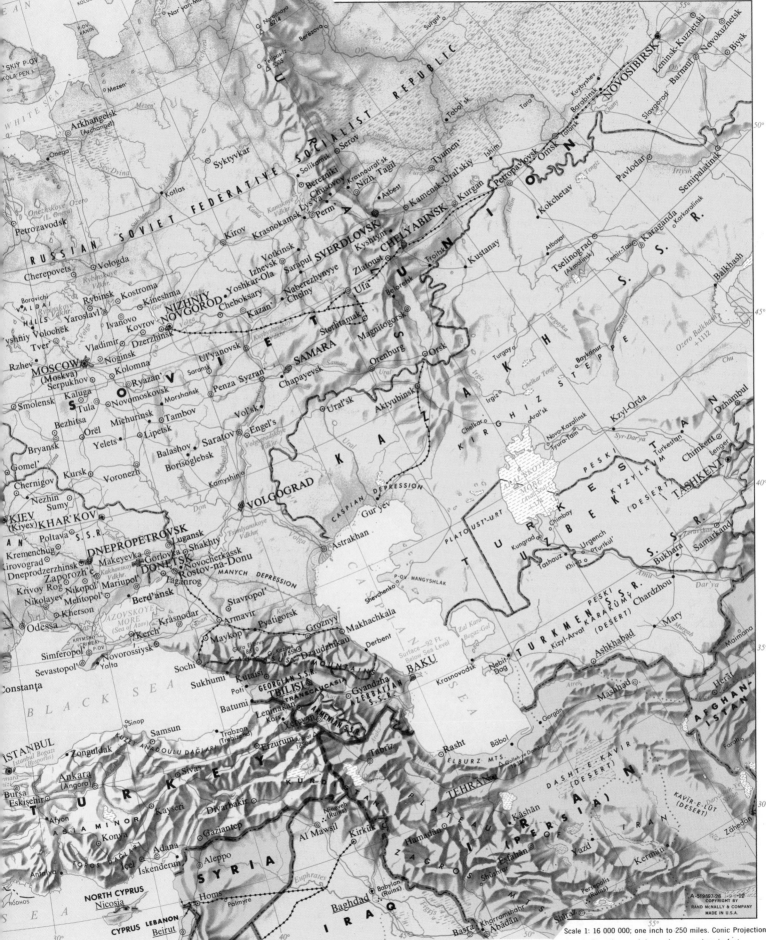

Scale 1: 16 000 000; one inch to 250 miles. Conic Projection
Elevations and depressions are given in feet

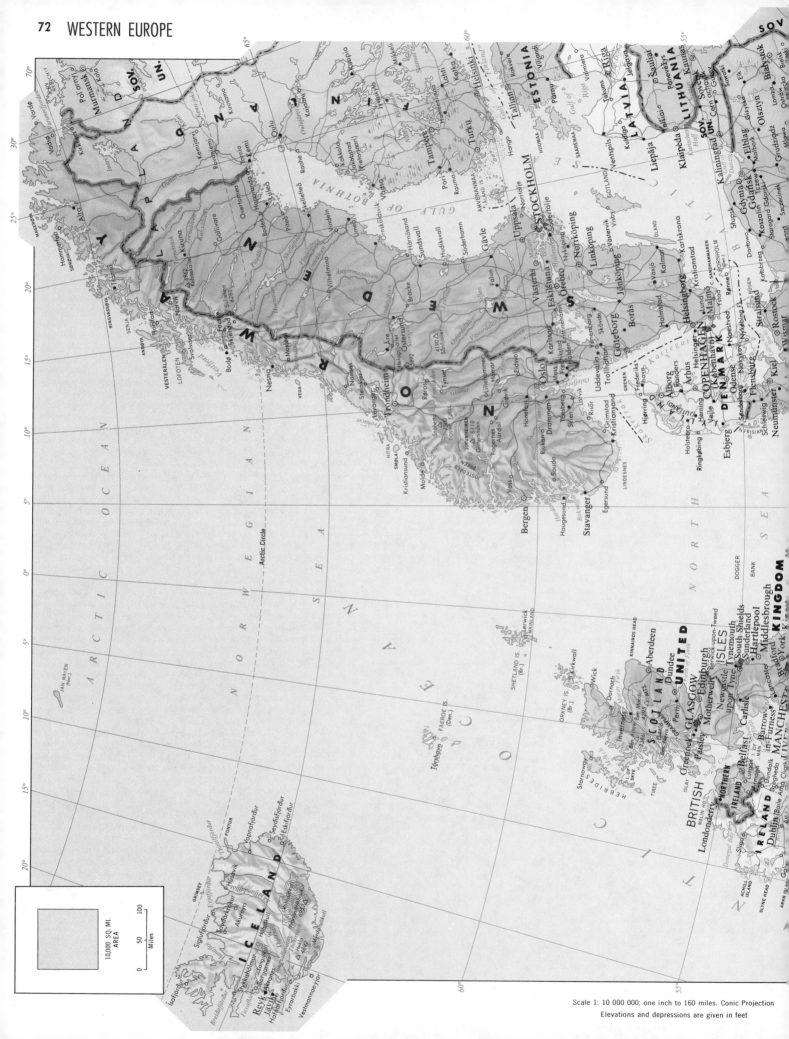

Scale 1: 10 000 000; one inch to 160 miles. Conic Projection
Elevations and depressions are given in feet

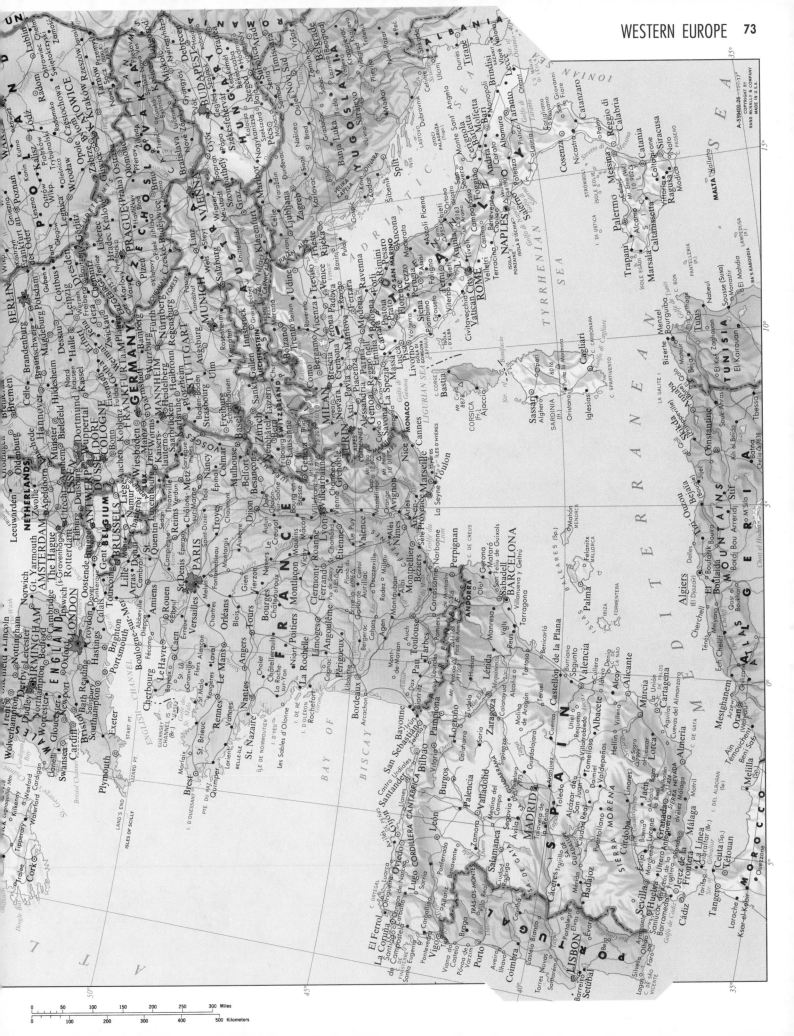

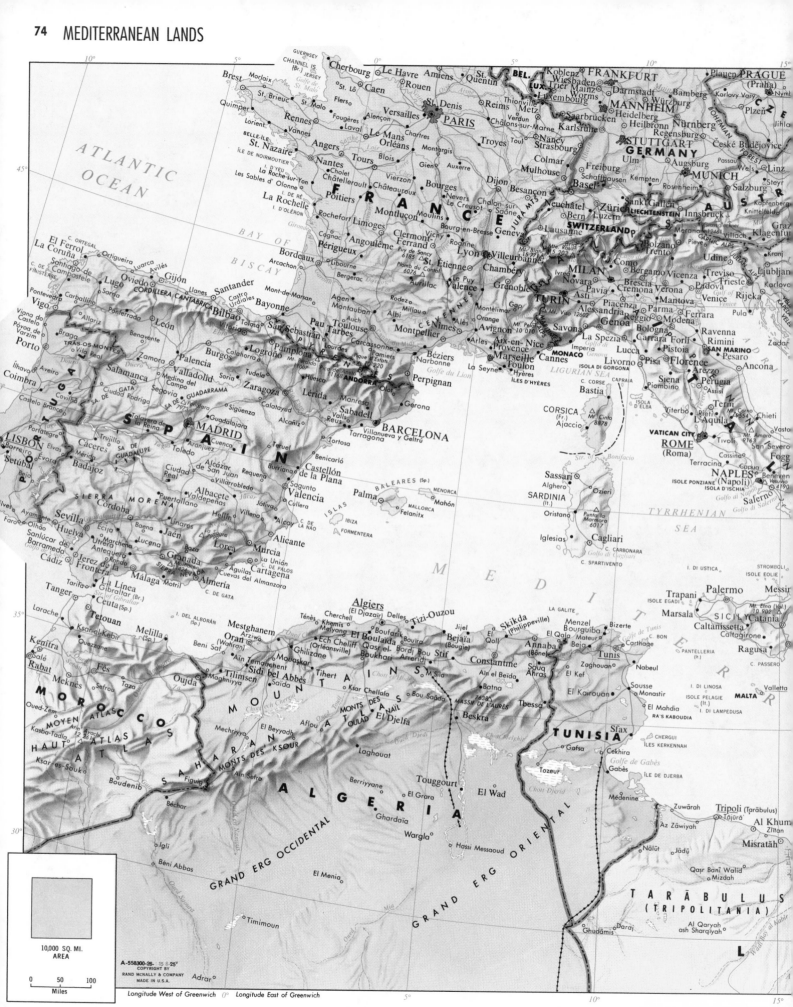

ATLANTIC
OCEAN

BAY
OF
BISCAY

FRANCE

GERMANY

SWITZERLAND

PARIS

PORTUGAL

SPAIN

MADRID

LISBON

BARCELONA

ANDORRA

LIGURIAN SEA

CORSICA
(Fr.)

SARDINIA
(It.)

TYRRHENIAN
SEA

ITALY

ROME
(Roma)

VATICAN CITY

NAPLES
(Napoli)

MEDITERRANEAN

MOROCCO

ALGERIA

TUNISIA

SICILY

MALTA

MOUNTAINS

ATLAS

SAHARAN

GRAND ERG OCCIDENTAL

GRAND ERG ORIENTAL

TARĀBULUS
(TRIPOLITANIA)

Tripoli (Tarābulus)

10,000 SQ. MI.
AREA

0   50   100
Miles

A-558300-26- 15 8-25
COPYRIGHT BY
RAND McNALLY & COMPANY
MADE IN U.S.A.

Longitude West of Greenwich   0°   Longitude East of Greenwich

Scale 1:10 000 000; one inch to 160 miles. Bonne's Projection
Elevations and depressions are given in feet

Cities, Towns, and Villages

0 to 25,000 ○	100,000 to 250,000 ⊙	1,000,000 and over ◉
25,000 to 100,000 •	250,000 to 1,000,000 ◎	Major urbanized area

Scale 1:20 000 000; one inch to 315 miles.
Lambert's Azimuthal, Equal Area Projection
Elevations and depressions are given in feet

40,000 SQ. MI.
AREA

0   150   300
Miles

O C E A N

SEVERNAYA ZEMLYA
(NORTHERN LAND)

TAYMYR
GORY BYRRANGA
P.-OV

M. CHELYUSKIN

BOL'SHOY BEGICHEV

DE-LONGA
FADDEYA
KOTEL'NYY
NOVOSIBIRSKIYE O-VA
(NEW SIBERIAN ISLANDS)
MALYY LYAKHOVSKIY
LYAKHOVSKIY
NOVAYA SIBIR

L A P T E V
S E A

E A S T   S I B E R I A N
S E A

VRANGELYA
(WRANGEL)

M. SHELAGSKIY

CHUKOTSKIY
P.-OV

M. DEZHNEV

Nordvik

Khatangskiy Zaliv

Taymyr

Ust'-Olenek

Tiksi

Bulun

M. SVYATOY NOS

M. BUOR-KHAYA

Kazach'ye

Abyy

Verkhoyansk

Allaykha

Nizhne-Kolymsk

Srednekolymsk

Zyryanka

Zashiversk

AYON

Ambarchik

Arctic Circle

Penzhino

Markovo

Anadyr'

Anadyrskiy Zaliv

CHUKOTSKOYE NAGORYE

KORYAKSKIY KHREBET

Noril'sk

GORY PUTORANA

Khatanga

Tura

Nizhnyaya Tunguska

Olenek

Zhigansk

KHREBET

VERKHOYANSKIY KHREBET

Gora Chen
3111

Y A K U T   A.S.S.R.

CHERSKOGO

Oymyakon

Gizhiga

Palana

M. OLYUTORSKIY

P.-OV

Klyuchevskaya (Vol.)
15,584

KAMCHATKA

Verkhne-Kamchatsk

Petropavlovsk-
Kamchatskiy

Ust'-Bol'sheretsk

M. LOPATKA

-urukhansk

Baykit

Podkamennaya Tunguska

Peleduy

Vitim

Yakutsk

Lena

Vilyuy

Vilyuysk

Mukhtuya

Suntar

Olekminsk

Aldan

Amga

Aldanskoye

Ust'-Maya

Nel'kan

Ayan

Magadan

Okhotsk

Yamsk

M. TAYGONOS

Shelekhova

M. ALEVINA

Zaliv

S E A
O F
O K H O T S K

M. YELIZAVETY

Okha

SAKHALIN
(Sov. Union)

M. TERPENIYA

Yartsevo

G. Polkan
3543

Yeniseysk

Ilimsk

Nizhneudinsk

Piramida
10801

Tulun

Cheremkhovo

Minusinsk

Abakan

SAYAN

Angarsk

Munku Sardyk
11457

Kyzyl

TANNU-OLA

Hovd

Har us Nuur

Uliastay

HANGAYN NURUU
(KHANGAI MTS.)

Tes Bogd
13419

MONGOLIA

Sayr Usa

G O B I   O R   S H A M O
(DESERT)

Hami

Kyren

Krasnoyarsk

Kansk

Tayshet

Bratsk

Bogotol

Balakhta

Nizhne-Angarsk

BAYKAL'SKIY KHREBET

Bratskoye Vdkhr.

Zhigalovo

Kirensk

Bodaybo

PATOM PLATEAU

G. Golets Purpula
5377

G. Golets Skalistyy
9186

Golets

VITIM

STANOVOY KHREBET

Tyndinskiy

Skovorodino

Zeya

Svobodnyy

Belogorsk

Ust'-Tygda

Bureya

DZHUGDZHUR KHREBET

Udskaya Guba

SHANTAR

Chumkan

Chumikan

Nikolayevsk-na-Amure

Komsomol'sk-
na-Amure

KHREBET BUREINSKIY

Amur

Birobidzhan

Khabarovsk

Aleksandrovsk

Poronaysk

Uglegorsk

Kholmsk

Sovetskaya Gavan'

Tatar Strait

Yuzhno-Sakhalinsk

Korsakov

Wakkanai

Soya Kaikyo

HOKKAIDŌ

Otaru

Sapporo

Esashi

DERATIVE   S O C I A L I S T   R E P U B L I C

TS K

-netski

BURYAT

Kachuga

Oz. Baykal (Lake Baikal)

BAYKAL'SKIY KHREBET

Barguzin

Surface elev. 1535 ft.
above sea level

B.A.S.S.R.

Ulan-Ude

Petrovsk-Zabaykal'skiy

Gorodok

Kyakhta

Selenge

Huvsgol Nuur

YABLONOVYY KHREBET

Aginskoye

Aksha

Borzya

Chita

Sretensk

Nerchinsk

Nerchinskiy Zavod

NERCHINSKIY KHREBET

STANOVOY KHREBET

Blagoveshchensk

LESSER KHINGAN RANGE

GREATER KHINGAN RANGE

Neijiang

Goukou

Qiqihar

Fuyu

Hailun

Suihua

Songari

Boli

Spassk-Dal'niy

Dal'nerechensk

Ussuriysk

Artem

USSURIYSKIY KHREBET

SIKHOTE ALIN'

Portizonsk

Nakhodka

S E A
O F
J A P A N

N

J A P A N

HONSHŪ

Kanazawa

KYŌTŌ

Tottori

KŌBE

Matsue

Okayama

OSAKA

Kōchi

Hiroshima

Kutulik

Irkutsk

Tulun

Sayan

MTS.

Uvs Nuur

Ulan Bator
(Ulaanbaatar)

Öndörhaan

Kerulen

Wenquan

Tao an

Jarud Qi

CHANGCHUN

Shuanghiao

Dunhua

Jilin

HARBIN

Mudanjiang

MANCHURIA

C H I N A

SHENYANG   FUSHUN

Ol'ga

Artem

Vladivostok

Najin

Chŏngjin

NORTH KOREA

SOUTH KOREA

SEOUL

P'yŏngyang

Kaesŏng

Andong

Taegu

PUSAN

Korea Strait

Tsushima

Chifeng

Weichang

Chengde

Korea Bay

Zhangjiakou

Fengzhen

BEIJING   TIANJIN

Baoding

Lüshun   Dalian

SHANDONG BANDAO

Bo Hai

Y E L L O W
S E A

Longitude East of Greenwich

100   200   300   400   500   600   Miles

200   400   600   800   1000   Kilometers

A-570000-26 -12-10-27°
COPYRIGHT BY
RAND McNALLY & COMPANY
MADE IN U.S.A.

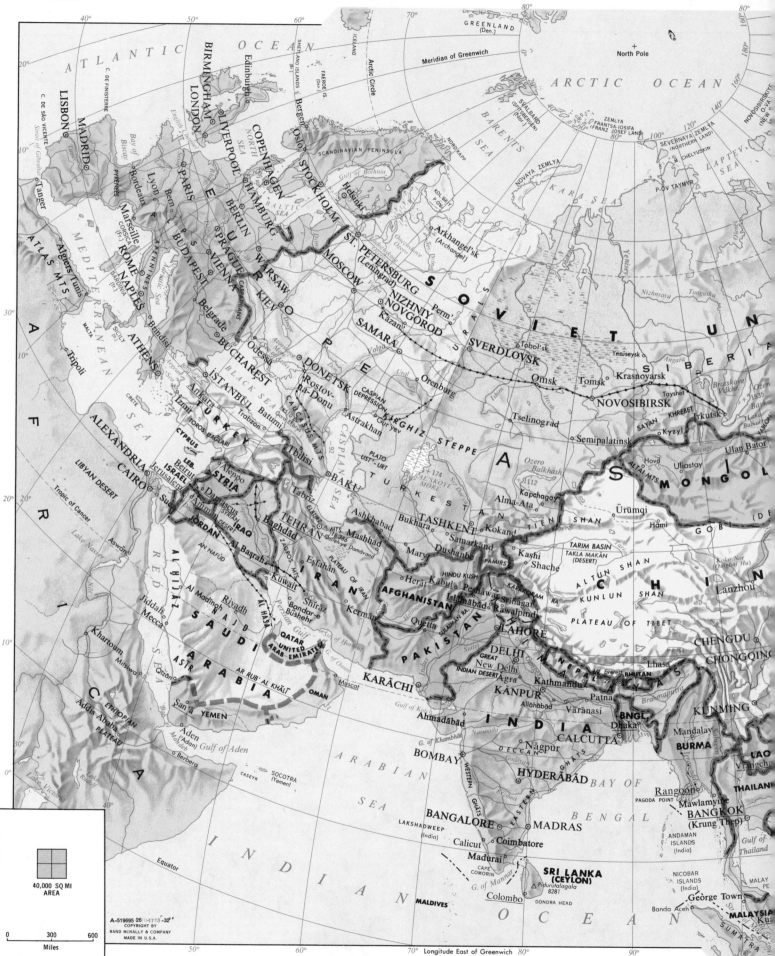

Scale 1:40 000 000; one inch to 630 miles. Lambert's Azimuthal, Equal Area Projection
Elevations and depressions are given in feet

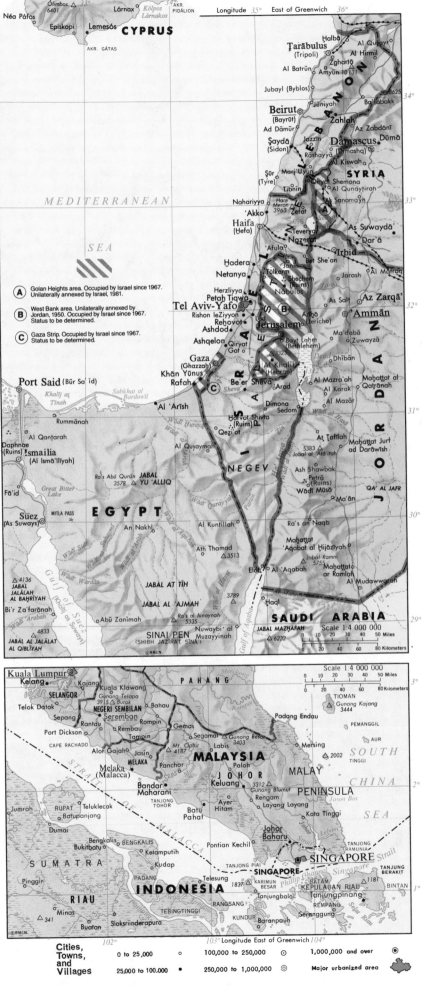

Map labels (left panel)

NORTH AMERICA

BERING SEA

SEA OF OKHOTSK

MANCHURIA

HARBIN
CHANGCHUN
SHENYANG
Zhangjiakou
BEIJING
TIANJIN
TAIYUAN
XI'AN
QIN LING
WUHAN
Yichang
Changsha
NAN LING
Wuzhou
Macao (Port.)
GUANGZHOU
HONG KONG (Br.)
Shantou
Xiamen
Fuzhou
NANJING
SHANGHAI
QINGDAO
Jinan
Dalian
Bo Hai

SEOUL
NORTH KOREA
SOUTH
P'yongyang
Pyongyang

TOKYO
YOKOHAMA
KYOTO
KOBE OSAKA
KITAKYUSHU
Nagasaki
KYUSHU
SHIKOKU
HONSHU
JAPAN
Sendai
Hakodate
HOKKAIDO
SAKHALIN (Sov. Union)
KURIL ISLANDS (Sov. Union)
Vladivostok
Komsomolsk
Khabarovsk
Blagoveshchensk
Sovetskaya Gavan
Okhotsk
Yakutsk
Petropavlovsk-Kamchatskiy
M. LOPATKA
KAMCHATKA

ALEUTIAN ISLANDS (U.S.A.)
ALEUTIAN TRENCH
PRIBILOF IS. (U.S.A.)
ST. LAWRENCE I.
M. DEZHNEVA (EAST CAPE)
Arctic Circle

PACIFIC OCEAN

EAST CHINA SEA

T'AIPEI
TAIWAN (FORMOSA)

PHILIPPINE SEA
Tropic of Cancer
PHILIPPINES
LUZON
Quezon City
MANILA
MINDORO
SAMAR
PANAY
LEYTE
NEGROS
PALAWAN
MINDANAO
SULU SEA
SULU IS.

HAINAN DAO
Hanoi
Hue
VIETNAM
CAMBODIA
Phnom Penh
HO CHI MINH CITY (Saigon)
MUI BAI BUNG

BORNEO
Kuching
BRUNEI
MALAYSIA
Kota Kinabalu
Sandakan
CELEBES SEA
HALMAHERA
NEW GUINEA
Equator
SINGAPORE
INDONESIA

Map labels (right panel — Cyprus / Levant)

Néa Páfos
Olimbos 6401
Lárnax
Lemesós
Larnakos
AKR. PIDALION
Episkopi
CYPRUS
AKR. GATAS

MEDITERRANEAN SEA

Ţarābulus (Tripoli)
Halbā
Al Qusayr
Al Hirmil
Zgharta
Amyun 10131
Al Batrūn
Jubayl (Byblos)
Ba'labakk
Juniyah
LEBANON
Beirut (Bayrūt)
Zahlah
Ad Dāmūr
Az Zabdānī
Şaydā (Sidon)
Jazzīn
Damascus (Dimashq)
Dūmā
Rāshayyā
Şūr (Tyre)
Marj 'Uyūn
Al Kiswah
Tibnīn
Qiryat Shemona
Al Qunayţirah
Naharivva
SYRIA
Nahariyya
Hare Meron 3963
Zefat
'Akko
As Sanamayn
696
Teverya
Haifa (Hefa)
Nazerat
Dar'ā
Irbid
'Afula
Bet She'an
Hadera
Jarash
Al Mafraq
Netanya
Janin
Tulkarm
Shechem (Ruins)
Nābulus
Herzliyya
Petah Tiqwa
As Salt
Az Zarqā'
Tel Aviv-Yafo
Rishon leZiyyon
Ariha (Jericho)
Amman
Ashdod
Jerusalem
Ma'daba
Rehovot
Qiryat Gat
Bayt Lahm (Bethlehem)
Zuwayza
Ashqelon
Al Khalil (Hebron)
Gaza (Ghazzah)
Dhībān
Khān Yūnus
Be'er Sheva
Al Mazra'ah
Rafah
Be'er Sheva
Arad
Al Karak
Mahattat al Qaţrānah
Dimona
Sedom
Al Mazār
Port Said (Būr Sa'īd)
Sabkhat al Bardawīl
Khalīj aţ Ţīnah
Ḩorvat Shivta (Ruins)
At Taftlah
Al 'Arīsh
Rummānah
Mahattat Jurf ad Darāwīsh
Al Qanţarah
Ismailia (Al Ismā'īlīyah)
Daphnae (Ruins)
Al Qusaymah
NEGEV
Ash Shawbak
Petra (Ruins)
Fā'id
Great Bitter Lake
Ra's Abū Qurūn
JABAL YU 'ALLIQ 3578
Wādī Mūsā
Qezi'ot
Ma'ān
Suez (As Suways)
An Nakhl
Al Kuntillah
Ra's an Naqb
MITLA PASS
QA' AL JAFR
EGYPT
Ath Thamad
5383 Jabal al 'Atā'itah
Mahattat 'Aqabat al Ḩijāzīyah
3513
Jabal Ramm 5755
Elat
Al 'Aqabah
Mahattat ar Ramlah
Bi'r Za'farānah
4136 JABAL JALĀLAH AL BAḨRĪYAH
Al Mudawwarah
JABAL AT ŢĪH
3789
JABAL AL 'AJMAH
Ra's al Junaynah 5335
Haql
SAUDI ARABIA
Abū Zanīmah
Nuwaybi' al Muzayyinah
JABAL MAZḨAFAH
4833 JABAL AL JALĀLAT AL QIBLĪYAH
SINAI PEN (SHIBH JAZĪRAT SĪNĀ)
6232
JORDAN
ISRAEL
Gulf of Suez
Gulf of Aqaba
Wādī 'Arabah

Legend (right panel)

Scale 1:4,000,000
0 10 20 30 40 50 Miles
0 20 40 60 80 Kilometers

Map labels (lower right — Malay Peninsula)

Scale 1:4,000,000
0 10 20 30 40 50 Miles
0 20 40 60 80 Kilometers

Kuala Lumpur
Kelang
PAHANG
Kajang
Kuala Klawang
SELANGOR
Gunong Telapa 3915 Burak
Telok Datok
NEGERI SEMBILAN
Bahau
TIOMAN
Sepang
Seremban
Rompin
Gunong Kajang 3444
Port Dickson
Rantau
Rembau
Gemas
Padang Endau
CAPE RACHADO
Tampin
Segamat
Gunong Besar 3403
PEMANGGIL
Alor Gajah
Jasin
Labis
Mersing
AUR
Melaka (Malacca)
Mt. Ophir 4187
MALAYSIA
2002
Panchor
Paloh
TINGGI
MELAKA
Bandar Maharani
JOHOR
Gunong Blumut 3312
Rengam
MALAY PENINSULA
Batu Pahat
Ayer Hitam
Layang Layang
Jumrah
RUPAT
Teluklecak
TANJONG TOHOR
Pontian Kechil
Kota Tinggi
Batupanjang
Johor Baharu
SOUTH CHINA SEA
Dumai
Bengkalis
BENGKALIS
Ketamputih
SINGAPORE
TANJONG RAMUNIA
Bukitbatu
Kudap
TANJONG PIAI
SINGAPORE
TANJUNG BERAKIT
Pinggir
SUMATRA
PADANG
Telesung
KARIMUN BESAR 1837
BATAM
KEPULAUAN RIAU
BINTAN
INDONESIA
RIAU
Rangsang
Tanjungbalai
Tanjungpinang
REMPANG
Minas
341
Buatan
Siaksriindrapura
KUNDUR
Baranpauh
Serangung

Legend (bottom)

Cities, Towns, and Villages			
0 to 25,000 ○	100,000 to 250,000 ◉	1,000,000 and over ◉	
25,000 to 100,000 •	250,000 to 1,000,000 ◎	Major urbanized area	

Scale at bottom left:
0 200 400 600 800 1000 Miles
0 400 800 1200 1600 Kilometers

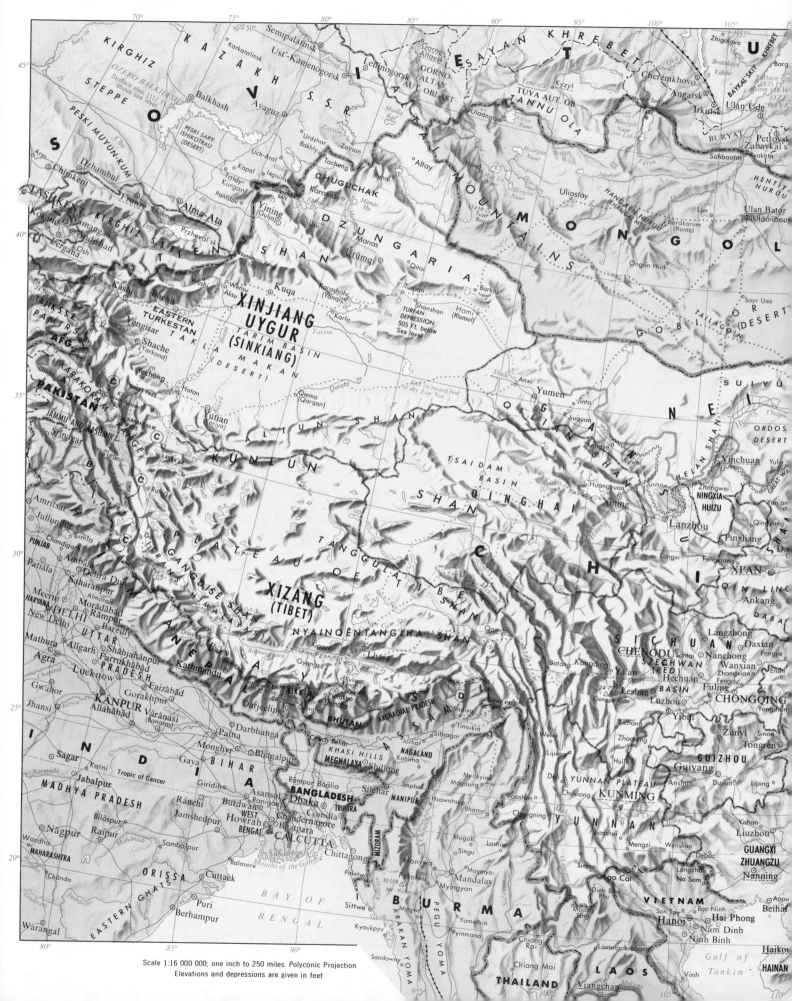

Scale 1:16 000 000; one inch to 250 miles. Polyconic Projection
Elevations and depressions are given in feet

Chinese Provinces, Autonomous Regions (AR) and Municipalities (M)

Conventional Form — Pinyin Form

Conventional Form	Pinyin Form
Anhwei	Anhui
Chekiang	Zhejiang
Fukien	Fujian
Heilungkiang	Heilongjiang
Honan	Henan
Hopeh	Hebei
Hunan	Hunan
Hupeh	Hubei
Inner Mongolia (AR)	Nei Monggol
Kansu	Gansu
Kiangsi	Jiangxi
Kiangsu	Jiangsu
Kirin	Jilin
Kwangsi (AR)	Guangxi Zhuangzu
Kwangtung	Guangdong
Kweichow	Guizhou
Liaoning	Liaoning
Ningsia Hui (AR)	Ningxia Huizu
Peking (M)	Beijing
Shanghai (M)	Shanghai
Shansi	Shanxi
Shantung	Shandong
Shensi	Shaanxi
Sinkiang (AR)	Xinjiang Uygur
Szechwan	Sichuan
Tibet (AR)	Xizang
Tientsin (M)	Tianjin
Tsinghai	Qinghai
Yunnan	Yunnan

Tropic of Cancer

A Area occupied by Pakistan and claimed by India.

B Area claimed and occupied by India; status disputed by Pakistan.

C Area occupied by China and claimed by India.

D Area occupied by India and claimed by China.

A-569700-26- 12-0-22

COPYRIGHT BY
RAND McNALLY & COMPANY
MADE IN U.S.A.

40,000 SQ MI
AREA

0   100   200
Miles

Longitude East of Greenwich

0   50 100   200   300   400   500 Miles

0   100   200   400   600   800 Kilometers

40,000 SQ MI
AREA

0   100   200
Miles

A-569400-26-0-17-13-31
COPYRIGHT BY
RAND McNALLY & COMPANY
MADE IN U.S.A.

Scale 1:16 000 000; one inch to 250 miles. Polyconic Projection
Elevations and depressions are given in feet

Longitude East of Greenwich

S. S. R.

Kzyl-Orda

Ozero Balkhash
+1112

Taldy-Kurgan

PESKI MUYUN-KUM

Turkestan   Dzhambul

Arys   Chimkent   Alma Ata

TASHKENT   Namangan Dzhalal-
Abad

Nurata   Kokand   Andizhan
Fergana   Osh

Khodzhent   Dzhizak

markand   KIRGHIZ S.S.R.

Katta-   Dushanbe   Garm
kurgan   Karshi   TAJIK S.S.R.   PAMIRS

Pik Kommunizma
24,590

Termez   Feyzabad   Khorog

Balkh   Mazar-e Sharif   HINDU KUSH

STAN   Kabul   Chitral   Gilgit
Qandahar   Ghazni   Peshawar   Islamabad   Srinagar

TAN   Chaman   Jhelum   Jammu   JAMMU AND KASHMIR
Quetta   Sialkot   Amritsar   HIMACHAL PRADESH
Loralai   Gujranwala   Jullundur   Simla
Kalat   Dera Ghazi   LAHORE   Ludhiana   Dehra Dun
Khan   Firozpur   Chandigarh
PAKISTAN   PUNJAB   Patiala   Ambala   Saharanpur

Nushki   Multan   Bhatinda   HARYANA Meerut   Moradabad
Shikarpur   Bahawalpur   DELHI Rampur   Bareilly
Mohenjo-Daro   Sukkur   Bikaner   New Delhi UTTAR   Shahjahanpur
(Ruins)   Alwar   Mathura   Agra   Farrukhabad   Lucknow
GREAT INDIAN DESERT   Bharatpur   PRADESH   Faizabad   Gorakhpur
Jaipur   Gwalior   KANPUR   Allahabad   Varanasi
RAJASTHAN   Ajmer   Tonk   Jhansi   (Benares)   Monghyr
Hyderabad   Jodhpur   Sheopur   Banda   Mirzapur   Sasaram   Gaya
Abu Road   Shivpuri   Sagar   Rewa   Son   BIHAR
ARACHI   Palanpur   Udaipur   Kota   Jhalawar

Rann of Kutch   Bhuj   GUJARAT   AHMADABAD   Ujjain   Bhopal
Rajkot   Indore   VINDHYA RA   Jabalpur   Bilaspur Raurkela
Jamnagar   KATHIAWAR   Baroda   Burhanpur   MADHYA PRADESH   Raigarh
Porbandar   Bhavnagar   Narmada   Amravati   Nagpur   Raipur
Veraval   Junagadh   PENINSULA   Dhule   Akola   Wardha
Diu   Surat   Tapti   Chandrapur
Daman   Nasik   Aurangabad   DECCAN   Indravati
BOMBAY   Ahmadnagar   MAHARASHTRA   Godavari
Pune   Nizamabad   Warangal   Vizianagaram
HYDERABAD   Vishakhapatnam
Sholapur   HYDERABAD   Rajahmundry
Sangli   Gulbarga   Vijayawada   Kakinada   Yanam
Kolhapur   Raichur   Guntur   Eluru
Belgaum   Kurnool   Krishna   Machilipatnam
Panaji   Hubli   ANDHRA   Pennar
(Panjim)   Bellary
GOA   KARNATAKA   EASTERN COASTAL
Cuddapah   Nellore
Mangalore   Kolar
BANGALORE   Vellore   MADRAS
Mysore   Kanchipuram
Pondicherry
Salem
Calicut   Mahe   Cuddalore
Coimbatore   TAMIL NADU   Kumbakonam
Tiruchchirappalli   Nagappattinam
Ernakulam   Thanjavur
Madurai

LAKSHADWEEP
(LACCADIVE IS.)
(India)

IAN
A

TIEN SHAN

KIRGHIZ S.S.R.
KIRGIZSKIY KHREBET

Panfilov
Ining   Wusu
Przheval'sk   (Akesu)   Kucha
Issyk Kul   (Kuche)
SINKIANG UIGHUR AUTONOMOUS REGION
Kashgar   Sufu   Yarkand
(Kashgar)   Shache   Yarkand
Yingchisha   (Yarkand)   TAKLA   MAKLAN (DESERT)
XINJIANG UYGUR   (SINKIANG)   Hotan
Yench'eng   (Karghalik)   Yutien
(Keriya)

Tihwa
(Urumchi) (T'ulufan)   Shanshan
TURFAN DEPRESSION 505 ft below level

EASTERN TURKESTAN

TARIM BASIN
Tarim   Cherchen
Salt incrusted bed of dry Lop Nor

KARAKORAM PASS   Rutag

ASTIN TAGH   KUNLUN SHAN   (KUN LUN MTS.)

K2 (Godwin Austen) 28,250

KUNLUN SHAN

PLATEAU OF

TIBET

XIZANG
(TIBET)

NYENCHEN

Brahmaputra   Gangdise Shan

NEPAL   Kathmandu   Lalitpur
Darjeeling
Cooch Behar
MEGHALAYA   Shillong   KHASI HILLS

BANGLADESH   Dhaka

WEST BENGAL   Burdwan   Khulna
Howrah   Bhatpara
CALCUTTA   Chittagong
Kharagpur   Mouths of the Ganges
Balasore
Sambalpur   Jaipur
ORISSA   Cuttack
Bhubaneswar
Puri
Berhampur

BAY OF
BENGAL

NAN SHAN
Yumen   Ch'ing Hai
(Koko Nor)
CHINGHAI

CHINA

Lhasa

THANGLHA

ARUNACHAL PRADESH

SIKKIM   BHUTAN   Thimphu
ASSAM   Gauhati
NAGALAND   Kohima
Mogaung
Myitkyina
Imphal   Bhamo
MANIPUR   Silchar
MIZORAM   Shwebo   Mandalay
TRIPURA   Monywa
Agartala   BURMA
Comilla   (MYANMAR)
Noakhali   Myingyan
Tropic of Cancer
Magwe   Yamethin
Sittwe   Yenangyaung
ARAKAN YOMA   Pyinmana
Kyaukpyu   Prome
Sandoway   PEGU YOMA
Henzada
PAGODA PT.   Pathein   Rangoon
Mouths of the   (Yangon)
Irrawaddy

(A) Area occupied by Pakistan
and claimed by India.

(B) Area claimed and occupied by India;
status disputed by Pakistan.

(C) Area occupied by China.

(D) Area occupied by India
and claimed by China.

Cities,
Towns,
and
Villages

0 to 25,000	100,000 to 250,000	1,000,000 and over
25,000 to 100,000	250,000 to 1,000,000	Major urbanized area

0   50   100   200   300   400   500 Miles
0   100   200   400   600   800 Kilometers

Tiruchchirappalli   Nagappattinam
Ernakulam   Thanjavur   TAMIL NADU
KERALA   Madurai   Jaffna
Alleppey   Tuticorin
Quilon   Tirunelveli   Trincomalee
Trivandrum   Mannar
CAPE COMORIN   Puttalam   Anuradhapura

SRI LANKA
(CEYLON)   Kandy
Colombo
INDIAN
OCEAN   Galle   Matara
DONDRA HEAD

Same scale as main map

CHINA

Wuzhou   Tropic of Cancer   Jieyang   Chao'an
Foshan   **GUANGZHOU**   Shantou
Xinhui   Kowloon   T'ainan   Yu Shan 12 714
Macao (Port.)   **HONG KONG** (Br.)   Kaohsiung   **TAIWAN**
Taiwan Strait

Monywa   Maymyo
Pakokku   Mandalay
Paletwa   Myingyan
Sittwe

Kyaukpyu   Pyinmana
RAMREE ISLAND
CHEDUBA ISLAND
Sandoway

BURMA (MYANMAR)

LAOS

Muong Sing
Chiang Rai
Louangphrabang
Chiang Mai
Phou Bia 9249
Viangchan

Lang Son
Hanoi
Ninh Binh
Hai Phong
Nam Dinh
Thanh Hoa

Beihai
Zhanjiang
LEIZHOU BANDAO
Haikou
Wuzhi Shan 6125
HAINAN DAO

GULF OF TONKIN

Moaming

Henzada   Bago
Rangoon (Yangon)
Pathein
Mouths of the Irrawaddy
Gulf of Martaban
Mawlamyine

Toungoo
Prome (Pyè)

Tak
Uttaradit
Udon Thani
Savannakhet
Vinh
Dong Hoi

Phitsanulok
Khon Kaen
VIETNAM
Hue
Da Nang

THAILAND
Nakhon Sawan
Ubon Ratchathani
Quang Ngai

PARACEL ISLANDS
(Claimed by China, Taiwan and Vietnam)

Ye
Dawei

Phra Nakhon
Si Ayutthaya
Prachin Buri
Nakhon Ratchasima
An Nhon
Qui Nhon

SOUTH

Mergui
Tenasserim
BANGKOK (Krung Thep)
Angkor (Ruins)
Siem Reap
Batdambang
Kâmpóng Thum
Stoeng Trêng
Krâchéh
Nha Trang
MUI KE GA

Chanthaburi
Tonlé Sap
CAMBODIA (KAMPUCHEA)
Phnum Pénh
Loc Ninh
Bien Hoa
Phan Thiet

CHINA

NORTH ANDAMAN
MERGUI
Gulf of Thailand
Kâmpóng Saôm
Kâmpôt
Chau-phu
Long Xuyen
HO CHI MINH CITY (Saigon)
Bac Lieu
DAO PHU QUOC
TIZARD BANK AND REEFS

Andaman Sea
MIDDLE ANDAMAN
SOUTH ANDAMAN
Port Blair
ISTHMUS OF KRA
MUI CA MAU
CON SON

PALAWAN
Puerto Princesa
CAGAYAN IS.

SEA

SPRATLY
(Claimed by China, Malaysia, Philippines, Taiwan and Vietnam)

LITTLE ANDAMAN

NICOBAR
ISLANDS (India)
Surat Thani
Nakhon Si Thammarat

Phuket
Thale Luang
MALAY
Songkhla
Pattani
PENINSULA
Kota Baharu

BALABAC ISLAND
Balabac Strait
PULAU BANGGI
Kudat
PULAU BANGGI
CAGAYAN SULU

SULU SEA

Zamboanga
Jolo
SULU ISLAND
JOLO ISLAND
SULU ARCHIPELAGO
SIBUTU ISLAND
TAWI-TAWI GROUP

GREAT NICOBAR
Sabang
Banda Aceh
Alor Setar
George Town (Pinang)
KEDAH
Idi
Langsa
Taiping
Ipoh 7174 G. Tahan

Kota Kinabalu
Gunong Kinabalu 13 455
Sandakan
Bandar Seri Begawan
Bukit Pagon 6070
SABAH

BRUNEI
Miri

Medan
Belawan
Pematangsiantar
MALAYSIA
Kelang
Kuala Lumpur
Melaka (Malacca)
Pahang

NATUNA BESAR
Binjai
KEPULAUAN BUNGURAN UTARA
KEPULAUAN ANAMBAS

MALAYSIA
Bintulu
SARAWAK
Kuching
TG. DATU
UPPER KAPUAS MTS.
Rajang
IRAN MTS.
Tarakan
TG. MANGKALIHAT

CELEB

PULAU SIMEULUE
KEPULAUAN BANYAK
Sibolga
Danau Toba
Strait of Malacca
Bengkalis
Batu Pahat
Johor Baharu
SINGAPORE
SINGAPORE
KEPULAUAN RIAU
Pakanbaru
KEPULAUAN TAMBELAN

PULAU NIAS
PULAU PINI
SUMATRA
Bukittinggi
Indragiri
(SUMATERA)
KEPULAUAN LINGA

Pontianak
B O R N E O
Sukadana
PEG. SCHWANER
Bukit Raya 7474
Samarinda
Donggala

Equator
PULAU TANAHMASA
KEPULAUAN BATU
PULAU TANAHBALA

Padang
Sawahlunto
Gunung Kerinci 12 467
PULAU SIBERUT
PULAU SIPURA
MENTAWAI
PULAU PAGAI UTARA
PULAU PAGAI SELATAN
KEPULAUAN

Jambi
Muntok
BANGKA
Pangkalpinang
Tanjungpandan
BELITUNG

Ketapang
KEPULAUAN KARIMATA
Selat Karimata

KALIMANTAN
PEGUNUNGAN MÜLLER
Kahayan
Barito
Mahakam
Balikpapan

CELEBES (SULAWESI)
Samarinda

Palembang
G. Dempo 10 365
Bengkulu
PEGUNUNGAN BARISAN

Musi
TG. PUTING
Sukadana
Banjarmasin
Martapura
TG. SELATAN
Kotabaru
PULAU LAUT

Majene
Bulu Raatekombolo 11 335
Parepare
Teluk Bone

GREATER
SUNDA

PULAU ENGGANO
Tanjungkarang-Telukbetung
Selat Sunda
KEPULAUAN KARIMUNJAWA
LAUT (JAVA SEA) JAWA
PULAU BAWEAN
MASALEMBO-BESAR

Ujungpandang (Makasar)
Bonthain
PULAU KABAENA
PULAU SELAYAR

I N D O N E

Serang
JAKARTA
Bogor
Cirebon
Semarang
Bangkalan
MADURA
Surakarta

ISLANDS
KEPULAUAN KANGEAN
LAUT FLORES (FLORES SEA)
PULAU KALAOT

Sukabumi
BANDUNG
G. Slamet 11 247
SURABAYA
Pasuruan
Malang
G. Semeru 12 060
G. Bromo
Banyuwangi
Denpasar
BALI
G. Agung 10 309
G. Rinjani 12 224
SUMBAWA-BESAR
Raba
FLORES

Yogyakarta
JAVA (JAWA)
LOMBOK
Mataram
LESSER
SUNDA
ISLANDS
SUMBA
PULAU SAWU
LAUT SA (SAVU SE

S I A

INDIAN OCEAN

JAVA TRENCH
24 442
CHRISTMAS ISLAND (Austl.)

Longitude East of Greenwich

LUZON
Laoag
Vigan
Aparri
Tuguegarao
San Fernando
Baguio
Lingayen
Tarlac
Quezon City
Olongapo
MANILA
Lipa
Batangas
LUBANG ISLANDS
MINDORO

Lamon
ESCARI
BABUYAN ISLANDS
BATA ISLAND
Balintang Channel
BABUY ISLAND

CALAMIAN GROUP
Culion
CUYO IS.
PANAY
Iloilo
Bacolod
NEGROS
MASBA ISLA
Roxa
MINDORO

20°
15°
10°
5°
0°
5°
10°

95°   100°   105°   110°   115°   120°

40,000 SQ MI AREA

0   100   200
Miles

A-569800-26
COPYRIGHT BY
RAND McNALLY & COMPANY
MADE IN U.S.A.

Scale 1:16 000 000; one inch to 250 miles. Polyconic Projection
Elevations and depressions are given in feet

Cities, Towns, and Villages

0 to 25,000 ○	100,000 to 250,000 ⊙	1,000,000 and over ◉
25,000 to 100,000 •	250,000 to 1,000,000 ◎	Major urbanized area

115°   120°   125°   130°   135°

INDONESIA

Pasuruan
G. Mahameru 10,932
12,060   G. Raung
JAVA   Rinjani 12,225
Singaraja
BALI   LOMBOK   Sumbawa-Besar   Rakao   FLORES   ALOR   LOMBLEN PANTAR   Dili   SELARU   TANJUNG VALS
SUMBAWA   Waingapu   SAVU SEA   Timor   ARAFURA   SEA
SUMBA   SAWU   ROTI   Kupang   TIMOR
SUNDA   ISLANDS
C. VAN DIEMEN   CROKER
COBURG PEN.
MELVILLE   Van Diemen Gulf
BATHURST   Clarence Str.   WESSEL IS.

10°   SUNDA TRENCH   TIMOR   SEA   CAPE ARNHEM

Darwin   ARNHEM LAND   Blue Mud Bay   GULF OF
Pine Creek   GROOTE EYLANDT
CAPE LONDONDERRY   Joseph Bonaparte Gulf   Katherine   Limmen Bight   CARPENTARIA

INDIAN   Anson Bay   SIR EDWARD PELLEW GROUP   WELLESLEY

15°   Wyndham   Victoria River Downs   Birdum   Daly Waters   Borroloola   Burketown
BUCCANEER ARCH.   Mt. Hann 2800   Newcastle Waters   **NORTHERN**
CAPE LEVEQUE   KING LEOPOLD RANGES   Woods   Alexandria   Dobby
DAMPIER   Derby   GEIKIE RANGE   Fitzroy Crossing   Camooweal   **QU**
LAND   Broome   Halls Creek   Tanami   Tennant Creek   Mount Isa   Malb
Roebuck Bay   Fitzroy   Sturt Cr.   **TERRITORY**   Dajarra
LaGrange   Barrow Creek   DI

20°   EIGHTY MILE BEACH   **OCEAN**   Mt. Ziel 4955   MACDONNELL RANGES   Arltunga   **QU**
LARREY POINT   **GREAT SANDY DESERT**   Mackay   Alice Springs   JAMES RANGE
DAMPIER ARCH.   RIPON   Port Hedland   DeGrey   **WESTERN**   Amadeus   SIMPSON   Birdsville
MONTE BELLO IS.   Roebourne   Marble Bar   MACDONNELL   Charlotte Waters   DESERT
BARROW   Fortescue   Nullagine   Macdonald
NORTH WEST CAPE   Millstream   HAMERSLEY RANGE   Jiggalong   MUSGRAVE RANGES
Onslow   Ashburton   Mt. Bruce 4024   Disappointment   Mt. Woodroffe 4970   EVERARD RANGES

Tropic of Capricorn   POINT CLOATES   **GIBSON DESERT**   Oodnadatta
CAPE FARQUHAR   Gascoyne   Peak Hill   Nabberu   Carnegie   Gillen   Everard   William Creek
Carnarvon   Geographe Channel   Wells   STUART RANGE   Marree
BERNIER   Murchison   Wiluna   Yeo   **SOUTH AUSTRALIA**   Farina
DORRE   Shark Bay   Meekatharra   **A U S T R A L I A**   Carey   Gregory
DIRK HARTOG   Nannine   Cue   Sandstone   **GREAT VICTORIA DESERT**   Woomera

25°   STEEP POINT   Austin   Mount Magnet   Laverton   Hughes   Ooldea Station   Pimba   Parachilna
Ajana   Ballard   Menzies   Rawlinna   Penong   Ceduna   Whyalla   Port Augusta
Northampton   Barlee   Kalgoorlie   Eucla   POINT FOWLER   Port Pirie   Peterbor
HOUTMAN ROCKS   Mingenew   Moore   Coolgardie   Boulder   Eyre   EYRE PENINSULA   Port Wakef
Geraldton   Pithara   Lake Brown   Southern Cross   Lefroy   Goddards Soak   **NULLARBOR PLAIN**   Wallaroo   Gawler
Dongara   Miling   Mopra   Cowan   Norseman   **GREAT AUSTRALIAN BIGHT**   Moonta   Adela

30°   Northam   York   Salmon Gums   Port Lincoln   KANGAROO
Perth   **DARLING RANGE**   Narrogin   Ravensthorpe   Esperance   Naraco
Fremantle   Collie   **SWANLAND**   Hopetoun   Kingston
Geographe Bay   Bunbury   Katanning   ARCHIPELAGO OF THE RECHERCHE   CAPE JAFFA
CAPE NATURALISTE   Busselton
CAPE LEEUWIN   Nornalup   Albany   Mt. Gam
PT. D'ENTRECASTEAUX   WEST CAPE HOWE   King George Sd.

INDIAN   OCEAN

35°

40°

A-590200 26 4-5-14
COPYRIGHT BY
RAND McNALLY & COMPANY
MADE IN U.S.A.

40,000 SQ MI AREA

0   100   200
Miles

110°   Longitude 115° East of Greenwich   120°   125°   130°   135°   140°

Scale 1:16 000 000; one inch to 250 miles. Lambert's Azimuthal, Equal Area Projection
Elevations and depressions are given in feet

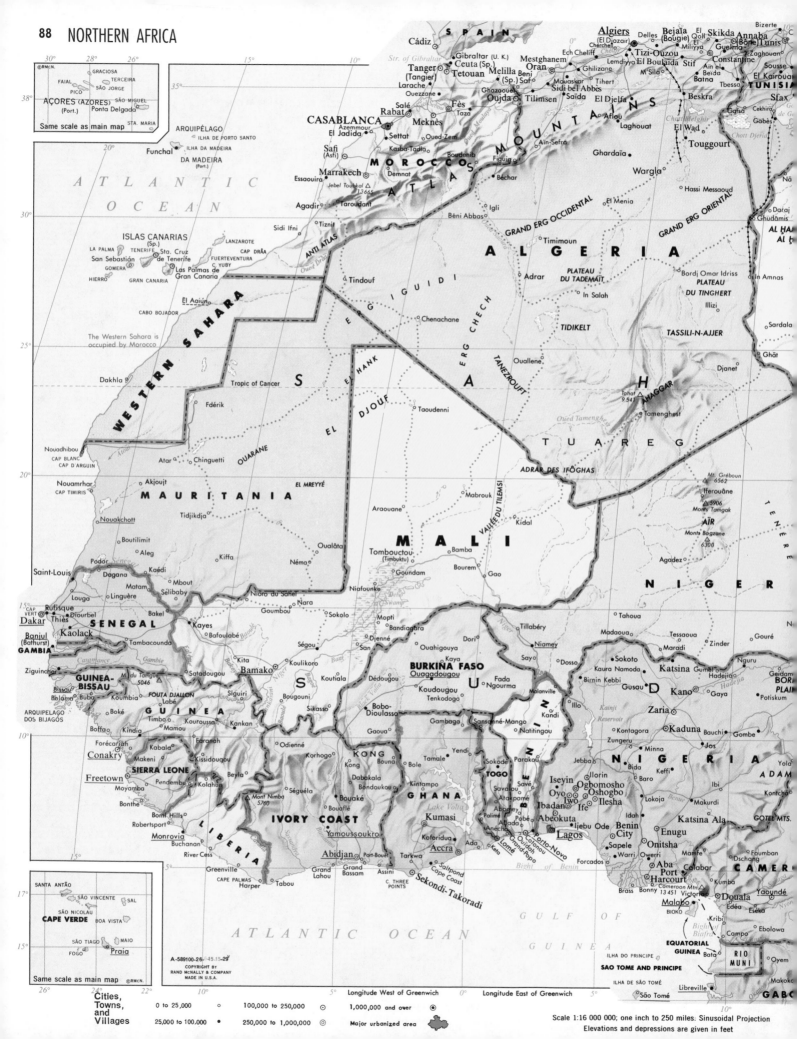

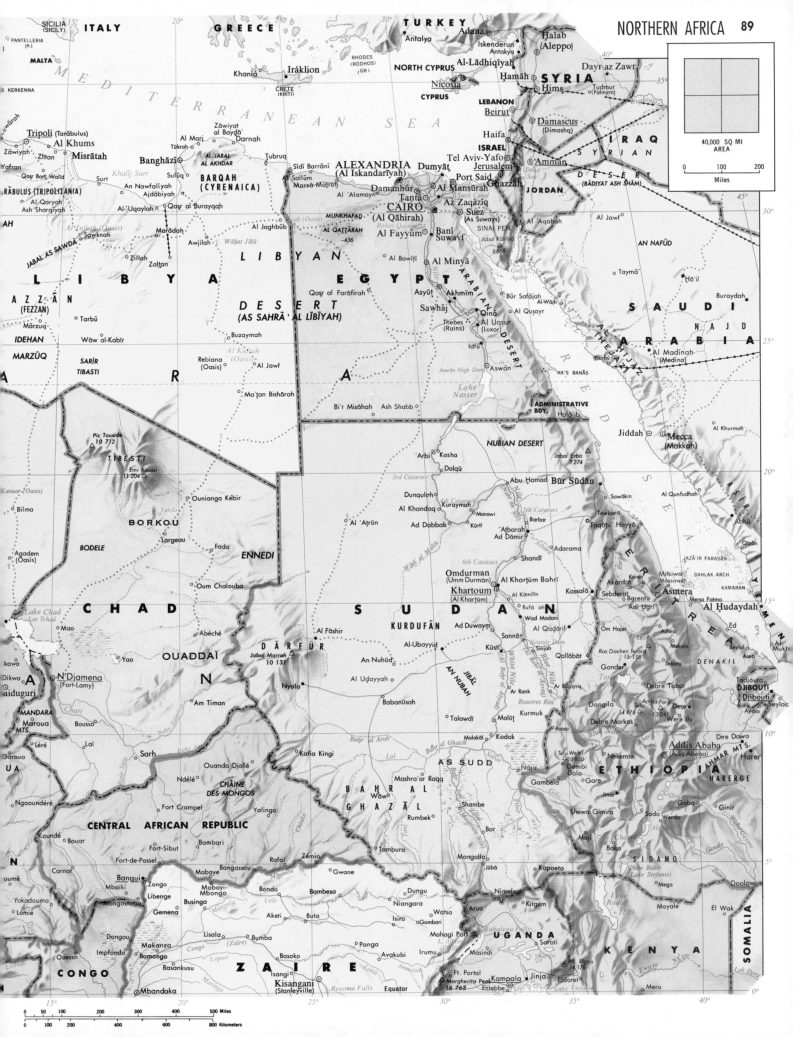

CAPE TOWN

Scale 1:1 000 000

10 Miles
16 Kilometers

The "Homelands" (Bophuthatswana, Ciskei, Transkei, Venda) were unilaterally created by South Africa and are not internationally recognized.

1 Bophuthatswana
2 Ciskei
3 Transkei
4 Venda

Scale 1:16 000 000; one inch to 250 miles. Sinusoidal Projection
Elevations and depressions are given in feet

A-589200-26
COPYRIGHT BY
RAND MCNALLY & COMPANY
MADE IN U.S.A.

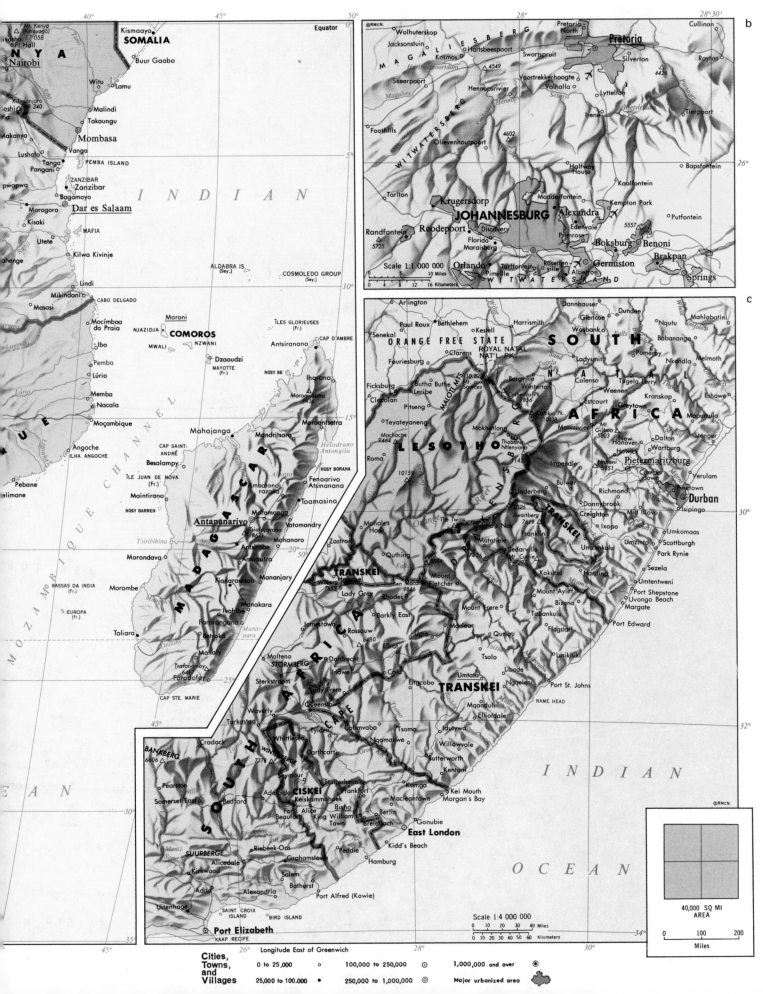

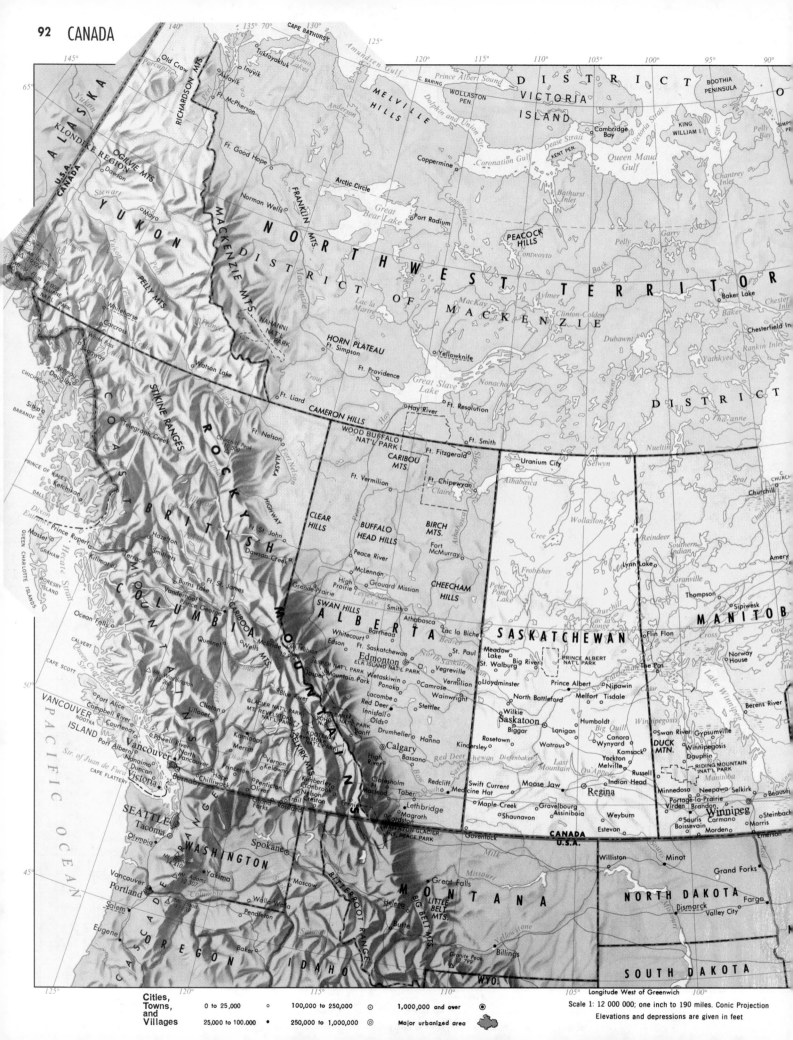

Cities,
Towns,
and
Villages

0 to 25,000   100,000 to 250,000   1,000,000 and over
25,000 to 100,000   250,000 to 1,000,000   Major urbanized area

Longitude West of Greenwich
Scale 1: 12 000 000; one inch to 190 miles. Conic Projection
Elevations and depressions are given in feet

Longitude West of Greenwich

QUEBEC

Same scale as main map

Gulf of St. Lawrence

NEWFOUNDLAND

ATLANTIC OCEAN

FRANKLIN

BAFFIN ISLAND

MELVILLE PENINSULA

Foxe Basin

Arctic Circle

Iqaluit

EVERETT MTS.

HUDSON BAY

KEEWATIN

PÉNINSULE D'UNGAVA

Ungava Bay

TORNGAT MTS.

NEWFOUNDLAND

LABRADOR

All islands within bays and straits lie within Northwest Territories.

James Bay

QUEBEC

MTS. OTISH

CHIC-CHOCS MTS.

ONTARIO

Gulf of St. Lawrence

NEW BRUNSWICK

NOVA SCOTIA

P.E.I.

Thunder Bay

Lake Superior

MICHIGAN

WISCONSIN

MINNESOTA

St. Paul

MINNEAPOLIS

Duluth

Sudbury

MONTRÉAL

Ottawa

Québec

MAINE

VERMONT

NEW HAMPSHIRE

BOSTON

MASS.

CONN.

R.I. Providence

Hartford

TORONTO

Hamilton

BUFFALO

NEW YORK

Albany

Rochester

DETROIT

CHICAGO

MILWAUKEE

ILL.

OHIO

PENNSYLVANIA

Scranton

NEW YORK

N.J.

Newark

ATLANTIC OCEAN

A-520200-26
COPYRIGHT BY
RAND McNALLY & COMPANY
MADE IN U.S.A.

40,000 SQ MI
AREA

0   100   200
Miles

0 25 50 75 100   200   300   400   500 Miles
0   100   200   400   600   800 Kilometers

Scale 1:12 000 000; one inch to 190 miles. Polyconic Projection
Elevations and depressions are given in feet

GULF OF MEXICO

ATLANTIC OCEAN

BAHAMAS

40,000 SQ MI
AREA
0   100   200
Miles

0 25 50 75 100   200   300   400   500 Miles
0   100   200   400   600   800 Kilometers

Scale 1:4 000 000; one inch to 64 miles.   Conic Projection
Elevations and depressions are given in feet

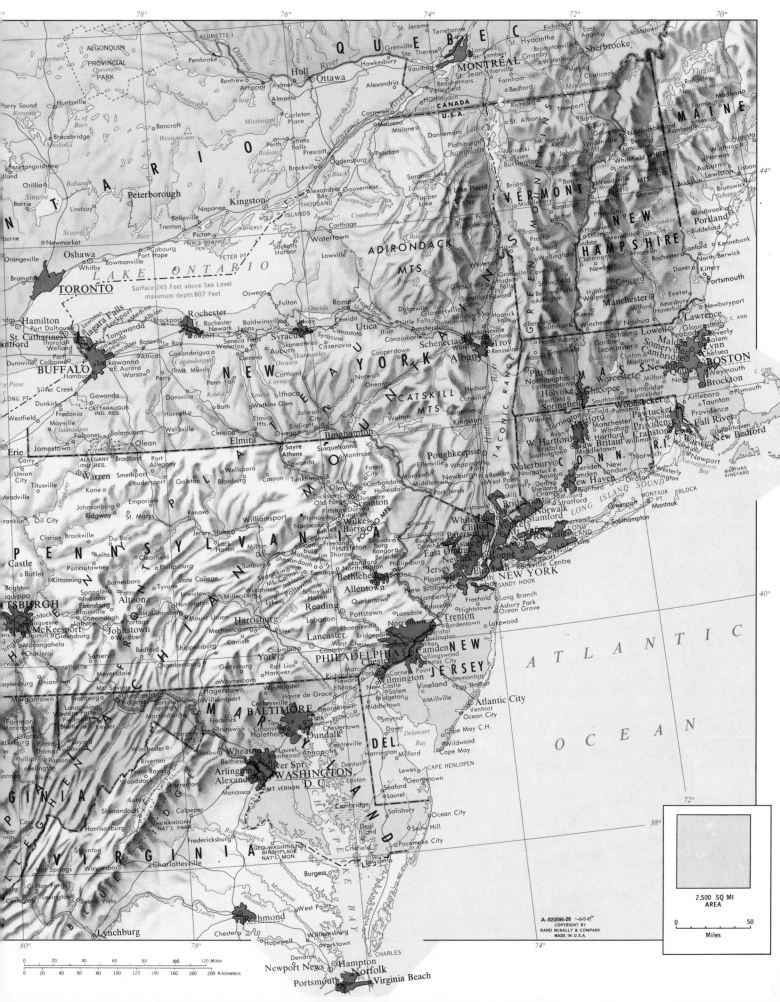

Scale 1:4 000 000; one inch to 64 miles. Conic Projection
Elevations and depressions are given in feet

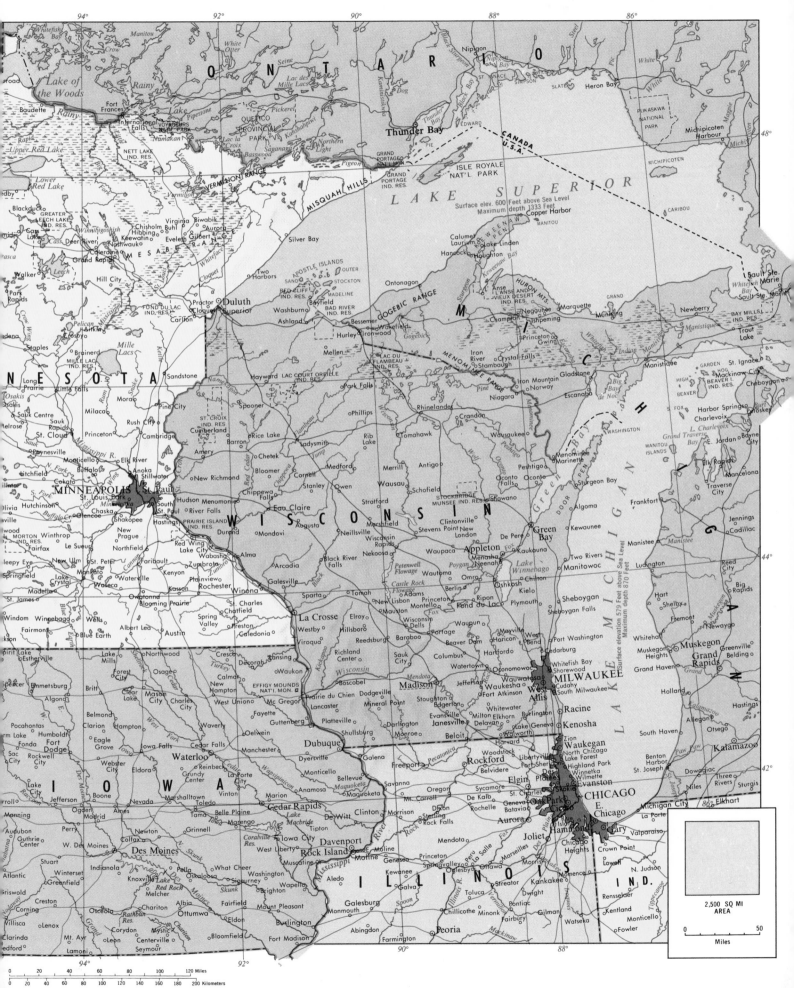

NORTHWESTERN U.S.A.

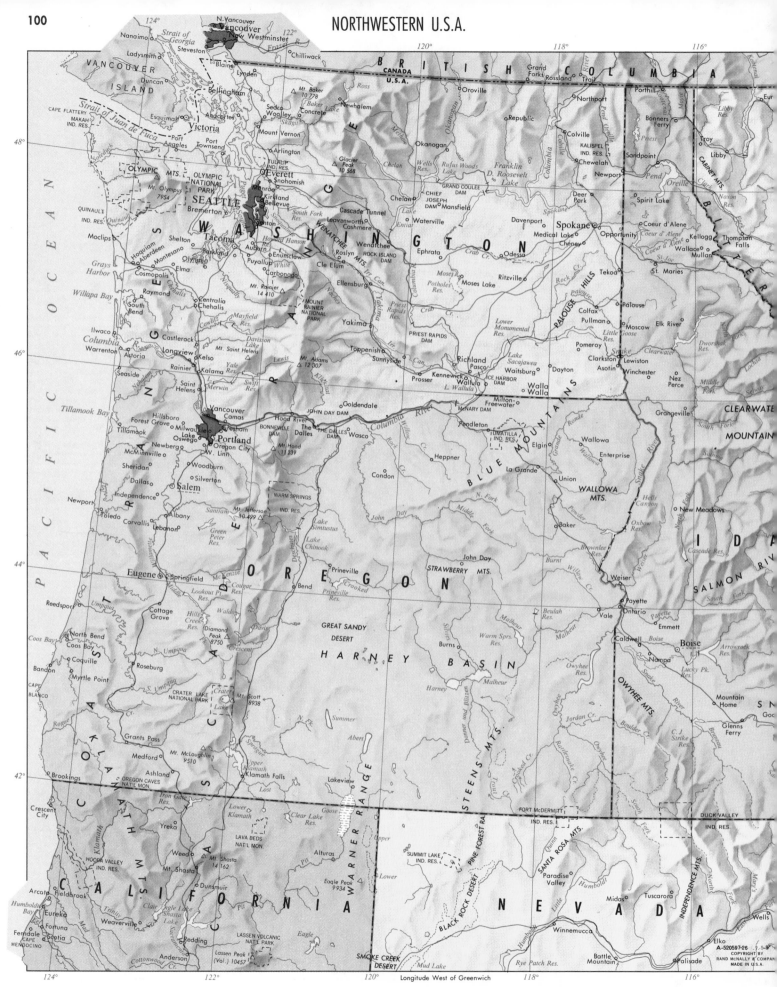

Scale 1 : 4,000 000; one inch to 64 miles. Conic Projection
Elevations and depressions are given in feet

A-520597-26
COPYRIGHT BY
RAND McNALLY & COMPANY
MADE IN U.S.A.

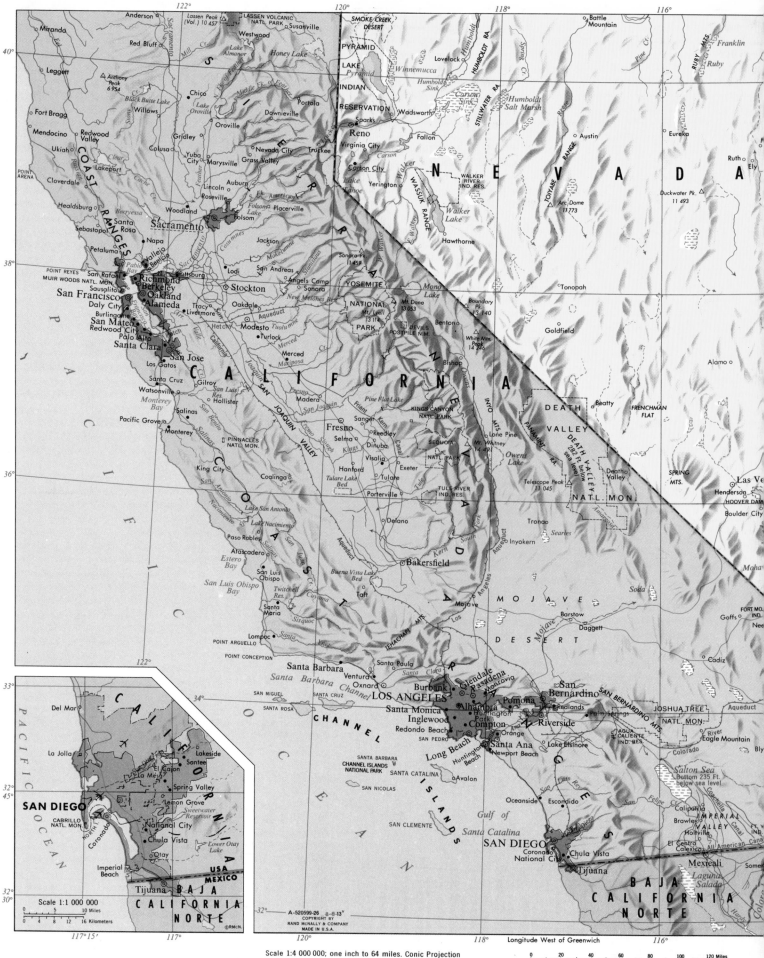

Scale 1:4 000 000; one inch to 64 miles. Conic Projection
Elevations and depressions are given in feet

Longitude West of Greenwich

Scale 1:1 000 000

A-520599-26   8-6-13
COPYRIGHT BY
RAND McNALLY & COMPANY
MADE IN U.S.A.

2,500 SQ MI
AREA

0   50
Miles

GREAT SALT LAKE DESERT

GREAT SALT LAKE DESERT

Great Salt Lake

Salt Lake City
Murray · Park City
Midvale
Tooele
West Jordan
Lehi · American Fork
Orem · Provo
Springville
Spanish Fork
Payson
Eureka
Nephi
Fairview
Moroni · Mount Pleasant
Ephraim
Manti
Delta
Gunnison
Fillmore
Salina
Milford
Monroe
Beaver
Richfield

IMPANOGOS CAVE N.M.
Heber City
UINTAH AND OURAY IND. RES.
Duchesne
Vernal
Roosevelt
WEST TAVAPUTS PLATEAU
Helper
Price
Hiawatha
Sunnyside
EAST TAVAPUTS PLATEAU
Castle Dale
Green River

Oak Creek
Meeker
Bond
Rifle
Glenwood Springs
Leadville
Mt. Massive 14,421
Aspen
Mt. Elbert 14,433
Castle Pk. 14,265
Plata Pk. 14,336
Mt. Harvard 14,420
Crested Butte
Buena Vista
Cripple Creek
Canon City

Grand Junction
COLORADO NATL. MON.
Fruita
Delta
Paonia
Montrose
UNCOMPAHGRE PLATEAU
Gunnison
Morrow Point Res.
BLACK CANYON OF THE GUNNISON NATL. MON.
Blue Mesa Res.
Crested Butte

COLORADO

Salida
SANGRE DE CRISTO MTS.
Saguache
ROCKY MTS.

UTAH

WASATCH PLATEAU

Castle Dale

San Rafael

ARCHES NATL. PARK
Moab
Mt. Peale 12,721
CANYONLANDS NATL. PARK
La Sal

Mt. Sneffels 14,150
Ouray
Uncompahgre Pk. 14,309
Telluride
Silverton
SAN JUAN MTS.

GREAT SAND DUNES N.M.
Del Norte
Blanca Pk. 14,345
Monte Vista
Alamosa

Delano Pk. 12,169
Little Salt Lake
Sevier Lake
GREAT BASIN NATL. PARK
Wheeler Peak

Parowan
Panguitch
Escalante
CAPITOL REEF NATL. PARK
Mt. Ellen 11,522
HENRY MTS.
Bullfrog
Abajo Pk. 11,360
Monticello
Blanding

HOVENWEEP NATL. MON.
Cortez
MESA VERDE NATL. PARK
Durango
Pagosa Springs
Summit Peak 13,300

Cedar City
CEDAR BREAKS NATL. MON.
BRYCE CANYON NATL. PARK
GLEN CANYON NATL. RECR. AREA
Lake Powell
NATURAL BRIDGES NATL. MON.

ZION NATL. PARK
Hurricane
Saint George
Kanab
RAINBOW BRIDGE NATL. MON.
San Juan
Mexican Hat
Bluff

SOUTHERN UTE IND. RES.
UTE MTN. IND. RES.
AZTEC RUINS NATL. MON.
Aztec
Farmington
APACHE
JICARILLA
El Vado Res.

Virgin
Mt. Bangs 8012
PIPE SPRING NATL. MON.
KAIBAB IND. RES.
Page
INSCRIPTION HOUSE RUIN
KEET SEEL RUIN
NAVAJO NATL. MON.
BETATAKIN RUIN
Navajo

INDIAN RESERVATION
CHACO CANYON NATL. MON.

Truchas Pk. 13,101
Santa Clara IND. RES.
Abiquiu Res.
Rio Chama

Lake Mead
MEAD RECR. AREA
Chloride
Kingman
Topock
Lake Havasu City
Lake Havasu
PARKER DAM
Bill Williams

SHIVWITS PLATEAU
UINKARET PLATEAU
KANAB PLATEAU
KAIBAB PLATEAU
GRAND CANYON NATIONAL PARK
Grand Canyon
MARBLE CANYON
HAVASUPAI IND. RES.
HUALAPAI IND. RES.

COCONINO PLATEAU
Moenkopi
NAVAJO INDIAN RES.
BLACK MESA
NAVAJO HOPI JOINT USE AREA
HOPI INDIAN RESERVATION
PAINTED DESERT
CANYON DE CHELLY NATL. MON.
CHUSKA MTS.

NAVAJO INDIAN RESERVATION

Gallup
Mt. Taylor 11,301
ZUNI
Los Alamos
BANDELIER NATL. MON.
JEMEZ IND. RES.
ZIA IND. RES.
SANTA FE
SANTO DOMINGO IND. RES.
SAN FELIPE IND. RES.
Galisteo
Bernalillo
SANDIA IND. RES.
Albuquerque
Canoncito IND. RES.

NEW MEXICO

HUALAPAI MTS.
Ash Fork
Williams
Humphreys Pk. 12,633
SUNSET CRATER N.M.
Flagstaff
WALNUT CANYON NATL. MON.
WUPATKI NATL. MON.
COLORADO

Winslow
Holbrook
PETRIFIED FOREST NATL. PARK
Sanders
Little Colorado

ZUNI IND. RES.
EL MORRO NATL. MON.
ZUNI MTS.
Rio San Jose
LAGUNA IND. RES.
ACOMA IND. RES.
Isleta
Belen
ISLETA IND. RES.

Prescott
Jerome
Clarkdale
TUZIGOOT N.M.
MONTEZUMA CASTLE NATL. MON.
MOGOLLON RIM

ARIZONA

Saint Johns
McNary
Springerville
FORT APACHE INDIAN RESERVATION
Mt. Ord 11,357
Baldy Peak 11,403
Maverick

Magdalena
ALAMO IND. RES.
Socorro

Wickenburg
Theodore Roosevelt Lake
Verde
Tonto
THEODORE ROOSEVELT DAM
TONTO NATL. MON.
Salt
SALT RIVER IND. RES.
Glendale
Phoenix
Tempe
Mesa
Miami
Superior
Globe
SAN CARLOS INDIAN RESERVATION
San Carlos Lake

Carrizozo
San Marcial
Elephant Butte
Sierra Blanca Peak 11,973
MESCALERO APACHE IND. RES.
Alamogordo
Tularosa

GILA RIVER IND. RES.
Painted Rock Res.
Gila Bend
Gila
Florence
CASA GRANDE N.M.
Hayden
Clifton
Morenci
Safford

Truth or Consequences
GILA CLIFF DWELLINGS NATL. MON.
Glenwood
BLACK RANGE
Caballo Res.
WHITE SANDS NATL. MON.
ANDRES MTS.
SAN

Casa Grande
PAPAGO INDIAN RESERVATION
San Manuel
San Pedro
PELONCILLO MTS.
Silver City
Bayard
Lordsburg
Deming
Las Cruces
Mesilla

Ajo
ORGAN PIPE CACTUS N.M.
Santa Cruz
Tucson
SAGUARO N.M.
SAN XAVIER IND. RES.
Willcox
Willcox Playa
Playa Lake
CHIRICAHUA NATL. MON.
Benson

FLORIDA MTS.
Columbus
Playas Lake

N. Franklin Mtn. 7192
TEXAS
El Paso
Ysleta
Ciudad Juárez

SONORA

TUMACACORI NATL. MON.
Nogales
Fort Huachuca
Tombstone
Bisbee
Lowell
Pirtleville
Douglas

USA
MEXICO

CHIHUAHUA

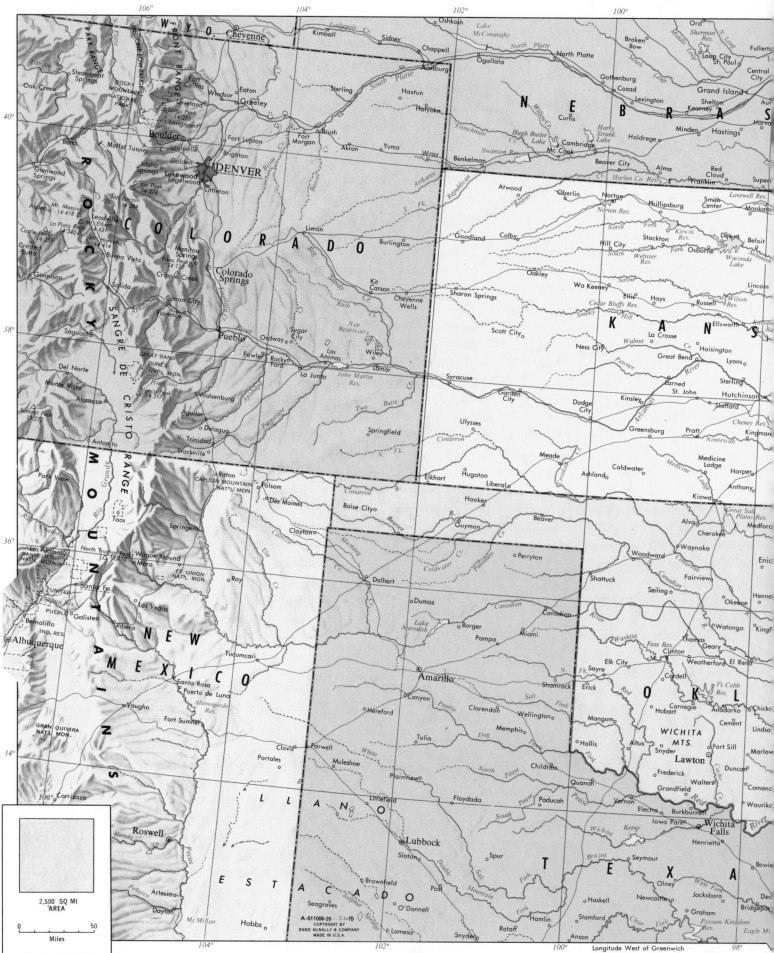

2,500 SQ MI AREA

0   50
Miles

Scale 1:4 000 000; one inch to 64 miles. Conic Projection
Elevations and depressions are given in feet.

Longitude West of Greenwich

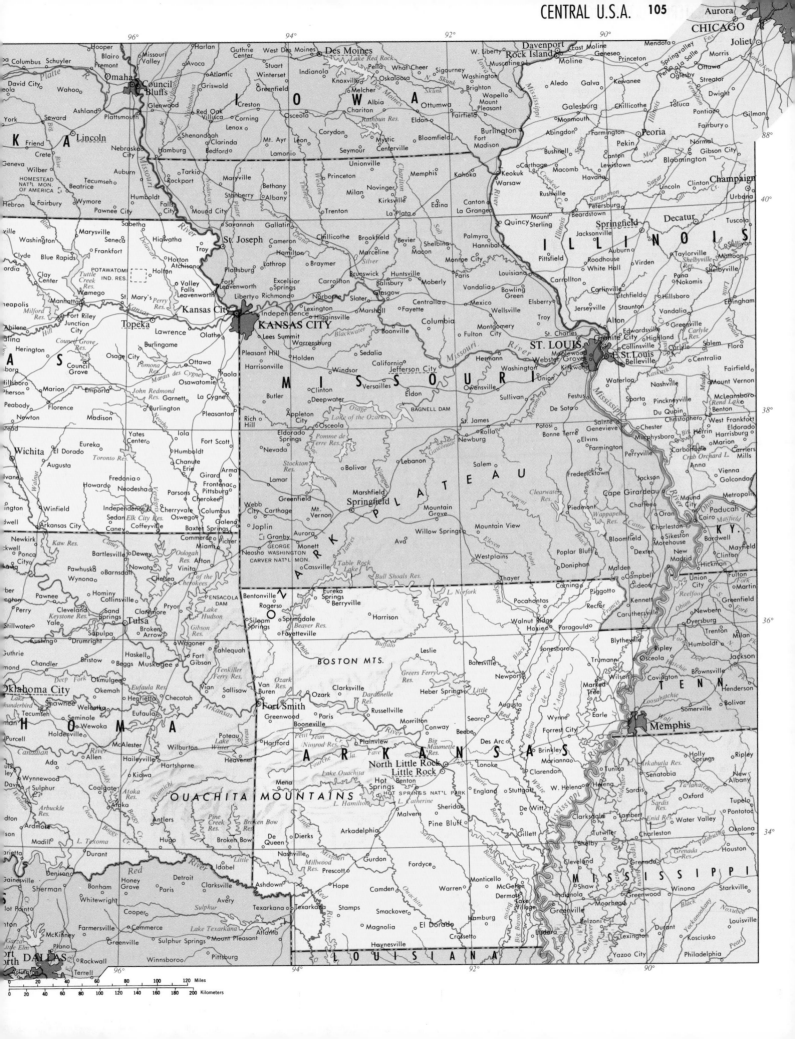

Scale 1:1 000 000

A-511007-26 56-6
COPYRIGHT BY
RAND McNALLY & COMPANY
MADE IN U.S.A.

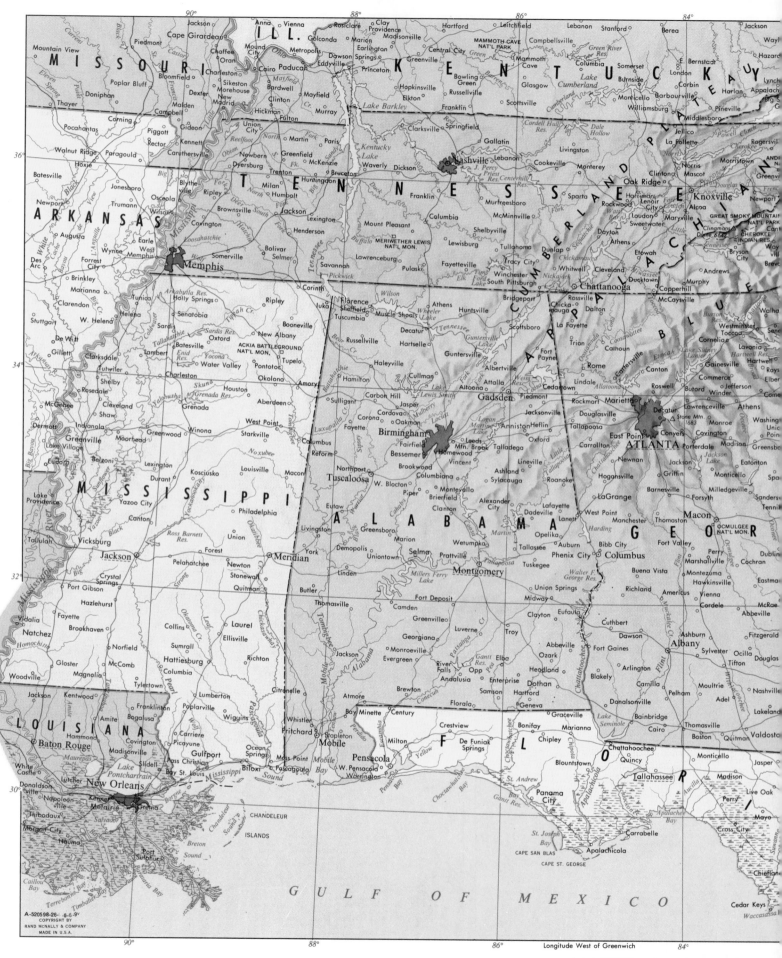

Scale 1:4 000 000; one inch to 64 miles. Conic Projection
Elevations and depressions are given in feet

Longitude West of Greenwich

2,500 SQ MI
AREA

0   50
Miles

Scale 1:16 000 000; one inch to 250 miles. Polyconic Projection
Elevations and depressions are given in feet

b

ATLANTIC OCEAN

Arecibo · San Juan · ST. THOMAS · TORTOLA (Br.)
Aguadilla · Bayamón · CABEZAS DE SAN JUAN · Charlotte Amalie · ST. JOHN (U.S.A.)
PTA. HIGUERO · Utuado · PUERTO RICO · Fajardo · CULEBRA · ST. JOHN (U.S.A.)
Mayagüez · Caguas · Vieques · VIEQUES
Coamo · Cayey · Humacao
Cabo Rojo · Ponce · Salinas · Guayama
Mona Passage · CARIBBEAN SEA · Christiansted · SAINT CROIX (U.S.A.)

Scale 1:4 000 000
0 10 20 30 40 Miles
0 10 20 30 40 50 60 Kilometers
©RMcN.

c

OUTER BRASS · LITTLE HANS LOLLICK
INNER BRASS · PICARA PT · HANS LOLLICK · GRASS CAY
STORMY PT. · THATCH CAY
ST. THOMAS · Crown Mt. (U.S.A.) 1558 · Charlotte Amalie (St. Thomas) · Nadir
WATER · FLAMINGO PT. · St. Thomas Harbor
Scale 1:500 000
©RMcN.

40 000 SQ MI
AREA

0 100 200
Miles

0 50 100 200 300 400 500 Miles
0 100 200 400 600 800 Kilometers

Longitude West of Greenwich

Inset map (Caracas region)

CARIBBEAN SEA

ISLA DE MARGARITA
Boca del Pozo · △ 2303
PUNTA ARENAS
Punta de Piedras
ISLA CUBAGUA

Tocuyo de la Costa
Chichiriviche
CAYO SOMBRERO
Tucacas

Golfo Triste

Maiquetía · La Guaira Naiguatá · La Sabana
Carayaca
Puerto Cabello
El Cambur · Pico Ceniza 7988 △
Montalbán Guacara
Morón
San Joaquín
Miranda
Tinaquillo

CARACAS
Petare · Santa Lucía
Los Teques
Maracay · El Consejo
VALENCIA
La Victoria
Cagua · La Victoria
Güigüe · Villa de Cura
Lago de Valencia

PUNTA DE ARAYA
Manicuare
Cumaná
Guanta

Higuerote
Río Chico
Caucagua
Boca de Uchire
El Guapo
Sabana de
Uchire
Clarines · San Miguel
El Pilar
Puerto Píritu
Barcelona

CABO CODERA
Pico Naiguatá 9072
Guatire

San Sebastián
San Juan de los Morros
Parapara
Camatagua

San Francisco de Macaira
Araguíta
Ocumare del Tuy
Casimiro

Soublette
San José de Gauribe
Valle de Guanape
Guanape

Aragua de Barcelona
Libertad de Orituco
Onoto
San Pablo
San Mateo
Anaco · Santa Rosa

Dos Caminos · Barbacoas

ISLA LA TORTUGA
ISLA LA BORRACHA

Puerto La Cruz
El Hatillo
Bergantín

8000 △

Scale 1:4 000 000
0 10 20 30 40 Miles
0 10 20 30 40 50 60 Kilometers
© RMcN.

Main map

TRINIDAD AND TOBAGO
Port of Spain
TOBAGO
TRINIDAD

Boca Grande
Morawhanna

Georgetown
New Amsterdam
Bartica Rosignol
Rockstone
Wismar
Skeldon
Nieuw Nickerie
Paranam
Totness
Paramaribo
Moengo
Albina
St. Laurent
Sinnamary
ILE DU DIABLE (DEVIL'S I.)
Cayenne
CABO ORANGE
Saint-Georges

GUYANA
SURINAME
FRENCH GUIANA

MERUME MTS.
Roraima 9094
KAIETEUR FALL
Kaieteur Fall
ACARAI MTS.
TUMUC-HUMAC MTS.
GEBERGTE
WILHELMINA
Dr. Ir. W. J. Van Blommestein Meer

Vista do Branco

CARIBBEAN

ATLANTIC OCEAN

Equator 0°

Amapá
Macapá
Mazagão
ILHA CAVIANA
ILHA DE MARAJO
Breves
Gurupá
Belém (Pará)
Abaetetuba
Cametá
Marapanim
Bragança
Cururupu
São Luís (Maranhão)
Alcântara
Tutóia
Parnaíba
Camocim
Acaraú
FORTALEZA (Ceará)
Maranguape
Baturité
Aracati
Areia Branca
Macau
CABO DE SÃO ROQUE
ARQUIPÉLAGO FERNANDO DE NORONHA (Brazil)
FERNANDO DE NORONHA
ATOL DAS ROCAS (Brazil)

Manaus (Manáos)
Itacoatiara
Parintins
Óbidos
Faro
Alenquer
Santarém
Amazonas
Itaituba
Maués
Borba
Manicoré

Óbidos
Brasília Legal (Fordlândia)

BRAZIL

SERRA DOS CARAJÁS
São João do Araguaia
Tucuruí
Altamira
Tocantinópolis
Araguatins
Carolina
Riachão
Loreto
Balsas

SERRA DO GURUPI
Grajaú
Barra do Corda
Miradoro
Floriano
Oeiras
Picos

Rosário
Viana
Itapecuru-Mirim
Brejo
Caxias
Codó
Pedreiras
Monção
Teresina
Campo Maior
Senador Pompeu
Iguatu
Icó
Crateús
Quixadá
Russas
Mossoró
Ceará-Mirim
Natal
Nova Cruz
Campina Grande
Guarabira
Cabedelo
João Pessoa (Paraíba)
Nazaré da Mata
Olinda
RECIFE (Pernambuco)

Currais Novos
Patos
Crato
Juazeiro do Norte
Flores
Sertânia
Caruaru
Jaboatão

SERRA DA IBIAPABA
SERRA DO ARARIPE
PLANALTO DA BORBOREMA

São Raimundo Nonato
Paulistana
Santa Filomena
CHAP. DAS MANGABEIRAS
Barreiras
Correntina
Carinhanha
SERRA GERAL DE GOIÁS

SERRA DO RONCADOR
SERRA DO ESTRONDO

Pôrto Nacional
Natividade
Parnaguá
SERRA DO PIAUÍ
Barra
Morro do Chapéu
Juazeiro
Petrolina
Jeremoabo
Senhor do Bonfim
Jacobina
Itabaiana
Aracaju
São Cristóvão
Estância
Inhambupe
Serrinha
Feira de Santana
Alagoinhas
Santo Amaro
Nazaré
Cachoeira
Lençóis
Mucugê
SALVADOR (Bahia)
Arauípe
Valença
Jequié
Vitória da Conquista
Condeúba
Caetité
Ilhéus
Itabuna
Canavieiras
Belmonte
Porto Seguro
ARQUIPÉLAGO DOS ABROLHOS
Caravelas
São Mateus

Garanhuns
Palmeira dos Índios
Pôrto de Pedras
Palmares
Maceió
Propriá
Penedo
Corurípe

SERRA DOS PARECIS
SERRA DO NORTE
SERRA DO TOMBADOR
SERRA FORMOSA
CHAPADA DE MATO GROSSO
Diamantino
Rosário Oeste
SA. DA TAQUARA
SERRA DA CHAPADA
Cuiabá
Barão de Melgaço
Cáceres
Mato Grosso

ILHA DO BANANAL
Cavalcante
Pilar de Goiás
Formosa
Brasília
São Francisco
Januária
Rio Pardo de Minas
SERRA DO ESPINHAÇO
Pedra Azul
SA. DOS AIMORÉS
Itabuna
Teófilo Otoni
Peçanha
Gov. Valadares
Colatina
Aracruz
Vitória
Espírito Santo
Guarapari
Cachoeiro do Itapemirim

Pirenópolis
Anápolis
Goiás
Goiânia
Bela Vista de Goiás
Silvânia
Luziânia
Paracatu
Ipameri
Catalão
Uberlândia
Uberaba
Araxá
SA. DE CANASTRA
Pará de Minas
Formiga
Divinópolis
Conselheiro Lafaiete
Barbacena
São João del Rei
Lavras
Três Corações
Poços de Caldas
Pouso Alegre

Montes Claros
Minas Novas
Grão Mogol
Araçuaí
Diamantina
Curvelo
Sete Lagoas
Patos de Minas
Patrocínio
Araguari
BELO HORIZONTE
Sta. Bárbara
Ponte Nova
Viçosa
Ubá
Juiz de Fora
Petrópolis
Nova Friburgo
Campos
CABO FRIO
Niterói
RIO DE JANEIRO
Tropic of Capricorn

MATO GROSSO DO SUL
Campo Grande
Aquidauana
Nioaque
SERRA DE AMAMBAI
Bahía Negra
Corumbá
Porto Murtinho
Mariscal Estigarribia
GRAN CHACO

PARAGUAY
Concepción
Fuerte Olimpo
Porto Murtinho
Bella Vista
Pedro Juan Caballero
Concepción
Belén
Horqueta

São José do Rio Prêto
Itapira
Barretos
Franca
Ribeirão Prêto
Catanduva
Araraquara
São Carlos
Rio Claro
Limeira
Campinas
Jundiaí
Piracicaba
Botucatu
Itu
Sorocaba
São Paulo
Santos
São Vicente
Mogi das Cruzes
Taubaté
Jacareí
Guaratinguetá
Cruzeiro
Redenção
Nova Iguaçu
Itajubá
Lorena
Barra Mansa
Resende

Araçatuba
Birigui
Lins
Marília
Assis
Presidente Epitácio
Presidente Prudente
Bauru
Ourinhos
Salto Grande
Jacarezinho
Londrina
Ibaiti
Tibagi
Castro
Ponta Grossa
Guarapuava
Curitiba

Três Lagoas
Paranaíba
Coxim
Rio Verde
Morrinhos
Ituiutaba
Paranaíba

PARANÁ
Rio Grande
Guaíra
IGUASSU FALLS
Iguaçu Falls
Porto Mendes

Represa de Três Marias
São Francisco
Pirapora
Corinto
Montes Claros

40,000 SQ MI AREA
0 100 200
Miles

0 50 100 200 300 400 500 Miles
0 100 200 400 600 800 Kilometers

Scale 1:16 000 000 one inch to 250 miles. Sinusoidal Projection
Elevations and depressions are given in feet

MAP INDEX

ABBREVIATIONS OF GEOGRAPHICAL NAMES AND TERMS

Afg. Afghanistan
Afr. Africa
Ala. Alabama
Alb. Albania
Alg. Algeria
Alsk. Alaska
Alta. Alberta
Ang. Angola
Arg. Argentina
Ariz. Arizona
Ark. Arkansas
Atl. O. Atlantic Ocean
Aus. Austria
Austl. Australia

B. Bay, Bahia
Barb. Barbados
B.C. British Columbia
Bdy. Boundary
Bel. Belgium
Bhu. Bhutan
Bngl. Bangladesh
Bol. Bolivia
Bots. Botswana
Br. British
Braz. Brazil
Bul. Bulgaria
Bur. Burma
Burkina Burkina Faso

C. Cape, Cerro
Calif. California
Cam. Cameroon
Camb. Cambodia
Can. Canada
Cen. Afr. Rep. Central African Republic
Chan. Channel
Col. Colombia
Colo. Colorado
Conn. Connecticut
C.R. Costa Rica
Cr. Creek
Ctry. Country

C.V. Cape Verde
Cyp. Cyprus
Czech. Czechoslovakia

D.C. District of Columbia
Del. Delaware
Den. Denmark
Des. Desert
D.F. Distrito Federal
Dom. Rep. Dominican Republic

E. East
Ec. Ecuador
Eg. Egypt
Eng. England
Equat. Gui. Equatorial Guinea
Est. Estonia
Eth. Ethiopia
Eur. Europe

Falk. Is. Falkland Is.
Fin. Finland
Fla. Florida
Fr. France
Fr. Gu. French Guiana
Ft. Fort

G. Gulf
Ga. Georgia
Gam. Gambia
Ger. Germany
Gib. Gibraltar
Grc. Greece
Gt. Great

Guad. Guadeloupe
Guat. Guatemala
Gui. Guinea
Gui.-B. Guinea-Bissau
Guy. Guyana

Har., Hbr. Harbor
Haw. Hawaii
Hd. Head
H.K. Hong Kong
Hond. Honduras
Hts. Heights
Hung. Hungary

I. Island
I.C. Ivory Coast
Ice. Iceland
Ill. Illinois
Ind. Indiana
Ind. O. Indian Ocean
Indon. Indonesia
Ind. Res. Indian Reservation
Int., Intl. International
Ire. Ireland
Is. Islands
Isr. Israel
Isr. Occ. Israeli Occupied Territories
Ist. Isthmus
It. Italy

Jam. Jamaica
Jc. Junction
Jor. Jordan

Kans. Kansas
Ken. Kenya
Kor. Korea
Kuw. Kuwait
Ky. Kentucky

L. Lake
La. Louisiana
Lat. Latvia
Leb. Lebanon
Leso. Lesotho
Lib. Liberia
Liech. Liechtenstein
Lith. Lithuania
Lux. Luxembourg

Mad. Madagascar
Mala. Malaysia
Man. Manitoba
Mart. Martinique
Mass. Massachusetts
Maur. Mauritania
Md. Maryland
Mex. Mexico
Mich. Michigan
Minn. Minnesota
Miss. Mississippi
Mo. Missouri
Mong. Mongolia
Mont. Montana
Mor. Morocco
Moz. Mozambique
Mt. Mount, Mountain
Mts. Mountains

N. North
N.A. North America
Nam. Namibia
Nat., Natl. National
Natl. Mon. National Monument
N.B. New Brunswick
N.C. North Carolina
N. Cal. New Caledonia
N. Dak. North Dakota
Neb. Nebraska
Nep. Nepal
Neth. Netherlands
Neth. Ant. Netherlands Antilles
Nev. Nevada
Newf. Newfoundland
N.H. New Hampshire

Nic. Nicaragua
Nig. Nigeria
N. Ire. Northern Ireland
N.J. New Jersey
N.Mex. New Mexico
Nor. Norway
N.S. Nova Scotia
N.W.T. Northwest Territories
N.Y. New York
N.Z. New Zealand

O. Ocean
Oc. Oceania
Ok. Oklahoma
Om. Oman
Ont. Ontario
Oreg. Oregon

P. Pass
Pa. Pennsylvania
Pac. O. Pacific Ocean
Pak. Pakistan
Pan. Panama
Pap. N. Gui. Papua New Guinea
Par. Paraguay
P.E.I. Prince Edward I.
Pen. Peninsula
Phil. Philippines
Pk. Park, Peak
Plat. Plateau
Pol. Poland
Polit. Reg. Political Region
Port. Portugal
P.R. Puerto Rico
Prov. Province

Pt. Point
Pta. Punta
Pte. Pointe

Que. Quebec

R. River, Río, Rvière
Ra. Range
Reg. Region
Rep. Republic
Res. Reservation, Reservoir
R.I. Rhode Island
Rom. Romania
Rw. Rwanda

S. San, Santo, South
Sa. Sierra
S.A. South America
S. Afr. South Africa
Sal. El Salvador
Sask. Saskatchewan
Sau. Ar. Saudi Arabia
S.C. South Carolina
Scot. Scotland
S.Dak. South Dakota
Sd. Sound
Sen. Senegal
S.L. Sierra Leone
Sol. Is. Solomon Islands
Som. Somalia
Sov. Un. Soviet Union
Sp. N. Afr. Spanish North Africa
Spr., Sprs. Spring, Springs
S.S.R. Soviet Socialist Republic
St. Saint, Station
Sta. Santa
Ste. Sainte
Str. Strait

St. Vin. St. Vincent and the Grenadines
Sud. Sudan
Sur. Suriname
Swaz. Swaziland
Swe. Sweden
Switz. Switzerland
Syr. Syria

Tan. Tanzania
Tenn. Tennessee
Ter. Territory
Tex. Texas
Thai. Thailand
Trin. Trinidad and Tobago
Tun. Tunisia
Tur. Turkey

U.A.E. United Arab Emirates
Ug. Uganda
U.K. United Kingdom
Ur. Uruguay
U.S. United States

Va. Virginia
Van. Vanuatu
Ven. Venezuela
Viet. Vietnam
Vir. Is. Virgin Islands
Vol. Volcano
Vt. Vermont

W. West
Wash. Washington
Wis. Wisconsin
W. Sah. Western Sahara
W. Va. West Virginia
Wyo. Wyoming

Yugo. Yugoslavia

Zimb. Zimbabwe

Page Place Lat.°' Long.°'

A

73 Aachen, Ger. 51N 6E
82 Ābādān, Iran 30N 48E
77 Abakan, Sov. Un. 54N 91E
76 Abdulino, Sov. Un. 54N 54E
72 Aberdeen, Scot. 57N 2W
98 Aberdeen, S. Dak. 45N 98W
100 Aberdeen, Wash. 47N 124W
88 Abidjan, I.C. 5N 4W
106 Abilene, Tex. 32N 100W
82 Abū Kamāl, Syr. 34N 41E
82 Abū Zaby, U.A.E. 24N 54E
110 Acapulco, Mex. 17N 100W
88 Accra, Ghana 6N 0
114 Aconcagua, C. (Mt.) Arg. 33S 70W
75 Acre, Isr. 33N 35E
75 Adana, Tur. 37N 35E
75 Adapazari, Tur. 41N 30E
82 Ad Dawhah, Qatar 25N 51E
82 Ad Dilam, Sau. Ar. 24N 47E
89 Addis Ababa, Eth. 9N 39E
86 Adelaide, Austl. 35S 139E
82 Aden, Yemen 13N 45E
82 Aden, Gulf of, Asia-Afr. 12N 46E
97 Adirondack Mts., N.Y. 44N 74W
74 Adriatic Sea, Eur. 44N 14E
75 Aegean Sea, Grc.-Tur. 39N 25E
82 Afghanistan (Ctry.) Asia 34N 65E
74 Aflou, Alg. 34N 2E
75 Afyon, Tur. 39N 30E
88 Agadir, Mor. 30N 10W
77 Aginskoye, Sov. Un. 51N 114E
83 Āgra, India 27N 78E
75 Agrínion, Grc. 39N 21E
110 Aguascalientes, Mex. 22N 102W
90 Agulhas, C., S. Afr. 35S 20E
88 Ahaggar (Mts.) Alg. 23N 6E
83 Ahmadābād, India 23N 73E
83 Ahmadnagar, India 19N 75E
82 Ahvāz, Iran 31N 49E
74 Aïn-Temouchent, Alg. 35N 1W
73 Aix-en-Provence, Fr. 44N 5E
73 Ajaccio, Fr. 42N 9E
82 Ajman, U.A.E. 25N 55E
83 Ajmer, India 26N 75E
75 Akhisar, Tur. 39N 28E
89 Akhmīm, Eg. 27N 32E
81 Akita, Japan 40N 140E
88 Akjoujt, Maur. 20N 15W
92 Aklavik, N.W. Ter., Can. 68N 135W
83 Akola, India 21N 77E
96 Akron, Ohio 41N 81W
80 Aksu, China 41N 80E
71 Aktyubinsk, Sov. Un. 50N 57E
95 Alabama (State) U.S. 33N 87W
102 Alameda, Calif. 38N 122W
103 Alamogordo, N. Mex. 33N 106W
75 Alanya, Tur. 37N 32E
76 Alapayevsk, Sov. Un. 58N 62E
94 Alaska (State) U.S. 65N 155W
76 Alatyr', Sov. Un. 55N 46E
74 Albacete, Sp. 39N 2W
75 Albania (Ctry.) Eur. 41N 20E
108 Albany, Ga. 32N 84W
97 Albany, N.Y. 43N 74W
100 Albany, Oreg. 45N 123W
93 Albany (R.) Ont., Can. 52N 84W
82 Al Başrah, Iraq 30N 48E
89 Albert, L., Ug.-Zaire 2N 30E
92 Alberta (Prov.) Can. 55N 117W
73 Albi, Fr. 44N 2E
72 Ålborg, Den. 57N 10E
103 Albuquerque, N. Mex. 35N 107W
82 Al Buraymī, Oman 24N 56E
74 Alcázar de San Juan, Sp. 39N 3W
74 Alcoy, Sp. 39N 1W
77 Aldan, Sov. Un. 59N 125E
77 Aledanskaya, Sov. Un. 62N 135E
77 Aleksandrovsk, Sov. Un. 51N 142E
82 Aleppo, Syr. 36N 37E
73 Alès, Fr. 44N 4E
73 Alessandria, It. 45N 9E
91 Alexandra, S. Afr. 26S 28E
89 Alexandria (Al Iskandarīyah), Eg. 31N 30E
107 Alexandria, La. 31N 92W
97 Alexandria, Va. 39N 77W
75 Alexandroúpolis, Grc. 41N 26E
89 Al Fāshir, Sud. 14N 25E
89 Al Fayyūm, Eg. 29N 31E
88 Algeria (Ctry.) Afr. 29N 1E
88 Algiers (El Djazaïr), Alg. 37N 3E
82 Al Ḩawṭah, Yemen 16N 48E
82 Al Ḩudaydah, Yemen 15N 43E
82 Al Hufūf, Sau. Ar. 25N 50E
74 Alicante, Sp. 38N 0
86 Alice Springs, Austl. 24S 134E
83 Alīgarh, India 28N 78E
97 Aliquippa, Pa. 41N 80W
75 Al Ismā'īlīyah, Eg. 31N 32E
82 Al Jawf, Sau. Ar. 30N 39E
75 Al Jīzah, Eg. 30N 31E
82 Al Khābūrah, Oman 24N 57E
89 Al Kharṭūm Bahrī, Sud. 16N 33E
89 Al Khums, Libya 33N 14E
82 Al Khurmah, Sau. Ar. 22N 42E
82 Al Lādhiqīyah (Latakia), Syr. 36N 36E
83 Allāhābād, India 26N 82E
77 Allaykha, Sov. Un. 71N 149E
97 Allegheny (R.) U.S. 42N 79W
97 Allentown, Pa. 41N 75W
83 Alleppey, India 10N 76E
98 Alliance, Nebr. 42N 103W
96 Alliance, Ohio 41N 81W
82 Al Luḩayyah, Yemen 16N 43E
76 Alma-Ata, Sov. Un. 43N 77E
82 Al Madīnah, Sau. Ar. 24N 40E
75 Al Maḩallah al Kubrā, Eg. 31N 31E
82 Al Manāmah, Bahrain 26N 51E
89 Al Manşūrah, Eg. 31N 31E
82 Al Mawşil, Iraq 36N 41E
74 Almería, Sp. 37N 2W
89 Al Minyā, Eg. 28N 31E
82 Al Mubarraz, Sau. Ar. 23N 46E
82 Al Mukallā, Yemen 14N 49E
82 Al Mukhā (Mocha), Yemen 14N 43E
84 Alor Setar, Mala. 6N 100E
96 Alpena, Mich. 45N 83W
73 Alps (Mts.) Eur. 46N 9E
89 Al Qaḑārif, Sud. 14N 35E
82 Al Qaṭīf, Sau. Ar. 27N 50E
82 Al Qayşūmah, Sau. Ar. 28N 46E
82 Al Qunfudhah, Sau. Ar. 19N 41E
80 Altai Mts., Asia 49N 87E
73 Altamura, It. 41N 17E
80 Altay, China 48N 88E
112 Altiplano (Plateau) Bol. 19S 68W
105 Alton, Ill. 39N 90W
97 Altoona, Pa. 40N 78W
89 Al Ubayyid, Sud. 13N 30E
89 Al Uqşur (Luxor), Eg. 26N 33E
82 Al Wajh, Sau. Ar. 26N 37E
83 Alwar, India 28N 77E
104 Amarillo, Tex. 35N 102W
113 Amazonas (Amazon) (R.) S.A. 2S 53W
83 Ambāla, India 31N 77E
77 Ambarchik, Sov. Un. 70N 162E
112 Ambato, Ec. 1S 79W
108 Americus, Ga. 32N 84W
92 Amery, Man., Can. 57N 94W
77 Amga, Sov. Un. 61N 132E
73 Amiens, Fr. 50N 2E
82 'Ammān, Jor. 32N 36E
83 Amrāvati, India 21N 78E
83 Amritsar, India 32N 75E
73 Amsterdam, Neth. 52N 5E
97 Amsterdam, N.Y. 43N 74W
82 Amu Darya (R.) Afg.-Sov. Un. 40N 62E
77 Amur (R.) China-Sov. Un. 52N 126E
101 Anaconda, Mont. 46N 113W
77 Anadyr', Sov. Un. 65N 177E
75 Anan'yev, Sov. Un. 48N 30E
114 Anchieta, Braz. 23S 43W
94 Anchorage, Alsk. 61N 150W
73 Ancona, It. 44N 14E
84 Andaman Is., India 12N 92E
84 Andaman Sea, Asia 13N 95E
96 Anderson, Ind. 40N 86W
109 Anderson, S.C. 34N 83W
112 Andes Mts., S.A. 11S 75W
76 Andizhan, Sov. Un. 41N 73E
81 Andong, Kor. 37N 129E
74 Andorra (Ctry.) Eur. 42N 1E
77 Angarsk, Sov. Un. 53N 104E
112 Angel, Salto (Falls) Ven. 6N 62W
73 Angers, Fr. 47N 1W
90 Angola (Ctry.) Afr. 12S 18E
73 Angoulême, Fr. 46N 0
111 Anguilla (Ctry.) N.A. 18N 63W
80 Ankang, China 33N 109E
75 Ankara (Angora), Tur. 40N 33E
88 Annaba, Alg. 37N 8E
82 An Nafūd (Des.) Sau. Ar. 28N 40E
82 An Najaf, Iraq 31N 45E
84 Annamese Cordillera (Mts.) Laos-Viet. 18N 106E
97 Annapolis, Md. 39N 76W
96 Ann Arbor, Mich. 42N 84W
108 Anniston, Ala. 34N 86W
81 Anqing, China 31N 117E
80 Anshun, China 26N 106E
75 Antakya, Tur. 36N 36E
75 Antalya (Adalia), Tur. 37N 31E
91 Antananarivo, Mad. 19S 48E
68 Antarctica 90S 60W
74 Antequera, Sp. 37N 5W
111 Antigua and Barbuda (Ctry.) N.A. 17N 62W
114 Antofagasta, Chile 24S 70W
114 Antofalla, Salar de (Dry L.) Arg. 26S 67W
91 Antsiranana, Mad. 12S 49E
73 Antwerp, Bel. 51N 4E
80 Anxi, China 41N 96E
76 Anzhero-Sudzhensk, Sov. Un. 56N 86E
81 Aomori, Japan 41N 141E
73 Apeldoorn, Neth. 52N 6E
95 Appalachian Mts., Can.-U.S 38N 80W
73 Appennino (Mts.), It. 44N 12E
99 Appleton, Wis. 44N 88W
75 Aqaba, Gulf of, Afr.-Asia 28N 35E
78 Arabian Sea, Asia 18N 63E
113 Aracaju, Braz. 11S 37W
85 Arafura Sea, Austl.-Indon. 9S 133E
113 Araguari, Braz. 19S 48W
82 Arak, Iran 34N 50E
76 Aral'sk, Sov. Un. 47N 62E
71 Aral'skoye More (L.) Sov. Un. 45N 60E
113 Araraquara, Braz. 22S 48W
73 Arcachon, Fr. 45N 1W
82 Ardabīl, Iran 38N 48E
73 Ardennes (Mts.) Bel. 50N 5E
105 Ardmore, Okla. 34N 97W
111 Arecibo, P.R. 18N 67W
112 Arequipa, Peru 16S 71W
73 Arezzo, It. 43N 12E
114 Argentina (Ctry.) S.A. 39S 67W
72 Århus, Den. 56N 10E
94 Arizona (State) U.S. 34N 112W
104 Arkansas (R.) U.S. 35N 95W
95 Arkansas (State) U.S. 35N 94W
71 Arkhangelsk (Archangel), Sov. Un. 64N 40E
107 Arlington, Tex. 33N 97W
97 Arlington, Va. 39N 77W
71 Armavir, Sov. Un. 45N 41E
112 Armenia, Col. 5N 76W
73 Arnhem, Neth. 52N 6E
73 Arras, Fr. 50N 3E
77 Arsen'yev, Sov. Un. 44N 134E
75 Árta, Grc. 39N 21E
77 Artëm, Sov. Un. 43N 132E
111 Aruba (Ctry.) N.A. 12N 70W
76 Arys, Sov. Un. 42N 68E
83 Asansol, India 24N 87E
71 Asbest, Sov. Un. 57N 61E
109 Asheville, N.C. 36N 83W
76 Ashkhabad, Sov. Un. 38N 58E
96 Ashland, Ky. 38N 83W
82 Ash Shaqrā, Sau. Ar. 25N 45E
82 Ash Shihr, Yemem 15N 50E
96 Ashtabula, Ohio 42N 81W
89 Asmera, Eth. 15N 39E
89 As Sallūm, Eg. 32N 25E
92 Assiniboia, Sask., Can. 50N 106W
82 As Sulaymānīyah, Iraq 36N 45E
75 As Suwaydā', Syr. 33N 37E
73 Asti, It. 45N 8E
100 Astoria, Oreg. 46N 124W
71 Astrakhan', Sov. Un. 46N 48E
114 Asunción, Par. 25S 57W
89 Aswān, Eg. 24N 33E
89 Asyūţ, Eg. 27N 31E
89 'Atbarah, Sud. 18N 30E
76 Atbasar, Sov. Un. 52N 68E
105 Atchison, Kans. 40N 95W
92 Athabasca, Alta., Can. 55N 113W
92 Athabasca (L.) Can. 59N 109W
92 Athabasca (R.) Alta., Can. 57N 112W
108 Athens, Ga. 34N 83W
75 Athens (Athínai), Grc. 38N 24E
108 Atlanta, Ga. 34N 84W
97 Atlantic City, N.J. 39N 74W

116

Atlas Mts., Afr.

Page	Place	Lat.°′	Long.°′
98	Atlas Mts., Afr.	33N	2W
92	Atlin (L.) Can.	60N	133W
82	Aṭ Ṭā'if, Sau. Ar.	21N	41E
97	Attleboro , Mass.	42N	71W
82	Aṭ Ṭurayf, Sau. Ar.	32N	38E
97	Auburn, Maine	44N	70W
87	Auckland, N.Z.	37S	175E
73	Augsburg, Ger.	48N	11E
109	Augusta, Ga.	33N	82W
95	Augusta, Maine	44N	70W
83	Aurangābād, India	20N	76E
73	Aurillac, Fr.	45N	2E
96	Aurora, Ill.	42N	88W
107	Austin, Tex.	30N	98W
86	Australia (Ctry.) Pac. O.	25S	135E
73	Austria (Ctry.) Eur.	47N	13E
73	Avignon, Fr.	44N	5E
76	Ayaguz, Sov. Un.	48N	80E
75	Aydin, Tur.	38N	28E
89	Aysha, Eth.	11N	43E
88	Azores (Açores) (Is.) Port.	38N	29W
75	Azovskoye More (Sea of Azov), Sov. Un.	46N	36E
82	Az Zahrān (Dhahran), Sau. Ar.	26N	50E
89	Az Zaqāzīq, Eg.	31N	32E

B

Page	Place	Lat.°′	Long.°′
89	Babanūsah, Sud.	12N	28E
82	Bābol, Iran	36N	53E
82	Babylon (Ruins) Iraq	32N	45E
75	Bacău, Rom.	47N	27E
80	Bachu, China	40N	78E
84	Bac Lieu, Viet.	10N	106E
84	Bacolod, Phil.	11N	123E
73	Baden-Baden, Ger.	49N	8E
93	Baffin I., N.W. Ter., Can.	67N	69W
82	Bāfq, Iran	32N	55E
114	Bagé, Braz.	31S	54W
82	Baghdād, Iraq	33N	44E
84	Bago, Bur.	17N	96E
85	Baguio, Phil.	16N	121E
111	Bahamas (Ctry.) N.A.	27N	77W
83	Bahāwalpur, Pak.	29N	72E
114	Bahía Blanca, Arg.	39S	62W
82	Bahrain (Ctry.) Asia	26N	51E
75	Baia-Mare, Rom.	48N	24E
100	Baker, Oreg.	45N	118W
102	Bakersfield, Calif.	35N	119W
82	Bakhtarān, Iran	34N	47E
71	Baku, Sov. Un.	40N	50E
71	Balashov, Sov. Un.	51N	43E
74	Baleares, Islas (Is.) Sp.	39N	3E
84	Bali (I.) Indon.	8S	115E
75	Balikesir, Tur.	40N	28E
76	Balkhash, Sov. Un.	47N	75E
76	Balkhash, Ozero (L.) Sov. Un.	47N	75E
87	Ballarat, Austl.	38S	144E
110	Balsas (R.) Mex.	18N	101W
75	Balta, Sov. Un.	48N	30W
72	Baltic Sea, Eur.	55N	17E
97	Baltimore, Md.	39N	77W
88	Bamako, Mali	13N	8W
73	Bamberg, Ger.	50N	11E
82	Bampūr, Iran	27N	60E
83	Bānda, India	26N	80E
85	Banda, Laut (Banda Sea), Indon.	6S	127E
82	Bandar-e 'Abbās, Iran	27N	56E
82	Bandar-e Anzalī, Iran	37N	49E
82	Bandar-e Būshehr, Iran	29N	51E
82	Bandar-e Khomeynī, Iran	30N	49E
82	Bandar-e Torkeman, Iran	37N	54E
75	Bandirma, Tur.	40N	28E
84	Bandung, Indon.	7S	107E
83	Bangalore, India	13N	75E
89	Banghāzī (Bengasi), Libya	32N	20E
84	Bangkok (Krung Thep), Thai.	14N	100E
83	Bangladesh (Ctry.) Asia	24N	90E
89	Bangui, Cen. Afr. Rep.	4N	19E
90	Bangweulu, L., Zambia	12S	30E
89	Banī Suwayf, Eg.	29N	31E
75	Banja Luka, Yugo.	45N	17E
84	Banjarmasin, Indon.	3S	115E
88	Banjul, Gam.	13N	17W
81	Baotou, China	40N	110E
70	Baranovichi, Sov. Un.	53N	26E
113	Barbacena, Braz.	21S	44W
111	Barbados (Ctry.) N.A.	14N	60W
96	Barberton, Ohio	41N	82W
74	Barcelona, Sp.	41N	2E
83	Bareilly, India	28N	79E
73	Bari, It.	41N	17E
80	Barkol, China	44N	93E
73	Barletta, It.	41N	16E
76	Barnaul, Sov. Un.	53N	83E
83	Baroda, India	22N	73E
112	Barquisimeto, Ven.	10N	69W
112	Barrancabermeja, Col.	7N	74W
112	Barranquilla, Col.	11N	75W
74	Barreiro, Port.	39N	9W
92	Barrhead, Alta., Can.	54N	114W
72	Barrow-in-Furness, Eng.	54N	3W
73	Basel, Switz.	48N	8E
111	Basse Terre, Guad.	16N	62W
87	Bass Str., Austl.	40S	145E
73	Bastia, Fr.	43N	9E
88	Bata, Eq. Gui.	2N	10E
80	Batang, China	30N	99E
85	Batangas, Phil.	14N	121E
84	Bătdâmbâng, Camb.	13N	103E
73	Bath, Eng.	51N	2W
88	Batna, Alg.	36N	6E
107	Baton Rouge, La.	30N	91W
96	Battle Creek, Mich.	42N	85W
71	Batumi, Sov. Un.	42N	41E
85	Bauang, Phil.	17N	120E
113	Bauru, Braz.	22S	49W
85	Bay, Laguna de (L.) Phil.	14N	121E
96	Bay City, Mich.	44N	84W
77	Baykal, Ozero (L. Baikal), Sov. Un.	53N	109E
77	Baykit, Sov. Un.	62N	97E
76	Baykonur, Sov. Un.	48N	66E
73	Bayonne, Fr.	43N	1W
97	Bayonne, N.J.	41N	74W
105	Beatrice, Nebr.	40N	97W
107	Beaumont, Tex.	30N	94W
73	Bedford, Eng.	52N	0
80	Beihai, China	21N	109E
81	Beijing (Peking), China	40N	116E
82	Beirut, Leb.	34N	35E
74	Beja, Tun.	37N	9E
88	Bejaïa, Alg.	37N	5E
93	Belcher Is. , N.W. Ter., Can.	56N	79W
113	Belém (Pará), Braz.	1S	48W
72	Belfast, N. Ire.	55N	6W
73	Belfort, Fr.	48N	7E
73	Belgium (Ctry.) Eur.	51N	3E
75	Belgrade (Beograd), Yugo.	45N	21E
110	Belize (Ctry.) N.A.	17N	89W
110	Belize City, Belize	17N	88W
83	Bellary, India	15N	77E
93	Belle Isle, Str. of, Can.	51N	56W
100	Bellingham, Wash.	49N	122W
110	Belmopan, Belize	16N	89W
77	Belogorsk, Sov. Un.	51N	129E
113	Belo Horizonte, Braz.	20S	44W
99	Beloit, Wis.	43N	89W
71	Beloretsk, Sov. Un.	54N	58E
75	Bel'tsy, Sov. Un.	48N	28E
100	Bend, Oreg.	44N	121W
75	Bendery, Sov. Un.	47N	29E
73	Benevento, It.	41N	15E
78	Bengal, Bay of, Asia	18N	88E
88	Benin (Ctry.) Afr.	8N	2E
88	Benin, Bight of (B.) Afr.	5N	2E
88	Benin City, Nig.	6N	6E
88	Beni Saf, Alg.	35N	1W
90	Benoni, S. Afr.	26S	28E
88	Benue (R.) Cam.-Nig.	8N	8E
82	Berbera, Som.	10N	45E
70	Berdichev, Sov. Un.	50N	29E
76	Berëzovo, Sov. Un.	64N	65E
73	Bergamo, It.	46N	10E
73	Bergen, Nor.	60N	5E
83	Berhampur, India	19N	85E
102	Berkeley, Calif.	38N	122W
73	Berlin, Ger.	52N	13E
111	Bermuda (Ctry.) N.A.	32N	65W
73	Bern, Switz.	47N	7E
114	Bernal, Arg.	34S	58W
96	Berwyn, Ill.	42N	88W
73	Besançon, Fr.	47N	6E
88	Beskra, Alg.	35N	6E
108	Bessemer, Ala.	33N	87W
94	Bethel, Alsk.	61N	162W
97	Bethelehem, Pa.	41N	75W
75	Bethlehem, Isr. Occ.	32N	35E
97	Beverly, Mass.	43N	71W
75	Beyşehir Gölü (L.) Tur.	38N	32E
71	Bezhitsa, Sov. Un.	53N	34E
73	Béziers, Fr.	43N	3E
83	Bhāgalpur, India	25N	87E
83	Bhātpāra, India	23N	89E
83	Bhaunagar, India	22N	73E
83	Bhopāl, India	23N	77E
83	Bhuj, India	24N	70E
83	Bhutan (Ctry.) Asia	27N	90E
88	Biafra, Bight of (B.) Afr.	3N	9E
72	Bialystok, Pol.	53N	23E
73	Bielefeld, Ger.	52N	9E
93	Bienville, Lac (L.) Que., Can.	56N	73W
83	Bilāspur, India	22N	82E
74	Bilbao, Sp.	43N	3W
101	Billings, Mont.	46N	108W
108	Biloxi, Miss.	30N	89W
97	Binghamton, N.Y.	42N	76W
88	Bioko (I.) Eq. Gui.	3N	8E
75	Bîrlad, Rom.	46N	28E
108	Birmingham, Ala.	34N	87W
73	Birmingham, Eng.	52N	2W
77	Birobidzhan, Sov. Un.	49N	133E
76	Birsk, Sov. Un.	55N	55E
103	Bisbee, Ariz.	31N	110W
74	Biscay, B. of,, Fr.-Sp.	45N	3W
90	Bisho, Ciskei	33S	27E
98	Bismarck, N. Dak.	47N	101W
88	Bissau, Gui-B.	12N	16W
75	Bitola, Yugo.	41N	21E
100	Bitterroot Range, U.S.	47N	115W
76	Biysk, Sov. Un.	53N	85E
88	Bizerte, Tun.	37N	10E
98	Black Hills, U.S.	44N	104W
75	Black Sea, Eur.	43N	33E
77	Blagoveshchensk, Sov. Un.	50N	128E
114	Blanca, B., Arg.	39S	61W
90	Blantyre, Malawi	16S	35E
90	Bloemfontein, S. Afr.	29S	26E
73	Blois, Fr.	48N	1E
96	Bloomington, Ind.	39N	87W
100	Blue Mts., U.S.	46N	118W
89	Blue Nile (R.) Eth.-Sud.	12N	34E
95	Blue Ridge, U.S.	37N	81W
88	Bobo-Dioulasso, Burkina	11N	4W
70	Bobruysk, Sov. Un.	53N	29E
77	Bodaybo, Sov. Un.	57N	115E
73	Boden See (L.) Ger.-Switz.	48N	9E
84	Bogor, Indon.	7S	107E
112	Bogotá, Col.	5N	74W
77	Bogotol, Sov. Un.	56N	89E
81	Bo Hai (B.) China	39N	119E
73	Bohemian Forest (Mts.) Ger.-Czech.	50N	12E
100	Boise, Idaho	44N	116W
92	Boissevain, Man., Can.	49N	100W
91	Boksburg, S. Afr.	26S	28E
112	Bolivia (Ctry.) S.A.	17S	64W
73	Bologna, It.	44N	11E
73	Bolzano, It.	46N	11E
83	Bombay, India	19N	73E
88	Bomi Hills, Lib.	7N	11W
89	Bomongo, Zaire	2N	18E
73	Bonn, Ger.	51N	7E
90	Bophuthatswana (Ctry.) Afr.	26S	26E
72	Borås, Swe.	58N	13E
82	Borāzjān, Iran	29N	51E
73	Bordeaux, Fr.	45N	1W
74	Bordj-Bou-Arreridj, Alg.	36N	5E
71	Borisoglebsk, Sov. Un.	51N	42E
84	Borneo (I.) Asia	1N	113E
76	Borovichi, Sov. Un.	58N	34E
82	Borūjerd, Iran	34N	49E
77	Borzya, Sov. Un.	51N	117E
81	Boshan, China	37N	118E
97	Boston, Mass.	42N	71W
72	Bothnia, Gulf of, Fin.-Swe.	62N	19E
75	Botosani, Rom.	48N	27E
90	Botswana (Ctry.) Afr.	22S	23E
88	Bouaké, I.C.	8N	5W
104	Boulder, Colo.	40N	105W
102	Boulder City, Nev.	36N	115W
73	Bourges, Fr.	47N	2E
96	Bowling Green , Ohio	41N	84W
101	Bozeman, Mont.	46N	111W
72	Bradford, Eng.	54N	2W
74	Braga, Port.	42N	8W
83	Brahmaputra (R.) Asia	27N	92E
75	Brăila, Rom.	45N	28E
91	Brakpan, S. Afr.	26S	28E
73	Brandenburg, Ger.	52N	13E
92	Brandon, Man., Can.	50N	100W
113	Brasília, Braz.	16S	48W
75	Braşov, Rom.	46N	26E
73	Bratislava, Czech.	48N	17E
77	Bratsk, Sov. Un.	56N	101E
73	Braunschweig, Ger.	52N	11E
102	Brawley, Calif.	33N	116W
113	Brazil (Ctry.) S.A.	8S	60W
90	Brazzaville, Congo	4S	15E
73	Bremen, Ger.	53N	9E
73	Bremerhaven, Ger.	54N	9E
100	Bremerton, Wash.	48N	123W
73	Brenner P., Aus.-It.	47N	11E
73	Brescia, It.	46N	10E
73	Brest, Fr.	48N	4W
70	Brest, Sov. Un.	52N	24E
97	Bridgeport, Conn.	41N	73W
111	Bridgetown, Barb.	13N	60W
73	Brig, Switz.	46N	8E
73	Brighton, Eng.	51N	0
87	Brisbane, Austl.	27S	153E
73	Bristol, Eng.	51N	3W
109	Bristol, Tenn.	37N	82W
73	Bristol Chan., U.K.	51N	4W
92	British Columbia (Prov.) Can.	56N	126W
72	British Isles, Eur.	55N	4W
73	Brno, Czech.	49N	17E
97	Brockton, Mass.	42N	71W
107	Brownsville, Tex.	26N	97W
106	Brownwood, Tex.	32N	99W
73	Brugge, Bel.	51N	3E
84	Brunei (Ctry.) Asia	5N	114E
109	Brunswick, Ga.	31N	81W
73	Brussels, Bel.	51N	4E
71	Bryansk, Sov. Un.	53N	34E
112	Bucaramanga, Col.	7N	73W
75	Bucharest, Rom.	44N	26E
73	Budapest, Hung.	47N	19E
112	Buenaventura, Col.	4N	77W
114	Buenos Aires, Arg.	34S	58W
97	Buffalo, N.Y.	43N	79W
72	Bug (R.) Pol.-Sov. Un.	52N	21E
76	Bugul'ma, Sov. Un.	55N	53E
90	Bujumbura, Burundi	3S	29E
90	Bukavu, Zaire	3S	29E
76	Bukhara, Sov. Un.	40N	64E
90	Bulawayo, Zimb.	20S	29E
75	Bulgaria (Ctry.) Eur.	43N	25E
77	Bulun, Sov. Un.	71N	127E
85	Buna, Pap. N. Gui.	9S	148E
82	Buraydah, Sau. Ar.	26N	44E
83	Burdwān, India	23N	88E
77	Bureya, Sov. Un.	50N	130E
75	Burgas, Bul.	42N	27E
74	Burgos, Sp.	42N	4W
83	Burhānpur, India	21N	76E
88	Burkina Faso (Ctry.) Afr.	13N	3W
99	Burlington, Iowa	41N	91W
97	Burlington, Vt.	44N	73W
80	Burma (Myanmar) (Ctry.) Asia	22N	95E
75	Bursa, Tur.	40N	28E
89	Būr Sūdān, Sud.	19N	37E
90	Burundi (Ctry.) Afr.	3S	30E
97	Butler, Pa.	41N	80W
101	Butte, Mont.	46N	113W
76	Buy, Sov. Un.	58N	42E
75	Buzău, Rom.	45N	27E
76	Buzuluk, Sov. Un.	53N	52E
72	Bydgoszcz, Pol.	53N	18E
73	Bytom, Pol.	50N	19E

C

Page	Place	Lat.°′	Long.°′
112	Cabimas, Ven.	10N	71W
90	Cabinda, Ang.	6S	12E
74	Cáceres, Sp.	39N	6W
74	Cádiz, Sp.	37N	6W
73	Caen, Fr.	49N	0
73	Cagliari, It.	39N	9E
111	Caguas, P.R.	18N	66W
89	Cairo (Al Qāhirah), Eg.	30N	31E
96	Cairo, Ill.	37N	89W
88	Calabar, Nig.	5N	8E
73	Calais, Fr.	51N	2E
75	Călărasi, Rom.	44N	27E
83	Calcutta, India	23N	88E
102	Calexico, Calif.	33N	115W
92	Calgary, Alta., Can.	51N	114W
112	Cali, Col.	3N	76W
83	Calicut, India	11N	76E
94	California (State) U.S.	38N	121W
110	California, G. de, Mex.	26N	110W
112	Callao, Peru	13S	77W
73	Caltanissetta, It.	37N	14E
111	Camagüey, Cuba	21N	78W
84	Cambodia (Ctry.) Asia	12N	104E
73	Cambridge, Eng.	52N	0
73	Cambrai, Fr.	50N	3E
97	Cambridge, Mass.	42N	71W
97	Camden, N.J.	40N	75W
88	Cameroon (Ctry.) Afr.	5N	12E
110	Campeche, Mex.	19N	90W
114	Campinas, Braz.	23S	47W
113	Campo Grande, Braz.	20S	55W
113	Campos, Braz.	22S	41W
92	Canada (Ctry.) N.A.	55N	100W
104	Canadian (R.) U.S.	35N	97W
75	Çanakkale Boğazı (Dardanelles) (Str.) Tur.	40N	26E
88	Canarias, Islas (Canary Is.), Sp.	29N	18W
109	Canaveral, C., Fla.	28N	81W
87	Canberra, Austl.	35S	149E
93	Caniapiscau (R.) Que., Can.	57N	69W
73	Cannes, Fr.	44N	7E
96	Canton, Ohio	41N	81W
105	Cape Girardeau, Mo.	37N	90W
90	Cape Town, S. Afr.	34S	18E
88	Cape Verde (Ctry.) Afr.	16N	25W
111	Cap-Haïtien, Hai.	20N	72W
90	Caprivi Strip (Reg.) Nam.	18S	23E
112	Caracas, Ven.	10N	67W
113	Caravelas , Braz.	18S	39W
73	Carcassonne, Fr.	43N	2E
73	Cardiff, Wales	51N	3W
111	Caribbean Sea, N.A.-S.A.	15N	67W
92	Cariboo Mts., B.C., Can.	54N	122W
72	Carlisle, Eng.	55N	3W
75	Carpathians (Mts.) Eur.	49N	22E
86	Carpentaria, Gulf of, Austl.	15S	138E
73	Carrara, It.	44N	10E
102	Carson City, Nev.	39N	120W
112	Cartagena, Col.	10N	76W
74	Cartagena, Sp.	38N	1W
74	Carthage, Tun.	37N	10E
113	Caruaru, Braz.	8S	36W
88	Casablanca, Mor.	34N	8W
100	Cascade Ra., N.A.	44N	122W
101	Casper, Wyo.	43N	106W
71	Caspian Sea, Iran-Sov. Un.	42N	49E
74	Castellón de la Plana, Sp.	40N	0
114	Catamarca, Arg.	28S	66W
73	Catania, It.	37N	15E
71	Caucasus Mts., Sov. Un.	43N	42E
114	Caxias do Sul, Braz.	29S	51W
113	Cayenne, Fr. Gui.	5N	52W
85	Cebu, Phil.	10N	124E
92	Cedar (L.) Man., Can.	53N	101W
99	Cedar Rapids, Iowa	42N	92W
73	Cegléd, Hung.	47N	20E
84	Celebes (Sulawesi) (I.) Indon.	2S	120E
84	Celebes Sea, Asia	4N	122E
73	Celle, Ger.	53N	10E
112	Central, Cordillera (Ra.) Bol.	21S	65W
89	Central African Republic (Ctry.) Afr.	7N	20E
73	České Budějovice, Czech.	49N	14E
74	Ceuta, Sp. N. Afr.	36N	5W
89	Chad (Ctry.) Afr.	15N	17E
89	Chad, L., Afr.	14N	14E
73	Chalon-sur-Saône, Fr.	47N	5E
83	Chaman, Pak.	31N	66E
96	Champaign, Ill.	40N	88W
97	Champlain, L., Can.-U.S.	45N	73W
81	Changchun, China	44N	125E
81	Changde, China	29N	112E
81	Changsha, China	28N	113E
81	Changzhou, China	32N	120E
73	Channel Is., Eur.	49N	3W
84	Chanthaburi, Thai.	13N	102E
105	Chanute, Kans.	38N	95W
81	Chao'an, China	24N	117E
84	Chao Phraya (R.) Thai.	14N	100E
110	Chapala, Lago de (L.) Mex.	20N	103W
109	Chapel Hill, N.C.	36N	79W
76	Chardzhou, Sov. Un.	39N	64E
73	Charleroi, Bel.	50N	5E
109	Charleston, S.C.	33N	80W
96	Charleston, W. Va.	38N	82W
109	Charlotte, N.C.	35N	81W
111	Charlotte Amalie (St. Thomas), Vir. Is.	18N	65W
97	Charlottesville, Va.	38N	78W
93	Charlottetown, P.E.I., Can.	46N	63W
73	Châteauroux, Fr.	47N	2E
73	Châtellerault, Fr.	47N	1E
108	Chattanooga, Tenn.	35N	85W
84	Chau-phu, Camb.	11N	105E
71	Cheboksary, Sov. Un.	56N	47E
76	Chelkar, Sov. Un.	48N	60E
73	Chełm, Pol.	51N	23E
97	Chelsea, Mass.	42N	71W
76	Chelyabinsk, Sov. Un.	55N	61E
73	Chemnitz, Ger.	51N	13E
81	Chengde, China	41N	118E
80	Chengdu, China	30N	104E
73	Cherbourg, Fr.	50N	2W
76	Cherdyn, Sov. Un.	60N	57E
76	Cherepanovo, Sov. Un.	54N	83E
71	Cherepovets, Sov. Un.	59N	36E
71	Chernigov, Sov. Un.	51N	31E
71	Chernobyl, Sov. Un.	51N	30E
70	Chernovtsy, Sov. Un.	48N	26E
72	Chernyakhovsk, Sov. Un.	55N	22E
97	Chesapeake Bay, U.S.	38N	76W
76	Chesnokovka, Sov. Un.	53N	84E
97	Chester, Pa.	40N	75W
104	Cheyenne, Wyo.	41N	105W
84	Chiang Rai, Thai.	20N	100E
93	Chibougamau, Que., Can.	50N	74W
96	Chicago, Ill.	42N	88W
96	Chicago Heights, Ill.	41N	88W
104	Chickasha, Okla.	35N	98W
112	Chiclayo, Peru	7S	80W
97	Chicopee, Mass.	42N	73W
93	Chicoutimi, Que., Can.	48N	71W
73	Chieti, It.	42N	14E
81	Chifeng, China	42N	119E
110	Chihuahua, Mex.	29N	106W

117

Germany (Ctry.) Eur.

Page Place Lat.°' Long.°'

82 Chikishlyar, Sov. Un. 38N 54 E
114 Chile (Ctry.) S.A. 38S 72W
114 Chillán, Chile 37S 72W
96 Chillicothe, Ohio 39N 83W
81 Chilung, Taiwan 25N 122 E
112 Chimbote, Peru 9S 78W
76 Chimkent, Sov. Un. 42N 70 E
80 China (Ctry.) Asia 34N 101 E
76 Chistopol', Sov. Un. 55N 50 E
77 Chita, Sov. Un. 52N 114 E
83 Chitrāl, Pak. 36N 72 E
83 Chittagong, Bngl. 22N 91 E
81 Chŏngjin, Kor. 42N 130 E
80 Chongqing, China 30N 107 E
81 Choybalsan, Mong. 48N 114 E
87 Christchurch, N.Z. 43S 173 E
84 Christmas I. (Ctry.) Ind. O. 10S 105 E
77 Chumikan, Sov. Un. 55N 135 E
114 Chuquicamata, Chile 22S 69W
92 Churchill, Man., Can. 59N 94W
92 Churchill (R.) Can. 58N 95W
71 Chusovoy, Sov. Un. 58N 58 E
76 Chust, Sov. Un. 41N 71 E
96 Cicero, Ill. 42N 88W
75 Cide, Tur. 42N 33 E
112 Ciénaga, Col. 11N 74W
111 Cienfuegos, Cuba 22N 80W
96 Cincinnati, Ohio 39N 84W
84 Cirebon, Indon. 7S 109 E
90 Ciskei (Ctry.) Afr. 33S 27 E
112 Ciudad Bolívar, Ven. 8N 64W
112 Ciudad Guayana, Ven. 9N 63W
110 Ciudad Juárez , Mex. 32N 106W
110 Ciudad Obregón, Mex. 28N 110W
74 Ciudad Real, Sp. 39N 4W
110 Ciudad Victoria, Mex. 24N 99W
97 Clarksburg, W. Va. 39N 80W
109 Clearwater, Fla. 28N 83W
107 Cleburne, Tex. 32N 97W
73 Clermont-Ferrand, Fr. 46N 3 E
96 Cleveland, Ohio 41N 82W
96 Cleveland Heights, Ohio 41N 82W
97 Clifton, N.J. 41N 74W
104 Clovis, N. Mex. 34N 103W
75 Cluj-Napoca, Rom. 47N 24 E
92 Coast Mts., Can.-U.S. 57N 131W
94 Coast Ranges, U.S. 40N 123W
97 Cod, Cape, Mass. 42N 70W
100 Coeur d'Alene, Idaho 48N 117W
105 Coffeyville, Kans. 37N 96W
74 Coimbra, Port. 40N 8W
110 Colima, Mex. 19N 104W
73 Colmar, Fr. 49N 7 E
73 Cologne (Köln), Ger. 51N 7 E
112 Colombia (Ctry.) S.A. 3N 74W
83 Colombo, Sri Lanka 7N 80 E
111 Colón, Pan. 9N 80W
112 Colon, Archipiélago de (Galápagos Is.), Ec. 0 90W
94 Colorado (R.) Mex.-U.S. 36N 113W
107 Colorado (R.) Tex. 30N 98W
94 Colorado (State) U.S. 39N 105W
114 Colorado, R., Arg. 39S 65W
104 Colorado Springs, Colo. 39N 105W
105 Columbia, Mo. 39N 92W
109 Columbia, S.C. 34N 81W
92 Columbia (R.) Can.-U.S. 46N 120W
108 Columbus, Ga. 32N 85W
96 Columbus, Ohio 40N 83W
83 Comilla, Bngl. 24N 91 E
73 Como, It. 46N 9 E
114 Comodoro Rivadavia, Arg. 46S 68W
91 Comoros (Ctry.) Afr. 12S 44 E
88 Conakry, Gui. 9N 14W
114 Concepción, Chile 37S 73W
97 Concord, N.H. 43N 71W
114 Concordia, Arg. 31S 58W
90 Congo (Ctry.) Afr. 3S 14 E
90 Congo (R.) Afr. 4S 16 E
97 Connecticut (R.) U.S. 44N 72W
95 Connecticut (State) U.S. 42N 73W
75 Constanța, Rom. 44N 29 E
88 Constantine, Alg. 36N 7 E
83 Cooch Behār, India 26N 90 E
72 Copenhagen (København), Den. 56N 12 E
109 Coral Gables, Fla. 26N 80W
87 Coral Sea, Oc. 14S 155 E
114 Córdoba, Arg. 32S 64W
110 Córdoba, Mex. 19N 97W
74 Córdoba, Sp. 38N 5W
73 Cork, Ire. 52N 8W
112 Coro, Ven. 11N 70W
107 Corpus Christi, Tex. 28N 97W
114 Corrientes, Arg. 27S 59W
73 Corsica (I.) Fr. 42N 9 E
107 Corsicana, Tex. 32N 96W
75 Çorum, Tur. 41N 35 E
100 Corvallis, Oreg. 45N 123W
111 Costa Rica (Ctry.) N.A. 10N 85W
73 Cottbus, Ger. 52N 14 E
98 Council Bluffs, Iowa 41N 96W
96 Covington, Ky. 39N 85W
75 Craiova, Rom. 44N 24 E
97 Cranston, R.I. 42N 71W
100 Crater L., Oreg. 43N 122W
73 Cremona, It. 45N 10 E
75 Crete (I.) Grc. 35N 25 E
73 Croydon, Eng. 51N 0
111 Cuba (Ctry.) N.A. 22N 79W
112 Cúcuta, Col. 8N 72W
83 Cuddalore, India 12N 80 E
112 Cuenca, Ec. 3S 79W
110 Cuernavaca, Mex. 19N 99W
113 Cuiabá, Braz. 16S 56W
110 Culiacán, Mex. 25N 107W
74 Cullera, Sp. 39N 0
112 Cumaná, Ven. 10N 64W
114 Curico, Chile 35S 71W
114 Curitiba, Braz. 26S 49W
83 Cuttack, India 21N 86 E
96 Cuyahoga Falls, Ohio 41N 81W
112 Cuzco, Peru 14S 72W
75 Cyprus (Ctry.) Asia 35N 33 E
75 Cyprus, North (Ctry.) Asia 36N 33 E
73 Czechoslovakia (Ctry.) Eur. 49N 19 E
73 Częstochowa, Pol. 51N 19 E

D

88 Dakar, Sen. 15N 17W
88 Dakhla, W. Sah. 24N 16W
80 Dali, China 35N 110 E
81 Dalian (Lüda), China 39N 121 E
107 Dallas, Tex. 33N 97W
77 Dalnerechensk, Sov. Un. 46N 134 E
83 Damān, India 21N 73 E
89 Damanhūr, Eg. 31N 31 E
82 Damascus (Dimashq), Syr. 34N 36 E
82 Dāmghān, Iran 36N 54 E
84 Da Nang (Tourane), Viet. 16N 108 E
81 Dandong, China 40N 124 E
75 Danube (R.) Eur. 43N 24 E
96 Danville, Ill. 40N 88W
109 Danville, Va. 37N 80W
72 Danzig, Gulf of, Pol.-Sov. Un. 54N 19 E
83 Darbhanga, India 26N 86 E
91 Dar es Salaam, Tan. 7S 39 E
83 Darjeeling, India 27N 88 E
87 Darling (R.) Austl. 33S 143 E
86 Darling Ra., Austl. 31S 116 E
73 Darmstadt, Ger. 50N 9 E
89 Darnah, Libya 33N 23 E
86 Darwin, Austl. 12S 131 E
70 Daugavpils, Lat. 56N 26 E
92 Dauphin, Man., Can. 51N 100W
85 Davao, Phil. 7N 125 E
99 Davenport, Iowa 42N 91W
111 David, Pan. 8N 82W
84 Dawei, Bur. 14N 98 E
92 Dawson, Yukon, Can. 64N 139W
92 Dawson Creek, B.C., Can. 56N 120W
80 Daxian, China 31N 107 E
82 Dayr az Zawr, Syr. 35N 40 E
96 Dayton , Ohio 40N 84W
109 Daytona Beach, Fla. 29N 81W
81 Da Yunhe (Grand Canal), China 35N 117 E
75 Dead Sea, Asia 32N 35 E
98 Deadwood, S. Dak. 44N 104W
96 Dearborn, Mich. 42N 83W
102 Death Valley, Calif. 36N 117W
73 Debrecen, Hung. 48N 22 E
108 Decatur, Ala. 34N 87W
96 Decatur, Ill. 40N 89W
83 Deccan Plat., India 19N 77 E
83 Dehra Dūn, India 30N 78 E
97 Delaware (R.) U.S. 42N 75W
95 Delaware (State) U.S. 39N 75W
97 Delaware Bay, U.S. 39N 75W
83 Delhi, India 29N 77 E
106 Del Rio, Tex. 29N 101W
103 Deming, N. Mex. 32N 108W
105 Denison, Tex. 34N 97W
75 Denizli, Tur. 38N 29 E
72 Denmark (Ctry.) Eur. 56N 10 E
104 Denver, Colo. 40N 105W
83 Dera Ghāzi Khān, Pak. 30N 71 E
83 Dera Ismāīl Khān, Pak. 32N 71 E
73 Derby, Eng. 53N 1W
89 Dese, Eth. 11N 40 E
99 DesMoines, Iowa 42N 94W
99 Des Moines (R.) U.S. 41N 93W
96 Des Plaines, Ill. 42N 88W
73 Dessau, Ger. 52N 12 E
96 Detroit, Mich. 42N 83W
98 Devils L., N. Dak. 48N 99W
82 Dezfūl, Iran 32N 49 E
83 Dhaka (Dacca), Bngl. 24N 90 E
83 Dhaulagiri (Mt.) Nepal 28N 84 E
83 Dhule, India 21N 75 E
98 Dickinson, N. Dak. 47N 103W
73 Dijon, Fr. 47N 5 E
76 Dikson, Sov. Un. 73N 80 E
85 Dili, Indon. 9S 126 E
89 Dire Dawa, Eth. 10N 42 E
97 District of Columbia, U.S. 39N 77W
83 Diu, India 21N 71 E
82 Diyarbakir, Tur. 38N 40 E
74 Djerid, Chott (L.) Tun. 33N 8 E
89 Djibouti, Djibouti 12N 43 E
89 Djibouti (Ctry.) Afr. 12N 43 E
71 Dnepropetrovsk, Sov. Un. 48N 34 E
75 Dnestr (Dniester) (R.) Sov. Un. 47N 28 E
85 Dobo, Indon. 6S 134 E
104 Dodge City, Kans. 38N 100W
111 Dominica (Ctry.) N.A. 15N 61W
111 Dominican Republic (Ctry.) N.A. 19N 71W
71 Don (R.) Sov. Un. 47N 40 E
71 Donetsk, Sov. Un. 48N 38 E
84 Dong Hoi, Viet. 17N 107 E
73 Dortmund, Ger. 52N 7 E
108 Dothan, Ala. 31N 85W
88 Douala, Cam. 4N 10 E
103 Douglas, Ariz. 31N 109W
74 Douro (Duero) (R.) Port.-Sp. 41N 8W
97 Dover, Del. 39N 75W
73 Dover, Eng. 51N 1 E
73 Dover, Str. of, Eng.-Fr. 50N 1 E
90 Drakensberg (Mts.) Afr. 29S 29 E
75 Dráma, Grc. 41N 24 E
73 Dresden, Ger. 51N 14 E
92 Drumheller, Alta., Can. 51N 113W
93 Dryden, Ont., Can. 50N 93W
82 Dubayy, U.A.E. 25N 55 E
72 Dublin (Baile Átha Cliath), Ire. 53N 6W
75 Dubrovnik, Yugo. 43N 18 E
99 Dubuque, Iowa 42N 91W
76 Dudinka, Sov. Un. 69N 86 E
73 Dudley, Eng. 53N 2W
73 Duisburg, Ger. 51N 7 E
99 Duluth, Minn. 47N 92W
89 Dumyāț (Damietta), Eg. 31N 32 E
72 Dundalk, Ire. 54N 6W
97 Dundalk, Md. 39N 77W
72 Dundee, Scot. 56N 3W
87 Dunedin, N.Z. 46S 171 E
72 Dun Laoghaire, Ire. 53N 6W
110 Durango, Mex. 24N 105W
114 Durazno, Ur. 33S 57W
90 Durban, S. Afr. 30S 31 E
109 Durham, N.C. 36N 79W
75 Durrës, Alb. 41N 19 E
76 Dushanbe, Sov. Un. 39N 69 E
73 Düsseldorf, Ger. 51N 7 E
70 Dvina (R.) Sov. Un. 55N 28 E
71 Dzerzhinsk, Sov. Un. 56N 44 E
76 Dzhambul, Sov. Un. 43N 71 E

E

106 Eagle Pass, Tex. 29N 100W
96 East Chicago, Ind. 42N 87W
81 East China Sea, Asia 29N 124 E
96 East Cleveland, Ohio 41N 82W
83 Eastern Ghāts (Mts.) India 16N 79 E
97 East Hartford, Conn. 42N 73W
96 East Liverpool, Ohio 41N 81W
90 East London, S. Afr. 33S 28 E
97 Easton, Pa. 41N 75W
97 East Orange, N.J. 41N 74W
97 East Providence, R.I. 42N 71W
105 East St. Louis, Ill. 39N 90W
74 Ebro (R.) Sp. 41N 0
88 Ech Cheliff, Alg. 36N 2 E
74 Écija, Sp. 37N 5W
112 Ecuador (Ctry.) S.A. 1S 79W
75 Édhessa, Grc. 41N 22 E
72 Edinburgh, Scot. 56N 3W
75 Edirne, Tur. 42N 27 E
92 Edmonton, Alta., Can. 54N 114W
92 Edson, Alta., Can. 54N 117W
90 Edward, L., Ug.-Zaire 0 29 E
89 Egypt (Ctry.) Afr. 27N 30 E
73 Eisenach, Ger. 51N 10 E
88 El Aaiún, W. Sah. 27N 13W
75 Elâzığ, Tur. 38N 39 E
72 Elblag, Pol. 54N 19 E
88 El Boulaïda, Alg. 37N 3 E
71 El'brus, Gora (Mt.) Sov. Un. 43N 42 E
82 Elburz Mts., Iran 37N 51 E
88 El Djelfa, Alg. 35N 3 E
105 El Dorado, Ark. 33N 93W
74 El Ferrol, Sp. 43N 8W
96 Elgin , Ill. 42N 88W
97 Elizabeth, N.J. 41N 74W
88 El Jadida, Mor. 33N 9W
88 El Kairouan, Tun. 36N 10 E
96 Elkhart, Ind. 42N 86W
100 Elko, Nev. 41N 116W
100 Ellensburg, Wash. 47N 120W
96 Elmhurst, Ill. 42N 88W
97 Elmira, N.Y. 42N 77W
112 El Pao, Ven. 8N 63W
106 El Paso, Tex. 32N 106W
74 El Qala, Alg. 37N 8 E
110 El Salvador (Ctry.) N.A. 14N 89W
83 Elūru, India 17N 80 E
88 El Wad, Alg. 33N 7 E
102 Ely, Nev. 39N 115W
96 Elyria, Ohio 41N 82W
82 Emāmshahr, Iran 36N 55 E
105 Emporia, Kans. 38N 96W
71 Engel's, Sov. Un. 51N 46 E
73 England (Polit. Reg.), U.K. 52N 2W
73 English Channel, Eur. 50N 2W
104 Enid, Okla. 36N 98W
73 Enschede, Neth. 52N 7 E
110 Ensenada, Mex. 32N 116W
89 Entebbe, Ug. 0 32 E
88 Enugu, Nig. 6N 7 E
73 Épinal, Fr. 48N 6 E
88 Equatorial Guinea (Ctry.) Afr. 3N 9 E
75 Ereğli, Tur. 38N 34 E
73 Erfurt, Ger. 51N 11 E
97 Erie, Pa. 42N 80W
96 Erie, L., Can.-U.S. 42N 81W
83 Ernākulam, India 10N 76 E
72 Erne, L., N. Ire. 55N 8W
82 Erzurum, Tur. 40N 41 E
72 Esbjerg, Den. 55N 8 E
82 Eşfahān, Iran 33N 51 E
72 Eskifjördur, Ice. 65N 14W
72 Eskilstuna, Swe. 59N 17 E
75 Eskişehir, Tur. 40N 30 E
114 Esquel, Arg. 43S 71W
73 Essen, Ger. 52N 7 E
76 Estonia (Ctry.) Eur. 59N 26 E
89 Ethiopia (Ctry.) Afr. 9N 38 E
73 Etna, Mt. (Vol.) It. 38N 15 E
90 Etoshapan (L.) Nam. 19S 16 E
96 Euclid, Ohio 42N 82W
100 Eugene, Oreg. 44N 123W
82 Euphrates (R.) Asia 36N 40 E
100 Eureka, Calif. 41N 124W
96 Evanston, Ill. 42N 88W
96 Evansville, Ind. 38N 87W
83 Everest, Mt., China-Nep. 28N 87 E
100 Everett, Wash. 48N 122W
74 Évora, Port. 39N 8W
73 Exeter, Eng. 51N 4W
86 Eyre (L.) Austl. 28S 136 E

F

72 Faeroe Is. (Ctry.) Eur. 62N 6W
97 Fairmont, W. Va. 39N 80W
83 Faisalabad, Pak. 31N 73 E
83 Faizābād, India 27N 83 E
114 Falkland Islands (Ctry.) S.A. 51S 59W
97 Fall River, Mass. 42N 71W
75 Famagusta, Cyp. 35N 34 E
82 Farāh, Afg. 32N 62 E
98 Fargo, N. Dak. 47N 97W
74 Faro, Port. 37N 8W
83 Farrukhābād, India 27N 80 E
109 Fayetteville, N.C. 35N 79W
74 Felanitx, Sp. 39N 3 E
81 Fenyang, China 37N 112 E
75 Feodosiya, Sov. Un. 45N 35 E
82 Ferdows, Iran 34N 58 E
76 Fergana, Sov. Un. 40N 72 E
98 Fergus Falls, Minn. 46N 96W
73 Ferrara, It. 45N 12 E
88 Fès, Mor. 34N 5W
83 Feyzābād, Afg. 37N 71 E
69 Fiji (Ctry.), Pac. O. 19S 175 E
96 Findlay, Ohio 41N 84W
72 Finland (Ctry.) Eur. 65N 27 E
70 Finland, Gulf of, Fin.-Sov. Un. 60N 24 E
97 Fitchburg, Mass. 43N 72W
103 Flagstaff, Ariz. 35N 112W
96 Flint, Mich. 43N 84W
108 Florence, Ala. 35N 88W
73 Florence (Firenze), It. 44N 11 E
84 Flores (I.) Indon. 8S 121 E
84 Flores, Laut (Flores Sea), Indon. 7S 120 E
114 Florianópolis, Braz. 27S 48W
95 Florida (State) U.S. 30N 84W
111 Florida, Strs. of, N.A. 25N 80W
109 Florida Keys (Is.) Fla. 25N 81W
75 Flórina, Grc. 41N 21 E
73 Foggia, It. 41N 16 E
99 Fond du Lac, Wis. 44N 88W
110 Fonseca, Golfo de (G.) N.A. 13N 88W
73 Forli, It. 44N 12 E
114 Formosa, Arg. 27S 58W
113 Formosa, Braz. 15S 47W
113 Fortaleza (Ceará), Braz. 4S 39W
104 Fort Collins, Colo. 41N 105W
111 Fort-de-France, Mart. 15N 61W
99 Fort Dodge, Iowa 43N 94W
72 Forth, Firth of (Str.) Scot. 56N 3W
109 Fort Lauderdale, Fla. 26N 80W
92 Fort Macleod, Alta., Can. 50N 113W
109 Fort Myers, Fla. 27N 82 S
92 Fort Nelson (R.) B.C., Can. 58N 122W
83 Fort Sandeman, Pak. 31N 69 E
105 Fort Scott, Kans. 38N 95W
93 Fort Severn, Ont., Can. 57N 88W
105 Fort Smith, Ark. 35N 94W
92 Fort Smith, N.W. Ter., Can. 60N 112W
96 Fort Wayne, Ind. 41N 85W
107 Fort Worth, Tex. 33N 97W
113 Franca, Braz. 21S 47W
73 France (Ctry.) Eur. 47N 2 E
96 Frankfort, Ky. 38N 85W
73 Frankfurt am Main, Ger. 50N 9 E
73 Frankfurt an der Oder, Ger. 52N 15 E
92 Fraser (R.) B.C., Can. 52N 122W
93 Fredericton, N.B., Can. 46N 67W
96 Freeport, Ill. 42N 89W
97 Freeport, N.Y. 41N 74W
88 Freetown, S.L. 8N 13W
73 Freiberg, Ger. 51N 13 E
113 French Guiana (Ctry.) S.A. 5N 53W
110 Fresnillo, Mex. 23N 103W
102 Fresno, Calif. 37N 120W
73 Fribourg, Switz. 47N 7 E
73 Frisian Is., Eur. 54N 5 E
81 Fujin, China 47N 132 E
81 Fuji San (Mt.) Japan 36N 139 E
81 Fukui, Japan 36N 136 E
81 Fukuoka, Japan 34N 130 E
73 Fulda, Ger. 51N 10 E
80 Fuling, China 30N 107 E
88 Funchal, Port. 33N 16W
93 Fundy, B. of, Can. 44N 67W
73 Fürth, Ger. 49N 11 E
81 Fushun, China 42N 125 E
81 Fuyang, China 33N 116 E
81 Fuzhou, China 26N 119 E

G

90 Gabon (Ctry.) Afr. 2S 12 E
90 Gaborone, Bots. 25S 25 E
108 Gadsden, Ala. 34N 86W
109 Gainesville, Fla. 30N 82W
75 Galați, Rom. 45N 28 E
83 Galle, Sri Lanka 6N 80 E
72 Gällivare, Swe. 68N 20 E
103 Gallup, N. Mex. 35N 109W
107 Galveston, Tex. 29N 95W
88 Gambia (Ctry.) Afr. 13N 17W
83 Ganges (R.) Bngl.-India 24N 98 E
83 Gangtok, India 27N 89 E
81 Ganzhou, China 26N 115 E
80 Gar, China 31N 81 E
114 Garin, Arg. 34S 59W
76 Garm, Sov. Un. 39N 70 E
73 Garonne (R.) Fr.-Sp. 45N 0
96 Gary, Ind. 42N 87W
110 Gatun, Pan. 9N 80W
72 Gävle, Swe. 61N 17 E
83 Gaya, India 25N 85 E
75 Gaziantep, Tur. 37N 37 E
72 Gdańsk (Danzig), Pol. 54N 19 E
72 Gdynia, Pol. 54N 18 E
87 Geelong, Austl. 38S 144 E
75 Gelibolu, Tur. 40N 27 E
89 Gemena, Zaire 3N 19 E
114 General San Martín, Arg. 34S 59W
73 Geneva, Switz. 46N 6 E
73 Geneva, L., Fr.-Switz. 46N 6 E
73 Genoa (Genova), It. 44N 9 E
73 Gent, Bel. 51N 4 E
86 Geographe Chan., Austl. 24S 113 E
113 Georgetown, Guy. 8N 58W
84 George Town (Pinang), Mala. 5N 100 E
95 Georgia (State), U.S. 33N 83W
93 Georgian B., Ont., Can. 46N 82W
73 Gera, Ger. 51N 12 E
96 Germantown, Ohio 40N 84W
73 Germany (Ctry.) Eur. 51N 10 E

118

Germiston, S. Afr.

Page	Place	Lat.°'	Long.°'
90	Germiston, S. Afr.	26S	28 E
74	Gerona, Sp.	42N	3 E
88	Ghana (Ctry.) Afr.	8N	2W
90	Ghanzi, Bots.	22S	22 E
88	Ghardaïa, Alg.	32N	4 E
88	Ghazaouet, Alg.	35N	2W
83	Ghaznī, Afg.	34N	68 E
89	Ghazzah (Gaza), Isr. Occ.	32N	34 E
88	Ghilizane, Alg.	36N	1 E
74	Gibraltar (Ctry.) Eur.	36N	5W
74	Gibraltar, Str. of, Afr.-Eur.	36N	6W
73	Gien, Fr.	48N	3 E
81	Gifu, Japan	35N	137 E
74	Gijón, Sp.	43N	6W
103	Gila (R.) U.S.	33N	114W
112	Girardot, Col.	4N	76W
77	Gizhiga, Sov. Un.	62N	161 E
72	Glama (R.) Nor.	61N	11 E
72	Glasgow, Scot.	56N	4W
76	Glazov, Sov. Un.	58N	53 E
102	Glendale, Calif.	34N	118W
73	Gliwice, Pol.	50N	19 E
103	Globe, Ariz.	33N	111W
73	Gloucester, Eng.	52N	2W
97	Gloucester, Mass.	43N	71W
97	Gloversville, N.Y.	43N	74W
73	Gniezno, Pol.	53N	18 E
80	Gobi (Shamo) (Des.) China-Mong.	43N	102 E
83	Godāvari (R.) India	19N	78 E
113	Goiânia, Braz.	17S	49W
71	Gomel', Sov. Un.	52N	31 E
110	Gómez Palacio, Mex.	26N	103W
111	Gonaïves, Hai.	19N	73W
89	Gonder, Eth.	13N	37 E
90	Good Hope, Cape of, S. Afr.	34S	19 E
90	Goodwood, S. Afr.	34S	19 E
83	Gorakhpur, India	27N	84 E
82	Gorgān, Iran	37N	54 E
73	Görlitz, Ger.	51N	15 E
71	Gorlovka, Sov. Un.	48N	38 E
76	Gorno-Altaysk, Sov. Un.	52N	86 E
77	Gorodok, Sov. Un.	51N	104 E
72	Göteborg, Swe.	58N	12 E
73	Gotha, Ger.	51N	11 E
72	Gotland (I.) Swe.	58N	19 E
81	Goukou, China	49N	122 E
75	Gradačac, Yugo.	45N	18 E
72	Grampian Mts., Scot.	57N	5W
74	Granada, Sp.	37N	4W
93	Granby, Que., Can.	45N	73W
114	Gran Chaco (Reg.) S.A.	24S	62W
92	Grande-Prairie, Alta., Can.	55N	119W
74	Grand Erg Occidental (Dunes) Alg.	30N	1W
74	Grand Erg Oriental (Dunes) Alg.	30N	6 E
98	Grand Forks, N. Dak.	48N	97W
104	Grand Island, Nebr.	41N	98W
103	Grand Junction, Colo.	39N	109W
96	Grand Rapids, Mich.	43N	86W
105	Granite City, Ill.	39N	90W
92	Granville (L.) Man., Can.	57N	100W
92	Gravelbourg , Sask., Can.	50N	107W
73	Graz, Aus.	47N	15 E
87	Great Artesian Basin, Austl.	23S	143 E
86	Great Australian Bight, Austl.	34S	127 E
87	Great Barrier Reef, Austl.	19S	148 E
92	Great Bear L., N.W. Ter., Can.	67N	120W
87	Great Dividing Ra., Austl.	25S	148 E
111	Greater Antilles (Is.) N.A.	18N	75W
81	Greater Khingan Range, China	46N	120 E
84	Greater Sunda Is., Asia	4S	110 E
101	Great Falls, Mont.	47N	111W
83	Great Indian (Thar) Des., India-Pak.	27N	71 E
90	Great Karroo (Plat.) S. Afr.	34S	21 E
86	Great Sandy Des., Austl.	22S	125 E
92	Great Slave L., N.W. Ter., Can.	62N	115W
101	Great Salt L., Utah	41N	113W
86	Great Victoria Des., Austl.	30S	127 E
80	Great Wall, China	38N	108 E
73	Great Yarmouth, Eng.	53N	2 E
75	Greece (Ctry.) Eur.	40N	22 E
104	Greeley, Colo.	40N	105W
94	Green (R.) U.S.	39N	110W
99	Green Bay, Wis.	44N	88W
68	Greenland (Ctry.), N.A.	75N	39W
97	Green Mts., Vt.	44N	73W
72	Greenock, Scot.	56N	5W
101	Green River, Wyo.	42N	110W
109	Greensboro, N.C.	36N	80W
108	Greenville, Miss.	33N	91W
109	Greenville, S.C.	35N	82W
111	Grenada (Ctry.) N.A.	12N	62W
73	Grenoble, Fr.	45N	6 E
73	Grimsby, Eng.	54N	0
70	Grodno, Sov. Un.	54N	24 E
73	Groningen, Neth.	53N	6 E
73	Grossglockner (Mt.) Aus.	47N	13 E
97	Groton, Conn.	41N	72W
110	Guadalajara, Mex.	21N	103W
111	Guadeloupe (Ctry.) N.A.	16N	62W
74	Guadiana (R.) Sp.-Port.	38N	8W
114	Gualeguaychú, Arg.	33S	58W
69	Guam (Ctry.), Pac. O.	14N	144 E
81	Guangzhou (Canton), China	23N	113 E
111	Guantánamo, Cuba	20N	75W
112	Guaporé (R.) Bol.-Braz.	12S	64W
110	Guatemala, Guat.	15N	91W
110	Guatemala (Ctry.) N.A.	15N	90W
112	Guayaquil, Ec.	2S	80W
112	Guayaquil, Golfo de (G.) Ec.	3S	83W
73	Guernsey (Ctry.) Eur.	50N	3W
81	Guilin, China	25N	110 E
88	Guinea (Ctry.) Afr.	11N	12W
88	Guinea, Gulf of, Afr.	3N	3 E
88	Guinea-Bissau (Ctry.) Afr.	12N	15W
80	Guiyang, China	27N	107 E
83	Gujrānwāla, Pak.	32N	74 E
83	Gulbarga, India	17N	77 E
108	Gulfport, Miss.	30N	89W
83	Guntūr, India	16N	80 E
71	Gur'yev, Sov. Un.	47N	52 E
76	Gur'yevsk, Sov. Un.	54N	86 E
88	Gusau, Nig.	12N	7 E
72	Gusev, Sov. Un.	55N	22 E
113	Guyana (Ctry.) S.A.	5N	59W
82	Gwādar, Pak.	25N	62 E
83	Gwalior, India	26N	78 E
71	Gyandzha, Sov. Un.	41N	46 E
80	Gyangzê, China	29N	89 E
73	Gyöngyös, Hung.	48N	20 E
73	Győr, Hung.	48N	18 E

H

Page	Place	Lat.°'	Long.°'
97	Hackensack, N.J.	41N	74W
82	Hadibū, Yemen	13N	54 E
97	Hagerstown, Md.	40N	78W
82	Haifa, Isr.	33N	35 E
84	Haikou, China	20N	110 E
82	Hā'il, Sau. Ar.	27N	42 E
81	Hailar, China	49N	119 E
81	Hainan Dao (I.) China	19N	110 E
84	Hai Phong, Viet.	21N	107 E
111	Haiti (Ctry.) N.A.	19N	73W
81	Hakodate, Japan	42N	141 E
97	Halethorpe, Md.	39N	77W
93	Halifax, N.S., Can.	45N	64W
73	Halle, Ger.	51N	12 E
85	Halmahera (I.) Indon.	1N	128 E
72	Halmstad, Swe.	57N	13 E
82	Hamadān, Iran	35N	48 E
72	Hamburg, Ger.	54N	10 E
97	Hamden, Conn.	41N	73W
81	Hamhŭng, Kor.	40N	128 E
80	Hami (Kumul), China	43N	93 E
96	Hamilton, Ohio	39N	85W
93	Hamilton, Ont., Can.	43N	80W
96	Hammond, Ind.	42N	88W
97	Hampton, Va.	37N	76W
96	Hamtramck, Mich.	42N	83W
81	Hangzhou, China	30N	120 E
105	Hannibal, Mo.	40N	91W
73	Hannover, Ger.	52N	10 E
84	Hanoi, Viet.	21N	106 E
81	Hanyang, China	30N	114 E
90	Harare, Zimb.	18S	31 E
81	Harbin, China	46N	126 E
83	Hardwār, India	30N	78 E
89	Harer, Eth.	10N	42 E
107	Harlingen, Tex.	26N	98W
97	Harrisburg, Pa.	40N	77W
97	Hartford, Conn.	42N	73W
72	Hartlepool, Eng.	55N	1W
96	Harvey, Ill.	42N	88W
73	Hastings, Eng.	51N	0
104	Hastings, Nebr.	41N	99W
109	Hatteras, C., N.C.	35N	76W
108	Hattiesburg, Miss.	31N	89W
111	Havana, Cuba	23N	82W
101	Havre, Mont.	49N	110W
94	Hawaii (State) U.S.	20N	157W
92	Hay River, N.W. Ter., Can.	61N	116W
97	Hazleton, Pa.	41N	76W
72	Hebrides (Is.) Scot.	58N	6W
75	Hebron, Jor.	32N	35 E
92	Hecate Str., B.C., Can.	54N	131W
80	Hechuan, China	30N	106 E
81	Hefei, China	32N	117 E
73	Heidelberg, Ger.	49N	9 E
73	Heilbronn, Ger.	49N	9 E
72	Hekla (Vol.) Ice.	64N	19W
105	Helena, Ark.	35N	91W
101	Helena, Mont.	47N	112W
74	Hellín, Sp.	38N	2W
72	Helsingborg, Swe.	56N	13 E
72	Helsingør, Den.	56N	13 E
72	Helsinki, Fin.	60N	25 E
81	Hengyang, China	27N	112 E
82	Herāt, Afg.	34N	62 E
110	Hermosillo, Mex.	29N	111W
99	Hibbing, Minn.	47N	93W
110	Hidalgo del Parral, Mex.	27N	106W
96	Highland Park, Ill.	42N	88W
92	High Prairie, Alta., Can.	55N	117W
80	Himalayas (Mts.) Asia	29N	85 E
82	Hims, Syr.	35N	36 E
83	Hindu Kush (Mts.) Afg.-Pak.	35N	69 E
81	Hirosaki, Japan	41N	141 E
81	Hiroshima, Japan	34N	132 E
87	Hobart, Austl.	43S	147 E
84	Ho Chi Minh City (Saigon), Viet.	11N	107 E
73	Hódmezővásárhely, Hung.	46N	20 E
81	Hohhot, China	41N	112 E
81	Hokkaidō (I.) Japan	43N	144 E
111	Holguín, Cuba	21N	76W
109	Hollywood, Fla.	26N	80W
97	Holyoke, Mass.	42N	72W
110	Honduras (Ctry.) N.A.	15N	87W
110	Honduras, Gulf of, N.A.	16N	87W
81	Hong Kong (Ctry.) Asia	22N	114 E
80	Hongshui (R.) China	25N	108 E
94	Honolulu, Haw.	21N	158W
81	Honshū (I.) Japan	34N	140 E
100	Hood, Mt., Oreg.	45N	122W
100	Hood River, Oreg.	46N	121W
82	Hormuz, Strait of, Asia	26N	56 E
114	Hornos, Cabo de (C. Horn), Chile	56S	67W
80	Hotan, China	37N	80 E
105	Hot Springs, Ark.	34N	93W
107	Houston, Tex.	30N	95W
80	Hovd, Mong.	48N	92 E
83	Howrah, India	23N	88 E
81	Huaiyin, China	34N	119 E
90	Huambo, Ang.	13S	16 E
112	Huancayo, Peru	12S	75W
81	Huang (Yellow) (R.) China	36N	116 E
80	Huangyuan, China	37N	101 E
112	Huaral, Peru	11S	77W
112	Huascarán, Nevs. (Pk.) Peru	9S	77W
83	Hubli, India	15N	75 E
97	Hudson (R.) U.S.	42N	74W
93	Hudson B., Can.	60N	85W
93	Hudson Str., Can.	63N	72W
84	Hue, Viet.	16N	108 E
74	Huelva, Sp.	37N	7W
81	Hulan, China	46N	127 E
93	Hull, Que., Can.	45N	76W
81	Huludao, China	41N	121 E
92	Humboldt, Sask., Can.	52N	105W
102	Humboldt (R.) Nev.	40N	118W
73	Hungary (Ctry.), Eur.	47N	19 E
96	Huntington, W. Va.	38N	82W
108	Huntsville, Ala.	35N	87W
98	Huron, S. Dak.	44N	98W
96	Huron, L., Can.-U.S.	45N	83W
104	Hutchinson, Kans.	38N	98W
83	Hyderābād, India	17N	79 E
83	Hyderābād, Pak.	25N	68 E
73	Hyères, Fr.	43N	6 E

I

Page	Place	Lat.°'	Long.°'
88	Ibadan, Nig.	7N	4 E
112	Ibagué, Col.	4N	75W
75	İçel. Tur.	37N	35 E
72	Iceland (Ctry.) Eur.	65N	19W
94	Idaho (State) U.S.	44N	115W
101	Idaho Falls, Idaho	43N	112W
88	Ife, Nig.	8N	5 E
77	Igarka, Sov. Un.	67N	86 E
73	Iglesias, It.	39N	9 E
76	Igriz, Sov. Un.	48N	61 E
114	Iguassu Falls, Arg.-Braz.	25S	54W
88	Ijebu Ode, Nig.	7N	4 E
88	Ilesha, Nig.	8N	5 E
77	Ilimsk, Sov. Un.	57N	104 E
95	Illinois (State) U.S.	40N	90W
84	Iloilo, Phil.	11N	123 E
73	Imperia, It.	44N	8 E
81	Inch'ŏn, Kor.	37N	127 E
83	India (Ctry.) Asia	24N	78 E
95	Indiana (State) U.S.	40N	86W
96	Indianapolis, Ind.	40N	86W
92	Indian Head, Sask., Can.	51N	104W
84	Indonesia (Ctry.) Asia	5S	115 E
83	Indore, India	23N	75 E
83	Indus (R.) Asia	27N	68 E
73	Inn (R.) Eur.	48N	13 E
73	Innsbruck, Aus.	47N	11 E
99	International Falls, Minn.	49N	93W
92	Inuvik, N.W. Ter., Can.	69N	134W
72	Inverness, Scot.	57N	4W
75	Ioánnina, Grc.	40N	21 E
75	Ionian Sea, Eur.	39N	18 E
95	Iowa (State) U.S.	42N	94W
99	Iowa City, Iowa	42N	92W
84	Ipoh, Mala.	5N	101 E
73	Ipswich, Eng.	52N	1 E
112	Iquique, Chile	20S	70W
112	Iquitos, Peru	4S	73W
75	Iráklion, Grc.	35N	25 E
82	Iran (Ctry.) Asia	33N	53 E
82	Iran, Plat. of, Iran	33N	56 E
82	Iraq (Ctry.) Asia	32N	44 E
76	Irbit, Sov. Un.	58N	63 E
72	Ireland (Ctry.) Eur.	53N	8W
77	Irkutsk, Sov. Un.	52N	104 E
99	Iron Mountain, Mich.	46N	88W
84	Irrawaddy (R.) Bur.	20N	95 E
76	Irtysh (R.) China-Sov. Un.	59N	70 E
76	Ishim, Sov. Un.	56N	69 E
81	Ishinomaki, Japan	38N	141 E
89	Isiro, Zaire	3N	28 E
75	Iskenderun, Tur.	37N	36 E
83	Islāmābād, Pak.	34N	73 E
72	Island (L.) Man., Can.	54N	96W
72	Isle of Man (Ctry.) Eur.	54N	5W
75	Isparta, Tur.	38N	31 E
82	Israel (Ctry.) Asia	32N	35 E
75	İstanbul , Tur.	41N	29 E
15	İstanbul Boğazı (Bosporus) (Str.) Tur.	41N	29 E
113	Itabuna, Braz.	15S	39W
73	Italy (Ctry.) Eur.	43N	13 E
97	Ithaca, N.Y.	42N	76W
70	Ivano-Frankovsk, Sov. Un.	49N	25 E
88	Ivory Coast (Ctry.) Afr.	7N	6W
88	Iwo, Nig.	8N	4 E
71	Izhevsk, Sov. Un.	57N	53 E
75	Izmail, Sov. Un.	45N	29 E
75	Izmir, Tur.	38N	27 E
75	Izmit, Tur.	41N	30 E

J

Page	Place	Lat.°'	Long.°'
83	Jabalpur, India	23N	80 E
113	Jaboatão, Braz.	8S	35W
96	Jackson, Mich.	42N	84W
108	Jackson, Miss.	32N	90W
108	Jackson, Tenn.	36N	89W
109	Jacksonville, Fla.	30N	82W
74	Jaén, Sp.	38N	4W
83	Jaffna, Sri Lanka	10N	80 E
83	Jaipur, India	27N	76 E
84	Jakarta, Indon.	6S	107 E
72	Jakobstad, Fin.	64N	23 E
110	Jalapa Enríquez, Mex.	20N	97W
111	Jamaica (Ctry.) N.A.	18N	77W
84	Jambi, Indon.	2S	103 E
98	James (R.) U.S.	45N	98W
97	James (R.) Va.	38N	78W
93	James B., Can.	54N	81W
97	Jamestown, N.Y.	42N	79W
98	Jamestown, N. Dak.	47N	99W
83	Jāmnagar, India	23N	70 E
83	Jamshedpur, India	23N	86 E
99	Janesville, Wis.	43N	89W
81	Japan (Ctry.) Asia	34N	139 E
81	Japan, Sea of, Asia	41N	132 E
73	Jaroslaw, Pol.	50N	23 E
82	Jāsk, Iran	26N	58 E
92	Jasper, Alta., Can.	53N	118W
84	Java (Jawa) (I.) Indon.	9S	111 E
84	Jawa, Laut (Java Sea), Indon.	5S	110 E
85	Jayapura, Indon.	3S	141 E
105	Jefferson City, Mo.	39N	92W
73	Jena, Ger.	51N	12 E
103	Jerome, Ariz.	35N	112W
73	Jersey (Ctry.) Eur.	49N	2W
97	Jersey City, N.J.	41N	74W
82	Jerusalem, Isr.-Jor.	32N	35 E
83	Jhelum, Pak.	33N	74 E
81	Ji'an, China	27N	115 E
81	Jiaoxian, China	36N	120 E
81	Jiaxing, China	31N	121 E
82	Jiddah, Sau. Ar.	21N	39 E
73	Jihlava, Czech.	49N	16 E
81	Jilin, China	44N	127 E
81	Jinan, China	37N	117 E
81	Jinhua, China	29N	120 E
81	Jining, China	35N	117 E
89	Jinja, Ug.	0	33 E
80	Jinta, China	40N	99 E
81	Jinzhou, China	41N	121 E
81	Jiujiang, China	30N	116 E
80	Jiuquan, China	40N	98 E
83	Jodhpur, India	26N	73 E
90	Johannesburg, S. Afr.	26S	28 E
109	Johnson City, Tenn.	36N	82W
97	Johnstown, Pa.	40N	79W
84	Johor Baharu, Mala.	1N	104 E
96	Joliet, Ill.	42N	88W
105	Jonesboro, Ark.	36N	91W
72	Jönköping, Swe.	58N	14 E
93	Jonquière, Que., Can.	48N	72W
105	Joplin, Mo.	37N	95W
82	Jordan (Ctry.) Asia	30N	36 E
100	Juan de Fuca, Str. of, Can.-U.S.	48N	124W
113	Juiz de Fora, Braz.	22S	43W
114	Jujuy, Arg.	23S	66W
83	Jullundur, India	31N	76 E
83	Junagādh, India	22N	70 E
94	Juneau, Alsk.	58N	134W
114	Junín, Arg.	35S	61W

K

Page	Place	Lat.°'	Long.°'
83	K2 (Mt.) China-Pak.	36N	76 E
89	Kabelega Falls, Ug.	3N	32 E
83	Kābul, Afg.	35N	69 E
77	Kachuga, Sov. Un.	54N	106 E
88	Kaduna, Nig.	10N	7 E
81	Kaesŏng (Kaijo), Kor.	38N	127 E
81	Kagoshima, Japan	32N	131 E
75	Kahramarimaraş, Tur.	38N	37 E
81	Kaifeng, China	35N	114 E
85	Kaimana, Indon.	4S	134 E
73	Kaiserslautern, Ger.	49N	8 E
75	Kakhovskoye Res., Sov. Un.	47N	34 E
83	Kākināda, India	17N	82 E
90	Kalahari Des., Afr.	23S	21 E
75	Kalámai, Grc.	37N	22 E
96	Kalamazoo, Mich.	42N	86W
83	Kalāt, Pak.	29N	67 E
90	Kalemie, Zaire	6S	29 E
70	Kaliningrad (Königsberg), Sov. Un.	55N	21 E
101	Kalispell, Mont.	48N	114W
73	Kalisz, Pol.	52N	18 E
71	Kaluga, Sov. Un.	54N	36 E
71	Kama (R.) Sov. Un.	55N	50 E
77	Kamchatka, Poluostrov (Pen.) Sov. Un.	55N	159 E
76	Kamen-na-Obi, Sov. Un.	54N	81 E
71	Kamensk-Ural'skiy, Sov. Un.	56N	62 E
92	Kamloops, B.C., Can.	51N	120W
89	Kampala, Ug.	0	33 E
84	Kâmpóng Thum, Camb.	13N	105 E
92	Kamsack, Sask., Can.	52N	102W
71	Kamyshin, Sov. Un.	50N	45 E
90	Kananga, Zaire	6S	22 E
81	Kanazawa, Japan	37N	137 E
83	Kānchipuram, India	13N	80 E
70	Kandalaksha, Sov. Un.	67N	33 E
80	Kanding, China	30N	102 E
83	Kandy, Sri Lanka	7N	81 E
82	Kangāvar, Iran	35N	47 E
96	Kankakee, Ill.	41N	88W
88	Kano, Nig.	12N	9 E
83	Kānpur, India	27N	80 E
94	Kansas (State) U.S.	39N	98W
105	Kansas City, Kans.	39N	95W
105	Kansas City, Mo.	39N	95W
77	Kansk , Sov. Un.	56N	96 E
81	Kaohsiung, Taiwan	23N	120 E
88	Kaolack, Sen.	14N	16W
93	Kapuskasing, Ont., Can.	49N	82W
76	Kara, Sov. Un.	69N	65 E
83	Karāchi, Pak.	25N	66 E
76	Karaganda, Sov. Un.	50N	73 E
83	Karakoram Ra., Asia	36N	76 E
75	Karaman, Tur.	37N	33 E
80	Karashahr (Yanqi), China	42N	86 E
82	Karbalā', Iraq	33N	44 E
76	Kargat, Sov. Un.	55N	80 E
76	Kargopol, Sov. Un.	61N	39 E
76	Karkaralinsk, Sov. Un.	49N	75 E
74	Karlovac, Yugo.	45N	15 E
73	Karlovy Vary, Czech.	50N	13 E
73	Karlsruhe, Ger.	49N	8 E
72	Karlstad, Swe.	59N	13 E
82	Kars, Tur.	41N	43 E
76	Karshi, Sov. Un.	38N	66 E
76	Karskoye More (Sea) Sov. Un.	72N	75 E
76	Kartaly, Sov. Un.	53N	61 E
90	Kasai (R.) Ang.-Zaire	4S	19 E
82	Kāshān, Iran	34N	51 E
80	Kashi, China	39N	76 E
89	Kassalā, Sud.	15N	36 E
73	Kassel, Ger.	51N	9 E

119

Marmara Denizi

Page	Place	Lat.°'	Long.°'
75	Kastoría, Grc.	40N	21 E
90	Katanga (Reg.) Zaire	9S	25 E
83	Kathmandu, Nepal	28N	85 E
73	Katowice, Pol.	50N	19 E
88	Katsina Ala, Nig.	7N	9 E
72	Kattegat (Str.) Den.-Swe.	57N	11 E
70	Kaunas (Kovno), Lith.	55N	24 E
75	Kavála, Grc.	41N	24 E
85	Kavieng, Pap. N. Gui.	3S	151 E
82	Kavīr, Dasht-e (Des.) Iran	34N	53 E
88	Kayes, Mali	14N	12W
75	Kayseri, Tur.	39N	35 E
77	Kazach'ye, Sov. Un.	71N	136 E
71	Kazan', Sov. Un.	56N	49 E
71	Kazbek, Gora (Mt.) Sov. Un.	43N	44 E
82	Kāzerūn, Iran	30N	52 E
73	Kecskemét, Hung.	47N	20 E
76	Kem, Sov. Un.	65N	35 E
76	Kemerovo, Sov. Un.	55N	86 E
72	Kemi, Fin.	66N	25 E
93	Kenora, Ont., Can.	50N	94W
99	Kenosha, Wis.	43N	88W
96	Kentucky (R.) Ken.	38N	85W
95	Kentucky (State) U.S.	37N	85W
91	Kenya (Ctry.) Afr.	2N	38 E
91	Kenya, Mt. (Kirinyaga), Ken.	0	37 E
105	Keokuk, Iowa	40N	92W
71	Kerch', Sov. Un.	45N	36 E
83	Kerki, Sov. Un.	38N	65 E
75	Kérkira (I.) Grc.	40N	20 E
82	Kermān, Iran	30N	57 E
96	Kettering, Ohio	40N	84W
109	Key West, Fla.	25N	82W
77	Khabarovsk, Sov. Un.	49N	135 E
75	Khalkís, Grc.	39N	24 E
76	Khal'mer-Yu, Sov. Un.	68N	64 E
83	Khambhāt, Gulf of, India	21N	72 E
75	Khaniá, Grc.	35N	24 E
83	Kharagpur, India	22N	87 E
71	Kharkov, Sov. Un.	50N	36 E
89	Khartoum, Sud.	16N	33 E
82	Khāsh, Iran	28N	61 E
83	Khasi Hills, India	26N	93 E
75	Khaskovo, Bul.	42N	26 E
77	Khatanga, Sov. Un.	72N	102 E
71	Kherson, Sov. Un.	47N	33 E
75	Khmel'nitskiy, Sov. Un.	49N	27 E
80	Khodzhent, Sov. Un.	40N	70 E
77	Kholmsk, Sov. Un.	47N	143 E
84	Khon Kaen, Thai.	17N	103 E
83	Khorog, Sov. Un.	37N	72 E
82	Khorramshahr, Iran	31N	48 E
83	Khulna, Bngl.	23N	90 E
82	Khvoy, Iran	39N	45 E
83	Khyber P., Afg.-Pak.	34N	70 E
72	Kiel, Ger.	54N	10 E
71	Kiev, Sov. Un.	50N	31 E
90	Kigali, Rwanda	2S	30 E
91	Kilimanjaro (Mt.) Tan.	3S	37 E
90	Kimberley, S. Afr.	29S	25 E
92	Kindersley, Sask., Can.	51N	109W
111	Kingston, Jam.	18N	77W
97	Kingston, N.Y.	42N	74W
93	Kingston, Ont., Can.	44N	76W
111	Kingstown, St. Vin.	13N	61W
90	Kinshasa (Léopoldville), Zaire	4S	15 E
77	Kirensk, Sov. Un.	58N	108 E
75	Kirklareli, Tur.	42N	27 E
105	Kirksville, Mo.	40N	93W
82	Kirkūk, Iraq	35N	44 E
72	Kirkwall, Scot.	59N	3W
71	Kirov, Sov. Un.	59N	50 E
71	Kirovograd, Sov. Un.	49N	32 E
70	Kirovsk, Sov. Un.	68N	34 E
83	Kīrthar Ra., Pak.	27N	67 E
72	Kiruna, Swe.	68N	20 E
89	Kisangani (Stanleyville), Zaire	1N	25 E
76	Kiselëvsk, Sov. Un.	54N	86 E
70	Kishinëv, Sov. Un.	47N	29 E
81	Kitayūshū, Japan	34N	130 E
93	Kitchener, Ont., Can.	43N	81W
90	Kivu (L.) Rwanda-Zaire	2S	28 E
75	Kizil Irmak (R.) Tur.	40N	34 E
72	Klaipėda, Lith.	56N	21 E
100	Klamath Falls, Oreg.	42N	122W
108	Knoxville, Tenn.	36N	84W
81	Kōbe, Japan	35N	135 E
73	Koblenz, Ger.	50N	8 E
81	Kōchi, Japan	34N	134 E
76	Kokand, Sov. Un.	40N	71 E
96	Kokomo, Ind.	41N	86W
80	Koko Nor (Qinghai Hu) (L.) China	37N	98 E
93	Koksoak (R.) Can.	58N	70W
83	Kolār, India	14N	79 E
83	Kolhāpur, India	17N	74 E
71	Kolomna, Sov. Un.	55N	39 E
75	Kolomyya , Sov. Un.	49N	25 E
76	Kolpashevo, Sov. Un.	58N	83 E
76	Kol'skiy Poluostrov (Kola Pen.), Sov. Un.	67N	37 E
90	Kolwezi, Zaire	11S	26 E
81	Kominato, Japan	28N	129 E
75	Komotiní, Grc.	41N	25 E
77	Komsomol'sk na-Amure, Sov. Un.	51N	137 E
75	Konya, Tur.	37N	32 E
75	Korçë, Alb.	41N	21 E
81	Korea (Ctry.) Asia	38N	127 E
81	Korea Str., Kor.-Japan	33N	128 E
80	Korla, China	42N	86 E
77	Korsakov, Sov. Un.	47N	143 E
87	Kosciusko, Mt., Austl.	36S	148 E
73	Košice, Czech.	49N	21 E
71	Kostroma, Sov. Un.	58N	41 E
72	Koszalin, Pol.	54N	16 E
84	Kota Baharu, Mala.	6N	102 E
84	Kota Kinabalu, Mala.	6N	116 E
72	Kotka, Fin.	60N	27 E
71	Kotlas, Sov. Un.	61N	47 E
88	Koudougou, Burkina	12N	2W
76	Kounradskiy, Sov. Un.	47N	75 E
89	Koussi, Emi (Mt.) Chad	20N	18 E
71	Kovrov, Sov. Un.	56N	41 E
81	Kowloon, H.K.	22N	114 E
75	Kozáni, Grc.	40N	22 E
84	Kra, Isthmus of, Bur.-Thai.	10N	99 E
75	Kragujevac, Yugo.	44N	21 E
73	Kraków, Pol.	50N	20 E
75	Kraljevo, Yugo.	44N	21 E
74	Kranj, Yugo.	46N	14 E
71	Krasnodar, Sov. Un.	45N	39 E
71	Krasnokamsk, Sov. Un.	58N	56 E
76	Krasnotur'insk, Sov. Un.	60N	60 E
71	Krasnoural'sk, Sov. Un.	58N	60 E
71	Krasnovodsk, Sov. Un.	40N	53 E
77	Krasnoyarsk, Sov. Un.	56N	93 E
71	Kremenchug, Sov. Un.	49N	33 E
72	Kristiansand, Nor.	57N	8 E
71	Krivoy Rog, Sov. Un.	48N	33 E
70	Kronshtadt, Sov. Un.	60N	30 E
75	Kropotkin, Sov. Un.	45N	41 E
90	Krugersdorp, S. Afr.	26S	28 E
71	Krymskiy Poluostrov (Crimean Pen.), Sov. Un.	45N	34 E
74	Ksar el Kebir, Mor.	35N	6W
84	Kuala Lumpur, Mala.	3N	102 E
84	Kuching, Mala.	1N	110 E
76	Kudymkar, Sov. Un.	59N	55 E
81	Kuji, Japan	40N	142 E
81	Kumamoto, Japan	33N	131 E
88	Kumasi, Ghana	7N	2W
76	Kungur, Sov. Un.	57N	57 E
80	Kunlun Shan (Mts.) China	36N	87 E
80	Kunming, China	25N	103 E
81	Kunsan, Kor.	36N	127 E
85	Kupang, Indon.	10S	124 E
76	Kupino, Sov. Un.	54N	78 E
76	Kurgan, Sov. Un.	55N	65 E
83	Kurgan-Tyube, Sov. Un.	38N	69 E
81	Kuril Is., Sov. Un.	46N	147 E
71	Kursk, Sov. Un.	52N	36 E
81	Kurume, Japan	33N	130 E
81	Kushiro, Japan	43N	144 E
76	Kushva, Sov. Un.	58N	60 E
76	Kustanay, Sov. Un.	53N	64 E
75	Kütahya, Tur.	39N	30 E
71	Kutaisi, Sov. Un.	42N	43 E
83	Kutch, Gulf of, India	22N	68 E
83	Kutch, Rann of (Swamp) India-Pak.	24N	69 E
77	Kutulik, Sov. Un.	53N	103 E
82	Kuwait (Al Kuwayt), Kuw.	29N	48 E
82	Kuwait (Ctry.) Asia	29N	48 E
71	Kuybyshevskoye (Res.) Sov. Un.	54N	47 E
77	Kyakhta, Sov. Un.	51N	107 E
81	Kyŏngju, Kor.	36N	129 E
81	Kyōto, Japan	35N	136 E
81	Kyūshū (I.) Japan	32N	132 E
75	Kyustendil, Bul.	42N	23 E
77	Kyzyl, Sov. Un.	52N	94 E
76	Kzyl-Orda, Sov. Un.	45N	66 E
	L		
97	Lackawanna, N.Y.	43N	79W
92	Lac la Biche, Alta., Can.	55N	112W
74	La Coruña, Sp.	43N	8W
99	La Crosse, Wis.	44N	91W
85	Lae, Pap. N. Gui.	6S	147 E
96	La Fayette, Ind.	40N	87W
107	Lafayette, La.	30N	92W
88	Laghouat, Alg.	34N	3 E
88	Lagos, Nig.	7N	3 E
100	La Grande, Oreg.	45N	118W
108	LaGrange, Ga.	33N	85W
83	Lahore, Pak.	32N	74 E
72	Lahti, Fin.	61N	26 E
107	Lake Charles, La.	30N	93W
96	Lake Forest, Ill.	42N	88W
109	Lakeland, Fla.	28N	82W
96	Lakewood, Ohio	41N	82W
74	La Línea, Sp.	36N	5W
83	Lalitpur, Nepal	27N	85 E
75	Lamia , Grc.	39N	22 E
114	Lanús, Arg.	34S	58W
72	Lancaster, Eng.	54N	3W
96	Lancaster, Ohio	40N	83W
97	Lancaster, Pa.	40N	76W
84	Lang Son, Viet.	22N	107 E
80	Langzhong, China	32N	106 E
92	Lanigan, Sask., Can.	52N	105W
96	Lansing, Mich.	43N	85W
80	Lanzhou, China	36N	104 E
84	Laoag, Phil.	18N	121 E
84	Laos (Ctry.) Asia	20N	102 E
112	La Paz, Bol.	17S	68W
110	La Paz, Mex.	24N	110W
72	Lapland (Reg.) Eur.	68N	25 E
114	La Plata, Arg.	35S	58W
77	Laptev Sea, Sov. Un.	75N	125 E
73	L'Aquila, It.	42N	13 E
88	Larache, Mor.	35N	6W
94	Laramie, Wyo.	41N	106W
106	Laredo, Tex.	28N	99W
114	La Rioja, Arg.	29S	67W
75	Lárisa, Grc.	40N	22 E
75	Larnaca, Cyp.	35N	34 E
103	Las Cruces, N. Mex.	32N	107W
114	La Serena, Chile	30S	71W
73	La Seyne, Fr.	43N	6 E
73	La Spezia, It.	44N	10 E
102	Las Vegas, Nev.	36N	115W
104	Las Vegas, N. Mex.	36N	105W
76	Latvia (Ctry.) Eur	57N	25 E
87	Launceston, Austl.	42S	147 E
108	Laurel, Miss.	32N	89W
73	Lausanne, Switz.	47N	7 E
73	Laval, Fr.	48N	1W
105	Lawrence, Kans.	39N	95W
97	Lawrence, Mass.	43N	71W
104	Lawton, Okla.	35N	98W
98	Lead, S. Dak.	44N	104W
105	Leavenworth, Kans.	39N	95W
97	Lebanon, Pa.	40N	76W
75	Lebanon (Ctry.) Asia	34N	36 E
73	Lecce, It.	40N	18 E
72	Leeds, Eng.	54N	2W
73	Leeuwarden, Neth.	52N	6 E
85	Legazpi, Phil.	13N	124 E
73	Legnica, Pol.	51N	16 E
73	Le Havre, Fr.	50N	0
73	Leicester, Eng.	53N	1W
73	Leipzig, Ger.	51N	12 E
73	Le Mans, Fr.	48N	0
88	Lemdiyya, Alg.	36N	3 E
77	Lena (R.) Sov. Un.	68N	123 E
71	Leninakan, Sov. Un.	41N	44 E
70	Leningrad, see St. Petersburg Sov. Un.	60N	30 E
76	Leninogorsk, Sov. Un.	50N	83 E
76	Lenkoran', Sov. Un.	39N	49 E
97	Leominster, Mass.	43N	72W
110	León, Mex.	21N	102W
74	León, Sp.	43N	6W
73	Le Puy, Fr.	45N	4 E
74	Lérida, Sp.	42N	1 E
72	Lerwick, Scot.	60N	1W
80	Leshan, China	30N	104 E
90	Lesotho (Ctry.) Afr.	30S	28 E
111	Lesser Antilles (Is.) N.A.-S.A.	15N	61W
81	Lesser Khingan Range (Xiao Hinggan Ling), China	48N	128 E
84	Lesser Sunda Is., Indon.	9S	120 E
100	Lewiston, Idaho	46N	117W
97	Lewiston, Maine	44N	70W
101	Lewistown, Mont.	47N	109W
96	Lexington, Ky.	38N	84W
80	Lhasa, China	30N	91 E
81	Liaoyang, China	41N	123 E
73	Liberec, Czech.	51N	15 E
88	Liberia (Ctry.) Afr.	6N	9W
90	Libreville, Gabon	0	9 E
89	Libya (Ctry.) Afr.	28N	18 E
89	Libyan Des., Afr.	28N	24 E
73	Liechtenstein (Ctry.) Eur.	47N	9 E
73	Liège, Bel.	51N	5 E
72	Liepāja, Lat.	57N	21 E
73	Ligurian Sea, Fr.-It.	43N	8 E
90	Likasi, Zaire	11S	27 E
73	Lille, Fr.	51N	3 E
96	Lima, Ohio	41N	84W
112	Lima, Peru	12S	77W
75	Limassol, Cyp.	35N	33 E
73	Limerick, Ire.	52N	9W
73	Limoges, Fr.	46N	1 E
90	Limpopo (R.) Afr.	23S	28 E
74	Linares, Sp.	38N	4W
73	Lincoln, Eng.	53N	1W
105	Lincoln, Nebr.	41N	97W
85	Lingayen, Phil.	16N	120 E
72	Linnköping, Swe.	58N	16 E
81	Linyi, China	35N	118 E
73	Linz, Aus.	48N	14 E
71	Lipetsk, Sov. Un.	52N	40 E
74	Lisbon, Port.	39N	9W
76	Lithuania (Ctry.) Eur.	56N	24 E
90	Little Karroo (Plat.) S. Afr.	34S	21 E
105	Little Rock, Ark.	35N	92W
80	Liuzhou, China	24N	109 E
72	Liverpool, Eng.	53N	3W
101	Livingston, Mont.	46N	111W
90	Livingstone, Zambia	18S	26 E
75	Livno, Yugo.	44N	17 E
73	Livorno, It.	44N	11 E
74	Ljubljana, Yugo.	46N	14 E
73	Llanelli, Wales	52N	4W
112	Llanos (Reg.) Col.-Ven.	5N	70W
92	Lloydminster, Sask., Can.	53N	110W
90	Lobatse, Bots.	25S	26 E
97	Lockport, N.Y.	43N	79W
84	Loc Ninh, Viet.	12N	107 E
73	Łódź, Pol.	52N	19 E
101	Logan, Utah	42N	112W
92	Logan, Mt., Yukon, Can.	61N	141W
74	Logroño, Sp.	42N	2W
73	Loire (R.) Fr.	48N	2 E
114	Lomas de Zamora, Arg.	34S	58W
88	Lomé, Togo	6N	1 E
73	London, Eng.	51N	0
93	London, Ont., Can.	43N	82W
72	Londonderry, N. Ire.	55N	7W
114	Londrina, Braz.	23S	51W
102	Long Beach, Calif.	34N	118W
97	Long I., N.Y.	41N	73W
84	Long Xuyen, Viet.	11N	105 E
96	Lorain, Ohio	41N	82W
83	Loralai, Pak.	31N	69 E
74	Lorca, Sp.	38N	2W
73	Lorient, Fr.	48N	3W
103	Los Alamos, N. Mex.	36N	106W
102	Los Angeles, Calif.	34N	118W
114	Los Angeles, Chile	37S	72W
113	Los Teques, Ven.	10N	67W
114	Lota, Chile	37S	73W
84	Louangphrabang, Laos	20N	102 E
95	Louisiana (State) U.S.	31N	92W
96	Louisville, Ky.	38N	86W
97	Lowell, Mass.	43N	71W
87	Lower Hutt, N.Z.	41S	175 E
75	Loznica, Yugo.	45N	19 E
90	Lualaba (R.) Zaire	10S	25 E
90	Luanda, Ang.	9S	13 E
104	Lubbock, Tex.	34N	102W
72	Lübeck, Ger.	54N	11 E
90	Lubilash (R.) Zaire	8S	24 E
73	Lublin, Pol.	51N	23 E
90	Lubumbashi (Elizabethville), Zaire	12S	28 E
73	Lucca, It.	44N	10 E
74	Lucena, Sp.	37N	4W
83	Lucknow, India	27N	81 E
83	Ludhiāna, India	31N	76 E
74	Lugo, Sp.	43N	8W
75	Lugoj, Rom.	46N	22 E
72	Luleå, Swe.	66N	22 E
80	Lun, Mong.	48N	105 E
72	Lund, Swe.	56N	13 E
81	Luoyang, China	35N	113 E
72	Lurgan, N. Ire.	54N	6W
90	Lusaka, Zambia	15S	28 E
81	Lüshun, China	39N	121 E
73	Luxembourg, Lux.	50N	6 E
73	Luxembourg (Ctry.) Eur.	50N	6 E
73	Luzern, Switz.	47N	8 E
80	Luzhou, China	29N	105 E
84	Luzon (I.) Phil.	17N	120 E
70	L'vov, Sov. Un.	50N	24 E
97	Lynchburg, Va.	37N	79W
97	Lynn, Mass.	42N	71W
92	Lynn Lake, Man., Can.	57N	101W
73	Lyon, Fr.	46N	5 E
71	Lys'va, Sov. Un.	58N	58 E
	M		
81	Macao (Ctry.) Asia	22N	114 E
113	Macapá, Braz.	0	51W
86	Macdonnell Ranges, Austl.	24S	133 E
113	Maceió, Braz.	10S	36W
92	Mackenzie (R.) N.W. Ter., Can.	63N	124W
92	Mackenzie Mts., Can.	64N	130W
96	Mackinaw City, Mich.	46N	85W
108	Macon, Ga.	33N	84W
91	Madagascar (Ctry.) Afr.	20S	46 E
112	Madeira (R.) Bol.-Braz.	7S	63W
88	Madeira, Arquipélago da (Is.) Port.	33N	16W
99	Madison, Wis.	43N	89W
83	Madras, India	13N	80 E
110	Madre del Sur, Sierra (Mts.) Mex.	18N	101W
110	Madre Occidental, Sierra (Mts.) Mex.	23N	105W
110	Madre Oriental, Sierra (Mts.) Mex.	23N	100W
74	Madrid, Sp.	40N	4W
83	Madurai, India	10N	78 E
81	Maebashi, Japan	36N	139 E
90	Mafeking, S. Afr.	26S	25 E
77	Magadan, Sov. Un.	60N	151 E
114	Magallanes, Estrecho de (Str.) Arg.-Chile	53S	69W
112	Magdalena (R.) Col.	8N	74W
73	Magdeburg, Ger.	52N	12 E
114	Magé, Braz.	23S	43W
74	Maghniyya, Alg.	35N	2W
71	Magnitogorsk, Sov. Un.	53N	59 E
91	Mahajanga, Mad.	15S	46 E
74	Mahón, Sp.	40N	4 E
89	Maiduguri, Nig.	12N	13 E
87	Main Barrier Ra., Austl.	31S	142 E
90	Mai-Ndombe (L.) Zaire	2S	19 E
95	Maine (State) U.S.	45N	69W
73	Mainz, Ger.	50N	8 E
113	Maiquetía, Ven.	11N	67W
84	Makasar, Selat (Str.) Indon.	3S	118 E
71	Makeyevka, Sov. Un.	48N	38 E
76	Makushino, Sov. Un.	55N	68 E
88	Malabo, Eq. Gui.	4N	9 E
74	Málaga, Sp.	37N	4W
75	Malatya, Tur.	38N	38 E
90	Malawi (Ctry.) Afr.	11S	34 E
76	Malaya Vishera, Sov. Un.	59N	32 E
84	Malay Pen., Asia	8N	101 E
84	Malaysia (Ctry.) Asia	4N	102 E
72	Malbork, Pol.	54N	19 E
97	Malden, Mass.	42N	71W
69	Maldives (Ctry.), Ind. O.	5N	70 E
88	Mali (Ctry.) Afr.	16N	2W
75	Mallawī, Eg.	28N	31 E
74	Mallorca (I.) Sp.	40N	3 E
72	Malmö, Swe.	56N	13 E
74	Malta (Ctry.) Eur.	36N	14 E
85	Maluku (Moluccas) (Is.) Indon.	3S	127 E
85	Maluku, Laut (Molucca Sea), Indon.	0	125 E
85	Manado, Indon.	1N	125 E
110	Managua, Nic.	12N	86W
91	Manakara, Mad.	22S	48 E
80	Manas, China	44N	86 E
113	Manaus (Manaos), Braz.	3S	60W
97	Manchester, Conn.	42N	72W
72	Manchester, Eng.	53N	2W
97	Manchester, N.H.	43N	71W
81	Manchuria (Reg.) China	46N	126 E
80	Mandalay, Bur.	22N	96 E
98	Mandan, N. Dak.	47N	101W
82	Mandeb, Bab el (Str.) Afr.-Asia	13N	43 E
83	Māndvi, India	23N	69 E
83	Mangalore, India	13	75 E
105	Manhattan, Kans.	39N	97W
85	Manila, Phil.	15N	121 E
75	Manisa, Tur.	39N	27 E
92	Manitoba (L.) Man., Can.	51N	99W
92	Manitoba (Prov.) Can.	55N	98W
99	Manitowoc, Wis.	44N	88W
112	Manizales, Col.	5N	76W
99	Mankato, Minn.	44N	94W
83	Mannar, G. of , India-Sri Lanka	9N	79 E
73	Mannheim, Ger.	49N	9 E
96	Mansfield, Ohio	41N	82W
111	Manzanillo, Cuba	20N	77W
81	Manzhouli, China	49N	117 E
90	Maputo, Moz.	26S	33 E
112	Maracaibo, Ven.	11N	72W
112	Maracaibo, Lago de (L.) Ven.	10N	72W
112	Maracay, Ven.	10N	68W
113	Marajó, Ilha de (I.) Braz.	1S	50W
112	Marañón (R.) Peru	5S	75W
114	Mar del Plata, Arg.	38S	58W
82	Mardin, Tur.	37N	41 E
111	Marianao, Cuba	23N	82W
75	Maribor, Yugo.	47N	16 E
113	Marília, Braz.	23S	50W
96	Marion, Ind.	41N	86W
96	Marion, Ohio	41N	83W
71	Mariupol', Sov. Un.	47N	38 E
85	Mariveles, Phil.	14N	120 E
77	Markovo, Sov. Un.	65N	170 E
75	Marmara Denizi (Sea) Tur.	41N	28 E

120

Maroua, Cam.

Page	Place	Lat.°′	Long.°′
89	Maroua, Cam.	11N	14 E
99	Marquette, Mich.	46N	88W
88	Marrakech, Mor.	32N	8W
73	Marsala, It.	38N	12 E
73	Marseille, Fr.	43N	5 E
107	Marshall, Tex.	33N	94W
69	Marshall Is. (Ctry.), Pac. O.	10N	170 E
97	Martha's Vineyard (I.) Mass.	41N	70W
111	Martinique (Ctry.) N.A.	15N	61W
76	Mary, Sov. Un.	38N	62 E
95	Maryland (State) U.S.	39N	76W
81	Masan, Kor.	35N	129 E
90	Maseru, Leso.	29S	27 E
82	Mashhad, Iran	36N	59 E
82	Masjed Soleymān, Iran	32N	49 E
99	Mason City, Iowa	43N	93W
95	Massachusetts (State) U.S.	42N	72W
92	Masset, B.C., Can.	54N	132W
96	Massillon, Ohio	41N	82W
90	Matadi, Zaire	6S	14 E
110	Matamoros, Mex.	26N	97W
111	Matanzas, Cuba	23N	82W
83	Matara, Sri Lanka	6N	81 E
84	Mataram, Indon.	9S	116 E
83	Mathura, India	28N	78 E
76	Matochkin Shar, Sov. Un.	74N	56 E
82	Maṭraḥ, Oman	24N	58 E
81	Matsue, Japan	35N	133 E
81	Matsuyama, Japan	34N	133 E
112	Maturín, Ven.	10N	63W
88	Mauritania (Ctry.) Afr.	19N	12W
69	Mauritius (Ctry.), Afr.	20S	58 E
84	Mawlamyine, Bur.	16N	98 E
111	Mayagüez, P.R.	18N	67W
71	Maykop, Sov. Un.	45N	40 E
92	Mayo, Yukon, Can.	64N	136W
110	Mayran, Laguna de (L.) Mex.	26N	103W
83	Mazār-e Sharīf, Afg.	37N	67 E
110	Mazatlán, Mex.	23N	106W
90	Mbabane, Swaz.	26S	31 E
90	Mbandaka, Zaire	0	18 E
90	M'banza Congo, Ang.	7S	14 E
105	McAlester, Okla.	35N	96W
106	McAllen, Tex.	26N	98W
94	McGrath, Alsk.	63N	155W
97	McKeesport, Pa.	40N	80W
94	McKinley, Mt., Alsk.	63N	150W
92	McLennan, Alta., Can.	56N	117W
82	Mecca (Makkah), Sau. Ar.	21N	40 E
84	Medan, Indon.	4N	99 E
112	Medellín, Col.	6N	76W
100	Medford, Oreg.	42N	123W
74	Mediterranean Sea, Afr.-Asia-Eur.	38N	10 E
76	Mednogorsk, Sov. Un.	51N	57 E
83	Meerut, India	29N	78 E
88	Meknès, Mor.	34N	6W
84	Mekong (R.) Asia	18N	104 E
84	Melaka, Mala.	2N	102 E
87	Melbourne, Austl.	38S	145 E
92	Melfort, Sask., Can.	53N	105W
74	Melilla, Afr.	35N	3W
71	Melitopol', Sov. Un.	47N	35 E
92	Melville, Sask., Can.	51N	103W
93	Melville Pen., N.W. Ter.Can.	68N	85W
108	Memphis, Tenn.	35N	90W
114	Mendoza, Arg.	33S	69W
74	Menorca (I.) Sp.	40N	4 E
74	Menzel Bourguiba, Tun.	37N	10 E
73	Merano, It.	46N	11 E
85	Merauke, Pap. N. Gui.	9S	140 E
114	Mercedes, Arg.	29S	58W
84	Mergui, Bur.	12N	99 E
110	Mérida, Mex.	21N	90W
112	Mérida, Ven.	8N	71W
97	Meriden, Conn.	41N	73W
108	Meridian, Miss.	32N	89W
73	Messina, It.	38N	16 E
107	Metairie, La.	30N	90W
72	Metz, Fr.	49N	6 E
110	Mexicali, Mex.	32N	115W
110	Mexico (Ctry.) N.A.	24N	102W
110	Mexico, G. of,, N.A.	25N	90W
110	Mexico City, Mex.	19N	99W
71	Mezen', Sov. Un.	66N	44 E
103	Miami, Ariz.	33N	111W
109	Miami, Fla.	26N	80W
109	Miami Beach, Fla.	26N	80W
95	Michigan (State) U.S.	44N	85W
96	Michigan City, Ind.	42N	87W
96	Michigan, L.,, U.S.	44N	87W
93	Michikamau (L.) Newf., Can.	54N	63W
71	Michurinsk, Sov. Un.	53N	41 E
69	Micronesia, Federated States of (Ctry.), Pac. O.	5N	153 E
72	Middlesbrough, Eng.	55N	1W
97	Middletown, Conn.	42N	73W
96	Middletown, Ohio	39N	84W
106	Midland, Tex.	32N	102W
68	Midway Is. (Ctry.), Pac. O.	30N	175W
73	Milan, It.	45N	9 E
101	Miles City, Mont.	46N	106W
99	Milwaukee, Wis.	43N	88W
114	Minas, Ur.	34S	55W
110	Minatitlán, Mex.	18N	95W
85	Mindanao (I.) Phil.	8N	125 E
85	Mindoro (I.) Phil.	13N	120 E
99	Minneapolis, Minn.	45N	93W
92	Minnedosa, Man., Can.	50N	100W
98	Minnesota (R.) Minn.	45N	96W
95	Minnesota (State) U.S.	46N	95W
98	Minot, N. Dak.	48N	101W
70	Minsk, Sov. Un.	54N	28 E
77	Minusinsk, Sov. Un.	54N	92 E
82	Mirbāṭ, Oman	17N	55 E
114	Mirim, L., Braz.-Ur.	33S	54W
83	Mirzāpur, India	25N	83 E
96	Mishawaka, Ind.	42N	86W
73	Miskolc, Hung.	48N	21 E
89	Misrātah, Libya	32N	15 E
95	Mississippi (R.) U.S.	32N	92W
95	Mississippi (State) U.S.	33N	90W
101	Missoula, Mont.	47N	114W
95	Missouri (R.) U.S.	41N	96W
95	Missouri (State) U.S.	38N	93W
112	Misti, Volcán (Vol.) Peru	16S	71W
98	Mitchell, S. Dak.	44N	98W
75	Mitilíni, Grc.	39N	27 E
89	Mitsiwa, Eth.	16N	39 E
90	Mmbatho, Bophuthatswana	26S	26 E
105	Moberly, Mo.	39N	92W
108	Mobile, Ala.	31N	88W
73	Modena, It.	45N	11 E
114	Mogi das Cruzes, Braz.	24S	46W
70	Mogilev, Sov. Un.	54N	30 E
75	Mogilëv Podol'skiy, Sov. Un.	48N	28 E
99	Moline, Ill.	42N	90W
91	Mombasa, Ken.	4S	40 E
73	Monaco (Ctry.) Eur.	44N	8 E
74	Monastir, Tun.	36N	11 E
93	Moncton, N.B., Can.	46N	65W
83	Monghyr, India	25N	87 E
80	Mongolia (Ctry.) Asia	46N	100 E
107	Monroe, La.	32N	92W
96	Monroe, Mich.	42N	83W
88	Monrovia, Lib.	6N	11W
73	Mons, Bel.	50N	4 E
94	Montana (State) U.S.	47N	109W
73	Montauban, Fr.	44N	1 E
111	Montego Bay, Jam.	18N	78W
102	Monterey, Calif.	37N	122W
112	Montería, Col.	9N	76W
110	Monterrey, Mex.	26N	100W
73	Monte Sant'Angelo, It.	42N	16 E
114	Montevideo, Ur.	35S	56W
108	Montgomery, Ala.	32N	86W
73	Montluçon, Fr.	46N	3 E
97	Montpelier, Vt.	44N	73W
73	Montpellier, Fr.	44N	4 E
93	Montréal, Que., Can.	45N	74W
111	Montserrat (Ctry.) N.A.	17N	63W
80	Monywa, Bur.	22N	95 E
92	Moose Jaw, Sask., Can.	50N	106W
93	Moosonee, Ont., Can.	51N	81W
83	Morādābād, India	29N	79W
92	Morden, Man., Can.	49N	98W
110	Morelia, Mex.	20N	101W
74	Morena, Sa. (Mts.) Sp.	38N	6W
107	Morgan City, La.	30N	91W
81	Morioka, Japan	40N	141 E
73	Morlaix, Fr.	49N	4W
88	Morocco (Ctry.) Afr.	32N	6W
91	Morombe, Mad.	22S	44 E
114	Morón, Arg.	34S	59W
92	Morris, Man., Can.	49N	98W
71	Morshansk, Sov. Un.	53N	42 E
100	Moscow, Idaho	47N	117W
71	Moscow (Moskva), Sov. Un.	56N	38 E
111	Mosquitos, Golfo de los (G.) Pan.	9N	81W
75	Mostar, Yugo.	43N	18 E
72	Motherwell, Scot.	56N	4W
88	Mouaskar, Alg.	35N	0
73	Moulins, Fr.	47N	3 E
96	Mount Carmel, Ill.	38N	88W
97	Mount Vernon, N.Y.	41N	74W
90	Mozambique (Ctry.) Afr.	18S	35 E
91	Mozambique Chan., Afr.	20S	40 E
75	Mukachevo, Sov. Un.	48N	23 E
77	Mukhtuya, Sov. Un.	61N	113 E
73	Mulhouse, Fr.	48N	7 E
83	Multān, Pak.	30N	71 E
96	Muncie, Ind.	40N	85W
73	Munich (München), Ger.	48N	12 E
73	Münster, Ger.	52N	8 E
74	Murcia, Sp.	38N	1W
70	Murmansk, Sov. Un.	69N	33 E
76	Murom, Sov. Un.	55N	42 E
81	Muroran, Japan	42N	141 E
86	Murray Bridge, Austl.	35S	140 E
82	Muscat, Oman	23N	58 E
96	Muskegon, Mich.	43N	86W
105	Muskogee, Okla.	36N	95W
80	Myitkyina, Bur.	26N	97 E
83	Mymensingh, Bngl.	25N	90 E
83	Mysore, India	13N	77 E

N

Page	Place	Lat.°′	Long.°′
71	Naberezhnyye Chelny, Sov. Un.	56N	53 E
88	Nabeul, Tun.	37N	11 E
75	Nabulus, Jor.	32N	35 E
91	Nacala, Moz.	15S	41 E
72	Naestved, Den.	55N	12 E
85	Naga, Phil.	14N	123 E
81	Nagano, Japan	37N	138 E
81	Nagaoka, Japan	37N	139 E
83	Nāgappattinam, India	11N	80 E
81	Nagasaki, Japan	33N	130 E
81	Nagoya, Japan	35N	137 E
83	Nāgpur, India	21N	79 E
73	Nagykanizsa, Hung.	46N	17 E
81	Naha, Japan	26N	128 E
112	Naiguatá, Ven.	11N	67W
91	Nairobi, Ken.	1S	37 E
81	Najin, Kor.	42N	130 E
77	Nakhodka, Sov. Un.	43N	133 E
84	Nakhon Ratchasima, Thai.	15N	102 E
72	Nakskov, Den.	55N	11 E
83	Namangan, Sov. Un.	41N	72 E
80	Nam Co (L.) China	31N	91 E
84	Nam Dinh, Viet.	20N	106 E
90	Namib Des., Nam.	24S	15 E
90	Namibia (Ctry.) Afr.	21S	16 E
100	Nampa, Idaho	44N	117W
81	Namp'o, Kor.	39N	125 E
73	Namur, Bel.	50N	5 E
81	Nanchang , China	29N	116 E
80	Nanchong, China	31N	106 E
73	Nancy, Fr.	49N	6 E
83	Nanda-Devi (Mt.) India	30N	80 E
81	Nanjing, China	32N	119 E
80	Nanning, China	23N	108 E
81	Nanping, China	26N	118 E
81	Nansei Shotō (Is.) Japan	28N	128 E
73	Nantes, Fr.	47N	2W
81	Nanyang, China	33N	113 E
102	Napa, Calif.	38N	122W
73	Naples, It.	41N	14 E
81	Nara, Japan	35N	136 E
73	Narbonne, Fr.	43N	3 E
72	Narvik, Nor.	68N	17 E
71	Nar'yan-Mar, Sov. Un.	68N	53 E
76	Narym, Sov. Un.	59N	82 E
76	Naryn, Sov. Un.	41N	76 E
97	Nashua, N.H.	43N	71W
108	Nashville, Tenn.	36N	87W
75	Našice, Yugo.	45N	18 E
83	Nāsik, India	20N	74 E
111	Nassau, Bahrain	25N	77W
113	Natal, Braz.	6S	35W
108	Natchez, Miss.	32N	91W
69	Nauru (Ctry.), Pac. O.	3S	170 E
75	Nazareth, Isr.	33N	35 E
89	N'Djamena, Chad	12N	15 E
90	Ndola, Zambia	13S	29 E
72	Neagh, L., N. Ire.	55N	7W
82	Nebit-Dag, Sov. Un.	39N	54 E
94	Nebraska (State) U.S.	42N	101W
112	Negro (R.), S.A.	0	64W
112	Neiva, Col.	3N	75W
92	Nelson, B.C., Can.	49N	117W
92	Nelson (R.) Can.	56N	94W
83	Nepal (Ctry.) Asia	28N	84 E
77	Nerchinsk, Sov. Un.	52N	116 E
73	Netherlands (Ctry.) Eur.	53N	5 E
73	Neuchâtel, Switz.	47N	7 E
72	Neumünster, Ger.	54N	10 E
114	Neuquén, Arg.	39S	68W
73	Neusiedler See (L.) Aus.-Hung.	48N	16 E
94	Nevada (State) U.S.	39N	117W
74	Nevada, Sa. (Mts.) Sp.	37N	3W
73	Nevers, Fr.	47N	3 E
76	Nev'yansk, Sov. Un.	57N	60 E
96	New Albany, Ind.	38N	86W
97	Newark, N.J.	41N	73W
96	Newark, Ohio	40N	82W
97	New Bedford, Mass.	42N	71W
109	New Bern, N.C.	35N	77W
97	New Britain, Conn.	42N	73W
97	New Brunswick, N.J.	40N	74W
93	New Brunswick (Prov.) Can.	47N	66W
87	New Caledonia (Ctry.) Pac. O.	21S	164 E
87	Newcastle, Austl.	33S	152 E
97	New Castle, Pa.	41N	80W
72	Newcastle upon Tyne, Eng.	55N	2W
83	New Delhi, India	29N	77 E
93	Newfoundland (Prov.) Can.	48N	56W
85	New Guinea (I.) Asia-Oc.	5S	140 E
95	New Hampshire (State) U.S.	44N	72W
97	New Haven, Conn.	41N	73W
95	New Jersey (State) U.S.	40N	74W
97	New London, Conn.	41N	72W
94	New Mexico (State) U.S.	35N	108W
107	New Orleans, La.	30N	90W
73	Newport, Eng.	51N	1W
97	Newport, R.I.	41N	71W
97	Newport News, Va.	37N	76W
97	Newton, Mass.	42N	71W
97	New York, N.Y.	41N	74W
95	New York (State) U.S.	43N	76W
87	New Zealand (Ctry.) Pac. O.	39S	170 E
82	Neyshābūr, Iran	36N	59 E
71	Nezhin, Sov. Un.	51N	32 E
84	Nha Trang, Viet.	12N	109 E
97	Niagara Falls, N.Y.	43N	79W
88	Niamey, Niger	14N	2 E
110	Nicaragua (Ctry.) N.A.	13N	86W
73	Nicastro, It.	39N	16 E
73	Nice, Fr.	44N	7 E
84	Nicobar Is., India	8N	94 E
75	Nicosia, Cyp.	35N	33 E
75	Niğde, Tur.	38N	35 E
88	Niger (Ctry.) Afr.	16N	8 E
88	Niger (R.) Afr.	8N	6 E
88	Nigeria (Ctry.) Afr.	9N	8 E
81	Niigata, Japan	38N	139 E
71	Nikolayev, Sov. Un.	47N	32 E
76	Nikol'sk, Sov. Un.	59N	46 E
75	Nikopol, Bul.	44N	25 E
71	Nikopol', Sov. Un.	48N	34 E
89	Nile (R.) Eg.-Sud.	28N	30 E
114	Nilopólis, Braz.	23S	43W
73	Nîmes, Fr.	44N	4 E
82	Nineveh (Ruins) Iraq	36N	43 E
81	Ningbo, China	30N	121 E
81	Ningde, China	26N	120 E
93	Nipigon, Ont., Can.	49N	88W
93	Nipigon (L.) Ont., Can.	50N	89W
75	Niš, Yugo.	43N	22 E
114	Niterói, Braz.	23S	43W
77	Nizhne-Angarsk, Sov. Un.	56N	109 E
77	Nizhne-Kolymsk, Sov. Un.	69N	161 E
71	Nizhniy Novgorod, Sov. Un.	56N	44 E
71	Nizhniy Tagil, Sov. Un.	58N	60 E
83	Noākhāli, Bngl.	23N	91 E
103	Nogales, Ariz.	31N	111W
110	Nogales, Mex.	31N	111W
71	Noginsk, Sov. Un.	56N	38 E
94	Nome, Alsk.	64N	165W
77	Nordvik, Sov. Un.	74N	111 E
98	Norfolk, Nebr.	42N	97W
97	Norfolk, Va.	37N	76W
77	Noril'sk, Sov. Un.	69N	87 E
97	Norristown, Pa.	40N	75W
72	Norrköping, Swe.	59N	16 E
73	Northampton, Eng.	52N	1W
97	Northampton, Mass.	42N	73W
95	North Carolina (State) U.S.	36N	79W
96	North Channel (B.) Can.	46N	83W
96	North Chicago, Ill.	42N	88W
94	North Dakota (State) U.S.	48N	100W
72	Northern Ireland (Polit. Reg.), U.K.	55N	7W
69	Northern Mariana Is. (Ctry.), Pac. O.	16N	146 E
110	North Gamboa, Pan.	9N	80W
87	North I., N.Z.	38S	171 E
96	North Judson, Ind.	41N	87W
105	North Little Rock, Ark.	35N	92W
104	North Platte (R.) Nebr.	41N	101W
92	North Saskatchewan (R.) Can.	54N	111W
72	North Sea, Eur.	56N	2 E
97	North Tonawanda, N.Y.	43N	79W
92	North Vancouver, B.C., Can.	49N	105W
92	Northwest Territories, Can.	65N	105W
97	Norwalk, Conn.	41N	73W
72	Norway (Ctry.) Eur.	65N	13 E
72	Norwegian Sea, Eur.	66N	1 E
97	Norwich, Conn.	41N	72W
73	Norwich, Eng.	53N	1 E
96	Norwood, Ohio	39N	84W
73	Nottingham, Eng.	53N	1W
88	Nouakchott, Maur.	18N	16W
87	Noumea, N. Cal.	22S	167 E
114	Nova Iguaçu, Braz.	23S	43W
73	Novara, It.	45N	9 E
93	Nova Scotia (Prov.) Can.	45N	64W
76	Novaya Zemlya (Is.) Sov. Un.	72N	54 E
73	Nové Zámky, Czech.	48N	18 E
70	Novgorod, Sov. Un.	59N	31 E
75	Novi-Pazar, Yugo.	43N	20 E
75	Novi Sad, Yugo.	45N	20 E
71	Novocherkassk, Sov. Un.	47N	40 E
76	Novo-Kazalinsk, Sov. Un.	46N	62 E
76	Novokuznetsk, Sov. Un.	54N	87 E
71	Novomoskovsk, Sov. Un.	54N	38 E
71	Novorossiysk, Sov. Un.	45N	38 E
76	Novosibirsk, Sov. Un.	55N	83 E
77	Novosibirskiye Ostrava (New Siberian Is.), Sov. Un.	75N	141 E
76	Novyy Port, Sov. Un.	67N	72 E
73	Nowy Sącz, Pol.	50N	21 E
90	Ntwetwe Pan (Basin) Bots.	20S	25 E
89	Nubian Des., Sud.	21N	33 E
110	Nuevo Laredo, Mex.	27N	99W
110	Nuevo San Juan, Pan.	9N	80W
86	Nullarbor Plain, Austl.	32S	128 E
76	Nurata, Sov. Un.	41N	65 E
73	Nürnberg, Ger.	49N	11 E
83	Nushki, Pak.	29N	66 E
89	Nyala, Sud.	12N	25 E
90	Nyasa, L., Afr.	12S	35 E
73	Nyíregyháza, Hung.	48N	22 E

O

Page	Place	Lat.°′	Long.°′
102	Oakland, Calif.	38N	122W
96	Oak Park, Ill.	42N	88W
108	Oak Ridge, Tenn.	36N	84W
110	Oaxaca, Mex.	17N	97W
76	Ob' (R.) Sov. Un.	63N	67 E
75	Ödemiş, Tur.	38N	28 E
72	Odense, Den.	55N	10 E
71	Odessa, Sov. Un.	46N	31 E
88	Ogbomosho, Nig.	8N	4 E
101	Ogden, Utah	41N	112W
92	Ogilvie Mts., Yukon, Can.	65N	139W
96	Ohio (R.), U.S.	37N	88W
95	Ohio (State) U.S.	40N	83W
81	Okayama, Japan	35N	134 E
77	Okha, Sov. Un.	54N	143 E
77	Okhotsk, Sea of, Japan-Sov. Un.	57N	147 E
94	Oklahoma (State) U.S.	36N	98W
105	Oklahoma City, Okla.	35N	98W
90	Okovango Swamp, Bots.	19S	23 E
114	Olavarría, Arg.	37S	60W
92	Old Crow, Yukon, Can.	68N	140W
73	Oldenburg, Ger.	53N	8 E
92	Olds, Alta., Can.	52N	114W
97	Olean, N.Y.	42N	78W
77	Olekminsk, Sov. Un.	61N	121 E
77	Ol'ga, Sov. Un.	44N	136 E
74	Olhão, Port.	37N	8W
113	Olinda, Braz.	8S	35W
114	Olivos, Arg.	34S	58W
73	Olomouc, Czech.	50N	17 E
74	Olot, Sp.	42N	3 E
72	Olsztyn, Pol.	54N	20 E
100	Olympia, Wash.	47N	123W
105	Omaha, Nebr.	41N	96W
82	Oman (Ctry.) Asia	19N	57 E
82	Oman, G. of, Asia	25N	57 E
89	Omdurman, Sud.	16N	32 E
76	Omsk, Sov. Un.	55N	73 E
81	Öndörhaan, Mong.	47N	111 E
71	Onega, Sov. Un.	64N	38 E
71	Onezhskoye Ozero (L. Onega), Sov. Un.	62N	37 E
88	Onitsha, Nig.	6N	6 E
93	Ontario (Prov.) Can.	50N	89W
97	Ontario, L., Can.-U.S.	44N	78W
73	Oostende, Bel.	51N	3 E
73	Opole, Pol.	51N	18 E
75	Oradea, Rom.	47N	22 E
88	Oran, Alg.	36N	1W
90	Orange (R.) Afr.	29S	18 E
90	Oranjemund, Nam.	29S	16 E
75	Ordu, Tur.	41N	38 E
82	Ordzhonikidze, Sov. Un.	43N	45 E
72	Örebro, Swe.	59N	15 E
94	Oregon (State) U.S.	44N	120W
76	Orekhovo-Zuyevo, Sov. Un.	56N	39 E
71	Orël, Sov. Un.	53N	36 E
71	Orenburg, Sov. Un.	52N	55 E
112	Oriental, Cordillera (Ra.) S.A.	14S	68W
112	Orinoco (R.) Col.-Ven.	8N	65W
73	Oristano, It.	40N	9 E
110	Orizaba, Mex.	19N	97W
72	Orkney Is., Scot.	59N	2W
109	Orlando, Fla.	29N	81W
91	Orlando, S. Afr.	26S	28 E
73	Orléans, Fr.	48N	2 E
71	Orsk, Sov. Un.	51N	59 E
112	Oruro, Bol.	18S	67W
81	Ōsaka, Japan	35N	135 E

121

San Fernando, Phil.

Page	Place	Lat.°′	Long.°′
76	Osh, Sov. Un.	40N	73 E
93	Oshawa, Ont., Can.	44N	79W
99	Oshkosh, Wis.	44N	89W
88	Oshogbo, Nig.	8N	4 E
75	Osijek, Yugo.	46N	19 E
72	Oslo, Nor.	60N	11W
114	Osorno, Chile	41S	73W
73	Ostrava, Czech.	50N	18 E
73	Ostrowiec Swiętokrzyski, Pol.	51N	21 E
73	Ostrów Wielkopolski, Pol.	52N	18 E
81	Otaru , Japan	43N	141 E
93	Ottawa, Ont., Can.	45N	76W
93	Ottawa (R.) Can.	46N	77W
99	Ottumwa, Iowa	41N	92W
88	Ouagadougou, Burkina	12N	2W
88	Oujda, Mor.	35N	2W
72	Oulu, Fin.	65N	26 E
74	Oviedo, Sp.	43N	6W
96	Owensboro, Ky.	38N	87W
73	Oxford, Eng.	52N	1W
96	Oxford, Ohio	39N	85W
88	Oyo, Nig.	8N	4 E
73	Ozieri, It.	41N	9 E
	P		
110	Pachuca, Mex.	20N	99W
69	Pacific Is., Trust Ter. of the (Ctry.), Pac. O.	10N	155 E
84	Padang, Indon.	1S	100 E
73	Padova, It.	45N	12 E
107	Padre I., Tex.	27N	97W
72	Paisley, Scot.	56N	4W
83	Pakistan (Ctry.) Asia	30N	71 E
77	Palana, Sov. Un.	59N	160 E
69	Palau (Ctry.), Pac. O.	8N	135 E
84	Palembang, Indon.	3S	105 E
74	Palencia, Sp.	42N	5W
73	Palermo, It.	38N	13 E
74	Palma, Sp.	40N	3 E
112	Palmira, Col.	4N	76W
112	Palúa, Ven.	9N	63W
82	Pamirs (Mts.) Asia	38N	73 E
104	Pampa, Tex.	36N	101W
114	Pampa (Reg.) Arg.	35S	64W
83	Panaji (Panjim), India	16N	74 E
111	Panamá, Pan.	9N	80W
111	Panama (Ctry.) N.A.	8N	80W
111	Panama, G. of, Pan.	8N	80W
108	Panama City, Fla.	30N	86W
75	Pančevo, Yugo.	45N	21 E
73	Pápa, Hung.	47N	17 E
75	Papua New Guinea (Ctry.) Pac. O.	7S	142 E
114	Paraguay (R.) S.A.	25S	58W
114	Paraguay (Ctry.) S.A.	24S	57W
113	Paramaribo, Sur.	5N	55W
114	Paraná, Arg.	32S	60W
114	Paraná (R.) S.A.	25S	54W
73	Paris, Fr.	49N	2 E
105	Paris, Tex.	34N	96W
96	Parkersburg, W. Va.	39N	82W
73	Parma, It.	45N	10 E
96	Parma, Ohio	41N	82W
113	Parnaíba, Braz.	3S	42W
72	Pärnu, Est.	58N	24 E
105	Parsons, Kans.	37N	95W
102	Pasadena, Calif.	34N	118W
97	Passaic, N.J.	41N	74W
112	Pasto, Col.	1N	77W
114	Patagonia (Reg.) Arg.	44S	46W
84	Pathein, Bur.	17N	95 E
83	Patiāla, India	30N	76 E
83	Patna, India	26N	85 E
114	Patos, Lago dos (L.) Braz.	31S	53W
75	Pátrai, Grc.	38N	22 E
97	Patterson, N.J.	41N	74W
73	Pau, Fr.	43N	0
73	Pavia, It.	45N	9 E
76	Pavlodar, Sov. Un.	52N	77 E
75	Pavlograd, Sov. Un.	49N	36 E
97	Pawtucket, R.I.	42N	71W
114	Paysandú, Ur.	32S	58W
97	Peabody, Mass.	43N	71W
92	Peace (R.) Can.	57N	117W
91	Pebane, Moz.	17S	38 E
73	Peć, Yugo.	43N	20 E
70	Pechenga, Sov. Un.	70N	31 E
94	Pecos (R.) U.S.	31N	103W
75	Pećs, Hung.	46N	18 E
77	Peleduy, Sov. Un.	60N	113 E
92	Pelly Mts., Yukon, Can.	62N	134W
114	Pelotas, Braz.	32S	52W
93	Pembroke, Ont., Can.	46N	77W
100	Pendleton, Oreg.	46N	119W
95	Pennsylvania (State) U.S.	41N	78W
108	Pensacola, Fla.	30N	87W
92	Penticton, B.C., Can.	49N	119W
71	Penza, Sov. Un.	53N	45 E
77	Penzhino, Sov. Un.	64N	168 E
96	Peoria, Ill.	41N	90W
112	Pereira, Col.	5N	76W
114	Pergamino, Arg.	34S	61W
73	Perigueux, Fr.	45N	1 E
71	Perm', Sov. Un.	58N	56 E
75	Pernik, Bul.	43N	23 E
73	Perpignan, Fr.	43N	3 E
82	Persian G., Asia	28N	50 E
86	Perth, Austl.	32S	116 E
72	Perth, Scot.	56N	3W
97	Perth Amboy, N.J.	41N	74W
112	Peru (Ctry.) S.A.	10S	75W
73	Perugia, It.	43N	12 E
75	Pervomaysk, Sov. Un.	48N	31 E
73	Pesaro, It.	44N	13 E
83	Peshāwar, Pak.	34N	72 E
93	Peterborough, Ont., Can.	44N	78W
109	Petersburg, Va.	37N	78W
75	Petrich, Bul.	41N	23 E
76	Petropavlovsk, Sov. Un.	55N	69 E
77	Petropavlovsk-Kamchatskiy, Sov. Un.	53N	159 E
114	Petrópolis, Braz.	23S	43W
71	Petrozavodsk, Sov. Un.	62N	34 E
108	Phenix City, Ala.	32N	85W
97	Philadelphia, Pa.	40N	75W
85	Philippines (Ctry.) Asia	14N	125 E
81	Philippine Sea, Asia	25N	129 E
84	Phnum Pénh, Camb.	12N	105 E
103	Phoenix, Ariz.	33N	112W
73	Piacenza, It.	45N	10 E
75	Piatra-Neamt, Rom.	47N	26 E
110	Piedras Negras, Mex.	29N	101W
98	Pierre, S. Dak.	44N	100W
90	Pietermaritzburg, S. Afr.	30S	30 E
74	Pieve, It.	46N	12 E
114	Pilcomayo (R.) S.A.	24S	60W
111	Pinar del Rio, Cuba	22N	84W
105	Pine Bluff, Ark.	34N	92W
76	Pinega, Sov. Un.	65N	43 E
70	Pinsk, Sov. Un.	52N	26 E
73	Piombino , It.	43N	11 E
73	Piotrkow Trybunalski, Pol.	51N	20 E
113	Piracicaba, Braz.	23S	48W
75	Piraiévs, Grc.	38N	24 E
75	Pirot, Yugo.	43N	23 E
73	Pisa, It.	44N	10 E
76	Pishpek, Sov. Un.	43N	75 E
73	Pistoia, It.	44N	12 E
68	Pitcairn (Ctry.), Pac. O.	25S	120W
75	Pitesti, Rom.	45N	25 E
105	Pittsburg, Kans.	37N	95W
97	Pittsburgh, Pa.	40N	80W
97	Pittsfield, Mass.	42N	73W
112	Piura, Peru	5S	81W
97	Plainfield, N.J.	41N	74W
114	Plata, R. de la, Arg.-Ur.	35S	58W
98	Platte (R.) Nebr.	41N	100W
73	Plauen, Ger.	50N	12 E
75	Pleven, Bul.	43N	24 E
75	Pljevlja, Yugo.	43N	19 E
75	Ploieşti, Rom.	45N	26 E
75	Plovdiv, Bul.	42N	25 E
73	Plymouth, Eng.	50N	4W
73	Plzeň, Czech.	50N	13 E
73	Po (R.) It.	45N	11 E
101	Pocatello, Idaho	43N	112W
111	Pointe-à-Pitre, Guad.	16N	62W
90	Pointe Noire, Congo	5S	12 E
73	Poitiers, Fr.	47N	0
73	Poland (Ctry.) Eur.	52N	18 E
71	Poltava, Sov. Un.	50N	35 E
102	Pomona, Calif.	34N	118W
111	Ponce, P.R.	18N	67W
83	Pondicherry, India	12N	80 E
88	Ponta Delgada, Port.	38N	26W
114	Ponta Grossa, Braz.	25S	50W
113	Ponta Pora, Braz.	22S	56W
96	Pontiac, Mich.	43N	83W
84	Pontianak, Indon.	0	109 E
112	Poopo, Lago de (L.) Bol.	18S	68W
112	Popayán, Col.	2N	77W
83	Porbandar, India	22N	70 E
72	Pori, Fin.	61N	22 E
77	Poronaysk, Sov. Un.	49N	143 E
92	Port Alice, B.C., Can.	50N	127W
100	Port Angeles, Wash.	48N	123W
111	Port Antonio, Jam.	18N	76W
107	Port Arthur, Tex.	30N	94W
111	Port-au-Prince, Hai.	19N	72W
90	Port Elizabeth, S. Afr.	34S	26 E
88	Port Harcourt, Nig.	5N	7 E
96	Port Huron, Mich.	43N	82W
97	Portland, Maine	44N	70W
100	Portland, Oreg.	46N	123W
85	Port Moresby, Pap. N. Gui.	10S	147 E
74	Porto, Port.	41N	9W
114	Porto Alegre, Braz.	30S	51W
111	Port of Spain, Trin.	11N	61W
88	Porto-Novo, Benin	7N	3 E
112	Porto Velho, Braz.	9S	64W
89	Port Said, Eg.	31N	32 E
73	Portsmouth, Eng.	51N	1W
97	Portsmouth, N.H.	43N	71W
96	Portsmouth, Ohio	39N	83W
97	Portsmouth, Va.	37N	76W
74	Portugal (Ctry.) Eur.	40N	8W
114	Posadas, Arg.	28S	56W
73	Potenza, It.	41N	16 E
71	Poti, Sov. Un.	42N	42 E
97	Potomac (R.) U.S.	38N	77W
112	Potosí, Bol.	20S	66W
73	Potsdam, Ger.	52N	13 E
97	Pottstown, Pa.	40N	76W
97	Pottsville, Pa.	41N	76W
97	Poughkeepsie, N.Y.	42N	74W
81	Poyang Hu (L.) China	29N	117 E
73	Poznan, Pol.	52N	17 E
73	Prague (Praha), Czech.	50N	14 E
88	Praia, C.V.	15N	23W
73	Přerov, Czech.	49N	17 E
103	Prescott, Ariz.	34N	112W
73	Prešov, Czech.	49N	21 E
90	Pretoria, S. Afr.	26S	28 E
75	Prilep, Yugo.	41N	22 E
92	Prince Albert, Sask., Can.	53N	106W
93	Prince Edward Island (Prov.) Can.	47N	63W
92	Prince George, B.C., Can.	54N	123W
92	Prince Rupert, B.C., Can.	54N	130W
75	Priština, Yugo.	43N	21 E
75	Prizren, Yugo.	42N	21 E
84	Prome (Pye), Bur.	19N	95 E
97	Providence, R.I.	42N	71W
103	Provo, Utah	40N	112W
73	Przemysl, Pol.	50N	23 E
80	Przheval'sk, Sov. Un.	42N	78 E
70	Pskov, Sov. Un.	58N	28 E
110	Puebla, Mex.	19N	98W
104	Pueblo, Col.	38N	105W
114	Puerto Aisén, Chile	46S	73W
112	Puerto Cabello, Ven.	10N	68W
114	Puerto Deseado, Arg.	48S	66W
112	Puerto la Cruz, Ven.	10N	65W
74	Puertollano, Sp.	39N	4W
114	Puerto Natales, Chile	52S	72W
111	Puerto Rico (Ctry.) N.A.	18N	67W
114	Puerto Santa Cruz, Arg.	50S	69W
113	Puerto Suárez, Bol.	19S	58W
100	Puget Sound, Wash.	48N	122W
74	Pula, Yugo.	45N	14 E
83	Punakha, Bhu.	28N	90 E
83	Pune, India	18N	72 E
114	Punta Arenas, Chile	53S	71W
112	Punto Fijo, Ven.	12N	70W
83	Puri, India	20N	86 E
81	Pusan, Kor.	35N	129 E
71	Pyatigorsk, Sov. Un.	44N	43 E
84	Pyinmana, Bur.	20N	96 E
81	P'yŏngyang, Kor.	39N	126 E
74	Pyrenees (Mts.) Fr.-Sp.	43N	0
	Q		
80	Qamdo, China	31N	97 E
83	Qandahār, Afg.	32N	66 E
89	Qaşr al Burayqah, Libya	30N	19 E
82	Qatar (Ctry.) Asia	25N	51 E
82	Qeshm, Iran	27N	56 E
89	Qinā, Eg.	26N	33 E
81	Qingdao, China	36N	120 E
81	Qiqihar, China	47N	124 E
80	Qitai , China	44N	89 E
82	Qom, Iran	34N	51 E
82	Qomsheh, Iran	32N	52 E
81	Quanzhou, China	25N	119 E
93	Québec, Que., Can.	47N	71W
93	Quebec (Prov.) Can.	52N	70W
92	Queen Charlotte Is., B.C., Can.	54N	133W
110	Querétaro, Mex.	21N	100W
83	Quetta, Pak.	30N	67 E
110	Quezaltenango, Guat.	15N	91W
85	Quezon City, Phil.	15N	121 E
112	Quibdó, Col.	6N	77W
114	Quilmes, Arg.	34S	58W
83	Quilon, India	9N	76 E
73	Quimper, Fr.	48N	4W
97	Quincy, Mass.	42N	71W
112	Quito, Ec.	0	79W
81	Quxian, China	29N	119 E
	R		
88	Rabat, Mor.	34N	7W
99	Racine, Wis.	43N	88W
73	Radom, Pol.	51N	21 E
114	Rafaela, Arg.	31S	61W
82	Rafḩā, Sau. Ar.	30N	43 E
74	Ragusa, It.	37N	15 E
83	Raigarh, India	22N	84 E
100	Rainier, Mt., Wash.	47N	122W
93	Rainy River, Ont., Can.	49N	94W
83	Raipur, India	21N	82 E
83	Rājahmundry, India	17N	82 E
83	Rājkot, India	22N	71 E
83	Rājshāhi, Pak.	24N	89 E
109	Raleigh, N.C.	36N	79W
83	Rāmpur, India	29N	79 E
114	Rancagua, Chile	34S	71W
83	Rānchī, India	23N	85 E
106	Ranger, Tex.	32N	99W
84	Rangoon (Yangon), Bur.	17N	96 E
83	Rangpur, Bngl.	26N	89 E
98	Rapid City, S. Dak.	44N	103W
75	Rashīd, Eg.	31N	30 E
82	Rasht, Iran	37N	50 E
104	Raton, N. Mex.	37N	104W
73	Ravenna, It.	44N	12 E
83	Rāwalpindi, Pak.	34N	73 E
82	Rawāndūz, Iraq	37N	44 E
101	Rawlins, Wyo.	42N	107W
114	Rawson, Arg.	43S	65W
73	Reading, Eng.	51N	1W
97	Reading, Pa.	40N	76W
113	Recife (Pernambuco), Braz.	8S	35W
92	Red (R.) Can.-U.S.	48N	97W
84	Red (R.) China-Viet.	21N	104 E
94	Red (R.) U.S.	32N	93W
92	Red Deer, Alta., Can.	52N	114W
100	Redding, Calif.	40N	122W
82	Red Sea, Afr.-Asia	24N	37 E
73	Regensburg, Ger.	49N	12 E
73	Reggio di Calabria, It.	38N	16 E
73	Reggio nell'Emilia, It.	45N	11 E
92	Regina, Sask., Can.	51N	104W
73	Reims, Fr.	49N	4 E
92	Reindeer L., Can.	58N	102W
73	Rennes, Fr.	48N	1W
102	Reno, Nev.	40N	120W
114	Resistencia, Arg.	27S	59W
69	Reunion (Ctry.), Ind. O.	22S	56 E
74	Reus, Sp.	41N	1 E
83	Rewa, India	25N	81 E
72	Reykajavik, Ice.	64N	22W
73	Rhein (R.) Eur.	51N	7 E
95	Rhode Island (State) U.S.	42N	72W
74	Rhône (R.) Fr.-Switz.	44N	5 E
113	Ribeirão Prêto, Braz.	21S	48W
100	Richland, Wash.	46N	119W
97	Richmond, Va.	38N	77W
73	Rieti, It.	42N	13 E
70	Rīga, Lat.	57N	24 E
82	Rīgān, Iran	29N	59 E
74	Rijeka, Yugo.	45N	13 E
73	Rimini, It.	44N	13 E
72	Ringkobing, Den.	56N	8 E
112	Riobamba, Ec.	2S	79W
112	Rio Branco, Braz.	10S	68W
114	Río Cuarto, Arg.	33S	64W
114	Rio de Janeiro, Braz.	23S	43W
114	Río Gallegos, Arg.	52S	68W
114	Rio Grande, Braz.	31S	52W
94	Rio Grande (R.) Mex.-U.S.	26N	98W
88	Rio Muni (Polit. Reg.), Eq. Gui.	2N	10 E
102	Riverside, Calif.	34N	117W
82	Riyadh, Sau. Ar.	25N	47 E
75	Rize, Tur.	41N	40 E
73	Roanne, Fr.	46N	4 E
109	Roanoke, Va.	37N	80W
114	Rocha, Ur.	34S	54W
73	Rochefort, Fr.	46N	1W
99	Rochester, Minn.	44N	92W
97	Rochester, N.Y.	43N	78W
96	Rockford, Ill.	42N	89W
87	Rockhampton, Austl.	23S	150 E
109	Rock Hill, S.C.	35N	81W
99	Rock Island, Ill.	42N	96W
101	Rock Springs, Wyo.	42N	109W
97	Rockville Centre, N.Y.	41N	74W
94	Rocky Mts., N.A.	45N	110W
75	Rodhós, Grc.	36N	28 E
75	Romania (Ctry.) Eur.	46N	23 E
108	Rome, Ga.	34N	85W
73	Rome, It.	42N	13 E
91	Roodepoort, S. Afr.	26S	28 E
114	Rosario, Arg.	33S	61W
100	Roseburg, Oreg.	43N	123W
73	Rosenheim, Ger.	48N	12 E
72	Rostock, Ger.	54N	12 E
71	Rostov-na-Donu, Sov. Un.	47N	40 E
104	Roswell, N. Mex.	33N	105W
73	Rotterdam, Neth.	52N	4 E
73	Rouen, Fr.	49N	22 E
96	Royal Oak, Mich.	42N	83W
76	Rubtsovsk, Sov. Un.	52N	81 E
89	Rudolf, L., Eth.-Ken.	4N	36 E
88	Rufisque, Sen.	15N	17W
75	Ruse, Bul.	44N	26 E
92	Russell, Man., Can.	51N	101W
90	Rwanda (Ctry.) Afr.	2S	30 E
71	Ryazan, Sov. Un.	55N	40 E
71	Rybinsk, Sov. Un.	58N	39 E
73	Rzeszow, Pol.	50N	22 E
71	Rzhev , Sov. Un.	56N	34 E
	S		
73	Saarbrücken, Ger.	49N	7 E
75	Šabac, Yugo.	45N	20 E
84	Sabah (Polit. Reg.), Mala.	5N	116 E
107	Sabine (R.) U.S.	30N	94W
102	Sacramento, Calif.	39N	121W
102	Sacramento (R.) Calif.	38N	122W
75	Safad, Isr.	33N	35 E
88	Safi (Asfi), Mor.	32N	9W
83	Sāgar, India	24N	79 E
96	Saginaw, Mich.	43N	84W
93	Saguenay (R.) Que., Can.	48N	71W
74	Sagunto, Sp.	40N	0
83	Sahāranpur, India	30N	78 E
88	Saïda, Alg.	35N	0
109	St. Agustine, Fla.	30N	81W
73	St. Brieuc, Fr.	49N	3W
93	St. Catharines, Ont., Can.	43N	79W
97	St. Clair, L., Can.-U.S.	42N	83W
99	St. Cloud, Minn.	46N	94W
73	St. Denis, Fr.	40N	2 E
73	St. Étienne, Fr.	45N	4 E
93	St. George's, Newf., Can.	48N	58W
73	St. George's Chan., Eur.	52N	7W
68	St. Helena (Ctry.), Atl. O.	15S	10W
100	St. Helens, Mt. (Vol.) Wash.	46N	122W
93	St. Hyacinthe, Que., Can.	46N	73W
93	St. John, N.B., Can.	45N	66W
93	St. John's, Newf., Can.	48N	53W
105	St. Joseph, Mo.	40N	95W
111	St. Kitts and Nevis (Ctry.) N.A.	17N	63W
93	St. Lawrence (R.) Can.-U.S.	48N	69W
93	St. Lawrence, G. of, Can.	48N	62W
105	St. Louis, Mo.	39N	90W
88	St. Louis, Sen.	16N	16W
111	St. Lucia (Ctry.) N.A.	14N	61W
73	St. Malo, Fr.	49N	2W
73	St. Nazaire, Fr.	48N	2W
92	St. Paul, Alta., Can.	54N	111W
99	St. Paul, Minn.	45N	93W
109	St. Petersburg, Fla.	28N	83W
70	St. Petersburg, Sov. Un.	60N	30 E
93	St. Pierre and Miquelon (Ctry.) N.A.	47N	57W
73	St. Quentin, Fr.	50N	3 E
111	St. Vincent and the Grenadines (Ctry.) N.A.	13N	61W
82	Sakākah, Sau. Ar.	30N	40 E
74	Salamanca, Sp.	41N	6W
88	Salé, Mor.	34N	7W
76	Salekhard, Sov. Un.	67N	67 E
83	Salem, India	12N	78 E
97	Salem, Mass.	43N	71W
100	Salem, Oreg.	45N	123W
73	Salerno, It.	40N	15 E
105	Salina, Kans.	39N	98W
110	Salina Cruz, Mex.	16N	95W
102	Salinas, Calif.	37N	122W
73	Salisbury, Eng.	51N	2W
114	Salta, Arg.	25S	65W
103	Salt Lake City, Utah	41N	112W
114	Salto, Ur.	31S	58W
102	Salton Sea (L.) Calif.	33N	116W
113	Salvador (Bahia), Braz.	13S	38W
84	Salween (R.), Asia	21N	98 E
73	Salzburg, Aus.	48N	13 E
71	Samara, Sov. Un.	53N	50 E
76	Samarkand, Sov. Un.	40N	67 E
75	Samsun, Tur.	41N	36 E
82	San'ā', Yemen	16N	44 E
82	Sanandaj, Iran	36N	47 E
106	San Angelo, Tex.	31N	100W
106	San Antonio, Tex.	29N	98W
114	San Antonio Oeste, Arg.	41S	65W
102	San Bernardino, Calif.	34N	117W
114	San Bernardo, Chile	34S	71W
112	San Cristóbal, Ven.	8N	72W
111	Sancti Spíritus, Cuba	22N	79W
102	San Diego, Calif.	33N	117W
100	Sandpoint, Idaho	48N	116W
96	Sandusky, Ohio	41N	83W
114	San Fernando, Arg.	34S	59W
85	San Fernando, Phil.	17N	120 E

Sanford, Fla.

FLAGS

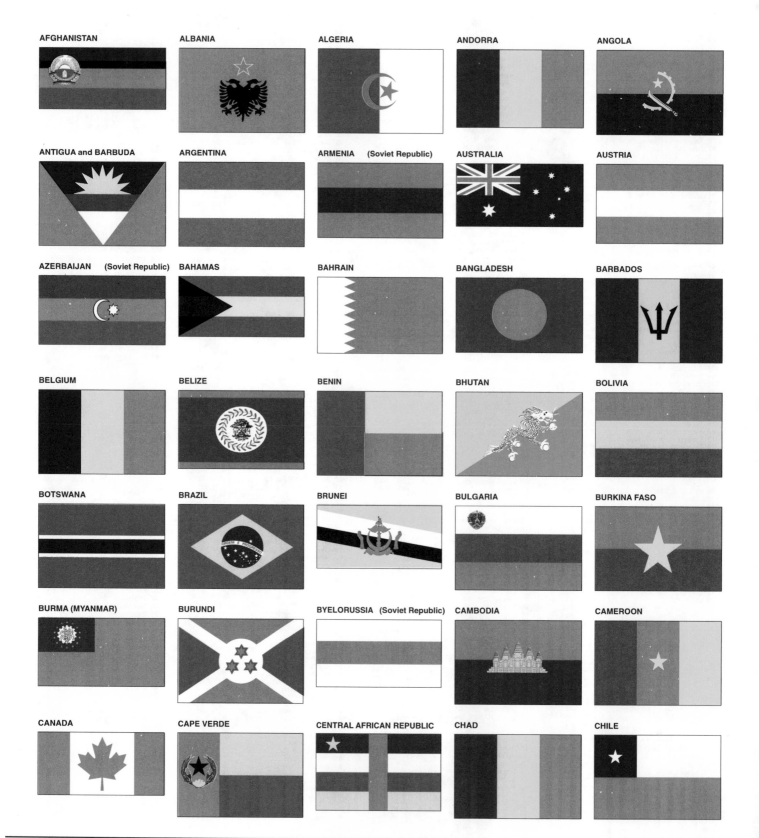

AFGHANISTAN ALBANIA ALGERIA ANDORRA ANGOLA

ANTIGUA and BARBUDA ARGENTINA ARMENIA (Soviet Republic) AUSTRALIA AUSTRIA

AZERBAIJAN (Soviet Republic) BAHAMAS BAHRAIN BANGLADESH BARBADOS

BELGIUM BELIZE BENIN BHUTAN BOLIVIA

BOTSWANA BRAZIL BRUNEI BULGARIA BURKINA FASO

BURMA (MYANMAR) BURUNDI BYELORUSSIA (Soviet Republic) CAMBODIA CAMEROON

CANADA CAPE VERDE CENTRAL AFRICAN REPUBLIC CHAD CHILE

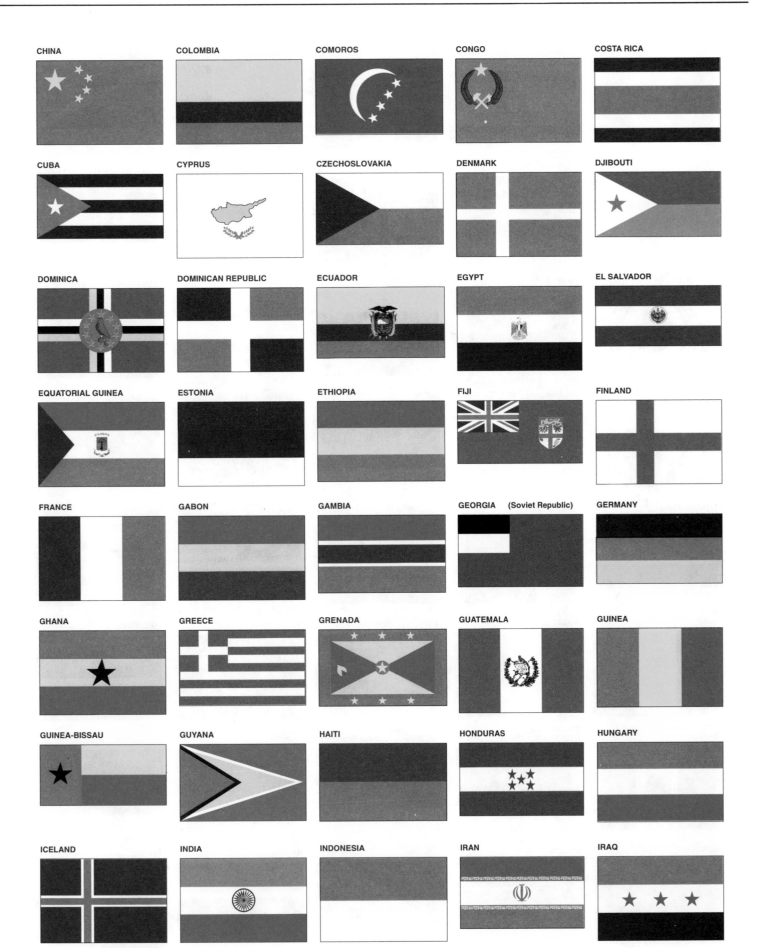

| CHINA | COLOMBIA | COMOROS | CONGO | COSTA RICA |

| CUBA | CYPRUS | CZECHOSLOVAKIA | DENMARK | DJIBOUTI |

| DOMINICA | DOMINICAN REPUBLIC | ECUADOR | EGYPT | EL SALVADOR |

| EQUATORIAL GUINEA | ESTONIA | ETHIOPIA | FIJI | FINLAND |

| FRANCE | GABON | GAMBIA | GEORGIA (Soviet Republic) | GERMANY |

| GHANA | GREECE | GRENADA | GUATEMALA | GUINEA |

| GUINEA-BISSAU | GUYANA | HAITI | HONDURAS | HUNGARY |

| ICELAND | INDIA | INDONESIA | IRAN | IRAQ |

FLAGS

IRELAND

ISRAEL

ITALY

IVORY COAST

JAMAICA

JAPAN

JORDAN

KENYA

KIRIBATI

KOREA, NORTH

KOREA, SOUTH

KUWAIT

LAOS

LATVIA

LEBANON

LESOTHO

LIBERIA

LIBYA

LIECHTENSTEIN

LITHUANIA

LUXEMBOURG

MADAGASCAR

MALAWI

MALAYSIA

MALDIVES

MALI

MALTA

MARSHALL ISLANDS

MAURITANIA

MAURITIUS

MEXICO

MICRONESIA, FEDERATED STATES of

MOLDAVIA   (Soviet Republic)

MONACO

MONGOLIA

MOROCCO

MOZAMBIQUE

NAMIBIA

NAURU

NEPAL

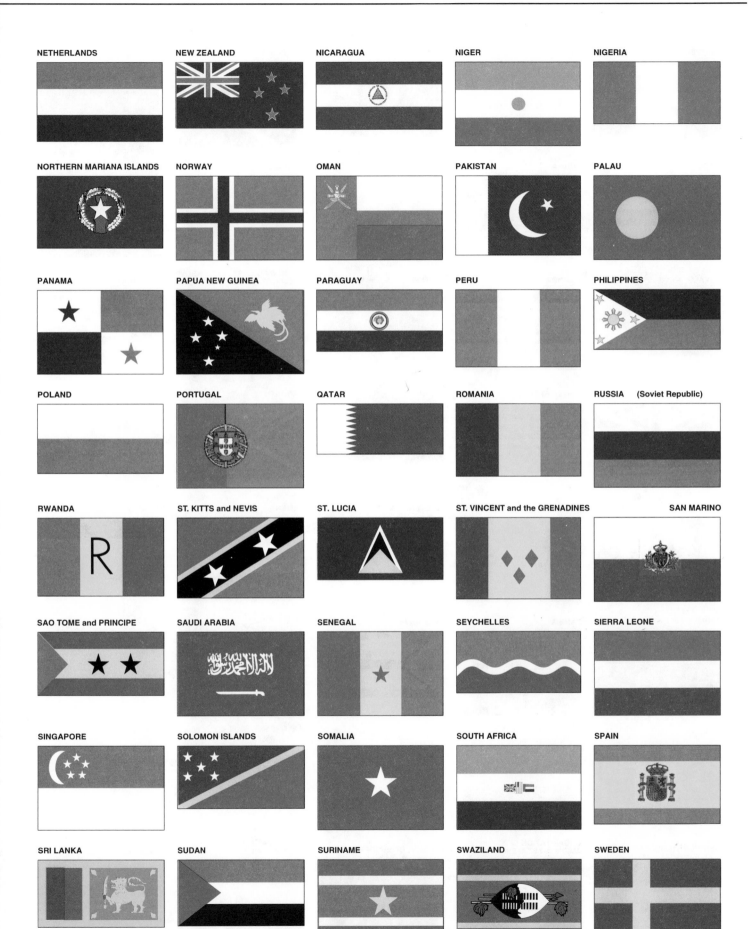

NETHERLANDS

NEW ZEALAND

NICARAGUA

NIGER

NIGERIA

NORTHERN MARIANA ISLANDS

NORWAY

OMAN

PAKISTAN

PALAU

PANAMA

PAPUA NEW GUINEA

PARAGUAY

PERU

PHILIPPINES

POLAND

PORTUGAL

QATAR

ROMANIA

RUSSIA   (Soviet Republic)

RWANDA

ST. KITTS and NEVIS

ST. LUCIA

ST. VINCENT and the GRENADINES

SAN MARINO

SAO TOME and PRINCIPE

SAUDI ARABIA

SENEGAL

SEYCHELLES

SIERRA LEONE

SINGAPORE

SOLOMON ISLANDS

SOMALIA

SOUTH AFRICA

SPAIN

SRI LANKA

SUDAN

SURINAME

SWAZILAND

SWEDEN

FLAGS

SWITZERLAND

SYRIA

TAIWAN

TANZANIA

THAILAND

TOGO
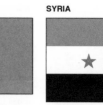

TONGA

TRINIDAD and TOBAGO

TUNISIA

TURKEY

TUVALU

UGANDA

UKRAINE   (Soviet Republic)

UNION OF SOVIET SOCIALIST REPUBLICS   (SOVIET UNION)

UNITED ARAB EMIRATES

UNITED KINGDOM

UNITED STATES

URUGUAY

VANUATU

VATICAN CITY

VENEZUELA

VIETNAM

WESTERN SAMOA

YEMEN

YUGOSLAVIA

ZAIRE

ZAMBIA

ZIMBABWE

UNITED NATIONS

ORGANIZATION OF AMERICAN STATES

COUNCIL OF EUROPE

ORGANIZATION OF AFRICAN UNITY

OLYMPICS

WORLD GAZETTEER
PROFILES OF NATIONS AND PLACES

The following World Gazetteer presents an up-to-date overview of the world's independent countries and their possessions. Geographic, political, and population-related information is derived from the most current Rand McNally data available. Ethnic groups, religions, trade partners, exports, and imports are listed in order of decreasing size and/or importance. Languages are similarly organized, with official language(s) listed first. Political parties are cited alphabetically, as are membership entries, which represent member nations of the following organizations:

Arab League (AL)
Association of South East Asian Nations (ASEAN)
Commonwealth of Nations (CW)
European Community (EC)
North Atlantic Treaty Organization (NATO)
Organization for Economic Cooperation and Development (OECD)
Organization of African Unity (OAU)
Organization of American States (OAS)
Organization of Petroleum Exporting Countries (OPEC)
United Nations (UN)

AFGHANISTAN

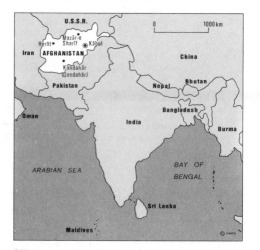

Official name Republic of Afghanistan
PEOPLE
Population 16,400,000. **Density** 65/mi² (25/km²).
Urban 22%. **Capital** Kabul, 1,424,400. **Ethnic groups**
Pathan 50%, Tajik 25%, Uzbek 9%, Hazara 9%.
Languages Dari, Pashto, Uzbek, Turkmen. **Religions**
Sunni Muslim 74%, Shiite Muslim 15%. **Life**
expectancy 44 female, 43 male. **Literacy** 20%.
POLITICS
Government Republic. **Parties** Homeland. **Suffrage**
Males, between 15 and 50. **Memberships** UN.
Subdivisions 29 provinces.
ECONOMY
GNP $3,520,000,000 **Per capita** $240. **Monetary unit**
Afghani. **Trade partners** Exports: U.S.S.R., Pakistan,
India. Imports: U.S.S.R., Japan. **Exports** Natural gas,
dried fruit, carpets. **Imports** Food, petroleum.
LAND
Description Southern Asia, landlocked. **Area**
251,826 mi² (652,225 km²). **Highest point** Nowshāk,
24,557 ft (7,485 m). **Lowest point** Along Amu Darya
River, 850 ft (259 m).

People. Afghanistan shares borders with the Soviet
Union, China, Pakistan, and Iran. This crossroads position has created a population that is ethnically and linguistically diverse. Religion, however, plays a strong unifying role. Most Afghans are Muslim, and Islamic laws
and customs determine lifestyles and beliefs, both religious and secular. The population is mainly rural, consisting primarily of farmers and a small nomadic group.

Economy and the Land. The main force of Afghanistan's underdevelopment is agriculture and the recent
civil war. Subsistence farming and animal husbandry account for much of the agricultural activity. Crop production has been aided by irrigation systems. A terrain of
mountains and valleys, including the Hindu Kush, separates the desert region of the southwest from the more
fertile north, an area of higher population density and the
site of natural gas deposits. Increased development has
made natural gas an important export. Winters are generally cold, and summers are hot and dry.

History and Politics. Once part of the Persian Empire,
the area of present-day Afghanistan saw invasions by
Persians, Macedonians, Greeks, Turks, Arabs, Mongols,
and other peoples. An Arab invasion in A.D. 652 introduced Islam. In 1747 Afghan tribes led by Ahmad Shah
Durrani united the area and established today's Afghanistan. Power remained with the Durrani tribe for more
than two centuries. In the nineteenth and early twentieth
centuries, Britain controlled Afghanistan's foreign affairs.
A Durrani tribe member and former prime minister led a
military coup in 1973 and set up a republic, ending the
country's monarchial tradition. The new government's
failure to improve economic and social conditions led to a
1978 revolution that established a Marxist government
and brought Soviet aid. Intraparty differences and citi-
zenry dissent resulted in a Soviet invasion in 1979. Fighting between government forces and the *mujahidin* (holy
warrior) guerrillas continued. In 1988 the Soviets agreed
to remove their military forces. Internal strife between
factions, which has resulted in the deaths of hundreds of
thousands of citizens, continues to plague the country. ■

ALBANIA

Official name People's Socialist Republic of Albania
PEOPLE
Population 3,318,000. **Density** 299/mi² (115/km²).
Urban 35%. **Capital** Tiranë, 255,700. **Ethnic groups**
Albanian (Illyrian) 96%. **Languages** Albanian, Greek.
Religions Muslim 20%, Christian 5%. **Life expectancy**
75 female, 70 male. **Literacy** 75%.
POLITICS
Government Socialist republic. **Parties** Labor.
Suffrage Universal, over 18. **Memberships** UN.
Subdivisions 26 districts.
ECONOMY
GNP $2,800,000,000 **Per capita** $936. **Monetary unit**
Lek. **Trade partners** Italy, Yugoslavia, Germany.
Exports Asphalt, bitumen, petroleum products, metals
and minerals. **Imports** Machinery, tools, iron and steel
products.
LAND
Description Southeastern Europe. **Area** 11,100 mi²
(28,748 km²). **Highest point** Korabit Peak, 9,026 ft
(2,751 m). **Lowest point** Sea level.

People. A homogeneous native population characterizes
Albania, where Greeks are the main minority. Five centuries of Turkish rule shaped much of the culture and led
many Albanians to adopt Islam. Since 1944, when the
current Communist regime was established, an increased emphasis on education has more than tripled
the literacy rate. In 1967 religious institutions were
banned. Albania claims to be the world's first atheist
state.

Economy and the Land. Reputedly one of the poorest
countries in Europe, Albania has tried to shift its economy from agriculture to industry. Farms employed about
60 percent of the work force in 1970, a significant decrease from more than 80 percent before 1944. Mineral
resources make mining the chief industrial activity. The
terrain consists of forested hills and mountains, and the
climate is mild.

History and Politics. Early invaders and rulers included
Greeks, Romans, Goths, and others. In 1468, the Ottoman Turks conquered the area and it remained part of
their empire until the First Balkan War in 1912. Albania
was invaded by Italy and occupied by Germany during
World War II. After the war, a Communist government
was established. Rioting and instability have begun to
result in some liberalization and increased contact with
the rest of the world. Free elections were held in April,
1991. ■

ALGERIA

Official name Democratic and Popular Republic of
Algeria
PEOPLE
Population 26,115,000. **Density** 28/mi² (11/km²).
Urban 45%. **Capital** Algiers, 1,507,241. **Ethnic groups**
Arab-Berber 99%. **Languages** Arabic, Berber dialects,
French. **Religions** Sunni Muslim 99%, Christian and
Jewish. **Life expectancy** 67 female, 63 male. **Literacy**
45%.

POLITICS
Government Socialist republic. **Parties** Islamic
Salvation Front, National Liberation Front, others.
Suffrage Universal, over 18. **Memberships** AL, OAU,
OPEC, UN. **Subdivisions** 48 departments.
ECONOMY
GDP $45,234,000,000 **Per capita** $2,125. **Monetary**
unit Dinar. **Trade partners** Exports: Netherlands,
Czechoslovakia, Romania. Imports: France, Germany,
Italy. **Exports** Petroleum, natural gas. **Imports**
Consumer goods, machinery, food.
LAND
Description Northern Africa. **Area** 919,595 mi²
(2,381,741 km²). **Highest point** Tahat, 9,541 ft (2,908
m). **Lowest point** Chott Melrhir, -131 ft (-40 m).

People. Indigenous Berbers and invading Arabs shaped
modern Algeria's culture, and today most of the population is Muslim and of Arab-Berber descent. European
cultural influences, evidence of over a century of French
control, exist in urban areas. Since independence in
1962, free medical care has been instituted and the educational system has been greatly improved.

Economy and the Land. A member of the Organization
of Petroleum Exporting Countries (OPEC), Algeria produces oil and natural gas. Agriculture is divided between
state and privately-owned farms. The government continues to emphasize gas production and exportation,
while it maintains a socialist economy and promotes
development of private business. Algeria's terrain is varied. The Tell, Arabic for hill, is a narrow Mediterranean
coastal region that contains the country's most fertile
land and highest population. South of this lie high
plateaus and the Atlas Mountains, which give way to the
Sahara Desert. The climate is temperate along the coast
and dry and cool in the plateau region.

History and Politics. In the eighth and eleventh centuries, invading Arabs brought their language and religion
to the native Berbers. The Berbers and Arabs together
became known as Moors, and conflicts between Moors,
Turks, and Spaniards erupted periodically over several
centuries. France began conquering Algeria in 1830, and
by 1902 the entire country was under French control.
The revolution against French rule began in 1954, but it
was not until 1962 that the country was declared independent. Since a bloodless coup in 1965, the political
situation has been relatively stable. A 1989 referendum
approved a new constitution allowing multiparty elections. The first free elections since independence were
held in 1990. The Islamic Salvation Front defeated the
ruling National Liberation Front. ■

AMERICAN SAMOA
See UNITED STATES.

ANDORRA

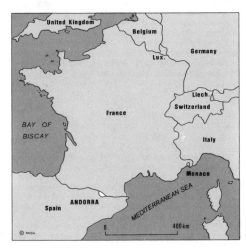

Official name Principality of Andorra
PEOPLE
Population 52,000. **Density** 297/mi² (115/km²). **Capital** Andorra, 18,463. **Ethnic groups** Spanish 61%, Andorran 30%, French 6%. **Languages** Spanish, French. **Religions** Roman Catholic. **Life expectancy** 81 female, 74 male. **Literacy** 100%.
POLITICS
Government Coprincipality (Spanish and French protection). **Parties** None. **Suffrage** Universal, over 18. **Memberships** None. **Subdivisions** 7 parishes. **Monetary unit** French franc, Spanish peseta. **Trade partners** France, Spain.
LAND
Description Southwestern Europe, landlocked. **Area** 175 mi² (453 km²). **Highest point** Pic de Coma Pedrosa, 9,665 ft (2,946 m). **Lowest point** Along Valira River, 2,756 ft (840 m).

People. Much of Andorran life and culture has been shaped by its mountainous terrain and governing countries, France and Spain. Population is concentrated in the valleys, and despite a tourism boom in past decades, the peaks and valleys of the Pyrenees have isolated the small country from many twentieth-century changes. Spanish is the official language, and cultural and historic ties exist with the Catalonian region of northern Spain. The majority of the population is Spanish; Andorran citizens are a minority.

Economy and the Land. The terrain has established Andorra's economy as well as its lifestyle. Improved transportation routes together with other factors have resulted in a thriving tourist industry—a dramatic shift from traditional sheepherding and tobacco growing. In addition, duty-free status has made the country a European shopping mecca. Tobacco is the main agricultural product, though only about 4 percent of the land is arable. Climate varies with altitude; winters are cold and summers are cool and pleasant.

History and Politics. Tradition indicates that Charlemagne freed the area from the Moors in A.D. 806. A French count and the Spanish bishop of Seo de Urgel signed an agreement in the 1200s to act as coprinces of the country, establishing the political status and boundaries that exist today. The coprincipality is governed by the president of France and the bishop of Seo de Urgel. The country has no formal constitution, no armed forces other than a small police force, and no political parties. ∎

ANGOLA

Official name People's Republic of Angola
PEOPLE
Population 10,155,000. **Density** 21/mi² (8.1/km²). **Urban** 28%. **Capital** Luanda, 1,459,900. **Ethnic groups** Ovimbundu 37%, Mbundu 25%, Kongo 13%, mulatto 2%, European 1%. **Languages** Portuguese, indigenous. **Religions** Animist 47%, Roman Catholic 38%, other Christian 15%. **Life expectancy** 48 female, 45 male. **Literacy** 20%.

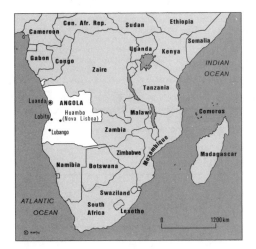

POLITICS
Government Socialist republic. **Parties** Popular Movement for Liberation-Labor. **Suffrage** Universal adult. **Memberships** OAU, UN. **Subdivisions** 18 provinces.
ECONOMY
GDP $2,541,000,000 **Per capita** $346. **Monetary unit** Kwanza. **Trade partners** U.S., U.S.S.R., Cuba, Portugal, Brazil. **Exports** Petroleum, coffee, diamonds. **Imports** Machinery, food, transportation equipment.
LAND
Description Southern Africa. **Area** 481,354 mi² (1,246,700 km²). **Highest point** Serra do Môco, 8,596 ft (2,620 m). **Lowest point** Sea level.

People. Angola today is made up mostly of various Bantu peoples—mainly Ovimbundu, Mbundu, Kongo, and others. Despite influences from a half-century of Portuguese rule, Angolan traditions remain strong, especially in rural areas. Each group has its own language, and although Portuguese is the official language, it is spoken by a minority. Many Angolans, retaining traditional indigenous beliefs, worship ancestral spirits.

Economy and the Land. A 1975 civil war, the resultant departure of skilled European labor, and continuing guerrilla activity have taken their toll on Angola's economy. The country has been working toward recovery, however, encouraging development of private industries and foreign trade. Although not a member of the Organization of Petroleum Exporting Countries (OPEC), Angola is a large oil producer. Cabinda, an enclave separated from the rest of the country by Zaire and the Zaire River, is the main site of oil production. Diamond mining remains an important activity, as does agriculture. Much of the land is forested, however, and is therefore not suited for commercial farming. The flat coastal area gives way to inland plateaus and uplands. The climate varies from tropical to subtropical.

History and Politics. Bantu groups settled in the area prior to the first century A.D. In 1483 a Portuguese explorer became the first European to arrive in Angola, and slave trade soon became a major activity. Portuguese control expanded and continued almost uninterrupted for several centuries. In the 1960s, ignored demands for popular rule led to two wars for independence. Three nationalist groups emerged, each with its own ideology and supporters. In 1974 a coup in Portugal resulted in independence for all Portuguese territories in Africa, and Angola became independent in 1975. A civil war ensued, with the three liberation groups fighting for power. By 1976, with the assistance of Cuban military personnel, the Popular Movement for the Liberation of Angola (PMLA) had established control. Angola, Cuba, and South Africa signed an accord in 1988 providing for Cuban troop withdrawals by July 1991. Despite continuing negotiations, there have been many casualties and much suffering as rival parties struggle for a share in the government. ∎

ANGUILLA See UNITED KINGDOM.

ANTARCTICA

Official name Antarctica **Capital** None. **Memberships** None.

LAND
Description Continent in Southern Hemisphere. **Area** 5,400,000 mi² (14,000,000 km²). **Highest point** Vinson Massif, 16,066 ft (4,897 m). **Lowest point** Deep Lake, -184 ft (-56 m).

People. Antarctica, which surrounds the South Pole, is the southernmost continent, the coldest place on earth, and one of the last frontiers. There are no native inhabitants, and its temporary population is made up mainly of scientists from various countries operating research stations.

Economy and the Land. Harsh climate and terrain have inhibited resource exploration and development. Antarctica's natural resources include coal, various ores, iron, offshore oil and natural gas. Fishing for krill, a marine protein source, is another activity. Crossed by several ranges collectively known as the Transantarctic Mountains, Antarctica can be roughly divided into a mountainous western region and a larger eastern sector consisting of an icy plain rimmed by mountains. With its tip about 700 miles (1,127 km) from southern South America, the mountainous Antarctic Peninsula and its offshore islands jut northward. Nearly all Antarctica is ice covered, precipitation is minimal, and the continent is actually a desert.

History and Politics. In the 1770s, Captain James Cook of Britain set out in search of the southernmost continent and sailed completely around Antarctica without sighting land. Explorations beginning in 1820 resulted in sightings of the mainland or offshore islands by the British, Russians, and Americans. British explorer Sir James C. Ross conducted the first extensive explorations. After a lull of several decades, interest in Antarctica was renewed in the late nineteenth and early twentieth centuries. Captain Robert F. Scott and Ernest Shackleton of Britain and Roald Amundsen of Norway led the renewed interest. Amundsen won the race to the South Pole in 1911. An Antarctic Treaty signed in 1959 permitted only peaceful scientific research to be conducted in the region. It also delayed settlement until 1989 of overlapping claims to the territory held by Norway, Australia, France, New Zealand, Chile, Britain, and Argentina. In 1988 several countries signed agreements to allow exploitation of Antarctica's natural resources. ∎

ANTIGUA AND BARBUDA

Official name Antigua and Barbuda

PEOPLE
Population 80,000. **Density** 468/mi² (181/km²). **Urban** 32%. **Capital** St. John's, Antigua I., 24,359. **Ethnic groups** Black. **Languages** English, local dialects. **Religions** Anglican, Protestant, Roman Catholic. **Life expectancy** 74 female, 70 male. **Literacy** 90%.
POLITICS
Government Parliamentary state. **Parties** Labor, United National Democratic. **Suffrage** Universal, over 18. **Memberships** CW, OAS, UN. **Subdivisions** 7 parishes.

ECONOMY
GDP $161,000,000 **Per capita** $2,013. **Monetary unit** East Caribbean dollar. **Trade partners** Exports: Trinidad and Tobago, Barbados. Imports: U.S., U.K.. **Exports** Petroleum, manufactures, food, machinery and transportation equipment. **Imports** Food, machinery and transportation equipment, manufactures, chemicals.
LAND
Description Caribbean islands. **Area** 171 mi² (443 km²). **Highest point** Boggy Pk., 1,319 ft (402 m). **Lowest point** Sea level.

People. Most Antiguans are descendants of black African slaves brought by the British to work sugarcane plantations. The largest urban area is St. John's, but most Antiguans live in rural areas. British rule has left its imprint; most people are Protestant and speak English.

Economy and the Land. The dry, tropical climate and white-sand beaches attract many visitors, making tourism the economic mainstay. Once dependent on sugar cultivation, the nation has shifted to a multicrop agriculture. The country is composed of three islands: Antigua, Barbuda, and uninhabited Redondo. Formed by volcanos, the low-lying islands are flat.

History and Politics. The original inhabitants of Antigua and Barbuda were the Carib Indians. Columbus arrived at Antigua in 1493, and after unsuccessful Spanish and French attempts at colonization, the British began settlement in the 1600s. The country remained a British colony until 1967, when it became an associated state of the United Kingdom. Antigua gained independence in 1981. ∎

ARGENTINA

Official name Argentine Republic

PEOPLE
Population 32,485,000. **Density** 30/mi² (12/km²). **Urban** 86%. **Capital** Buenos Aires, 2,922,829. **Ethnic groups** White 85%, mestizo, Amerindian, and others 15%. **Languages** Spanish, English, Italian, German, French. **Religions** Roman Catholic 90%, Jewish 2%, Protestant 2%. **Life expectancy** 75 female, 68 male. **Literacy** 94%.

POLITICS
Government Republic. **Parties** Justicialist (Peronista), Radical Civic Union, Union of the Democratic Center. **Suffrage** Universal, over 18. **Memberships** OAS, UN. **Subdivisions** 22 provinces, 1 district, 1 national territory.

ECONOMY
GDP $64,829,000,000 **Per capita** $2,263. **Monetary unit** Austral. **Trade partners** Exports: U.S., U.S.S.R., Netherlands. Imports: U.S., Brazil, Germany. **Exports** Meat, wheat, corn, oilseed, hides, wool. **Imports** Machinery, chemicals, metals, fuel.

LAND
Description Southern South America. **Area** 1,073,400 mi² (2,780,092 km²). **Highest point** Cerro Aconcagua, 22,831 ft (6,959 m). **Lowest point** Salinas Chicas, -138 ft (-42 m).

People. An indigenous Indian population, Spanish settlement, and a turn-of-the-century influx of immigrants have made Argentina an ethnically diverse nation. Today, most Argentines are descendants of Spanish and Italian immigrants. Other Europeans, mestizos of mixed Indian-Spanish blood, Indians, Middle Easterners, and Latin American immigrants diversify the population further. Spanish influence is evident in the major religion, Roman Catholicism; the official language, Spanish; and many aspects of cultural life.

Economy and the Land. Political difficulties beginning in the 1930s have resulted in economic problems and have kept this one-time economic giant from realizing its potential. The most valuable natural resource is the rich soil of the pampas, fertile plains in the east-central region. The greatest contributors to the economy, however, are manufacturing and services. The second largest country in South America, Argentina has a varied terrain, with northern lowlands, the east-central pampas, the Andes Mountains in the west, and the southern Patagonian steppe. The climate likewise varies, from subtropical in the north to subarctic in the south.

History and Politics. The earliest inhabitants of the area were Indians. In the 1500s silver-seeking Spaniards arrived, and by 1580 they had established a colony on the site of present-day Buenos Aires. In 1816 Argentina officially announced its independence from Spain. A successful struggle for independence ensued, and in 1853 a

constitution was adopted and a president elected. Prosperity continued through the 1920s, and immigration and foreign investment increased. Unsatisfactory power distribution and concern over foreign investment resulted in a military coup in 1930. Thus began a series of civil and military governments; coups; the election, overthrow, and reelection of Juan Perón; and controversial human-rights violations. In 1982 Argentina lost a war with Britain over the Falkland Islands. Years of struggling with human rights transgressions followed. Since winning the election in 1989, the Peronistas are attempting to deal with severe economic problems. ∎

ARUBA See NETHERLANDS.

ASCENSION ISLAND
See UNITED KINGDOM.

AUSTRALIA

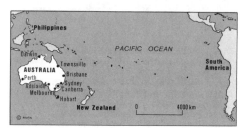

Official name Commonwealth of Australia
PEOPLE
Population 17,260,000. **Density** 5.8/mi² (2.2/km²). **Urban** 86%. **Capital** Canberra, 247,194. **Ethnic groups** European 95%, Asian 4%, Aboriginal and other 1%. **Languages** English, indigenous. **Religions** Anglican 24%, Roman Catholic 26%, other Christian 23%. **Life expectancy** 80 female, 74 male. **Literacy** 100%.

POLITICS
Government Parliamentary state. **Parties** Democratic, Labor, Liberal, National. **Suffrage** Universal, over 18. **Memberships** CW, OECD, UN. **Subdivisions** 6 states, 2 territories.

ECONOMY
GDP $167,441,000,000 **Per capita** $10,758. **Monetary unit** Dollar. **Trade partners** Exports: Japan, U.S., New Zealand. Imports: U.S., Japan, U.K.. **Exports** Wheat, barley, beef, lamb, dairy products, wool, coal, iron ore. **Imports** Manufactures, machinery, consumer goods.

LAND
Description Continent between South Pacific and Indian oceans. **Area** 2,966,155 mi² (7,682,300 km²). **Highest point** Mt. Kosciusko, 7,310 ft (2,228 m). **Lowest point** Lake Eyre (North), -52 ft (-16 m).

People. Australia's culture reflects a unique combination of British, other European, and aboriginal influences. Settlement and rule by the United Kingdom gave the country

a distinctly British flavor, and many Australians trace their roots to early British settlers. Planned immigration also played a major role in Australia's development, bringing more than three million Europeans since World War II. Refugees, most recently from Southeast Asia, make up another group of incoming peoples. The country is home to a small number of aborigines. The nation's size and a relatively dry terrain have resulted in uneven settlement patterns, with people concentrated in the rainier southeastern coastal area. The population is mainly urban, though overall population density remains low.

Economy and the Land. Australia's economy is similar to economies in other developed nations, and is characterized by a postwar shift from agriculture to industry and services, as well as inflation and unemployment. Wool is a major export, and livestock raising takes place on relatively flat, wide grazing lands surrounding an arid central region. Commercial crop raising is concentrated on a fertile southeastern plain. Plentiful mineral resources provide for a strong mining industry. Australia is the world's smallest continent but one of its largest countries. The climate is varied, and part of the country lies within the tropics. Because it is south of the equator, Australia has seasons the reverse of those in the Northern Hemisphere.

History and Politics. Aboriginal peoples probably arrived about forty thousand years ago and established a hunter-gatherer society. The Dutch explored the area in the seventeenth century, but no claims were made until the eighteenth century, when British Captain James Cook found his way to the fertile east and annexed the land to Britain. The first colony, New South Wales, was founded in 1788, and many of the early settlers were British convicts. During the 1800s, a squatter movement spread the population to other parts of the island, and the discovery of gold led to a population boom. Demands for self-government soon began, and by the 1890s all the colonies were self-governing, with Britain maintaining control of foreign affairs and defense. Nationalism continued to increase, and a new nation, the Commonwealth of Australia, was created in 1901. Australia fought on the side of the British during both world wars, and postwar years saw increased attention paid to the rights of the dwindling aboriginal population. Since World War II, participation in international affairs has expanded, with attention turned particularly to Asian countries. ∎

AUSTRIA

Official name Republic of Austria

PEOPLE
Population 7,681,000. **Density** 237/mi² (92/km²). **Urban** 58%. **Capital** Vienna, 1,482,800. **Ethnic groups** German 99%. **Languages** German. **Religions** Roman Catholic 85%, Protestant 6%. **Life expectancy** 79 female, 72 male. **Literacy** 99%.

POLITICS
Government Republic. **Parties** Freedom, People's, Socialist, others. **Suffrage** Universal, over 19. **Memberships** OECD, UN. **Subdivisions** 9 states.

Places and Possessions of AUSTRALIA

Entity	Status	Area	Population	Capital/Population
Ashmore and Cartier Islands (Indian Ocean; north of Australia)	External territory	1.9 mi² (5.0 km²)	None	None
Christmas Island (Indian Ocean)	External territory	52 mi² (135 km²)	1,500	The Settlement
Cocos (Keeling) Islands (Indian Ocean)	Part of Australia	5.4 mi² (14 km²)	700	West Island
Coral Sea Islands (South Pacific)	External territory	1.0 mi² (2.6 km²)	None	None
Heard and McDonald Islands (Indian Ocean)	External territory	154 mi² (400 km²)	None	None
Norfolk Island (South Pacific)	External territory	14 mi² (36 km²)	2,000	Kingston
Tasmania (South Pacific island; south of Australia)	State	26,178 mi² (67,800 km²)	461,000	Hobart, 47,356

ECONOMY

GDP $66,053,000,000 **Per capita** $8,714. **Monetary unit** Schilling. **Trade partners** Germany, Italy, Switzerland. **Exports** Machinery and equipment, iron and steel, wood, textiles. **Imports** Petroleum, food, machinery, transportation equipment, chemicals.

LAND

Description Central Europe, landlocked. **Area** 32,377 mi² (83,855 km²). **Highest point** Grossglockner, 12,457 ft (3,797 m). **Lowest point** Neusiedler See, 377 ft (115 m).

People. The majority of Austrians are native born, German speaking, and Roman Catholic, a homogeneity belying a history of invasions by diverse peoples. With a long cultural tradition, the country has contributed greatly to music and the arts—Vienna, the capital, is one of the great cultural centers of Europe.

Economy and the Land. Austria's economy is a blend of state and privately-owned industry. After World War II the government began nationalizing industries, returning many to the private sector as the economy stabilized. Unemployment is low, and the economy remains relatively strong. The economic mainstays are services and manufacturing. Agriculture is limited because of the overall mountainous terrain, with the Danube River basin in the east containing the most productive soils. In addition to the country's cultural heritage, the alpine landscape also attracts many tourists. The climate is generally moderate.

History and Politics. Early in its history, Austria was settled by Celts, ruled by Romans, and invaded by Germans, Slavs, Magyars, and others. Long rule by the Hapsburg family began in the thirteenth century, and in time Austria became the center of a vast empire. In 1867 Hungarian pressure resulted in the formation of the dual monarchy of Austria-Hungary. Nationalist movements against Austria culminated in the 1914 assassination of the heir to the throne, Archduke Francis Ferdinand, and set off the conflict that became World War I. In 1918 the war ended, the Hapsburg emperor was overthrown, Austria became a republic, and present-day boundaries were established. Political unrest and instability followed. In 1938 Adolf Hitler incorporated Austria into the German Reich. A period of occupation after World War II was followed by Austria's declaration of neutrality and ongoing political stability. Today Austria enjoys economic prosperity with strong ties to the western European community. ∎

AZORES See PORTUGAL.

BAHAMAS

Official name The Commonwealth of the Bahamas

PEOPLE

Population 256,000. **Density** 48/mi² (18/km²). **Urban** 59%. **Capital** Nassau, New Providence I., 135,000. **Ethnic groups** Black 85%, white 15%. **Languages** English, Creole. **Religions** Baptist 29%, Anglican 23%, Roman Catholic 22%. **Life expectancy** 75 female, 68 male. **Literacy** 89%.

POLITICS

Government Parliamentary state. **Parties** Free National Movement, Progressive Liberal. **Suffrage** Universal, over 18. **Memberships** CW, OAS, UN. **Subdivisions** 21 districts.

ECONOMY

GDP $2,258,000,000 **Per capita** $9,817. **Monetary unit** Dollar. **Trade partners** Exports: U.S., U.K. Imports: Iran, Nigeria, U.S.. **Exports** Petroleum, chemicals. **Imports** Crude petroleum, manufactures, food, chemicals.

LAND

Description Caribbean islands. **Area** 5,380 mi² (13,934 km²). **Highest point** Mt. Alvernia, 206 ft (63 m). **Lowest point** Sea level.

People. Only about 29 of the 700 Bahamian islands are inhabited, and most of the people live on Grand Bahama and New Providence. The majority blacks are mainly descendants of slaves routed through the area or brought by British Loyalists fleeing the American colonies during the revolutionary war.

Economy and the Land. Because the thin soils of these flat coral islands are not suited for agriculture, for years the country struggled to develop a strong economic base. The solution was tourism, which capitalizes on the islands' most valuable resource—a semitropical climate. Because it is a tax haven, the country is also an international finance center.

History and Politics. Christopher Columbus's first stop on his way to America in 1492, the Bahamas were originally the home of the Lucayo Indians, whom the Spaniards took for slave trade. The British arrived in the 1600s, and the islands became a British colony in 1717. Independence was achieved in 1973. ∎

BAHRAIN

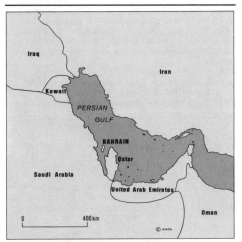

Official name State of Bahrain

PEOPLE

Population 501,000. **Density** 1,876/mi² (725/km²). **Urban** 83%. **Capital** Manama, Bahrain I., 115,054. **Ethnic groups** Bahraini 68%, Asian 25%, other Arab 4%, European 3%. **Languages** Arabic, English, Farsi, Urdu. **Religions** Muslim 85%, Christian 7%. **Life expectancy** 74 female, 70 male. **Literacy** 63%.

POLITICS

Government Monarchy. **Parties** None. **Suffrage** None. **Memberships** AL, UN. **Subdivisions** 12 regions.

ECONOMY

GDP $5,133,000,000 **Per capita** $12,369. **Monetary unit** Dinar. **Trade partners** Exports: United Arab Emirates, Singapore, Japan. Imports: U.S., U.K., Japan. **Exports** Refined petroleum, chemicals, aluminum. **Imports** Crude petroleum, machinery, manufactured goods, transportation equipment.

LAND

Description Southwestern Asian islands (in Persian Gulf). **Area** 267 mi² (691 km²). **Highest point** Mt. Dukhan, 440 ft (134 m). **Lowest point** Sea level.

People. Most residents of Bahrain are native-born Muslims, with the Sunni sect predominating in urban areas and Shiites in the countryside. Many of the country's thirty-three islands are barren, and population is concentrated in the capital city—Manama, on Bahrain Island—and on the smaller island of Muharraq. The oil economy has resulted in an influx of foreign workers and considerable westernization, and Bahrain is a Persian Gulf leader in free health care and education.

Economy and the Land. The one-time pearl-and-fish economy was reshaped by exploitation of oil and natural gas, careful management, and diversification. A major refinery processes crude oil piped from Saudi Arabia as well as the country's own oil, and Bahrain's aluminum industry is the Gulf's largest non-oil activity. Because of its location, Bahrain is able to provide Gulf countries with services such as dry docking, and the country has become a Middle Eastern banking center. Agriculture exists on northern Bahrain Island, where natural springs provide an irrigation source. Much of the state is desert. Summers are hot and dry and winters are mild.

History and Politics. From about 2000 to 1800 B.C. the area of Bahrain flourished as a center for trade. After early periods of Portuguese and Iranian rule, the Al Khalifa family came to power in the eighteenth century, and it has governed ever since. Bahrain became a British protectorate in the nineteenth century, and independence was gained in 1971. Friendly international relations and political allegiance to the Arab League characterize the current government. ∎

BALEARIC ISLANDS See SPAIN.

BANGLADESH

Official name People's Republic of Bangladesh

PEOPLE

Population 109,540,000. **Density** 1,970/mi² (761/km²). **Urban** 14%. **Capital** Dhaka, 2,365,695. **Ethnic groups** Bengali 98%. **Languages** Bangla, English. **Religions** Muslim 84%, Hindu 15%. **Life expectancy** 53 female, 53 male. **Literacy** 29%.

POLITICS

Government Islamic republic. **Parties** Awami League, Jamaat-e-Islami, Jatiya, others. **Suffrage** Universal, over 18. **Memberships** CW, UN. **Subdivisions** 4 divisions.

ECONOMY

GDP $17,204,000,000 **Per capita** $170. **Monetary unit** Taka. **Trade partners** Exports: U.S., Italy, Japan. Imports: Japan, Singapore, U.S.. **Exports** Jute, tea, leather, shrimp, manufactures. **Imports** Food, petroleum, consumer goods, manufactures.

LAND

Description Southern Asia. **Area** 55,598 mi²

(143,998 km²). **Highest point** Reng Mtn., 3,141 ft (957 m). **Lowest point** Sea level.

People. Bangladesh's population is characterized by extremes. The people, mostly peasant farmers, are among Asia's poorest and most rural. With a relatively small area and a high birthrate, the country is also one of the world's most densely populated. Many Bangladeshis are victims of disease, floods, and ongoing medical and food shortages. Islam, the major religion, has influenced almost every aspect of life. Bangla is the official language.

Economy and the Land. Fertile flood plain soil is the chief resource of this mostly flat, river-crossed country, and farming is the main activity. Rice and jute are among the major crops. Farm output fluctuates greatly, however, subject to the frequent monsoons, floods, and droughts of a semitropical climate. Because of this and other factors, foreign aid, imports, and an emphasis on agriculture have not assuaged the continuing food shortages. In 1988, floods put 75 percent of the country under water and left twenty-five million people in dire straits.

History and Politics. Most of Bangladesh lies in eastern Bengal, an Asian region whose western sector encompasses India's Bengal province. Early religious influences in Bengal included Buddhist rulers in the eighth century and Hindus in the eleventh. In 1200 Muslim rule introduced the religion to which the majority of eastern Bengalis eventually converted, while most western Bengalis retained their Hindu beliefs. British control in India, beginning in the seventeenth century, expanded until all Bengal was part of British India by the 1850s. When British India gained independence in 1947, Muslim population centers were united into the single nation of Pakistan in an attempt to end Hindu-Muslim hostilities. More than 1,000 miles (1,600 km) separated West Pakistan, formed from northwest India, from East Pakistan, comprised mostly of eastern Bengal. The bulk of Pakistan's population resided in the eastern province and felt the west wielded political and economic power at its expense. A civil war began in 1971, and the eastern province declared itself an independent nation called Bangladesh, or ''Bengal nation.'' That same year, West Pakistan surrendered to eastern guerrillas joined with Indian troops. The state has seen political crises since independence, including two leader assassinations and several coups. In 1982 General Ershad took control in a bloodless coup, assuming the office of president in 1983. Violent protests led to Ershad's resignation in December 1990. Buddhist tribal groups, which claim religious persecution, are agitating for autonomy. ■

BARBADOS

Official name Barbados

PEOPLE
Population 259,000. **Density** 1,560/mi² (602/km²). **Urban** 45%. **Capital** Bridgetown, 7,466. **Ethnic groups** Black 92%, white 3%, mixed 3%, East Indian 1%. **Languages** English. **Religions** Anglican 40%, Pentecostal 8%, Methodist 7%, Roman Catholic 4%. **Life expectancy** 78 female, 72 male. **Literacy** 99%.
POLITICS
Government Parliamentary state. **Parties** Democratic Labor, Labor, National Democratic. **Suffrage** Universal, over 18. **Memberships** CW, OAS, UN. **Subdivisions** 11 parishes.
ECONOMY
GDP $1,230,000,000 **Per capita** $4,920. **Monetary unit** Dollar. **Trade partners** Exports: U.S., U.K., Germany. Imports: U.S., U.K., Trinidad and Tobago. **Exports** Sugar, electrical equipment, clothing. **Imports** Food, consumer goods, raw materials, petroleum.
LAND
Description Caribbean island. **Area** 166 mi² (430 km²). **Highest point** Mt. Hillaby, 1,115 ft (340 m). **Lowest point** Sea level.

People. A history of British rule is reflected in the Anglican religion and English language of this easternmost West Indian island. It is one of the world's most densely populated countries, and most citizens are black descendants of African slaves.

Economy and the Land. Barbados's pleasant tropical climate and its land have determined its economic mainstays: tourism and sugar. Sunshine and year-round warmth attract thousands of visitors and, in conjunction with the soil, provide an excellent environment for sugar cane cultivation. Manufacturing consists mainly of sugar processing. The coral island's terrain is mostly flat, rising to a central ridge.

History and Politics. Originally settled by South American Arawak Indians, followed by Carib Indians, Barbados was uninhabited when the first British settlers arrived in the 1600s. More colonists followed, developing sugar plantations and bringing slaves from Africa to work them. The country remained under British control until it became independent in 1966. ■

BELGIUM

Official name Kingdom of Belgium
PEOPLE
Population 9,927,000. **Density** 842/mi² (325/km²). **Urban** 97%. **Capital** Brussels, 136,920. **Ethnic groups** Fleming 55%, Walloon 33%, mixed and others 12%. **Languages** Dutch (Flemish), French, German. **Religions** Roman Catholic 75%. **Life expectancy** 79 female, 72 male. **Literacy** 99%.
POLITICS
Government Constitutional monarchy. **Parties** Flemish: Liberal, Social Christian, Socialist. Walloon: Liberal, Socialist. **Suffrage** Universal, over 18. **Memberships** EC, NATO, OECD, UN. **Subdivisions** 9 provinces.
ECONOMY
GDP $79,076,000,000 **Per capita** $8,008. **Monetary unit** Franc. **Trade partners** Exports: France, Germany, Netherlands. Imports: Germany, Netherlands, France. **Exports** Iron and steel, transportation equipment, diamonds, petroleum. **Imports** Fuel, grains, chemicals, food.
LAND
Description Western Europe. **Area** 11,783 mi² (30,518 km²). **Highest point** Botrange, 2,277 ft (694 m). **Lowest point** Sea level.

People. Language separates Belgium into two main regions. Northern Belgium, known as Flanders, is dominated by Flemings, Flemish-speaking descendants of Germanic Franks. French-speaking Walloons, descendants of the Celts, inhabit southern Belgium, or Wallonia. Both groups are found in centrally located Brussels. In addition, a small German-speaking population is concentrated in the east. Flemish and French divisions often result in discord, but diversity has also been a source of cultural richness. Belgium has often been at the hub of European cultural movements.

Economy and the Land. The economy, as well as the population, was affected by Belgium's location at the center of European activity. Industry was early established as the economic base, and today the country is heavily industrialized. Although agriculture plays a minor economic role, Belgium is nearly self-sufficient in food production. The north and west are dominated by a flat fertile plain, the central region by rolling hills, and the south by the Ardennes Forest, often a tourist destination. The climate is cool and temperate.

History and Politics. Belgium's history began with the settlement of the Belgae tribe in the second century B.C. The Romans invaded the area around 50 B.C. and were overthrown by Germanic Franks in the A.D. 400s. Trade, manufacturing, and art prospered as various peoples invaded, passed through, and ruled the area. In 1794 Napoleon annexed Belgium to France. He was defeated at Waterloo in Belgium in 1815, and the country passed into Dutch hands. Dissatisfaction under Netherlands rule led to revolt and, in 1830, the formation of the independent country of Belgium. Germans overthrew the country during both world wars. Linguistic divisions mark nearly all political activity, from parties split by language to government decisions based on linguistic rivalries. ■

BELIZE

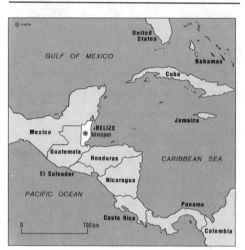

Official name Belize
PEOPLE
Population 204,000. **Density** 23/mi² (8.9/km²). **Urban** 52%. **Capital** Belmopan, 4,500. **Ethnic groups** Creole 40%, mestizo 33%, Amerindian 16%. **Languages** English, Spanish, Garifuna, Mayan. **Religions** Roman Catholic 62%, Anglican 12%, Methodist 6%, Mennonite 4%. **Life expectancy** 72 female, 67 male. **Literacy** 91%.
POLITICS
Government Parliamentary state. **Parties** People's United, United Democratic. **Suffrage** Universal, over 18. **Memberships** CW, OAS, UN. **Subdivisions** 6 districts.
ECONOMY
GDP $195,000,000 **Per capita** $1,219. **Monetary unit** Dollar. **Trade partners** Exports: U.S., Mexico, U.K. Imports: U.S., U.K., Netherlands. **Exports** Sugar, clothing, seafood, molasses, citrus, wood. **Imports** Machinery and transportation equipment, food, manufactures.
LAND
Description Central America. **Area** 8,866 mi² (22,963 km²). **Highest point** Victoria Pk., 3,675 ft (1,120 m). **Lowest point** Sea level.

People. With the lowest population of any Central American country, Belize has a mixed populace, including descendants of black Africans, mestizos of Spanish-Indian ancestry, and Indians. Population is concentrated in six urban areas along the coast. Most people are poor, but participation in the educational system has led to a high literacy rate.

Economy and the Land. An abundance of timberland resulted in an economy based on forestry until woodlands began to be depleted in the twentieth century. Today the economy focuses on agriculture, with sugar the major crop and export. Arable land is the primary resource, but only a small portion has been cultivated. Industrial activity is limited. The recipient of much foreign aid, Belize hopes to expand export of agricultural surpluses and to develop a tourist industry based on its climate and sandy beaches. The coastal region consists of swampy lowlands rising to the Maya Mountains inland. The hot, humid climate is offset by sea breezes.

History and Politics. Until about the eleventh century A.D., Belize was the site of a flourishing Mayan civilization. Spain claimed the region in the sixteenth century. A British shipwreck in 1638 resulted in the first European settlement and began a process of British colonization, accompanied by extensive logging, piracy, and occasional Spanish and Indian attacks. In 1862 the area officially became the crown colony of British Honduras. Its name was changed to Belize in 1973, and independence was achieved in 1981. To assist economic and political development, Belize seeks closer relations with Spanish-speaking Central American countries and English-speaking Caribbean states. ■

BENIN

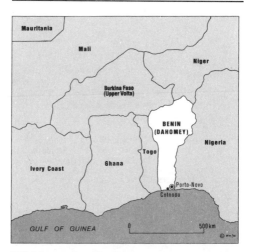

Official name Republic of Benin

PEOPLE
Population 4,819,000. **Density** 111/mi² (43/km²). **Urban** 42%. **Capital** Porto-Novo (designated), 164,000; Cotonou (de facto), 215,000. **Ethnic groups** Fon 39%, Yoruba 12%, Adja 10%, others. **Languages** French, Fon, Adja, indigenous. **Religions** Fetishism 70%, Muslim 15%, Christian 15%. **Life expectancy** 50 female, 47 male. **Literacy** 17%.

POLITICS
Government Republic. **Parties** People's Revolutionary. **Suffrage** Universal, over 18. **Memberships** OAU, UN. **Subdivisions** 6 provinces.

ECONOMY
GDP $1,153,000,000 **Per capita** $307. **Monetary unit** CFA franc. **Trade partners** Exports: Nigeria, Netherlands, France. Imports: France, U.K., Netherlands. **Exports** Oil, cotton, palm products, cocoa. **Imports** Food, beverages, tobacco, petroleum, manufactures.

LAND
Description Western Africa. **Area** 43,475 mi² (112,600 km²). **Highest point** 2,235 ft (681 m). **Lowest point** Sea level.

People. The mostly black population of Benin is composed of numerous peoples. The main groups are the Fon, the Adja, the Yoruba, and the Bariba. The nation's linguistic diversity reflects its ethnic variety; French is the official language, a result of former French rule. Most Beninese are farmers, although urban migration is increasing. Indigenous beliefs predominate, but there are also Christians, especially in the south, and Muslims in the north.

Economy and the Land. Political instability has been both the cause and effect of Benin's economic problems. The agricultural economy is largely undeveloped, and palm trees and their by-products provide the chief source of income and activity for both farming and industry. Some economic relief may be found in the exploitation of offshore oil. The predominately flat terrain features coastal lagoons and dense forests, with mountains in the northwest. Heat and humidity characterize the coast, with less humidity and varied temperatures in the north.

History and Politics. In the 1500s, Dahomey, a Fon kingdom, became the power center of the Benin area. European slave traders came to the coast in the seventeenth and eighteenth centuries, establishing posts and bartering with Dahomey royalty for slaves. As the slave trade prospered, the area became known as the Slave Coast. In the 1890s France defeated Dahomey's army and subsequently made the area a territory of French West Africa. In 1960, the country gained independence, followed by political turmoil, various coups, and a military overthrow which installed a socialist government in 1972. In 1975 the nation changed its name from Dahomey to Benin. Economic difficulties in the late 1980s have led the country away from socialism and towards private enterprise. ■

BERMUDA

Official name Bermuda

PEOPLE
Population 60,000. **Density** 2,857/mi² (1,111/km²). **Urban** 100%. **Capital** Hamilton, Bermuda I., 1,676. **Ethnic groups** Black 61%, white 37%. **Languages** English. **Religions** Anglican 37%, Roman Catholic 14%, African Methodist Episcopal 10%. **Life expectancy** 76 female, 69 male. **Literacy** 98%.

POLITICS
Government Dependent territory (U.K.). **Parties** Progressive Labor, United. **Suffrage** Universal, over 21. **Memberships** None. **Subdivisions** 9 parishes, 2 municipalities.

ECONOMY
GDP $1,148,000,000 **Per capita** $16,400. **Monetary unit** Dollar. **Trade partners** Exports: U.S., Italy, Canada. Imports: U.S., U.K., Canada. **Exports** Food, manufactures. **Imports** Fuel, food, machinery.

LAND
Description North Atlantic islands (east of North Carolina). **Area** 21 mi² (54 km²). **Highest point** Town Hill, 259 ft (79 m). **Lowest point** Sea level.

People. The population of this British colony is mainly black descendants of African slaves, but also includes Portuguese, British, Canadian, Caribbean peoples, and some United States military staff.

Economy and the Land. A mild climate, beautiful beaches, and a scenic, hilly terrain make tourism Bermuda's economic mainstay. Foreign businesses, attracted by tax exemptions, provide additional economic contributions. There is limited light manufacturing, agriculture, and fishing, and no heavy industry. Situated about 650 miles (1,046 km) east of North Carolina in the United States, the archipelago consists of many small islands and islets. About twenty are inhabited, several of which are connected by bridges and collectively known as the Island of Bermuda.

History and Politics. The colony received its name from Juan de Bermudez, a Spanish explorer who sailed past the islands in 1503, not landing because of the dangerous coral reefs. Colonization began following a British shipwreck in 1609. Racial inequality resulted in unrest in the late 1960s and 1970s. As a British colony, Bermuda recognizes Great Britain's queen as the head of state. ■

BHUTAN

Official name Kingdom of Bhutan

PEOPLE
Population 1,580,000. **Density** 88/mi² (34/km²). **Urban** 5%. **Capital** Thimphu, 12,000. **Ethnic groups** Bhotia 60%, Nepalese 25%, indigenous 15%. **Languages** Dzongkha, Tibetan and Nepalese dialects. **Religions** Buddhist 75%, Hindu 25%. **Life expectancy** 47 female, 49 male. **Literacy** 5%.

POLITICS
Government Monarchy (Indian protection). **Parties** None. **Suffrage** One vote per family. **Memberships** UN. **Subdivisions** 18 districts.

ECONOMY
GDP $187,000,000 **Per capita** $130. **Monetary unit** Ngultrum, Indian rupee. **Trade partners** India. **Exports** Cement, forestry products, food. **Imports** Fuel, rice, tires, machinery and manufactures.

LAND
Description Southern Asia, landlocked. **Area** 17,954 mi² (46,500 km²). **Highest point** Kula Kangri, 24,784 ft (7,554 m). **Lowest point** Along Manās River, 318 ft (97 m).

People. A mountainous terrain long isolated Bhutan from the outside world and limited internal mingling of its peoples. The population is ethnically divided into the Bhotia, Nepalese, and various tribes. Of Tibetan ancestry, the Bhotes are a majority and as such have determined the major religion, Buddhism, and language, Dzongkha, a Tibetan dialect. The Nepalese are mostly Hindu and speak Nepalese; tribal dialects diversify language further. A largely rural population, many villages grew up around *dzongs*, monastery fortresses built in strategic valley locations during Bhutan's past. Training programs have been instituted to improve the country's low literacy rate and skilled labor shortage.

Economy and the Land. Partially due to physical isolation, Bhutan has one of the world's least developed economies and remains dependent on foreign aid. There is potential for success, however. Forests cover much of the land, limiting agricultural area but offering opportunity for the expansion of forestry. Farming is concentrated in the more densely populated, fertile valleys of the Himalayas, and the country is self-sufficient in food production. The climate varies with altitude; the icy Himalayas in the north give way to temperate central valleys and a subtropical south.

History and Politics. Bhutan's early history remains mostly unknown, but it is thought that by the early sixteenth century, descendants of Tibetan invaders were ruling their lands from strategically located dzongs. In the 1600s a Tibetan lama consolidated the area and became political and religious leader. Proximity to and interaction with British India resulted in British control of Bhutan's foreign affairs in the nineteenth and early twentieth centuries. In 1907 the current hereditary monarchy was established. India gained independence from Britain in 1947 and soon assumed the role of adviser in Bhutan's foreign affairs. Indian ties were strengthened in the late 1950s to counter Chinese influence. At the same time, modernization programs were instituted, improving primitive transportation and communication systems, and bringing Bhutan further into the twentieth-century mainstream. ■

BOLIVIA

Official name Republic of Bolivia

PEOPLE
Population 7,507,000. **Density** 18/mi² (6.8/km²). **Urban** 51%. **Capital** La Paz (seat of government), 992,592; Sucre (seat of judiciary), 86,609. **Ethnic groups** Quechua 30%, Aymara 25%, mixed 25-30%, European 5-15%. **Languages** Spanish, Quechua, Aymara. **Religions** Roman Catholic 95%, Methodist and other

BOTSWANA

BRAZIL

Protestant. **Life expectancy** 58 female, 54 male. **Literacy** 63%.

POLITICS
Government Republic. **Parties** Movement of the Revolutionary Left, Nationalist Democratic Action, Nationalist Revolutionary Movement, others. **Suffrage** Universal adult (married, 18; single, 21). **Memberships** OAS, UN. **Subdivisions** 9 departments.

ECONOMY
GDP $6,266,000,000 **Per capita** $1,025. **Monetary unit** Boliviano. **Trade partners** Exports: Argentina, U.S. U.K. Imports: U.S., Brazil, Argentina. **Exports** Natural gas, tin alloys, minerals, food. **Imports** Food, petroleum, consumer goods, capital goods.

LAND
Description Central South America, landlocked. **Area** 424,165 mi² (1,098,581 km²). **Highest point** Nevado Illimani, 22,579 ft (6,882 m). **Lowest point** Along Paraguay River, 226 ft (69 m).

People. Indians compose the majority of Bolivia's population, while minorities include mestizos, of Spanish-Indian descent, and Europeans. Although most people are poor, Bolivia has a rich cultural heritage, evidenced by early Aymaran and Quechuan artifacts; Spanish-influenced Indian and mestizo art; and twentieth-century achievements. Roman Catholicism is the major religion, and is frequently combined with Indian beliefs.

Economy and the Land. Although the underdeveloped Bolivia is among South America's poorest nations, it is rich in natural resources. While farming is the main activity, mining makes the largest contribution to the gross national product. Population, industry, and major cities are concentrated on the western altiplano, an Andean high plateau where many continue to practice agriculture according to ancestral methods. The eastern llano, or lowland plain, contains fuel deposits and is the site of commercial farming. The yungas, hills, and valleys between the altiplano and the llano form the most developed agricultural region. Successful development of Bolivia's rich resources is partially dependent upon political stability. The climate varies from tropical to semiarid and cool, depending on altitude.

History and Politics. The Aymara Indian culture flourished in the area that is now Bolivia between the seventh and tenth centuries. In the mid-1400s the area was absorbed into the expanding empire of the Incas, who controlled the region until ousted by the Spanish in 1535. Simón Bolívar, the Venezuelan organizer of the South American movement to free Spanish colonies, helped lead the way to independence, which was gained in 1825. As Bolivia developed economically, the Indian population remained ensconced in poverty and enjoyed few rights. After years of turmoil, a 1952 revolution installed a government that introduced suffrage, land and educational reforms. Several military coups followed, and civilian control was re-established in 1982. Although economic instability and high inflation rates have long troubled Bolivia, the economy has shown signs of growth since 1987. ■

Official name Republic of Botswana
PEOPLE
Population 1,324,000. **Density** 5.9/mi² (2.3/km²). **Urban** 24%. **Capital** Gaborone, 107,677. **Ethnic groups** Tswana 95%; Kalanga, Baswara, and Kgalagadi 4%; white 1%. **Languages** English, Tswana. **Religions** Tribal religionist 50%, Roman Catholic and other Christian 50%. **Life expectancy** 64 female, 58 male. **Literacy** 41%.

POLITICS
Government Republic. **Parties** Democratic, National Front. **Suffrage** Universal, over 21. **Memberships** CW, OAU, UN. **Subdivisions** 11 districts.

ECONOMY
GDP $1,165,000,000 **Per capita** $1,104. **Monetary unit** Pula. **Trade partners** Switzerland, U.S., U.K., Southern African countries. **Exports** Diamonds, copper, nickel, meat. **Imports** Food, motor vehicles, textiles, petroleum.

LAND
Description Southern Africa, landlocked. **Area** 224,711 mi² (582,000 km²). **Highest point** 4,969 ft (1,515 m). **Lowest point** Confluence of Shashi and Limpopo rivers, 1,684 ft (513 m).

People. The population of this sparsely-populated country is composed mostly of Tswana, Bantu peoples of various groups. Following settlement patterns laid down centuries ago, Tswana predominate in the more fertile eastern region, and the minority Bushmen are concentrated in the Kalahari Desert. There is also a white minority population. English is an official language, reflecting years of British rule, but the majority speak Tswana. Half the people follow traditional beliefs, while the rest are Christian.

Economy and the Land. Agriculture and livestock raising are the primary activities, although they are limited by the southwestern Kalahari Desert. The most productive farmland lies in the east and north, where rainfall is higher and grazing lands are plentiful. Since the early seventies, when increased exploitation of natural resources began, the economy has developed rapidly. Diamond mining is the main focus of this growth, together with development of copper, nickel, and coal. The climate is mostly subtropical.

History and Politics. In Botswana's early history, Bushmen, the original inhabitants, retreated into the Kalahari region when the Tswana invaded and established their settlements in the more fertile east. Intertribal wars in the early nineteenth century were followed by conflicts with the Boers, settlers of Dutch or Huguenot descent. These conflicts led the Tswana to seek British assistance, and the area of present-day Botswana became part of the British protectorate of Bechuanaland. When the Union of South Africa was created in 1910, those living in Bechuanaland (later Botswana), Basutoland (later Lesotho), and Swaziland requested and were granted exclusion from the Union. British rule continued until 1966, when the protectorate of Bechuanaland became the Republic of Botswana. The country seeks to expand relations with other nations. In addition, Botswana would like to reduce its economic dependence on South Africa, whose apartheid policy it opposes. ■

Official name Federative Republic of Brazil
PEOPLE
Population 152,050,000. **Density** 46/mi² (18/km²). **Urban** 77%. **Capital** Brasília, 1,567,709. **Ethnic groups** White 54%, mixed 39%, black 6%. **Languages** Portuguese, Spanish, English, French. **Religions** Roman Catholic 96%. **Life expectancy** 69 female, 64 male. **Literacy** 74%.

POLITICS
Government Republic. **Parties** Democratic Movement, Liberal Front, Social Democratic, others. **Suffrage** Universal, over 16. **Memberships** OAS, UN. **Subdivisions** 24 states, 2 territories, 1 federal district.

ECONOMY
GDP $226,787,000,000 **Per capita** $1,688. **Monetary unit** Cruzado. **Trade partners** Exports: U.S., Netherlands, Japan. Imports: U.S., Iraq, Germany. **Exports** Coffee and other food, metals, chemicals, food, iron ore. **Imports** Petroleum, machinery, chemicals, wheat and other food, coal.

LAND
Description Eastern South America. **Area** 3,286,488 mi² (8,511,965 km²). **Highest point** Pico da Neblina, 9,888 ft (3,014 m). **Lowest point** Sea level.

People. The largest South American nation, Brazil is also the most populous. Indigenous Indians, Portuguese colonists, black African slaves, and European and Japanese immigrants shaped the mixed population. Today, native Indians compose less than 1 percent of the population, and the group is disappearing rapidly due to contact with modern cultures and other factors. Brazil is the only Portuguese-speaking nation in the Americas, and Roman Catholicism is the major religion.

Economy and the Land. Brazil's prosperous economy stems from a diversified base of agriculture, mining, and industry. Most commercial farms and ranches lie in the southern plateau region, and coffee, cocoa, soybeans, and beef are important products. Mineral resources include iron-ore deposits, many found in the central and southern plateau regions. Additional mineral deposits have recently been discovered in the Amazon area. During and after World War II, the country focused on industrial expansion in the southeast, and in 1960 it moved the capital from Rio de Janeiro to Brasília to redistribute activity. Undeveloped states have been targeted for development, but such programs may require displacement of the Indian population. Forests cover about half the country, and the Amazon River basin is the site of the world's largest rain forest. The northeast consists of semiarid grasslands, and the central-west and south are marked by hills, mountains, and rolling plains. Overall the climate is semitropical to tropical, with heavy rains.

History and Politics. Portugal obtained rights to the region in a 1494 treaty with Spain and claimed Brazil in 1500. As the native Indian population died out, blacks were brought from Africa to work the plantations. In the 1800s, during the Napoleonic Wars, the Portuguese royal family fled to Rio de Janeiro, and in 1815 the colony became a kingdom. In 1821 the Portuguese king departed for Portugal, leaving Brazil's rule to his son, who declared Brazil an independent country and himself emperor in 1822. Economic development in the mid-1800s brought an influx of Europeans. Following a military takeover in 1889, Brazil became a republic. Economic problems resulted in a 1930 military coup, a dictatorship that lasted until 1945, and military takeovers in 1954 and 1964. The country returned to civilian rule in 1985. Key political issues have been the massive foreign debt and worldwide concern over the destruction of the rain forest. ∎

BRITISH INDIAN OCEAN TERRITORY See UNITED KINGDOM.

BRUNEI

Official name Negara Brunei Darussalam

PEOPLE
Population 261,000. **Density** 117/mi² (45/km²). **Urban** 58%. **Capital** Bandar Seri Begawan, 64,000. **Ethnic groups** Malay 65%, Chinese 20%, indigenous 8%, Tamil 3%. **Languages** Malay, English, Chinese. **Religions** Muslim 63%, Buddhist 14%, Roman Catholic and other Christian 10%. **Life expectancy** 73 female, 70 male. **Literacy** 78%.

POLITICS
Government Monarchy. **Parties** None. **Suffrage** None. **Memberships** ASEAN, CW, UN. **Subdivisions** 4 districts.

ECONOMY
GDP $3,032,000,000 **Per capita** $13,782. **Monetary unit** Dollar. **Trade partners** Exports: Japan, Thailand, Thailand. Imports: Singapore, Japan, U.S.. **Exports** Petroleum, natural gas. **Imports** Machinery and transportation equipment, manufactures, food.

LAND
Description Southeastern Asia (island of Borneo). **Area** 2,226 mi² (5,765 km²). **Highest point** Mt. Pagon, 6,070 ft (1,850 m). **Lowest point** Sea level.

People. The majority of Brunei's population is Malay, with minorities of Chinese and indigenous peoples. Most Malays are Muslim, and the Chinese are mainly Christian or Buddhist. Many Chinese, although wealthy, are unable to become citizens due to language-proficiency exams and strict residency requirements. The standard of living is high because of Brunei's oil-based economy, yet wealth is not equally distributed.

Economy and the Land. Oil and natural gas are the economic mainstays, giving Brunei a high per capita gross domestic product. Much food is imported, however, and diversification is a current goal. Situated on northeastern Borneo, Brunei is generally flat and covered with dense rain forests. The climate is tropical.

History and Politics. Historical records of Brunei date back to the seventh century. The country was an important trading center, and by the sixteenth century the sultan of Brunei ruled Borneo and parts of nearby islands. In 1888 Brunei became a British protectorate. In 1984, it gained independence from Great Britain. The nation is ruled by a sultan. ∎

BULGARIA

Official name Republic of Bulgaria

PEOPLE
Population 9,008,000. **Density** 210/mi² (81/km²). **Urban** 70%. **Capital** Sofia, 1,119,152. **Ethnic groups** Bulgarian (Slavic) 85%, Turkish 9%, Gypsy 3%, Macedonian 3%. **Languages** Bulgarian. **Religions** Bulgarian Orthodox, Muslim. **Life expectancy** 76 female, 70 male. **Literacy** 93%.

POLITICS
Government Republic. **Parties** National Agrarian Union, Socialist, Turkish Rights Movement, Union of Democratic Forces. **Suffrage** Universal, over 18. **Memberships** UN. **Subdivisions** 28 provinces.

ECONOMY
GNP $57,800,000,000 **Per capita** $6,437. **Monetary unit** Lev. **Trade partners** U.S.S.R., Germany, Czechoslovakia. **Exports** Machinery and equipment, agricultural products, manufactures. **Imports** Fuel and minerals, machinery and equipment, manufactures.

LAND
Description Eastern Europe. **Area** 42,823 mi² (110,912 km²). **Highest point** Musala, 9,596 ft (2,925 m). **Lowest point** Sea level.

People. Bulgaria's ethnic composition was determined early in its history when Bulgar tribes conquered the area's Slavic inhabitants. Bulgarians, descendants of these peoples, are a majority today, while Turks, Gypsies, and Macedonians compose the main minority groups. Postwar development is reflected in an agriculture-to-industry shift in employment and a resultant rural-to-urban population movement.

Economy and the Land. Following World War II, the Bulgarian government began a program of expansion, turning the undeveloped agricultural nation into an industrial state modeled after the Soviet Union. Today the industrial sector is the greatest economic contributor and employer. Farming, however, continues to play an economic role. Rich soils in river valleys, as well as a climate similar to that of the American Midwest, make the area well suited for raising livestock, growing grain and other crops. The overall terrain is mountainous.

History and Politics. The area of modern Bulgaria was absorbed by the Roman Empire by A.D. 15 and was subsequently invaded by the Slavs. In the seventh century Bulgars conquered the region and settled alongside Slavic inhabitants. Rule by the Ottoman Turks began in the late fourteenth century and lasted until 1878, when the Bulgarians defeated the Turks with the aid of Russia and Romania. The Principality of Bulgaria emerged in 1885, with boundaries approximating those of today, and in 1908 Bulgaria was declared an independent kingdom. Increased territory and a desire for access to the Aegean Sea were partially responsible for Bulgaria's involvement in the Balkan Wars of 1912 and 1913 and alliances with Germany during both world wars. Following Bulgaria's declaration of war on the United States and Britain in World War II, the Soviet Union declared war on Bulgaria. Defeat came in 1944, when the monarchy was overthrown and a Communist government was established shortly thereafter. In 1989, pressure from the people for more participation in the government resulted in the resignation of General Zhivkov, Bulgaria's leader for thirty-five years. The rights of Bulgaria's ethnic Turks have become a major political issue. A severe economic

downturn forced multiparty elections in 1990, with the Bulgarian Socialist (formerly Communist) party retaining control. Worsening economic conditions in late 1990 led to the collapse of the governing party. Negotiations continued into 1991. ∎

BURKINA FASO

Official name Burkina Faso

PEOPLE
Population 9,247,000. **Density** 87/mi² (34/km²). **Urban** 9%. **Capital** Ouagadougou, 441,514. **Ethnic groups** Mossi 30%, Fulani, Lobi, Malinke, Bobo, Senufo, Gurunsi, others. **Languages** French, indigenous. **Religions** Animist 65%, Muslim 25%, Roman Catholic and other Christian. **Life expectancy** 51 female, 48 male. **Literacy** 9%.

POLITICS
Government Provisional military government. **Parties** None. **Suffrage** None. **Memberships** OAU, UN. **Subdivisions** 30 provinces.

ECONOMY
GDP $833,000,000 **Per capita** $128. **Monetary unit** CFA franc. **Trade partners** Exports: Ivory Coast, France, Japan. Imports: France, Ivory Coast, U.S.. **Exports** Oilseed, cotton, live animals, gold. **Imports** Grain and other food, petroleum, manufactures, machinery.

LAND
Description Western Africa, landlocked. **Area** 105,869 mi² (274,200 km²). **Highest point** Téna Kourou, 2,451 ft (747 m). **Lowest point** Along Pendjari River, 443 ft (135 m).

People. The agricultural Mossi, descendants of warrior migrants, are Burkina Faso's majority population. Other groups include the Fulani, Lobi, Malinke, Bobo, Senufo, and Gurunsi. Ethnic languages vary, although French is the official language.

Economy and the Land. Burkina Faso's agricultural economy suffers from frequent droughts and an underdeveloped transportation system. Most people engage in subsistence farming or livestock raising, and industrialization is minimal. Resources are limited but include gold and manganese. The country remains dependent on foreign aid, much of it from France. The land is marked by northern desert, central savanna, and southern forests, while the climate is generally tropical.

History and Politics. The Mossi arrived from central or eastern Africa during the eleventh century and established their kingdom in the area of Burkina Faso. The French came in the late nineteenth century. In 1919 France united various provinces and created the colony of Upper Volta. The colony was divided among other French colonies in 1932, reinstituted in 1937 as an administrative unit called the Upper Coast, and returned to territorial status as Upper Volta in 1947. It gained independence in 1960. Economic problems and accusations of government corruption led to leadership changes and military rule, including numerous coups. In 1984, the country changed its name from Upper Volta to Burkina Faso. ∎

BURMA (MYANMAR)

Official name Union of Burma
PEOPLE
Population 41,690,000. **Density** 160/mi² (62/km²).
Urban 25%. **Capital** Rangoon (Yangon), 2,705,039.
Ethnic groups Bamar (Burmese) 69%, Shan 9%, Kayin 6%, Rakhine 5%. **Languages** Burmese, indigenous.
Religions Buddhist 89%, Muslim 4%, Christian 5%.
Life expectancy 64 female, 61 male. **Literacy** 67%.
POLITICS
Government Provisional military government. **Parties** National League for Democracy, National Unity Party, others. **Suffrage** Universal, over 18. **Memberships** UN. **Subdivisions** 7 divisions, 7 states.
ECONOMY
GDP $6,812,000,000 **Per capita** $185. **Monetary unit** Kyat. **Trade partners** Exports: Southeast Asian countries, India, China. Imports: Japan, Western European countries. **Exports** Teak, rice, oilseed, metals, rubber, gems. **Imports** Machinery and transportation equipment, food.
LAND
Description Southeastern Asia. **Area** 261,228 mi² (676,577 km²). **Highest point** Hkakabo Razi, 19,296 ft (5,881 m). **Lowest point** Sea level.

People. The population of Burma is highly diverse, with many ethnic groups including Tibetan-related Bamar, who compose the majority; Kayin, who inhabit mainly the south and east; and Thai-related Shan, found on the eastern plateaus. Diversity results in many languages, although Burmese predominates. Buddhist monasteries and pagodas dot the landscape, and minority religions include Christianity, indigenous beliefs, and Islam. The primarily rural population is concentrated in the fertile valleys and on the delta of the Irrawaddy River.

Economy and the Land. Fertile soils, dense woodlands, and mineral deposits provide a resource base for agriculture, forestry, and mining. Burma has been beset with economic problems, however, caused mainly by the destruction of World War II, as well as postindependence instability. Today agriculture continues as the economic mainstay. The hot, wet climate is ideal for rice production. In addition, dense forests provide for a timber industry, and resource deposits include petroleum and various minerals. Burma's economic future most likely depends on exploitation of natural resources and political stability. The terrain is marked by mountains, rivers, and forests, and the climate is tropical.

History and Politics. Burma's Chinese and Tibetan settlers were first united in the eleventh century. Independence ended with the invasion of Mongols led by Kublai Khan, followed by national unification in the fifteenth and eighteenth centuries. Annexation to British India in the nineteenth century ended Burma's monarchy. During World War II, Japanese occupation and subsequent Allied-Japanese conflicts caused much economic and physical damage. Burma officially became independent in 1948. After initial stability, the government was unable to withstand separatist and political revolts, and military rule alternated with civilian governments. In 1974, a new government was installed and a new constitution adopted. Yet another military coup in 1988 was widely protested, forcing concessions and the promise of elections from the military. Elections in May 1990 resulted in an overwhelming victory for the opposition, but the military government refused to relinquish power. ∎

BURUNDI

Official name Republic of Burundi
PEOPLE
Population 5,541,000. **Density** 516/mi² (199/km²).
Urban 7%. **Capital** Bujumbura, 273,000. **Ethnic groups** Hutu 85%, Tutsi 14%, Twa 1%. **Languages** French, Kirundi, Swahili. **Religions** Roman Catholic 62%, Animist 32%, Protestant 5%, Muslim 1%. **Life expectancy** 53 female, 49 male. **Literacy** 23%.
POLITICS
Government Provisional military government. **Parties** Unity and Progess. **Suffrage** Universal adult. **Memberships** OAU, UN. **Subdivisions** 15 provinces.
ECONOMY
GDP $1,032,000,000 **Per capita** $219. **Monetary unit** Franc. **Trade partners** Exports: Germany, Finland. Imports: Belgium, Germany, Iran. **Exports** Coffee, tea, hides and skins. **Imports** Manufactures, machinery, petroleum, food, chemicals, automobiles.
LAND
Description Eastern Africa, landlocked. **Area** 10,745 mi² (27,830 km²). **Highest point** Mont Heha 8,760 ft (2,670 m). **Lowest point** Lake Tanganyika, 2,534 ft (772 m).

People. One of Africa's most densely populated nations, Burundi has a populace composed mainly of three Bantu groups. The Hutu are a majority, while the Tutsi, descendants of invaders from Ethiopia, wield most of the power. The Twa are Pygmy hunters, probably descended from the area's inhabitants prior to the influx of the Hutu. Most Burundians are subsistence farmers and Roman Catholic, evidence of foreign influence and rule.

Economy and the Land. An undeveloped country, Burundi relies mainly on agriculture, although undependable rainfall, depleted soil, and erosion occasionally combine for famine. Coffee is a major export. Exploitation of nickel deposits, industrial development through foreign investment, and expansion of tourism offer potential for growth. Although the country is situated near the equator, its high altitude and hilly terrain result in a pleasant climate.

History and Politics. In the fourteenth century, invading pastoral Tutsi warriors conquered the Hutu and Pygmy Twa and established themselves as the region's power base. The areas of modern Burundi and Rwanda were absorbed into German East Africa in the 1890s. Following Belgian occupation during World War I, in 1919 the League of Nations placed present-day Burundi and Rwanda under Belgian rule as part of Ruanda-Urundi. After World War II Ruanda-Urundi was made a United Nations trust territory under Belgian administration. In 1962 Urundi became Burundi, an independent monarchy, and political turmoil soon followed. A Tutsi-dominated government replaced the monarchy in 1966. A 1976 coup installed a government that sought a redistribution of power, but was overthrown by the Army in 1987. The Constitution was suspended and thousands of Burundians have since died in ethnic clashes between the Tutsi and the Hutu. ∎

CAMBODIA

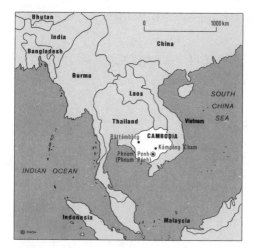

Official name Cambodia
PEOPLE
Population 8,345,000. **Density** 119/mi² (46/km²).
Urban 12%. **Capital** Phnom Penh, 700,000. **Ethnic groups** Khmer 90%, Chinese 5%. **Languages** Khmer, French. **Religions** Buddhist 95%, Animist, Muslim. **Life expectancy** 52 female, 50 male. **Literacy** 48%.
POLITICS
Government Socialist republic. **Parties** People's Revolutionary. **Suffrage** Universal, over 18. **Memberships** UN. **Subdivisions** 20 provinces. **Monetary unit** Riel. **Trade partners** Exports: Western European countries, U.S. Imports: France, Japan, U.S.. **Exports** Petroleum, coffee, cocoa, wood, manufactures. **Imports** Machinery and electrical equipment, transportation equipment, chemicals.
LAND
Description Southeastern Asia. **Area** 69,898 mi² (181,035 km²). **Highest point** Mt. Aoral, 5,948 ft (1,813 m). **Lowest point** Sea level.

People. The Khmer, one of the oldest peoples in Southeast Asia, constitute the major ethnic group in Cambodia. The population has declined significantly since the mid-1970s due to war, famine, human-rights abuses, and emigration. Because of an urban-evacuation campaign initiated by the Khmer Rouge, Cambodia's previous regime, most Cambodians live in rural areas, working as farmers or laborers. Although the new government does not encourage religion (an activity often punished by death during the Khmer Rouge era), the practice of Buddhism, the main religion, is on the rise.

Economy and the Land. Cambodia's flat central region and wet climate make it well suited for rice production. Along with rubber, rice was the mainstay of the economy before the seventies, but the Vietnam and civil wars all but destroyed agriculture. This sector of the economy has begun to recover recently, but a shortage of skilled labor, combined with the effects of war, have held back industry. The terrain is marked by the central plain, forests, and mountains in the south, west, and along the Thai border. The climate is tropical, with high rainfall and humidity.

History and Politics. Cambodia traces its roots to the Hindu kingdoms of Funan and Chenla, which reigned in the early centuries A.D. The Angkor Empire dominated until the fifteenth century, incorporating much of present-day Laos, Thailand, and Vietnam and constructing the stone temples of Angkor Wat, considered one of Southeast Asia's greatest architectural achievements. By 1431 the Siamese had overrun the region, and subsequent years saw the rise of the Siamese, Vietnamese, and Lao. By the mid-1700s Cambodia's boundaries approximated those of today. During the 1800s, as French control in Indochina expanded, the area became a French protectorate. Cambodia gained independence in 1953 under King Sihanouk, who, after changing his title to ''prince,'' became prime minister in 1955 and head of state in 1960. In 1970, after Sihanouk was ousted, Lon Nol was installed as prime minister, and the monarchy of Cambodia changed to the Khmer Republic. During this time the Vietnam War spilled over the Khmer Republic's borders, as United States forces made bombing raids against what they claimed were North Vietnamese bases. Resulting anti-American sentiment gave rise to discontent with Lon Nol's pro-United States regime. The Khmer Communists, or Khmer Rouge, seized power in 1975 and, led by Pol Pot, exiled most Cambodians to the countryside. An estimated three million died under the Khmer Rouge, many were executed because they were educated or had links to the former government. Vietnamese troops supported by some Cambodian Communists invaded Cambodia in late 1978, and by early 1979 they had overthrown the Khmer Rouge. Withdrawal of Vietnam in 1989 has renewed fears that the Khmer Rouge may regain power. ■

CAMEROON

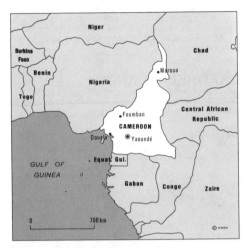

Official name Republic of Cameroon
PEOPLE
Population 12,110,000. **Density** 66/mi² (25/km²).
Urban 49%. **Capital** Yaoundé, 653,670. **Ethnic groups** Cameroon Highlander 31%, Equatorial Bantu 19%, Kirdi 11%, Fulani 10%. **Languages** English, French, indigenous. **Religions** Animist 51%, Christian 33%, Muslim 16%. **Life expectancy** 55 female, 51 male. **Literacy** 41%.
POLITICS
Government Republic. **Parties** People's Democratic Movement. **Suffrage** Universal, over 21. **Memberships** OAU, UN. **Subdivisions** 10 provinces.
ECONOMY
GDP $8,385,000,000 **Per capita** $941. **Monetary unit** CFA franc. **Trade partners** Exports: Netherlands, France, Italy. Imports: France, Germany, Japan. **Exports** Petroleum, coffee, cocoa, aluminum, cotton, wood. **Imports** Machinery, manufactures, transportation equipment, pharmaceuticals, alumina.
LAND
Description Central Africa. **Area** 183,569 mi² (475,442 km²). **Highest point** Cameroon Mtn., 13,451 ft (4,100 m). **Lowest point** Sea level.

People. Immigration and foreign rule shaped Cameroon's diverse population, composed of some two hundred groups speaking twenty-four major African languages. Both English and French are official languages, resulting from the merging of former French-ruled eastern and British-ruled western territories. Population is concentrated in the French-speaking eastern region. The majority of people practice indigenous beliefs that often influence Islamic and Christian practices as well.

Economy and the Land. Recent economic plans have focused on agriculture, industry, and the development of oil deposits. Agriculture is still the country's economic base, but oil is a major export. A varied terrain features southern coastal plains and rain forests, central plateaus, mountainous western forests, and northern savanna and marshes. Although this has hindered transportation development and thus slowed economic growth, improvements are being made. Climate varies from a hot, humid coastal region to fluctuating temperatures and less humidity northward.

History and Politics. The Sao people reached the Cameroon area in the tenth century. The Portuguese arrived in the 1500s, and the following three centuries saw an influx of European and African peoples and an active slave trade along the coast. In 1884 Germany set up a protectorate that included modern Cameroon by 1914. During World War I British and French troops occupied the area, and in 1919, following the war, the League of Nations divided Cameroon into eastern French and western British mandates. The Cameroons became trust territories in 1946, and French Cameroon became an independent republic in 1960. In 1961 the northern region of British Cameroon elected to join Nigeria, and the southern area chose to unite with the eastern Republic of Cameroon. This resulted in a two-state Federal Republic of Cameroon. A 1972 referendum combined the states into the United Republic of Cameroon, and in 1984, the official name became the Republic of Cameroon. In September 1990, the country reached an agreement in principle for an interim government and subsequent elections. ■

CANADA

Official name Canada
PEOPLE
Population 26,710,000. **Density** 6.9/mi² (2.7/km²).
Urban 76%. **Capital** Ottawa, 300,763. **Ethnic groups** British origin 40%, French origin 27%, other European 23%, native Canadian 2%. **Languages** English, French. **Religions** Roman Catholic 47%, United Church 16%, Anglican 10%, other Christian. **Life expectancy** 81 female, 74 male. **Literacy** 93%.
POLITICS
Government Parliamentary state. **Parties** Liberal, New Democratic, Progressive Conservative. **Suffrage** Universal, over 18. **Memberships** CW, NATO, OAS, OECD, UN. **Subdivisions** 10 provinces, 2 territories.
ECONOMY
GDP $348,291,000,000 **Per capita** $13,783. **Monetary unit** Dollar. **Trade partners** U.S., Japan, U.K.. **Exports** Newsprint, wood pulp, timber, grain, petroleum, natural gas, ores. **Imports** Food, beverages, petroleum, chemicals, machinery, motor vehicles.
LAND
Description Northern North America. **Area** 3,849,674 mi² (9,970,610 km²). **Highest point** Mt. Logan, 19,524 ft (5,951 m). **Lowest point** Sea level.

People. Canada was greatly influenced by French and British rule, and its culture reflects this dual nature. Descendants of British and French settlers compose the two main population groups, and languages include both English and French. French-speaking inhabitants are concentrated in the Province of Québec. Minorities include descendants of various European groups, indigenous Indians, and Inuit. Because of the rugged terrain and harsh climate of northern Canada, population is concentrated near the United States border.

Economy and the Land. Rich natural resources—including extensive mineral deposits, fertile land, forests, and lakes—helped shape Canada's diversified economy, which ranks among the world's most prosperous. Economic problems are those common to most modern industrial nations. Agriculture, mining, and industry are highly developed. Canada is a major wheat producer; mineral output includes asbestos, zinc, silver, and nickel; and crude petroleum is an important export. The service sector is also active. Second only to the Soviet Union in land area, Canada has a terrain that varies from eastern rolling hills and plains to mountains in the west. The Canadian Shield consists of ancient rock and extends from Labrador to the Arctic Islands. It is covered by thick forests in the south and tundra in the north. Overall, summers are moderate and winters long and cold.

History and Politics. Canada's first inhabitants were Asian Indians and Inuit, an Arctic people. Around the year 1000, Vikings were the first Europeans to reach North America, and in 1497 John Cabot claimed the Newfoundland coastal area for Britain. Jacques Cartier established French claim when he landed at the Gaspé Peninsula in the 1500s. Subsequent French and British rivalry culminated in several wars during the late seventeenth and eighteenth centuries. The wars ended with the 1763 Treaty of Paris, by which France lost Canada and other North American territory to Britain. To aid in resolving the continued conflict between French and English residents, the British North America Act of 1867 united the colonies into the Dominion of Canada. Canada fought on the side of the British during World War I. In 1926, along with other dominions, Canada declared itself an independent member of the British Commonwealth, and in 1931 Britain recognized the declaration through the Statute of Westminster. Canada once again allied itself with Britain during World War II. In 1988, Canada saw vigorous debate over a free trade pact with the United States, which narrowly won approval. The Québec separatist movement is striving for independent status for French-speaking Québec.

CANARY ISLANDS See SPAIN.

CAPE VERDE

Official name Republic of Cape Verde

PEOPLE
Population 381,000.
Density 245/mi² (94/km²).
Urban 52%. **Capital** Praia, São Tiago I., 61,797.
Ethnic groups Creole (mulatto) 71%, African 28%, European 1%.
Languages Portuguese, Crioulo. **Religions** Roman Catholic, Nazarene and other Protestant. **Life expectancy** 65 female, 61 male. **Literacy** 37%.
POLITICS
Government Republic.
Parties African Party for Independence, Movement for Democracy. **Suffrage** Universal, over 15.
Memberships OAU, UN.
Subdivisions 14 districts.

ECONOMY
GNP $135,100,000 **Per capita** $450. **Monetary unit** Escudo. **Trade partners** Exports: Algeria, Italy, Portugal. Imports: Portugal, Netherlands, France. **Exports** Fish, bananas, vegetables, salt. **Imports** Grain and other food, manufactures, machinery, petroleum, chemicals.
LAND
Description Western African islands. **Area** 1,557 mi² (4,033 km²). **Highest point** Pico, 9,281 ft (2,829 m). **Lowest point** Sea level.

People. The Portuguese-African heritage of Cape Verde's population is a result of Portuguese rule and the forced transmigration of Africans for slavery. Although Portuguese is an official language, the majority speaks Crioulo, a creole dialect. Most people are Roman Catholic, but indigenous practices exist, sometimes in combination with Catholicism. The mainly poor population is largely undernourished and plagued by unemployment. The country consists of five islets and ten main islands, and all but one are inhabited.

Economy and the Land. The volcanic, mountainous islands have few natural resources and low rainfall; thus the country's economy remains underdeveloped. Fishing and agriculture are important for both subsistence and commercial purposes. Much of the land is too dry for farming, and drought is a frequent problem. Cape Verde's location on air and sea routes and its tropical climate offer potential for expansion into services and tourism. However, Cape Verde will most likely continue to rely on foreign aid for some time.

History and Politics. The islands that make up Cape Verde were uninhabited when the Portuguese arrived around 1460. Settlement began in 1462, and by the sixteenth century Cape Verde had become a shipping center for the African slave trade. Until 1879 Portugal ruled Cape Verde and present-day Guinea-Bissau as a single colony. A movement for the independence of Cape Verde and Guinea-Bissau began in the 1950s, and a 1974 coup in Portugal ultimately resulted in autonomy for both countries, with Cape Verde proclaiming independence in 1975. Plans to unify Cape Verde and Guinea-Bissau were abandoned following a 1980 coup in Guinea-Bissau. Cape Verde follows a foreign policy of nonalignment and takes a special interest in African affairs. ∎

CAYMAN ISLANDS
See UNITED KINGDOM.

CENTRAL AFRICAN REPUBLIC

Official name Central African Republic
PEOPLE
Population 2,917,000. **Density** 12/mi² (4.7/km²). **Urban** 47%. **Capital** Bangui, 473,817. **Ethnic groups** Baya 34%, Banda 27%, Mandja 21%, Sara 10%. **Languages** French, Sango, Arabic, indigenous. **Religions** Protestant 25%, Roman Catholic 25%, Animist 24%, Muslim 15%. **Life expectancy** 49 female, 46 male. **Literacy** 18%.
POLITICS
Government Republic. **Parties** Democratic Rally. **Suffrage** Universal, over 21. **Memberships** OAU, UN. **Subdivisions** 16 prefectures, 1 autonomous commune.
ECONOMY
GDP $641,000,000 **Per capita** $245. **Monetary unit** CFA franc. **Trade partners** Exports: France, Belgium, Israel. Imports: France, Zaire, Japan. **Exports** Wood, coffee, diamonds, cotton. **Imports** Food, textiles, petroleum, machinery, electrical equipment.
LAND
Description Central Africa, landlocked. **Area** 240,535 mi² (622,984 km²). **Highest point** Mont Ngaoui, 4,626 ft (1,410 m). **Lowest point** Along Ubangi River, 1,100 ft (335 m).

People. Lying near Africa's geographical center, the Central African Republic was the stopping point for many precolonial nomadic groups. The resultant multiethnic populace was further diversified by migrations during the slave-trade era. Of the country's many languages, Sango is most widely used. Overall, the population is rural and suffers from poverty and a low literacy rate.

Economy and the Land. Fertile land, extensive forests, and mineral deposits provide adequate bases for agriculture, forestry, and mining. Economic development remains minimal, however, impeded by poor transportation routes, a landlocked location, lack of skilled labor, and political instability. Subsistence farming continues as the major activity, and agriculture is the chief contributor to

the economy. The country consists of a plateau region with southern rain forests and a northeastern semidesert. The climate is temperate, and ample rainfall sometimes results in impassable roads.

History and Politics. Little is known of the area's early history except that it was the site of many migrations. European slave trade in the nineteenth century led to the 1894 creation of a French territory called the Ubangi-Chari. This in turn combined with the areas of the present-day Congo, Chad, and Gabon in 1910 to form French Equatorial Africa. The Central African Republic gained independence in 1960. A 1966 military coup installed military chief Jean-Bedel Bokassa, who in 1976 assumed the title of emperor, changed the republic to a monarchy, and renamed the nation the Central African Empire. A 1979 coup ended the monarchy and reinstated the name Central African Republic. The country enacted a new constitution in 1986. ∎

CHAD

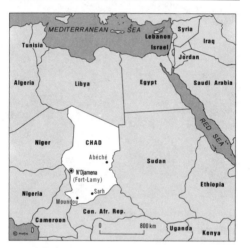

Official name Republic of Chad
PEOPLE
Population 5,122,000. **Density** 10/mi² (4.0/km²). **Urban** 33%. **Capital** N'Djamena, 303,000. **Ethnic groups** Sara and other African, Arab. **Languages** Arabic, French, indigenous. **Religions** Muslim 44%, Christian 33%, Animist 23%. **Life expectancy** 49 female, 46 male. **Literacy** 17%.
POLITICS
Government Republic. **Parties** National Union for Independence and Revolution. **Suffrage** Universal adult. **Memberships** OAU, UN. **Subdivisions** 14 prefectures.
ECONOMY
GDP $630,000,000 **Per capita** $135. **Monetary unit** CFA franc. **Trade partners** Exports: France, Nigeria, Cameroon. Imports: U.S., France. **Exports** Cotton, cattle, textiles, fish. **Imports** Machinery and transportation equipment, industrial goods, petroleum, food.
LAND
Description Central Africa, landlocked. **Area** 495,755 mi² (1,284,000 km²). **Highest point** Mt. Koussi, 11,204 ft (3,415 m). **Lowest point** Bodélé Depression, 525 ft (160 m).

People. Centuries ago Islamic Arabs mixed with indigenous black Africans and established Chad's diverse population. This variety has led to a rich but often troubled culture. Descendants of Arab invaders mainly inhabit the north, where Islam predominates and nomadic farming is the major activity. In the south—traditionally the economic and political center—the black Sara predominate, operating small farms and practicing indigenous or Christian beliefs. Chad's many languages also reflect its ethnic variety.

Economy and the Land. Natural features and instability arising from ethnic and regional conflict have combined to prevent Chad from prospering. Agriculture and fishing are economic mainstays and are often conducted at subsistence levels. The Sahara extends into Chad's northern region, and the southern grasslands with their heavy rains compose the primary agricultural area. The relative

prosperity of the region, in conjunction with its predominantly Sara population, has fueled much of the political conflict. Future growth is greatly dependent on political equilibrium. Climate varies from the hot, dry northern desert to the semiarid central region and rainier south.

History and Politics. African and Arab societies began prospering in the Lake Chad region around the eighth century A.D. Subsequent centuries saw the landlocked area become an ethnic crossroads for Muslim nomads and African groups. European traders arrived in the late 1800s, and by 1900 France had gained control. When created in 1910, French Equatorial Africa's boundaries included modern Chad, Gabon, the Congo, and the Central African Republic. Following Chad's independence in 1960, the southern Sara gained dominance over the government. A northern rebel group has emerged and government-rebel conflict has continued. Libyan troops entered Chad in 1980, and conflict continued until a cease-fire was agreed to in 1987. Isolated incursions continue. The pro-Western government fell to rebel forces in December 1990, which led to the concern that Libya's influence will grow. ∎

CHANNEL ISLANDS
See UNITED KINGDOM.

CHILE

Official name Republic of Chile

PEOPLE
Population 13,270,000. **Density** 45/mi² (18/km²). **Urban** 86%. **Capital** Santiago, 232,667. **Ethnic groups** White and mestizo 95%, Amerindian 3%. **Languages** Spanish. **Religions** Roman Catholic 89%, Pentecostal and other Protestant 11%. **Life expectancy** 76 female, 69 male. **Literacy** 91%.
POLITICS
Government Republic. **Parties** Christian Democratic, National Renovation, Radical, Social Democratic, others. **Suffrage** Universal, over 18. **Memberships** OAS, UN. **Subdivisions** 12 regions, 1 metropolitan region.
ECONOMY
GDP $15,996,000,000 **Per capita** $1,363. **Monetary unit** Peso. **Trade partners** Exports: U.S., Japan, Germany. Imports: U.S., Japan, Brazil, Germany. **Exports** Copper, manufactures, molybdenum, iron ore, wood pulp. **Imports** Manufactures, machinery, transportation equipment, petroleum, food.
LAND
Description Southern South America. **Area** 292,135 mi² (756,626 km²). **Highest point** Nevado Ojos del Salado 22,615 ft (6,893 m). **Lowest point** Sea level.

People. Chile's land barriers—the eastern Andes, western coastal range, and northern desert—have resulted in a mostly urban population concentrated in a central valley. Mestizos, of Spanish-Indian heritage, and descendants of Spanish immigrants predominate. In addition to an Indian minority, the population includes those who trace their roots to Irish and English colonists or nineteenth-century German immigrants. The country enjoys a relatively high literacy rate, but poverty remains a problem.

Economy and the Land. Chile's land provides the natural resources necessary for a successful economy, but longtime instability has taken its toll. The northern desert region is the site of mineral deposits, and mining is a major component of trade, making Chile vulnerable to outside market forces. An agricultural zone lies in the central valley, while the south offers forests, grazing land, and some petroleum deposits. The climate varies from region to region but is generally mild.

History and Politics. Upon their arrival in the 1500s, the Spanish defeated the northern Inca Indians, although many years were spent in conflict with Araucanian Indians of the central and southern regions. From the sixteenth through nineteenth centuries, Chile received little attention from ruling Spain, and colonists established a successful agriculture. In 1818 Bernardo O'Higgins led the way to victory over the Spanish and became ruler of independent Chile. By the 1920s, dissent arising from unequal power and land distribution united the middle and working classes but social-welfare, education, and economic programs were unable to eliminate inequalities rooted in the past. A 1960 earthquake and tidal wave added to the country's problems. Leftist Salvador Allende Gossens was elected to power in 1970, governing until his death in 1973 in a military coup, which installed Augusto Pinochet. Civil disturbances and grave human-rights abuses marked his right-wing government. This dictatorship ended with the election of a new leader in December 1989. Pinochet's continued control of the military has dashed hopes for a more democratic government. ■

CHINA

Official name People's Republic of China
PEOPLE
Population 1,141,530,000. **Density** 309/mi² (119/km²). **Urban** 21%. **Capital** Beijing (Peking), 6,710,000. **Ethnic groups** Han Chinese 93%, Zhuang, Hui, Uygur, Yi, Miao, Manchu, Tibetan, others. **Languages** Chinese dialects. **Religions** Confucian, Taoist, Buddhist, Muslim. **Life expectancy** 73 female, 69 male. **Literacy** 66%.
POLITICS
Government Socialist republic. **Parties** Communist. **Suffrage** Universal, over 18. **Memberships** UN. **Subdivisions** 22 provinces, 5 autonomous regions, 3 municipalities.
ECONOMY
GNP $262,000,000,000 **Per capita** $251. **Monetary unit** Yuan. **Trade partners** Exports: Hong Kong, Japan, U.S. Imports: Japan, Hong Kong, U.S.. **Exports** Textiles and other manufactures, petroleum, food, crude materials. **Imports** Manufactures, machinery, chemicals, wood and other crude materials.
LAND
Description Eastern Asia. **Area** 3,689,631 mi² (9,556,100 km²). **Highest point** Mt. Everest, 29,028 ft (8,848 m). **Lowest point** Turfan Depression, -505 ft (-154 m).
The above information excludes Taiwan.

People. Population is concentrated in the east, and Han Chinese are the majority group. Zhuang, Hui, Uygur, Yi, Miao, Manchu, and Tibetan peoples compose minorities. Many Chinese languages are spoken, but the national language is Modern Standard Chinese, or Mandarin, based on a northern dialect. Following a Communist revolution in 1949, religious activity was discouraged. It is now on the increase, and religions include Confucianism, Taoism, and Buddhism, plus Islam and Christianity. China ranks first in the world in population, and family-planning programs have been implemented to aid population control. With a recorded civilization going back about 3,500 years, China has contributed much to world culture.

Economy and the Land. Most economic progress dates from 1949, when the new People's Republic of China faced a starving, war-torn, and unemployed population. Industry is expanding, but agriculture continues as the major activity. Natural resources include coal, oil, natural gas, and minerals, many of which remain to be explored. A current economic plan focuses on growth in agriculture, industry, science and technology, and national defense. China's terrain is varied: two-thirds consists of mountainous or semiarid land, with fertile plains and deltas in the east. The climate is marked by hot, humid summers, while the dry winters are often cold.

History and Politics. China's civilization ranks among the world's oldest. The first dynasty, the Shang, began sometime during the second millennium B.C. Kublai Khan's thirteenth-century invasion brought China the first of its various foreign rulers. In the nineteenth century, despite government efforts to the contrary, foreign influence and intervention grew. The government was weakened by the Opium War with Britain in the 1840s; the Taiping Rebellion, a civil war; and a war with Japan from 1894 to 1895. Opposition to foreign influences erupted in the anti-foreign and anti-Christian Boxer Rebellion of 1900. After China became a republic in 1912, the death of the president in 1916 triggered the warlord period, in which conflicts were widespread and power was concentrated among military leaders. Attempts to unite the nation began in the 1920s with Sun Yat-sen's Nationalist party, initially allied with the Communist party. Under the leadership of Chiang Kai-shek, the Nationalist party overcame the warlords, captured Beijing, and executed many Communists. Remaining Communists reorganized under Mao Zedong, and the Communist-Nationalist conflict continued, along with Japanese invasion and occupation. By 1949 the Communists controlled most of the country, and the People's Republic of China was proclaimed. Chiang Kai-shek fled to Taiwan, proclaiming T'aipei as China's provisional capital. After Mao's death in 1976, foreign trade and contact expanded. In 1979 the United States recognized Beijing, rather than T'aipei, as China's capital. When a retrenchment of the government from liberalization erupted violently in student demonstrations in 1989, many people were killed or arrested. See also TAIWAN. ■

CHRISTMAS ISLAND See AUSTRALIA.

COCOS ISLANDS See AUSTRALIA.

COLOMBIA

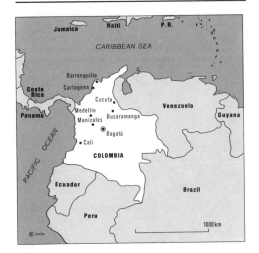

Official name Republic of Colombia
PEOPLE
Population 31,370,000. **Density** 71/mi² (27/km²). **Urban** 70%. **Capital** Bogotá, 3,982,941. **Ethnic groups** Mestizo 58%, white 20%, mulatto 14%, black 4%. **Languages** Spanish. **Religions** Roman Catholic 95%. **Life expectancy** 68 female, 64 male. **Literacy** 88%.
POLITICS
Government Republic. **Parties** Conservative, Liberal, others. **Suffrage** Universal, over 18. **Memberships**

OAS, UN. **Subdivisions** 23 departments, 5 commissariats, 4 intendencies, 1 federal district.
ECONOMY
GDP $34,187,000,000 **Per capita** $1,198. **Monetary unit** Peso. **Trade partners** Exports: U.S., Japan, Germany. Imports: U.S., Japan, Venezuela. **Exports** Coffee, petroleum, bananas and other food, manufactures. **Imports** Machinery and transportation equipment, food, chemicals, paper products.
LAND
Description Northern South America. **Area** 440,831 mi² (1,141,748 km²). **Highest point** Pico Cristóbal Colón, 19,029 ft (5,800 m). **Lowest point** Sea level.

People. Colombia's mixed population traces its roots to indigenous Indians, Spanish colonists, and black African slaves. Most numerous today are mestizos, those of Spanish-Indian descent. Roman Catholicism, the Spanish language, and Colombia's overall culture evidence the long-lasting effect of Spanish rule. Over the past decades the population has shifted from mainly rural to urban as the economy has expanded into industry.

Economy and the Land. Industry now keeps pace with traditional agriculture in economic contributions, and mining is also important. Natural resources include oil, coal, natural gas, most of the world's emeralds, plus fertile soils. The traditional coffee crop also remains important for Colombia, a leading coffee producer. The terrain is characterized by a flat coastal region, central highlands, and wide eastern llanos, or plains. The climate is tropical on the coast and in the west, with cooler temperatures in the highlands.

History and Politics. In the 1500s Spaniards conquered the native Indian groups and established the area as a Spanish colony. In the early 1700s, Bogotá became the capital of the viceroyalty of New Granada, which included modern Colombia, Venezuela, Ecuador, and Panama. Rebellion in Venezuela in 1796 sparked revolts elsewhere in New Granada, including Colombia, and in 1813 independence was declared. In 1819 the Republic of Greater Colombia was formed and included all the former members of the Spanish viceroyalty. Independence leader Simón Bolívar became president. By 1830 Venezuela and Ecuador had seceded from the republic, followed by Panama in 1903. The Conservative and Liberal parties, dominating forces in Colombia's political history, arose from differences between supporters of Bolívar and Santander. Conservative-Liberal conflict led to a violent civil war from 1899 to 1902, as well as to *La Violencia*, The Violence, a civil disorder that continued from the 1940s to the 1960s and resulted in about three hundred thousand deaths. From the late fifties through the seventies, the government alternated between conservative and liberal rule. Political unrest reduced the effectiveness of both parties. By the 1980s, growing drug traffic presented Colombia with new problems. In 1989 the government declared war on the drug cartels after antigovernment terrorism increased. ■

COMOROS

Official name Federal Islamic Republic of the Comoros
PEOPLE
Population 498,000. **Density** 577/mi² (223/km²). **Urban**

28%. **Capital** Moroni, Njazidja I., 23,432. **Ethnic groups** African-Arab descent (Antalote, Cafre, Makua, Oimatsaha, Sakalava). **Languages** Arabic, French, Shaafi Islam (Swahili), Malagasy. **Religions** Sunni Muslim 86%, Roman Catholic 14%. **Life expectancy** 56 female, 52 male. **Literacy** 15%.

POLITICS
Government Islamic republic. **Parties** National Union for Democracy, Union for Progress. **Suffrage** Universal, over 18. **Memberships** OAU, UN. **Subdivisions** 3 islands.

ECONOMY
GNP $114,000,000 **Per capita** $248. **Monetary unit** Franc. **Trade partners** Exports: U.S., France. Imports: France, Madagascar, Somalia. **Exports** Cloves, perfume oils, vanilla. **Imports** Petroleum, rice, meat, sugar and honey.

LAND
Description Southeastern African islands. **Area** 863 mi² (2,235 km²). **Highest point** Kartala, 7,746 ft (2,361 m). **Lowest point** Sea level.
The above information excludes Mayotte.

People. The ethnic groups of Comoros' Njazidja, Nzwani, and Mwali islands are mainly of Arab-African descent, practice Islam, and speak a Swahili dialect. Arab culture, however, predominates throughout the island group. Poverty, disease, a shortage of medical care, and low literacy continue to plague the nation.

Economy and the Land. The economic mainstay of Comoros is agriculture, and most Comorans practice subsistence farming and fishing. Plantations employ workers to produce the main cash crops, which include spices and essential (perfume) oils. Of volcanic origin, the islands have soils of varying quality, and some are unsuited for farming. Terrain varies from the mountains of Njazidja to the hills and valleys of Mwali. The climate is cool and dry, with a winter rainy season.

History and Politics. The Comoro Islands saw invasions by coastal African, Persian Gulf, Indonesian, and Malagasy peoples. Portuguese explorers landed in the 1500s, around the same time Arab Shirazis, most likely from Persia, introduced Islam. The French took Mayotte in 1843 and had established colonial rule over the four main islands by 1912. Comoros declared unilateral independence in 1975. Mayotte, however, voted to remain under French administration. ■

CONGO

Official name People's Republic of the Congo
PEOPLE
Population 2,346,000. **Density** 18/mi² (6.9/km²). **Urban** 42%. **Capital** Brazzaville, 585,812. **Ethnic groups** Kongo 52%, Bateke 17%, Mbochis 12%. **Languages** French, indigenous. **Religions** Christian 50%, Animist 42%, Muslim 2%. **Life expectancy** 52 female, 49 male. **Literacy** 80%.
POLITICS
Government Socialist republic. **Parties** Labor. **Suffrage** Universal, over 18. **Memberships** OAU, UN. **Subdivisions** 9 regions, 1 federal district.
ECONOMY
GDP $2,194,000,000 **Per capita** $1,276. **Monetary**

unit CFA franc. **Trade partners** Exports: U.S., Spain, France. Imports: France, Italy, U.S.. **Exports** Petroleum, diamonds, wood products. **Imports** Manufactured goods, machinery, fish and other food, petroleum chemicals.

LAND
Description Central Africa. **Area** 132,047 mi² (342,000 km²). **Highest point** Mt. Nabeba, 3,219 ft (981 m). **Lowest point** Sea level.

People. The Congo's main groups, the Kongo, Bateke, and Mbochi create an ethnically and linguistically diverse populace. The official language, French, reflects former colonial rule. Population is concentrated in the south, away from the dense forests, heavy rainfall, and hot climate of the north. Educational programs have improved, although rural inhabitants remain relatively isolated.

Economy and the Land. Brazzaville was the commercial center of the former colony called French Equatorial Africa. The Congo now benefits from the early groundwork laid for service and transport industries. Subsistence farming occupies most Congolese, however, and takes most of the cultivated land. Low productivity and a growing populace create a need for foreign aid, much of it from France. Offshore petroleum is the most valuable mineral resource and a major economic contributor. The land is marked by coastal plains, a south-central valley, a central plateau, and the Congo River basin in the north. The climate is tropical.

History and Politics. Several tribal kingdoms existed in the area during its early history. The Portuguese arrived on the coast in the 1400s, and slave trade flourished until it was banned in the 1800s. A Teke king then signed a treaty placing the area, known as Middle Congo, under French protection. In 1910 Middle Congo, the present-day Central African Republic, Gabon, and Chad were joined to form French Equatorial Africa. The Republic of the Congo became independent in 1960. Subsequent years saw unrest, including coups, a presidential assassination, and accusations of corruption and human-rights violations. In 1969, the country became "The People's Republic of the Congo" under the leadership of a single political party, the Workers' Party. In 1979, a newly-elected president granted amnesty to political prisoners, and opposition political parties were legalized in 1991. ■

COOK ISLANDS See NEW ZEALAND.

CORSICA See FRANCE.

COSTA RICA

Official name Republic of Costa Rica

PEOPLE
Population 3,032,000. **Density** 154/mi² (59/km²). **Urban** 54%. **Capital** San José, 278,600. **Ethnic groups** White and mestizo 96%, black 3%, Amerindian 1%. **Languages** Spanish. **Religions** Roman Catholic 95%. **Life expectancy** 78 female, 73 male. **Literacy** 88%.

POLITICS
Government Republic. **Parties** National Liberation, Social Christian Unity, others. **Suffrage** Universal, over 18. **Memberships** OAS, UN. **Subdivisions** 7 provinces.
ECONOMY
GDP $3,814,000,000 **Per capita** $1,400. **Monetary unit** Colon. **Trade partners** Exports: U.S., Germany, Guatemala. Imports: U.S., Venezuela, Mexico. **Exports** Coffee, bananas, textiles, sugar. **Imports** Petroleum, machinery, manufactures, chemicals, fertilizer, food.
LAND
Description Central America. **Area** 19,730 mi² (51,100 km²). **Highest point** Cerro Chirripó, 12,530 ft (3,819 m). **Lowest point** Sea level.

People. Compared with most other Central American countries, Costa Rica has a relatively large population of European descent, mostly Spanish with minorities of German, Dutch, and Swiss ancestry. Together with mestizos, people of Spanish-Indian heritage, they compose the bulk of the population. Descendants of black Jamaican immigrants inhabit mainly the Caribbean coastal region. Indigenous Indians in scattered enclaves continue traditional lifestyles; some, however, have been assimilated into the country's majority culture.

Economy and the Land. Costa Rica's economy, one of the most prosperous in Central America, has not been without problems, some resulting from falling coffee prices and rising oil costs. Agriculture remains important, producing traditional coffee and banana crops, while the country attempts to expand industry. Population and agriculture are concentrated in the central highlands. Much of the country is forested, and the mountainous central area is bordered by coastal plains on the east and west. The climate is semitropical to tropical.

History and Politics. In 1502 Christopher Columbus arrived and claimed the area for Spain. Spaniards named the region Rich Coast, and settlers soon flocked to the new land to seek their fortune. Rather than riches, they found an Indian population unwilling to surrender its land. But many Spaniards remained, establishing farms in the central area. In 1821 the Central American provinces of Costa Rica, Guatemala, El Salvador, Honduras, and Nicaragua declared themselves independent from Spain, and by 1823 they had formed the Federation of Central America. Despite efforts to sustain it, the federation was in a state of virtual collapse by 1838, and Costa Rica became an independent republic. Since the first free elections in 1889, Costa Rica has experienced a presidential overthrow in 1919 and a civil war in 1948, which arose over a disputed election. In the 1980s the country worked to promote peaceful solutions to armed conflicts in the region. ■

CUBA

Official name Republic of Cuba
PEOPLE
Population 10,805,000. **Density** 252/mi² (97/km²). **Urban** 75%. **Capital** Havana, 2,036,800. **Ethnic groups** White 66%, mixed 22%, black 12%. **Languages** Spanish. **Religions** Roman Catholic, Pentecostal, Baptist. **Life expectancy** 77 female, 73 male. **Literacy** 98%.

POLITICS

Government Socialist republic. **Parties** Communist. **Suffrage** Universal, over 16. **Memberships** UN. **Subdivisions** 13 provinces, 1 city, 1 municipality.

ECONOMY

GNP $18,000,000,000 **Per capita** $1,767. **Monetary unit** Peso. **Trade partners** U.S.S.R., Germany. **Exports** Sugar, nickel, shellfish, fruit, tobacco, coffee. **Imports** Machinery, grain and other food, manufactures.

LAND

Description Caribbean island. **Area** 42,804 mi² (110,861 km²). **Highest point** Pico Turquino, 6,470 ft (1,972 m). **Lowest point** Sea level.

People. Most Cubans are descendants of Spanish colonists, African slaves, or a blend of the two. The government provides free education and health care, and although religious practices are discouraged, most people belong to the Roman Catholic church. Personal income, health, education, and housing have improved since the 1959 revolution, but most food products and consumer goods remain in short supply.

Economy and the Land. Cuba's economy is largely dependent on sugar, although other forms of agriculture are also important. The most fertile soils lie in the central region between mountain ranges, while mineral deposits, including oil and nickel, are found in the northeast. In addition to agriculture and mining, industry is an economic contributor. Most economic activity is nationalized, and Cuba remains dependent on aid from the Soviet Union. Mountains, plains, and a scenic coastline make Cuba one of the most beautiful islands in the West Indies. The climate is tropical.

History and Politics. Christopher Columbus claimed Cuba for Spain in 1492, and Spanish settlement began in 1511. When the native Indian population died out, African slaves were brought to work plantations. The United States joined with Cuba against Spain in the Spanish-American War in 1898. Cuba gained full independence in 1902. Unrest continued, however, and the United States again intervened from 1906 to 1909 and in 1917. A 1933 coup ousted a nine-year dictatorship, and a subsequent government overthrow in 1934 ushered in an era dominated by Sergeant Fulgencio Batista. After ruling through other presidents and serving an elected term himself, Batista seized power in a 1952 coup that established an unpopular and oppressive regime. Led by lawyer Fidel Castro, a revolutionary group opposed to Batista gained quick support, and Batista fled the country on January 1, 1959, leaving the government to Castro. Early United States support of Castro soured when nationalization of American businesses began. American aid soon ceased, and Cuba looked to the Soviet Union for assistance. The United States ended diplomatic relations with Cuba in 1961. In 1962 the United States and the Soviet Union became embroiled in a dispute over Soviet missile bases in Cuba that ended with removal of the missiles. In the early 1980s more than one hundred thousand Cubans were allowed to emigrate to the United States. Fidel Castro remains in power despite a weakening economy and the collapse of communism throughout the world. ■

CURAÇAO See NETHERLANDS.

CYPRUS

Official name Republic of Cyprus

PEOPLE
Population 528,000. **Density** 232/mi² (90/km²). **Urban** 53%. **Capital** Nicosia (Levkosia), 48,221. **Ethnic groups** Greek. **Languages** Greek, English. **Religions** Greek Orthodox. **Life expectancy** 79 female, 74 male. **Literacy** 89%.
POLITICS
Government Republic. **Parties** Democratic, Democratic Rally, Progressive Party of the Working People. **Suffrage** Universal, over 18. **Memberships** CW, UN. **Subdivisions** 6 districts.
ECONOMY
GDP $2,337,000,000

Per capita $3,462. **Monetary unit** Pound. **Trade partners** Exports: U.K., Libya, Lebanon. Imports: U.K., Italy, Japan. **Exports** Clothing and shoes, fruit and vegetables, machinery, petroleum, manufactures. **Imports** Textiles and other manufactures, machinery, food, motor vehicles, petroleum.

LAND
Description Southern part of the island of Cyprus. **Area** 2,276 mi² (5,896 km²). **Highest point** Olimbos, 6,401 ft (1,951 m). **Lowest point** Sea level.

People. Most Cypriots occupying the southern two thirds of the island are of Greek ancestry, and their religion, language, and general culture reflect this heritage. Family and religion are a dominant influence in the community. Decades of British rule had little impact.

Economy and the Land. Conflict between the Greek and Turkish Cypriots has severely disrupted the economy of the island. With foreign assistance, Greek Cypriots have made considerable progress, expanding traditional southern agriculture to light manufacturing and tourism. Known for its scenic beauty and tourist appeal, southern Cyprus is marked by a fertile southern plain bordered by the rugged Troodos Mountains to the southwest. Sandy beaches dot the coastline. The Mediterranean climate brings hot, dry summers and damp, cool winters.

History and Politics. History of Cyprus and North Cyprus follows NORTH CYPRUS. ■

CYPRUS, NORTH

Official name Turkish Republic of Northern Cyprus
PEOPLE
Population 176,000. **Density** 136/mi² (52/km²). **Capital** Nicosia (Lefkoşa), 37,400. **Ethnic groups** Turkish 99%, Greek, Maronite, and others 1%. **Languages** Turkish. **Religions** Sunni Muslim.

POLITICS
Government Republic. **Parties** Democratic Struggle, National Unity. **Memberships** None.

ECONOMY
GDP $185,000,000 **Per capita** $1,156. **Monetary unit** Turkish lira. **Trade partners** Turkey, U.K., Germany. **Exports** Food and livestock, manufactured goods, crude materials. **Imports** Manufactured goods, machinery and transportation equipment, mineral fuels.

LAND
Description Northern part of the island of Cyprus. **Area** 1,295 mi² (3,355 km²). **Highest point** 3,360 ft (1,024 m). **Lowest point** Sea level.

People. The northern part of the island is occupied by Cypriots of Turkish ancestry who speak Turkish and are Sunni Muslims. The 1974 Turkish invasion resulted in a formal segregation of this settlement pattern. The Turk-

ish Cypriot ancestors arrived on the island during the three centuries of Ottoman rule.

Economy and the Land. Since the partition of the island, North Cyprus has become somewhat isolated. Lacking in capital, experience, foreign aid, and official recognition, it remains agriculturally based and dependent upon Turkey for tourism, trade, and assistance. North Cyprus is dominated by the mostly barren Kyrenia Range.

History and Politics. In the Late Bronze Age—from 1600 to 1050 B.C.—a Greek culture flourished in Cyprus. Rule by various peoples followed, including Assyrians, Egyptians, Persians, Romans, Byzantines, French, and Venetians. The Ottoman Turks invaded in 1571. In the nineteenth century, Turkey ceded the island to the British as security for a loan. Although many Turks remained on Cyprus, the British declared it a crown colony in 1925. A growing desire for *enosis*, or union, with Greece led to rioting and guerrilla activity by Greek Cypriots. The Turkish government, opposed to absorption by Greece, desired separation into Greek and Turkish sectors. The present Greek government is committed to absolute separation between Greece and Cyprus. Cyprus became independent in 1960, with treaties forbidding either enosis or partition, but Greek-Turkish conflicts continued. A 1974 coup by pro-enosis forces led to an invasion by Turkey. The resulting partition runs east-west across the island dividing Nicosia, which serves as a capital for both countries. North Cyprus, which is not recognized internationally, maintains a separate government with a prime minister and a president. ■

CZECHOSLOVAKIA

Official name Czech and Slovak Federative Republic
PEOPLE
Population 15,690,000. **Density** 318/mi² (123/km²). **Urban** 69%. **Capital** Prague, 1,215,656. **Ethnic groups** Czech 64%, Slovak 31%, Hungarian 4%. **Languages** Czech, Slovak, Hungarian. **Religions** Roman Catholic 77%, Protestant 20%, Orthodox 2%. **Life expectancy** 76 female, 69 male. **Literacy** 99%.
POLITICS
Government Republic. **Parties** Civic Forum, Communist, Public Against Violence, others. **Suffrage** Universal, over 18. **Memberships** UN. **Subdivisions** 2 republics.
ECONOMY
GNP $135,600,000,000 **Per capita** $8,754. **Monetary unit** Koruna. **Trade partners** U.S.S.R., Germany, Poland. **Exports** Machinery, iron and steel and other manufactures, railway vehicles. **Imports** Machinery, petroleum, manufactures, crude materials, chemicals, food.

LAND
Description Eastern Europe, landlocked. **Area** 49,382 mi² (127,899 km²). **Highest point** Gerlachovka, 8,711 ft (2,655 m). **Lowest point** Along Bodrog River, 308 ft (94 m).

People. Czechs and Slovaks, descendants of Slavic tribes, predominate in Czechoslovakia. Characterized by a German-influenced culture, Czechs are concentrated in the regions of Bohemia and Moravia. Slovaks, whose culture was influenced by Hungarian Magyars, reside mainly in Slovakia. Czech and Slovak are official languages. Minorities include Hungarians, or Magyars; Ukrainians; Germans; Poles; and Gypsies, a rapidly growing group concentrated in Slovakia. Most people are Roman Catholic; the government licenses and pays clergy.

Economy and the Land. An industrial nation, Czechoslovakia has a centralized economy and one of the highest standards of living in Eastern-bloc countries. Coal deposits in Bohemia form the base for industrial development, and Bohemia remains an economically important region. Nearly all agriculture is collectivized; despite high farm outputs, some food must be imported. Farming areas are found in the river valleys of north-central Bohemia and central Moravia, and Slovakia remains largely agricultural. A rolling western area, central hills, low mountains in the north and south, and the Carpathian Mountains in the east characterize Czechoslovakia's terrain. The climate is temperate.

History and Politics. Slavic tribes were established in the region by the sixth century. By the tenth century Hungarian Magyars had conquered the Slovaks in the region of Slovakia. Bohemia and Moravia became part of the Holy Roman Empire, and by the twelfth century Bohemia had become a strong kingdom that included Moravia and parts of Austria and Poland. Austria gained control of the area in 1620, and later became part of Austria-Hungary. With the collapse of Austria-Hungary at the end of World War I, an independent Czechoslovakia, consisting of Bohemia, Moravia, and Slovakia, was formed. Nazi Germany invaded Czechoslovakia in 1939, and the Soviet Union liberated the nation from German occupation in the winter and spring of 1944 to 1945. By 1948 Communists controlled the government, and political purges continued from 1949 to 1952. A 1968 invasion by the Soviet Union and Bulgaria, Hungary, Poland, and East Germany resulted when the Czechoslovakian Communist party leader introduced liberal reforms. Demonstrations forced the Communist party to agree to a coalition government in 1989. Vaclav Havel, a longtime opposition leader, was elected president in 1990. Rising nationalism has resulted in tensions between the Czech, Slovak, and Hungarian ethnic groups. ∎

DENMARK

Official name Kingdom of Denmark
PEOPLE
Population 5,138,000. **Density** 309/mi² (119/km²).
Urban 86%. **Capital** Copenhagen, 466,723. **Ethnic groups** Danish (Scandinavian), German. **Languages** Danish. **Religions** Lutheran 90%. **Life expectancy** 79 female, 73 male. **Literacy** 99%.
POLITICS
Government Constitutional monarchy. **Parties** Conservative, Liberal, Social Democratic, Socialist People's, others. **Suffrage** Universal, over 18.
Memberships EC, NATO, OECD, UN. **Subdivisions** 14 counties, 2 independent cities.
ECONOMY
GDP $58,062,000,000 **Per capita** $11,589. **Monetary unit** Krone. **Trade partners** Germany, Sweden, U.K.. **Exports** Manufactures, machinery, meat, chemicals, furskins and other crude materials. **Imports** Manufactures, machinery, petroleum, chemicals, transportation equipment, food.
LAND
Description Northern Europe. **Area** 16,638 mi² (43,093 km²). **Highest point** Yding Skovhøj, 568 ft (173 m). **Lowest point** Lammefjord, -23 ft (-7 m).
The above information excludes Greenland and the Faeroe Is.

People. Denmark is made up of the Jutland Peninsula and more than four hundred islands, about one hundred of which are inhabited. Greenland, which is situated northeast of Canada, and the Faeroe Islands, which are located between Scotland and Iceland in the North Atlantic, are also part of Denmark. Lutheran, Danish-speaking Scandinavians constitute the homogenous population of the peninsula and surrounding islands, although a German minority is concentrated near the West German border. The government provides extensive social services and programs. The literacy rate is high, and Denmark has made significant contributions to science, literature, and the arts.

Economy and the Land. Despite limited natural resources, Denmark has a diversified economy. Agriculture contributes to trade, and pork and bacon are important products. Postwar expansion focused on industry, and the country now imports the raw materials it lacks and exports finished products. The North Sea is the site of oil and natural gas deposits. On the Faeroe Islands, traditional fishing continues as the economic mainstay. Most of Denmark's terrain is rolling, with hills covering much of the peninsula and the nearby islands. Coastal regions are marked by fjords and sandy beaches, especially in the west. The climate is temperate, with North Sea winds moderating temperatures. The rugged Faeroe Islands are damp, cloudy, and windy.

History and Politics. By the first century, access to the sea had brought contact with other civilizations. This led to the Viking area, which lasted from the ninth to eleventh centuries and resulted in temporary Danish rule of England. In the fourteenth century, Sweden, Norway, Finland, Iceland, the Faeroe Islands, and Greenland were united under Danish rule. Sweden and Finland withdrew from the union in the 1500s, and Denmark lost Norway to Sweden in 1814. A constitutional monarchy was instituted in 1849. Late nineteenth-century social reform, reflected in a new constitution in 1915, laid the groundwork for Denmark's current welfare state. The country remained neutral in World War I. Iceland gained independence following the war but maintained its union with Denmark until 1944. Despite declared neutrality in World War II, Denmark was invaded and occupied by Germany from 1940 to 1945. Compromise and gradual change characterize Danish politics. Its foreign policy stresses ties with developing nations and peaceful solutions to international problems. ∎

DJIBOUTI

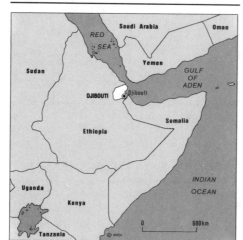

Official name Republic of Djibouti
PEOPLE
Population 341,000. **Density** 38/mi² (15/km²). **Urban** 81%. **Capital** Djibouti, 120,000. **Ethnic groups** Somali (Issa) 60%, Afar 35%. **Languages** French, Somali, Afar, Arabic. **Religions** Muslim 94%, Christian 6%. **Life expectancy** 51 female, 47 male. **Literacy** 20%.
POLITICS
Government Republic. **Parties** People's Progress Assembly. **Suffrage** Universal adult. **Memberships** AL, OAU, UN. **Subdivisions** 5 districts.
ECONOMY
GDP $339,000,000 **Per capita** $969. **Monetary unit** Franc. **Trade partners** Exports: France, Yemen, Somalia. Imports: France, Ethiopia, Japan. **Exports** Grain, transportation equipment, tobacco. **Imports** Textiles and other manufactures, transportation equipment, tobacco, food.

LAND
Description Eastern Africa. **Area** 8,958 mi² (23,200 km²). **Highest point** Moussa Ali, 6,768 ft (2,063 m). **Lowest point** Lake Assal, -502 ft (-153 m).

People. Characterized by strong cultural unity, Islam, and ethnic ties to Somalia, Somali Issas compose Djibouti's majority. Afars, who make up another main group, are also mostly Muslim and are linked ethnically with Ethiopia. Rivalry between the two groups has marked the nation's history. Because of unproductive land, much of the population is concentrated in the capital city of Djibouti.

Economy and the Land. Traditional nomadic herding continues as a way of life for many Djiboutians, despite heat, aridity, and limited grazing area. Several assets promote Djibouti as a port and trade center: a strategic position on the Gulf of Aden, an improved harbor, and a railway linking the city of Djibouti with Addis Ababa in Ethiopia. Marked by mountains that divide a coastal plain from a plateau region, the terrain is mostly desert. The climate is extremely hot and dry.

History and Politics. In the ninth century Arab missionaries introduced Islam to the population, and by the 1800s a pattern of conflict between the Issas and Afars had developed. The French purchased the port of Obcock from Afar sultans in 1862, and their territorial control expanded until the region became French Somaliland. The goal of the pro-independence Issas was defeated in elections in 1958 and 1967 when the majority voted for continued French control. The country became the French Territory of Afars and Issas in 1967, and as the Issa population grew, so did demands for independence. A 1977 referendum resulted in the independent Republic of Djibouti. ∎

DOMINICA

Official name Commonwealth of Dominica

PEOPLE
Population 89,000.
Density 292/mi²
(113/km²). **Urban** 27%.
Capital Roseau, 9,348.
Ethnic groups Black 91%,
mixed 6%, West Indian
2%. **Languages** English,
French. **Religions** Roman
Catholic 77%, Methodist
5%, Pentecostal 3%. **Life
expectancy** 79 female, 73
male. **Literacy** 94%.
POLITICS
Government Republic.
Parties Freedom, Labor.
Suffrage Universal, over
18. **Memberships** CW,
OAS, UN. **Subdivisions**
10 parishes.
ECONOMY
GDP $85,000,000 **Per
capita** $1,149. **Monetary
unit** East Caribbean dollar.

Trade partners Exports: U.K., Jamaica. Imports: U.S., U.K., Trinidad and Tobago. **Exports** Bananas, soap, copra. **Imports** Manufactures, food, machinery, chemicals, fuel.
LAND
Description Caribbean island. **Area** 305 mi² (790 km²).
Highest point Morne Diablotins, 4,700 ft (1,433 m).
Lowest point Sea level.

People. Dominica's population consists of descendants of black Africans, brought to the island as slaves, and Carib Indians descended from early inhabitants. The Carib population is concentrated in the northeastern part of the island and maintains its own customs and lifestyle. English is widely spoken in urban areas, but villagers, who compose a majority, speak mainly a French-African blend, resulting from French rule and the importation of Africans.

Economy and the Land. Of volcanic origin, the island has soils suitable for farming, but a mountainous and densely-forested terrain limits land accessible to cultivation. Agriculture is the economic mainstay, although hurricanes have hindered production. Forestry and fishing offer potential for expansion, and a tropical climate and scenic landscape create a basis for tourism.

History and Politics. In the fourteenth century Carib Indians conquered the Arawak who originally inhabited the island. Although Christopher Columbus arrived at Dominica in 1493, Spanish settlement was discouraged by Carib hostilities. French and British rivalry for control of the island followed, and British possession was recognized in 1783. Dominica gained independence in 1978. ■

DOMINICAN REPUBLIC

Official name Dominican Republic
PEOPLE
Population 7,245,000. **Density** 387/mi² (150/km²).
Urban 60%. **Capital** Santo Domingo, 1,313,172.
Ethnic groups Mulatto 73%, white 16%, black 11%.
Languages Spanish. **Religions** Roman Catholic 95%.
Life expectancy 70 female, 65 male. **Literacy** 67%.
POLITICS
Government Republic. **Parties** Liberation, Revolutionary, Social Christian Reformist, others.
Suffrage Universal, over 18 or married. **Memberships** OAS, UN. **Subdivisions** 29 provinces, 1 district.
ECONOMY
GDP $4,651,000,000 **Per capita** $750. **Monetary unit** Peso. **Trade partners** Exports: U.S., Netherlands. Imports: U.S., Venezuela, Mexico. **Exports** Sugar, coffee, cocoa, gold. **Imports** Petroleum, machinery, manufactures, chemicals, grain and other food.
LAND
Description Caribbean island (eastern Hispaniola). **Area** 18,704 mi² (48,442 km²). **Highest point** Pico Duarte, 10,417 ft (3,175 m). **Lowest point** Lago Enriquillo, -131 ft (-40 m).

People. Occupying eastern Hispaniola Island, the Dominican Republic borders Haiti and has a population of mixed ancestry. Haitians, other blacks, Spaniards, and European Jews compose minority groups. Population growth has resulted in unemployment and made it difficult for the government to meet food and service needs.

Economy and the Land. Agriculture remains important, with sugar a main component of trade, and sugar refining a major manufacturing activity. Farmland is limited, however, by a northwest-to-southeast mountain range and an arid region west of the range. Mineral exploitation and iron and steel exports contribute to trade, and a number of American firms have subsidiaries here. Tourism is growing, aided by the warm, tropical climate.

History and Politics. In 1492 Christopher Columbus arrived at Hispaniola Island. Spanish colonists followed, and the Indian population was virtually wiped out, although some intermingling with Spanish probably occurred. In 1697 the western region of the island, which would become Haiti, was ceded to France. The entire island came under Haitian control as the Republic of Haiti in 1822, and an 1844 revolution established the independent Dominican Republic. Since independence the country has experienced periods of instability, evidenced by military coups and rule, United States military intervention and occupation, and human-rights abuses. Economic instability continues as the government attempts to diversify the economy and lessen dependence on the export of sugar. ■

ECUADOR

Official name Republic of Ecuador

PEOPLE
Population 10,930,000. **Density** 100/mi² (39/km²).
Urban 57%. **Capital** Quito, 1,137,705. **Ethnic groups** Mestizo 55%, Amerindian 25%, Spanish 10%, black 10%. **Languages** Spanish, Quechua, indigenous.
Religions Roman Catholic 95%. **Life expectancy** 69 female, 65 male. **Literacy** 84%.
POLITICS
Government Republic. **Parties** Democratic Left, Popular Democracy, Roldosist, Social Christian, others.
Suffrage Universal, over 18. **Memberships** OAS, OPEC, UN. **Subdivisions** 21 provinces.
ECONOMY
GDP $15,982,000,000 **Per capita** $1,731. **Monetary unit** Sucre. **Trade partners** Exports: U.S., Panama. Imports: U.S., Japan, Brazil. **Exports** Petroleum, bananas, fish, coffee. **Imports** Machinery, iron and steel and other manufactures, chemicals.
LAND
Description Western South America. **Area** 109,484 mi² (283,561 km²). **Highest point** Chimborazo, 20,702 ft (6,310 m). **Lowest point** Sea level.

People. Ecuador's ethnicity was established by an indigenous Indian population and Spanish colonists. Minority whites, of Spanish or other European descent, live mainly in urban areas or operate large farms called haciendas. Of mixed Spanish-Indian blood, mestizos compose over half the population, although economic and political power is concentrated among whites. Minority Indians speak Quechua or other Indian languages and maintain traditional customs in Andean villages or nomadic jungle tribes. Blacks are concentrated on the northern coastal plain. Recent trends show a movement from the interior highlands to the fertile coastal plain and a rural-to-urban shift. A history of economic inequality has produced a literary and artistic tradition that has focused on social reform.

Economy and the Land. Despite an oil boom in the 1970s, Ecuador remains underdeveloped. Minor oil production began in 1911, but since a 1967 petroleum discovery in the *oriente*, a jungle region east of the Andes, Ecuador has become an oil exporter and a member of the Organization of Petroleum Exporting Countries (OPEC). Agriculture remains important for much of the population, although primitive and inefficient practices continue among the poor. Rich soils of the *costa*, extending from the Pacific to the Andes, support most of the export crops. Forestry and fishing have growth potential, and the waters around the Galápagos Islands are rich in tuna. Manufacturing is mainly devoted to meeting domestic needs. The oriente and costa lie on either side of the sierra, a region of highland plateaus between the two Andean chains. Varied altitudes result in a climate ranging from tropical in the lowlands to temperate in the plateaus and cold in the high mountains. A variety of wildlife inhabits the Galápagos Islands, five large and nine small islands about 600 miles (966 km) off Ecuador's coast in the Pacific Ocean.

History and Politics. In the fifteenth century Incas conquered and subsequently united the area's various tribes. In the 1500s the Spanish gained control, using Indians and African slaves to work the plantations. Weakened by the Napoleonic Wars, Spain lost control of Ecuador in 1822, and Simón Bolívar united the independent state with the Republic of Greater Colombia. Ecuador left the union as a separate republic in 1830, and

subsequent years saw instability and rule by presidents, dictators, and juntas. From 1925 to 1948 no leader was able to complete a full term in office. A new constitution was established in 1978, and a 1979 election installed a president who died in a plane crash in 1981. A 1988 election brought a leftward shift in the government, which is now challenged by a large foreign debt. ■

EGYPT

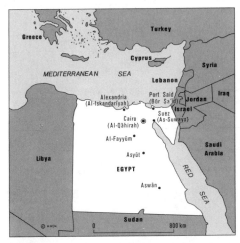

Official name Arab Republic of Egypt
PEOPLE
Population 54,910,000. **Density** 142/mi² (55/km²).
Urban 49%. **Capital** Cairo, 6,052,836. **Ethnic groups** Egyptian (Eastern Hamitic) 90%. **Languages** Arabic.
Religions Muslim 94%, Coptic Christian and others 6%. **Life expectancy** 65 female, 62 male. **Literacy** 38%.
POLITICS
Government Socialist republic. **Parties** National Democratic, Muslim Brotherhood, New Wafd, Socialist Labor, Socialist Liberal. **Suffrage** Universal, over 18. **Memberships** AL, OAU, UN. **Subdivisions** 26 governorates.
ECONOMY
GDP $39,421,000,000 **Per capita** $848. **Monetary unit** Pound. **Trade partners** Exports: Italy, Soviet Union, Israel. Imports: U.S., Germany, France. **Exports** Petroleum, cotton, textiles, food. **Imports** Manufactures, machinery, grain and other food, chemicals.
LAND
Description Northeastern Africa. **Area** 386,662 mi² (1,001,449 km²). **Highest point** Mt. Katrina, 8,668 ft (2,642 m). **Lowest point** Qattara Depression, -436 ft (-133 m).

People. Egypt's population is relatively homogenous, and Egyptians compose the largest group. Descended from ancient Nile Valley inhabitants, Egyptians have intermixed somewhat with Mediterranean and Asiatic peoples in the north and with black Africans in the south. Minorities include Bedouins, Arabic-speaking desert nomads; Nubians, black descendants of migrants from the Sudan; and Copts, a Christian group. Islam, the major religion, is also a cultural force, and many Christians as well as Muslims follow Islamic lifestyles. A desert terrain confines about 99 percent of the population to less than 4 percent of the land, in the fertile Nile River valley and along the Suez Canal.

Economy and the Land. Egypt's economy has suffered from wars, shifting alliances, and limited natural resources. Government-sponsored expansion and reform in the 1950s concentrated on manufacturing, and most industry was nationalized during the 1960s. Agriculture, centered in the Nile Valley, remains an economic mainstay, and cotton, a principal crop, is both exported and processed. Petroleum, found mainly in the Gulf of Suez, will most likely continue its economic role, and tourism will remain a contributor. Much of Egypt is desert, with hills and mountains in the east and along the Nile River, while the climate is warm and dry.

History and Politics. Egypt's recorded history began when King Menes united the region in about 3100 B.C., beginning a series of Egyptian dynasties. Art and architecture flourished during the Age of the Pyramids, from

2700 to 2200 B.C. In time native dynasties gave way to foreign conquerors, including Alexander the Great in the fourth century B.C. The Coptic Christian church emerged between the fourth and sixth centuries A.D., but in the 600s Arabs conquered the area and established Islam as the main religion. Ruling parties changed frequently, and in 1517 the Ottoman Turks added Egypt to their empire. Upon completion of the strategically important Suez Canal in 1869, foreign interest in Egypt increased. In 1875 Egypt sold its share of the canal to Britain, and a rebellion against foreign intervention ended with British occupation in 1882. Turkey sided with Germany in World War I, and the United Kingdom made Egypt a British protectorate in 1914. The country became an independent monarchy in 1922, but the British presence remained. In 1945 Egypt and six other nations formed the Arab League. The founding of Israel in 1948 initiated an era of Arab-Israeli hostilities, including periodic warfare in which Egypt often had a major role. Dissatisfaction over dealings with Israel and continued British occupation of the Suez Canal led to the overthrow of the king, and Egypt became a republic in 1953. Following a power struggle, Gamal Abdel Nasser was elected president in 1956, and the British agreed to remove their troops. Upon the death of Nasser in 1970, Vice President Anwar Sadat came to power. Negotiations between Egyptian president Sadat and Israeli prime minister Menachem Begin began in 1977, and in 1979 the leaders signed a peace treaty ending conflicts between Egypt and Israel. As a result, Egypt was suspended from the Arab League until 1989. In 1981 President Sadat was assassinated and was succeeded by Hosni Mubarek, who is faced with pressure from Muslim fundamentalists and discontent over the economy. ∎

EL SALVADOR

Official name Republic of El Salvador
PEOPLE
Population 5,363,000. **Density** 660/mi² (255/km²).
Urban 44%. **Capital** San Salvador, 462,652. **Ethnic groups** Mestizo 89%, Amerindian 10%, white 1%.
Languages Spanish, Nahua. **Religions** Roman Catholic 97%. **Life expectancy** 69 female, 64 male.
Literacy 62%.
POLITICS
Government Republic. **Parties** Authentic Christian Movement, Christian Democratic, National Republican Alliance, others. **Suffrage** Universal, over 18.
Memberships OAS, UN. **Subdivisions** 14 departments.
ECONOMY
GDP $5,732,000,000 **Per capita** $1,169. **Monetary unit** Colon. **Trade partners** Exports: U.S., Germany, Guatemala. Imports: U.S., Mexico, Venezuela. **Exports** Coffee and other food, cotton, textiles, paper, clothing.
Imports Petroleum, pharmaceuticals and other chemicals, manufactures, food.
LAND
Description Central America. **Area** 8,124 mi² (21,041 km²). **Highest point** Cerro El Pital, 8,957 ft (2,730 m). **Lowest point** Sea level.

People. Most Salvadorans are Spanish-speaking mestizos, people of Spanish-Indian descent. An Indian minority is mainly descended from the Pipil, a Nahuatl group

related to the Aztecs. The Nahuatl dialect is still spoken among some Indians. El Salvador, the smallest Central American country in area, has the highest population density in mainland Latin America, with inhabitants concentrated in a central valley-and-plateau region.

Economy and the Land. El Salvador's economy has been plagued by political instability, low literacy, high population density, and high unemployment. Agriculture remains the economic mainstay, and most arable land has been cultivated. Coffee, cotton, and sugar are produced on large commercial plantations, while subsistence farmers rely on corn, bean, and sorghum crops. East-to-west mountain ranges divide El Salvador into a southern coastal region, central valleys and plateaus, and northern mountains. The climate is subtropical.

History and Politics. Maya and Pipil predominated in the area of El Salvador prior to Spanish arrival. In the 1500s Pipil defeated invading Spaniards but were conquered in a subsequent invasion. In 1821 the Spanish-controlled Central American colonies declared independence, and in 1823 they united as the Federation of Central America. By 1838 the problem-ridden federation was in a state of collapse, and as the union dissolved, El Salvador became independent. Instability and revolution soon followed. The expansion of the coffee economy in the late 1800s exacerbated problems by further concentrating wealth and power among large-estate holders. A dictatorship from 1931 to 1944 was followed by instability under various military rulers. In 1969 a brief war with Honduras arose from resentment toward land-ownership laws, border disputes, and nationalist feelings following a series of soccer games between the two countries. Discontent increased throughout the seventies until a civil war erupted between leftist guerrillas and government forces, accompanied by right-wing death squads and human-rights abuses by the government. During the 1980s, the United States provided extensive military and economic aid in an attempt to moderate the government. However, the election of rightist Alfredo Cristiani in 1989 escalated guerrilla activity. ∎

EQUATORIAL GUINEA

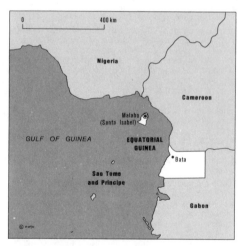

Official name Republic of Equatorial Guinea
PEOPLE
Population 353,000. **Density** 33/mi² (13/km²). **Urban** 65%. **Capital** Malabo, Bioko I., 31,630. **Ethnic groups** Fang 80%, Bubi 15%. **Languages** Spanish, indigenous, English. **Religions** Roman Catholic 83%, other Christian, tribal religionist. **Life expectancy** 50 female, 47 male. **Literacy** 55%.
POLITICS
Government Republic. **Parties** Democratic. **Suffrage** Universal adult. **Memberships** OAS, UN. **Subdivisions** 7 provinces.
ECONOMY
GDP $90,000,000 **Per capita** $321. **Monetary unit** CFA franc. **Trade partners** Exports: Spain, Germany, Italy, Netherlands. **Exports** Coffee, wood, cocoa. **Imports** Petroleum, food, beverages, clothing, machinery.
LAND
Description Central Africa. **Area** 10,831 mi² (28,051 km²). **Highest point** Pico de Santa Isabel, 9,869 ft (3,008 m). **Lowest point** Sea level.

People. Several ethnic groups inhabit Equatorial Guinea's five islands, as well as the mainland region of Río Muni. Although the majority Fang, a Bantu people, are concentrated in Río Muni, they also inhabit Bioko, the largest island. Found mainly on Bioko Island are the minority Bubi, also a Bantu people. Coastal groups known as *playeros*, or "those who live on the beach," live on both the mainland and the small islands. The Fernandino, of mixed African heritage, are concentrated on Bioko. Equatorial Guinea is the only black African state with Spanish as its official language.

Economy and the Land. Equatorial Guinea's economy is based on agriculture and forestry; cocoa, coffee, and wood are the main products. Cocoa production is centered on fertile Bioko Island, and coffee in Río Muni. The mainland's rain forests also provide for forestry. Mineral exploration has revealed petroleum and natural gas in the waters north of Bioko, and petroleum, iron ore, and radioactive materials exist in Río Muni. Bioko is of volcanic origin, and Río Muni consists of a coastal plain and interior hills. The climate is tropical, with high temperatures and humidity.

History and Politics. Pygmies most likely inhabited the Río Muni area prior to the thirteenth century, when mainland Bubi came to Bioko. From the seventeenth to the nineteenth centuries, Bantu migrations brought first the coastal tribes and then the Fang. Portugal claimed Bioko and part of the mainland in the 1400s, then ceded them to Spain in 1778. From 1827 to 1843, British antislavery activities were based on Bioko, which became the home of many former slaves, the ancestors of the Fernandino population. In 1959 the area became the Spanish Territory of the Gulf of Guinea, and the name was changed to Equatorial Guinea in 1963. Independence was achieved in 1968, and a subsequent dictatorship resulted in human-rights violations, the flight of many residents, and a general deterioration of the economy. A 1979 military coup ended the regime, but ethnic power rivalries continue. ∎

ESTONIA

Official name Republic of Estonia
PEOPLE
Population 1,602,000. **Density** 92/mi² (36/km²).
Capital Tallinn, 482,000. **Ethnic groups** Estonian 65%, Russian 28%, Ukranian 3%, Byelorussian 2%.
Languages Estonian, Russian. **Religions** Lutheran.
POLITICS
Government Republic. **Parties** Popular Front, others.
Suffrage Universal, over 18.
LAND
Description Eastern Europe. **Area** 17,413 mi² (45,100 km²). **Highest point** Suur Munamägi, 1,043 ft (318 m). **Lowest point** Sea level.

People. The Estonians have retained their own unique language and culture for centuries despite almost continuous foreign intervention. Before the Soviet invasion in 1940 the Estonians, who are related to the Finns, accounted for almost all of the population. Since that time massive immigration has increased the Russians' share of the population to almost one-third. Estonia has a relatively high urban population, and most people are engaged in industry.

Economy and the Land. Most of Estonia's industry is centered on oil shale, its only major industrial raw material. Oil shale has permitted Estonia to develop a chemical industry and also to become an exporter of electricity. Agriculture is based on livestock production and most crops are grown to supply animal feed. Estonia's natural landscape is low hills and poorly drained marshes, although much of the land has been drained for agriculture. About one-third of the land is forested.

History and Politics. Prior to incorporation into the Soviet Union, Estonia enjoyed only twenty years of independence during its long history. Danes conquered the territory in 1219 and sold it to the Teutonic Knights in 1346. The Swedes invaded in 1561 and held Estonia until it was conquered by Peter the Great of Russia in 1721. The country was granted independence in 1920, but freedom lasted only until the Soviet invasion of 1940, after which Estonia was forced to become a Soviet Socialist Republic. Estonians enjoyed the highest overall standard of living in the Soviet Union. Estonia's 'home rule' legislation led the Baltic states' drive for independence following the introduction of glasnost in the Soviet Union. International recognition as an independent nation was achieved in 1991. ∎

ETHIOPIA

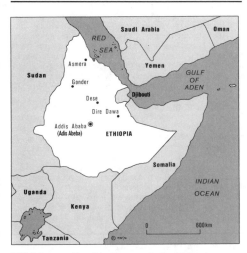

Official name People's Democratic Republic of Ethiopia
PEOPLE
Population 52,206,000. **Density** 108/mi² (42/km²). **Urban** 13%. **Capital** Addis Ababa, 1,686,300. **Ethnic groups** Oromo (Galla) 40%, Amhara and Tigrean 32%, Sidamo 9%, Shankella 6%, Somali 6%. **Languages** Amharic, Tigrinya, Orominga, Arabic. **Religions** Muslim 45%, Ethiopian Orthodox 35%, Animist 15%. **Life expectancy** 45 female, 41 male. **Literacy** 4%.
POLITICS
Government Socialist republic. **Parties** Workers'. **Suffrage** Universal, over 18. **Memberships** OAU, UN. **Subdivisions** 25 administrative regions, 5 autonomous regions.
ECONOMY
GDP $4,857,000,000 **Per capita** $153. **Monetary unit** Birr. **Trade partners** Exports: Germany, Netherlands, U.S. Imports: U.S.S.R., U.S., Germany. **Exports** Coffee, animal hides and other crude materials, petroleum. **Imports** Food, manufactures, machinery, petroleum, transportation equipment.
LAND
Description Eastern Africa. **Area** 483,123 mi² (1,251,282 km²). **Highest point** Ras Dashen Mtn., 15,158 ft (4,620 m). **Lowest point** Asālē, -410 ft (-125 m).

People. Ethiopia is ethnically, linguistically, and religiously diverse, but the Oromo, Amhara, and Tigre predominate. The Oromo include agricultural Muslims, Christians, and nomadic herders with traditional religions. Mainly Christian and also agricultural, the Amhara have dominated the country politically. The official language is Amharic; Arabic and indigenous languages are also spoken. Ethiopia's boundaries encompass over forty ethnic groups.

Economy and the Land. In addition to problems caused by political instability, drought has plagued Ethiopia's agricultural economy. Existing problems of soil erosion and deforestation resulted in disaster in 1982 when planting-season rains failed to fall in much of the country. The consequences of drought are especially severe in the north and west. Subsistence farming remains a major activity, and much arable land is uncultivated. Mines produce gold, copper, and platinum, and there is potential for expansion. A central plateau is split diagonally by the Great Rift Valley, with lowlands on the west and plains in the southeast. The climate is temperate on the plateau and hot in the lowlands.

History and Politics. Ethiopia's history is one of the oldest in the world. Its ethnic patterns were established by indigenous Cushites and Semite settlers, who probably arrived from Arabia about three thousand years ago. Christianity was introduced in the early fourth century. During the 1800s modern Ethiopia began to develop under Emperor Menelik II. Ras Tafari Makonnen became emperor in 1930, taking the name Haile Selassie. Italians invaded in the 1930s and occupied the country until 1941, when Selassie returned to the throne. Discontent with the feudal society increased until Selassie was ousted by the military in 1974. Reform programs and the change in leadership have done little to ease political tensions, which have sometimes erupted in governmental and civilian violence. Government troops continue their battle with separatists in Eritrea, a former Italian colony and autonomous province incorporated into Ethiopia in 1962. Since the 1980s, widespread famine and drought aggravated political problems. Internal strife between the Marxist government and secessionist factions hampered worldwide relief efforts. The government has since relaxed its policies, however, to attempt reconciliation with the rest of the world. ∎

FAEROE ISLANDS See DENMARK.

FALKLAND ISLANDS

Official name Falkland Islands
PEOPLE
Population 2,200. **Density** 0.5/mi² (0.2/km²). **Urban** 59%. **Capital** Stanley, East Falkland I., 1,200. **Ethnic groups** British descent. **Languages** English. **Religions** Anglican, United Free Church, Roman Catholic.
POLITICS
Government Dependent territory (U.K.). **Suffrage** Universal, over 18. **Memberships** None. **Subdivisions** None. **Monetary unit** Pound. **Trade partners** Exports: U.K., Netherlands, Japan. Imports: U.K., Netherlands Antilles, Japan. **Exports** Wool, animal hides. **Imports** Food, clothing, fuel, machinery.
LAND
Description South Atlantic islands (east of Argentina). **Area** 4,700 mi² (12,173 km²). **Highest point** Mt. Usborne, 2,312 ft (705 m). **Lowest point** Sea level.
The above information excludes dependencies.

People. Most Falkland Island inhabitants are of British descent, an ancestry reflected in their official language, English, and majority Anglican religion.

Economy and the Land. Sheep raising is the main activity, supplemented by fishing. In 1982 Britain funded the Falkland Islands Development Corporation, which began operation in 1984. Situated about 300 miles (482 km) east of southern Argentina, East and West Falkland compose the main and largest islands. Numerous small islands are also part of the Falklands. The climate is cool, damp, and windy.

History and Politics. Although the British sighted the islands in 1592, the French established the first settlement in 1764, on East Falkland. The British settled on West Falkland the next year. Spain, which ruled the Argentine territories to the west, purchased the French area and drove out the British in 1770. When Argentina gained independence from Spain in 1816, it claimed Spain's right to the islands. Britain reasserted its rule over the islands in the 1830s. The Falklands became a British colony in 1892, with dependencies annexed in 1908. Continued Argentine claim resulted in a 1982 Argentine invasion and occupation. The British won the subsequent battle and continue to govern the Falklands. The dependencies of South Georgia and the South Sandwich Islands became a separate British colony in 1985. ∎

FIJI

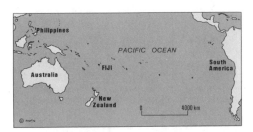

Official name Republic of Fiji
PEOPLE
Population 732,000. **Density** 103/mi² (40/km²). **Urban** 44%. **Capital** Suva, Viti Levu I., 69,665. **Ethnic groups** Indian 49%, Fijian 46%. **Languages** English, Fijian, Hindustani. **Religions** Methodist and other Christian 53%, Hindu 38%, Muslim 8%. **Life expectancy** 74 female, 69 male. **Literacy** 79%.
POLITICS
Government Republic. **Parties** Alliance, Labor, National Federation. **Suffrage** Universal adult. **Memberships** UN. **Subdivisions** 4 divisions.
ECONOMY
GDP $1,162,000,000 **Per capita** $1,672. **Monetary unit** Dollar. **Trade partners** Exports: U.K., Malaysia, New Zealand. Imports: Australia, New Zealand, Japan. **Exports** Sugar, copra, fish. **Imports** Textiles and other manufactures, petroleum, food, machinery, chemicals.
LAND
Description South Pacific islands. **Area** 7,078 mi² (18,333 km²). **Highest point** Tomanivi (Victoria), 4,341 ft (1,323 m). **Lowest point** Sea level.

People. Fiji's majority population is descended from laborers brought from British India between 1879 and 1916. Most Indians are Hindu, but a Muslim minority exists. Native Fijians are of Melanesian and Polynesian heritage, and most are Christian. English is the official language, a result of British rule; but Indians speak Hindustani, and the main Fijian dialect is Bauan. Tensions between the two groups occasionally arise because plantation owners, who are mainly Indian, must often lease their land from Fijians, the major landowners. About a hundred of the several hundred islands are inhabited.

Economy and the Land. The traditional sugar cane crop continues as the basis of Fiji's economy, and agricultural diversification is a current goal. Tourism is another economic contributor, and expansion of forestry is planned. Terrain varies from island to island and is characterized by mountains, valleys, rain forests, and fertile plains. The tropical islands are cooled by ocean breezes.

History and Politics. Little is known of Fiji's history prior to the arrival of Europeans. Melanesians probably migrated from Indonesia, followed by Polynesian settlers in the second century. After a Dutch navigator sighted Fiji in 1643, Captain James Cook of Britain visited the island in the eighteenth century. The nineteenth century saw the arrival of European missionaries, traders, and whalers, and several native wars. In 1874 tribal chiefs ceded Fiji to the British, who established sugar plantations and brought indentured Indian laborers. The country became independent in 1970. Fiji was ejected from the British Commonwealth, after declaring itself a republic and limiting participation by Indians in the government. ∎

FINLAND

Official name Republic of Finland
PEOPLE
Population 4,984,000. **Density** 38/mi² (15/km²). **Urban** 68%. **Capital** Helsinki, 490,034. **Ethnic groups** Finnish (mixed Scandinavian and Baltic), Swedish, Lappic, Gypsy, Tatar. **Languages** Finnish, Swedish. **Religions** Lutheran 89%, Eastern Orthodox 1%. **Life expectancy** 80 female, 72 male. **Literacy** 99%.
POLITICS
Government Republic. **Parties** Center-Liberal, National Coalition, People's Democratic League, Social

Democratic, others. **Suffrage** Universal, over 18. **Memberships** OECD, UN. **Subdivisions** 12 provinces.

ECONOMY

GDP $54,113,000,000 **Per capita** $11,077. **Monetary unit** Markka. **Trade partners** Exports: U.S.S.R., Sweden, U.K. Imports: Germany, U.S.S.R., Sweden. **Exports** Paper and other manufactures, machinery, wood and other crude materials. **Imports** Manufactures, machinery, petroleum, transportation equipment, crude materials.

LAND

Description Northern Europe. **Area** 130,559 mi² (338,145 km²). **Highest point** Haltiatunturi, 4,357 ft (1,328 m). **Lowest point** Sea level.

People. The mainly Finnish population includes minorities of Swedes—a result of past Swedish rule—and indigenous Lapps. As part of northern Finland lies within the Arctic Circle, population is concentrated in the south. Finland's rich cultural tradition has contributed much to the arts. Its highly developed social-welfare programs provide free education through the university level, as well as national health insurance.

Economy and the Land. Much of Finland's economy is based on its rich forests, which support trade and manufacturing activities. The steel industry is also important. Agriculture focuses on dairy farming and livestock raising; hence many fruits and vegetables must be imported. Coastal islands and lowlands, a central lake region, and northern hills mark Finland's scenic terrain. Summers in the south and central regions are warm, and winters long and cold. Northern Finland—located in the "Land of the Midnight Sun"—has periods of uninterrupted daylight in the summer and darkness in the winter.

History and Politics. The indigenous nomadic Lapps migrated north in the first century when the Finns arrived, probably from west-central Russia. A Russian-Swedish struggle for control of the area ended with Swedish rule in the 1100s. Finland was united with Denmark from the fourteenth through the sixteenth centuries. Russia and Sweden fought several wars for control of the country. In 1809 Finland became an autonomous grand duchy within the Russian Empire. After the Russian czar was overthrown in the 1917 Bolshevik Revolution, the new Russian government recognized Finland's declaration of independence. During World War II, Finland fought against the Soviets and, by the peace treaty signed in 1947, lost a portion of its land to the Soviet Union. During the postwar years, Finland and Russia renewed their economic and cultural ties and signed an agreement of friendship and cooperation. Foreign policy emphasizes friendly relations with the Soviet Union and Scandinavia. ■

FRANCE

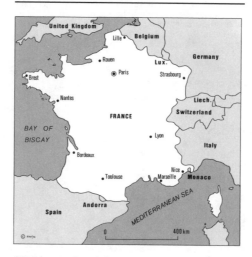

Official name French Republic

PEOPLE

Population 56,580,000. **Density** 268/mi² (103/km²). **Urban** 74%. **Capital** Paris, 2,078,900. **Ethnic groups** French (mixed Celtic, Latin, and Teutonic). **Languages** French. **Religions** Roman Catholic 90%, Protestant 2%, Jewish 1%, Muslim 1%. **Life expectancy** 81 female, 73 male. **Literacy** 99%.

POLITICS

Government Republic. **Parties** Left Radical Movement, Rally for the Republic, Socialist, Union for Democracy, others. **Suffrage** Universal, over 18. **Memberships** EC, NATO, OECD, UN. **Subdivisions** 95 departments, 1 territory.

ECONOMY

GDP $510,333,000,000 **Per capita** $9,275. **Monetary unit** Franc. **Trade partners** Germany, Italy, Belgium. **Exports** Manufactures, machinery, chemicals, transportation equipment, food. **Imports** Manufactures, machinery, petroleum, chemicals, food.

LAND

Description Western Europe. **Area** 211,208 mi² (547,026 km²). **Highest point** Mt. Blanc, 15,771 ft (4,807 m). **Lowest point** Lac de Cazaux et de Sanguinet, -10 ft (-3 m).

The above information excludes French overseas departments

People. Many centuries ago, Celtic and Teutonic tribes and Latins established France's current ethnic patterns. The French language developed from the Latin of invading Romans but includes Celtic and Germanic influences as well. Language and customs vary somewhat from region to region, but most people who speak dialects also speak French. France has long contributed to learning and the arts, and Paris is a world cultural center. In addition to mainland divisions, the country has overseas departments and territories.

Economy and the Land. The French economy is highly developed. The nation is a leader in agriculture and industry; its problems of inflation and unemployment are common to other modern countries. Soils in the north and northeast are especially productive, and grapes are grown in the south. Minerals include iron ore and bauxite. Industry is diversified, centered in the Paris manufacturing area, and tourism is important. About two-thirds of the country is flat to rolling, and about one-third is mountainous, including the Pyrenees in the south and the Alps in the east. In the west and north, winters are cool and summers mild. Climate varies with altitude. The southern coast has a Mediterranean climate with hot summers and mild winters.

History and Politics. In ancient times Celtic tribes inhabited the area that encompasses present-day France. The Romans, who called the region Gaul, began to invade about 200 B.C., and by the 50s B.C. the entire region had come under Roman rule. Northern Germanic tribes—including the Franks, Visigoths, and Burgundians—spread throughout the region as Roman control weakened, and the Franks defeated the Romans in A.D. 486. In the 800s Charlemagne greatly expanded Frankish-controlled territory, which was subsequently divided into three kingdoms. The western kingdom and part of the central kingdom included modern France. In 987 the Capetian dynasty began when Hugh Capet came to the throne, an event which is often considered the start of the French nation. During subsequent centuries, the power of the kings increased and France became a leading world power. Ambitious projects, such as the palace built by Louis XIV at Versailles, and several military campaigns, resulted in financial difficulties. The failing economy and divisions between rich and poor led to the French Revolution in 1789 and the First French Republic in 1792. Napoleon Bonaparte, who had gained prominence during the revolution, overthrew the government in 1799 and established the First Empire, which ended in 1815 with his defeat at Waterloo in Belgium. The subsequent monarchy resulted in discontent, and an 1848 revolution established the Second French Republic with an elected president, who in turn proclaimed himself emperor and set up the Second Empire in 1852. Following a war with Prussia in 1870, the emperor was ousted, and the Third Republic began. This republic ended Germany's invasion in World War I but ended in 1940 when invading Germans defeated the French. By 1942 the Nazis had control of the entire country. The Allies liberated France in 1944, and General Charles de Gaulle headed a provisional government until 1946, when the Fourth Republic was established. Colonial revolts in Africa and French Indochina took their toll on the economy during the fifties. Controversy over a continuing Algerian war for independence brought de Gaulle to power once more and resulted in the Fifth Republic in 1958. Dissension and national strikes erupted during the 1960s, a result of dissatisfaction with the government, and de Gaulle resigned in 1969. In 1987 François Mitterand was re-elected, giving the Socialists a plurality. ■

FRENCH GUIANA

Official name Department of Guiana
PEOPLE
Population 100,000. **Density** 2.8/mi² (1.1/km²). **Urban** 75%. **Capital** Cayenne, 38,091. **Ethnic groups** Black or mulatto 66%; white 12%; East Indian, Chinese, and Amerindian 12%. **Languages** French. **Religions** Roman Catholic. **Life expectancy** 76 female, 68 male. **Literacy** 82%.

Places and Possessions of FRANCE

Entity	Status	Area	Population	Capital/Population
Corsica (Mediterranean island)	Part of France	3,367 mi² (8,720 km²)	251,000	None
French Guiana (Northeastern South America)	Overseas department	35,135 mi² (91,000 km²)	100,000	Cayenne, 38,091
French Polynesia (South Pacific islands)	Overseas territory	1,544 mi² (4,000 km²)	199,000	Papeete, 23,496
French Southern and Antarctic Territories (Indian Ocean islands)	Overseas territory	3,000 mi² (7,770 km²)	175	Port-aux-Français
Guadeloupe (Caribbean islands)	Overseas department	687 mi² (1,780 km²)	350,000	Basse-Terre, 13,656
Kerguelen Islands (Indian Ocean)	Territory	2,700 mi² (6,993 km²)	75	None
Martinique (Caribbean island)	Overseas department	425 mi² (1,100 km²)	341,000	Fort-de-France, 99,844
Mayotte (Southeastern African islands)	Territorial collectivity	144 mi² (374 km²)	85,000	Dzaoudzi (de facto) and Mamoudzou (future), 5,865
New Caledonia (South Pacific islands)	Overseas territory	7,358 mi² (19,058 km²)	170,000	Nouméa, 65,110
Reunion (Indian Ocean island)	Overseas department	969 mi² (2,510 km²)	600,000	Saint-Denis, 84,400
St. Pierre and Miquelon (North Atlantic islands; south of Newfoundland)	Territorial collectivity	93 mi² (242 km²)	6,800	Saint-Pierre, 5,371
Wallis and Futuna (South Pacific islands)	Overseas territory	98 mi² (255 km²)	16,000	Mata-Utu, 815

POLITICS
Government Overseas department (France). **Parties** Democratic Action, Rally for the Republic, Socialist, Union for French Democracy. **Suffrage** Universal, over 18. **Memberships** None. **Subdivisions** 2 arrondissements.

ECONOMY
GDP $181,000,000 **Per capita** $2,742. **Monetary unit** French franc. **Trade partners** Exports: France, U.S., Guadeloupe. Imports: France, Trinidad and Tobago, U.S. **Exports** Shrimp, manufactures, wood, rice. **Imports** Manufactures, food, machinery, petroleum, transportation equipment.

LAND
Description Northeastern South America. **Area** 35,135 mi² (91,000 km²). **Highest point** 2,723 ft (830 m). **Lowest point** Sea level.

People. French Guiana has a majority population of black descendants of African slaves and people of mixed African-European ancestry. Population is concentrated in the more accessible coastal area, but the interior wilderness is home to minority Indians and the descendants of slaves who fled to pursue traditional African lifestyles. French is the predominant language, but a French-English creole is also spoken. Two Indo-Chinese refugee settlements were established in 1977 and 1979.

Economy and the Land. Shrimp production and a growing timber industry are French Guiana's economic mainstays. The land remains largely undeveloped, however, and reliance on French aid continues. Agriculture is limited by wilderness, but mineral deposits offer potential for mining. The fertile coastal plains of the north give way to hills and mountains along the Brazilian border. Rain forests cover much of the landscape, which features a tropical climate.

History and Politics. Indigenous Indians and a hot climate defeated France's attempt at settlement in the early 1600s. The first permanent French settlement was established in 1634, and the area became a French colony in 1667. For almost one hundred years, beginning in the 1850s, penal colonies such as Devils Island brought an influx of European prisoners. The region became a French overseas department in 1946. A minority nationalist group strives for greater autonomy. ∎

FRENCH POLYNESIA

Official name Territory of French Polynesia
PEOPLE
Population 199,000. **Density** 129/mi² (50/km²). **Urban** 65%. **Capital** Papeete, Tahiti I., 23,555. **Ethnic groups** Polynesian 69%, European 12%, Chinese 10%. **Languages** French, Tahitian, Chinese. **Religions** Evangelical and other Protestant 55%, Roman Catholic 32%. **Life expectancy** 71 female, 66 male. **Literacy** 98%.
POLITICS
Government Overseas territory (France). **Parties** Amuitahiraa Mo Porinesia, Ia Mana, Pupu Here Ai'a, Tahoeraa Huiraatira. **Suffrage** Universal, over 18. **Memberships** None. **Subdivisions** 5 circumscriptions.
ECONOMY
GDP $1,146,000,000 **Per capita** $7,640. **Monetary unit** CFP franc. **Trade partners** Exports: France, U.S., Italy. Imports: France, U.S., New Zealand. **Exports** Pearls, machinery, copra, precision instruments.

Imports Manufactures, meat and other food, machinery, transportation equipment.
LAND
Description South Pacific islands. **Area** 1,544 mi² (4,000 km²). **Highest point** Mont Orohena, 7,352 ft (2,241 m). **Lowest point** Sea level.

People. Most inhabitants are Polynesian, with minorities including Chinese and French. More than one hundred islands compose the five archipelagoes, and population and commercial activity is concentrated in Papeete on Tahiti. Although per capita income is relatively high, wealth is not equally distributed. Emigration from the poorer islands to Tahiti is common. Polynesia's reputation as a tropical paradise has attracted European and American writers and artists, including French painter Paul Gauguin.

Economy and the Land. The islands' economy is based on natural resources; coconut, mother-of-pearl, and tourism contribute to the economy. This South Pacific territory, located south of the equator and midway between South America and Australia, is spread over roughly 1.5 million square miles (3.9 million square km) and is made up of the Marquesas Islands, the Society Islands, the Tuamotu Archipelago, the Gambier Islands, and the Austral Islands. The Marquesas, known for their beauty, form the northernmost group. The Society Islands, southwest of the Marquesas, include Tahiti and Bora-Bora, both popular tourist spots. The Tuamoto Archipelago lies south of the Marquesas and east of the Society Islands, the Gambier Islands are situated at the southern tip of the Tuamotu group, and the Austral Islands lie to the southwest. The region includes both volcanic and coral islands, and the climate is tropical, with a rainy season extending from November to April.

History and Politics. The original settlers probably came from Micronesia and Melanesia in the east. Europeans began arriving around the sixteenth century. By the late 1700s they had reached the five major island groups, and visitors to the area included mutineers from the British vessel *Bounty*. By the 1880s the islands had come under French rule, although they did not become an overseas territory until 1946. During European settlement, many Polynesians died as a result of exposure to foreign diseases. The French use several of the islands for nuclear testing. ∎

GABON

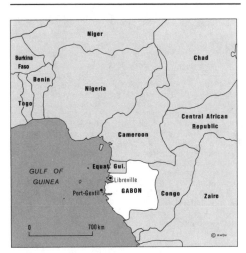

Official name Gabonese Republic
PEOPLE
Population 1,074,000. **Density** 10/mi² (4.0/km²). **Urban** 46%. **Capital** Libreville, 235,700. **Ethnic groups** Fang, Eshira, Bapounou, Teke. **Languages** French, Fang, indigenous. **Religions** Roman Catholic and other Christian 55-75%, Fetishism, Muslim. **Life expectancy** 55 female, 52 male. **Literacy** 65%.
POLITICS
Government Republic. **Parties** Social Democratic Rally. **Suffrage** Universal, over 21. **Memberships** OAU, OPEC, UN. **Subdivisions** 9 provinces.
ECONOMY
GDP $3,142,000,000 **Per capita** $5,561. **Monetary unit** CFA franc. **Trade partners** Exports: France, U.S., Spain. Imports: France, U.S., Japan. **Exports**

Petroleum, wood, manganese. **Imports** Manufactures, machinery, transportation equipment, food, chemicals.
LAND
Description Central Africa. **Area** 103,347 mi² (267,667 km²). **Highest point** 3,360 ft (1,024 m). **Lowest point** Sea level.

People. Of Gabon's more than forty ethnic groups, the Fang are a majority and inhabit the area north of the Ogooué River. Other major groups include the Eshira, Bapounou, and Teke. The French, who colonized the area, compose a larger group today than during colonial times. Each of the groups has its own distinct language as well as culture, but French remains the official language.

Economy and the Land. Gabon is located astride the equator, and its many resources include petroleum, manganese, uranium, and dense rain forests. The most important activities are oil production, forestry, and mining. The economy depends greatly on foreign investment and imported labor, however, and many native Gabonese continue as subsistence farmers. While the labor shortage hinders economic development, the country has a high per capita income. The terrain is marked by a coastal plain, inland forested hills, and savanna in the east and south. The climate is hot and humid.

History and Politics. First inhabited by Pygmies, Gabon was the site of migrations by numerous Bantu peoples during its early history. The thick rain forests isolated the migrant groups from one another and thus preserved their individual cultures. The Portuguese arrived in the fifteenth century, followed by the Dutch, British, and French in the 1700s. The slave and ivory trades flourished, and the Fang, drawn by the prosperity, migrated to the coast in the 1800s. A group of freed slaves founded Libreville, which later became the capital. By 1885 France had gained control of the area, and in 1910 it was united with present-day Chad, the Congo, and the Central African Republic as French Equatorial Africa. Gabon became independent in 1960, and in 1964 French assistance thwarted a military takeover. During the 1970s, Gabon developed major economic ties with the United States and with China. After anti-government protests, 1990 elections ended one-party rule. ∎

GALAPAGOS ISLANDS
See ECUADOR.

GAMBIA

Official name Republic of the Gambia
PEOPLE
Population 831,000. **Density** 191/mi² (74/km²). **Urban** 23%. **Capital** Banjul, 44,536. **Ethnic groups** Malinke 40%, Fulani 19%, Wolof 15%, Jola 10%, Serahuli 8%. **Languages** English, Malinke, Wolof, Fula, indigenous. **Religions** Muslim 90%, Christian 9%, tribal religionist 1%. **Life expectancy** 47 female, 34 male. **Literacy** 12%.
POLITICS
Government Republic. **Parties** National Convention, People's, People's Progressive. **Suffrage** Universal, over 21. **Memberships** CW, OAU, UN. **Subdivisions** 5 divisions, 1 city.

ECONOMY

GDP $212,000,000 **Per capita** $348. **Monetary unit** Dalasi. **Trade partners** Exports: Ghana, European countries, Japan. Imports: European countries, Asian countries, U.S.. **Exports** Peanuts, fish, cotton, palm kernels. **Imports** Food, manufactures, raw materials, fuel.

LAND

Description Western Africa. **Area** 4,361 mi^2 (11,295 km^2). **Highest point** 174 ft (53 m). **Lowest point** Sea level.

People. Gambia's population includes the Mandingo, or Malinke; Fulani; Wolof; Jola; and Serahuli. Most people are Muslim, and language differs from group to group, although the official language is English. Gambians are mainly rural farmers, and literacy is low, with educational opportunities focused in the Banjul area. The population's size varies with the arrival and departure of seasonal Senegalese farm laborers.

Economy and the Land. Gambia's economy relies on peanut production, and crop diversification is a current goal. Subsistence crops include rice, and the government hopes increased rice production will decrease dependence on imports and foreign aid. Fishing and tourism have expanded in the past years. In addition, the Gambia River, which provides a route to the African interior, offers potential for an increased role in trade. Dense mangrove swamps border the river, giving way to flat ground that floods in the rainy season. Behind this lie sand hills and plateaus. Low-lying Gambia, with its subtropical climate, is virtually an enclave within Senegal.

History and Politics. From the thirteenth to the fifteenth centuries the flourishing Mali Empire included the Gambia area. The Portuguese arrived in the fifteenth century, established slave trading posts, and sold trade rights to Britain in 1588. During the seventeenth and eighteenth centuries France and Britain competed for control of the river trade. By the late 1800s, the Banjul area had become a British colony and the interior a British protectorate. Gambia achieved independence as a monarchy in 1965, and the country became a republic in 1970. ∎

GERMANY

Official name Federal Republic of Germany

PEOPLE

Population 79,220,000. **Density** 575/mi^2 (222/km^2). **Urban** 84%. **Capital** Berlin (designated), 3,115,473; Bonn (de facto), 282,190. **Ethnic groups** German (Teutonic). **Languages** German. **Religions** Evangelical and other Protestant 45%, Roman Catholic 37%. **Life expectancy** 76 female, 70 male. **Literacy** 99%.

POLITICS

Government Republic. **Parties** Christian Democratic-Christian Social Union, Free Democratic, Social Democratic, others. **Suffrage** Universal, over 18. **Memberships** EC, NATO, OECD, UN. **Subdivisions** 16 states.

ECONOMY

GDP $798,000,000,000 **Per capita** $10,224. **Monetary unit** Mark. **Trade partners** Western European countries, U.S.. **Exports** Manufactures, machinery, transportation equipment, chemicals. **Imports** Manufactures, machinery, petroleum, food, chemicals, transportation equipment.

LAND

Description Northern Europe. **Area** 108,333 mi^2 (357,040 km^2). **Highest point** Zugspitze, 9,718 ft (2,962 m). **Lowest point** Freepsum Lake, -7 ft (-2 m).

People. Germany has a homogeneous, German-speaking population with very small Danish and Slavic minorities. Roman Catholics, Evangelicals, and other Protestants are the largest religious groups. Germans are well-educated and boast a rich cultural heritage of achievements in music, literature, philosophy, and science. Germany has the largest population of any European nation, excluding the Soviet Union.

Economy and the Land. Despite the devastating effects of World War II and Germany's forty-five year division into two countries, the country has one of the world's strongest economies. Industry is the basis of its prosperity, with mining, manufacturing, construction, and utilities as important contributors. The Ruhr district, which is the nation's most important industrial region, is located near the Rhine River in west-central Germany and includes cities such as Essen and Dortmund. Agriculture remains important in the southern and central regions. Germany's terrain varies from northern plains to central uplands and hills that rise to the southern Bavarian Alps. A mild climate is tempered by the sea in the north; in the south the winters are colder because of the Alps.

History and Politics. In ancient times Germanic tribes overcame Celtic inhabitants in the area of Germany and established a northern stronghold against Roman expansion of Gaul. As the Roman Empire weakened, the Germanic peoples invaded, deposing the Roman governor of Gaul in the fifth century A.D. The Franks composed the strongest tribe, and in the ninth century Frankish-controlled territory was expanded and united under Charlemagne. Unity did not last, however, and Germany remained a disjointed territory of warring feudal states, duchies, and independent cities. The Reformation, a movement led by German monk Martin Luther, began in 1517 and evolved into the Protestant branch of Christianity. The rise of Prussian power and growing nationalism eventually united the German states into the German Empire in 1871, and Prussian chancellor Otto von Bismarck installed Prussian King Wilhelm I as emperor. In a few short years, Germany rose to become Europe's foremost industrial and military power. In 1914 Germany allied with Austria; their subsequent invasions of France and Russia led to World War I. Hardships imposed by the victors against Germany led to instability and economic collapse. Promising prosperity, Adolph Hitler and his National Socialists, or Nazi, party rose to power in 1933. Hitler's ruthless nationalist policies included a genocidal program to eliminate Jews and many other peoples, and his ambitions to conquer all of Europe led to World War II. The Allied Forces defeated Germany in 1945 only after enormous casualties had been inflicted on both sides. The United States, Britain, the Soviet Union, and France subsequently divided Germany into four zones of occupation. The eastern, Soviet-occupied zone became a Communist country called the German Democratic Republic, or East Germany. The three remaining zones of Germany were combined to form the capitalist Federal Republic of Germany, or West Germany. Berlin, not included in occupation zones, was divided between the east and west. The Berlin Wall became a symbol of the Cold War between the United States and the Soviet Union. In the late 1980s the Soviet Union began to loosen its grip on its satellite nations, and in 1989 East Germans began a mass exodus to West Germany. In October 1990 East Germany was officially absorbed into West Germany, despite concerns by the Soviet Union and other nations that a reunified Germany could once again threaten to dominate its European neighbors. ∎

GHANA

Official name Republic of Ghana

PEOPLE

Population 15,550,000. **Density** 169/mi^2 (65/km^2). **Urban** 33%. **Capital** Accra, 859,640. **Ethnic groups** Akan 44%, Moshi-Dagomba 16%, Ewe 13%, Ga 8%. **Languages** English, Akan, indigenous. **Religions** Tribal religionist 38%, Muslim 30%, Christian 24%. **Life expectancy** 58 female, 54 male. **Literacy** 30%.

POLITICS

Government Provisional military government. **Parties**

None. **Suffrage** None. **Memberships** CW, OAU, UN. **Subdivisions** 10 regions.

ECONOMY

GDP $6,900,000,000 **Per capita** $492. **Monetary unit** Cedi. **Trade partners** Exports: Switzerland, U.K., U.S.S.R., Japan. Imports: Nigeria, U.K., Germany. **Exports** Cocoa, aluminum, petroleum, wood. **Imports** Petroleum, manufactures, machinery, transportation equipment, chemicals.

LAND

Description Western Africa. **Area** 92,098 mi^2 (238,533 km^2). **Highest point** Afadjoto, 2,905 ft (885 m). **Lowest point** Sea level.

People. Nearly all Ghanaians are black Africans. The Akan, the majority group, are further divided into the Fanti, who live mainly along the coast, and the Ashanti, who inhabit the forests north of the coast. The Ewe and Ga live in the south and southeast. Other groups include the Guan, living on the Volta River plains, and the Moshi-Dagomba in the north. Ghana's more than fifty languages and dialects reflect this ethnic diversity, and English, the official language, is spoken by a minority. Islam and traditional African religions predominate, but a Christian minority also exists. Most people live in rural areas, and the literacy rate is low.

Economy and the Land. Agriculture is the economic base, but Ghana's natural resources are diverse. Production of cocoa, the most important export, is concentrated in the Ashanti region, a belt of tropical rain forest extending north from the coastal plain. Resources include forests and mineral deposits, and exploitation of bauxite, gold, diamonds, and manganese ore is currently underway. Ghana's coastal lowlands give way to scrub and plains, the Ashanti rain forest, and northern savanna. The climate is tropical.

History and Politics. The ancestors of today's Ghanaians probably migrated from the northern areas of Mauritania and Mali in the thirteenth century. The Portuguese reached the shore around 1470 and called the area the Gold Coast. Many countries competed for the region, but in 1874 the Gold Coast was made a British colony. By 1901 Britain had extended its control to the inland Ashanti area, which became a colony, and the northern territories, which became a protectorate. The three regions were merged with British Togoland, a onetime German colony under British administration since 1922. In 1957 the four regions united as independent Ghana. Instability resulted, arising from a history of disunity and economic problems. The parliamentary state became a republic in 1960, and civilian rule has alternated with military governments. Although Ghanaians' loyalties are based on community rather than national allegiance, they are in general agreement on foreign affairs. ∎

GIBRALTAR

Official name Gibraltar

PEOPLE

Population 33,000. **Density** 14,348/mi^2 (5,500/km^2). **Urban** 100%. **Capital** Gibraltar, 33,000. **Ethnic groups** Gibraltarian (mixed Italian, English, Maltese, Portuguese, and Spanish) 75%, British 14%. **Languages** English, Spanish. **Religions** Roman Catholic 75%, Anglican 9%, Muslim 8%, Jewish 2%,

Hindu 1%. **Life expectancy** 77 female, 72 male. **Literacy** 99%.
POLITICS
Government Dependent territory (U.K.). **Parties** Labor/Association for the Advancement of Civil Rights, Socialist Labor. **Suffrage** Universal, over 18. **Memberships** None. **Subdivisions** None.
ECONOMY
GNP $129,000,000 **Per capita** $4,300. **Monetary unit** Pound. **Trade partners** U.K., Morocco, Portugal, Netherlands. **Exports** Petroleum, beverages and tobacco, manufactures. **Imports** Manufactures, fuel, food.
LAND
Description Southwestern Europe (peninsula on Spain's southern coast). **Area** 2.3 mi² (6.0 km²). **Highest point** 1,398 ft (426 m). **Lowest point** Sea level.

People. Occupying a narrow peninsula on Spain's southern coast, the British colony of Gibraltar has a mixed population of Italian, English, Maltese, Portuguese, and Spanish descent. A number of British residents—many of which are military personnel—also reside here. Most are bilingual in English and Spanish.

Economy and the Land. With land unsuited for agriculture and a lack of mineral resources, Gibraltar depends mainly on the British military and tourism. Shipping-related activities and a growing service industry also provide jobs and income. Connected to Spain by an isthmus, Gibraltar consists mainly of the limestone-and-shale ridge known as the Rock of Gibraltar. The climate is mild.

History and Politics. Drawn by Gibraltar's strategic location at the Atlantic entrance to the Mediterranean Sea, Phoenicians, Carthaginians, Romans, Vandals, Visigoths, and Moors all played a role in the land's history. After nearly three hundred years under Spanish control, Gibraltar was captured by Britain in 1704, during the War of the Spanish Succession. It was officially ceded to the British in the 1713 Peace of Utrecht. In a 1967 referendum, residents voted to remain under British control. British-Spanish competition for the colony continues. ■

GREECE

Official name Hellenic Republic
PEOPLE
Population 10,075,000. **Density** 198/mi² (76/km²). **Urban** 63%. **Capital** Athens, 885,737. **Ethnic groups** Greek 98%, Turkish 1%. **Languages** Greek. **Religions** Greek Orthodox 98%, Muslim 1%. **Life expectancy** 79 female, 74 male. **Literacy** 91%.
POLITICS
Government Republic. **Parties** New Democracy, Left Alliance, Panhellenic Socialist Movement, others. **Suffrage** Universal, over 18. **Memberships** EC, NATO, OECD, UN. **Subdivisions** 13 administrative regions.
ECONOMY
GDP $33,407,000,000 **Per capita** $3,331. **Monetary unit** Drachma. **Trade partners** Germany, Italy, France. **Exports** Food, clothing, petroleum, textiles, minerals and other crude materials. **Imports** Petroleum, manufactures, machinery, transportation equipment, chemicals.

LAND
Description Southeastern Europe. **Area** 50,962 mi² (131,990 km²). **Highest point** Mt. Olympus, 9,570 ft (2,917 m). **Lowest point** Sea level.

People. Greece has played a central role in European, African, and Asian cultures for thousands of years, but today its population is almost homogeneous. Native Greek inhabitants are united by a language that dates back three thousand years and a religion that influences many aspects of everyday life. Athens, the capital, was the cultural center of an ancient civilization that produced masterpieces of art and literature and broke ground in philosophy, political thought, and science.

Economy and the Land. The economy of Greece takes its shape from terrain and location. Dominated by the sea and long a maritime trading power, Greece has one of the largest merchant fleets in the world and depends greatly on commerce. The mountainous terrain and poor soil limit agriculture, although Greece is a leading producer of lemons and olives. The service sector, including tourism, provides most of Greece's national income. Inhabitants enjoy a temperate climate, with mild, wet winters, and hot, dry summers.

History and Politics. Greece's history begins with the early Bronze Age cultures of the Minoans and the Mycenaeans. The city-state, or *polis*, began to develop around the tenth century B.C., and Athens, a democracy, and Sparta, an oligarchy, gradually emerged as Greece's leaders. The Persian Wars, in which the city-states united to repel a vastly superior army, ushered in the Golden Age of Athens, a cultural explosion in the fifth century B.C. The Parthenon, perhaps Greece's most famous building, was built at this time. Athens was defeated by Sparta in the Peloponnesian War, and by 338 B.C. Philip II of Macedon had conquered all of Greece. His son, Alexander the Great, defeated the Persians and spread Greek civilization and language all over the known world. Greece became a Roman province in 146 B.C. and part of the Byzantine Empire in A.D. 395, but its traditions had a marked influence on these empires. Absorbed into the Ottoman Empire in the 1450s, Greece had gained independence by 1830 and became a constitutional monarchy about fifteen years later. For much of the twentieth century the nation was divided between republicans and monarchists. During World War II Germany occupied Greece, and postwar instability led to a civil war, which Communist rebels eventually lost. A repressive military junta ruled Greece from 1967 until 1974, when the regime relinquished power to a civilian government. The Greeks then voted for a republic over a monarchy. A Socialist government ruled until 1989. Indecisive election results forced the scheduling of a new election in 1990, when a narrow victory gave support to the first conservative government in nine years. ■

GREENLAND

Official name Greenland
PEOPLE
Population 57,000. **Density** 0.07/mi² (0.03/km²). **Urban** 78%. **Capital** Godthåb, 12,217. **Ethnic groups** Greenlander (Inuit and native-born whites) 86%, Danish 14%. **Languages** Danish, Greenlandic, Inuit dialects.

Religions Lutheran. **Life expectancy** 66 female, 60 male. **Literacy** 99%.
POLITICS
Government Self-governing territory (Danish protection). **Parties** Forward (Siumut), Inuit Movement, Polar (Issittrup), Unity (Atassut). **Suffrage** Universal, over 18. **Memberships** None. **Subdivisions** 3 municipalities. **Monetary unit** Danish krone. **Trade partners** Exports: Denmark, France, Germany. Imports: Denmark, Norway, Sweden. **Exports** Fish and shellfish, lead and zinc. **Imports** Manufactures, machinery, petroleum, ships and other transportation equipment.
LAND
Description North Atlantic island. **Area** 840,004 mi² (2,175,600 km²). **Highest point** Gunnbjorn Mtn., 12,139 ft (3,700 m). **Lowest point** Sea level.

People. Most Greenlanders are native-born descendants of mixed Inuit-Danish ancestry. Lutheranism, the predominant religion, reflects Danish ties. Descended from an indigenous Arctic people, pure Inuit are a minority and usually follow traditional lifestyles. Most of the island lies within the Arctic Circle, and population is concentrated along the southern coast.

Economy and the Land. Fishing is the state's economic backbone. Despite a difficult arctic environment, mining of zinc and lead continues; but iron, coal, uranium, and molybdenum deposits remain undeveloped. The largest island in the world, Greenland is composed of an inland plateau, coastal mountains and fjords, and offshore islands. More than 80 percent of the island lies under permanent ice cap. Greenland is situated in the "Land of the Midnight Sun," and certain areas have twenty-four consecutive hours of daylight in summer and darkness in winter. The climate is cold, with warmer temperatures and more precipitation in the southwest.

History and Politics. Following early migration of Arctic Inuit, Norwegian Vikings sighted Greenland in the ninth century, and in the tenth century Erik the Red brought the first settlers from Iceland. Greenland united with Norway in the 1200s, and the two regions, along with several others, came under Danish rule in the 1300s. Denmark retained control of Greenland when Norway left the union in 1814. American troops defended the island during World War II. In 1953 the island became a province of Denmark and in 1979 it gained home rule. ■

GRENADA

Official name Grenada

PEOPLE
Population 114,000. **Density** 857/mi² (331/km²). **Urban** 15%. **Capital** St. George's, 4,788. **Ethnic groups** Black 82%, mixed 13%, East Indian 3%. **Languages** English, French. **Religions** Roman Catholic 59%, Anglican 17%, Seventh Day Adventist 6%. **Life expectancy** 74 female, 69 male. **Literacy** 98%.
POLITICS
Government Parliamentary state. **Parties** National, National Democratic Congress, New National, United Labor. **Suffrage** Universal, over 18. **Memberships** CW, OAS, UN. **Subdivisions** 7 parishes.

ECONOMY
GDP $96,000,000 **Per capita** $842. **Monetary unit** East Caribbean dollar. **Trade partners** Exports: U.K., Trinidad and Tobago. Imports: U.S., Trinidad and Tobago, U.K.. **Exports** Cocoa, spices, bananas, clothing. **Imports** Machinery, food, manufactures, petroleum.
LAND
Description Caribbean island. **Area** 133 mi² (344 km²). **Highest point** Mt. St. Catherine, 2,757 ft (840 m). **Lowest point** Sea level.

People. Grenada's culture bears the influences of former British and French rule. The most widely spoken language is English, although a French patois is also spoken, and the majority of the population is Roman Catholic. Most Grenadians are black, descended from African slaves brought to the island by the British, but there are small East Indian and European populations.

Economy and the Land. Rich volcanic soils and heavy rainfall have made agriculture the chief economic activity. Also known as the Isle of Spice, Grenada is one of the world's leading producers of nutmeg and mace. Many tropical fruits are also raised, and the small plots of peasant farmers dot the hilly terrain. Another mainstay of the economy is tourism, with visitors drawn by the beaches and tropical climate. Grenada has little industry; high unemployment has plagued the nation in recent years.

History and Politics. The Carib Indians resisted European attempts to colonize Grenada for more than one hundred years after Christopher Columbus discovered the island in 1498. The French established the first settlement in 1650 and slaughtered the Caribs, but the British finally gained control in 1783. In 1974 Grenada achieved full independence under Prime Minister Eric Gairy, despite widespread opposition to his policies. In 1979 foes of the regime staged a coup and installed a Marxist government headed by Maurice Bishop. Power struggles resulted, and a military branch of the government seized power in 1983 and executed Bishop, along with several of his ministers. The United States led a subsequent invasion that deposed the Marxists. A new centrist government was installed in 1984 elections. ∎

GUADELOUPE See FRANCE.

GUAM See UNITED STATES.

GUATEMALA

Official name Republic of Guatemala
PEOPLE
Population 9,324,000. **Density** 222/mi² (86/km²).
Urban 42%. **Capital** Guatemala, 1,057,210. **Ethnic groups** Ladino (mestizo and westernized Maya) 56%, Maya 44%. **Languages** Spanish, indigenous. **Religions** Roman Catholic, Protestant, tribal religionist. **Life expectancy** 67 female, 62 male. **Literacy** 55%.
POLITICS
Government Republic. **Parties** Christian Democratic, Democratic Party of National Cooperation, National Centrist Union, Revolutionary, others. **Suffrage** Universal, over 18. **Memberships** OAS, UN. **Subdivisions** 22 departments.
ECONOMY
GDP $11,130,000,000 **Per capita** $1,377. **Monetary unit** Quetzal. **Trade partners** Exports: U.S., El Salvador. Imports: U.S., Venezuela, Mexico. **Exports** Coffee, bananas, sugar, cardamom. **Imports** Petroleum, manufactures, chemicals, machinery, food.
LAND
Description Central America. **Area** 42,042 mi² (108,889 km²). **Highest point** Volcán Tajumulco, 13,845 ft (4,220 m). **Lowest point** Sea level.

People. Guatemala's population is made up of majority ladinos and minority Indians. Ladinos include both mesti-

zos, those of Spanish-Indian origin, and westernized Indians of Mayan descent. Classified on the basis of culture rather than race, ladinos follow a Spanish-American lifestyle and speak Spanish. Nonladino Indians are also of Mayan descent; they generally speak Mayan dialects. Many are poor, uneducated, and isolated from the mainstream of Guatemalan life. Roman Catholicism often combines with traditional Mayan religious practice. Population is concentrated in the central highlands.

Economy and the Land. Most Guatemalans practice agriculture in some form. Indians generally operate small, unproductive subsistence farms. Export crops are mainly produced on large plantations on the fertile southern plain that borders the Pacific. Although light industry is growing, it is unable to absorb rural immigrants seeking employment in the cities. Much of the landscape is mountainous, with the Pacific plain and Caribbean lowlands bordering central highlands. Northern rain forests and grasslands are sparsely populated and largely undeveloped. The climate is tropical in low areas and temperate in the highlands.

History and Politics. Indians in the region were absorbed into the Mayan civilization that flourished in Central America by the fourth century. In 1523 the Spanish defeated the indigenous Indians and went on to establish one of the most influential colonies in Central America. Guatemala joined Costa Rica, El Salvador, Nicaragua, and Honduras in 1821 to declare independence from Spain, and the former Spanish colonies formed the Federation of Central America in 1823. Almost from the start, the federation was marked by dissension, and by 1838 it had, in effect, been dissolved. Following a series of dictatorships, social and economic reform began in 1944 and continued under two successive presidents. The government was ousted in a United States-backed 1954 coup and military rule established. A presidential assassination, accusations of government corruption and human-rights violations, guerrilla activities, and violence followed. A 1976 earthquake resulted in heavy loss of life and property. Military rule continued until 1985, when the nation returned to civilian rule under Marco Vinicio Cerezo. Leftist guerrillas continue to pressure the government, which is accused of the worst human rights abuses in Central America. In an upset victory, opposition candidate Jorge Serrano was elected president in 1991 and vowed to end the abuses. ∎

GUERNSEY See UNITED KINGDOM.

GUINEA

Official name Republic of Guinea
PEOPLE
Population 7,364,000. **Density** 78/mi² (30/km²). **Urban** 26%. **Capital** Conakry, 800,000. **Ethnic groups** Fulani, Malinke, Susu, others. **Languages** French, indigenous. **Religions** Muslim 85%, Christian 10%, Animist 5%. **Life expectancy** 46 female, 43 male. **Literacy** 48%.
POLITICS
Government Provisional military government. **Parties** None. **Suffrage** None. **Memberships** OAU, UN. **Subdivisions** 29 provinces.
ECONOMY
GNP $1,600,000,000 **Per capita** $291. **Monetary unit** Franc. **Trade partners** Exports: U.S., European

countries, U.S.S.R. Imports: U.S., France, Brazil.
Exports Alumina, bauxite, diamonds, coffee, pineapples, bananas, palm kernels. **Imports** Petroleum, metals, machinery and transportation equipment, food.
LAND
Description Western Africa. **Area** 94,926 mi² (245,857 km²). **Highest point** Mont Nimba, 5,748 ft (1,752 m). **Lowest point** Sea level.

People. Guinea's population is composed of several ethnic groups, with three—the Fulani, Malinke, and Susu—forming nearly half the total. Most Guineans are rural farmers, living in hamlets, and the only true urban center is Conakry. Mortality as well as emigration rates are high. Eight languages besides French, the language of the colonial power, are taught in the schools.

Economy and the Land. Rich soil and a varied terrain suited for diverse crop production have made agriculture an important economic activity. Guinea also has vast mineral reserves, including one of the world's largest bauxite deposits. Centralized economic planning and state enterprise have characterized the republic, but Guinea now encourages private and foreign investments. The terrain is mostly flat along the coast and mountainous in the interior. The climate is tropical on the coast, hot and dry in the north and northeast, and cooler with less humidity in the highlands.

History and Politics. As part of the Ghana, Mali, and Songhai empires that flourished in West Africa between the fourth and fifteenth centuries, Guinea was a trading center for gold and slaves. The Portuguese arrived on the coast in the 1400s, and European competition for Guinean trade soon began. In the 1890s France declared the area a colony and named it French Guinea. A movement for autonomy began after World War II with a series of reforms by the French and the growth of a labor movement headed by Sékou Touré, later the nation's first president. The first of the French colonies in West Africa to attain independence, in 1958 Guinea was also the only colony to reject membership in the French Community. In recent years the military set up a provisional government and banned political parties. ∎

GUINEA-BISSAU

Official name Republic of Guinea-Bissau
PEOPLE
Population 1,011,000. **Density** 72/mi² (28/km²). **Urban** 31%. **Capital** Bissau, 125,000. **Ethnic groups** Balanta 30%, Fulani 20%, Manjaca 14%, Malinke 13%, Papel 7%. **Religions** Portuguese, Crioulo, indigenous. **Religions** Tribal religionist 65%, Muslim 30%, Christian 5%. **Life expectancy** 49 female, 45 male. **Literacy** 20%.
POLITICS
Government Republic. **Parties** African Party for Independence. **Suffrage** Universal, over 15. **Memberships** OAU, UN. **Subdivisions** 9 regions.
ECONOMY
GDP $190,000,000 **Per capita** $228. **Monetary unit** Peso. **Trade partners** Exports: Spain, Portugal. Imports: Portugal, Sweden, U.S., Senegal. **Exports** Peanuts and palm kernels, fish, plywood, cashews. **Imports** Manufactures, transportation equipment, machinery, food, petroleum, chemicals.
LAND
Description Western Africa. **Area** 13,948 mi² (36,125 km²). **Highest point** 860 ft (262 m). **Lowest point** Sea level.

People. Guinea-Bissau's largest ethnic group, the Balanta, mainly inhabit the coastal area. Most practice traditional beliefs, although some are Christian. Predominately Muslim peoples, the Fulani and Malinke are concentrated in the northwest. The Manjaca inhabit the northern and central coastal regions. Although the official language is Portuguese, many speak Crioulo, a creole dialect also spoken in Cape Verde.

Economy and the Land. Guinea-Bissau's economy is underdeveloped and dependent upon agriculture. Peanuts, cotton, corn, and sorghum are grown in the north, and palm-oil production is concentrated along the coast. Timber is produced primarily in the south. Fishing, especially shrimp production, has increased since 1976. Bauxite deposits have been located, and exploration for additional resources continues. Mineral exploitation is hindered by a lack of transportation routes, however. A swamp-covered coastal plain rises to an eastern savanna. The climate is tropical. The country includes the Bijagos Archipelago, which lies just off the coast.

History and Politics. The area of Guinea-Bissau was inhabited by diverse peoples prior to the arrival of the Portuguese in 1446. Ruled as a single colony with Cape Verde, the region soon developed into a base for the Portuguese slave trade. In 1879 it was separated from Cape Verde as Portuguese Guinea, and its status changed to overseas province in 1951. A movement for the independence of Guinea-Bissau and Cape Verde developed in the 1950s, and a coup in Portugal in 1974 resulted in independence the same year. Attempts to unite Guinea-Bissau and Cape Verde were unsuccessful, and a 1980 coup installed an anti-unification government. ∎

GUYANA

Official name Co-operative Republic of Guyana
PEOPLE
Population 1,000,000. **Density** 12/mi² (4.7/km²). **Urban** 35%. **Capital** Georgetown, 78,500. **Ethnic groups** East Indian 51%, black 30%, mixed 11%, Amerindian 5%. **Languages** English, indigenous. **Religions** Anglican and other Christian 57%, Hindu 33%, Muslim 9%. **Life expectancy** 74 female, 69 male. **Literacy** 92%.

POLITICS
Government Republic. **Parties** People's National Congress, People's Progressive, others. **Suffrage** Universal, over 18. **Memberships** CW, OAS, UN. **Subdivisions** 10 districts.

ECONOMY
GDP $462,000,000 **Per capita** $550. **Monetary unit** Dollar. **Trade partners** Exports: U.K., U.S., Venezuela. Imports: Trinidad and Tobago, U.S., U.K.. **Exports** Bauxite, sugar, rice. **Imports** Manufactures, petroleum, machinery, dairy products and other food, chemicals.

LAND
Description Northeastern South America. **Area** 83,000 mi² (214,969 km²). **Highest point** Mt. Roraima, 9,432 ft (2,875 m). **Lowest point** Sea level.

People. Guyana's population includes descendants of black African slaves and East Indian, Chinese, and Portuguese laborers who were brought to work sugar plantations. Amerindians, the indigenous peoples of Guyana, are a minority. Ninety percent of the people live along the fertile coastal plain, where farming and manufacturing are concentrated.

Economy and the Land. Agriculture and mining com-

pose the backbone of the Guyanese economy. Sugar and rice continue to be important crops, and mines produce bauxite, manganese, diamonds, and gold. Guyana's inland forests give way to savanna and a coastal plain. The climate is tropical.

History and Politics. First gaining European notice in 1498 with the voyages of Christopher Columbus, Guyana was the stage for competing colonial interests—British, French, and Dutch—until it officially became British Guiana in 1831. Slavery was abolished several years later, causing the British to import indentured laborers, the ancestors of today's majority group. A constitution, adopted in 1953, was suspended when Britain feared a Communist victory at the polls. In the early 1960s, racial tensions erupted into riots between East Indians and blacks. In 1966, the country gained independence, and adopted the name Guyana. Guyana became a republic in 1970 and has pursued socialist policies. The two main political parties continue to reflect its ethnic divisions: the People's National Congress is supported by blacks, and the People's Progressive party by East Indians. ∎

HAITI

Official name Republic of Haiti
PEOPLE
Population 5,745,000. **Density** 536/mi² (207/km²). **Urban** 30%. **Capital** Port-au-Prince, 797,000. **Ethnic groups** Black 95%, mulatto and white 5%. **Languages** Creole, French. **Religions** Roman Catholic 80%, Baptist 10%, Pentecostal 4%. **Life expectancy** 58 female, 55 male. **Literacy** 21%.

POLITICS
Government Republic. **Parties** Christian Democratic, Movement to Install Democracy, National Alliance Front, Social Christian. **Suffrage** Universal, over 18. **Memberships** OAS, UN. **Subdivisions** 9 departments.

ECONOMY
GDP $2,009,000,000 **Per capita** $379. **Monetary unit** Gourde. **Trade partners** Exports: U.S., France. Imports: U.S., Netherlands Antilles, Japan. **Exports** Textiles and other manufactures, coffee and other food, aluminum ore. **Imports** Manufactures, food, petroleum, machinery, chemicals, vegetable oil.

LAND
Description Caribbean island (western Hispaniola). **Area** 10,714 mi² (27,750 km²). **Highest point** Morne La Selle, 8,773 ft (2,674 m). **Lowest point** Sea level.

People. The world's oldest black republic, Haiti has a population composed mainly of descendants of African slaves. Most people are poor and rural. Although French is an official language, Haitian Creole, a combination of French and West African languages, is more widely spoken. Roman Catholicism is the major religion. Voodooism, which blends Christian and African beliefs, is also practiced.

Economy and the Land. Haiti's economy remains underdeveloped. Most people rely on subsistence farming, though productivity is hampered by high population den-

sity in productive regions. Coffee is a main commercial crop and export. Recent growth of light industry is partially attributable to tax exemptions and low labor costs. Occupying the western third of Hispaniola Island, Haiti has an overall mountainous terrain and a tropical climate.

History and Politics. Christopher Columbus reached Hispaniola in 1492, and the indigenous Arawak Indians almost completely died out during subsequent Spanish settlement. Most Spanish settlers had gone to seek their fortunes in other colonies by the 1600s, and western Hispaniola came under French control in 1697. Slave importation increased rapidly, and in less than a hundred years black Africans far outnumbered the French. In a 1791 revolution led by Toussaint L'Ouverture, Jean Jacques Dessalines, and Henri Christophe, the slaves rose against the French. By 1804 the country achieved independence from France, and the area was renamed Haiti. In the 1820s, Haitians conquered the eastern region of the island, now the Dominican Republic, and it remained part of Haiti until 1844. Instability increased under various dictatorships from 1843 to 1915, and United States marines occupied the country from 1915 to 1934. After a time of alternating military and civilian rule, François Duvalier came to office in 1957, declaring himself president-for-life in 1964. His rule was marked by repression, corruption, and human-rights abuses. His son, Jean-Claude, succeeded him as president-for-life in 1971. The Duvalier dictatorship ended in 1986 when Jean-Claude fled the country. Continued unrest resulted in six different governments between 1987 and 1990. International observers monitored a December 1990 election, which marked the first democratically elected government in Haiti's history. ∎

HONDURAS

Official name Republic of Honduras
PEOPLE
Population 5,181,000. **Density** 120/mi² (46/km²). **Urban** 44%. **Capital** Tegucigalpa, 551,606. **Ethnic groups** Mestizo 90%, Amerindian 7%, black 2%, white 1%. **Languages** Spanish, indigenous. **Religions** Roman Catholic 97%. **Life expectancy** 68 female, 64 male. **Literacy** 57%.

POLITICS
Government Republic. **Parties** Liberal, National, others. **Suffrage** Universal, over 18. **Memberships** OAS, UN. **Subdivisions** 18 departments.

ECONOMY
GDP $3,480,000,000 **Per capita** $773. **Monetary unit** Lempira. **Trade partners** Exports: U.S., Germany, Italy. Imports: U.S., Venezuela, Japan. **Exports** Bananas, coffee, minerals, shrimp and lobster, lumber. **Imports** Paper and other manufactures, petroleum, chemicals, machinery, food.

LAND
Description Central America. **Area** 43,277 mi² (112,088 km²). **Highest point** Cerro Las Minas, 9,347 ft (2,849 m). **Lowest point** Sea level.

People. Most Hondurans are mestizos—people of Spanish-Indian descent. Other groups include Indians and descendants of black Africans and Europeans. Most Indians have been assimilated into the majority culture, but a minority continues to practice a traditional Indian lifestyle. The Spanish language predominates, and English is spoken by a small population of British descent on the northern coast and Bay Islands. Poverty is an ongoing problem for the mainly rural population, and economic and educational improvements mostly affect urban inhabitants.

Economy and the Land. Honduras has an underdeveloped economy based on banana cultivation. Other activities include livestock raising, coffee production, forestry, and some mining. Honduras's terrain is mostly mountainous, with lowlands along some coastal regions. The climate varies from tropical in the lowlands to temperate in the mountains.

History and Politics. Early in its history Honduras was part of the Mayan Empire. By 1502, when Christopher Columbus arrived to claim the region for Spain, the decline of the Maya had rendered the Indians weakened and unable to stave off Spanish settlement. The Spanish colonial period introduced gold and silver mines, cattle ranches, and African slaves. In 1821 Honduras, El Salvador, Nicaragua, Costa Rica, and Guatemala declared independence from Spain and, in 1823, formed the Federation of Central America. The unstable union had virtually collapsed by 1838, and the member states became independent as the federation dissolved. Instability, Guatemalan political influence, and the development of a banana economy based on United States-owned plantations marked the 1800s and early 1900s. Frequent revolutions have characterized the twentieth century, and a dictator governed from 1933 to 1948. Since the 1950s civilian governments have alternated with military coups and rule. Controversies focus on issues of poverty and land distribution. An elected civilian government has ruled since 1982. The country has become an important base for United States activities in Central America, evidenced by ongoing American military maneuvers in the area. ∎

HONG KONG

Official name Hong Kong
PEOPLE
Population 6,009,000. **Density** 14,514/mi² (5,605/km²). **Urban** 93%. **Capital** Victoria (Hong Kong), Hong Kong I., 1,175,860. **Ethnic groups** Chinese 95%. **Languages** Chinese (Cantonese), English. **Religions** Buddhist and Taoist 90%, Christian 10%. **Life expectancy** 80 female, 74 male. **Literacy** 77%.
POLITICS
Government Chinese territory under British administration. **Parties** United Democrats. **Suffrage** Professional or skilled persons. **Memberships** None. **Subdivisions** 4 areas.
ECONOMY
GDP $34,186,000,000 **Per capita** $6,290. **Monetary unit** Dollar. **Trade partners** Exports: U.S., China. Imports: China, Japan, U.S.. **Exports** Clothing, textiles, toys, watches, clocks, and other manufactures. **Imports** Textiles and other manufactures, machinery, chemicals, food.
LAND
Description Eastern Asia (islands and mainland area on China's southeastern coast). **Area** 414 mi² (1,072 km²). **Highest point** Tai Mo Mtn., 3,140 ft (957 m). **Lowest point** Sea level.

People. Hong Kong has a majority Chinese population. Cantonese, a Chinese dialect, is spoken by most of the people, and English and Chinese are the official languages. Major religions are Taoism, Christianity, and Buddhism. Hong Kong is one of the world's most densely populated areas.

Economy and the Land. Low taxes, duty-free status, an accessible location, and an excellent natural harbor have helped make Hong Kong an Asian center of trade, finance, manufacturing, and transportation. Situated on the coast of China, Hong Kong borders Guangdong province. The colony consists of the islands of Hong Kong and Lantau, the Kowloon Peninsula, and the New Territories, which include a mainland area and many islands. In addition to mountains, the New Territories contain some level areas suitable for agriculture, while the islands are hilly. The climate is tropical, with hot, rainy summers and cool, humid winters.

History and Politics. Inhabited since ancient times, Hong Kong came under Chinese rule around the third century B.C. In 1839 British opium smuggling led to the Opium War between Britain and China, and a victorious Britain received the island of Hong Kong in an 1842 treaty. In 1860 the British gained control of the Kowloon Peninsula, and in 1898 the New Territories came under British

rule through a ninety-nine-year lease with China. Hong Kong will be returned to China in 1997 under a negotiated agreement whereby the present economic system will be retained for fifty years. Recent events in China, however, have made many residents uneasy about Hong Kong's future. ∎

HUNGARY

Official name Republic of Hungary
PEOPLE
Population 10,540,000. **Density** 293/mi² (113/km²). **Urban** 60%. **Capital** Budapest, 2,016,132. **Ethnic groups** Hungarian (Magyar) 99%. **Languages** Hungarian. **Religions** Roman Catholic 68%, Calvinist 20%, Lutheran 5%. **Life expectancy** 75 female, 68 male. **Literacy** 99%.
POLITICS
Government Republic. **Parties** Democratic Forum, Free Democrats, Independent Smallholders, Socialist, others. **Suffrage** Universal, over 18. **Memberships** UN. **Subdivisions** 19 counties, 1 autonomous city.
ECONOMY
GNP $80,100,000,000 **Per capita** $7,504. **Monetary unit** Forint. **Trade partners** U.S.S.R., Germany. **Exports** Manufactures, machinery, food, transportation equipment, chemicals, petroleum. **Imports** Machinery, manufactures, fuel, chemicals.
LAND
Description Eastern Europe, landlocked. **Area** 35,920 mi² (93,033 km²). **Highest point** Kékes, 3,327 ft (1,014 m). **Lowest point** Along Tisza River, 256 ft (78 m).

People. Hungary's major ethnic group and language evolved from Magyar tribes who settled the region in the ninth century. Gypsies, Germans, and other peoples compose minorities. Most people are Roman Catholic and the literacy rate is high. Growth of industry since the 1940s has caused a rural-to-urban population shift.

Economy and the Land. Following World War II, Hungary pursued a program of industrialization, and the one-time agricultural nation now looks to industry as its main economic contributor. Agriculture was almost completely socialized under Communist rule and farming remains important, with productivity aided by fertile soils and a mild climate. Economic planning was decentralized in 1968, thus Hungary's economy differed from that of other Soviet-bloc nations, permitting some private enterprise. A flat plain dominates the landscape, and the lack of varied terrain results in a temperate climate throughout the country.

History and Politics. In the late 800s Magyar tribes from the east overcame Slavic and Germanic residents and settled the area. Invading Mongols caused much destruction in the thirteenth century. In the early 1500s, after repeated attacks, the Ottoman Turks dominated central Hungary. By the late seventeenth century, the entire region had come under the rule of Austria's Hapsburgs. Hungary succeeded in obtaining equal status with Austria in 1867, and the dual monarchy of Austria-Hungary emerged. Discontent and nationalistic demands increased until 1914, when a Bosnian Serb killed the heir to the Austro-Hungarian throne. Austria-Hungary de-

clared war on Serbia, and World War I began, resulting in both territory and population losses for Hungary. At the end of the war, in 1918, Hungary became a republic, only to revert to monarchical rule in 1919. Hungary entered World War II on the side of Germany, and Adolf Hitler set up a pro-Nazi government in Hungary in 1944. The Soviet Union invaded that same year, and a Hungarian-Allied peace treaty was signed in 1947. Coalition rule evolved into a Communist government in 1949. In 1956 discontent erupted into rebellion, a new premier declared Hungary neutral, and Soviet forces entered Budapest to quell the uprising. A new constitution, which goes into effect in 1990, will help move the nation away from Communist domination. A center-right government elected in 1990 inherited a country in economic crisis. ∎

ICELAND

Official name Republic of Iceland
PEOPLE
Population 260,000. **Density** 6.5/mi² (2.5/km²). **Urban** 91%. **Capital** Reykjavík, 93,425. **Ethnic groups** Icelander (mixed Norwegian and Celtic). **Languages** Icelandic. **Religions** Lutheran 95%, other Christian 3%. **Life expectancy** 81 female, 75 male. **Literacy** 100%.
POLITICS
Government Republic. **Parties** Independence, Progressive, Social Democratic, others. **Suffrage** Universal, over 18. **Memberships** NATO, OECD, UN. **Subdivisions** 23 counties, 14 independent towns.
ECONOMY
GDP $2,663,000,000 **Per capita** $249. **Monetary unit** Krona. **Trade partners** Exports: U.K., U.S., Germany. Imports: Germany, Denmark, Norway. **Exports** Fish and shellfish, aluminum and other manufactures. **Imports** Manufactures, machinery, petroleum, food, chemicals, crude materials.
LAND
Description North Atlantic island. **Area** 39,769 mi² (103,000 km²). **Highest point** Hvannadalshnúkur, 6,952 ft (2,119 m). **Lowest point** Sea level.

People. Most Icelanders are of Norwegian or Celtic ancestry, live in coastal cities, and belong to the Lutheran church. Icelandic, the predominant language, has changed little from the Old Norse of the original settlers and still resembles the language of twelfth-century Nordic sagas.

Economy and the Land. Fish, found in the island's rich coastal waters, are the main natural resource and export. Iceland has a long tradition based on fishing, but the industry has recently suffered from decreasing markets and catches. Glaciers, lakes, hot springs, volcanoes, and a lava desert limit agricultural land but provide a scenic terrain. Although the island lies just south of the Arctic Circle, the climate is moderated by the Gulf Stream. Summers are damp and cool, and winters relatively mild but windy. Proximity to the Arctic Circle puts Iceland in the "Land of the Midnight Sun," resulting in periods of twenty-four-hour daylight in June.

History and Politics. Norwegians began settlement of Iceland around the ninth century. The world's oldest parliament, the Althing, was established in Iceland in A.D. 930. Civil wars and instability during the thirteenth century led to the end of independence in 1262, when Iceland came under Norwegian rule. In the fourteenth century Norway was joined to Denmark's realm, and rule of Iceland passed to the Danes. The Althing was abolished in 1800 but re-established in 1843. In the 1918 Act of Union, Iceland became a sovereign state but retained its union with Denmark under a common king. Germany occupied Denmark in 1940 during World War II; and British troops, replaced by Americans in 1941, protected Iceland from invasion. Following a 1944 plebiscite, Iceland left its union with Denmark and became an independent republic. ∎

INDIA

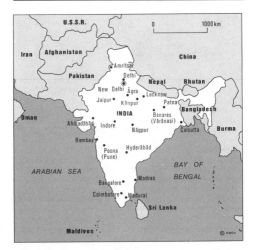

Official name Republic of India
PEOPLE
Population 836,170,000. **Density** 676/mi² (261/km²). **Urban** 28%. **Capital** New Delhi, 273,036. **Ethnic groups** Indo-Aryan 72%, Dravidian 25%, Mongoloid and other 3%. **Languages** English, Hindi, Telugu, Bengali, indigenous. **Religions** Hindu 83%, Muslim 11%, Christian 2%, Sikh 2%. **Life expectancy** 61 female, 60 male. **Literacy** 41%.
POLITICS
Government Republic. **Parties** Congress (I), Communist (Marxist), Janata, Janata Dal, others. **Suffrage** Universal, over 18. **Memberships** CW, UN. **Subdivisions** 25 states, 7 union territories.
ECONOMY
GDP $196,904,000,000 **Per capita** $261. **Monetary unit** Rupee. **Trade partners** Exports: U.S.S.R., U.S., Japan. Imports: Iran, U.S., Germany. **Exports** Clothing and other manufactures, food, crude materials, machinery, chemicals. **Imports** Petroleum, iron and steel and other manufactures, machinery, chemicals.
LAND
Description Southern Asia. **Area** 1,237,062 mi² (3,203,975 km²). **Highest point** Kānchenjunga, 28,208 ft (8,598 m). **Lowest point** Sea level.
The above information includes part of Jammu and Kashmir.

People. India's population is composed of two main ethnic groups: the Indo-Aryans and the Dravidians. Found mostly in the north are the Indo-Aryans, a central Asian people who arrived in India around 1500 B.C., pushing the Dravidians to the south, where they remain concentrated today. A Mongoloid minority inhabits the mountains of the far north, and aboriginal groups live in the central forests and mountains. There are fifteen official indigenous languages, as well as English, which is spoken by the majority of educated people. India is second only to China in population, and although Hindus are the religious majority, the country also has one of the world's largest Muslim populations. Christians, Sikhs, Jains, and Buddhists comprise additional religious minorities.

Economy and the Land. Economic conditions have improved since India became independent in 1947. Agriculture, upon which most Indians depend, is now more efficient, a result of modernization programs. Industry has expanded as well, and the country ranks high in its number of scientists and skilled laborers. Poverty, unemployment, and underemployment continue to plague the nation, however, partly due to rapid population growth and improved life expectancy. Many natural resources,

including coal, iron ore, bauxite, and manganese, remain undeveloped. India comprises three land regions: the Himalayas along the northern border; the Gangetic plain, a fertile northern region; and the peninsula, made up mostly of the Deccan, a plateau region. The climate ranges from temperate to tropical monsoon.

History and Politics. India's civilization dates back to 2500 B.C., when the Dravidians flourished in the region. Aryan tribes invaded about one thousand years later, bringing the indigenous beliefs that evolved into Hinduism, and various empires followed. In the sixth or fifth century B.C., Siddhārtha Gautama, who came to be called Buddha, founded Buddhism, a major influence on Indian life until about A.D. 800. Invasions beginning around A.D. 450 brought the Huns, and during the seventh and eighth centuries Arab conquerors introduced Islam. The Mogul Empire, under a series of Muslim rulers, began in the 1500s, and the British East India Company established trading posts in the 1600s. By 1757 the East India Company had become India's major power, and by the 1850s the company controlled nearly all present-day India, Pakistan, and Bangladesh. An Indian rebellion in 1857 caused Britain to take over the East India Company's rule. Demands for independence increased after a controversial massacre of Indians by British troops in 1919. By 1920 Mohandas Gandhi had emerged as the leader of an independence campaign based on nonviolent disobedience and noncooperation. The nation gained independence in 1947, establishing Pakistan as a separate Muslim state because of Muslim-Hindu hostilities. Recent disputes included a border conflict with China that erupted into fighting in 1959 and 1962 and a disagreement with Pakistan over the mainly Muslim region of Kashmir. Internal dissension and a high birth rate continue to inhibit India's development. ∎

INDONESIA

Official name Republic of Indonesia
PEOPLE
Population 193,080,000. **Density** 261/mi² (101/km²). **Urban** 29%. **Capital** Jakarta, Java I., 9,200,000. **Ethnic groups** Javanese 45%, Sundanese 14%, Madurese 8%, coastal Malay 8%. **Languages** Indonesian, Javanese, Sundanese, Madurese, other indigenous. **Religions** Muslim 87%, Protestant 7%, Catholic 3%, Hindu 2%. **Life expectancy** 60 female, 57 male. **Literacy** 67%.
POLITICS
Government Republic. **Parties** Democracy, Golkar, United Development. **Suffrage** Universal, over 17 or married. **Memberships** ASEAN, OPEC, UN. **Subdivisions** 27 provinces.
ECONOMY
GDP $85,081,000,000 **Per capita** $512. **Monetary unit** Rupiah. **Trade partners** Japan, U.S., Singapore. **Exports** Petroleum, natural gas, rubber and other crude materials, manufactures. **Imports** Machinery, petroleum, chemicals, iron and steel and other manufactures.
LAND
Description Southeastern Asian islands. **Area** 741,101 mi² (1,919,443 km²). **Highest point** Jaya Pk., 16,503 ft (5,030 m). **Lowest point** Sea level.

People. Indonesia is the fifth most populous nation in the

world. The majority of the people are of Malay stock, which includes several subgroups, such as Javanese, Sundanese, Madurese, and coastal Malay. More than two hundred indigenous languages are spoken, but the official, unifying language is Indonesian. Most people live in small farm villages and follow ancient customs stressing cooperation. Muslim traders brought Islam to Indonesia, and most of the population is Muslim. Many Indonesians combine spirit worship with Islam or Christianity. Indonesia's rich cultural heritage includes many ancient temples.

Economy and the Land. Indonesia is a leading producer of petroleum in the Far East. The area also has large deposits of minerals and natural gas. Agriculture is still a major economic activity, and rice remains an important crop, though overpopulation threatens the economy and food supply. The nation's more than 13,600 islands form a natural barrier between the Indian and Pacific oceans, making the straits between the islands important for world trade and military strategy. Java, the most industrial and heavily populated island, is characterized by volcanic mountains and narrow fertile plains along the northern coast. Indonesia includes most of Borneo, the third largest island in the world. Other major Indonesian islands are Sulawesi, Sumatra, and Irian Jaya (the western half of New Guinea), which also feature inland mountains and limited coastal plains. The climate is tropical, with seasonal monsoons.

History and Politics. Indonesian civilization is more than 2,500 years old and has produced two major empires with influence throughout Southeast Asia. The Portuguese arrived in the sixteenth century but were outnumbered by the Dutch, who eventually gained control of most of the islands and established a plantation colony. An independence movement began early in the twentieth century and slowly gained momentum. Japan encouraged Indonesian nationalism during World War II. Shortly after the Japanese surrendered in 1945, Indonesia proclaimed itself an independent republic. Economic and political instability led to an attempted Communist coup in 1965. The government has outlawed the Communist party and strengthened relations with the West, at the same time establishing trade talks with China. Concerns continue over reported human-rights abuses in East Timor. ∎

IRAN

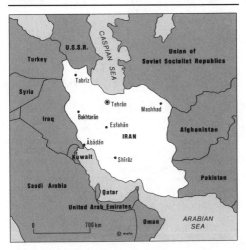

Official name Islamic Republic of Iran
PEOPLE
Population 56,810,000. **Density** 89/mi² (34/km²). **Urban** 55%. **Capital** Tehrān, 6,042,584. **Ethnic groups** Persian 63%, Turkish 18%, other Iranian 13%, Kurdish 3%. **Languages** Farsi, Turkish, Kurdish, Arabic, English, French. **Religions** Shiite Muslim 93%, Sunni Muslim 5%. **Life expectancy** 68 female, 67 male. **Literacy** 37%.
POLITICS
Government Islamic republic. **Parties** Militant Clerics Association, Fedaiyin Islam Organization. **Suffrage** Universal, over 15. **Memberships** OPEC, UN. **Subdivisions** 24 provinces.
ECONOMY
GDP $168,100,000,000 **Per capita** $3,778. **Monetary unit** Rial. **Trade partners** Exports: Japan, Turkey, Italy. Imports: Germany, Japan, Turkey. **Exports** Petroleum, carpets, fruit and nuts, hides. **Imports** Machinery, military supplies, metal works, food, pharmaceuticals.

LAND

Description Southwestern Asia. **Area** 636,372 mi² (1,648,196 km²). **Highest point** Mt. Demavend, 18,386 ft (5,604 m). **Lowest point** Caspian Sea, -92 ft (-28 m).

People. Most Iranians are of Aryan ancestry, descended from an Asiatic people who migrated to the area in ancient times. The Aryan groups include majority Persians and minority Gilani, Mazanderani, Kurds, Lur, Bakhtiari, and Baluchi. Turks are the major non-Aryan minority. Until 1935, when the shah officially changed its name, Iran was known as Persia. Farsi, or Persian, remains the main language. Nearly all Iranians are Muslim, mainly of the Shiite sect, and the country is an Islamic republic, with law based on Islamic teachings. Minority religious groups, especially Baha'is, have been victims of persecution. Due to aridity and a harsh mountain-and-desert terrain, the population is concentrated in the west and north.

Economy and the Land. Iran's previously rapid economic development has slowed as a result of a 1979 revolution and a war with Iraq. Small-scale farming, manufacturing, and trading appear to be current economic trends. Oil remains the most important export, although output has decreased due to changes in economic policy and other factors. Persian carpets also continue as elements of trade. Iran's terrain consists mainly of a central plateau marked by desert and surrounded by mountains; thus agriculture is limited, and the country remains dependent on imported food. The central region is one of the most arid areas on Earth, and summers throughout most of the country are long, hot, and dry, with higher humidity along the Persian Gulf and Caspian coast. Winters are cold in the mountains of the northwest, but mild on the plain. The Caspian coastal region is generally subtropical.

History and Politics. Iran's history is one of the world's oldest, with a civilization dating back several thousand years. Around 1500 B.C., Aryan immigrants began arriving from central Asia, calling the region Iran, or land of the Aryans, and splitting into two groups: the Medes and the Persians. In the sixth century B.C., Cyrus the Great founded the Persian, or Achaemenian, Empire, which came to encompass Babylonia, Palestine, Syria, and Asia Minor. Alexander the Great conquered the region in the fourth century B.C. Various dynasties followed, and Muslim Arabs invaded in the A.D. 600s and established Islam as the major religion. The following centuries saw Iran's boundaries expand and recede under various rulers, and increasing political awareness resulted in a 1906 constitution and parliament. In 1908 oil was discovered in the region, and modernization programs began during the reign of Reza Shah Pahlavi, who came to power in 1925. Despite Iran's declared neutrality in World War II, the Allies invaded, obtaining rights to use the country as a supply route to the Soviet Union. The presence of foreign influences caused nationalism to increase sharply after the war. Mohammad Reza Pahlavi—who succeeded his father, Reza Shah Pahlavi, as shah—instituted social and economic reforms during the sixties, although many Muslims felt the reforms violated religious law, and resented the increasing Western orientation of the country and the absolute power of the shah. Led by Muslim leader Ayatollah Ruholla Khomeini, revolutionaries seized the government in 1979, declaring Iran an Islamic republic based upon fundamental Islamic principles. Khomeini remained the religious leader of Iran until his death in 1989. In 1990 Iran elected the first president of the republic. The country has been involved for many years in conflicts in Lebanon and the Persian Gulf. A cease-fire halted the war with Iraq in 1988. ∎

IRAQ

Official name Republic of Iraq

PEOPLE

Population 18,920,000. **Density** 112/mi² (43/km²). **Urban** 74%. **Capital** Baghdād, 3,841,268. **Ethnic groups** Arab 75%-80%; Kurdish 15-20%; Turkoman, Assyrian, or other 5%. **Languages** Arabic, Kurdish, Assyrian, Armenian. **Religions** Shiite Muslim 60-65%, Sunni Muslim 32-37%, Christian and others 3%. **Life expectancy** 68 female, 65 male. **Literacy** 45%.

POLITICS

Government Republic. **Parties** National Progressive Front. **Suffrage** Universal, over 18. **Memberships** AL, OPEC, UN. **Subdivisions** 15 governorates, 3 autonomous regions.

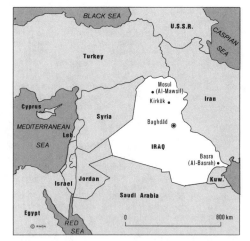

ECONOMY

GDP $42,338,000,000 **Per capita** $3,144. **Monetary unit** Dinar. **Trade partners** Exports: U.S., Brazil, U.S.S.R., Italy. Imports: Turkey, U.S., Germany, U.K.. **Exports** Petroleum, machinery, chemicals, dates. **Imports** Manufactures, food.

LAND

Description Southwestern Asia. **Area** 169,235 mi² (438,317 km²). **Highest point** 11,835 ft (3,607 m). **Lowest point** Sea level.

People. Descendants of the founders of one of the world's oldest civilizations inhabit Iraq. Most Iraqis are Muslim Arabs and Arabic speaking. The minority Kurds, also mainly Muslim, are concentrated in the northwest; speak their own language, Kurdish; and follow a non-Arab lifestyle. Kurdish demands for self-rule have led to occasional rebellion.

Economy and the Land. Oil is the mainstay of Iraq's economy, and nearly all economic development has focused on the petroleum industry, nationalized in the 1970s. Despite its oil wealth, the Iraqi economy, like the Iranian, was drained by the Iran-Iraq war. Most farmland lies near the Tigris and Euphrates rivers. The terrain is marked by northeastern mountains, southern and western deserts, and the plains of upper and lower Iraq, which lie between the Tigris and Euphrates rivers. The climate is generally hot and dry.

History and Politics. Civilizations such as the Sumerian, Babylonian, and Parthian flourished in the area of the Tigris and Euphrates in ancient times. Once known as Mesopotamia, the region was the setting for many biblical events. After coming under Persian rule in the sixth century B.C., Mesopotamia fell to Alexander the Great in the fourth century B.C. Invading Arabs brought the Muslim religion in the seventh century A.D., and for a time Baghdād was the capital and cultural center of the Arab empire. Thirteenth-century Mongol invaders were followed by Ottoman Turks in the sixteenth century. Ottoman rule continued, and following a British invasion during World War I, Mesopotamia became a British mandate at the end of the war. In 1921 the monarchy of Iraq was established, and independence was gained in 1932. Iraq and other nations formed the Arab League in 1945 and participated in a war against Israel in 1948. Opposition to monarchical rule increased during the 1950s; and after a 1958 military coup, the country was declared a republic. Instability, evidenced by coups, continued into the 1970s. The political climate was further complicated by occasional uprisings by Kurds demanding autonomy. War with Iran, which caused heavy losses on both sides, continued intermittently through the early 1980s, ending in a 1988 cease-fire agreement. In August 1990, Iraq invaded Kuwait and forced the government into exile. Historic United Nations resolutions imposed economic sanctions against Iraq and demanded that the country withdraw from Kuwait by January 15, 1991. On January 16, a coalition of countries under the military direction of the United States began military action against Iraq and forced it to relinquish Kuwait. ∎

IRELAND

Official name Republic of Ireland

PEOPLE

Population 3,471,000. **Density** 128/mi² (49/km²). **Urban** 59%. **Capital** Dublin, 502,749. **Ethnic groups** Irish (Celtic), English. **Languages** English, Irish Gaelic.

Religions Roman Catholic 93%, Church of Ireland 3%. **Life expectancy** 78 female, 73 male. **Literacy** 98%.

POLITICS

Government Republic. **Parties** Fianna Fail, Fine Gael, Labor, others. **Suffrage** Universal, over 18. **Memberships** EC, OECD, UN. **Subdivisions** 26 counties.

ECONOMY

GDP $18,394,000,000 **Per capita** $5,117. **Monetary unit** Pound (punt). **Trade partners** Exports: U.K., Germany, France Imports: U.K., U.S., Germany. **Exports** Machinery, food, chemicals, manufactures. **Imports** Machinery, manufactures, chemicals, food, petroleum.

LAND

Description Northwestern European island (five-sixths of island of Ireland). **Area** 27,137 mi² (70,285 km²). **Highest point** Carrauntoohil, 3,406 ft (1,038 m). **Lowest point** Sea level.

People. Most of Ireland's population is descended from the Celts, a people who flourished in Europe and Great Britain in ancient times. Irish Gaelic, a form of ancient Celtic, and English are official languages. Most people are Roman Catholic. Protestants mainly belong to the Church of Ireland, a member of the Anglican Communion. With a long literary tradition, the country has contributed greatly to world literature.

Economy and the Land. Ireland's economy was agricultural until the 1950s, when a program of rapid industrialization began. This expansion resulted in significant foreign investment, especially by the United States. Most of the Irish labor force is unionized. Agriculture continues to play an important role, however, and food is produced for domestic and foreign consumption. The country of Ireland occupies most of the island but excludes Northern Ireland, which is part of the United Kingdom. The fertile central region features green, rolling hills, suitable for farming and pastureland, and is surrounded by coastal highlands. The climate is temperate maritime, with mild summers and winters and plentiful rainfall.

History and Politics. Around the fourth century B.C., Ireland's indigenous population was conquered by Gaels, a Celtic tribe, from continental Europe and Great Britain. Christianity was introduced by St. Patrick in A.D. 432, and periodic Viking raids began near the end of the eighth century. In the twelfth century the pope made the Norman king of England, Henry II, overlord of the island; the English intervened in a dispute between Irish kings; and centuries of British influence began. As British control grew, so did Irish Catholic hostility, arising from seizure of land by English settlers, the Protestant Reformation, and the elimination of political and religious freedoms. The Protestant majority of present-day Northern Ireland was established in the 1600s, when land taken from the Irish was distributed to English and Scottish Protestants. In 1801 the British Act of Union established the United Kingdom of Great Britain, and Northern Ireland. Religious freedom was regained in 1829, but the struggle for independence continued. Most of the Irish depended upon potatoes as a staple food, and hundreds of thousands died or emigrated in the 1840s when the crop failed because of a plant disease. Following an armed rebellion, the Irish Free State, a dominion of Great Britain, was created in 1921, with the predominantly Protestant countries in the north remaining under British rule. The nation became a republic in 1949. Many Irish citizens and Catholics in Northern Ireland continue to demand unification of the country, and the struggle occasionally erupts into violence. Neutrality remains the basis of foreign policy, and the nation is a strong supporter of European unity. ∎

ISLE OF MAN See UNITED KINGDOM.

ISRAEL

Official name State of Israel
PEOPLE
Population 4,518,000. **Density** 563/mi² (218/km²).
Urban 92%. **Capital** Jerusalem, 493,500. **Ethnic
groups** Jewish 83%, Arab and others 17%.
Languages Hebrew, Arabic, Yiddish. **Religions** Jewish
82%, Muslim 14%, Christian 2%, Druze 2%. **Life
expectancy** 78 female, 74 male. **Literacy** 88%.

POLITICS
Government Republic. **Parties** Labor, Likud, others.
Suffrage Universal, over 18. **Memberships** UN.
Subdivisions 6 districts.

ECONOMY
GDP $24,559,000,000 **Per
capita** $5,889. **Monetary
unit** Shekel. **Trade
partners** Exports: U.S.,
U.K., Japan. Imports: U.S.,
Belgium, Germany.
Exports Diamonds and
other manufactures,
chemicals, machinery, fruit
and other food. **Imports**
Machinery, rough
diamonds, manufactures,
chemicals, petroleum,
food.
LAND
Description Southwestern
Asia. **Area** 8,019 mi²
(20,770 km²). **Highest
point** Mt. Meron, 3,963 ft
(1,208 m). **Lowest point**
Dead Sea, -1,322 ft
(-403 m).
*The above information
excludes Israeli-occupied
areas.*

People. Most Israelis are Jewish immigrants or descendants of Jews who settled in the region in the late 1800s. The two main ethnic groups are the Ashkenazim of central and eastern European origin and the Sephardim of the Mediterranean and Middle East. The non-Jewish population is predominantly Arab and Muslim, and many Palestinians inhabit the Israeli-occupied West Bank, whose status is still in dispute. Hebrew and Arabic are the official languages, and both are used on documents and currency. Conflict between conservative and liberal Jewish groups has spilled over into the nation's political life.

Economy and the Land. Despite drastic levels of inflation and a constant trade deficit, Israel has experienced continuous economic growth. Skilled labor supports the market economy based on services, manufacturing, and commerce. Taxes are a major source of revenue, as are grants and loans from other countries, and income from tourism. The country is poor in natural resources, but through improved irrigation and soil conservation, Israel now produces much of its own food. Because of its limited natural resources, Israel must import most of the raw materials it needs for industry. The region's varied terrain includes coastal plains, central mountains, the Jordan Rift Valley, and the desert region of the Negev. Except in the Negev, the climate is temperate.

History and Politics. Israel comprises much of the historic region of Palestine, known in ancient times as Canaan and the site of most biblical history. Hebrews arrived in this region about 1900 B.C. The area experienced subsequent immigration and invasion by diverse peoples, including Assyrians, Babylonians, and Persians. In 63 B.C. it became part of the Roman Empire, was renamed Judaea and finally, Palestine. In the A.D. 600s, invading Arabs brought Islam to the area, and by the early 1500s, when Ottoman Turks conquered the region, Muslims comprised a majority. During the late 1800s, as a result of oppression in eastern Europe, many Jews immigrated to Palestine, hoping to establish a Jewish

state. This movement, called Zionism, and the increasing Jewish population, led to Arab-Jewish tensions. Turkey sided with Germany in World War I, and after the war the Ottoman Empire collapsed. Palestine became a mandated territory of Britain in 1920. Jewish immigration and Arab-Jewish hostility increased during the years of Nazi Germany. Additional unrest arose from conflicting interpretations of British promises and the terms of the mandate. In 1947 Britain turned to the United Nations for help, and in 1948 the nation of Israel was established. Neighboring Arab countries invaded immediately, and war ensued, during which Israel gained some land. A truce was signed in 1949, but Arab-Israeli wars broke out periodically throughout the fifties, sixties, and seventies. Israel signed a peace treaty with Egypt in 1979, annexed the Golan Heights in 1981, and returned the Sinai to Egypt the following year. The years since have seen increasing trouble with the Palestinian refugee problem and the administration of the occupied territories of the West Bank and the Gaza Strip. In January 1991, Israel once again became involved in Arab hostilities. Iraq's first response to the United Nations sanctioned attempts to force it to withdraw from Kuwait was to send missiles into Israel. ∎

ITALY

Official name Italian Republic
PEOPLE
Population 57,630,000. **Density** 495/mi² (191/km²).
Urban 69%. **Capital** Rome, 2,815,457. **Ethnic groups**
Italian (Latin). **Languages** Italian. **Religions** Roman
Catholic 99%. **Life expectancy** 80 female, 73 male.
Literacy 97%.

POLITICS
Government Republic. **Parties** Christian Democratic,
Democratic Party of the Left, Socialist, others.
Suffrage Universal, over 18. **Memberships** EC, NATO,
OECD, UN. **Subdivisions** 20 regions.

ECONOMY
GDP $358,669,000,000 **Per capita** $6,299. **Monetary
unit** Lira. **Trade partners** Exports: Germany, France,
U.S. Imports: Germany, France, Netherlands. **Exports**
Machinery, clothing and other manufactures, motor
vehicles, chemicals. **Imports** Petroleum, iron and steel
and other manufactures, machinery, food, chemicals.
LAND
Description Southern Europe. **Area** 116,324 mi²
(301,277 km²). **Highest point** Mont Blanc (Monte
Bianco), 15,771 ft (4,807 m). **Lowest point** Sea level.

People. Italy is populated mainly by Italian Roman Catholics. Most speak Italian; however, dialects often differ from region to region. Despite an ethnic homogeneity, the people exhibit diversity in terms of politics and culture. The country has about twelve political parties, and northern inhabitants are relatively prosperous, employed primarily in industry, whereas southerners are generally farmers and often poor. The birthplace of the Renaissance, Italy has made substantial contributions to world culture.

Economy and the Land. The Italian economy is based on private enterprise, although the government is involved in some industrial and commercial activities. Industry and commercial agriculture are centered in the

north, which produces steel, textiles, and chemicals. A hilly terrain makes parts of the south unsuited for crop raising, and livestock grazing is a main activity. Tourism is also important; visitors are drawn by the northern Alps, the sunny south, and the Italian cultural tradition. The island of Sicily, lying off the southwest coast, produces fruits, olives, and grapes. Sardinia, a western island, engages in some sheep and wheat raising. Except for the northern Po Valley, narrow areas along the coast, and a small section of the southern peninsula, Italy's terrain is mainly rugged and mountainous. In 1987, landslides in the Alps destroyed Sant'Antonio Morignone, isolating it from the rest of the country. The climate varies from cold in the Alps to mild and Mediterranean in other regions.

History and Politics. Early influences in Italy included Greeks, Etruscans, and Celts. From the fifth century B.C. to the fifth century A.D., the dominant people were Romans descended from Sabines and neighboring Latins, who inhabited the Latium coast. Following the demise of the Roman Empire, rulers and influences included Byzantines; Lombards, an invading Germanic tribe; and the Frankish King Charlemagne, whom the pope crowned emperor of the Romans in 800. During the eleventh century, Italy became a region of city-states, and its cultural life led to the Renaissance, which started in the 1300s. As the city-states weakened, Italy fell victim to invasion and rule by France, Spain, and Austria, with these countries controlling various regions at different times. In 1861 Victor Emmanuel II, the king of Sardinia, proclaimed Italy a kingdom, and by 1871 the nation included the entire peninsula, with Rome as the capital and Victor Emmanuel as king. In 1922 Benito Mussolini, the leader of Italy's Fascist movement, came to power. By 1925 Mussolini was ruling as dictator, and an almost continuous period of warfare followed. In World War II the country allied with Germany, and a popular resistance movement evolved. The monarchy was ended by plebiscite in 1946, and the country became a republic. Italy's Communist party, which was renamed the Democratic Party of the Left, is the world's largest nonruling Communist party. ∎

IVORY COAST

Official name Republic of the Ivory Coast
PEOPLE
Population 12,305,000. **Density** 99/mi² (38/km²).
Urban 47%. **Capital** Abidjan (de facto), 1,950,000;
Yamoussoukro (future), 80,000. **Ethnic groups** Baule
23%, Bete 18%, Senoufou 15%, Malinke 11%, other
African. **Languages** French, indigenous. **Religions**
Animist 63%, Muslim 25%, Christian 12%. **Life
expectancy** 56 female, 53 male. **Literacy** 25%.

POLITICS
Government Republic. **Parties** Democratic. **Suffrage**
Universal, over 21. **Memberships** OAU, UN.
Subdivisions 49 departments.

ECONOMY
GDP $6,980,000,000 **Per capita** $807. **Monetary unit**
CFA franc. **Trade partners** Exports: France, U.S.,
Netherlands. Imports: France, Nigeria, U.S.. **Exports**
Cocoa, coffee, wood and other crude materials,
petroleum. **Imports** Manufactures, petroleum,
machinery, fish and other food, chemicals.
LAND
Description Western Africa. **Area** 124,518 mi²

(322,500 km²). **Highest point** Mont Nimba, 5,748 ft (1,752 m). **Lowest point** Sea level.

People. Ivory Coast is composed almost entirely of black Africans from more than sixty ethnic groups. French is the nation's official language, a result of former French rule, but many indigenous languages are spoken as well. Traditional religions predominate, though a significant number of Ivorians are Muslim or Christian. Most Ivorians live in huts in small villages, but increased numbers have moved to the cities to find work. Overcrowding is a major problem in the cities.

Economy and the Land. Once solely dependent upon the export of cocoa and coffee, Ivory Coast now produces and exports a variety of agricultural goods. Forest land, when cleared, provides rich soil for agriculture—still the country's main activity. Petroleum, textile, and apparel industries also contribute to the strong economy. Ivory Coast pursues a policy of economic liberalism in which foreign investment is encouraged. As a result, foreigners hold high-level positions in most Ivory Coast industries. The hot, humid coastal region gives way to inland tropical forest. Beyond the forest lies savanna, and to the northwest are highlands.

History and Politics. Ivory Coast once consisted of many African kingdoms. French sailors gave the region its present name when they began trading for ivory and other goods in 1483. Missionaries arrived in 1637, but European settlement was hindered by the rugged coastline and intertribal conflicts. Ivory Coast became a French colony in 1893. Movements toward autonomy began after World War II, and in 1960 Ivory Coast declared itself an independent republic. The nation has enjoyed political stability since independence and has maintained close economic ties with France. The nation enjoyed many years of political stability under the rule of President Houphouet-Boigny. However, protests against the government and against one-party rule led to Ivory Coast's first multiparty election in 1990. The ruling party won an overwhelming victory, leading to charges of fraud by the opposition. Foreign policy stresses favorable relations with the West. ∎

JAMAICA

Official name Jamaica
PEOPLE
Population 2,425,000. **Density** 571/mi² (221/km²). **Urban** 52%. **Capital** Kingston, 646,400. **Ethnic groups** Black 75%, mixed 13%, East Indian 1%. **Languages** English, Creole. **Religions** Church of God and other Protestant, Anglican, Roman Catholic. **Life expectancy** 78 female, 72 male. **Literacy** 96%.
POLITICS
Government Parliamentary state. **Parties** Labor, People's National. **Suffrage** Universal, over 18. **Memberships** CW, OAS, UN. **Subdivisions** 14 parishes.
ECONOMY
GDP $2,026,000,000 **Per capita** $934. **Monetary unit** Dollar. **Trade partners** Exports: U.S., Canada, U.K. Imports: U.S., Netherlands Antilles, Venezuela. **Exports** Alumina and bauxite, sugar and other food, manufactures. **Imports** Petroleum, grain and other food, manufactures, machinery, chemicals.

LAND
Description Caribbean island. **Area** 4,244 mi² (10,991 km²). **Highest point** Blue Mountain Pk., 7,402 ft (2,256 m). **Lowest point** Sea level.

People. Most Jamaicans are of African or Afro-European descent, and the majority are Christian. English is the official language, but many Jamaicans also speak Creole. Population is concentrated on the coastal plains, where the main commercial crops are also grown.

Economy and the Land. Agriculture is the traditional mainstay, and more than a third of the population is engaged in farming. Sugar cane and bananas are principal crops. Mining is also important, and Jamaica is a leading producer of bauxite. The tropical climate, tempered by ocean breezes, makes the island a popular tourist destination. A mountainous inland region is surrounded by coastal plains and beaches.

History and Politics. Christopher Columbus claimed the island for Spain in 1494. As the enslaved native population died out, blacks were brought from Africa to work plantations. Britain invaded and gained control of Jamaica in the seventeenth century, and for a time the island was one of the most important sugar and slave centers of the New World. In 1838 the British abolished slavery, the plantation economy broke down, and most slaves became independent farmers. Local political control began in the 1930s, and the nation became fully independent in 1962. Since independence the nation has faced problems of unemployment, inflation, and poverty, with periodic social unrest. ∎

JAPAN

Official name Japan
PEOPLE
Population 123,850,000. **Density** 849/mi² (328/km²). **Urban** 77%. **Capital** Tōkyō, Honshū I., 8,354,615. **Ethnic groups** Japanese 99%, Korean. **Languages** Japanese. **Religions** Buddhist and Shinto. **Life expectancy** 82 female, 76 male. **Literacy** 99%.
POLITICS
Government Constitutional monarchy. **Parties** Clean Government (Komeito), Communist, Liberal Democratic, Socialist, others. **Suffrage** Universal, over 20. **Memberships** OECD, UN. **Subdivisions** 47 prefectures.
ECONOMY
GDP $1,325,203,000,000 **Per capita** $11,025. **Monetary unit** Yen. **Trade partners** Exports: U.S., Korea, Germany. Imports: U.S., Indonesia, Korea. **Exports** Machinery, motor vehicles and other transportation equipment, manufactures. **Imports** Fuels, manufactures, minerals and other crude materials, food, machinery.
LAND
Description Eastern Asian islands. **Area** 145,870 mi² (377,801 km²). **Highest point** Mt. Fuji, 12,388 ft (3,776 m). **Lowest point** Hachiro-gata reclamation area, Honshū I., -13 ft (-4 m).

People. The Japanese constitute Japan's major ethnic group, while minorities include Koreans and Chinese. Shintoism and Buddhism are the principal religions. Almost all the population lives on the coastal plains. Japan's culture blends East and West, with karate, tea ceremonies, and kimonos balanced by baseball, fast food, and business suits. Although its arts have been greatly influenced by China, Japan has developed distinctive music, literature, and painting.

Economy and the Land. One of the world's leading industrial powers, Japan is remarkable for its economic growth rate since World War II, considering it has few natural resources. It has also become famous for its innovative technology and continues to be a major user of robots in industry. Manufacturing is the basis of the economy, and Japan is a leading producer of ships, machinery, cars, and electronic equipment. Its chemical, iron, and steel industries are extremely profitable. Agriculture's part in the economy is small, since little of the rugged island terrain is arable. Fishing still plays a significant role in Japan's economy, though exports in this area have not been as high in recent years. Overseas trade has expanded rapidly since the 1960s, as Japan requires raw materials for its many industries. Trade barriers and the competitiveness of Japanese products overseas have led to trade deficits among Western nations. Japan's mountainous terrain includes both active and dormant volcanoes; earthquakes occasionally occur. The climate ranges from subtropical to temperate.

History and Politics. Legend states that Japan's first emperor was descended from the sun goddess and came to power around 600 B.C. The arrival of Buddhism, Confucianism, and new technologies from China in the fifth and sixth centuries A.D. revolutionized society. Feuding nobles controlled Japan between 1192 and 1867 and ruled as *shoguns*, or generals, in the name of the emperor. The warrior class, or *samurai*, developed early in this period. The arrival of Europeans in the sixteenth century caused fear of an invasion among the shoguns, and in the 1630s they dissolved all foreign contacts. Japan's isolation lasted until 1854, when Commodore Matthew Perry of the United States opened the nation to the West with a show of force. The subsequent Meiji Restoration modernized Japan by adopting Western technologies and legal systems, and by stressing industrialization and education. Japan embarked on military expansion in the late nineteenth century, annexing Korea in 1910 and adding to its holdings after participating in World War I as a British ally. It occupied Manchuria in 1931 and invaded China in 1937. As part of the Axis powers in World War II, Japan attacked United States military bases in Pearl Harbor, Hawaii, in 1941. After the United States dropped atomic bombs on Hiroshima and Nagasaki in 1945, Japan surrendered. Allied forces occupied the nation until 1952. By that time the Japanese approved a constitution that shifted political power from the emperor to the people and also abolished the military. In the years since, Japan has emerged as one of the world's fastest growing economies. ∎

JERSEY See UNITED KINGDOM.

JORDAN

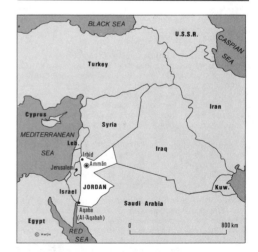

Official name Hashemite Kingdom of Jordan
PEOPLE
Population 3,112,000. **Density** 89/mi² (34/km²). **Urban** 68%. **Capital** Àmmān, 936,300. **Ethnic groups** Arab 98%, Circassian 1%, Armenian 1%. **Languages** Arabic. **Religions** Sunni Muslim 95%, Christian 5%. **Life expectancy** 70 female, 66 male. **Literacy** 65%.

POLITICS

Government Constitutional monarchy. **Parties** Muslim Brotherhood. **Suffrage** Universal, over 20. **Memberships** AL, UN. **Subdivisions** 8 governorates.

ECONOMY

GDP $4,067,000,000 **Per capita** $1,643. **Monetary unit** Dinar. **Trade partners** Exports: Iraq, Saudi Arabia, India. Imports: Saudi Arabia, U.S., Iraq. **Exports** Fertilizer, chemicals, vegetables and other food, manufactures. **Imports** Manufactures, food, petroleum, machinery, chemicals, transportation equipment.

LAND

Description Southwestern Asia. **Area** 35,135 mi^2 (91,000 km^2). **Highest point** Mt. Ramm, 5,755 ft (1,754 m). **Lowest point** Dead Sea, -1,322 ft (-403 m).

People. Most Jordanians are Arabs, but there are Circassian, Armenian, and Kurdish minorities, as well as a small nomadic population, the Bedouins, in desert areas. A large number of Jordanians are Palestinian refugees, displaced by Arab-Israeli wars, who have been granted citizenship by the government. Many Palestinians also live on the West Bank, a disputed area occupied by Jordan until Israel gained control in 1967. Arabic is the official language, and most people are Sunni Muslim, legacies of the Muslim conquest in A.D. 600s.

Economy and the Land. A nation with few natural resources, limited rainfall, and little arable land, Jordan has suffered further economic damage from an influx of refugees and the chronic political instability of the Middle East. In a 1967 war with Israel, Jordan lost the economically active West Bank, which made up about half the country's farmland. Agriculture remains the most important activity, and tourism has helped boost a weak economy that relies heavily on foreign aid and investment from the United States and Arab nations. There is some light industry and mining. The Jordan River forms the country's westernmost boundary, and the terrain is marked by deserts, mountains, and rolling plains. The climate ranges from Mediterranean in the west to desert in the east.

History and Politics. Jordan is the site of one of the world's oldest settlements, dating back to about 8000 B.C. The area came under the rule of the Hebrews, Assyrians, Egyptians, Persians, Greeks, and Romans, and, around A.D. 636 Arab Muslims. Rule by the Ottoman Turks began in the sixteenth century, and in World War I Arab armies helped the British defeat Turkey. At the end of the war present-day Israel and Jordan became the British mandate of Palestine, which in 1922 was divided into the mandates of Transjordan, lying east of the Jordan River, and Palestine, lying to the west. Transjordan gained full independence in 1946. In 1948 the Palestine mandate created Israel, and Arab-Israeli fighting ensued. After capturing the West Bank, Transjordan was renamed Jordan in 1949. During the Arab-Israeli Six-Day War in 1967, this region and the Jordanian section of Jerusalem fell to Israel. After each war, Jordan's Palestinian-refugee population grew. A 1970 civil war pitted the government against Palestinian guerrillas, who, like Jordan, desired control of the West Bank. The guerrillas were expelled following the war, but subsequent Arab-Israeli hostilities led to Jordan's recognition of the Palestine Liberation Organization. In 1988, Jordan relinquished all claims to the Israeli-held West Bank area, although it continues to be involved in discussions on the fate of the Palestinians. Jordan is a constitutional monarchy headed by a king. After Iraq's occupation of Kuwait in 1990, a rush of refugees presented Jordan with severe economic pressures. ■

KAMPUCHEA See CAMBODIA.

KENYA

Official name Republic of Kenya

PEOPLE

Population 26,400,000. **Density** 117/mi^2 (45/km^2). **Urban** 24%. **Capital** Nairobi, 1,505,000. **Ethnic groups** Kikuyu 21%, Luhya 14%, Luo 13%, Kamba 11%, Kalenjin 11%, Kisii 6%, Meru 5%. **Languages** English, Swahili, indigenous. **Religions** Protestant 38%, Roman Catholic 28%, Animist 26%, Muslim 6%. **Life expectancy** 63 female, 59 male. **Literacy** 47%.

POLITICS

Government Republic. **Parties** African National Union. **Suffrage** Universal, over 18. **Memberships** CW, OAU, UN. **Subdivisions** 7 provinces, 1 capital district.

ECONOMY

GDP $5,769,000,000 **Per capita** $304. **Monetary unit** Shilling. **Trade partners** Exports: U.K., Germany, Netherlands. Imports: U.K., Japan, Germany. **Exports** Coffee, tea, petroleum, crude materials, fruit and vegetables. **Imports** Machinery, chemicals, petroleum, manufactures, transportation equipment.

LAND

Description Eastern Africa. **Area** 224,961 mi^2 (582,646 km^2). **Highest point** Kirinyaga (Mt. Kenya), 17,058 ft (5,199 m). **Lowest point** Sea level.

People. Nearly all Kenyans are black Africans belonging to one of more than forty different groups, each with its own language and culture. Some groups are nomadic, like the Masai. Arab and European minorities—found mostly along the coast—reflect Kenya's history of foreign rule. Most Kenyans live in the southwestern highlands, raising crops or livestock. Over half of the citizens practice a form of Christianity, while the rest pursue indigenous beliefs or Islam. Swahili, a blend of Bantu and Arabic, is an official language; it serves as a communication link among Kenya's many ethnic groups. English is also an official language. The national slogan of *harambee*, or "pull together," illustrates the need for cooperation among Kenya's diverse groups. The government promotes such national unity.

Economy and the Land. Scenic terrain, tropical beaches, and abundant wildlife have given Kenya a thriving tourist industry, and land has been set aside for national parks and game preserves. Agriculture is the primary activity, even though the northern three-fifths of the country is semidesert. The most productive soils are found in the southwestern highlands, and coffee is the main export crop. Much of the land is also used for raising livestock, another leading economic contributor. Oil from other nations is refined in Kenya, and food processing and cement production are also significant activities. Kenya's climate varies from arid in the north to temperate in the highlands and tropical along the coast.

History and Politics. Remains of early humans dating back more than two million years have been found in Kenya. Settlers from other parts of Africa arrived about 1000 B.C. A thousand years later Arab traders reached the coast, and controlled the area by the eighth century A.D. The Portuguese ruled the coast between 1498 and the late 1600s. Kenya came under British control in 1895 and was known as the East African Protectorate. Opposition to British rule began to mount in the 1940s as Kenyans demanded a voice in government. The Mau Mau rebellion of the fifties, an armed revolt, was an outgrowth of this discontent. Kenya gained independence from Britain in 1963 and became a republic in 1964. Its first president was Jomo Kenyatta, a Kikuyu who had been an active leader in the previous revolt. Recent administrations have pursued a policy of Africanization, under which land and other holdings have been transferred from European to African hands. There is rising opposition to the autocratic one-party rule that has existed since 1978. ■

KERGUELEN ISLANDS See FRANCE.

KIRIBATI

Official name Republic of Kiribati

PEOPLE

Population 74,000. **Density** 264/mi^2 (102/km^2). **Urban** 36%. **Capital** Bairiki, Tarawa Atoll, 2,230. **Ethnic groups** Kiribatian (Micronesian) 99%. **Languages** English, Gilbertese. **Religions** Roman Catholic 53%, Congregationalist 41%, Bahai 2%. **Life expectancy** 57 female, 52 male. **Literacy** 90%.

POLITICS

Government Republic. **Parties** Christian Democratic, Gilbertese National. **Suffrage** Universal, over 18. **Memberships** CW. **Subdivisions** 6 districts.

ECONOMY

GDP $28,000,000 **Per capita** $475. **Monetary unit** Australian dollar. **Trade partners** Exports: Netherlands, Fiji, U.S. Imports: Australia, Japan, Fiji. **Exports** Copra, fish. **Imports** Food, machinery and transportation equipment, manufactures, fuel.

LAND

Description Central Pacific islands. **Area** 280 mi^2 (726 km^2). **Highest point** 246 ft (75 m). **Lowest point** Sea level.

People. The people of Kiribati, a nation of thirty-three islands in the central Pacific, are mostly Micronesian. Almost all the population lives on the Gilbert Islands in small villages and practices Roman Catholicism or Protestantism. English, the official language, and Gilbertese are spoken.

Economy and the Land. A small, unskilled work force combined with small land area and few natural resources have given Kiribati a subsistence economy. Copra and fish are the main exports. Kiribati depends on economic aid from Australia, New Zealand, and Great Britain. The islands of Kiribati are almost all coral reefs, composed of hard sand and little soil; many surround a lagoon. The climate is tropical.

History and Politics. Kiribati was invaded by Samoa in the 1400s. From 1916 the islands were part of the British Gilbert and Ellice Islands Colony. Fighting between the United States and Japan took place during World War II on Tarawa Island. The Ellice Islands became independent in 1978 as the nation of Tuvalu and the Republic of Kiribati came into existence a year later. ■

KOREA, NORTH

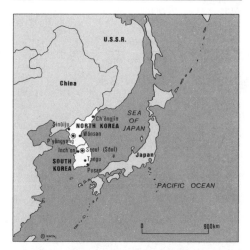

Official name Democratic People's Republic of Korea

PEOPLE

Population 23,335,000. **Density** 501/mi^2 (194/km^2). **Urban** 67%. **Capital** Pyŏngyang, 1,283,000. **Ethnic groups** Korean 100%. **Languages** Korean. **Religions** Shamanist, Chondoist, Buddhist. **Life expectancy** 74 female, 68 male. **Literacy** 95%.

POLITICS

Government Socialist republic. **Parties** Workers'. **Suffrage** Universal, over 17. **Memberships** None. **Subdivisions** 9 provinces, 4 special cities.

ECONOMY

GNP $24,000,000,000 **Per capita** $1,209. **Monetary unit** Won. **Trade partners** U.S.S.R., Japan, China,

Germany. **Exports** Minerals, metal products, food, manufactures. **Imports** Petroleum, machinery, coal, grain.

LAND
Description Eastern Asia. **Area** 46,540 mi² (120,538 km²). **Highest point** Paektu Mtn., 9,003 ft (2,744 m). **Lowest point** Sea level.

People. Despite a history of invasions, North Korea has a homogeneous population with virtually no minorities. Several dialects of Korean are spoken, and North Koreans use the Hankul, or Korean, alphabet exclusively. Korean religions have included Shamanism and Buddhism with Chondoist sects, though the government discourages religious activity. Urban population has grown rapidly since 1953 due to an emphasis on manufacturing. The nation remains more sparsely populated than South Korea.

Economy and the Land. The division of the Korean peninsula after World War II left North Korea with most of the industry and natural resources but little agricultural land and few skilled workers. The country has succeeded in becoming one of the most industrialized nations in Asia and in overcoming its agricultural problems. Most industry is government owned, and mines produce a variety of minerals. Farming is collectivized, and output has been aided by irrigation and other modern practices. The Soviet Union and China aided North Korea's development, but the theory of self-reliance was the government's guiding principle. A central mountainous region is bounded by coastal plains, and the climate is temperate.

History and Politics. History of North and South Korea follows SOUTH KOREA. ∎

KOREA, SOUTH

Official name Republic of Korea
PEOPLE
Population 42,975,000. **Density** 1,124/mi² (434/km²). **Urban** 72%. **Capital** Seoul, 10,522,000. **Ethnic groups** Korean. **Languages** Korean. **Religions** Buddhist 20%, Roman Catholic 16%, Protestant 5%, Confucian 1%. **Life expectancy** 74 female, 68 male. **Literacy** 88%.
POLITICS
Government Republic. **Parties** Democratic Justice, New Democratic Republican, Peace and Democracy, Reunification Democratic, others. **Suffrage** Universal, over 20. **Memberships** None. **Subdivisions** 9 provinces, 6 special cities.
ECONOMY
GDP $86,180,000,000 **Per capita** $2,037. **Monetary unit** Won. **Trade partners** Exports: U.S., Japan, Hong Kong. Imports: Japan, U.S., Germany. **Exports** Clothing and other manufactures, machinery, ships and boats. **Imports** Machinery, manufactures, petroleum, textiles and other crude materials.
LAND
Description Eastern Asia. **Area** 38,230 mi² (99,016 km²). **Highest point** Halla Mtn., 6,398 ft (1,950 m). **Lowest point** Sea level.

People. The homogeneous quality of South Korea's population is similar to that of North Korea. Population density, however, is much greater in South Korea, where two million Koreans migrated following World War II. The major language, Korean, is written predominantly in the Hankul, or Korean, alphabet, with some Chinese characters. Buddhism is practiced by most South Koreans, although Confucianism has influenced much of life.

Economy and the Land. South Korea was traditionally the peninsula's agricultural zone, and following the 1945 partition of the country, the south was left with little industry and few resources but abundant manpower. The economy has advanced rapidly since 1953, and today agriculture and industry are of almost equal importance. Rice, barley, and beans are principal crops; machinery and textiles are significant manufactured products. Central mountains give way to plains in the south and west, and the climate is temperate.

History and Politics. Korea's strategic location between Russia, China, and Japan has made it prey to foreign powers. China conquered the northern part of the peninsula in 108 B.C., influencing culture, religion, and government. Mongols controlled Korea for most of the thirteenth and fourteenth centuries. The rule of the Yi dynasty lasted from 1392 to 1910, when Japan annexed Korea. In 1945, following Japan's defeat in World War II,

Soviet troops occupied northern Korea while the United States military occupied the south. The Soviet Union, the United States, and Great Britain tried to aid unification of the country but failed. The Soviets opposed a subsequent plan for United Nations-supervised elections. Separate governments were formed in 1948: the northern Democratic People's Republic of Korea and the southern Republic of Korea. Both governments claimed the peninsula, and relations became strained. After several border clashes, North Korea invaded South Korea in 1950. Chinese Communists fought on the side of North Korea, and United States/United Nations forces aided the south. An armistice ended the war in 1953, but a permanent peace treaty has never been signed. Both countries continue to claim the entire peninsula. Sporadic fighting has broken out between the north and south in recent years, and tense relations have stalled steps toward reunification.

North Korea. The Democratic People's Republic of Korea was established in 1948, several months after the formation of South Korea. The country incurred about three million casualties during the war with South Korea. Following the war, the government moved quickly to modernize industry and the military; North Korea maintains one of the world's largest armies. Despite its ties to the Soviet Union and China, North Korea strives for an independent foreign policy based on self-reliance. ∎

South Korea. The Republic of Korea was established on August 15, 1948. The country has since experienced a presidential overthrow, military rule, and a presidential assassination. In 1980 it adopted its fifth constitution since 1948, which initiated the Fifth Republic. Students have since pressed for free elections, withdrawal of United States troops, and reunification with North Korea. ∎

KUWAIT

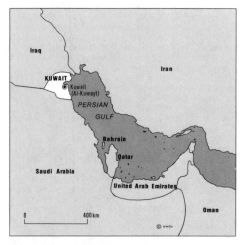

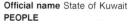

Official name State of Kuwait
PEOPLE
Population 2,189,000. **Density** 318/mi² (123/km²). **Urban** 96%. **Capital** Kuwait, 44,335. **Ethnic groups** Kuwaiti 40%, other Arab 39%, Southern Asian 9%, Iranian 4%. **Languages** Arabic, English. **Religions** Sunni Muslim 45%, Shiite Muslim 30%, Christian 6%. **Life expectancy** 76 female, 72 male. **Literacy** 68%.
POLITICS
Government Constitutional monarchy. **Parties** None. **Suffrage** Limited adult male. **Memberships** AL, OPEC, UN. **Subdivisions** 5 governorates.
ECONOMY
GDP $19,744,000,000 **Per capita** $10,878. **Monetary unit** Dinar. **Trade partners** Exports: Japan, Netherlands, Italy. Imports: Japan, U.S., Germany. **Exports** Petroleum, chemicals, manufactures. **Imports** Manufactures, machinery, transportation equipment, food.
LAND
Description Southwestern Asia. **Area** 6,880 mi²

(17,818 km²). **Highest point** 922 ft (281 m). **Lowest point** Sea level.

People. Kuwait's recent prosperity has drawn emigrants from the Persian Gulf and beyond, giving it a diverse population; there are Palestinian, Iranian, and Pakistani minorities. The population has risen dramatically since the thirties, when the oil industry began. Arabic is the official language; English is also taught and widely spoken. Almost all residents of Kuwait observe Islam, the state religion. Most belong to the Sunni branch, but there is a sizable Shiite community.

Economy and the Land. The economy centers on the largely government-controlled petroleum industry. Kuwait is one of the world's largest oil producers, and its oil reserves are among the world's most extensive. Iraq's 1990 invasion of Kuwait brought the economy to a standstill when many Kuwaitis and virtually all of the large foreign work force fled the country. During 1991, burning oil fields, oil slicks, and massive aerial bombardments threatened the environment. Despite the destruction, the Kuwaiti government continues to profit from its many foreign investments.

History and Politics. Arab nomads settled Kuwait Bay around A.D. 1700. The Al Sabah dynasty has ruled the nation since the mid-1700s. Alarmed by Turk and Arabic expansion, in 1899 Kuwait signed an agreement with Britain to guarantee Kuwait's defense. Drilling for oil began in 1936, and by 1945 Kuwait had become a major exporter. Independence came in 1961. Iraq immediately made a claim to the state but was discouraged from attacking by the arrival of British troops. Official border agreements have never been made between Kuwait and Iraq. Kuwait briefly cut off oil shipments to Western nations in retaliation for their support of Israel in the 1967 and 1973 Arab-Israeli wars. Kuwait's remarkable oil wealth, which transformed it from a poor nation into an affluent one, has enabled it to offer its citizens a wide range of benefits and to aid other Arab states. Poised at the tip of the Persian Gulf, Kuwait must always be sensitive to the interests of its many neighbors. Kuwait allied itself with Iraq in the 1980-1988 Iran/Iraq war. This did not, however, prevent Iraq from invading Kuwait in August 1990. International outrage resulted in allied military action against Iraq in January 1991. Less than two months later Iraq was forced to withdraw. ∎

LAOS

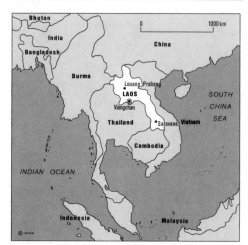

Official name Lao People's Democratic Republic
PEOPLE
Population 4,069,000. **Density** 45/mi² (17/km²). **Urban** 19%. **Capital** Viangchan (Vientiane), 377,409. **Ethnic groups** Lao 50%; Thai 20%; Phoutheung 15%; Miao, Hmong, Yao, and others 15%. **Languages** Lao, French, Thai, indigenous. **Religions** Buddhist 85%, Animist and others 15%. **Life expectancy** 53 female, 50 male. **Literacy** 85%.
POLITICS
Government Socialist republic. **Parties** People's Revolutionary. **Suffrage** Universal, over 18. **Memberships** UN. **Subdivisions** 16 provinces, 1 municipality.
ECONOMY
GNP $765,000,000 **Per capita** $190. **Monetary unit**

Kip. **Trade partners** Exports: Thailand, Malaysia, Vietnam. Imports: Thailand, U.S.S.R, Japan, France. **Exports** Electricity, wood, coffee, tin. **Imports** Food, petroleum, consumer goods, manufactures.

LAND

Description Southeastern Asia, landlocked. **Area** 91,429 mi² (236,800 km²). **Highest point** Mt. Bia, 9,249 ft (2,819 m). **Lowest point** Along Mekong River, 230 ft (70 m).

People. Laos is populated by many ethnic groups, each with its own customs, religion, and language. Its history of culturally diverse communities is mirrored in the political divisions of recent years. The Lao are numerically and politically dominant, and Lao is the official language. Small Vietnamese and Chinese minorities exist. Most of Lao's residents are rice farmers.

Economy and the Land. Years of warfare, a landlocked position, and a poor transportation system have hindered the development of Laos's economy. Although agriculture is the basis of the economy, very little of the fertile land is cultivated. Substantial mineral deposits and large timber reserves also have not been exploited to their potential. Manufacturing is limited, partly because of an unskilled work force. Situated in a mountainous, densely-forested region, Laos has a tropical climate and experiences seasonal monsoons.

History and Politics. By A.D. 900 the forerunners of the Lao had arrived from southern China. The first united Lao kingdom was founded in 1353 and included much of modern Thailand. It dissolved into three rival states by the early 1700s, setting the stage for interference by Burma, Vietnam, and Sigam, present-day Thailand. In 1899 France made Laos part of French Indochina. Laos gained some autonomy in 1949, but this period saw the growth of Communist and anti-Communist factions whose rivalry would prevent any unified government until 1975. Although Geneva peace agreements declared Laos neutral in 1954 and 1962, the nation became increasingly embroiled in the Vietnam War as both sides in that conflict entered Laos. A protracted civil war began in 1960 between the Pathet Lao, a Communist faction aided by the North Vietnamese, and government forces backed by the Thai and South Vietnamese. A cease-fire was signed in 1973 and a new coalition government was formed a year later. Following Communist victories in Vietnam and Cambodia, the Pathet Lao gained control in 1975 and established the Lao People's Democratic Republic. Opposed to Communist rule, many Lao fled the country for refuge in Thailand and the United States. Laos retains close ties with Vietnam. ∎

LATVIA

Official name Republic of Latvia
PEOPLE
Population 2,738,000. **Density** 111/mi² (43/km²). **Capital** Rīga, 915,000. **Ethnic groups** Latvian 54%, Russian 33%, Byelorussian 5%, Polish 3%, Ukranian 3%. **Languages** Latvian, Russian. **Religions** Roman Catholic, Lutheran.
POLITICS
Government Republic. **Parties** Popular Front, others. **Suffrage** Universal, over 18.
LAND
Description Eastern Europe. **Area** 24,595 mi² (63,700 km²). **Highest point** Gaizina Kalns, 1,020 ft (311 m). **Lowest point** Sea level.

People. The Latvians are closely related to the neighboring Lithuanians, and the Latvian language is one of the oldest in Europe. Many Latvians were killed or deported during World War II and the subsequent Soviet invasion. Today about one-third of the people are Russian. Most Latvians are Lutherans or Roman Catholics.

Economy and the Land. The Latvian economy is based primarily on light industry. It is also known for the manufacture of railroad cars. Latvia depends on imported coal because the country has no natural energy resources other then peat. Latvia is self-sufficient in grain production. Most of the land is gently rolling hills, and much is forested. The capital city of Rīga is one of the Baltic region's busiest important ports.

History and Politics. Latvian history was profoundly affected by the Teutonic Knights, who ruled the country for more than two hundred years starting in the mid-1300s. They established themselves as landowners and forced the Latvians into serfdom. Latvia was subsequently captured by Poland, Sweden, and Russia. After one hundred years of Russian rule, serfdom in Latvia was eliminated in the early 1800s. An independent Latvian state was established in 1918. Political instability followed and the country descended into fascism. Latvia was invaded by the Soviet Union in 1940, ending 22 years of Latvian independence. The Latvians resisted Soviet domination and regained their independence in 1991. ∎

LEBANON

Official name Republic of Lebanon

PEOPLE
Population 3,360,000. **Density** 837/mi² (323/km²). **Urban** 84%. **Capital** Beirut, 509,000. **Ethnic groups** Arab 93%, Armenian 6%. **Languages** Arabic, French, Armenian, English. **Religions** Muslim 75%, Christian 25%, Jewish. **Life expectancy** 71 female, 67 male. **Literacy** 68%.
POLITICS
Government Republic. **Parties** Progressive Socialist, Liberal Nationalist, Phalangist, others. **Suffrage** Females, over 21 (with elementary education); males, over 21. **Memberships** AL, UN. **Subdivisions** 6 governorates.

ECONOMY
GDP $2,656,000,000 **Per capita** $811. **Monetary unit** Pound. **Trade partners** Exports: Saudi Arabia, Switzerland, Jordan. Imports: Italy, France, U.S., Turkey. **Exports** Agricultural products, chemicals, textiles, jewelry. **Imports** Food, textiles and clothing, machinery and transportation equipment, metals.

LAND
Description Southwestern Asia. **Area** 4,015 mi² (10,400 km²). **Highest point** Mt. Sawda, 10,115 ft (3,083 m). **Lowest point** Sea level.

People. Traditionally home to many diverse groups, Lebanon has recently been shaken by the conflicting demands of its population. Almost all Lebanese are of Arab stock, and Arabic and French are the official languages. Palestinian refugees have settled here since the creation of Israel in 1948, many of them living in refugee camps. Lebanon's religious makeup is notable for its variety, encompassing seventeen recognized sects. Islam is now the majority religion, although Christianity continues to be a strong presence. Muslims are divided among the majority Shiite, minority Sunni, and Druze sects, while most Christians are Maronites.

Economy and the Land. Situated strategically between the West and the Middle East, Lebanon has long been a center of commerce. Its economy is fueled by the service sector, particularly banking. Prolonged fighting, beginning with the 1975 civil war, has greatly damaged all economic activity. Much of the work force is engaged in agriculture, and various crops are grown. The coastal area consists of a plain, behind which lie mountain ranges separated by a fertile valley. The climate is Mediterranean.

History and Politics. The Phoenicians settled parts of Lebanon about 3000 B.C. and were followed by Egyptian, Assyrian, Persian, Greek, and Roman rulers. Christianity came to the area during the Byzantine Empire, around A.D. 325, and Islam followed in the seventh century. In 1516 Lebanon was incorporated into the Ottoman Empire. Between the end of World War I, when the Ottoman Empire collapsed, and 1943, when Lebanon became independent, the nation was a French mandate. After independence, Muslims and Christians shared government power. Opposition to Lebanon's close ties to the West led to a 1958 insurrection, which United States marines put down at the government's request. The Palestine Liberation Organization (PLO), a group working to establish a Palestinian state, began operating from bases in Lebanon. This led to clashes with Israel in the late 1970s and early 1980s. The presence of the PLO divided Muslims, who generally supported it, from Christians, who opposed it. The increasing Muslim population also demanded a greater voice in the government. Civil war between Muslims and Christians broke out in 1975, and fighting slowed the next year with the requested aid of Syrian deterrent forces. Internal instability continued, however, along with Israeli-Palestinian hostilities. In June 1982 Israel invaded Lebanon, driving the PLO from Beirut and the south. Hundreds of Palestinian refugees were killed by the Christian Lebanese forces in September. A multinational peacekeeping force left after falling victim to terrorist attacks. Israel began a gradual withdrawal from Lebanon in 1985, but maintains a buffer zone in southern Lebanon. Syrian troops also occupy parts of the country. International attempts to reconcile warring factions are ongoing. ∎

LESOTHO

Official name Kingdom of Lesotho
PEOPLE
Population 1,764,000. **Density** 151/mi² (58/km²). **Urban** 20%. **Capital** Maseru, 109,382. **Ethnic groups** Sotho 99%. **Languages** English, Sesotho, Zulu, Xhosa. **Religions** Roman Catholic and other Christian 80%, tribal religionist 20%. **Life expectancy** 63 female, 54 male. **Literacy** 60%.

POLITICS
Government Constitutional monarchy. **Parties** Basotho National, Basutoland Congress, Democratic Alliance, others. **Suffrage** Universal, over 21. **Memberships** CW, OAU, UN. **Subdivisions** 10 districts.

ECONOMY
GDP $401,000,000 **Per capita** $281. **Monetary unit** Loti. **Trade partners** South Africa, Western European countries. **Exports** Wool, mohair, wheat, cattle, peas, beans, corn, hides and skins. **Imports** Corn, building materials, clothing, vehicles, machinery, pharmaceuticals.

LAND
Description Southern Africa, landlocked. **Area** 11,720 mi² (30,355 km²). **Highest point** Mt. Ntlenyana, 11,425 ft (3,482 m). **Lowest point** Along Orange River, 5,000 ft (1,524 m).

People. The Sotho, a black African group, comprise almost all of Lesotho's population. Most Sotho live in the lowlands and raise livestock and crops. The official languages are Sesotho, a Bantu tongue, and English, and the traditional religion is based on ancestor worship, though many Sotho are Christian. A system of tribal chieftaincy is followed locally.

Economy and the Land. Surrounded by South Africa and having few resources, Lesotho is almost entirely dependent on South Africa for economic survival. Much of the male population must seek employment there, usually spending several months a year in South African mines or industries. Agriculture remains at the subsistence level, and soil erosion threatens production. Livestock raising represents a significant part of Lesotho's economy. Wool and mohair are among the chief exports. Diamond mining, one of the few industries, employs a small portion of the population. Most of the terrain is mountainous; the fairly high elevations give Lesotho a temperate climate.

History and Politics. Refugees from tribal wars in southern Africa arrived in what is now Lesotho between the sixteenth and nineteenth centuries A.D. Chief Moshoeshoe united the Sotho tribes in 1818 and led them in war against the Boers, settlers of Dutch or Huguenot descent. At Moshoeshoe's request, Basutoland came under British protection in 1868. It resisted attempts at absorption by the Union of South Africa and became the independent kingdom of Lesotho in 1966. The government of Prime Minister Leabua Jonathan, threatened by an apparent defeat at the polls, suspended the constitution in 1970 and set up a provisional assembly in 1973. Opposition to the Jonathan administration has erupted in periodic violence. Lesotho, although unforgiving of South Africa's racial policies, is forced by its geographic and economic situation to cooperate with its powerful neighbor. After claims by South Africa that Lesotho was harboring rebel groups, Lesotho agreed to expel rebels opposing South African policies. ∎

LIBERIA

Official name Republic of Liberia

PEOPLE

Population 2,689,000. **Density** 70/mi² (27/km²). **Urban** 44%. **Capital** Monrovia, 465,000. **Ethnic groups** Indigenous black 95%, descendants of freed American slaves 5%. **Languages** English, indigenous. **Religions** Animist 70%, Muslim 20%, Christian 10%. **Life expectancy** 58 female, 55 male. **Literacy** 21%.

POLITICS

Government Republic. **Parties** Action, National Democratic, others. **Suffrage** Universal, over 18. **Memberships** OAU, UN. **Subdivisions** 11 counties, 2 territories.

ECONOMY

GDP $811,000,000 **Per capita** $369. **Monetary unit** Dollar. **Trade partners** Exports: Germany, U.S., Italy. Imports: U.S., Germany, Netherlands. **Exports** Iron ore, rubber, wood, cocoa, coffee. **Imports** Rice and other food, petroleum, manufactures, machinery.

LAND

Description Western Africa. **Area** 38,250 mi² (99,067 km²). **Highest point** Mt. Wuteve, 4,528 ft (1,380 m). **Lowest point** Sea level.

People. Most Liberians belong to about twenty indigenous black groups. Few are descended from the freed American slaves who founded modern Liberia, but this group—known as Americo-Liberians—has traditionally been politically dominant. The official language is English, and more than twenty other tongues are also spoken. Most people are farmers and practice traditional religious beliefs, although Islam and Christianity also have adherents. Liberia is the only black African state to escape colonialism.

Economy and the Land. Liberia owes its healthy economy largely to an open-door policy, which has made its extensive resources attractive to foreign nations. Two of the most important activities, iron-ore mining and rubber production, were developed by Western firms. Large timber reserves have not yet been fully exploited. Liberia also profits from the vast merchant fleet registered under its flag. The land is characterized by a coastal plain,

plateaus, and low mountains, while the hot, humid climate is marked by distinct wet and dry seasons.

History and Politics. Early settlers are thought to have migrated from the north and east between the twelfth and seventeenth centuries A.D. Trade between Europeans and coastal groups developed after the Portuguese visited the area in the late 1400s. The American Colonization Society, a private United States organization devoted to resetting freed slaves, purchased land in Liberia, and in 1822 the first settlers landed at the site of Monrovia. The settlers declared their independence in 1847, setting up a government based on the United States model and creating Africa's first independent republic. For the next century, the Liberian government endured attempts at colonization by France and Britain, as well as internal tribal opposition. The string of Americo-Liberian rulers was broken in 1980, when a small group of soldiers of African descent toppled the government and imposed martial law. Civilian rule and some degree of harmony were restored in a 1985 election. Dissatisfaction with the growing corruption and waste of this government led to civil war in early 1990, resulting in the president's assassination. Peacekeeping forces of five West African nations negotiated a cease-fire in November 1990. ∎

LIBYA

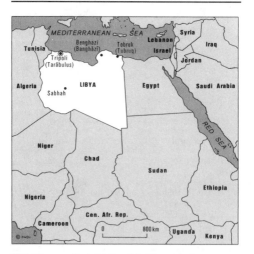

Official name Socialist People's Libyan Arab Jamahiriya

PEOPLE

Population 4,271,000. **Density** 6.3/mi² (2.4/km²). **Urban** 70%. **Capital** Tripoli, 990,697. **Ethnic groups** Arab-Berber 97%. **Languages** Arabic. **Religions** Sunni Muslim 97%. **Life expectancy** 65 female, 62 male. **Literacy** 39%.

POLITICS

Government Socialist republic. **Parties** None. **Suffrage** Universal, over 18. **Memberships** AL, OAU, OPEC, UN. **Subdivisions** 13 municipalities.

ECONOMY

GDP $29,884,000,000 **Per capita** $9,472. **Monetary unit** Dinar. **Trade partners** Italy, U.S.S.R., Germany. **Exports** Petroleum. **Imports** Metal goods and other manufactures, machinery, food, motor vehicles.

LAND

Description Northern Africa. **Area** 679,362 mi² (1,759,540 km²). **Highest point** Bīkkū Bīttī, 7,438 ft (2,267 m). **Lowest point** Sabkhat Ghuzzayil, -154 ft (-47 m).

People. Libya, originally settled by Berbers, is largely a mix of Arab and Berber today. Almost all Libyans live along the coast, with some nomadic groups in desert areas. Large migrations from rural areas to the cities have accompanied Libya's oil-based prosperity. Islam is the majority religion, and nearly all Libyans speak Arabic. Traditional social orders still exist, despite centuries of foreign rule.

Economy and the Land. The discovery of oil in 1959 propelled Libya from the ranks of the world's poorest nations to one of its leading oil producers. It has used these revenues to develop industry and agriculture to diversify its economy. Most of Libya is covered by the

Sahara Desert, and the limited agriculture has been further hurt by Libyan farmers migrating to the cities. The climate is desert except for the coast, which has moderate temperatures.

History and Politics. For much of its history, Libya was dominated by Mediterranean empires: Phoenician, Carthaginian, Greek, and Roman. In the seventh century A.D. the area was taken by Muslim Arabs, whose language and religion transformed Libyan culture. Although the Ottoman Turks conquered the region in the sixteenth century, local rulers remained virtually autonomous. Italy invaded Libya in 1911, and the country became an Italian colony in 1912. Following World War II, British and French forces occupied the area until a United Nations resolution made Libya an independent nation in 1951. A monarchy ruled until 1969, when a military coup established a republic headed by Colonel Mu'ammar al-Qadhafi. Under his leadership, Libya has backed Arab unity and the Palestinian cause, opposed foreign influences, and created a welfare system. Libya's support of terrorist activities led to a controversial United States air strike against the country in 1986, and several nations have instituted economic sanctions against Libya. ∎

LIECHTENSTEIN

Official name Principality of Liechtenstein

PEOPLE

Population 31,000. **Density** 500/mi² (194/km²). **Urban** 26%. **Capital** Vaduz, 4,874. **Ethnic groups** Liechtensteiner (Alemannic) 66%, Swiss 15%, Austrian 7%, German 4%. **Languages** German. **Religions** Roman Catholic 85%, Protestant 9%. **Life expectancy** 73 female, 66 male. **Literacy** 100%.

POLITICS

Government Constitutional monarchy. **Parties** Fatherland Union, Progressive Citizens'. **Suffrage** Universal, over 18. **Memberships** UN. **Subdivisions** 11 communes. **Monetary unit** Swiss franc. **Trade partners** Switzerland and other European countries. **Exports** Machinery, dental products, stamps, hardware, pottery. **Imports** Machinery, metal goods, textiles, food, motor vehicles.

LAND

Description Central Europe, landlocked. **Area** 62 mi² (160 km²). **Highest point** Vorder-Grauspitz, 8,527 ft (2,599 m). **Lowest point** Ruggleller Riet, 1,411 ft (430 m).

People. In spite of its location at the crossroads of Europe, Liechtenstein has retained a largely homogeneous ethnicity. Almost all Liechtensteiners are descended from the Alemanni, a Germanic tribe, and many speak the Alemanni dialect. German, however, is the official language. Roman Catholicism is the most widely practiced religion but a Protestant minority also exists. Most of the country is mountainous, and population is concentrated on the fertile plains adjacent to the Rhine River, which forms the country's western boundary. Most Liechtensteiners work in factories or in trades.

Economy and the Land. The last few decades have seen the economy shift from agricultural to highly industrialized. Despite this growth in industry, Liechtenstein has not experienced a serious pollution problem, and the government continues its work to prevent the problem from occurring. An economic alliance with Switzerland dating from 1923 has been profoundly beneficial to Liechtenstein: the two nations form a customs union and use the same currency. Other important sources of revenue are tourism, the sale of postage stamps, and taxation of foreign businesses headquartered here. Most of Liechtenstein, one of the world's smallest nations, is covered by the Alps; nonetheless, its climate is mild.

History and Politics. Early inhabitants of what is now Liechtenstein included the Celts, Romans, and Alemanni, who arrived about A.D. 500. The area became part of the empire of the Frankish King Charlemagne in the late 700s, and following Charlemagne's death, it was divided into the lordships of Vaduz and Schellenberg. By 1719, when the state became part of the Holy Roman Empire, the Austrian House of Liechtenstein had purchased both lordships, uniting them as the Imperial Principality of Liechtenstein. The nation's independence dates from the abolition of the empire by France's Napoleon Bonaparte in 1806. Liechtenstein was neutral in both world wars and has remained unaffected by European conflicts. The government is a hereditary constitutional monarchy; the prince is the head of the House of Liechtenstein, thus chief of state, and the prime minister is the head of government. In 1984, women gained the right to vote. ∎

LITHUANIA

Official name Republic of Lithuania

PEOPLE
Population 3,760,000. **Density** 149/mi² (58/km²). **Capital** Vilnius, 582,000. **Ethnic groups** Lithuanian 80%, Russian 9%, Polish 7%, Byelorussian 2%. **Languages** Lithuanian, Russian, Polish. **Religions** Roman Catholic.

POLITICS
Government Republic. **Parties** Sajudis, others. **Suffrage** Universal, over 18.

LAND
Description Eastern Europe. **Area** 25,174 mi² (65,200 km²). **Highest point** 945 ft (288 m). **Lowest point** Sea level.

People. Lithuanians are a Baltic people related to the Latvians. Although about 80% of the people are ethnic Lithuanians, Russian immigrants held many key positions in Lithuania under Soviet rule. Lithuanians also chafed under Soviet rules restricting religion because most are devoutly Roman Catholic. Lithuanians are known for their fine singing and splendid choral festivals.

Economy and the Land. Prior to Soviet rule, Lithuania was predominately rural with an agricultural economy. Today the Lithuanian economy is dependent on industrial production although it lacks significant mineral fuel deposits. Agriculture is based on meat and dairy products. The land is generally flat. There are fine white sand beaches along the coastline of the Baltic Sea.

History and Politics. Unlike its neighboring Soviet republics of Latvia and Estonia, Lithuania has had a long tradition of independence. By the mid-1300s, Lithuania extended from the Baltic to the Black Seas and was a major regional power. Close political association with Poland led to a merger in 1569 and eventual annexation by Russia in the late 19th century. In 1918 Lithuania again claimed its independence until it was overtaken by the Soviets in 1940. Stalin killed or deported about one-third of the Lithuanian population. Friction between Lithuania and the Soviet Union increased after the introduction of glasnost fueled Lithuanian aspirations for independence. A Soviet invasion in early 1991 was followed by international recognition as an independent state later in the year. ∎

LUXEMBOURG

Official name Grand Duchy of Luxembourg

PEOPLE
Population 379,000. **Density** 380/mi² (147/km²). **Urban** 84%. **Capital** Luxembourg, 76,130. **Ethnic groups** Luxembourger (mixed Celtic, French, and German). **Languages** French, Luxembourgish, German. **Religions** Roman Catholic 97%, Jewish and Protestant

3%. **Life expectancy** 79 female, 72 male. **Literacy** 99%.

POLITICS
Government Constitutional monarchy. **Parties** Christian Socialist, Liberal, Socialist Workers, others. **Suffrage** Universal, over 18. **Memberships** EC, NATO, OECD, UN. **Subdivisions** 3 districts.

ECONOMY
GDP $3,567,000,000 **Per capita** $9,773. **Monetary unit** Franc. **Trade partners** Germany, Belgium, France. **Exports** Iron and steel products, chemicals, rubber products, glass. **Imports** Minerals, metals, foodstuffs, consumer goods.

LAND
Description Western Europe, landlocked. **Area** 998 mi² (2,586 km²). **Highest point** Buurgplaatz, 1,834 ft (559 m). **Lowest point** Confluence of Moselle and Sûre rivers, 427 ft (130 m).

People. Luxembourg's population bears the imprint of foreign influences, yet retains an individual character. Most Luxembourgers are a blend of Celtic, French, and German stock. French is an official language, as is Luxembourgish, an indigenous German dialect. Roman Catholicism is observed by virtually all the population. There are significant communities of guest workers from several European nations.

Economy and the Land. Luxembourg's steel industry forms the basis of its economy, and the country has compensated for a worldwide drop in the steel market by developing financial services, notably banking. Manufacturing of plastics and chemicals is also important, as is tourism. Luxembourg's trade benefits from the country's membership in the European Community and the Benelux union. Luxembourg has two distinct regions: the mountainous, wooded north and the open, rolling south, known as Bon Pays. The climate is temperate.

History and Politics. The present city of Luxembourg developed from a castle built in A.D. 963 by Count Siegfried of Ardennes. Several heavily fortified towns grew up around the castle, and the area became known as the "Gibraltar of the North" because of those fortifications. The duchy remained semiautonomous until the Burgundians conquered the area in 1443. Various European powers ruled Luxembourg for most of the next four centuries, and in 1815 the duchy was elevated to a grand duchy. It became autonomous in 1839 and was recognized in 1867 as an independent state. Despite Luxembourg's declaration of neutrality, Germany occupied the country in both world wars. Luxembourg maintains a pro-Western, pan-European stance in its foreign relations. ∎

MACAO

Official name Macao

PEOPLE
Population 462,000. **Density** 70,000/mi² (27,176/km²). **Urban** 99%. **Capital** Macao, Macao I., 429,000. **Ethnic groups** Chinese 95%, Portuguese 3%. **Languages** Portuguese, Chinese (Cantonese). **Religions** Buddhist 45%, Roman Catholic 16%, other Christian 3%. **Life expectancy** 79 female, 75 male. **Literacy** 79%.

POLITICS
Government Chinese territory under Portuguese administration. **Parties** Association to Defend the Interests of Macau, Democratic Center, others. **Suffrage** Universal, over 18. **Memberships** None. **Subdivisions** 2 districts.

ECONOMY
GNP $1,030,000,000 **Per capita** $3,323. **Monetary unit** Pataca. **Trade partners** Exports: U.S., Hong Kong, Germany. Imports: Hong Kong, China, Japan. **Exports** Clothing, textiles, toys, and other manufactures. **Imports** Textiles and other manufactures, food, machinery, crude materials.

LAND
Description Eastern Asia (islands and peninsula on China's southeastern coast). **Area** 6.6 mi² (17 km²). **Highest point** Coloane Alto, 571 ft (174 m). **Lowest point** Sea level.

People. Situated on the southeastern China coast, 17 miles (27.4 km) west of Hong Kong, Macao is populated almost entirely by Chinese. A former overseas province of Portugal, the island includes people of Portuguese and mixed Chinese-Portuguese descent. Several Chinese dialects are widely spoken, and Portuguese is the official language. Buddhism is Macao's principal religion; a small percentage of its population are Roman Catholics.

Economy and the Land. Tourism, gambling, and light industry help make up Macao's economy; however, its leading industries are textiles and light manufacturing, which employ the majority of the labor force. Macao has been likened to Hong Kong because of its textile exports, yet it remains a heavy importer, relying on China for drinking water and much of its food supply. The province consists of the city of Macao, located on a peninsula, and the nearby islands of Taipa and Coloane. The climate is maritime tropical, with cool winters and warm summers.

History and Politics. Macao became a Portuguese trading post in 1557. It flourished as the midpoint for trade between China and Japan but declined when Hong Kong became a trading power in the mid-1800s. Macao remained a neutral port during World War II and was economically prosperous. Although the government is nominally directed by Portugal, any policies relating to Macao are subject to China's approval. Macao is the oldest European settlement in the Far East. It will be returned to China in 1999 under a negotiated agreement whereby the present capitalist system will be maintained for 50 years. ∎

MADAGASCAR

Official name Democratic Republic of Madagascar

PEOPLE
Population 11,995,000. **Density** 53/mi² (20/km²). **Urban** 25%. **Capital** Antananarivo, 663,000. **Ethnic groups** Merina 15%, Betsimisaraka 9%, Betsileo 7%, Tsimihety 4%, Antaisaka 4%, other tribes. **Languages** Malagasy, French. **Religions** Animist 52%, Christian 41%, Muslim 7%. **Life expectancy** 57 female, 54 male. **Literacy** 81%.

POLITICS

Government Republic. **Parties** Advance Guard of the Revolution, Militants for the Establishment of a Proletarian Regime, others. **Suffrage** Universal, over 18. **Memberships** OAU, UN. **Subdivisions** 6 provinces.

ECONOMY

GDP $2,345,000,000 **Per capita** $240. **Monetary unit** Franc. **Trade partners** Exports: France, U.S., Japan. Imports: France, U.S., U.S.S.R. **Exports** Coffee, vanilla, cloves, shellfish. **Imports** Machinery, petroleum, manufactures, rice and other grains, chemicals.

LAND

Description Southeastern African island. **Area** 226,658 mi² (587,041 km²). **Highest point** Maromokotro, 9,436 ft (2,876 m). **Lowest point** Sea level.

People. Most of the population is of mixed African and Indonesian descent. Those who live on the coast, the *cotiers*, are of predominantly African origin, while those on the inland plateau have Asian roots. There is a long-standing rivalry between the *cotiers* and the inland groups, most of whom belong to the Merina people. The official language is Malagasy. Sizable Christian communities exist, but most Malagasy practice indigenous Animist beliefs.

Economy and the Land. Madagascar is chiefly an agricultural nation, with the majority of the work force engaged in farming or herding. Overpopulation and outmoded cultivation have recently cut into yields of rice, an important crop, and other products. Varied mineral resources, including oil, point to possible expansion. The climate is tropical on the coastal plains and moderate in the inland highlands.

History and Politics. Madagascar's first settlers are thought to be Indonesians, who brought African wives and slaves around two thousand years ago. Arab traders established themselves on the coast in the seventh century. The Portuguese first sighted the island in the 1500s, and other Europeans followed. The Merina kingdom, based in the central plateau, gained control over most of the island in the 1790s. French influence grew throughout the nineteenth century, and in 1896 France made the island a colony after subduing the Merina. Resentment of French rule continued, culminating in an armed revolt in 1947. Full independence came in 1960. After twelve years of rule by the same president, a coup placed the military in power. A new constitution was adopted in 1975 that established the Democratic Republic of Madagascar. ∎

MADEIRA ISLANDS See PORTUGAL.

MALAWI

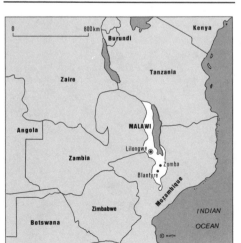

Official name Republic of Malawi
PEOPLE
Population 8,432,000. **Density** 184/mi² (71/km²). **Urban** 15%. **Capital** Lilongwe, 233,973. **Ethnic groups** Chewa, Nyanja, Tumbuka, Yao, Lomwe, others. **Languages** Chichewa, English, Tombuka. **Religions** Protestant 55%, Roman Catholic 20%, Muslim 20%. **Life expectancy** 50 female, 48 male. **Literacy** 25%.

POLITICS

Government Republic. **Parties** Congress. **Suffrage** Universal, over 21. **Memberships** CW, OAU, UN. **Subdivisions** 3 regions.

ECONOMY

GDP $1,203,000,000 **Per capita** $185. **Monetary unit** Kwacha. **Trade partners** Exports: U.K., Germany, Netherlands. Imports: South African countries, Germany, Japan. **Exports** Tobacco, sugar, tea, textiles, peanuts. **Imports** Textiles and other manufactures, machinery, chemicals, petroleum, food.

LAND

Description Southern Africa, landlocked. **Area** 45,747 mi² (118,484 km²). **Highest point** Sapitwa, 9,849 ft (3,002 m). **Lowest point** Along Shire River, 120 ft (37 m).

People. Almost all Malawians are black Africans descended from Bantu peoples. The Chewa constitute the majority in the central area, while the Nyanja are dominant in the south and the Tumbuka in the north. Chichewa and English are official languages. The majority of the population is rural, and traditional village customs are prevalent. For the most part, the society is matriarchal. Many Malawians combine Christian or Muslim beliefs with traditional religious practices.

Economy and the Land. A landlocked nation with limited resources and a largely unskilled work force, Malawi relies almost entirely on agriculture. A recent series of poor harvests, combined with a tripling of the population between 1950 and 1989, has contributed to the decline in agricultural output. Among the main exports are tea and tobacco. Many Malawians work part of the year as miners in South Africa, Zambia, and Zimbabwe. Malawi, situated along the Great Rift Valley, has a varied terrain with highlands, plateaus, and lakes. The climate is subtropical, and rainfall varies greatly from north to south.

History and Politics. Archaeological findings indicate that Malawi has been inhabited for at least fifty thousand years. Bantu-speaking peoples, ancestors of the Malawians, immigrated from the north around A.D. 1400 and soon formed centralized kingdoms. In the 1830s, other Bantu groups, involved in the slave trade, invaded the region. The arrival of Scottish missionary David Livingstone in 1859 began a period of British influence; in 1891 the territory became the British protectorate of Nyasaland. Beginning in 1953, Nyasaland was part of the larger Federation of Rhodesia and Nyasaland. Malawi attained independence in 1964 and became a republic in 1966, with nationalist leader Dr. Hastings Banda as its first president. The Malawi Congress party appointed Banda as president-for-life in 1970. ∎

MALAYSIA

Official name Malaysia
PEOPLE
Population 17,915,000. **Density** 139/mi² (54/km²). **Urban** 42%. **Capital** Kuala Lumpur, 919,610. **Ethnic groups** Malay and other indigenous 60%, Chinese 31%, Indian 8%. **Languages** Malay, Chinese dialects, English, Tamil. **Religions** Muslim 53%, Buddhist 17%, Chinese religions 12%, Hindu 7%. **Life expectancy** 73 female, 69 male. **Literacy** 83%.

POLITICS

Government Constitutional monarchy. **Parties** Democratic Action, Islamic, National Front. **Suffrage** Universal, over 21. **Memberships** ASEAN, CW, UN. **Subdivisions** 13 states, 2 federal territories.

ECONOMY

GDP $31,231,000,000 **Per capita** $2,015. **Monetary unit** Ringgit. **Trade partners** Exports: Japan, Singapore, U.S. Imports: Japan, U.S., Singapore. **Exports** Machinery, petroleum, tin and other manufactures, wood, rubber, palm oil. **Imports** Machinery, manufactures, food, chemicals, petroleum, transportation equipment.

LAND

Description Southeastern Asia (includes part of the island of Borneo). **Area** 129,251 mi² (334,758 km²). **Highest point** Mt. Kinabalu, 13,455 ft (4,101 m). **Lowest point** Sea level.

People. Malaysia's location at one of Southeast Asia's maritime crossroads has left it with a diverse population, including Malays, Chinese, Indians, and native non-Malay groups. The mostly rural Malays dominate politically, while the predominantly urban Chinese are very active in economic life. Considerable tension exists between the two groups. Although most Malays speak Malay and practice Islam, Malaysia's ethnic groups have resisted assimilation; Chinese, Indian, and Western languages and beliefs are also part of the culture. Most Malaysians live in Peninsular Malaysia.

Economy and the Land. The economy is one of the healthiest in the region, supported by multiple strengths in agriculture, mining, forestry, and fishing. The nation is one of the world's leading producers of rubber, palm oil, and tin, and one of the Far East's largest petroleum exporters. Manufacturing is also being developed. Malaysia consists of the southern portion of the Malay Peninsula and the states of Sarawak and Sabah on northern Borneo. The land is characterized by swampy areas, mountains, and rain forests. The climate is tropical and very humid.

History and Politics. The Malay Peninsula has been inhabited since the late Stone Age. Hindu and Buddhist influences were widespread from the ninth through the fourteenth centuries A.D., after which Islam was introduced. In 1511 the Portuguese seized Melaka, a trading center, but were soon replaced, first by the Dutch in 1641 and then by the British in 1795. By the early 1900s, Britain was in control of present-day Malaysia and Singapore, the areas which were occupied by Japan during World War II. Following the war, the Federation of Malaya was created, a semiautonomous state under British authority. A guerrilla war ensued, waged by Chinese Communists and others who opposed the British. The country gained full independence in 1963 with the unification of Malaysia. Singapore seceded in 1965. As a result of the impact of large numbers of Vietnamese refugees, Malaysia announced that as of April 1989 it could accept no more.

MALDIVES

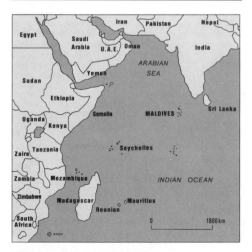

Official name Republic of Maldives
PEOPLE
Population 215,000. **Density** 1,870/mi² (721/km²).

Urban 21%. **Capital** Male, Male I., 46,334. **Ethnic groups** Maldivian (mixed Sinhalese, Dravidian, Arab, and black). **Languages** Divehi. **Religions** Sunni Muslim. **Life expectancy** 59 female, 62 male. **Literacy** 82%.

POLITICS
Government Republic. **Parties** None. **Suffrage** Universal, over 21. **Memberships** CW, UN. **Subdivisions** 19 districts, 1 capital city.

ECONOMY
GDP $84,000,000 **Per capita** $480. **Monetary unit** Rufiyaa. **Trade partners** Exports: Thailand, Western European countries, Sri Lanka. Imports: Japan, Western European countries, Thailand. **Exports** Fish, clothing. **Imports** Fuel, food, machinery, transportation equipment, textiles.

LAND
Description Indian Ocean islands. **Area** 115 mi² (298 km²). **Highest point** 10 ft (3 m). **Lowest point** Sea level.

People. Most Maldivians are descended from Sinhalese peoples from Sri Lanka; southern Indians, or Dravidians; and Arabs. Nearly all Maldivians are Sunni Muslims and speak Divehi. The population is concentrated on Male, the capital island.

Economy and the Land. The nation draws on its advantages as a union of twelve hundred islands to fuel its economy: tourism, shipping, and fishing are the mainstays. With limited arable land and infertile soil, agriculture is marginal. The Maldives, flat coral islands, form a chain of nineteen atolls. Seasonal monsoons mark the tropical climate.

History and Politics. The Maldives are believed to have been originally settled by southern Indian peoples. Arab sailors brought Islam to the islands in the twelfth century A.D. Although a Muslim sultanate remained in power with only two interruptions from 1153 until 1968, the Portuguese and Dutch controlled the islands intermittently between the 1500s and the 1700s. The Maldives were a British protectorate from 1887 to 1965, when they achieved independence. They declared the country a republic three years later. The Republic of Maldives is nonaligned and maintains close ties with other Islamic nations. ∎

MALI

Official name Republic of Mali
PEOPLE
Population 8,205,000. **Density** 17/mi² (6.6/km²). **Urban** 19%. **Capital** Bamako, 646,163. **Ethnic groups** Malinke 50%, Fulani 17%, Voltaic 12%, Songhai 6%. **Languages** French, Bambara, indigenous. **Religions** Sunni Muslim 90%, Animist 9%, Christian 1%. **Life expectancy** 48 female, 44 male. **Literacy** 9%.
POLITICS
Government Republic. **Parties** Democratic Union of the People. **Suffrage** Universal, over 21. **Memberships** OAU, UN. **Subdivisions** 7 regions, 1 capital district.
ECONOMY
GDP $538,000,000 **Per capita** $70. **Monetary unit** CFA franc. **Trade partners** Exports: Ivory Coast, France, Senegal. Imports: France, Senegal. **Exports** Cotton, livestock and other food, textiles, peanut oil.

Imports Petroleum, manufactures, machinery, rice and other food.
LAND
Description Western Africa, landlocked. **Area** 478,767 mi² (1,240,000 km²). **Highest point** Hombori Mtn., 3,789 ft (1,155 m). **Lowest point** Along Senegal River, 72 ft (22 m).

People. The majority of Malians belong to one of several black groups, although there is a small non-black nomadic population. Most Malians are farmers who live in small villages. The official language is French, but most people communicate in Bambara, a market language. The population is concentrated in the basins of the Niger and Senegal rivers in the south. Heirs of three ancient empires, Malians have produced a distinct culture.

Economy and the Land. One of the world's poorest nations, Mali depends primarily on agriculture but is limited by a climate that produces drought and a terrain that is almost half desert. Mineral reserves have not been exploited because of poor transportation and power facilities. Food processing and textiles account for most industry. A landlocked country, Mali faces a growing national debt due to its dependence on foreign goods. The climate is hot and dry, with alternating dry and wet seasons.

History and Politics. Parts of present-day Mali once belonged to the Ghana, Mali, and Songhai empires. These wealthy empires, which ruled from about A.D. 300 to 1600, traded with the Mediterranean world and were centers of Islamic learning. Fierce native resistance delayed colonization by the French until 1904, when French Sudan, as the area was called, was made part of French West Africa. In 1959 it joined Senegal to form the Federation of Mali. Senegal soon withdrew from the union, and French Sudan declared itself the Republic of Mali in 1960. A military coup overthrew the republic, a socialist state, in 1968. In 1979, the country reestablished civilian rule. ∎

MALTA

Official name Republic of Malta
PEOPLE
Population 354,000. **Density** 2,902/mi² (1,120/km²). **Urban** 87%. **Capital** Valletta, 9,210. **Ethnic groups** Maltese (mixed Arab, Sicilian, Norman, Spanish, Italian, and English). **Languages** English, Maltese. **Religions** Roman Catholic 98%. **Life expectancy** 76 female, 72 male. **Literacy** 88%.
POLITICS
Government Republic. **Parties** Labor, Nationalist. **Suffrage** Universal, over 18. **Memberships** CW, UN. **Subdivisions** 6 regions.
ECONOMY
GDP $1,017,000,000 **Per capita** $2,825. **Monetary unit** Lira. **Trade partners** Exports: Germany, Italy, U.K. Imports: Italy, Germany, U.K.. **Exports** Clothing, eyeglasses, and other manufactures; electrical machinery. **Imports** Textiles and other manufactures, machinery, food, chemicals, petroleum.
LAND
Description Mediterranean island. **Area** 122 mi² (316 km²). **Highest point** 829 ft (253 m). **Lowest point** Sea level.

People. Malta's diverse population reflects centuries of rule by Arabs, Normans, and British. The official languages are English and Maltese, the latter a blend of Arabic and a Sicilian dialect of Italian. Roman Catholicism is practiced by the majority of residents. Malta is one of the world's most densely populated nations.

Economy and the Land. Situated strategically between Europe and Africa, Malta became an important military site for foreign powers with the opening of the Suez Canal in 1869. Its economy, shaped by the patterns of war and peace in the Mediterranean, has recently turned toward commercial shipbuilding, construction, manufacturing, and tourism. Its soil is poor, and most food is imported. Although there are many natural harbors and hundreds of miles of coastline, fishing is not a major source of income. Malta, with its hilly terrain, is subtropical in summer and temperate the rest of the year.

History and Politics. The Phoenicians and Carthaginians first colonized the island of Malta between 1000 and 600 B.C. After becoming part of the Roman and Byzantine empires, Malta was ruled successively by Arabs, Normans, and various feudal lords. In the 1500s the Holy Roman Emperor Charles V ceded Malta to the Knights of St. John of Jerusalem, an order of the Roman Catholic church. The Knights' reign, marked by cultural and architectural achievements, ended with surrender to France's Napoleon Bonaparte in 1798. The Maltese resisted French rule, however, and offered control to Britain, becoming part of the United Kingdom in 1814. Throughout both world wars, Malta was a vital naval base for the Allied forces. It achieved independence from Britain in 1964 and became a republic ten years later. In 1979 the last British and North Atlantic Treaty Organization (NATO) military forces departed, and Malta declared its neutrality. ∎

MARSHALL ISLANDS
See UNITED STATES.

MARTINIQUE See FRANCE.

MAURITANIA

Official name Islamic Republic of Mauritania
PEOPLE
Population 2,070,000. **Density** 5.2/mi² (2.0/km²). **Urban** 42%. **Capital** Nouakchott, 285,000. **Ethnic groups** Mixed Moor and black 40%, Moor 30%, black 30%. **Languages** Arabic, French, indigenous. **Religions** Sunni Muslim 100%. **Life expectancy** 50 female, 46 male. **Literacy** 17%.
POLITICS
Government Provisional military government. **Parties** None. **Suffrage** None. **Memberships** AL, OAU, UN. **Subdivisions** 12 regions, 1 capital district.
ECONOMY
GDP $697,000,000 **Per capita** $386. **Monetary unit** Ouguiya. **Trade partners** Exports: Japan, France, Spain. Imports: France, Spain, Senegal. **Exports** Iron ore, fish. **Imports** Food, manufactures, petroleum.

LAND

Description Western Africa. **Area** 395,956 mi² (1,025,520 km²). **Highest point** Mt. Jill, 3,002 ft (915 m). **Lowest point** Sebkha de Ndrhamcha, -10 ft (-3 m).

People. Most Mauritanians are Moors, descendants of Arabs and Berbers, or of mixed Arab, Berber, and black descent. The Moors, who speak Arabic, are mostly nomadic herdsmen. The remainder of the population is composed of black Africans, who speak several languages and farm in the Senegal River valley. Virtually all Mauritanians are Muslim. Proportionally, the nomadic population has declined recently because of long periods of drought, although overall population is increasing.

Economy and the Land. Mauritania's economy is based on agriculture, with many farmers producing only subsistence-level outputs. Crop production, confined chiefly to the Senegal River valley, has recently fallen because of drought and outmoded cultivation methods. Mining of high-grade iron-ore deposits is the main industrial activity, although fishing and fish processing are also important. Inadequate transportation and communication systems have crippled the economy. In addition to the river valley, land regions include a northern desert and southeastern grasslands. Mauritania has a hot, dry climate.

History and Politics. Berbers began settling in parts of the area around A.D. 300 and established a network of caravan trading routes. From this time until the late 1500s, sections of the south were dominated by the Ghana, the Mali, and finally the Songhai empires. Contact with Europeans grew between the 1600s and 1800s, and in 1920 France made Mauritania a colony. Mauritania attained independence in 1960, although Morocco claimed the area and did not recognize the state until 1970. During the late seventies, Mauritania became embroiled in a war with Morocco and the Polisario Front, a Western Saharan nationalist group, for control of Western Sahara. Mauritania withdrew its claim to the area in 1979. A coup in 1978 ended seventeen years of presidential rule and established a military government. Local elections were held in the late 1980s in a first step towards democratization. ∎

MAURITIUS

Official name Mauritius

PEOPLE

Population 1,091,000. **Density** 1,385/mi² (535/km²). **Urban** 42%. **Capital** Port Louis, Mauritius I., 139,730. **Ethnic groups** Indo-Mauritian 68%, Creole 27%, Sino-Mauritian 3%, Franco-Mauritian 2%. **Languages** English, Creole, Bhojpuri, Hindi. **Religions** Hindu 31%, Muslim 13%, Sanatanist 10%. **Life expectancy** 73 female, 68 male. **Literacy** 67%.

POLITICS

Government Parliamentary state. **Parties** Labor, Militant Socialist Movement, Militant Movement, Social Democratic, others. **Suffrage** Universal, over 18. **Memberships** CW, OAU, UN. **Subdivisions** 9 districts.

ECONOMY

GDP $1,061,000,000 **Per capita** $1,035. **Monetary unit** Rupee. **Trade partners** Exports: U.K., France, U.S. Imports: Bahrain, South African countries, U.K.. **Exports** Sugar, clothing and other manufactures. **Imports** Textiles and other manufactures, grain and other food, petroleum, machinery.

LAND

Description Indian Ocean island. **Area** 788 mi² (2,040 km²). **Highest point** Piton de la Petite Rivière Noire, 2,717 ft (828 m). **Lowest point** Sea level. *The above information includes dependencies.*

People. Mauritius's diverse ethnicity is largely the product of its past as a sugar-producing colony. Creoles are descendants of African slaves and European plantation owners, while the Indian community traces its roots to laborers who replaced the Africans after slavery was abolished. There are also people of Chinese and French descent. Franco-Mauritians now compose most of the nation's elite. English is the official tongue, although a French creole and many other languages are also spoken. Religious activity is similarly varied and includes followers of Hinduism, Christianity, Islam, and Tamil.

Economy and the Land. Sugar remains fundamental to the economy: almost all arable land is covered by sugar cane, and sugar and its by-products make up the majority of exports. Attempts have been made at diversification, with tea and tobacco recently introduced. Inflation, unemployment, overpopulation, and low sugar prices cloud the economic outlook. The nation includes the island of Mauritius, Rodrigues Island, Agalega Islands, and Cargados Carajos Shoals. The climate is tropical.

History and Politics. Although visited by Arab, Malay, and Portuguese sailors between the tenth and sixteenth centuries A.D., Mauritius was uninhabited until 1598, when the Dutch claimed it. They abandoned the island in 1710, and five years later the French made it their colony. During the 1700s, the French used Mauritius, which they called Île de France, as a naval base and established plantations worked by imported slaves. The British ousted the French in 1810 and outlawed slavery soon afterward. In the nineteenth century indentured workers from India replaced the slaves. Mauritius began its history as an independent state in 1968 with a system of parliamentary democracy. In 1982, the Militant Socialist Movement succeeded the Labor Party, which had been in power for fourteen years. ∎

MAYOTTE See FRANCE.

MEXICO

Official name United Mexican States

PEOPLE

Population 86,675,000. **Density** 115/mi² (44/km²). **Urban** 73%. **Capital** Mexico City, 8,831,079. **Ethnic groups** Mestizo 60%, Amerindian 30%, white 9%. **Languages** Spanish, indigenous. **Religions** Roman Catholic 93%, Protestant 3%. **Life expectancy** 74 female, 67 male. **Literacy** 83%.

POLITICS

Government Republic. **Parties** Cardenist Front of the Nationalist Reconstruction, Institutional Revolutionary, National Action, others. **Suffrage** Universal, over 18. **Memberships** OAS, UN. **Subdivisions** 31 states, 1 federal district.

ECONOMY

GDP $177,475,000,000 **Per capita** $2,256. **Monetary unit** Peso. **Trade partners** Exports: U.S., Japan, Spain. Imports: U.S., Germany, Japan. **Exports** Petroleum, coffee and other food, manufactures,

machinery. **Imports** Machinery, chemicals, manufactures, hides and other crude materials, food.

LAND

Description Southern North America. **Area** 756,066 mi² (1,958,201 km²). **Highest point** Pico de Orizaba, 18,406 ft (5,610 m). **Lowest point** Laguna Salada, -26 ft (-8 m).

People. Most Mexicans are mestizos, descended from Indians and the Spaniards who conquered Mexico in the 1500s. Spanish is spoken by most inhabitants, and Roman Catholicism is the most popular religion. Another major ethnic group is comprised of indigenous Indians, or Amerindians, some of whom speak only Indian languages and hold traditional religious beliefs. Mexico's rapid population growth has contributed to poverty among rural dwellers, spurring a migration to the cities. Due to its mild climate and fertile soils, Mexico's central plateau is home to most of the population.

Economy and the Land. Mexico is a leading producer of petroleum and silver, a growing manufacturer of iron, steel, and chemicals, and an exporter of coffee and cotton. Foreign visitors—drawn by archaeological sites and warm, sunny weather—make tourism an important activity. Despite economic gains made since the mid-1900s in agriculture and industry, Mexico recently has been troubled by inflation, declining oil prices, rising unemployment, and a trade deficit that has grown with the need for imported materials. In recent years the peso has been significantly devalued, and banks have been nationalized to help reduce a massive international debt. Austerity plans and foreign aid are expected to help revitalize the economy. Terrain and climate are greatly varied, ranging from tropical jungles along the coast to desert plains in the north. A temperate central plateau is bounded by rugged mountains in the south, east, and west.

History and Politics. Farm settlements grew in the Valley of Mexico between 6500 and 1500 B.C., and during the subsequent three thousand years Mexico gave birth to the great civilizations of the Olmec, Maya, Toltec, and Aztec Indians. The Aztec Empire was overthrown by the Spanish in 1521, and Mexico became the viceroyalty of New Spain. Although there was much dissatisfaction with Spanish rule, rebellion did not begin until 1810. Formal independence came in 1821. Mexico lost considerable territory, including Texas, to the United States during the Mexican War, from 1846 to 1848. During subsequent years, power changed hands frequently as liberals demanding social and economic reforms battled conservatives. A brief span of French imperial rule, from 1864 to 1867, interrupted the struggle. Following a revolution that started in 1910, a new constitution was adopted in 1917, and progress toward reform began, culminating in the separation of church and state and the redistribution of land. A 1988 election was won by the Institutional Revolutionary candidate but parties on both the right and the left showed significant strength. ∎

MICRONESIA, FEDERATED STATES OF See UNITED STATES.

MIDWAY ISLANDS
See UNITED STATES.

MONACO

Official name Principality of Monaco

PEOPLE

Population 29,000. **Density** 41,429/mi² (15,263/km²). **Urban** 100%. **Capital** Monaco, 29,000. **Ethnic groups** French 47%, Monegasque 17%, Italian 16%, English 4%, Belgian 2%, Swiss 1%. **Languages** French, English, Italian, Monegasque. **Religions** Roman Catholic 95%. **Life expectancy** 80 female, 72 male. **Literacy** 99%.

POLITICS

Government Constitutional monarchy. **Parties** Action, Democractic Union Movement, National and Democratic Union, Socialist. **Suffrage** Universal, over 25. **Memberships** None. **Subdivisions** 3 communes. **Monetary unit** French franc.

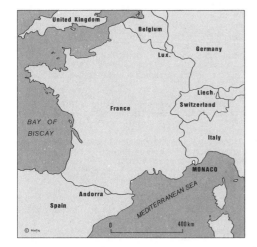

LAND

Description Southern Europe (on the southeastern coast of France). **Area** 0.7 mi² (1.9 km²). **Highest point** 459 ft (140 m). **Lowest point** Sea level.

People. Monaco is inhabited mostly by French citizens, while Monegasques—citizens of indigenous descent—and various Europeans form the rest of the population. Many foreigners have taken up residence, drawn by the country's tax benefits. French is the official language. Monegasque, a blend of French and Italian, is also spoken, as are French, Italian and English. Most residents are Roman Catholic.

Economy and the Land. Monaco's beautiful seaside location, mild Mediterranean climate, and famous gambling casino in Monte Carlo make it a popular tourist haven. Consequently, tourism forms the backbone of the economy. Production of chemicals, food products, and perfumes, among other light industries, are additional sources of income. Monaco also profits from many foreign businesses, which are attracted by the favorable tax climate and headquartered in the principality. France and Monaco form a customs union for a mutually beneficial trade system; the French franc is Monaco's official currency. The world's second smallest independent state in area—after Vatican City—Monaco has four regions: the old city of Monaco-Ville, site of the royal palace; Monte Carlo, the resort and major tourist center; La Condamine, the port area; and Fontvieille, the rapidly growing industrial section.

History and Politics. Known to the Phoenicians, Greeks, and Romans, the region became a Genoese colony in the twelfth century A.D. Around the turn of the fourteenth century, the area was granted to the Grimaldi family of Genoa. France, Spain, and Sardinia had intermittent control of Monaco from 1400 until 1861, when its autonomy was recognized by the Franco-Monegasque Treaty. Another treaty, providing for French protection of Monaco, was signed in 1918. The absolute rule of Monaco's princes ended with the 1911 constitution. ∎

MONGOLIA

Official name Mongolian People's Republic
PEOPLE
Population 2,203,000. **Density** 3.6/mi² (1.4/km²).
Urban 51%. **Capital** Ulan Bator, 548,400. **Ethnic**

groups Mongol 90%, Kazakh 4%, Chinese 2%, Russian 2%. **Languages** Khalkha Mongol, Kazakh, Russian, Chinese. **Religions** Shamanic, Tibetan Buddhist, Muslim. **Life expectancy** 67 female, 63 male. **Literacy** 80%.
POLITICS
Government Socialist republic. **Parties** Democratic, National Progress, People's Revolutionary, Social Democratic. **Suffrage** Universal, over 18.
Memberships UN. **Subdivisions** 18 provinces, 3 municipalities.
ECONOMY
GDP $1,670,000,000 **Per capita** $886. **Monetary unit** Tughrik. **Trade partners** U.S.S.R.. **Exports** Livestock, animal products, wool, hides, minerals, metals. **Imports** Machinery, fuel, food, consumer goods, chemicals, building materials.
LAND
Description Central Asia, landlocked. **Area** 604,829 mi² (1,566,500 km²). **Highest point** Nayramadlin Orgil, 14,291 ft (4,356 m). **Lowest point** Höh Lake, 1,814 ft (553 m).

People. Mongols, a central Asian people, make up the vast majority of Mongolia's population. Khalkha Mongol is the predominant language. Turkic-speaking Kazakhs, as well as Russians and Chinese, comprise minorities. Tibetan Buddhism was once the most common religion; however, the government has discouraged religious practice. The traditional nomadic way of life is becoming less common, as recent government policies have led to urbanization and settled agriculture.

Economy and the Land. Mongolia's economy, long based on the raising of livestock, has been shaped by the ideal grazing land found in most of the country. But significant economic changes have occurred since 1924, including the collectivization and modernization of farming, the introduction of industry, and the exploitation of mineral resources. Although dependent on Soviet aid, Mongolia has made considerable progress toward diversifying and developing its economy. Mongolia's terrain varies from mountains in the north and west to steppe in the east and desert in the south. Located in the heart of Asia, remote from any moderating body of water, Mongolia has a rigorous continental climate with little precipitation.

History and Politics. Mongolian tribes were united under the warlord Genghis Khan around A.D. 1200, and he and his successors built one of history's largest land empires. In 1691 the Manchu dynasty of China subdued Outer Mongolia, as the area was then known, but allowed the Mongol rulers autonomy. Until the Mongols ousted the Chinese in 1911, Outer Mongolia remained a Chinese province. In 1912 the state accepted Russian protection but was unable to prevent a subsequent Chinese advance, and in 1919 Outer Mongolia again became a Chinese province. In 1921 a combined Soviet and Mongolian force defeated Chinese and Belorussian, or White Russian, troops, and the Mongolian People's Republic was declared in 1924. A mutual-assistance pact was signed by Mongolia and Russia in 1966. In 1989, the Soviets agreed to withdraw most of their troops from Mongolia. Increasing pressure for democratization led to the country's first free, multiparty elections in August 1990. Previous to the election, the Communist party had renounced its monopoly but managed to win 85 percent of the vote. ∎

MONTSERRAT See UNITED KINGDOM.

MOROCCO

Official name Kingdom of Morocco
PEOPLE
Population 26,575,000. **Density** 154/mi² (60/km²).
Urban 49%. **Capital** Rabat, 518,616. **Ethnic groups** Arab-Berber 99%. **Languages** Arabic, Berber dialects, French. **Religions** Sunni Muslim 99%. **Life expectancy** 65 female, 62 male. **Literacy** 30%.
POLITICS
Government Constitutional monarchy. **Parties** Constitutional Union, Istiqlal, National Assembly of Independents, Popular Movement, others. **Suffrage** Universal, over 21. **Memberships** AL, UN.
Subdivisions 36 provinces, 2 prefectures.
ECONOMY
GDP $11,892,000,000 **Per capita** $547. **Monetary unit** Dirham. **Trade partners** Exports: France, India, Germany, Spain. Imports: France, U.S., Spain. **Exports** Manufactures, food, phosphates. **Imports** Machinery, manufactures, raw materials, fuel, food.

LAND
Description Northwestern Africa. **Area** 172,414 mi² (446,550 km²). **Highest point** Mt. Toubkal, 13,665 ft (4,165 m). **Lowest point** Sebkha Tah, -180 ft (-55 m). *The above information excludes Western Sahara.*

People. Moroccans, virtually homogeneous in race and culture, are mostly a mix of Arab and Berber stocks and speak Arabic. A few Berber dialects are spoken in rural mountain areas, and French and Spanish, the colonial tongues, are common in business and government. The majority of people are Sunni Muslim. The population is concentrated west of the Atlas Mountains, which border the Sahara Desert. Rural people are migrating to cities, where the standard of living is higher.

Economy and the Land. Although agriculture employs much of the work force and is an important activity, the nation depends on mining for most of its income. Morocco is a leading exporter of phosphates, but has other mineral reserves as well. Fishing and tourism are growing sources of revenue. Recently, severe drought, rising dependency on imported oil, and a costly war in Western Sahara have slowed productivity, while investments by Arab countries have bolstered the economy. Morocco, with its varied terrain of desert, forests, and mountains, has an equally varied climate that is semitropical along the coast, and desert beyond the Atlas Mountains.

History and Politics. In ancient times, Morocco was a province of Carthage and Rome. Vandals and Byzantine Greeks, the subsequent rulers, were followed in the A.D. 700s by Arabs, who brought Islam. Morocco's strategic position awakened the interest of colonial powers in the 1800s, and by 1912 the area was divided into French and Spanish protectorates. A nationalist movement began in the 1920s, occasionally bringing violence, but not until 1956 did Morocco become independent from France. The last of Spain's holdings in Morocco were returned in 1969. War broke out in 1976, when Morocco claimed the northern part of Western Sahara and was challenged by the Saharan nationalist Polisario Front. Although Mauritania, which had been involved in the war and had been fighting for southern Western Sahara, surrendered its claim in 1979, Morocco has continued to battle the Polisario Front. ∎

MOZAMBIQUE

Official name Republic of Mozambique
PEOPLE
Population 15,785,000. **Density** 51/mi² (20/km²).
Urban 27%. **Capital** Maputo, 1,069,727. **Ethnic groups** Makua, Lomwe, Thonga, others. **Languages** Portuguese, indigenous. **Religions** Tribal religionist 60%, Roman Catholic and other Christian 30%, Muslim. **Life expectancy** 50 female, 47 male. **Literacy** 27%.
POLITICS
Government Republic. **Parties** Front for the Liberation of Mozambique. **Suffrage** Universal, over 18.
Memberships OAU, UN. **Subdivisions** 10 provinces, 1 independent city.
ECONOMY
GDP $1,840,000,000 **Per capita** $142. **Monetary unit** Metical. **Trade partners** Exports: U.S., Germany, Japan. Imports: U.S.S.R., South African countries, Portugal. **Exports** Shrimp, cashews, sugar, copra, citrus. **Imports** Food, clothing, machinery, petroleum.

LAND

Description Southern Africa. **Area** 308,642 mi² (799,379 km²). **Highest point** Monte Binga, 7,992 ft (2,436 m). **Lowest point** Sea level.

People. Black Africans belonging to about ten groups compose the vast majority of the population. Most black Mozambicans live in rural areas, while small European and Asian minorities live primarily in urban centers. Traditional African religions are followed by a majority, while others practice Islam and Christianity. Although Portuguese is the official language, most blacks speak Bantu tongues.

Economy and the Land. Mozambique's underdeveloped economy is largely the product of its colonial past, during which its human and natural resources were neglected. Recent political developments in southern Africa have created more economic woes, as lucrative trade agreements with racially divided neighbors have ceased. While the mainstays of the economy are agriculture and transport services, fishing and mining are also being developed. The Marxist government has allowed some private enterprise, and foreign aid is important. The climate is tropical or subtropical along the coastal plain that covers nearly half of the country, with cooler conditions in the western high plateaus and mountains.

History and Politics. Bantu-speaking peoples settled in present-day Mozambique around the first century A.D. Subsequent immigrants included Arab traders in the 800s and the Portuguese in the late 1400s. European economic interest in the area was hindered by lucrative trading with other colonies, and Mozambique wasn't recognized as a Portuguese colony until 1885. Policies instituted by the Portuguese benefitted European settlers and Portugal while overlooking the welfare of Mozambique and its native inhabitants. In the early 1960s, the country made clear its opposition to foreign rule, with the formation of the Front for the Liberation of Mozambique, a Marxist nationalist group that initiated an armed campaign against the Portuguese. In 1975 Mozambique became an independent state dedicated to eliminating white-minority rule in the area. Nevertheless, Mozambique has economic ties to South Africa, and in 1984 the two nations pledged to deny refuge to each other's foes. A new constitution passed in 1990 marked the end of single-party rule in Mozambique. Elections are scheduled for mid-1991. Continued guerrilla fighting and food shortages have created a crisis situation in Mozambique. ∎

NAMIBIA

Official name Republic of Namibia
PEOPLE
Population 1,904,000. **Density** 6.0/mi² (2.3/km²). **Urban** 57%. **Capital** Windhoek, 114,500. **Ethnic groups** Ovambo 49%, Kavango 9%, Damara 8%, Herero 7%, white 7%, mixed 7%. **Languages** Afrikaans, English, German, indigenous. **Religions** Lutheran and other Protestant, Roman Catholic, Animist. **Life expectancy** 60 female, 58 male. **Literacy** 23%.
POLITICS
Government Republic. **Parties** Democratic Turnhalle Alliance, South West Africa People's Organization, United Democratic Front, others. **Suffrage** Universal, over 18. **Memberships** CW, OAU, UN. **Subdivisions** 26 districts.

ECONOMY

GDP $860,000,000 **Per capita** $782. **Monetary unit** South African rand. **Trade partners** South Africa, Germany, U.K., U.S.. **Exports** Diamonds, uranium, zinc, copper, meat, fish. **Imports** Food, consumer goods, machinery.
LAND
Description Southern Africa. **Area** 317,818 mi² (823,144 km²). **Highest point** Brandberg, 8,461 ft (2,579 m). **Lowest point** Sea level.
The above information excludes Walvis Bay.

People. The largest ethnic group is black African, composed of many indigenous peoples. South Africans, Britons, and Germans constitute the white minority. Black Namibians speak various native dialects, while the majority of whites speak Afrikaans. Blacks still follow traditional customs and religions, but a considerable number have converted to Christianity.

Economy and the Land. Namibia's economy is based on the mining of diamonds, copper, lead, and other minerals. Agriculture makes a marginal contribution, but livestock raising is important. Manufacturing remains undeveloped because of an unskilled work force, and Namibia imports most of its finished goods from South Africa, its partner in a customs union. A variety of factors, including continuing drought and political instability, have held back economic growth. Namibia consists of a high plateau that encompasses the Namib Desert and part of the Kalahari Desert. The climate is subtropical.

History and Politics. Bushmen were probably the area's first inhabitants, followed by other African peoples. European exploration of the coast began in the A.D. 1500s, but the coastal desert prevented foreign penetration. In 1884 Germany annexed all of the territory except for the coastal enclave of Walvis Bay, which had been claimed by Britain in 1878. After South African troops ousted the Germans from the area during World War I, the League of Nations mandated Namibia, then known as South West Africa, to South Africa. Following World War II, the United Nations requested that the territory become a trusteeship. South Africa refused to cooperate. In 1966 the United Nations revoked South Africa's mandate, yet South Africa kept control of Namibia. Beginning in the sixties, the South West Africa People's Organization, a Namibian nationalist group with Communist support, made guerrilla raids on South African forces from bases in Zambia and, later, from Angola. In 1989, after years of continued pressure, an assembly was elected to draft a constitution. Independence was achieved in March 1990. ∎

NAURU

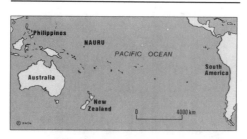

Official name Republic of Nauru

PEOPLE
Population 9,000. **Density** 1,111/mi² (429/km²). **Capital** Yaren District. **Ethnic groups** Nauruan 58%, other Pacific Islander 26%, Chinese 8%, European 8%. **Languages** Nauruan, English. **Religions** Congregationalist and other Protestant 67%, Roman Catholic 33%. **Life expectancy** 69 female, 64 male. **Literacy** 99%.
POLITICS
Government Republic. **Parties** None. **Suffrage** Universal, over 20. **Memberships** CW. **Subdivisions** 14 districts.
ECONOMY
GNP $160,000,000 **Per capita** $20,513. **Monetary unit** Australian dollar. **Trade partners** Exports: Australia, New Zealand. Imports: Australia, U.K., New Zealand, Japan. **Exports** Phosphates. **Imports** Food, fuel, manufactures, building materials, machinery.
LAND
Description South Pacific island. **Area** 8.1 mi² (21 km²). **Highest point** 210 ft (64 m). **Lowest point** Sea level.

People. Indigenous Nauruans are a mix of Polynesian, Micronesian, and Melanesian stock, and many residents are from other Pacific islands. Nauruan is the language of most inhabitants, but English is widely spoken. Nearly all Nauruans are Christian.

Economy and the Land. The economy depends primarily on its sole resource, phosphates; the government is establishing trust funds to support islanders when the resource is depleted. With limited agriculture, nearly all food must be imported. Nauru is one of the smallest countries in the world. Most of the coral island is a plateau, and the climate is tropical.

History and Politics. Nauru was most likely settled by castaways from nearby islands. Noted by a British explorer in 1798, Nauru remained autonomous until it came under German control in 1881. In 1914 Germany surrendered the island, and it was subsequently mandated to Australia, Britain, and New Zealand. World War II brought occupation by Japan. Nauru reverted to Australian rule in 1947 as a trusteeship. It became independent in 1968 and gained control of European interests in the phosphate industry in 1970. ∎

NEPAL

Official name Kingdom of Nepal
PEOPLE
Population 19,390,000. **Density** 341/mi² (132/km²). **Urban** 10%. **Capital** Kathmandu, 235,160. **Ethnic groups** Newar, Indian, Tibetan, Gurung, Magar, Tamang, Bhotia, others. **Languages** Nepali, Maithali, Bhojpuri, other indigenous. **Religions** Hindu 90%, Buddhist 5%, Muslim 3%. **Life expectancy** 53 female, 54 male. **Literacy** 21%.
POLITICS
Government Constitutional monarchy. **Parties** Congress, others. **Suffrage** Universal, over 21. **Memberships** UN. **Subdivisions** 14 zones.
ECONOMY
GDP $2,288,000,000 **Per capita** $136. **Monetary unit** Rupee. **Trade partners** Exports: India, U.S. Imports: India, Japan. **Exports** Rice and other food, carpets and other textiles, clothing, leather goods. **Imports** Textiles and other manufactures, machinery, chemicals, food, petroleum.
LAND
Description Southern Asia, landlocked. **Area**

56,827 mi² (147,181 km²). **Highest point** Mt. Everest, 29,028 ft (8,848 m). **Lowest point** 197 ft (60 m).

People. Nepal's mixed population results from migrations over the centuries from India, Tibet, and central Asia. Most of Nepal's ruling families have been of Indian descent, and Nepali, the official language, is derived from Sanskrit, an ancient Indian language. Although the majority of the population practices Hinduism, Nepal is the birthplace of Buddha and has been greatly influenced by Buddhism as well. The importance of both religions is reflected in the more than twenty-seven hundred shrines in the Kathmandu Valley. Most Nepalese are rural farmers.

Economy and the Land. Because of geographic remoteness and a political policy of isolation lasting until the 1950s, Nepal's economy is one of the least developed in the world. Agriculture, concentrated chiefly in the south, is the most significant activity, even though most of Nepal is covered by the Himalayas, the world's highest mountains. This range—which includes Mount Everest, the world's highest peak—has made tourism increasingly lucrative. Nepal has potential in hydroelectricity and forestry, but inadequate transportation routes, overpopulation, and deforestation present obstacles to development. Nepal has received financial aid from many nations, partly because of its strategic location between India and China. The climate varies from subtropical in the flat, fertile south to temperate in the central hill country. Himalayan summers are cool and winters severe.

History and Politics. Several small Hindu-Buddhist kingdoms had emerged in the Kathmandu Valley by about A.D. 300. These states were unified in the late 1700s by the founder of the Shah dynasty. The Rana family wrested control from the Shahs in 1846 and pursued an isolationist course, which thwarted foreign influence but stunted economic growth. Opposition to the Ranas mounted during the 1930s and 1940s, and in 1951 the Shah monarchy was restored by a revolution. In 1962 the king established a government that gave the crown dominance and abolished political parties. A 1980 referendum narrowly upheld this system. In November 1990, a pro-democracy movement forced the king to approve a new constitution providing for a multiparty structure and the country's new status as a constitutional monarchy. Elections are scheduled for 1991. ∎

NETHERLANDS

Official name Kingdom of the Netherlands
PEOPLE
Population 14,980,000. **Density** 929/mi² (359/km²). **Urban** 89%. **Capital** Amsterdam (designated), 696,500; The Hague (seat of government), 443,900. **Ethnic groups** Dutch (mixed Scandinavian, French, and Celtic)

99%, Indonesian and others 1%. **Languages** Dutch. **Religions** Roman Catholic 40%, Dutch Reformed and other Protestant 31%. **Life expectancy** 81 female, 74 male. **Literacy** 99%.
POLITICS
Government Constitutional monarchy. **Parties** Christian Democratic Appeal, Labor, Liberal, others. **Suffrage** Universal, over 18. **Memberships** EC, NATO, OECD, UN. **Subdivisions** 12 provinces.
ECONOMY
GDP $124,983,000,000 **Per capita** $8,640. **Monetary unit** Guilder. **Trade partners** Exports: Germany, Belgium, France. Imports: Germany, Belgium, U.K.. **Exports** Textiles and other manufactures, food, chemicals, machinery, petroleum. **Imports** Clothing and other manufactures, machinery, food, petroleum, chemicals.
LAND
Description Western Europe. **Area** 16,133 mi² (41,785 km²). **Highest point** Vaalserberg, 1,053 ft (321 m). **Lowest point** Prins Alexander polder, -23 ft (-7 m).

People. The major ethnic group is the Dutch, for the most part a mixture of French, Scandinavian, and Celtic peoples. There are small minorities from the former Dutch possessions of Indonesia and Suriname. Dutch is the official language, but many Netherlanders also speak English or German. Although most Dutch are Christian, the nation has a history of religious tolerance that has drawn countless refugees.

Economy and the Land. A variety of manufacturing strengths—notably the metal, chemical, and food-processing industries—fuels the prosperous economy. Tourism and the production of natural gas are also important. Due to a lack of natural resources, the Netherlands must import many goods. The country benefits from its strategic position and has enjoyed success in shipping and trade. Much of the Netherlands, including most farmland, has been reclaimed from the sea through artificial drainage. The land is almost uniformly flat, and proximity to the sea produces a mild, damp climate. The Kingdom of the Netherlands includes the Netherlands Antilles, two groups of Caribbean islands, and Aruba.

History and Politics. The Germanic tribes of the area were conquered in 58 B.C. by the Romans, who were driven out in the A.D. 400s by the Franks. As part of the Low Countries with Belgium and Luxembourg, the Netherlands was dominated successively by Charlemagne, the dukes of Burgundy, the Hapsburgs, and rulers of Spain. Spanish persecution of Dutch Protestants led to a revolt that in 1581 created the Republic of the United Netherlands. In the 1600s the Netherlands became a maritime as well as a colonial power and produced many masterpieces in painting. But a series of wars with England and France ending in 1714 spelled the end of Dutch influence, and the nation fell to France in 1795. With the defeat of Napoleon Bonaparte of France in 1815, the Netherlands was united with Belgium and became an independent kingdom. Belgium seceded in 1830. The Netherlands declared its neutrality in both world wars but was occupied by Germany from 1940 to 1945. The war cost the country many lives and much of its economic strength. Membership in several international economic unions aided recovery. Since the war, the Netherlands has abandoned neutrality and now maintains a pro-Western stance in foreign affairs. ∎

NETHERLANDS ANTILLES
See NETHERLANDS.

NEW CALEDONIA

Official name Territory of New Caledonia and Dependencies

PEOPLE
Population 170,000. **Density** 23/mi² (8.9/km²). **Urban** 81%. **Capital** Nouméa, New Caledonia I., 65,110. **Ethnic groups** Melanesian 43%, French 37%, Wallisian 8%, Polynesian 4%, Indonesian 4%, Vietnamese 2%. **Languages** French, Malay-Polynesian languages. **Religions** Roman Catholic 60%, Protestant 30%. **Life expectancy** 71 female, 64 male. **Literacy** 91%.
POLITICS
Government Overseas territory (France). **Parties** Kanak Socialist National Liberation Front, National Front, Rally for the Republic, others. **Suffrage** Universal adult. **Memberships** None. **Subdivisions** 3 autonomous provinces.
ECONOMY
GDP $824,000,000 **Per capita** $5,644. **Monetary unit** CFP franc. **Trade partners** Exports: France, Japan. Imports: France, Australia, U.S.. **Exports** Nickel. **Imports** Manufactures, coal, food, machinery, automobiles, chemicals.
LAND
Description South Pacific islands. **Area** 7,358 mi² (19,058 km²). **Highest point** Mont Panié, 5,341 ft (1,628 m). **Lowest point** Sea level.

People. The largest ethnic group in New Caledonia, a group of Pacific islands northeast of Australia, is the Melanesian, or Kanak. People of French descent make up the second largest group, with Asians and Polynesians composing significant minorities. New Caledonia's status as an overseas French territory is reflected in its languages, which include French as well as regional dialects, and in a population that is largely Christian.

Economy and the Land. The principal economic activity, the mining and smelting of nickel, has fallen off in recent years. Small amounts of coffee and copra are exported, and tourism is important in the capital. Possessing few resources, New Caledonia imports almost all finished products from France. The main island, also called New Caledonia, is mountainous and accounts for almost 90 percent of the territory's land area. Smaller islands include the Isle of Pines, Loyalty and Bélep islands. The climate is tropical.

History and Politics. New Caledonia was settled by Melanesians about 2000 B.C. Europeans first reached the main island in 1774, when Captain James Cook of Britain gave it its present name. In 1853 France annexed New Caledonia and used the main island as a penal colony until the turn of the century. During World War II the islands served as a base for the United States military. Officially a French overseas territory since 1946, New Caledonia experienced violence in the 1980s, stemming from the desire of the Kanak population for independence. ∎

NEW ZEALAND

Official name New Zealand
PEOPLE
Population 3,483,000. **Density** 34/mi² (13/km²). **Urban** 84%. **Capital** Wellington, North I., 137,495. **Ethnic groups** European origin 86%, Maori 9%, Samoan and other Pacific islander 3%. **Languages** English, Maori. **Religions** Anglican 24%, Presbyterian 18%, Roman Catholic 15%, Methodist 5%. **Life expectancy** 79 female, 73 male. **Literacy** 99%.
POLITICS
Government Parliamentary state. **Parties** Green, Labor, National, New Labor, others. **Suffrage** Universal, over 18. **Memberships** CW, OECD, UN. **Subdivisions** 85 counties.
ECONOMY
GDP $23,367,000,000 **Per capita** $7,406. **Monetary unit** Dollar. **Trade partners** Australia, Japan, U.S.. **Exports** Wool and other crude materials, meat,

Places and Possessions of THE NETHERLANDS

Entity	Status	Area	Population	Capital/Population
Aruba (Caribbean island)	Self-governing territory	75 mi² (193 km²)	66,000	Oranjestad, 19,800
Curaçao (Caribbean island)	Division of Netherlands Antilles	171 mi² (444 km²)	153,000	Willemstad, 31,883
Netherlands Antilles (Caribbean islands)	Self-governing territory	309 mi² (800 km²)	194,000	Willemstad, 31,883

Places and Possessions of NEW ZEALAND

Entity	Status	Area	Population	Capital/Population
Cook Islands (South Pacific)	Self-governing territory	91 mi² (236 km²)	18,000	Avarua, 9,678
Niue (South Pacific island)	Self-governing territory	102 mi² (263 km²)	1,800	Alofi, 811
Tokelau (South Pacific islands)	Island territory	4.6 mi² (12 km²)	1,800	None

manufactures, dairy products, fish. **Imports** Textiles and other manufactures, machinery, chemicals, automobiles, petroleum.

LAND
Description South Pacific islands. **Area** 103,519 mi² (268,112 km²). **Highest point** Mt. Cook, 12,349 ft (3,764 m). **Lowest point** Sea level.

People. The majority of New Zealanders are descended from Europeans, mostly Britons, who arrived in the 1800s. Of Polynesian descent, the indigenous Maori form the largest minority. After a period of decline following the arrival of the Europeans, the Maori population has been increasing. The major languages are English, the official tongue, and Maori. Most New Zealanders live on North Island. Christian religions are observed by many residents, and the Maori have incorporated some Christian elements into their beliefs.

Economy and the Land. Success in agriculture and trade has allowed New Zealand to overcome its small work force, remoteness from major markets, and a relative lack of natural resources. A terrain with much ideal grazing land and a climate that is temperate year-round have encouraged cattle and sheep farming. Manufacturing, including the food-processing and paper industries, is an expanding sector, as is tourism. New Zealand consists of two large islands—North Island and South Island—and many smaller islands scattered throughout the South Pacific. The nation administers several island territories. The scenic terrain is greatly varied, ranging from fjords and mountains to a volcanic plateau.

History and Politics. The Maori, the original settlers, are thought to have arrived around A.D. 1000. In 1642 they fought off the Dutch, the first Europeans to reach the area. Captain James Cook of Britain charted the islands in the late 1700s. Soon after, European hunters and traders, drawn by the area's whales, seals, and forests, began to arrive. Maori chiefs signed the 1840 Treaty of Waitangi, establishing British sovereignty, and British companies began to send settlers to New Zealand. Subsequent battles between settlers and Maori ended with the Maori's defeat in 1872, but European diseases and weapons continued to reduce the Maori population. In 1907 New Zealand became a self-governing dominion of Britain; formal independence came forty years later. New Zealand supported Britain in both world wars, but foreign policy has recently focused on Southeast Asia and the South Pacific. The country has banned vessels carrying nuclear weapons through its waters, which has strained relations with the United States. ∎

NICARAGUA

Official name Republic of Nicaragua
PEOPLE
Population 3,659,000. **Density** 73/mi² (28/km²). **Urban** 60%. **Capital** Managua, 682,000. **Ethnic groups** Mestizo 69%, white 17%, black 9%, Amerindian 5%. **Languages** Spanish, English, indigenous. **Religions** Roman Catholic 95%. **Life expectancy** 68 female, 65 male. **Literacy** 58%.

POLITICS
Government Republic. **Parties** National Opposition Union, Sandinista National Liberation Front. **Suffrage** Universal, over 16. **Memberships** OAS, UN. **Subdivisions** 6 administrative regions, 3 special zones.

ECONOMY
GDP $3,560,000,000 **Per capita** $1,203. **Monetary unit** Cordoba. **Trade partners** Exports: Japan, Germany, U.S. Imports: U.S., U.S.S.R., Mexico. **Exports** Coffee, textile fibers, sugar and honey, meat, shellfish, chemicals. **Imports** Pharmaceuticals and other chemicals, machinery, manufactures, petroleum.

LAND
Description Central America. **Area** 50,054 mi² (129,640 km²). **Highest point** Mogotón, 6,913 ft (2,107 m). **Lowest point** Sea level.

People. Nicaraguan society closely reflects the nation's history as a Spanish colony: most of its inhabitants are Spanish speaking, Roman Catholic, and mestizo, a mix of Indian and European stocks. Indian and black communities are found mostly in the Caribbean region. The educational level has improved in the past decade.

Economy and the Land. Nicaragua is chiefly an agricultural nation, relying on the production of textiles, coffee, and sugar. Years of instability before a 1979 revolution, a large foreign debt inherited from the previous regime, and a continuing civil war have severely hindered economic prosperity. The nation also suffers from a reliance on imported goods. In 1985 the currency was sharply devalued, and the United States, formerly a chief trading partner, announced a trade embargo. Basic consumer goods are in short supply. The terrain includes a low-lying Pacific region, central highlands, and a flat Caribbean area. The climate is tropical.

History and Politics. Spanish conquistadores, who came via Panama in 1522 to what is now Nicaragua, found a number of independent Indian states. Nicaragua was ruled by Spain as part of Guatemala until it became independent in 1821. In 1823 the former Spanish colonies of the region formed the Federation of Central America, a union which collapsed in 1838, resulting in the independent Republic of Nicaragua. For the next century, Nicaragua was the stage both for conflict between the Liberal and Conservative parties and for United States military and economic involvement. Members of the Somoza family, who had close ties to America, directed a repressive regime from 1936 to 1979, when the widely-supported Sandinistas overthrew the government. The Sandinistas, led by Daniel Ortega, were opposed by rival political parties and the Contras, rebels linked to the former Somoza administration and backed by the United States. Five Central American countries reached an agreement in 1987 on a plan to dismantle Contra forces. In 1990 elections, Ortega was defeated by Violeta Chamorro of the National Opposition Union. Despite the disbanding of the Contras in 1990, the situation remains unstable as Chamorro tries to placate the still powerful Sandinistas and revise the moribund economy. ∎

NIGER

Official name Republic of Niger

PEOPLE
Population 7,848,000. **Density** 16/mi² (6.2/km²). **Urban** 20%. **Capital** Niamey, 398,265. **Ethnic groups** Hausa 56%, Djerma 22%, Fulani 9%, Taureg 8%, Beriberi 4%. **Languages** French, Hausa, Djerma, indigenous. **Religions** Muslim 80%, Animist and Christian 20%. **Life expectancy** 48 female, 45 male. **Literacy** 10%.

POLITICS
Government Provisional military government. **Parties** National Movement for the Development of Society. **Suffrage** Universal, over 18. **Memberships** OAU, UN. **Subdivisions** 7 departments.

ECONOMY
GDP $1,830,000,000 **Per capita** $320. **Monetary unit** CFA franc. **Trade partners** Exports: France, Japan, Nigeria. Imports: France, Nigeria. **Exports** Uranium, textiles, livestock. **Imports** Textiles and other manufactures, food, petroleum, machinery.

LAND
Description Western Africa, landlocked. **Area** 489,191 mi² (1,267,000 km²). **Highest point** Indoukâl-n-Taghès, 6,634 ft (2,022 m). **Lowest point** Along Niger River, 650 ft (198 m).

People. Nearly all Nigerois are black Africans belonging to culturally diverse groups. The Hausa and the Djerma, farmers who live mostly in the south, constitute the two largest groups. The remaining Nigerois are nomadic herders who inhabit the northern desert regions. Although the official language is French, most inhabitants speak indigenous tongues. Islam is the most commonly observed religion, but some Nigerois follow indigenous and Christian beliefs.

Economy and the Land. Niger's economy is chiefly agricultural, although arable land is scarce and drought common. The raising of livestock, grain, beans, and peanuts accounts for most farming activity. Uranium mining, a growing industry, has become less productive recently due to a slump in the world uranium market. Mountains and the Sahara Desert cover most of northern Niger, while the south is savanna. The climate is hot and dry.

History and Politics. Because of its central location in northern Africa, Niger was a crossroads for many peoples during its early history and was dominated by several African empires before European explorers arrived in the 1800s. The area was placed within the French sphere of influence in 1885, but not until 1922 did France make Niger a colony of French West Africa. Gradual moves toward autonomy were made during the forties and fifties, and Niger became fully independent in 1960. Unrest caused in part by a prolonged drought led to a coup in 1974 and the establishment of a military government. Civilians now have some part in the political system. Niger maintains close ties to France. ∎

NIGERIA

Official name Federal Republic of Nigeria
PEOPLE
Population 112,830,000. **Density** 316/mi² (122/km²). **Urban** 35%. **Capital** Lagos (de facto), 1,213,000; Abuja (future). **Ethnic groups** Hausa, Fulani, Yoruba, Ibo, others. **Languages** English, Hausa, Fulani, Yorbua, Ibo, indigenous. **Religions** Muslim 50%, Christian 40%, Animist 10%. **Life expectancy** 54 female, 51 male. **Literacy** 38%.

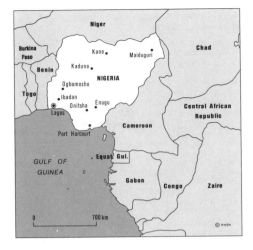

POLITICS
Government Provisional military government. **Parties** National Republican Convention, Social Democratic. **Suffrage** Universal, over 21. **Memberships** CW, OAU, OPEC, UN. **Subdivisions** 21 states, 1 capital territory.

ECONOMY
GDP $67,291,000,000 **Per capita** $805. **Monetary unit** Naira. **Trade partners** Exports: France, Italy, U.S. Imports: U.K., France, U.S.. **Exports** Petroleum, cocoa. **Imports** Manufactures, machinery, food, chemicals, transportation equipment.

LAND
Description Western Africa. **Area** 356,669 mi² (923,768 km²). **Highest point** Mt. Waddi, 7,936 ft (2,419 m). **Lowest point** Sea level.

People. Nigeria, Africa's most populous nation, contains more than two hundred distinct black African groups. The largest groups are the Hausa and the Fulani, who dominate the north; the Yoruba, found primarily in the southwest; and the Ibo, who live in the southeast and have historically been active in government and trade. Most Hausa and Fulani are Muslim, and a sizable Christian community is found mainly in the south. Nigerians commonly combine traditional beliefs with Islam or Christianity. Indigenous tongues are more widely spoken than English, the official language. Competition among Nigeria's many ethnic groups has threatened national unity.

Economy and the Land. Nigeria's economy is based on mining and agriculture. Petroleum is very important to the Nigerian economy, but a number of factors—including unskilled labor, poor power facilities, and the worldwide dip in oil prices—have silenced the oil boom of the 1970s and slowed development in other areas. In 1983 and 1985 the government expelled millions of illegal aliens in an effort to revive the economy. The terrain is diverse, encompassing tropical forest, savanna, and semi-desert. The climate is predominantly tropical.

History and Politics. From around 500 B.C. to about A.D. 200 the region was home to the sophisticated Nok civilization. Later cultures that dominated parts of the area included the Hausa, Fulani, and Yoruba. The Portuguese arrived in the 1400s, but the British gained control over the following centuries, uniting the region in 1914 as the Colony and Protectorate of Nigeria. Nigerian calls for self-rule culminated in independence in 1960. Internal tensions began to wrack the new nation, and in 1966 two military coups took place. After subsequent massacres of Ibo, that group declared eastern Nigeria the autonomous state of Biafra. A three-year civil war followed, ending in 1970 with Biafra's surrender. Government development and the oil boom speeded economic recovery. Subsequent years have seen coups and elections install short-lived regimes, and political instability continues. ∎

NIUE See NEW ZEALAND.

NORFOLK ISLAND See AUSTRALIA.

NORTHERN MARIANA ISLANDS See UNITED STATES.

NORWAY

Official name Kingdom of Norway
PEOPLE
Population 4,271,000. **Density** 29/mi² (11/km²). **Urban** 74%. **Capital** Oslo, 452,415. **Ethnic groups** Norwegian (Scandinavian), Lappic. **Languages** Norwegian, Lapp. **Religions** Lutheran 94%, other Protestant and Roman Catholic 4%. **Life expectancy** 81 female, 74 male. **Literacy** 99%.

POLITICS
Government Constitutional monarchy. **Parties** Conservative, Labor, Progress, Socialist Left, others. **Suffrage** Universal, over 18. **Memberships** NATO, OECD, UN. **Subdivisions** 19 counties.

ECONOMY
GDP $58,371,000,000 **Per capita** $14,065. **Monetary unit** Krone. **Trade partners** Exports: U.K., Germany, Sweden. Imports: Sweden, Germany, U.K.. **Exports** Petroleum, natural gas, aluminum and other manufactures, ships and boats. **Imports** Machinery, manufactures, transportation equipment, chemicals, crude materials.

LAND
Description Northern Europe. **Area** 149,412 mi² (386,975 km²). **Highest point** Galdhøppigen, 8,100 ft (2,469 m). **Lowest point** Sea level.
The above information includes Svalbard and Jan Mayen.

People. Because of its relatively remote location in far northern Europe, Norway has seen few population migrations and possesses a virtually homogeneous population, which is predominantly Germanic, Norwegian speaking, and Lutheran. Small communities of Lapps and Finns live in the far north, while most Norwegians live in the south and along the coast. The people enjoy many government-provided social services and programs.

Economy and the Land. Norway's economy, based on shipping, trade, and the mining of offshore oil and natural gas, takes its shape from the nation's proximity to several seas. Shipbuilding, fishing, and forestry are also important activities. Norway is a leading producer of hydroelectricity. Combined with some government control of the economy, these lucrative activities have given the nation a high standard of living and fairly low unemployment. Most of Norway is a high plateau covered with mountains. The Gulf Stream gives the nation a much milder climate than other places at the same latitude.

History and Politics. Parts of present-day Norway were inhabited by about 9000 B.C. Germanic tribes began immigrating to the area about 2000 B.C. Between A.D. 800 and 1100, Viking ships from Norway raided coastal towns throughout Western Europe and also colonized Greenland and Iceland. Unified around 900, Norway was subsequently shaken by civil war, plague, and the end of its royal line. It entered a union with Denmark in 1380, becoming a Danish province in 1536. Around the end of the Napoleonic Wars, in 1814, Norway became part of Sweden. A long struggle against Swedish rule ended in 1905 as Sweden recognized Norwegian independence, and a Danish prince was made king. Norway was neutral in World War I but endured German occupation during World War II. In 1967 the government initiated a wide-ranging social-welfare system. Norway retains relations with Western nations and the Soviet Union, but does not allow foreign military bases or nuclear arms on its soil. ∎

OMAN

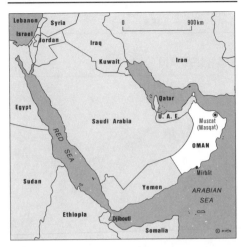

Official name Sultanate of Oman
PEOPLE
Population 1,366,000. **Density** 17/mi² (6.4/km²). **Urban** 11%. **Capital** Muscat, 50,000. **Ethnic groups** Arab, Baluchi, Zanzibari, Indian. **Languages** Arabic, English, Baluchi, Urdu, Indian dialects. **Religions** Ibadite Muslim 75%, Sunni Muslim, Shiite Muslim, Hindu. **Life expectancy** 60 female, 57 male. **Literacy** 20%.

POLITICS
Government Monarchy. **Parties** None. **Suffrage** None. **Memberships** AL, UN. **Subdivisions** 10 provinces.

ECONOMY
GDP $10,019,000,000 **Per capita** $9,775. **Monetary unit** Rial. **Trade partners** Exports: United Arab Emirates, U.K. Imports: United Arab Emirates, Japan, U.K.. **Exports** Motor vehicles, fish and other food, machinery, manufactures, aircraft parts. **Imports** Machinery, manufactures, transportation equipment, food.

LAND
Description Southwestern Asia. **Area** 82,030 mi² (212,457 km²). **Highest point** Mt. Sham, 9,957 ft (3,035 m). **Lowest point** Sea level.

People. Most of Oman's population is Arab, Arabic speaking, and belongs to the Ibadite sect of Islam. Other forms of Islam are also practiced. There is a significant foreign community that includes Indians, Pakistanis, and East African blacks. Many of them are guest workers in the oil industry.

Economy and the Land. Once a mainstay of Oman's economy, oil revenues declined as prices fell throughout the 1980s. The mining of natural gas and copper is being developed, as are agriculture and fishing. A central position in the politically volatile Persian Gulf and revolutionary internal strife have led Oman to devote a considerable portion of its budget to defense. Land regions include a coastal plain and interior mountains and desert. Oman's land borders are undefined and in dispute. A desert climate prevails over most areas except the coast, which has humid conditions.

History and Politics. Islam came to Muscat and Oman, as the nation was known before 1970, in the seventh century A.D. The Portuguese gained control of parts of the coast in 1508 but were driven out in 1650 by the Arabs. At about this time the hereditary sultanate—which absorbed the political power formerly held by the Ibadite religious leaders, or imams—was founded. Close relations with Britain, cemented in a 1798 agreement and subsequent treaties, have continued to the present. Conflicts between the sultan and Omanis, who wanted to be ruled exclusively by their imam, erupted intermittently after 1900, and in 1959 the sultan defeated the rebels with British help and outlawed the office of imam. Marxist insurgency was put down in 1975. Sultan Qaboos bin Said, who overthrew his father's regime in 1970, has liberalized some policies and worked to modernize the nation. Oman is still somewhat isolated and discourages foreign contacts. ∎

ORKNEY ISLANDS
See UNITED KINGDOM.

PACIFIC ISLANDS, TRUST TERRITORY OF THE
See UNITED STATES.

PAKISTAN

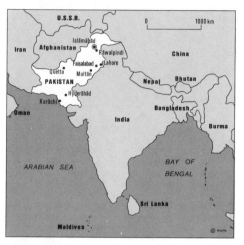

Official name Islamic Republic of Pakistan
PEOPLE
Population 114,380,000. **Density** 337/mi² (130/km²).
Urban 32%. **Capital** Islāmābād, 204,364. **Ethnic groups** Punjabi, Sindhi, Pathan, Baluchi. **Languages** English, Urdu, Punjabi, Pashto, Sindhi, Saraiki.
Religions Sunni Muslim 77%, Shiite Muslim 20%, Christian 1%, Hindu 1%. **Life expectancy** 59 female, 59 male. **Literacy** 26%.
POLITICS
Government Islamic republic. **Parties** Muslim League, People's, others. **Suffrage** Universal, over 21.
Memberships CW, UN. **Subdivisions** 4 provinces, 1 tribal area, 1 capital territory.
ECONOMY
GDP $33,136,000,000 **Per capita** $327. **Monetary unit** Rupee. **Trade partners** Exports: U.S., Japan, Saudi Arabia. Imports: Japan, U.S., Germany. **Exports** Cotton fabric and other textiles, rice and other food, raw cotton, clothing. **Imports** Machinery, manufactures, chemicals, petroleum, food, transportation equipment.
LAND
Description Southern Asia. **Area** 339,732 mi² (879,902 km²). **Highest point** K2, 28,250 ft (8,611 m). **Lowest point** Sea level.
The above information includes part of Jammu and Kashmir.

People. Pakistan's varied ethnicity is the product of centuries of incursions by different races. Today each people is concentrated in a different region and speaks its own language; English and Urdu, official languages, are not widely spoken. The Punjabis compose the largest ethnic group and traditionally have been influential in government and commerce. Virtually all of Pakistan, which was created as a Muslim homeland, follows Islam. Spurred by poor living conditions and a lack of jobs, many Pakistanis work abroad.

Economy and the Land. Despite recent progress in manufacturing, agriculture remains the economic mainstay. Improvement in farming techniques has increased productivity. Government planning and foreign assistance have aided all sectors, but Pakistan remains troubled by population growth, unskilled labor, a trade deficit, and an influx of refugees fleeing the war in Afghanistan. Pakistan's terrain includes mountains, fertile plains, and desert. The climate is continental, with extremes in temperature.

History and Politics. Around 2500 B.C., the Indus Valley civilization flourished in the area of modern Pakistan. Various empires and immigrants followed, including Aryans, Persians, and Greeks. Invading Arabs introduced Islam to the region in the A.D. 700s. In the 1500s, the Mogul Empire of Afghanistan came to include nearly all of present-day Pakistan, India, and Bangladesh, and as that empire declined, various peoples ruled the area. Through wars and treaties, the British presence in Asia expanded, and by the early twentieth century British India included all of modern Pakistan. Because of hostili-ties between British India's Muslims and Hindus, the separate Muslim nation of Pakistan was created when British India gained independence in 1947. With its boundaries drawn around the Muslim population centers, Pakistan was formed from the northeastern and northwestern parts of India, and its eastern region was separated from the west by more than 1,000 miles (1,600 km). East Pakistanis felt that power was unfairly concentrated in the west, and in 1971 a civil war erupted. Aided by India, East Pakistan won the war and became the independent nation of Bangladesh. After the death of President Mohammed Zia in 1988, the people elected Benazir Bhutto, who has revived the People's party of her father, a previous president. In 1990 she was ousted, amidst charges of governmental corruption. ∎

PALAU See UNITED STATES.

PANAMA

Official name Republic of Panama
PEOPLE
Population 2,445,000. **Density** 84/mi² (32/km²). **Urban** 55%. **Capital** Panamá, 411,549. **Ethnic groups** Mestizo 70%, West Indian 14%, white 10%, Amerindian 6%. **Languages** Spanish, English, indigenous. **Religions** Roman Catholic 93%, Protestant 6%. **Life expectancy** 75 female, 71 male. **Literacy** 87%.
POLITICS
Government Republic. **Parties** Christian Democrat, Nationalist Republican Liberal Movement, Authentic Liberal, others. **Suffrage** Universal, over 18.
Memberships OAS, UN. **Subdivisions** 9 provinces, 1 intendency.
ECONOMY
GDP $4,881,000,000 **Per capita** $2,265. **Monetary unit** Balboa. **Trade partners** Exports: U.S., Costa Rica, Germany. Imports: U.S., Japan, Mexico. **Exports** Bananas and other fruit, shrimp, sugar, petroleum, coffee. **Imports** Manufactures, petroleum, machinery, chemicals, food, transportation equipment.
LAND
Description Central America. **Area** 29,157 mi² (75,517 km²). **Highest point** Volcán Barú, 11,401 ft (3,475 m). **Lowest point** Sea level.

People. Most Panamanians are mestizos, a mixture of Spanish and Indian stocks. Indigenous Indians, blacks from the West Indies, and whites form the remaining population. A Spanish legacy is reflected in the official language, Spanish, and the predominance of Roman Catholicism. Most people live near the Panama Canal. A wealthy elite has traditionally directed the government and economy.

Economy and the Land. Because of its location, Panama has been a strategic center for trade and transportation. The 1914 opening of the Panama Canal, connecting the Atlantic and Pacific oceans, accentuated these strengths and has provided additional revenue and jobs; the canal area is now Panama's most economically developed region. Agriculture is an important activity; and oil refining, food processing, fishing, and financial services all contribute to the economy as well. Panama will have to adjust to the economic and technical losses that will accompany the end of United States operation of the canal in 1999. The country has a mountainous interior and a tropical climate.

History and Politics. Originally inhabited by Indians, Panama became a Spanish colony in the early 1500s and served as a vital transportation center. In 1821 it overcame Spanish rule and entered the Republic of Greater Colombia. After Colombia vetoed a United States plan to build a canal across the narrow isthmus, Panama, encouraged by the United States, seceded from the republic and became independent in 1903. Eleven years later, America completed the canal and established control over it and the Panama Canal Zone. Dissatisfaction with this arrangement resulted in several anti-American riots in the fifties and sixties. A 1968 coup placed the Panamanian National Guard in power, and the movement to end American control of the Canal Zone gained momentum. In 1979, the sovereignty of the Canal Zone was transferred to Panama; it will gain control of the canal in 1999. Some representation has been returned to civilians, but the military, under General Manuel Noriega, exercised repressive control until United States military forces invaded and overthrew Noriega in December 1989. ∎

PAPUA NEW GUINEA

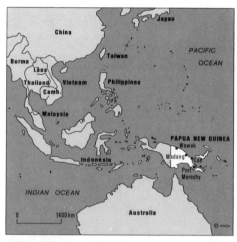

Official name Papua New Guinea
PEOPLE
Population 3,641,000. **Density** 20/mi² (7.9/km²). **Urban** 16%. **Capital** Port Moresby, New Guinea I., 152,100. **Ethnic groups** Melanesian, Papuan, Negrito, Micronesian, Polynesian. **Languages** English, Motu, Pidgin, indigenous. **Religions** Roman Catholic 35%, Lutheran 26%, United Church 13%, Evangelical 9%. **Life expectancy** 57 female, 55 male. **Literacy** 32%.
POLITICS
Government Parliamentary state. **Parties** Pangu, People's Democratic Movement, People's Progress, others. **Suffrage** Universal, over 18. **Memberships** CW, UN. **Subdivisions** 19 provinces, 1 capital district.
ECONOMY
GDP $2,292,000,000 **Per capita** $674. **Monetary unit** Kina. **Trade partners** Exports: Japan, U.K., Australia. Imports: Australia, Japan, U.S.. **Exports** Copper, gold, coffee, copra products, cocoa, palm oil, wood, tea. **Imports** Manufactures, machinery, food, petroleum, transportation equipment, chemicals.
LAND
Description South Pacific islands. **Area** 178,704 mi² (462,840 km²). **Highest point** Mt. Wilhelm, 14,793 ft (4,509 m). **Lowest point** Sea level.

People. Almost all inhabitants are Melanesians belonging to several thousand culturally diverse and geographically isolated communities. More than seven hundred languages are spoken, but most people also speak Motu or a dialect of English. European missionaries brought Christianity, but faiths based on spirit and ancestor worship predominate. The traditions of village life remain strong.

Economy and the Land. The economic supports are agriculture, which employs most of the work force, and copper and gold mining. Papua New Guinea has other mineral resources, as well as potential for forestry. The nation consists of the eastern half of New Guinea Island, plus New Britain, New Ireland, Bougainville, and six hundred smaller islands. Terrain includes mountains, volcanoes, broad valleys, and swamps; the climate is tropical.

History and Politics. Settlers from Southeast Asia are thought to have arrived as long as fifty thousand years ago. Isolated native villages were found by the Spanish and Portuguese in the early 1500s. In 1884 Germany annexed the northeastern part of the island of New Guinea and its offshore islands, and Britain took control of the southeastern section and its islands. Australia assumed administration of the British territory, known as Papua, in 1906 and seized the German regions, or German New Guinea, during World War I. The League of Nations granted Australia a mandate to New Guinea in 1920. After being occupied by Japan in World War II, Papua and New Guinea were united as an Australian territory from 1945 to 1946. Papua New Guinea gained independence in 1975. A separatist movement in Bougainville continues to plague the central government. Papua New Guinea has close ties with Australia and a moderate foreign policy. ∎

PARAGUAY

Official name Republic of Paraguay

PEOPLE
Population 4,338,000. **Density** 28/mi² (11/km²). **Urban** 48%. **Capital** Asunción, 477,100. **Ethnic groups** Mestizo 95%, white and Amerindian 5%. **Languages** Spanish, Guarani. **Religions** Roman Catholic 90%, Mennonite and other Protestant. **Life expectancy** 70 female, 65 male. **Literacy** 88%.

POLITICS
Government Republic. **Parties** Authentic Radical Liberal, Colorado, others. **Suffrage** Universal, over 18. **Memberships** OAS, UN. **Subdivisions** 20 departments.

ECONOMY
GDP $5,808,000,000 **Per capita** $1,798. **Monetary unit** Guarani. **Trade partners** Exports: Brazil, Argentina, Netherlands. Imports: Brazil, Argentina, U.S.. **Exports** Cotton, soybeans, wood, vegetable oil, animal food, chemicals. **Imports** Machinery, manufactures, petroleum, transportation equipment, chemicals.

LAND
Description Central South America, landlocked. **Area** 157,048 mi² (406,752 km²). **Highest point** 2,625 ft (800 m). **Lowest point** Confluence of Paraná and Paraguay rivers, 151 ft (46 m).

People. Paraguay's population displays a homogeneity unusual in South America; most people are a mix of Spanish and Guarani Indian ancestry, are Roman Catholic, and speak both Spanish and Guarani. The small number of unassimilated Guarani live mostly in western Paraguay, known as the Gran Chaco. There are some foreign communities, mostly German, Japanese, and Brazilian. Culture combines Spanish and Indian traditions.

Economy and the Land. Agriculture—based on cotton, soybeans, and cattle—forms the keystone of the economy. Forestry also contributes significantly to Paraguay's exports. The lack of direct access to the sea, unskilled labor, and a history of war and instability have resulted in an underdeveloped economy; manufacturing in particular has suffered. The world's largest hydroelectric project, the Itaipu Dam, was completed in 1988. Paraguay has two distinct regions, divided by the Paraguay River: the semiarid Gran Chaco plains in the west, and the temperate, fertile east, where most farming takes place.

History and Politics. The indigenous Guarani formed an agricultural society centered around what is now Asunción. Portuguese and Spanish explorers arrived in the early 1500s, and the region subsequently gained importance as the center of Spanish holdings in southern South America. During the 1700s, Jesuit missionaries worked to convert thousands of Indians to Roman Catholicism. After gaining independence in 1811, Paraguay was ruled until 1870 by three successive dictators: José Gaspar Rodríguez de Francia, who held power from 1814 to 1840 and sealed Paraguay off from foreign influence; Carlos Antonio López, who reversed this isolationism during his rule from 1841 to 1862; and his son, Francisco Solano López, who led Paraguay into a disastrous war against Uruguay, Argentina, and Brazil that cost the nation half its population. A war against Bolivia from 1932 to 1935 increased Paraguay's territory but further weakened its stability. Alternating weak and repressive regimes followed until 1989, when a military coup ended the thirty-five year regime of General Stroessner. His successor, General Rodriguez, then won a multi-candidate election and promised to turn over the government to an elected civilian in 1993. ∎

PERU

Official name Republic of Peru
PEOPLE
Population 22,610,000. **Density** 46/mi² (18/km²). **Urban** 70%. **Capital** Lima, 371,122. **Ethnic groups** Amerindian 45%, mestizo 37%, white 15%. **Languages** Quechua, Spanish, Aymara. **Religions** Roman Catholic 89%, Protestant 5%. **Life expectancy** 67 female, 63 male. **Literacy** 83%.

POLITICS
Government Republic. **Parties** American Popular Revolutionary Alliance, Popular Action, United Left. **Suffrage** Universal, over 18. **Memberships** OAS, UN. **Subdivisions** 24 departments, 1 constitutional province.

ECONOMY
GDP $14,394,000,000 **Per capita** $737. **Monetary unit** Inti. **Trade partners** Exports: U.S., Japan, Belgium. Imports: U.S., Germany, Japan. **Exports** Petroleum, copper and other metals, mineral ores, coffee and other food. **Imports** Machinery, food, chemicals, manufactures, transportation equipment.

LAND
Description Western South America. **Area** 496,225 mi² (1,285,216 km²). **Highest point** Nevado Huascarán, 22,133 ft (6,746 m). **Lowest point** Sea level.

People. Peru's Indian population constitutes the nation's largest ethnic group and the largest Indian concentration in North or South America. Although whites make up the third largest group after Indians and mestizos, they have historically controlled much of the wealth. The Indians are often geographically and culturally remote from the ruling classes and generally live in poverty. Most Peruvians practice Roman Catholicism, a Spanish inheritance.

Economy and the Land. Considerable natural resources have made Peru a leader in the production of minerals—notably copper, lead, and silver—and in fishing. The food-processing, textile, and oil-refining industries also contribute. Productivity has been slowed by a mountainous terrain that impedes transport and communication, earthquakes and other natural disasters, a largely unskilled work force, and years of stringent military rule. Climate varies from arid and mild in the coastal desert to temperate but cool in the Andean highlands and hot and humid in the eastern jungles and plains.

History and Politics. Several Indian cultures arose in the region between 900 B.C. and A.D. 1200, the last of which was the Incan. Excavation began in 1987 of the richest burial ground of a pre-Hispanic ruler ever discovered, further documenting the sophistication of these cultures. Builders of an empire stretching from Colombia to Chile, the Inca were conquered by the Spanish by 1533. For almost the next three hundred years, Peru was a harshly ruled Spanish colony and center for colonial administration. Peru achieved independence from Spain in 1821, largely through the efforts of José de San Martín of Argentina and Simón Bolívar of Venezuela, although Spain did not formally recognize Peruvian independence until 1879. Military officers ruled the country through the rest of the century. In 1883, Chile and Bolivia defeated Peru in the War of the Pacific, and the country lost its valuable southern nitrate region. A reform party, despite being banned by the government, gained momentum in the 1930s and 1940s. Fernando Belaúnde Terry, a moderate reformer, was elected in 1963. A military junta ousted him in 1968, nationalizing some industries and instituting land reform. Inflation and unemployment caused dissatisfaction and a 1975 coup. Elections in 1980 and 1985 restored democratic leadership. However, economic chaos has since destabilized the government and allowed the growth of the Shining Path, a terrorist guerrilla movement. The new government, elected in June 1990, inherits formidable economic and political problems. A cholera epidemic in 1991 threatened millions. ∎

PHILIPPINES

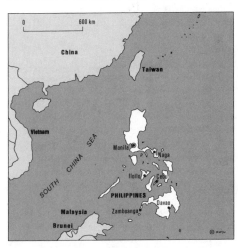

Official name Republic of the Philippines
PEOPLE
Population 62,170,000. **Density** 537/mi² (207/km²). **Urban** 42%. **Capital** Manila, Luzon I., 1,587,000. **Ethnic groups** Christian Malay 92%, Muslim Malay 4%, Chinese 2%. **Languages** English, Pilipino, Tagalog. **Religions** Roman Catholic 83%, Protestant 9%, Muslim 5%, Buddhist and others 3%. **Life expectancy** 67 female, 63 male. **Literacy** 83%.

POLITICS
Government Republic. **Parties** Nationalist, PDP-Laban, Struggle of Philippine Democrats, Union for National Action. **Suffrage** Universal, over 15. **Memberships** ASEAN, UN. **Subdivisions** 73 provinces.

ECONOMY
GDP $32,787,000,000 **Per capita** $595. **Monetary unit** Peso. **Trade partners** Exports: U.S., Japan, Germany. Imports: U.S., Japan, Kuwait. **Exports** Clothing and other manufactures, food, raw materials, machinery, copra oil. **Imports** Petroleum, manufactures, chemicals, machinery, food.

LAND
Description Southeastern Asian islands. **Area** 115,831 mi² (300,000 km²). **Highest point** Mt. Apo, 9,692 ft (2,954 m). **Lowest point** Sea level.

People. Nearly all Filipinos are descended from Malay peoples. The majority are Roman Catholic, a reflection of centuries of Spanish rule. A Muslim minority has begun agitating for autonomy. Although nearly ninety native languages and dialects are spoken, Pilipino and English are the official languages. The wide gap between rich and poor, inherited from a plantation economy, has concentrated wealth in the hands of the landowners.

Economy and the Land. Philippines is a primarily agricultural nation, relying on rice, sugar, coconuts, and wood. Fishing is an important activity. Considerable reserves of copper, nickel, and chromite make mining important. Manufacturing is developing through government incentives. A dependence on imported goods, along with inadequate but growing power and transport systems, has hampered growth. The archipelago of more than seven thousand islands is marked by mountains, volcanoes, forests, and inland plains. The climate is tropical and includes a typhoon season.

History and Politics. The islands are thought to have been settled by Negritos about thirty thousand years ago. Beginning about 3000 B.C., Malay immigrants arrived. By 1565 the area was under Spanish control, and the Roman Catholic church had considerable influence throughout the Spanish period. In the late 1800s, a movement for independence developed but was put down first by the Spanish and then by the United States, which gained the islands in 1898 after defeating Spain in the Spanish-American War. During World War II Japan occupied the Philippines. Independence came in 1946 and was followed by a rebellion by Communists demanding land reform; the rebels were defeated in 1954. Ferdinand Marcos was elected president in 1965 and, in the face of opposition from many quarters, declared martial law in 1972. Marcos lifted martial law in 1981 but was defeated in a 1986 presidential election by Corazon Aquino, wife of assassinated opposition leader Benigno Aquino. Marcos eventually fled the island, and Aquino assumed power. Reforms have been instituted; but coup attempts, leftist insurgency groups, and unresolved social and economic problems still plague the country. ■

PITCAIRN See UNITED KINGDOM.

POLAND

Official name Republic of Poland
PEOPLE
Population 38,010,000. **Density** 315/mi² (122/km²).
Urban 63%. **Capital** Warsaw, 1,651,200. **Ethnic groups** Polish (mixed Slavic and Teutonic) 99%, Ukrainian, Byelorussian. **Languages** Polish. **Religions** Roman Catholic 95%. **Life expectancy** 76 female, 68 male. **Literacy** 99%.
POLITICS
Government Republic. **Parties** Democratic, Polish Peasant, Social Democracy, Solidarity. **Suffrage** Universal, over 18. **Memberships** UN. **Subdivisions** 49 provinces.
ECONOMY
GNP $240,600,000,000 **Per capita** $6,493. **Monetary unit** Zloty. **Trade partners** U.S.S.R., Germany, Czechoslovakia. **Exports** Machinery, manufactures, coal, transportation equipment, crude materials. **Imports** Machinery, manufactures, petroleum, crude materials, food, chemicals.
LAND
Description Eastern Europe. **Area** 120,728 mi² (312,683 km²). **Highest point** Rysy, 8,199 ft (2,499 m). **Lowest point** Raczki Elbląskie, -7 ft (-2 m).

People. Poland's homogeneous population is partially a result of Nazi persecution during World War II, which virtually obliterated the Jewish community and led to the emigration of most minorities. Roman Catholicism, prac-

ticed by almost all Poles, remains a unifying force. The urban population has risen in the postwar period because of government emphasis on industrialization.

Economy and the Land. Government policies since the war have transformed Poland from an agricultural nation into an industrial one. It is a leading producer of coal and has several metal-processing industries. Machinery and textiles are important products. Although most industries are government controlled, the majority of farms are privately owned. Poland's poor soil and short growing season have kept it from achieving agricultural self-sufficiency. Shortages in consumer goods have been chronic since the 1970s, when the failure of Polish goods in world markets compounded debts to the West. Poland has a mostly flat terrain—except for mountains in the south—and a temperate climate.

History and Politics. Slavic tribes inhabited the region of modern Poland several thousand years ago. The Piast dynasty began in the A.D. 900s and established Roman Catholicism as the official religion. In the sixteenth century, the Jagiellonian dynasty guided the empire to its height of expansion. A subsequent series of upheavals and wars weakened Poland, and from the 1770s to the 1790s it was partitioned three times, finally disappearing as an independent state. In 1918, following the Allies' World War I victory, Poland regained its independence and, through the 1919 Treaty of Versailles, much of its former territory. World War II began with Germany's invasion of Poland in 1939. With the end of the war, Poland came under Communist control and Soviet domination. Antigovernment strikes and riots, some spurred by rising food prices, erupted periodically. In the first free election since Communist control, the trade union, Solidarity, won an overwhelming victory in 1989. In 1990, the country elected Lech Walesa as president. ■

PORTUGAL

Official name Portuguese Republic
PEOPLE
Population 10,560,000. **Density** 297/mi² (115/km²).
Urban 33%. **Capital** Lisbon, 807,167. **Ethnic groups** Portuguese (Mediterranean), black. **Languages** Portuguese. **Religions** Roman Catholic 81%, Protestant 1%. **Life expectancy** 78 female, 71 male. **Literacy** 71%.
POLITICS
Government Republic. **Parties** Communist, Social

Democratic, Socialist, others. **Suffrage** Universal, over 18. **Memberships** EC, NATO, OECD, UN. **Subdivisions** 18 districts, 2 autonomous regions.
ECONOMY
GDP $20,687,000,000 **Per capita** $2,055. **Monetary unit** Escudo. **Trade partners** Exports: France, Germany, U.K. Imports: Germany, Spain, France. **Exports** Clothing and other manufactures, machinery, crude materials, chemicals. **Imports** Manufactures, machinery, chemicals, petroleum, food, crude materials.
LAND
Description Southwestern Europe. **Area** 35,516 mi² (91,985 km²). **Highest point** Ponta do Pico, 7,713 ft (2,351 m). **Lowest point** Sea level.

People. Although many foreign invaders have been drawn by Portugal's long coastline, today the population is relatively homogeneous. One group of invaders, the Romans, laid the basis for the chief language, Portuguese, which developed from Latin. The only significant minority is composed of black Africans from former colonies. Most Portuguese are rural and belong to the Roman Catholic church, which has had a strong influence on society.

Economy and the Land. The mainstays of agriculture and fishing were joined in the mid-1900s by manufacturing, chiefly of textiles, clothing, cork products, metals, and machinery. A variety of social and political ills contributing to Portugal's status as one of Europe's poorest nations include: past wars with African colonies, an influx of colonial refugees, and intraparty violence. Tourism is increasingly important, but agriculture has suffered from outdated techniques and a rural-to-urban population shift. The terrain is mostly plains and lowlands, with some mountains; the climate is mild and sunny.

History and Politics. Inhabited by an Iberian people about five thousand years ago, the area was later visited by Phoenicians, Celts, and Greeks before falling to the Romans around the first century B.C. The Romans were followed by Germanic Visigoths and in A.D. 711 by North African Muslims, who greatly influenced Portuguese art and architecture. Spain absorbed Portugal in 1094, and Portugal declared its independence in 1143. About one hundred years later, the last of the Muslims were expelled. Portugal's golden age—during which its navigators explored the globe and founded colonies in South America, Africa, and the Far East—lasted from 1385 to the late 1500s. Rival European powers soon began to seize Portuguese holdings. In 1580, Spain invaded Portugal, ruling until 1640, when the Spanish were driven out and independence reestablished. After the 1822 loss of Brazil, Portugal's most valuable colony, and decades of opposition, a weakened monarchy was overthrown in 1910. The hardships of World War I battered the newly-established republic, and in 1926 its parliamentary democracy fell to a military coup. Antonio Salazar became prime minister in 1932, ruling as a virtual dictator until 1968. Salazar's favored treatment of the rich and his refusal to relinquish Portugal's colonies aggravated the economic situation. A 1974 coup toppled Salazar's successor and set up a military government, events that sparked violence among political parties. Almost all Portuguese colonies gained independence during the next two years. A democratic government was adopted in 1976; varying coalitions have since ruled the nation. Elections in 1987 resulted in the first majority government won by the Social Democrats. ■

Places and Possessions of PORTUGAL

Entity	Status	Area	Population	Capital/Population
Azores (North Atlantic islands)	Autonomous region	868 mi² (2,247 km²)	260,000	Ponta Delgada, 21,187
Macao (Eastern Asia; islands and peninsula on China's southeastern coast)	Chinese territory under Portuguese administration	6.6 mi² (17 km²)	462,000	Macao, 462,000
Madeira Islands (North Atlantic; northwest of Africa)	Autonomous region	307 mi² (794 km²)	277,000	Funchal, 44,111

PUERTO RICO

Official name Commonwealth of Puerto Rico

PEOPLE
Population 3,604,000. **Density** 1,025/mi^2 (396/km^2).
Urban 74%. **Capital** San Juan, 424,600. **Ethnic groups** Puerto Rican (mixed Spanish and black).
Languages Spanish. **Religions** Roman Catholic 85%.
Life expectancy 79 female, 73 male. **Literacy** 88%.

POLITICS
Government Commonwealth (U.S. protection). **Parties** New Progressive, Popular Democratic, others.
Suffrage Universal, over 18. **Memberships** None.
Subdivisions 78 municipalities.

ECONOMY
GDP $21,109,000,000 **Per capita** $6,301. **Monetary unit** U.S. dollar. **Trade partners** Exports: U.S., Virgin Is., Dominican Republic. Imports: U.S., Venezuela, Iran. **Exports** Sugar, coffee, petroleum, chemicals, metal products, textiles. **Imports** Chemicals, clothing, food, fish, petroleum.

LAND
Description Caribbean island. **Area** 3,515 mi^2 (9,104 km^2). **Highest point** Cerro de Punta, 4,389 ft (1,338 m). **Lowest point** Sea level.

People. Puerto Rico's chief language, Spanish, and religion, Roman Catholicism, reflect this American Commonwealth's past under Spanish rule. Most of the population is descended from Spaniards and black African slaves. A rising population has caused housing shortages and unemployment. Many Puerto Ricans live in the United States, mostly in New York City.

Economy and the Land. Once dependent on such plantation crops as sugar and coffee, Puerto Rico is now a manufacturing nation, specializing in food processing and electrical equipment. Commonwealth incentives for foreign investors aided this transformation, also known as Operation Bootstrap, after World War II. Foreign visitors, attracted by the tropical climate, make tourism another important activity. Economic development has been hurt by a lack of natural resources and by fluctuations in the United States economy. The island's terrain is marked by mountains, lowlands, and valleys.

History and Politics. The original inhabitants, the Arawak Indians, were wiped out by Spanish colonists, who first settled the island in 1508. Despite successive attacks by the French, English, and Dutch, Puerto Rico remained under Spanish control until 1898, when the United States took possession after the Spanish-American War. A civil government under a United States governor was set up in 1900; seventeen years later Puerto Ricans were made United States citizens. In 1952 the island became a self-governing Commonwealth. This status was upheld in a referendum in 1967, but fierce, occasionally violent internal debate continues over whether Puerto Rico should be a state, a Commonwealth, or an independent nation. ∎

QATAR

Official name State of Qatar
PEOPLE
Population 514,000. **Density** 116/mi^2 (45/km^2). **Urban**

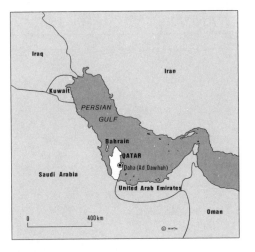

90%. **Capital** Doha, 217,294. **Ethnic groups** Arab 40%, Pakistani 18%, Indian 18%, Iranian 10%. **Languages** Arabic, English. **Religions** Muslim 95%. **Life expectancy** 73 female, 68 male. **Literacy** 34%.

POLITICS
Government Monarchy. **Parties** None. **Suffrage** None. **Memberships** AL, OPEC, UN. **Subdivisions** None.

ECONOMY
GDP $6,532,000,000 **Per capita** $23,329. **Monetary unit** Riyal. **Trade partners** Exports: France, Germany, Italy. Imports: European countries, Japan, Arab countries. **Exports** Petroleum, steel, fertilizer. **Imports** Food, animal and vegetable oils, chemicals, machinery.

LAND
Description Southwestern Asia. **Area** 4,416 mi^2 (11,437 km^2). **Highest point** Aba al Bawl Hill, 344 ft (105 m). **Lowest point** Sea level.

People. Qatar's population is distinguished by a relatively high proportion of Iranians, Pakistanis, and Indians, who began arriving during the oil boom of the 1950s. Most Qataris are Sunni Muslims and live in or near Doha, the capital. In recent years, the government has encouraged the nomadic Bedouins to take up settled lifestyles. Despite a political trend toward a modern welfare state, Qatar retains many elements of a traditional Islamic society.

Economy and the Land. Oil provides the great majority of Qatar's income, while extensive reserves of natural gas await exploitation. The government has made moves toward economic diversification, investing in agriculture and industry; fertilizer and cement are important new products. Most of Qatar is stony desert, and the climate is hot and arid.

History and Politics. No strong central government existed in Qatar before Saudi Muslims gained control in the late eighteenth century. Ottoman Turks occupied the region from 1872 to 1916, when Qatar became a British protectorate. Although oil was discovered in 1940 on the western side of Qatar's peninsula, the outbreak of World War II postponed exploitation for another nine years. Qatar became independent in 1971 after failing to agree on the terms of a union with eight Persian Gulf sheikdoms—today the United Arab Emirates and Bahrain. Oil revenues have been used to improve housing, transportation, and public health. Qatar maintains friendly relations with the West. ∎

REUNION

Official name Department of Reunion

PEOPLE
Population 600,000. **Density** 619/mi^2 (239/km^2). **Urban** 64%. **Capital** St. Denis, 84,400. **Ethnic groups** Reunionese (mixed French, African, Malagasy, Chinese, Pakistani, and Indian). **Languages** French, Creole. **Religions** Roman Catholic 94%. **Life expectancy** 76 female, 68 male. **Literacy** 79%.

POLITICS
Government Overseas department (France). **Parties** Communist, Rally for the Republic, Union for Democracy, others. **Suffrage** Universal, over 18. **Memberships** None. **Subdivisions** 4 arrondissements.

ECONOMY
GDP $1,709,000,000 **Per capita** $3,165. **Monetary unit** French franc. **Trade partners** Exports: France, Portugal. Imports: France, Italy. **Exports** Sugar, rum, fish and shellfish. **Imports** Manufactures, food, machinery, transportation equipment, chemicals.

LAND
Description Indian Ocean island. **Area** 969 mi^2 (2,510 km^2). **Highest point** Piton des Neiges, 10,072 ft (3,070 m). **Lowest point** Sea level.

People. Reunion has a racially mixed population, mainly descended from French settlers, African slaves, and Asian laborers. French is the official language, but most inhabitants speak a creole dialect. The mainly Roman Catholic population is densely concentrated in the lowland areas along the coast. Social stratification is rigid.

Economy and the Land. Reunion's traditional sugar crop continues as its economic mainstay, although commercial fishing and shellfish are also important. Unemployment is a problem, and the island remains dependent upon French aid. Volcanoes, including one active and several extinct, mark the mountainous terrain. The tropical climate is subject to occasional cyclones and trade winds, which bring high rainfall to the south and southeast.

History and Politics. Although known to the Arabs and the Portuguese, Reunion was uninhabited when French settlement began in the 1660s. First called Île Bourbon, the island originally served as a stopover on the French shipping route to India. The French soon developed coffee and sugar plantations, bringing slaves from Africa to work them. British-French rivalry for control of the area led to brief British rule during the early 1800s. The name was changed to Reunion in 1848, and after the abolition of slavery, indentured laborers were brought from Indochina, India, and eastern Africa. Reunion was a French colony until 1946, when it became an overseas department. ∎

ROMANIA

Official name Romania

PEOPLE
Population 23,325,000. **Density** 254/mi^2 (98/km^2).
Urban 50%. **Capital** Bucharest, 1,989,823. **Ethnic groups** Romanian (mixed Latin, Thracian, Slavic, and Celtic) 89%, Hungarian 8%, German 2%. **Languages** Romanian, Hungarian, German. **Religions** Romanian Orthodox 80%, Roman Catholic 6%. **Life expectancy** 74 female, 69 male. **Literacy** 96%.

POLITICS
Government Republic. **Parties** Hungarian Democratic Union, National Liberal, National Salvation Front. **Suffrage** Universal, over 18. **Memberships** UN. **Subdivisions** 40 counties, 1 municipality.

ECONOMY

GNP $123,700,000,000 **Per capita** $5,411. **Monetary unit** Leu. **Trade partners** Exports: U.S.S.R., Italy, Germany. Imports: U.S.S.R., Iran, Egypt. **Exports** Machinery and transportation equipment; fuel, minerals, and metals. **Imports** Fuel, minerals, and metals; machinery and transportation equipment; chemicals.

LAND

Description Eastern Europe. **Area** 91,699 mi² (237,500 km²). **Highest point** Moldoveanu, 8,346 ft (2,544 m). **Lowest point** Sea level.

People. The majority population of Romania belongs to the Romanian Orthodox church and traces its roots to Latin-speaking Romans, Thracians, Slavs, and Celts. Minorities, concentrated in Transylvania and areas north and west of Bucharest, are mainly Roman Catholic Hungarians and Germans. Other minorities include Gypsies, Serbs, Croats, Ukrainians, Greeks, Turks, and Armenians. Almost all inhabitants speak Romanian, although minority groups often speak other languages.

Economy and the Land. When Romania became a Communist country in the 1940s, the government began to turn the country from agriculture to industry. The economy is now based on such major products as iron and steel. Although Romania remains less developed than many other European countries, it has experienced post-war growth in its gross national product. Most agriculture is collectivized, and corn and wheat are major crops. The terrain is marked by a south-to-northeast plateau that curves around several mountain ranges, including the Carpathians, found in the northern and central regions. The climate is continental, with cold, snowy winters and warm summers.

History and Politics. First colonized by the Dacians, a Thracian tribe, around the fourth century B.C., the area became the Roman province of Romania in the second century A.D. Invading Bulgars, Goths, Huns, Magyars, Slavs, and Tartars followed the Romans. Between 1250 and 1350, the independent Romanian principalities of Walachia and Moldavia emerged. In the fifteenth and sixteenth centuries, Ottoman Turks conquered the principalities, and following a Russian-Turkish war, Russians occupied the states. In 1861 Walachia and Moldavia were united as Romania, in 1878 they gained independence, and in 1881 Romania was proclaimed a kingdom. Oppression and a concentration of land and wealth among the aristocracy marked the nation's government, and in 1907 its army quelled a rebellion. In 1919, after a World War I alliance with the Allies, Romania gained Transylvania and other territories. Instability and dissatisfaction, spurred by worldwide economic depression, continued through the 1930s. With the cooperation of Romanian leadership, Germany occupied the country in World War II. In 1944 Soviet troops entered Romania, and the nation subsequently joined the Allies. A Communist government was established in 1945, and in 1947 the king was forced to abdicate and Romania officially became a Communist country. Initially Romania's policies were closely tied to those of the Soviet Union; but renewed nationalism in the sixties led to several independent policy decisions. Nicolae Ceausescu's twenty-four years of harsh, repressive leadership led to a popular revolt and his execution in 1989. An interim government held elections in 1990, which were won by the National Salvation Front (former Communists). Force used in June riots resulted in hundreds of injuries and damaged international relations. ∎

RWANDA

Official name Republic of Rwanda

PEOPLE

Population 7,748,000. **Density** 762/mi² (294/km²). **Urban** 8%. **Capital** Kigali, 181,600. **Ethnic groups** Hutu 89%, Tutsi 10%, Twa. **Languages** French, Kinyarwanda. **Religions** Roman Catholic 52%, Protestant 21%, Animist 9%. **Life expectancy** 52 female, 49 male. **Literacy** 35%.

POLITICS

Government Provisional military government. **Parties** National Revolutionary Movement for Development. **Suffrage** Universal adult. **Memberships** OAU, UN. **Subdivisions** 10 prefectures.

ECONOMY

GDP $1,587,000,000 **Per capita** $295. **Monetary unit** Franc. **Trade partners** Exports: Kenya. Imports: Japan, Belgium, Germany. **Exports** Coffee, tea, tin and other minerals, crude vegetable materials. **Imports** Textiles and other manufactures, petroleum, food, transportation equipment.

LAND

Description Eastern Africa, landlocked. **Area** 10,169 mi² (26,338 km²). **Highest point** Volcan Karisimbi, 14,787 ft (4,507 m). **Lowest point** Along Ruzizi River, 3,117 ft (950 m).

People. Most Rwandans are Hutu, mainly farmers of Bantu stock. Minorities include the Tutsi, a pastoral people that dominated politically until a Hutu rebellion in 1959, and the Twa, Pygmies descended from the original population. Both French and Kinyarwanda are official languages, but most speak Kinyarwanda, a Bantu tongue. Roman Catholicism is the major religion, and minority groups practice indigenous beliefs as well as Protestantism and Islam. A high population density and a high birthrate characterize Rwanda.

Economy and the Land. Agriculture is the major activity, although plagued by the erosion and overpopulation of arable land. Many Rwandans practice subsistence farming, while coffee and tea are major export crops. The production and export of minerals, partly fueled by foreign investment, is also important. Tourism is small but growing; Rwanda is one of the last refuges of the mountain gorilla. The country's landlocked position and underdeveloped transportation system hinder economic growth. The terrain consists mainly of grassy uplands and hills, with volcanic mountains in the west and northwest, while the climate is mild.

History and Politics. The Twa, the region's original inhabitants, were followed by the Hutu. The Tutsi most likely arrived about the fourteenth century, subjugating the weaker Hutu and becoming the region's dominant force. The areas of present-day Rwanda and Burundi became part of German East Africa in the 1890s. In 1919, following World War I, the region was mandated to Belgium as Ruanda-Urundi, and following World War II, Ruanda-Urundi was made a United Nations trust territory under Belgian administration. In 1959 a Hutu revolt against Tutsi domination resulted in the death of many Tutsi and the flight of many more. After gaining independence in 1962, the former territory split into the countries of Rwanda and Burundi. The military overthrew the nation's first president in 1973. Demographic pressures have forced the emigration of a large number of citizens. An attempted coup in October 1990, led by Rwandan

refugees living in Uganda, was countered by government and foreign troops. In November the ruling president announced he would permit a multiparty political system. ∎

ST. HELENA See UNITED KINGDOM.

ST. KITTS AND NEVIS

Official name Federation of St. Kitts and Nevis

PEOPLE

Population 44,000. **Density** 423/mi² (164/km²). **Urban** 49%. **Capital** Basseterre, St. Christopher I., 14,725. **Ethnic groups** Black 94%, mixed 3%, white 1%. **Languages** English. **Religions** Anglican 33%, Methodist 29%, Moravian 9%, Roman Catholic 7%. **Life expectancy** 70 female, 66 male. **Literacy** 98%.

POLITICS

Government Parliamentary state. **Parties** Labor, People's Action Movement, Nevis Reformation. **Suffrage** Universal, over 18. **Memberships** CW, OAS, UN. **Subdivisions** 14 parishes.

ECONOMY

GDP $65,000,000 **Per capita** $1,444. **Monetary unit** East Caribbean dollar. **Trade partners** U.S., U.K., Trinidad and Tobago. **Exports** Sugar, clothing and other manufactures, machinery. **Imports** Manufactures, meat and other food, machinery, petroleum, chemicals.

LAND

Description Caribbean islands. **Area** 104 mi² (269 km²). **Highest point** Mt. Liamuiga, 3,792 ft (1,156 m). **Lowest point** Sea level.

People. Most of the inhabitants of the islands of St. Kitts, often called St. Christopher, and Nevis are of black African descent. The primarily rural population is concentrated along the coast. English is spoken throughout the islands, and most people are Protestant, especially Anglican, evidence of former British rule.

Economy and the Land. Agriculture and tourism are the economic mainstays of St. Kitts and Nevis. Sugar cane is a major crop, cultivated mainly on St. Kitts Island, while Nevis Island produces cotton, fruits, and vegetables. Agriculture also provides for sugar processing, the major industrial activity. A tropical climate, beaches, and a scenic mountainous terrain provide an ideal setting for tourism.

History and Politics. The islands were first inhabited by Arawak Indians, who were displaced by the warlike Caribs. In 1493 Christopher Columbus sighted the islands, and in the 1600s British settlement of both islands began, along with French settlement on St. Christopher. Sugar plantations were soon established, and slaves were imported from Africa. Britain's control of the islands was recognized by the 1783 Treaty of Paris, and for a time St. Kitts, Nevis, and Anguilla were ruled as a single colony. Anguilla became a separate dependency of Britain in 1980, and St. Kitts and Nevis gained independence in 1983. ∎

ST. LUCIA

Official name St. Lucia

PEOPLE

Population 152,000. **Density** 639/mi² (247/km²). **Urban** 46%. **Capital** Castries, 53,933. **Ethnic groups** Black

87%, mixed 9%, East Indian 3%. **Languages** English, French. **Religions** Roman Catholic 86%, Seventh Day Adventist 4%, Anglican 3%. **Life expectancy** 75 female, 68 male. **Literacy** 67%.

POLITICS

Government Parliamentary state. **Parties** Labor, United Workers'. **Suffrage** Universal, over 18. **Memberships** CW, OAS, UN. **Subdivisions** 11 quarters.

ECONOMY

GDP $151,000,000 **Per capita** $1,258. **Monetary unit** East Caribbean dollar. **Trade partners** Exports: U.K., Jamaica, U.S. Imports: U.S., U.K., Trinidad and Tobago. **Exports** Bananas, cocoa, vegetables, fruit, coconut oil, clothing. **Imports** Manufactures, machinery and transportation equipment, food, fuel.

LAND

Description Caribbean island. **Area** 238 mi² (616 km²). **Highest point** Mt. Gimie, 3,117 ft (950 m). **Lowest point** Sea level.

People. St. Lucia's population is composed mainly of descendants of black African slaves, and minority groups include people of African-European descent, whites, and East Indians. During the colonial period, the island frequently shifted from British to French control, and its culture reflects both British and French elements. Although English is widely spoken, many St. Lucians speak a French dialect. Roman Catholicism is the main religion, and the Protestant minority includes Anglicans.

Economy and the Land. Agriculture remains important, and principal crops include bananas and cocoa. Tax incentives and relative political stability have caused an increase in industrial development and foreign investment, mainly from the United States. Tourism is becoming increasingly important, with visitors drawn by the tropical climate, scenic mountainous terrain, and beaches.

History and Politics. Arawak Indians arrived between the A.D. 200s and 400s, and were conquered by the Caribs between the ninth and eleventh centuries. Dutch, French, and British rivalry for control began in the seventeenth century, but the Europeans were unable to subdue the Caribs. The first successful settlement was established by the French in 1651. After many years of alternating French and British control, St. Lucia came under British rule through the 1814 Treaty of Paris. The island gained full independence in 1979. ∎

ST. PIERRE AND MIQUELON
See FRANCE.

ST. VINCENT AND THE GRENADINES

Official name St. Vincent and the Grenadines

PEOPLE

Population 115,000. **Density** 767/mi² (296/km²). **Urban** 21%. **Capital** Kingstown, St. Vincent I., 19,028. **Ethnic groups** Black 82%, mixed 14%, East Indian 2%, white 1%. **Languages** English, French. **Religions** Anglican 42%, Methodist 21%, Roman Catholic 12%, Baptist

6%. **Life expectancy** 72 female, 68 male. **Literacy** 96%.

POLITICS

Government Parliamentary state. **Parties** Labor, New Democratic. **Suffrage** Universal, over 18. **Memberships** CW, OAS, UN. **Subdivisions** 5 parishes.

ECONOMY

GDP $102,000,000 **Per capita** $729. **Monetary unit** East Caribbean dollar. **Trade partners** Exports: U.K., Trinidad and Tobago. Imports: U.S., U.K., Trinidad and Tobago. **Exports** Bananas, root crops, copra. **Imports** Food, machinery, chemicals, fuel.

LAND

Description Caribbean islands. **Area** 150 mi² (388 km²). **Highest point** Soufrière, 4,048 ft (1,234 m). **Lowest point** Sea level.

People. The people of St. Vincent are mainly descended from black African slaves. The colonial influences of Britain and France are evident in the languages and religions. English is the official language, though a French patois is also spoken. Most people are Anglican, Methodist, or Roman Catholic.

Economy and the Land. St. Vincent's economy is based on agriculture, especially banana production. Tourism also plays a role, both on the main island of St. Vincent and in the Grenadines. St. Vincent is the largest island, and about one hundred smaller islands make up the Grenadines. The terrain is mountainous, with coastlines marked by sandy beaches, and the climate is tropical.

History and Politics. The indigenous Arawak Indians were conquered by the Caribs about 1300. Christopher Columbus probably reached the area in 1498. Although the Caribs fought the Europeans, the British began settling St. Vincent in the 1760s. A period of French control began in 1779, and the islands were returned to the British in 1783. St. Vincent and the Grenadines remained under British rule until they gained independence in 1979. ∎

SAN MARINO

Official name Republic of San Marino

PEOPLE

Population 24,000. **Density** 1,000/mi² (393/km²). **Urban** 74%. **Capital** San Marino, 2,777. **Ethnic groups** Sanmarinese (mixed Latin, Adriatic, and Teutonic), Italian. **Languages** Italian. **Religions** Roman Catholic. **Life expectancy** 79 female, 73 male. **Literacy** 96%.

POLITICS

Government Republic. **Parties** Christian Democratic, Communist, Socialist, Socialist Unity. **Suffrage** Universal, over 18. **Memberships** None. **Subdivisions** 9 municipalities. **Monetary unit** Italian lira. **Trade partners** Italy. **Exports** Building materials, wood, chestnuts, wheat, wine, hides, ceramics. **Imports** Consumer goods.

LAND

Description Southern Europe, landlocked. **Area** 24 mi² (61 km²). **Highest point** Monte Titano, 2,425 ft (739 m). **Lowest point** 164 ft (50 m).

People. San Marino, completely surrounded by Italy, has strong ethnic ties to the Italians, combining Latin, Adriatic, and Teutonic roots. Italian is the main language, and Roman Catholicism the major religion. Despite San Marino's similarities to Italy, its tradition of independence has given its citizens a strong national identity.

Economy and the Land. Close economic ties between San Marino and Italy have produced a mutually beneficial customs union: Italians have no customs restrictions at San Marino's borders, and San Marino receives annual budget subsidiary payments from Italy. Most San Marinese are employed in agriculture; livestock raising is a main activity, and crops include wheat and grapes. Tourism and the sale of postage stamps are major economic contributors, as is industry, which produces construction materials for export. Located in the Apennine Mountains, San Marino has a rugged terrain and a generally moderate climate.

History and Politics. San Marino is considered the world's oldest republic. Tradition has it that Marinus, a Christian stonecutter seeking religious freedom in a time of repressive Roman rule, founded the state in the fourth century A.D. Partly because of the protection afforded by its mountainous terrain, San Marino has been able to maintain continuous independence despite attempted invasions. In the 1300s the country became a republic, and the pope recognized its independent status in 1631. San Marino signed its first treaty of friendship with Italy in 1862. In its foreign relations, the country maintains a distinct identity and status. ∎

SAO TOME AND PRINCIPE

Official name Democratic Republic of Sao Tome and Principe

PEOPLE

Population 127,000. **Density** 341/mi² (132/km²). **Urban** 42%. **Capital** São Tomé, São Tomé I., 17,380. **Ethnic groups** Black, mixed black and Portuguese, Portuguese. **Languages** Portuguese, Fang. **Religions** Roman Catholic, African Protestant, Seventh Day Adventist. **Life expectancy** 67 female, 64 male. **Literacy** 57%.

POLITICS

Government Republic. **Parties** Democratic Convergence-Reflection Group, Movement for the Liberation. **Suffrage** Universal, over 18. **Memberships** OAU, UN. **Subdivisions** 7 districts.

ECONOMY

GDP $37,700,000 **Per capita** $428. **Monetary unit** Dobra. **Trade partners** Exports: Germany,

Netherlands, China. Imports: Portugal, Germany, Angola, China. **Exports** Cocoa, copra, coffee, palm oil. **Imports** Machinery and electrical equipment, food, fuel.

LAND

Description Western African islands. **Area** 372 mi² (964 km²). **Highest point** Pico de São Tomé, 6,640 ft (2,024 m). **Lowest point** Sea level.

People. Descendants of African slaves and people of Portuguese-African heritage compose most of Sao Tome and Principe's population. Colonial rule by Portugal is evidenced by the predominance of the Portuguese language and Roman Catholicism. The majority of the population lives on São Tomé.

Economy and the Land. Cocoa dominates Sao Tome and Principe's economy. Copra and palm-oil production are also important, and fishing plays an economic role as well. Through the development of vegetable crops, the government hopes to diversify agricultural output, as much food must now be imported. Part of an extinct volcanic mountain range, Sao Tome and Principe have a mostly mountainous terrain. The climate is tropical.

History and Politics. When Portuguese explorers arrived in the 1400s, Sao Tome and Principe were uninhabited. Early settlers included Portuguese convicts and exiles. Cultivation of the land and importation of slaves led to a thriving sugar economy by the mid-1500s. In the 1800s, following slave revolts and the decline of sugar production, coffee and cocoa became the islands' mainstays, and soon large Portuguese plantations called *rocas* were established. Slavery was abolished by Portugal in 1876, but an international controversy arose in the early 1900s when it was found that Angolan contract workers were being treated as virtual slaves. Decades of unrest led to the 1953 Batepa Massacre, in which Portuguese rulers killed several hundred rioting African workers. A movement for independence began in the late 1950s, and following a 1974 change of government in Portugal, Sao Tome and Principe became independent in 1975. The country has established ties with other former Portuguese colonies in northern Africa since gaining independence. In March 1990, the first presidential elections were held. ∎

SAUDI ARABIA

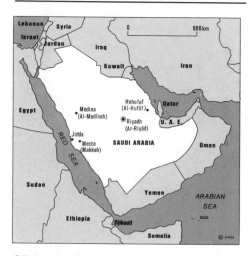

Official name Kingdom of Saudi Arabia
PEOPLE
Population 15,285,000. **Density** 18/mi² (7.1/km²). **Urban** 77%. **Capital** Riyadh, 1,250,000. **Ethnic groups** Arab 90%, Afro-Asian 10%. **Languages** Arabic. **Religions** Muslim 100%. **Life expectancy** 68 female, 64 male. **Literacy** 35%.

POLITICS
Government Monarchy. **Parties** None. **Suffrage** None. **Memberships** AL, OPEC, UN. **Subdivisions** 14 emirates.

ECONOMY
GDP $79,152,000,000 **Per capita** $7,215. **Monetary unit** Riyal. **Trade partners** Exports: Japan, U.S., France. Imports: U.S., Japan, U.K.. **Exports** Petroleum, natural gas. **Imports** Manufactures, transportation equipment, food.

LAND

Description Southwestern Asia. **Area** 830,000 mi² (2,149,690 km²). **Highest point** Mt. Sawda, 10,522 ft (3,207 m). **Lowest point** Sea level.

People. Saudi Arabia is inhabited primarily by Arab Muslims descended from Semitic peoples who settled in the region several thousand years ago. The petroleum industry has attracted a sizable minority of Arabs from other nations, Europeans, and non-Arab Muslims from Africa and Asia. The country's official language is Arabic, although English is used among educated Saudis in business and international affairs. Islam dominates Saudi life, and nearly all the people belong to the religion's Sunni branch. Various forms of Christianity and traditional religions are practiced among foreign workers and indigenous minority groups. Most live in urban areas, but some Bedouin tribes preserve their nomadic way of life.

Economy and the Land. The economy of Saudi Arabia has been shaped by its vast deserts and huge petroleum and natural gas reserves. The hot, mostly arid climate has prevented agricultural abundance and stability: the country must import nearly all its food. Oil was discovered in the 1930s, but the country did not begin rapid economic development until the reserves were aggressively exploited following World War II. Saudi Arabia is one of the world's leading exporters of petroleum, possessing the largest concentration of known oil reserves in the world. The government is seeking to diversify the economy, improve transportation and communication lines, and build agricultural output. Private enterprise and foreign investment are encouraged. Saudi Arabia is divided into the western highlands bordering the Red Sea, a central plateau, northern deserts, the huge Rub al Khali desert in the south, and the eastern lowlands. Only the coastal regions receive appreciable rainfall, and some inland desert areas may go without rain for several years.

History and Politics. Even though what is now Saudi Arabia established prosperous trade routes thousands of years ago, its history begins with the founding of Islam by Muhammad in the early 600s A.D. By the end of that century, Mecca and Medina were established as political and religious centers of Islam and remain so today. The territory split into numerous states that warred among themselves for over a thousand years. The Ottoman Turks gained control over the coastal region of Hejaz in the early 1500s, while Britain set up protectorates along the southern and eastern coasts of Arabia during the 1800s. The Saud family dynasty, founded in the 1400s, managed to remain a dominant religious and political force. Members of the dynasty fought to establish the supremacy of Islamic law and unite the various clans into one nation. In 1932 Ibn Saud proclaimed the Kingdom of Saudi Arabia and established a Saud monarchy that has continued despite dissension within the royal family. Since the 1960s Saudi Arabia has aggressively sought to upgrade local governments, industry, education, the status of women, and the standard of living, while maintaining Islamic values and traditions. Saudi Arabia is a dominant member of the Organization of Petroleum Exporting Countries (OPEC). Despite disagreements with the West and continuing conflicts with Israel, the country maintains strong diplomatic and economic ties with Western nations. When Iraq invaded Kuwait in August 1990, Saudi Arabia called upon United States troops to prevent incursion into its territory. ∎

SENEGAL

Official name Republic of Senegal
PEOPLE
Population 7,257,000. **Density** 96/mi² (37/km²). **Urban** 38%. **Capital** Dakar, 1,447,642. **Ethnic groups** Wolof 41%, Serer 15%, Fulani 12%, Tukulor 11%, Diola 5%, Malinke 6%. **Languages** French, Wolof, indigenous. **Religions** Muslim 92%, Animist and other Christian 2%. **Life expectancy** 50 female, 46 male. **Literacy** 47%.

POLITICS
Government Republic. **Parties** Democratic, Socialist, others. **Suffrage** Universal, over 21. **Memberships** OAU, UN. **Subdivisions** 10 regions.

ECONOMY
GDP $2,642,000,000 **Per capita** $397. **Monetary unit** CFA franc. **Trade partners** Exports: France, U.K., Ivory Coast. Imports: France, Nigeria. **Exports** Manufactures, fish, peanuts, petroleum products, phosphates. **Imports** Manufactures, food, petroleum, machinery.

LAND

Description Western Africa. **Area** 75,951 mi² (196,712 km²). **Highest point** 1,906 ft (581 m). **Lowest point** Sea level.

People. Most Senegalese are black Africans from many ethnic groups, each with its own customs and language. The country has many immigrants from other African nations. While French is the official language, Wolof is widely spoken. Islam is the major religion, followed by Animist and Christian beliefs. Senegal is mainly a rural nation of subsistence farmers.

Economy and the Land. The mainstays of the economy are petroleum, agriculture, fishing, and mining. Tourism is a rapidly growing new industry. Petroleum, chemicals, phosphates, and fish products rank as Senegal's primary exports. Agricultural output is often hurt by irregular weather patterns, and the country must import nearly all its energy. Senegal has one of the finest transportation systems in Africa. Small plateaus, low massifs, marshy swamps, and a sandy coast highlight the terrain, which is mainly flat. The climate is marked by dry and rainy seasons, with differing precipitation patterns in the south and the more arid north.

History and Politics. The area that is now Senegal has been inhabited by black Africans since prehistoric times. When Europeans first established trade ties with the Senegalese in the mid-1400s, the country had been divided into several independent kingdoms. By the early 1800s, France had gained control of the region and in 1895 made Senegal part of French West Africa. In 1959 Senegal joined with French Sudan, or present-day Mali, to form the Federation of Mali, which became independent in 1960. However, Senegal withdrew from the federation later in the year to found the independent Republic of Senegal. The new parliamentary government was plagued by coup attempts and an economy crippled by the severe droughts of the late 1960s and early 1970s. Senegal maintains close ties to France and follows a pro-Western foreign policy.

SEYCHELLES

Official name Republic of Seychelles
PEOPLE
Population 68,000. **Density** 389/mi² (150/km²). **Urban** 59%. **Capital** Victoria, Mahé I., 23,000. **Ethnic groups** Seychellois (mixed Asian, African, and European). **Languages** English, French, Creole. **Religions** Roman Catholic 90%, Anglican 8%. **Life expectancy** 74 female, 65 male. **Literacy** 58%.

POLITICS
Government Republic. **Parties** People's Progressive Front. **Suffrage** Universal, over 17. **Memberships** CW, OAU, UN. **Subdivisions** 21 districts.

ECONOMY
GDP $152,000,000 **Per capita** $2,338. **Monetary unit** Rupee. **Trade partners** Exports: Pakistan, Japan, U.K., U.S. Imports: U.K., Italy, South African countries. **Exports** Petroleum products, fish, copra. **Imports** Petroleum, manufactures, machinery, food, transportation equipment.

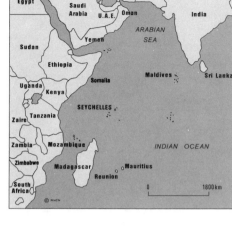

LAND
Description Indian Ocean islands. **Area** 175 mi² (453 km²). **Highest point** Morne Seychellois, 2,969 ft (905 m). **Lowest point** Sea level.

People. The majority of Seychellois are of mixed African, European, and Asian ancestry. The islands' culture combines French and African elements, and although the official languages of French and English are widely spoken, most also speak a creole dialect of French. Many of the more than one hundred islands are coral atolls, unable to support human life. The population is concentrated on Mahé, the largest island, while the remainder live mainly on Praslin and La Digue islands.

Economy and the Land. The basis of the economy is tourism, with foreign visitors attracted by the tropical climate, white-sand beaches, and exotic flora and wildlife found on the granite islands. Mountainous granite islands, which contain fertile soils for growing cinnamon and coconuts, and flat coral islands comprise Seychelles.

History and Politics. The Portuguese reached the uninhabited islands in the early 1500s. For more than two hundred years, the islands served as little more than pirates' havens. France claimed them in 1756; by the 1770s white planters and African slaves had begun to settle Mahé. After a French-English war, France ceded the islands to Britain in 1814. Seychelles achieved independence in 1976. ∎

SHETLAND ISLANDS
See UNITED KINGDOM.

SIERRA LEONE

Official name Republic of Sierra Leone
PEOPLE
Population 4,222,000. **Density** 151/mi² (58/km²). **Urban** 32%. **Capital** Freetown, 469,776. **Ethnic groups** Temne 30%, Mende 30%, Creole 2%, other African. **Languages** English, Krio, indigenous.

Religions Muslim 30%, Animist 30%, Christian 10%. **Life expectancy** 45 female, 41 male. **Literacy** 15%.
POLITICS
Government Republic. **Parties** All People's Congress. **Suffrage** Universal, over 21. **Memberships** CW, OAU, UN. **Subdivisions** 3 provinces, 1 area.
ECONOMY
GDP $1,627,000,000 **Per capita** $438. **Monetary unit** Leone. **Trade partners** Exports: Belgium, Netherlands, U.K. Imports: U.K., U.S., Germany. **Exports** Bauxite ad other minerals, cocoa, diamonds, coffee. **Imports** Machinery, food, petroleum, manufactures.
LAND
Description Western Africa. **Area** 27,925 mi² (72,325 km²). **Highest point** Bintimani, 6,381 ft (1,945 m). **Lowest point** Sea level.

People. The population of Sierra Leone is divided into nearly twenty main ethnic groups. The two major groups are the Temne in the north and west and the Mende in the south. Descendants of freed American slaves, who settled in Freetown on the coast, make up a sizable Creole minority. English is the official language, but most of the people speak local African tongues. The Creoles speak Krio, a dialect of English. Most people practice Islam or various local religions, and a small number are Christian.

Economy and the Land. Sierra Leone is one of the world's largest producers of industrial and commercial diamonds. The nation also mines bauxite and rutile. Poor soil, a fluctuating tropical climate, and traditional farming methods keep crop yields low. Rice, coffee, and cocoa are important crops. To improve agricultural production, the government is clearing some of the coastal mangrove swamplands. The interior of Sierra Leone is marked by a broad coastal plain in the north and by mountains and plateaus that rise along the country's northern and eastern borders. During the wet season Sierra Leone receives heavy rainfall in the Freetown area and significantly less in the north.

History and Politics. When the Portuguese reached the region in 1460, they found the area inhabited by the Temne. The British followed the Portuguese in the 1500s. Europeans took slaves from the area for the New World until Britain abolished the slave trade. In 1787 Englishman Granville Sharp settled nearly four hundred freed black American slaves in what is now Freetown. Britain declared the peninsula a colony in 1808 and a protectorate in 1896. In 1961, Sierra Leone became an independent nation with a constitution and parliamentary form of government. A military takeover in 1967 was short lived, and the constitution was rewritten in 1971 to make the country a republic. Though officially nonaligned, Sierra Leone maintains close ties to Britain and other Western nations. ∎

SINGAPORE

Official name Republic of Singapore
PEOPLE
Population 2,757,000. **Density** 11,207/mi² (4,335/km²). **Urban** 100%. **Capital** Singapore, 2,757,000. **Ethnic groups** Chinese 76%, Malay 15%, Indian 6%. **Languages** Chinese (Mandarin), English, Malay, Tamil. **Religions** Taoist 29%, Buddhist 27%, Muslim 16%,

Christian 10%, Hindu 4%. **Life expectancy** 77 female, 71 male. **Literacy** 83%.
POLITICS
Government Republic. **Parties** Democratic, People's Action, Workers', others. **Suffrage** Universal, over 20. **Memberships** ASEAN, CW, UN. **Subdivisions** None.
ECONOMY
GDP $17,510,000,000 **Per capita** $6,880. **Monetary unit** Dollar. **Trade partners** Exports: U.S., Malaysia, Japan. Imports: Japan, U.S., Malaysia. **Exports** Machinery, petroleum, manufactures, chemicals, rubber. **Imports** Petroleum, machinery, manufactures, food, transportation equipment, chemicals.
LAND
Description Southeastern Asian island. **Area** 246 mi² (636 km²). **Highest point** Timah Hill, 545 ft (166 m). **Lowest point** Sea level.

People. Singapore is one of the most densely populated nations in the world. Most of the population is Chinese. A significant minority is Malay, and the remainder is European or Indian. Singapore's languages include Chinese, English, Malay, and Tamil. The main religions—Taoism, Buddhism, Islam, Christianity, and Hinduism—reflect the cultural diversity of the nation. A mixture of Western and traditional customs and dress characterize Singapore's society. Nearly all the population lives in the city of Singapore on Singapore Island.

Economy and the Land. Singapore is a leading Asian economic power. The city of Singapore is well known as a financial center and major harbor for trade. The nation's factories produce a variety of goods, such as chemicals, electronic equipment, and machinery, and are among the world leaders in petroleum refining. Singapore has few natural resources, however, and little arable land. Most agricultural output is consumed domestically; the country must import much of its raw materials and food. The nation consists of one main island, which is characterized by wet lowlands, and many small offshore islets. Cool sea breezes and a tropical climate make Singapore an attractive spot for tourists.

History and Politics. Present-day Singapore has been inhabited since prehistoric times. From the 1100s to the 1800s, Singapore served mainly as a trading center and refuge for pirates. The British East India Company, the major colonial force in India, realized Singapore's strategic importance to British trade and gained possession of the harbor in 1819. Singapore became a crown colony in 1826. As the port prospered, the island's population grew rapidly. Following World War II, the people of Singapore moved from internal self-government to independence in 1965. The government continues to work in partnership with the business community to further Singapore's growth. In foreign policy, the nation remains nonaligned, but as a small country dependent on trade, Singapore is interested in maintaining wide contacts. ∎

SOLOMON ISLANDS

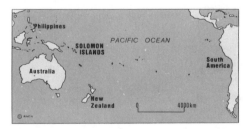

Official name Solomon Islands
PEOPLE
Population 322,000. **Density** 29/mi² (11/km²). **Urban** 11%. **Capital** Honiara, Guadalcanal I., 30,413. **Ethnic groups** Melanesian 93%, Polynesian 4%, Micronesian 2%. **Languages** English, Malay-Polynesian languages. **Religions** Church of Melanesia 34%, Roman Catholic 19%, South Sea Evangelical 17%. **Life expectancy** 61 female, 60 male. **Literacy** 60%.
POLITICS
Government Parliamentary state. **Parties** Nationalist Front for Progress, People's Alliance, United, others. **Suffrage** Universal, over 21. **Memberships** CW, UN. **Subdivisions** 7 provinces, 1 town.
ECONOMY
GDP $152,000,000 **Per capita** $608. **Monetary unit** Dollar. **Trade partners** Exports: Japan, U.K., Netherlands. Imports: Australia, Japan, Singapore. **Exports** Fish, wood, copra, palm oil. **Imports** Machinery, fuel, food.

LAND

Description South Pacific islands. **Area** 10,954 mi² (28,370 km²). **Highest point** Mt. Makarakomburu, 8,028 ft (2,447 m). **Lowest point** Sea level.

People. Over 90 percent of the people are Melanesian, and the remainder are Polynesian, European, Chinese, and Micronesian. English is the official language, but some ninety local languages are also spoken. The dominant religion is Protestantism, and religious minorities include Roman Catholics and followers of local traditions. The population is primarily rural, and much of its social structure is patterned on traditional village life.

Economy and the Land. The economy is based on subsistence farming and exports of fish, wood, copra, and some spices and palm-oil. Food, machinery, gasoline, and manufactured goods must be imported. Terrain ranges from forested mountains to low-lying coral atolls. The climate is warm and moist, with heavy annual rainfall.

History and Politics. Hunter-gatherers lived on the islands as early as 1000 B.C. Because of disease and native resistance, early attempts at colonization failed, and Europeans did not firmly establish themselves until the mid-1800s. Britain declared the islands a protectorate in 1893. The area was the site of fierce battles between the Japanese and Allied forces during World War II, and following the war, moves were made toward independence. In 1978, the Solomon Islands adopted a constitution and became a sovereign nation. ∎

SOMALIA

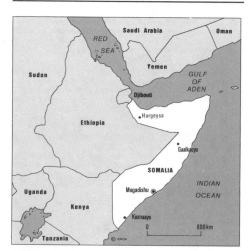

Official name Somali Democratic Republic
PEOPLE
Population 8,499,000. **Density** 35/mi² (13/km²). **Urban** 36%. **Capital** Mogadishu, 600,000. **Ethnic groups** Somali 85%. **Languages** Arabic, Somali, English, Italian. **Religions** Sunni Muslim. **Life expectancy** 49 female, 45 male. **Literacy** 60%.
POLITICS
Government Provisional military government. **Parties** Revolutionary Socialist. **Suffrage** Universal, over 18. **Memberships** AL, OAU, UN. **Subdivisions** 16 regions.
ECONOMY
GDP $2,551,000,000 **Per capita** $563. **Monetary unit** Shilling. **Trade partners** Exports: Saudi Arabia, United Arab Emirates. Imports: U.K., Italy, Germany. **Exports** Livestock, bananas, fish. **Imports** Telecommunications equipment and other machinery, transportation equipment.
LAND
Description Eastern Africa. **Area** 246,201 mi² (637,657 km²). **Highest point** Shimbiris, 7,897 ft (2,407 m). **Lowest point** Sea level.

People. Unlike the population in many African nations, the people of Somalia are remarkably homogeneous in their language, culture, and identity. Most are nomadic or seminomadic herders; only a quarter of the people have settled in permanent communities in southern Somalia. While Arabic and Somali are official languages, English and Italian are also spoken. Nearly all the Somali people are Sunni Muslims.

Economy and the Land. Somalia is a developing country that has not exploited its rich deposits of iron ore and gypsum. There is little manufacturing. The economy is agricultural, though activity is restricted to the vicinity of

the rivers and certain coastal districts. A hot climate with recurring droughts, as well as a lack of railroads and paved highways, hamper economic development. The terrain ranges from central and southern flatlands to northern hills.

History and Politics. In the A.D. 800s or 900s, Arabs converted the ancestors of the Somalis who settled the region to Islam. They fought many religious wars with the Christian kingdom of Ethiopia between the 1300s and 1500s. The British, Italians, and French arrived in the region in the latter half of the 1800s and divided the Somali territory among themselves, with Ethiopia seizing Ogaden in the west. After World War II, Italy was made administrator of its former colony to prepare it for independence. In 1960 British Somaliland and Italian Somalia joined to form an independent republic. Since that time, Somalia has had many border clashes with Kenya and Ethiopia over the rights of Somalis living in these countries to determine their own destiny. Military leaders staged a successful coup in 1969, and subsequently changed the nation's name to Somali Democratic Republic and abolished all political parties. In 1976, however, the Somali Revolutionary Socialist party was formed. Military activity has since resulted in a civil war and the killing of thousands of civilians. Destruction of the rural economy has further aggravated famine conditions. Human rights abuses caused the suspension of United States military aid in 1990. In January 1991, rebel forces overcame the government. The new regime promised elections at an unspecified date. ∎

SOUTH AFRICA

Official name Republic of South Africa
PEOPLE
Population 40,055,000. **Density** 92/mi² (36/km²). **Urban** 59%. **Capital** Pretoria (administrative), 443,059; Cape Town (legislative), 776,617; Bloemfontein (judicial), 104,381. **Ethnic groups** Black 69%, white 18%, mulatto (coloured) 10%, Indian 3%. **Languages** Afrikaans, English, Zulu, Xhosa, other indigenous. **Religions** Black Independent 21%, Dutch Reformed 14%, Roman Catholic 10%. **Life expectancy** 66 female, 60 male. **Literacy** 59%.
POLITICS
Government Republic. **Parties** African National Congress, Conservative, Democratic, National, others. **Suffrage** Coloreds, Indians, and whites, over 18. **Memberships** UN. **Subdivisions** 4 provinces.
ECONOMY
GDP $54,834,000,000 **Per capita** $2,042. **Monetary unit** Rand. **Trade partners** Exports: Germany, Japan, U.K., U.S. Imports: U.S., Germany, Japan, U.K.. **Exports** Gold, food, coal, iron and steel, diamonds, metals, minerals. **Imports** Machinery, manufactures, transportation equipment, chemicals.
LAND
Description Southern Africa. **Area** 433,680 mi² (1,123,226 km²). **Highest point** eNjesuthi, 11,306 ft (3,446 m). **Lowest point** Sea level.
The above information excludes Bophuthatswana, Ciskei, Transkei, and Venda.

People. The government of South Africa classifies the country's population into four groups: black, white, colored, and Asian. Black African groups make up the majority population. The minority whites are either

Afrikaners—of Dutch, German, and French descent— or British. Coloreds, people of mixed white, black, and Asian heritage, and Asians, primarily from India, make up the remaining population. Afrikaans and English are the official languages, although the blacks, coloreds, and Asians speak their own languages as well. The dominant religions are Christian; however, many groups follow traditional practices. The South African government enforces apartheid, a policy of racial segregation widely criticized for violating the rights of blacks, coloreds, and Asians.

Economy and the Land. The discovery of gold and diamonds in South Africa in the late 1800s shaped the nation's prosperous economy. Revenues from mining promoted industry, and today South Africa is one of the richest and most highly developed countries in Africa. Mining remains a mainstay, as does agriculture; the nation is almost self-sufficient in food production. Many effects of apartheid, including discriminatory systems of education and job reservation, have kept the majority population from the benefits of national prosperity. The varied landscape features coastal beaches, plateaus, mountains, and deep valleys. The climate is temperate. The Republic of South Africa includes the enclave of Walvis Bay, situated on Africa's southwest coast.

History and Politics. Southern Africa has been inhabited for many thousands of years. Ancestors of the area's present African population had settled there by the time Portuguese explorers reached the Cape of Good Hope in the late 1400s. The first white settlers, ancestors of today's Afrikaners, established colonies in the seventeenth century. Britain gained control of the area in the late eighteenth century, and relations between Afrikaners and the British soon became strained. To escape British rule, many Afrikaners migrated northward to lands occupied by black Africans. The discovery of gold and diamonds in the late 1800s brought an influx of Europeans and further strained relations between Afrikaners and the British, with both groups striving for control of valuable mineral deposits. Two wars broke out, and in 1902 the British defeated the Afrikaners, or Boers, and incorporated the Boer territories into the British Empire. The British also subdued black Africans, and in 1910 they formed the white-controlled Union of South Africa. Afrikaner nationalism grew in the early twentieth century and led to the formation of the National party, which gained control in 1924 and again in 1948. The party began the apartheid system of separation of the races in the late forties, and subsequent decades saw increasing apartheid legislation and racial tension. In 1951 South Africa embarked on a program to create a white majority by setting up "independent" black republics within its borders. Transkei, the largest of these homelands, became independent in 1976. Transkei was established as a homeland for the Xhosa, Pondo, and Thembu people and is located along South Africa's southeast coast. South of Transkei is Ciskei, also a homeland for the Xhosa. Established in 1981, Ciskei was the last of the homelands to gain independence. Bophuthatswana is an odd political entity consisting of seven separate land blocks. As a home for the Tswana people, Bophuthatswana boasts the healthiest economy of the four independent homelands. Venda is the smallest homeland and was founded in the northeast corner of South Africa. Six other homelands were established but remain under South African administration. During the 1980s, the government began to force blacks to move into the homelands and to thereby renounce their citizenship, sparking international outcry. Foreign and internal pressure has forced the government to respond with reforms and to begin to dismantle apartheid. The future status of the homelands is uncertain, with many people favoring reincorporation into South Africa. ∎

SOUTH GEORGIA
See UNITED KINGDOM.

SOVIET UNION

Official name Union of Soviet Socialist Republics
PEOPLE
Population 283,210,000. **Density** 33/mi² (13/km²). **Urban** 68%. **Capital** Moscow, 8,769,000. **Ethnic groups** Russian 52%, Ukrainian 16%, Uzbek 5%, Byelorussian 4%. **Languages** Russian and other Slavic languages, various ethnic languages. **Religions** Russian Orthodox 18%, Muslim 9%. **Life expectancy** 75 female, 67 male. **Literacy** 100%.

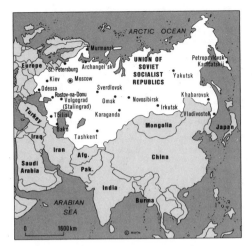

many Eastern European nations. Following Stalin's death in 1953, the Soviet Union experienced a liberalization of policies under Nikita Krushchev. In 1964 Leonid Brezhnev worked to consolidate and strengthen the power of the Secretariat and Politburo of the Communist party. Mikhail S. Gorbachev took office in 1985 and introduced a new era of leadership, reform, and government restructure. Although Gorbachev received a Nobel Peace Prize in 1990, the political and economic upheaval brought about by his policies have threatened his political future. Economic restructuring has failed to improve the lives of the people and chronic shortages are more serious than ever. Rising nationalism has led to violence and growing independence movements throughout the country, threatening both the existence of the union and the Communist party. In August, 1991 an unsuccessful coup against Gorbachev ultimately increased the power of his liberal rival, Boris Yeltsin. Under Yeltsin's direction, the country moved to speed up the reform process while most of the constituent republics asserted their desire for independence within a loose economic and military federation. ∎

SPAIN

Official name Kingdom of Spain
PEOPLE
Population 40,190,000. **Density** 206/mi² (80/km²). **Urban** 78%. **Capital** Madrid, 3,102,846. **Ethnic groups** Spanish (mixed Mediterranean and Teutonic). **Languages** Spanish (Castilian), Catalan, Galician, Basque. **Religions** Roman Catholic 99%. **Life expectancy** 80 female, 74 male. **Literacy** 93%.
POLITICS
Government Constitutional monarchy. **Parties** Convergence and Unity, Popular, Social Democratic Center, Socialist Workers, United Left, others. **Suffrage** Universal, over 18. **Memberships** EC, NATO, OECD, UN. **Subdivisions** 17 autonomous communities.
ECONOMY
GDP $164,254,000,000 **Per capita** $4,265. **Monetary unit** Peseta. **Trade partners** Exports: France, Germany, U.K. Imports: Germany, France, Italy. **Exports** Manufactures, machinery, food, transportation equipment, chemicals, petroleum. **Imports** Machinery, manufactures, petroleum, food, crude materials.
LAND
Description Southwestern Europe. **Area** 194,885 mi² (504,750 km²). **Highest point** Pico de Teide, 12,188 ft (3,715 m). **Lowest point** Sea level.

People. The population of Spain is a mixture of ethnic groups from northern Europe and the area surrounding the Mediterranean Sea. Spanish is the official language;

however, several regional dialects of Spanish are commonly spoken. The Basque minority, one of the oldest surviving ethnic groups in Europe, lives mainly in the Pyrenees in northern Spain, preserving its own language and traditions. Since the 1978 constitution, Spain has not had an official religion, yet nearly all its people are Roman Catholic. Spain has a rich artistic tradition, blending Moorish and Western cultures.

Economy and the Land. Spain has benefitted greatly from an economic-restructuring program that began in the 1950s. The nation has concentrated on developing industry, which now employs over 30 percent of the population. The chemical industry, high technology, electronics, and tourism are important sources of revenue. The agricultural contribution to the economy has declined to about half of peak production. Spain's terrain is mainly composed of a dry plateau area; mountains cover the northern section, and plains extend down the country's eastern coast. The climate in the eastern and southern regions is Mediterranean, while the northwest has more rainfall and less sunshine throughout the year.

History and Politics. Spain is among the oldest inhabited regions in Europe. A Roman province for centuries, Spain was conquered by the Visigoths in the A.D. 500s, only to change hands again in the 700s when the Arab-Berbers, or Moors, seized control of all but a narrow strip of northern Spain. Christian kings reclaimed the country from the eleventh to the fourteenth centuries. Controlled by the three kingdoms of Navarre, Aragon, and Castile, Spain was united in the late 1400s under King Ferdinand and Queen Isabella. At the height of its empire, Spain claimed territory in North and South America, northern Africa, Italy, and the Canary Islands. However, a series of wars burdened Spain financially, and in the 1500s, under King Philip II, the country entered a period of decline. Throughout the 1700s and 1800s, the nation lost most of its colonial possessions through treaty or revolution. In 1936 a bitter civil war erupted between an insurgent fascist group and supporters of the republic. General Francisco Franco, leader of the successful insurgent army, ruled as dictator of Spain from the end of the war until his death in 1975. Spain enjoyed phenomenal economic growth during the 1950s and 1960s; however, that growth declined in the 1970s. Since Franco's death, King Juan Carlos has led the country toward a more democratic form of government. ∎

SRI LANKA

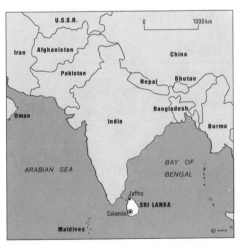

Official name Democratic Socialist Republic of Sri Lanka

POLITICS
Government Socialist republic. **Parties** Communist, others. **Suffrage** Universal, over 18. **Memberships** UN. **Subdivisions** 12 soviet socialist republics.
ECONOMY
GNP $2,062,600,000,000 **Per capita** $7,484. **Monetary unit** Ruble. **Trade partners** Exports: Germany, Czechoslovakia, Poland. Imports: Germany, Czechoslovakia, Bulgaria. **Exports** Petroleum, machinery and transportation equipment, natural gas. **Imports** Machinery, grain, transportation equipment, chemicals, sugar, iron and steel.
LAND
Description Eastern Europe and northern Asia. **Area** 8,533,205 mi² (22,100,900 km²). **Highest point** Communism Pk., 24,590 ft (7,495 m). **Lowest point** Vpadina Karagije (near Caspian Sea), -433 ft (-132 m).

People. The varied population of the Soviet Union is composed of more than one hundred distinct groups. Nearly three-quarters of the people are Eastern Slavs, and more than 70 percent of this group are Russians. The remaining Slavs are Ukrainians, Byelorussians, and Uzbek. The rest of the population belongs to Turkic, Finno-Ugric, Caucasian, other Indo-European groups, and a mixture of peoples, including Inuit. Each group speaks its own language, although Russian is the most widely used. Until recently, religious practice was discouraged by the state, and churches have no legal status—although Russian Orthodox, Islam, Catholicism, Protestantism, Judaism, and other religions are actively practiced.

Economy and the Land. The Soviet Union is one of the world's leading industrial powers. Mining, steel production, and other heavy industries predominate. The economy is controlled by the state, and economic policies are administered through a series of five-year plans, which emphasize industrial and technological growth. The Soviet economy suffers from low productivity, energy shortages, and a lack of skilled labor, problems the government hopes can be eased by greater use of technology and science. The Soviet Union traded primarily with members of the eastern-bloc Council for Mutual Economic Assistance until the late 1980s, when economic reform led to increased trade with the West and the subsequent dissolution of CMEA in 1991. Geographically, the Soviet Union is the largest nation in the world. Its terrain is widely varied and richly endowed with minerals. Though the country contains some of the world's most fertile land, long winters and hot, dry summers keep many crop yields low.

History and Politics. Inhabited as early as the Stone Age, what is now the Soviet Union was much later invaded successively by Scythians, Sarmatians, Goths, Huns, Bulgars, Slavs, and others. By A.D. 989 Byzantine cultural influence had become predominant. Various groups and regions were slowly incorporated into a single state. In 1547 Ivan IV was crowned czar of all Russia, beginning a tradition of czarist rule that lasted until the 1917 Russian Revolution, when the Bolsheviks came to power and named Vladimir Ilyich Lenin as head of the first Soviet government. The Bolsheviks established a Communist state and weathered a bitter civil war. Joseph Stalin succeeded Lenin as head of state in 1924 and initiated a series of political purges that lasted through the 1930s. The Soviet Union became embroiled in World War II, siding with the Allies, losing over twenty million people, and suffering widespread destruction of its cities and countryside. It emerged from the war with extended influence, however, having annexed part of Finland and

Places and Possessions of SPAIN

Entity	Status	Area	Population	Capital/Population
Balearic Islands (Mediterranean Sea)	Province	1,936 mi² (5,014 km²)	723,000	Palma, 242,900
Canary Islands (North Atlantic; northwest of Africa)	Part of Spain	2,808 mi² (7,273 km²)	1,467,000	None
Spanish North Africa (Cities on northern coast of Morocco)	Five possessions	12 mi² (32 km²)	121,000	None

PEOPLE
Population 17,135,000. **Density** 686/mi² (265/km²).
Urban 21%. **Capital** Colombo (de facto), 683,000; Sri
Jayawardenapura (future). **Ethnic groups** Sinhalese
74%, Ceylon Tamil 10%, Ceylon Moor 7%, Indian
Tamil 6%. **Languages** English, Sinhala, Tamil.
Religions Buddhist 69%, Hindu 15%, Muslim 8%,
Christian 7%. **Life expectancy** 74 female, 70 male.
Literacy 86%.

POLITICS
Government Socialist republic. **Parties** Freedom, Tamil
Independents, United National, others. **Suffrage**
Universal, over 18. **Memberships** CW, UN.
Subdivisions 8 provinces.

ECONOMY
GDP $5,808,000,000 **Per capita** $361. **Monetary unit**
Rupee. **Trade partners** Exports: U.S., Germany, U.K.
Imports: Japan, U.S., U.K. **Exports** Tea, clothing,
petroleum, rubber. **Imports** Petroleum, textiles and
other manufactures, machinery, food, chemicals.

LAND
Description Southern Asian island. **Area** 24,962 mi²
(64,652 km²). **Highest point** Pidurutalagala, 8,281 ft
(2,524 m). **Lowest point** Sea level.

People. The two principal groups in Sri Lanka are the
majority Sinhalese and the minority Tamils. Other minorities include the Moors; Burghers, who are descendants
of Dutch, Portuguese, and British colonists; Malays; and
Veddah aborigines. Sinhala, Tamil, and English are official languages. Most Sinhalese are Buddhist, most
Tamils are Hindu, and the majority of the Moors and
Malays are Muslims.

Economy and the Land. Sri Lanka's economy is based
on agriculture, which employs nearly half the people in
producing tea, rubber, and coconuts. Sri Lanka also
hopes to become self-sufficient in rice, thus reducing
imports of this staple. Industrial production has increased, and major exports include rubber and textile
products. The country also sponsors several internal-
development programs. However, continuing high government subsidy and welfare policies threaten economic
growth. A low coastal plain, mountainous and forested
southern interior, and tropical climate characterize Sri
Lanka.

History and Politics. The Sinhalese dynasty was found-
ed by a northern Indian prince in about 500 B.C. Later, the
Tamils from southern India settled in the north of Sri
Lanka. European control began in the 1500s, when the
Portuguese and Dutch ruled the island. It became a Brit-
ish possession in 1796 and the independent nation of
Ceylon in 1948. In 1972 it changed its name to Sri Lanka.
Tensions between the ruling Sinhalese and the minority
Tamils have often erupted in violence. Sri Lanka pursues
a policy of nonalignment in foreign affairs. ■

SUDAN

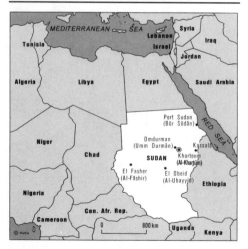

Official name Republic of the Sudan
PEOPLE
Population 25,515,000. **Density** 26/mi² (10/km²).
Urban 22%. **Capital** Khartoum, 476,218. **Ethnic
groups** Black 52%, Arab 39%, Beja 6%. **Languages**
Arabic, indigenous, English. **Religions** Sunni Muslim
70%, indigenous 20%, Christian 5%. **Life expectancy**
53 female, 51 male. **Literacy** 31%.
POLITICS
Government Islamic Republic. **Parties** None. **Suffrage**

None. **Memberships** AL, OAU, UN. **Subdivisions** 6
regions, 1 capital territory.
ECONOMY
GDP $7,678,000,000 **Per capita** $375. **Monetary unit**
Pound. **Trade partners** Exports: Saudi Arabia, China,
Germany. Imports: Saudi Arabia, U.K., U.S. **Exports**
Cotton, grain, livestock, sesame and other oil seeds,
gum arabic, peanuts. **Imports** Petroleum,
manufactures, machinery, pharmaceuticals and other
chemicals.
LAND
Description Eastern Africa. **Area** 967,500 mi²
(2,505,813 km²). **Highest point** Kinyeti, 10,456 ft
(3,187 m). **Lowest point** Sea level.

People. Sudan's population is composed of two distinct
cultures—black African and Arab. African blacks of diverse ethnicity are a majority and are concentrated in the
south, where they practice traditional lifestyles and beliefs and speak indigenous languages. Arabic-speaking
Muslims, belonging to several ethnic groups, live mainly
in northern and central regions.

Economy and the Land. The economy is based on agriculture; and irrigation has made arid Sudan a leading
producer of cotton, although the land is vulnerable to
drought. Forests provide for production of gum arabic,
used in making candy and perfumes, while other crops
include peanuts and sesame seeds. Economic activity is
concentrated near the Nile River and its branches, as
well as near water holes and wells. The mostly flat terrain
is marked by eastern and western mountains; southern
forests and savanna give way to swampland, scrubland,
and northern desert. The climate varies from desert in
the north to tropical in the south.

History and Politics. Egypt mounted repeated invasions
of what is now northern Sudan beginning about 300 B.C.
Sudan remained a collection of small independent states
until 1821, when Egypt conquered and unified the northern portion. Egypt was unable to establish control over
the south, which was often raided by slavers. In 1881 a
Muslim leader began uniting various groups in a revolt
against Egyptian rule, and success came four years later. His successor ruled until 1898, when British and
Egyptian forces reconquered the land. Renamed the An-
glo-Egyptian Sudan, the region was ruled jointly by
Egypt and Britain, with British administration dominating.
Since gaining independence in 1956, a series of military
coups, a continuing civil war, and severe famine have
burdened Sudan with political and economic instability. ■

SURINAME

Official name Republic of Suriname
PEOPLE
Population 412,000. **Density** 6.5/mi² (2.5/km²). **Urban**
48%. **Capital** Paramaribo, 241,000. **Ethnic groups**
East Indian 37%, Creole 31%, Javanese 15%, black
10%, Amerindian 3%, Chinese 2%. **Languages** Dutch,
Sranan Tongo, English, Hindustani, Javanese.
Religions Hindu 27%, Protestant 25%, Roman
Catholic 23%, Muslim 20%. **Life expectancy** 74
female, 68 male. **Literacy** 65%.
POLITICS
Government Republic. **Parties** New Democratic, Front
for Democracy and Development, others. **Suffrage**
Universal, over 18. **Memberships** OAS, UN.
Subdivisions 10 districts.
ECONOMY
GDP $963,000,000 **Per capita** $2,568. **Monetary unit**

Guilder. **Trade partners** Exports: Netherlands, U.S.,
Norway. Imports: U.S., Netherlands, Trinidad and
Tobago. **Exports** Alumina, bauxite, aluminum, rice,
wood. **Imports** Machinery, petroleum, food, cotton,
consumer goods.
LAND
Description Northeastern South America. **Area**
63,251 mi² (163,820 km²). **Highest point** Juliana Mtn.,
4,035 ft (1,230 m). **Lowest point** Sea level.

People. Descendants of East Indians and Creoles—of
mixed European-black African heritage—compose Suriname's two major groups. Black African slaves and contract laborers, imported from the east, resulted in various
ethnic populations. Minority groups include the Javanese; Bush Negroes, a black group; Amerindians, descendants of Arawak and Caribs; Chinese; and Europeans. Dutch is the official language, but most groups have
preserved their distinct language, culture, and religion.

Economy and the Land. The economy is based on mining and metal processing, and bauxite and alumina are
the major exports. Agriculture plays an economic role as
well and, together with fishing and forestry, offers potential for expansion. A narrow coastal swamp, central forests and savanna, and southern jungle-covered hills
mark the country's terrain. The climate is tropical.

History and Politics. Prior to the arrival of Europeans,
present-day Suriname was inhabited by indigenous Indians. Christopher Columbus sighted the coast in 1498,
but the area's lack of gold slowed Spanish and Portuguese exploration. The British established the first settlement in 1651, and in 1665 Jews from Brazil erected the
first synagogue in the Western Hemisphere. In 1667 the
British traded the area to the Netherlands for the Dutch
colony of New Amsterdam—present-day Manhattan,
New York. Subsequent wars and treaties shifted owner-
ship of Suriname among the British, French, and Dutch
until 1815, when the Netherlands regained control. In
1954, Suriname became an autonomous part of the
Netherlands, with status equal to that of the Netherlands
and the Netherlands Antilles. Suriname gained independence in 1975. In 1980, the military seized power and
established a military-civilian government soon after. In
1987 a new coalition and election led to hopes for
greater political stability. However, the military retained
considerable control and in December 1990 overthrew
the elected president in a bloodless coup. ■

SWAZILAND

Official name Kingdom of Swaziland
PEOPLE
Population 791,000. **Density** 118/mi² (46/km²). **Urban**
33%. **Capital** Mbabane (de facto), 38,290; Lobamba
(future). **Ethnic groups** Swazi 95%, European 2%,
Zulu 1%. **Languages** English, siSwati. **Religions**
African Protestant and other Christian 57%, tribal
religionist 43%. **Life expectancy** 60 female, 56 male.
Literacy 64%.
POLITICS
Government Monarchy. **Parties** None. **Suffrage** None.
Memberships CW, OAU, UN. **Subdivisions** 4 districts.
ECONOMY
GDP $571,000,000 **Per capita** $960. **Monetary unit**
Lilangeni. **Trade partners** South Africa, U.K., U.S.
Exports Sugar, asbestos, wood, fruit. **Imports**
Transportation equipment, chemicals, petroleum, food.
LAND
Description Southern Africa, landlocked. **Area**
6,704 mi² (17,364 km²). **Highest point** Emlembe,
6,109 ft (1,862 m). **Lowest point** Along Usutu River,
70 ft (21 m).

People. About 95 percent of the people of Swaziland are black Africans called Swazi, though small minorities of white Europeans and Zulus also live in the country. The two official languages are English and siSwati. Government and official business is conducted primarily in English. More than half the Swazi belong to Christian churches, while others practice traditional African religions.

Economy and the Land. Most Swazi are subsistence farmers. Cattle are highly prized for their own sake but are being used increasingly for milk, meat, and profit. Europeans own nearly half the land in Swaziland and raise most of the cash crops, including fruits, sugar, tobacco, cotton, and wood. About half the nation's income comes from European-owned mining operations, and major exports include asbestos. Swaziland also has deposits of coal, pottery clay, gold, and tin. The country's mountains and forests have brought a growing tourist industry. The climate is temperate.

History and Politics. According to legend, the Swazi originally came from the area near Maputo. British traders and Dutch farmers from South Africa first reached Swaziland in the 1830s; more whites arrived in the 1880s when gold was discovered. Swazi leaders unknowingly granted many concessions to the whites at this time. After the Boer War, Britain assumed administration of Swaziland and ruled until 1967. Swaziland became independent in 1968. The British designed a constitution, but many Swazi thought it disregarded their traditions and interests. In 1973, King Sobhuza abolished this constitution, suspended the legislature, and appointed a commission to produce a new constitution. Sobhuza ruled until his death in 1982, and King Mswati III was installed in 1986. ∎

SWEDEN

Official name Kingdom of Sweden
PEOPLE
Population 8,602,000. **Density** 50/mi² (19/km²). **Urban** 84%. **Capital** Stockholm, 672,187. **Ethnic groups** Swedish (Scandinavian) 92%, Finnish, Lappic. **Languages** Swedish. **Religions** Lutheran (Church of Sweden) 94%, Roman Catholic 2%. **Life expectancy** 81 female, 75 male. **Literacy** 99%.
POLITICS
Government Constitutional monarchy. **Parties** Center, Moderate, Liberal, Social Democratic, others. **Suffrage** Universal, over 18. **Memberships** OECD, UN. **Subdivisions** 24 counties.
ECONOMY
GDP $100,247,000,000 **Per capita** $12,027. **Monetary unit** Krona. **Trade partners** Exports: Germany, U.S., Norway. Imports: Germany, U.K., Finland. **Exports** Paper and other manufactures, machinery, transportation equipment, wood. **Imports** Manufactures, machinery, transportation equipment, crude materials, chemicals.
LAND
Description Northern Europe. **Area** 173,732 mi² (449,964 km²). **Highest point** Kebnekaise, 6,926 ft (2,111 m). **Lowest point** Sea level.

People. The most significant minorities in the largely urban Swedish population are Swedes of Finnish origin and a small number of Lapps. Sweden is also the home of immigrants from other Nordic countries, Yugoslavia, Greece, and Turkey. Swedish is the main language, although Finns and Lapps often speak their own tongues. English is the leading foreign language, especially among students and younger people.

Economy and the Land. Sweden has one of the highest standards of living in the world. Taxes are also high, but the government provides exceptional benefits for most citizens, including free education and medical care, pension payments, four-week vacations, and payments for child care. The nation is industrial and bases its economy on its three most important natural resources—timber, iron ore, and water power. The iron and steel industry produces high-quality steel used in ball bearings, precision tools, agricultural machinery, aircraft, automobiles, and ships. Swedish farmers rely heavily on dairy products and livestock, and most farms are part of Sweden's agricultural-cooperative movement. Sweden's varied terrain includes mountains, forests, plains, and sandy beaches. The climate is temperate, with cold winters in the north. Northern Sweden lies in the "Land of the Midnight Sun" and experiences periods of twenty-four hours of daylight in summer and darkness in winter.

History and Politics. Inhabitants of what is now Sweden began to trade with the Roman Empire about 50 B.C. Sailing expeditions by Swedish Vikings began about A.D. 800. In the fourteenth century the kingdom came under Danish rule, but declared its independence in 1523. The Swedish king offered protection to the followers of Martin Luther, and Lutheranism was soon declared the state religion. By the late 1660s, Sweden had become one of the great powers of Europe; it suffered a military defeat by Russia in 1709, however, and gradually lost most of its European possessions. An 1809 constitution gave most of the executive power of the government to the king. Despite this, the power of the Parliament gradually increased, and parliamentary rule was adopted in 1917. A 1975 constitution reduced the king's role to a ceremonial one. Sweden remained neutral during both world wars. Except for 1976-82, when Sweden was run by a conservative coalition, the country had a Socialist government until February 1990, when it failed to carry Parliament in an economic reform bill. Elections are scheduled for 1991. ∎

SWITZERLAND

Official name Swiss Confederation
PEOPLE
Population 6,737,000. **Density** 423/mi² (163/km²). **Urban** 60%. **Capital** Bern, 134,393. **Ethnic groups** German 65%, French 18%, Italian 10%, Romansch 1%. **Languages** German, French, Italian, Romansch. **Religions** Roman Catholic 48%, Protestant 44%. **Life expectancy** 81 female, 75 male. **Literacy** 99%.
POLITICS
Government Republic. **Parties** Christian Democratic People's, People's, Radical Democratic, Social Democratic, others. **Suffrage** Universal, over 20. **Memberships** OECD. **Subdivisions** 26 cantons.
ECONOMY
GDP $92,776,000,000 **Per capita** $14,306. **Monetary unit** Franc. **Trade partners** Exports: Germany, France, France. Imports: Germany, France, Italy. **Exports** Watches and other manufactures, machinery, chemicals. **Imports** Manufactures, machinery, chemicals, transportation equipment, food.
LAND
Description Central Europe, landlocked. **Area** 15,943 mi² (41,293 km²). **Highest point** Dufourspitze, 15,203 ft (4,634 m). **Lowest point** Lago Maggiore, 633 ft (193 m).

People. About seven hundred years ago, the Swiss began joining together for mutual defense, but preserved their regional differences in language and customs. The country has four official languages—German, French, and Italian—and the fourth, Romansch, is spoken by a minority. Dialects often differ from community to community. The population is concentrated on a central plain located between mountain ranges.

Economy and the Land. The Alps and Jura Mountains cover nearly 70 percent of Switzerland, making much of the land unsuited for agriculture but a good basis for a thriving tourist industry. The central plain contains rich cropland and holds Switzerland's major cities and manufacturing facilities, many specializing in high-quality, precision products. Switzerland is also an international banking and finance center. Straddling the ranges of the central Alps, Switzerland features mountains, hills, and plateaus. The temperate climate varies with altitude.

History and Politics. Helvetic Celts inhabited the area of present-day Switzerland when Julius Caesar conquered the region, annexing it to the Roman Empire. As the Roman Empire declined, northern and western Germanic tribes began a series of invasions, and in the 800s the region became part of the empire of the Frankish king Charlemagne. In 1291 leaders of the three Swiss cantons, or regions, signed an agreement declaring their freedom and promising mutual aid against any foreign ruler. The confederation was the beginning of modern Switzerland. Over the next few centuries Switzerland became a military power, expanding its territories until 1515, when it was defeated by France. Soon after, Switzerland adopted a policy of permanent neutrality. The country was again conquered by France during the French Revolution; however, after Napoleon's final defeat in 1815, the Congress of Vienna guaranteed Switzerland's neutrality, a guarantee that has never been broken. ∎

SYRIA

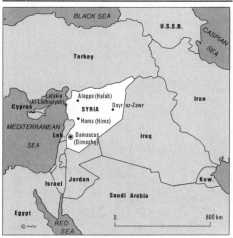

Official name Syrian Arab Republic
PEOPLE
Population 12,315,000. **Density** 172/mi² (67/km²). **Urban** 52%. **Capital** Damascus, 1,326,000. **Ethnic groups** Arab 90%, Kurdish, Armenian, and others 10%. **Languages** Arabic, Kurdish, Armenian, Aramaic, Circassian. **Religions** Sunni Muslim 74%, other Muslim 16%, Christian 10%. **Life expectancy** 69 female, 65 male. **Literacy** 40%.
POLITICS
Government Socialist republic. **Parties** Arab Socialist, Arab Socialist Resurrectionist (Baath), Communist. **Suffrage** Universal, over 18. **Memberships** AL, UN. **Subdivisions** 14 districts.
ECONOMY
GDP $20,267,000,000 **Per capita** $1,933. **Monetary unit** Pound. **Trade partners** Exports: Italy, U.S.S.R., France. Imports: France, U.S.S.R., Germany. **Exports** Petroleum, cotton, textiles. **Imports** Petroleum, manufactures, food, machinery, chemicals, crude materials.
LAND
Description Southwestern Asia. **Area** 71,498 mi² (185,180 km²). **Highest point** Mt. Hermon, 9,232 ft (2,814 m). **Lowest point** Near Sea of Galilee, -656 ft (-200 m).

People. Most Syrians are Arabic-speaking descendants of Semites, a people who settled the region in ancient times. The majority are Sunni Muslim, and Islam is a powerful cultural force. Only a small percentage are Christian. Non-Arab Syrians include Kurds and Armenians, who speak their own languages and maintain their own customs. French is widely understood, and English is spoken in larger cities. The population is evenly divided between urban and rural settlements.

Economy and the Land. Syria is a developing country with great potential for economic growth. Textile manufacturing is a major industry, and oil, the main natural resource, provides for expanding activity in oil refining. The plains and river valleys are fertile, but rainfall is irregular and irrigation is necessary to sustain agriculture. Most farms are small; cotton and wheat are their major products. The terrain is marked by mountains, the Euphrates River valley, and a semiarid plateau. The climate is hot and dry, with relatively cold winters.

History and Politics. Syria was the site of one of the world's most ancient civilizations, and Damascus and other Syrian cities were centers of world trade as early as 2500 B.C. Greater Syria, as the area was called until the end of World War I, originally included much of modern Israel, Jordan, Lebanon, and parts of Turkey. The region was occupied and ruled by several empires, including the Phoenician, Assyrian, Babylonian, Persian, and Greek, before coming under Roman rule in 64 B.C. During subsequent years, Christianity arose in the part of Greater Syria called Palestine. In 636 the region fell to Arab Muslims, who governed until 1260, when Egypt gained control. Syria became part of the Turkish Ottoman Empire in 1516. During World War I, Syria aided Britain in defeating the Turks and Germans in return for independence. After the war, however, the League of Nations divided Greater Syria into four mandates—Syria, Lebanon, Palestine, and Transjordan—and placed Syria under French control. When Syria gained independence in 1946, many nationals wanted to reunite Greater Syria, but the United Nations made part of Palestine into the Jewish state of Israel. Tensions between Israel and Syria erupted in war in 1967 and 1973 and remain unresolved. In the 1980s, Syria assumed a role in Lebanon's affairs and maintains a military presence there. In 1990 it joined in a coalition of countries united against Iraq's occupation of Kuwait. ■

1949, when the Communists came to power in mainland China, many educated Chinese fled to Taiwan. A small group of aborigines, which lives in the mountains in central Taiwan, is most likely of Malay-Polynesian origin. Taiwan's languages are mainly various dialects of Chinese, a Fujian dialect, and a dialect known as "Hakka." Most religious practices combine Buddhist and Taoist beliefs with the Confucian ethical code.

Economy and the Land. Since World War II, Taiwan's economy has changed from agriculture to industry. A past emphasis on light industry, producing mainly consumer goods, has shifted to technology and heavy industry. Although only one-quarter of the island is arable, farmland is intensely cultivated, with some areas producing two and three crops a year. Even though rice, sugar cane, fruits, tea, and fishing are important, much food must be imported. The island's terrain is marked by steep eastern mountains sloping to a fertile western region. The capital of T'aipei administers the Penghu Islands and about twenty offshore islands as well as the island of Taiwan. The climate is maritime subtropical.

History and Politics. Chinese migration to Taiwan began as early as A.D. 500. Dutch traders claimed the island in 1624 as a base for trade with China and Japan. It was ruled by China's Manchu dynasty from 1683 until 1895, when China ceded Taiwan to Japan after the first Sino-Japanese war. Following World War II, China regained possession of Taiwan. A civil war in mainland China between Nationalist and Communist forces ended with the victory of the Communists in 1949. Nationalist leader Chiang Kai-shek fled to Taiwan, proclaiming T'aipei the provisional capital of Nationalist China. In 1971 the People's Republic of China replaced Taiwan in the United Nations. Even though the Republic of China still maintains it is the legitimate ruler of all China, nearly all nations now recognize the mainland's People's Republic of China. ■

distinct language. Religious beliefs are nearly evenly divided among Christian, Muslim, and traditional religions.

Economy and the Land. Agriculture accounts for the most export earnings and employs 80 percent of the work force. Yet two-thirds of the land cannot be cultivated because of lack of water and tsetse-fly infestation. Mainland farmers grow cassava, corn, and beans, while other cash crops include coffee and cashews. Zanzibar and Pemba islands are famous sources of cloves. Diamonds, salt, and iron are important mineral resources. Hot, humid coastal plains; an arid central plateau; and temperate lake and highland areas characterize mainland Tanzania. The climate is equatorial and includes monsoons.

History and Politics. The northern mainland has fossil remains of some of humanity's earliest ancestors. Subsequent early inhabitants were gradually displaced by Bantu farmers and Nilotes. Arabs were trading with coastal groups as early as the eighth century, and by the early 1500s the Portuguese had claimed the coastal region. They were displaced in the 1700s by Arabs, who subsequently established a lucrative slave trade. Germans began colonizing the coast in 1884 and six years later signed an agreement with Great Britain, which secured German dominance along the coast and made Zanzibar a British protectorate. After World War I, Britain received part of German East Africa from the League of Nations as a mandate and renamed it Tanganyika. The area became a trust territory under the United Nations following World War II. The country achieved independence in 1961, and two years later Zanzibar received its independence as a constitutional monarchy under the sultan. A 1964 revolt by the African majority overthrew the sultan, and Zanzibar and Tanganyika subsequently united and became known as Tanzania. ■

TAIWAN

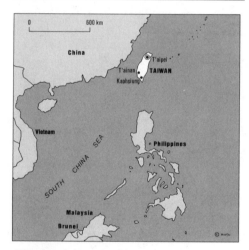

Official name Republic of China

PEOPLE
Population 20,565,000. **Density** 1,479/mi² (571/km²). **Urban** 66%. **Capital** T'aipei, 2,637,100. **Ethnic groups** Taiwanese 84%, Chinese 14%, aborigine 2%. **Languages** Chinese dialects. **Religions** Buddhist, Confucian, and Taoist 93%, Christian 5%. **Life expectancy** 77 female, 72 male. **Literacy** 86%.

POLITICS
Government Republic. **Parties** Democratic Progressive, Kuomintang, Labor. **Suffrage** Universal, over 20. **Memberships** None. **Subdivisions** 16 counties, 7 municipalities.

ECONOMY
GNP $60,000,000,000 **Per capita** $3,143. **Monetary unit** Dollar. **Trade partners** Exports: U.S., Japan. Imports: Japan, U.S., Saudi Arabia. **Exports** Machinery, textiles, electronic equipment, metals. **Imports** Machinery, petroleum, chemicals, metals, food.

LAND
Description Eastern Asian island. **Area** 13,900 mi² (36,002 km²). **Highest point** Yu Mtn., 13,114 ft (3,997 m). **Lowest point** Sea level.

People. The majority of Taiwan's inhabitants are descendants of Chinese who migrated from the coast of China in the eighteenth and nineteenth centuries. In

TANZANIA

Official name United Republic of Tanzania

PEOPLE
Population 26,065,000. **Density** 71/mi² (28/km²). **Urban** 33%. **Capital** Dar es Salaam (de facto), 1,300,000; Dodoma (future), 54,000. **Ethnic groups** African 99%. **Languages** English, Swahili, indigenous. **Religions** Animist 35%, Muslim 35%, Christian 30%. **Life expectancy** 57 female, 53 male. **Literacy** 46%.

POLITICS
Government Republic. **Parties** Revolutionary. **Suffrage** Universal, over 18. **Memberships** CW, OAU, UN. **Subdivisions** 25 regions.

ECONOMY
GDP $6,401,000,000 **Per capita** $297. **Monetary unit** Shilling. **Trade partners** Exports: Germany, U.K. Imports: U.K., Japan, Germany. **Exports** Coffee, cotton, nuts, diamonds, cloves, sisal, tobacco. **Imports** Manufactures, machinery and transportation equipment, cotton, petroleum, food.

LAND
Description Eastern Africa. **Area** 364,900 mi² (945,087 km²). **Highest point** Kilimanjaro, 19,340 ft (5,895 m). **Lowest point** Sea level.

People. The largely rural African population of Tanzania consists of more than 130 ethnic groups; most speak a

TASMANIA See AUSTRALIA.

THAILAND

Official name Kingdom of Thailand

PEOPLE
Population 56,860,000. **Density** 287/mi² (111/km²). **Urban** 23%. **Capital** Bangkok, 5,716,779. **Ethnic groups** Thai 84%, Chinese 12%. **Languages** Thai, indigenous. **Religions** Buddhist 98%, Muslim 1%. **Life expectancy** 69 female, 65 male. **Literacy** 88%.

POLITICS
Government Constitutional monarchy. **Parties** Citizens, Democratic, Social Action, Thai Nation (Chart Thai), United. **Suffrage** Universal, over 21. **Memberships** ASEAN, UN. **Subdivisions** 73 provinces.

ECONOMY
GDP $38,343,000,000 **Per capita** $734. **Monetary unit** Baht. **Trade partners** Exports: U.S., Japan, Singapore. Imports: Japan, U.S., Singapore. **Exports** Clothing and other manufactures, rice, tapioca, machinery, fish, rubber. **Imports** Machinery, manufactures, chemicals, petroleum, crude materials.

LAND
Description Southeastern Asia. **Area** 198,115 mi² (513,115 km²). **Highest point** Mt. Inthanon, 8,530 ft (2,600 m). **Lowest point** Sea level.

People. Thailand's society is relatively homogeneous. More than 80 percent of its people speak varying dialects of Thai and share a common culture and common religion, Buddhism. Malay-speaking Muslims and Chinese immigrants compose small minorities. Thai society is rural, with most people living in the rice-growing regions. The government has sponsored a successful family-planning program, which has greatly reduced the annual birth rate.

Economy and the Land. With an economy based on agriculture, Thailand exports large quantities of rice each year. Forests produce teak and rattan, and tin is another valuable natural resource. Tourism is the largest source of foreign income. Future industrialization may hinge on deposits of coal and natural gas. The cost of caring for thousands of refugees from Vietnam, Laos, and Cambodia has been a major drain on the Thai economy. A mountainous and heavily forested nation, Thailand has a tropical climate, dominated by monsoons, high temperatures, and humidity.

History and Politics. Thai communities were established as early as 4000 B.C., although a Thai kingdom founded in the thirteenth century A.D. began the history of modern Thailand. In the late 1700s Burmese armies overwhelmed the kingdom. Rama I, founder of the present dynasty, helped to drive the invaders from the country in 1782. He subsequently renamed the nation Siam and established a capital at Bangkok. Siam allowed Europeans to live within its borders during the period of colonial expansion, but the nation never succumbed to foreign rule. As a result, Siam was the only South and Southeast Asian country never colonized by a European power. In 1932 a revolt changed the government from an absolute monarchy to a constitutional monarchy. Military officers assumed control in 1938, and the nation reverted to its former name, Thailand, in 1939. The country was invaded by Japan in World War II. Following the war, Thailand was ruled by military officers until 1973, when civilians seized control and instigated a period of democracy that ended in 1976, when the military again took control. A new constitution was passed in 1978, followed by another coup in 1991. ∎

TOGO

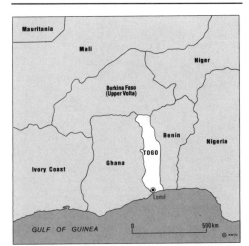

Official name Republic of Togo
PEOPLE
Population 3,627,000. **Density** 165/mi² (64/km²). **Urban** 26%. **Capital** Lomé, 400,000. **Ethnic groups** Ewe, Mina, Kabye, others. **Languages** French, indigenous. **Religions** Animist 70%, Christian 20%, Muslim 10%. **Life expectancy** 57 female, 53 male. **Literacy** 16%.
POLITICS
Government Republic. **Parties** Rally of the People. **Suffrage** Universal adult. **Memberships** OAU, UN. **Subdivisions** 21 prefectures.
ECONOMY
GDP $747,000,000 **Per capita** $267. **Monetary unit** CFA franc. **Trade partners** Exports: France, Netherlands, Germany. Imports: France, Germany, Netherlands. **Exports** Phosphates, coffee, cotton, cocoa. **Imports** Food, textiles, chemicals, transportation equipment, petroleum products.
LAND
Description Western Africa. **Area** 21,925 mi² (56,785 km²). **Highest point** Mont Agou, 3,235 ft (986 m). **Lowest point** Sea level.

People. Almost all the people of Togo are black Africans, coming primarily from the Ewe, Kabye, and Mina ethnic groups. Most of the population lives in the south and

practices traditional religions. Significant Christian and Muslim minorities exist.

Economy and the Land. Togo is an agricultural country, but productive land is scarce. Fishing is a major industry in the coastal areas. Togo has one of the world's largest phosphate reserves. Much of Togo is mountainous, with a sandy coastal plain. The climate is hot and humid.

History and Politics. Togo's original inhabitants were probably the ancestors of the present-day central mountain people. Ewes entered the south in the 1300s, and refugees from war-torn northern countries settled in the north between the 1500s and 1800s. For two hundred years, European ships raided the coastal region in search of slaves. In 1884 Germany claimed the territory. After World War I, Togoland became a League of Nations mandate governed by Britain and France. The mandate was made a United Nations trust territory following World War II and remained under British and French administration. British Togoland voted to join the Gold Coast and nearby British-administered territories in 1957 and became the independent nation of Ghana. French Togoland voted to become a republic in 1956 with internal self-government within the French Union, although the United Nations did not accept this method of ending the trusteeship. Togo peacefully severed its ties with France in 1960 and gained independence the same year. Internal political strife and military dominance of the government have characterized Togo's years of independence. ∎

TOKELAU See NEW ZEALAND.

TONGA

Official name Kingdom of Tonga
PEOPLE
Population 102,000. **Density** 352/mi² (136/km²). **Urban** 21%. **Capital** Nuku'alofa, Tongatapu I., 21,265. **Ethnic groups** Tongan (Polynesian) 98%. **Languages** Tongan, English. **Religions** Methodist 47%, Roman Catholic 16%, Free Church 14%, Church of Tonga 9%. **Life expectancy** 70 female, 65 male. **Literacy** 100%.
POLITICS
Government Constitutional monarchy. **Parties** None. **Suffrage** Literate adults, over 21 (males must be taxpayers). **Memberships** CW. **Subdivisions** 3 island groups.
ECONOMY
GDP $61,000,000 **Per capita** $570. **Monetary unit** Pa'anga. **Trade partners** Exports: New Zealand, Australia, Fiji. Imports: New Zealand, Australia, Japan. **Exports** Copra, manufactures, bananas, fish, nuts. **Imports** Manufactures, meat and other food, petroleum, transportation equipment.
LAND
Description South Pacific islands. **Area** 290 mi² (750 km²). **Highest point** 3,432 ft (1,046 m). **Lowest point** Sea level.

People. Almost all Tongans are Polynesian and follow Methodist and other Christian religions. About two-thirds of the population lives on the main island of Tongatapu.

Economy and the Land. Tonga's economy is dominated by both subsistence and plantation agriculture, while manufacturing is almost nonexistent. Most of the islands are coral reefs, and many have fertile soil. The climate is subtropical.

History and Politics. Tonga has been settled since at least 500 B.C. In the late 1700s, a civil war broke out among three lines of kings who sought to establish rulership. In 1822 Wesleyan Methodist missionaries converted one of the warring kings to Christianity. His faction prevailed, and he ruled as George Tupou I, founder of the present dynasty. Tonga came under British protection in 1900 but retained its autonomy in internal matters. The nation became fully independent in 1970 and maintains close relations with Great Britain, as well as its Pacific neighbors. ∎

TRINIDAD AND TOBAGO

Official name Republic of Trinidad and Tobago
PEOPLE
Population 1,242,000. **Density** 627/mi² (242/km²). **Urban** 69%. **Capital** Port of Spain, Trinidad I., 59,200. **Ethnic groups** Black 41%, East Indian 41%, mixed 16%, white 1%. **Languages** English, Hindi, French, Spanish. **Religions** Roman Catholic 33%, Anglican and

other Protestant 29%, Hindu 25%. **Life expectancy** 74 female, 69 male. **Literacy** 95%.
POLITICS
Government Republic. **Parties** National Alliance for Reconstruction, People's National Movement. **Suffrage** Universal, over 18. **Memberships** CW, OAS, UN. **Subdivisions** 10 administrative areas.
ECONOMY
GDP $7,558,000,000 **Per capita** $6,095. **Monetary unit** Dollar. **Trade partners** Exports: U.S., Barbados, U.K. Imports: U.S., U.K., Canada. **Exports** Petroleum, chemicals. **Imports** Manufactures, machinery, food, chemicals, transportation equipment.
LAND
Description Caribbean islands. **Area** 1,980 mi² (5,128 km²). **Highest point** El Cerro Del Aripo, 3,085 ft (940 m). **Lowest point** Sea level.

People. The two islands of Trinidad and Tobago form a single country, but Trinidad has nearly all the land mass and population. About 80 percent of all Trinidadians are either black African or East Indian, and about 20 percent are European, Chinese, and of mixed descent. Most Tobagonians are black African. The official language is English, and Christianity and Hinduism are the major religions.

Economy and the Land. Agriculture and tourism are important, but the economy is based on oil, which accounts for about 80 percent of the nation's exports. Trinidad is also one of the world's chief sources of natural asphalt and possesses supplies of natural gas. Tropical rain forests, scenic beaches, and fertile farmland characterize the islands.

History and Politics. Trinidad was occupied by Arawak Indians when Christopher Columbus arrived and claimed the island for Spain in 1498. The island remained under Spanish rule until 1797, when the British captured it and ruled for more than 150 years. Tobago changed hands among the Dutch, French, and British until 1814, when Britain took control. In 1888 Trinidad and Tobago became a single British colony and achieved independence in 1962. The racially diverse society is beginning to agitate for a more balanced representation in the government. In August 1990, Muslim militants kidnapped a large number of government officials in an unfocused and failed attempt to force the Prime Minister to resign. ∎

TUNISIA

Official name Republic of Tunisia
PEOPLE
Population 8,188,000. **Density** 130/mi² (50/km²). **Urban** 54%. **Capital** Tunis, 596,654. **Ethnic groups** Arab 98%, European 1%. **Languages** Arabic, French. **Religions** Muslim 98%, Christian 1%. **Life expectancy** 68 female, 67 male. **Literacy** 46%.
POLITICS
Government Republic. **Parties** Constitutional

Democratic Rally, others. **Suffrage** Universal, over 20. **Memberships** AL, OAU, UN. **Subdivisions** 23 governorates.

ECONOMY

GDP $8,214,000,000 **Per capita** $1,126. **Monetary unit** Dinar. **Trade partners** France, Germany, Italy. **Exports** Clothing, petroleum, fertilizer and other chemicals, manufactures, food. **Imports** Textiles and other manufactures, machinery, crude materials, food, petroleum.

LAND

Description Northern Africa. **Area** 63,170 mi² (163,610 km²). **Highest point** Mt. Chambi, 5,066 ft (1,544 m). **Lowest point** Chott el Gharsa, -56 ft (-17 m).

People. Tunisians are descended from a mix of Berber and Arab ethnic groups. Nearly all Tunisians are Muslim. Arabic is the official language, but French is widely spoken. Tunisia is a leader in the Arab world in promoting rights for women. A large middle class and equitable land distribution characterize its society.

Economy and the Land. Tunisia is an agricultural country; wheat, barley, citrus fruits, and olives are important crops. Oil from deposits discovered in the 1960s supplies domestic needs and serves as a major export, along with phosphates and other chemicals. Tourism is a growing industry, and despite an unemployment problem, Tunisia has a more balanced economy than many of its neighbors. Tunisia's terrain ranges from a well-watered and fertile northern area to more arid central and southern regions.

History and Politics. Phoenicians began the Carthaginian Empire in Tunisia about 1100 B.C. In 146 B.C. Romans conquered Carthage and ruled Tunisia for six hundred years. Arab Muslims from the Middle East gained control of most of North Africa in the seventh century, influencing the religion and overall culture of the region. Tunisia became part of the Turkish Ottoman Empire in the late 1500s, and in 1881 France succeeded in establishing a protectorate in the area. Nationalistic calls for Tunisian independence began before World War I and gained momentum by the 1930s. When Tunisia gained independence in 1956, more than half of the European population emigrated, severely damaging the economy. A year later Tunisia abolished its monarchy and became a republic. After a thirty-year rule, Habib Bourguiba was deposed in 1987. Tunisia continues to maintain a balance between pro-Western and Arab positions. ∎

TURKEY

Official name Republic of Turkey

PEOPLE

Population 63,720,000. **Density** 212/mi² (82/km²). **Urban** 48%. **Capital** Ankara, 2,553,209. **Ethnic groups** Turkish 85%, Kurdish 12%. **Languages** Turkish, Kurdish, Arabic. **Religions** Muslim 98%. **Life expectancy** 68 female, 65 male. **Literacy** 69%.

POLITICS

Government Republic. **Parties** Correct Way, Motherland, Social Democratic Populist. **Suffrage** Universal, over 21. **Memberships** NATO, OECD, UN. **Subdivisions** 67 provinces.

ECONOMY

GDP $52,701,000,000 **Per capita** $1,039. **Monetary unit** Lira. **Trade partners** Exports: Germany, Iraq, Italy. Imports: Germany, U.S., Iraq. **Exports** Clothing and other manufactures, fruits and other food, machinery, tobacco. **Imports** Machinery, petroleum, manufactures, chemicals, crude materials.

LAND

Description Southeastern Europe and southwestern Asia. **Area** 300,948 mi² (779,452 km²). **Highest point** Mt. Ararat, 16,804 ft (5,122 m). **Lowest point** Sea level.

People. Most Turks are descended from an Asian people who migrated from Russia and Mongolia around A.D. 900. About half the Turkish population lives in cities and half in rural areas. Kurds, the largest minority, live in the country's mountainous regions. Arabs and whites compose smaller minorities. The population is mainly Sunni Muslim. The changing status of women and the influence of Islam on daily life are key issues in Turkish society.

Economy and the Land. More than half the workers in this developing country are farmers, but industrialization has increased greatly since 1950. The most productive lands are in the mild coastal regions, although wheat and barley are grown in the desertlike plateau area. The government owns or controls many important industries, transportation services, and utilities, while most small farms and manufacturing companies are privately owned. The climate is Mediterranean along the coast, but temperature extremes are typical in the inland plateau.

History and Politics. Hittites began to migrate to the area from Europe or central Asia around 2000 B.C. Successive dominant groups included Phrygians, Greeks, Persians, and Romans. Muslims and Christians battled in the area during the Crusades of the eleventh and twelfth centuries. In the 1300s, Ottoman Turks began to build what would become a vast empire for six hundred years. Mustafa Kemal founded the Republic of Turkey in 1923, after the collapse of the Ottoman Empire. In 1960 the Turkish government was overthrown by Turkish military forces, who subsequently set up a provisional government, adopted a new constitution, and held free elections. In the sixties and seventies, disputes with Greece over Cyprus, populated by majority Greeks and minority Turks, flared into violence, and radical groups committed terrorist acts against the government. Turkey's generals assumed power in 1980 and restored order to the country. The government returned to civilian rule in 1984 under Prime Minister Turgut Ozal, who was re-elected in 1987. Iraq's 1991 attacks on its Kurdish population brought hundreds of thousands of refugees to the Turkish border. ∎

TURKS AND CAICOS ISLANDS
See UNITED KINGDOM.

TUVALU

Official name Tuvalu

PEOPLE

Population 8,900. **Density** 890/mi² (342/km²). **Capital** Funafuti, Funafuti I., 2,191. **Ethnic groups** Tuvaluan (Polynesian) 91%, Kiribatian 5%. **Languages** Tuvaluan, English. **Religions** Tuvalu Church 97%. **Life expectancy** 63 female, 60 male. **Literacy** 50%.

POLITICS

Government Parliamentary state. **Parties** None. **Suffrage** Universal, over 18. **Memberships** CW. **Subdivisions** 1 town council, 7 island councils.

ECONOMY

GNP $4,000,000 **Per capita** $513. **Monetary unit** Dollar, Australian dollar. **Trade partners** Australia, Fiji, New Zealand. **Exports** Copra, developed cinema film. **Imports** Grain and other food, manufactures, petroleum, machinery, chemicals.

LAND

Description South Pacific islands. **Area** 10 mi² (26 km²). **Highest point** 16 ft (5 m). **Lowest point** Sea level.

People. The small island nation of Tuvalu has a largely Polynesian population centered in rural villages. Tuvaluans speak the Tuvaluan language, derived from Polynesian, and many also speak English, reflecting ties with England.

Economy and the Land. The soil of the Tuvaluan coral-reef islands is poor, and there are few natural resources other than coconut palms. Copra and developed film are the primary exports, and many Tuvaluans weave mats and baskets for export. Tuvalu has minimal manufacturing and no mining. The nation consists of nine islands, most of them atolls surrounding lagoons. The climate is tropical.

History and Politics. Tuvalu's first inhabitants were probably Samoan immigrants. The islands were not seen by Europeans until 1568 and came under British control in the 1890s. Then called the Ellice Islands by Europeans, they were combined with the nearby Gilbert Islands

in 1916 to form the Gilbert and Ellice Islands Colony. The island groups were separated in 1975. The Ellice Islands were renamed Tuvalu and gained independence in 1978. One year later, the Gilbert Islands became independent Kiribati. ∎

UGANDA

Official name Republic of Uganda

PEOPLE

Population 17,890,000. **Density** 192/mi² (74/km²). **Urban** 10%. **Capital** Kampala, 1,008,707. **Ethnic groups** Ganda, Nkole, Gisu, Soga, Turkana, Chiga, Lango, Acholi. **Languages** English, Luganda, Swahili, indigenous. **Religions** Roman Catholic 33%, Protestant 33%, Muslim 16%, Animist. **Life expectancy** 55 female, 51 male. **Literacy** 52%.

POLITICS

Government Republic. **Parties** National Resistance Movement. **Suffrage** Universal, over 18. **Memberships** CW, OAU, UN. **Subdivisions** 10 provinces.

ECONOMY

GDP $5,900,000,000 **Per capita** $422. **Monetary unit** Shilling. **Trade partners** Exports: U.S., U.K., France. Imports: Kenya, U.K., Italy. **Exports** Coffee, cotton, tea. **Imports** Petroleum products, machinery, textiles, metals, transportation equipment.

LAND

Description Eastern Africa, landlocked. **Area** 93,104 mi² (241,139 km²). **Highest point** Margherita Pk., 16,763 ft (5,109 m). **Lowest point** Along Albert Nile River, 2,000 ft (610 m).

People. Primarily a rural nation, Uganda has a largely African population, which is composed of various ethnic groups. Numerous differences divide Uganda's peoples and have traditionally inspired conflict. Though English is the official language, Luganda and Swahili are widely used, along with indigenous Bantu and Nilotic languages. Most Ugandans are Christian, but Muslims and followers of traditional beliefs compose significant minorities.

Economy and the Land. Despite attempts to diversify the economy, the country remains largely agricultural. Uganda meets most of its own food needs and grows coffee, cotton, and tea commercially. Copper deposits account for most mining activity. Though Uganda straddles the equator, temperatures are modified by altitude. Most of the country is plateau, and Uganda benefits from its proximity to several major lakes.

History and Politics. Arab traders who traveled to the interior of Uganda in the 1830s found sophisticated kingdoms that had developed over several centuries. Trying to track the source of the Nile River, British explorers arrived in the 1860s and were followed by European missionaries. Britain quickly became a dominant force in eastern Africa, and part of modern Uganda became a British protectorate in 1894. Subsequent border adjustments brought Uganda to its present boundaries in 1926. After increasing demands for independence, moves toward autonomy began in the mid-1950s. Independence came in 1962, followed by internal conflicts and power struggles. In 1971 Major General Idi Amin Dada led a successful coup against President Obote and declared himself president. His dictatorship was rife with corruption, economic decline, and disregard for human rights. A force of Tanzanian troops and Ugandan exiles drove Amin out of Uganda in 1979. President Obote returned to power in 1980 but was forced from office in a

1985 military coup. A military-civilian government is in the process of drafting a new constitution. ∎

UNITED ARAB EMIRATES

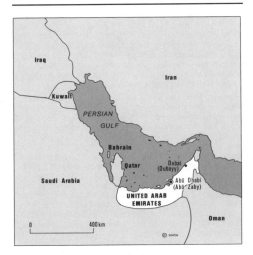

Official name United Arab Emirates

PEOPLE

Population 2,321,000. **Density** 72/mi² (28/km²). **Urban** 78%. **Capital** Abu Dhabi, 242,975. **Ethnic groups** South Asian 50%, native Emirian 19%, other Arab 23%. **Languages** Arabic, English, Farsi, Hindi, Urdu. **Religions** Muslim 89%, Christian 6%. **Life expectancy** 74 female, 70 male. **Literacy** 68%.

POLITICS

Government Federation of monarchs. **Parties** None. **Suffrage** None. **Memberships** AL, OPEC, UN. **Subdivisions** 7 emirates.

ECONOMY

GDP $27,081,000,000 **Per capita** $16,926. **Monetary unit** Dirham. **Trade partners** Exports: Japan, France, U.S. Imports: Japan, U.S., U.K. **Exports** Petroleum. **Imports** Iron and steel and other manufactures, machinery, transportation equipment.

LAND

Description Southwestern Asia. **Area** 32,278 mi² (83,600 km²). **Lowest point** Sea level.

People. The United Arab Emirates is a predominantly urban federation of seven independent states, each with its own ruling emir. The indigenous population is mostly Arab and Muslim, but only a small percentage of residents are United Arab Emirates citizens. Other groups include foreigners attracted by jobs in industry, especially Asians and Western Europeans. Arabic is the official language, but Farsi and English are widely spoken. The nation's population enjoys one of the highest per capita incomes in the world, as well as free medical and educational facilities.

Economy and the Land. Most of the United Arab Emirates is desert, which explains agriculture's small economic role. However, the federation is rich in oil, and major deposits—primarily in Abu Dhabi—account for nearly all of the Emirian national budget. The United Arab Emirates has tried to diversify its economy through production of natural gas, ammonia, and building materials. To attract tourists, airport expansion and hotel development are also on the rise.

History and Politics. Centuries ago, Arab rulers gained control of the region, formerly called the Trucial Coast, and Islam spread to the area in the A.D. 600s. In 1820 Arabian emirs signed the first of a number of treaties with the United Kingdom. Mutual self-interest led to an 1892 treaty that granted Britain exclusive rights to Trucial territory and government activity in return for military protection. Britain formally withdrew from Trucial affairs in 1971, and six of the Trucial emirates entered into a loose federation called the United Arab Emirates, which included Abu Dhabi, Dubai, Ash Shāriqah, 'Ajmān, Umm al Qaywayn, and Al Fujayrah. The seventh, Ra's al Khaymah, joined in early 1972. Because each emirate has a great deal of control over its internal affairs and economic development, the growth of federal powers has been slow. Defense spending is on the increase, however, and growing Arab nationalism may lead to a more centralized government. ∎

UNITED KINGDOM

Official name United Kingdom of Great Britain and Northern Ireland

PEOPLE

Population 57,380,000. **Density** 609/mi² (235/km²). **Urban** 93%. **Capital** London, England, 6,574,009.

Ethnic groups English 82%, Scottish 10%, Irish 2%, Welsh 2%. **Languages** English, Welsh, Gaelic. **Religions** Anglican 45%, Roman Catholic 9%, Presbyterian 3%, Methodist 1%. **Life expectancy** 79 female, 73 male. **Literacy** 99%.

POLITICS

Government Constitutional monarchy. **Parties** Conservative, Labor, Social and Liberal Democratic, others. **Suffrage** Universal, over 18. **Memberships** CW, EC, NATO, OECD, UN. **Subdivisions** 4 political divisions (England, Northern Ireland, Scotland, and Wales).

ECONOMY

GDP $454,540,000,000 **Per capita** $8,111. **Monetary unit** Pound sterling. **Trade partners** Exports: U.S., Germany, France. Imports: Germany, U.S., France. **Exports** Manufactures, machinery, petroleum, chemicals, transportation equipment. **Imports** Manufactures, machinery, transportation equipment, petroleum, food, chemicals.

LAND

Description Northwestern European islands. **Area** 94,248 mi² (244,100 km²). **Highest point** Ben Nevis, 4,406 ft (1,343 m). **Lowest point** Holme Fen, England, -9 ft (-3 m).

People. The ancestry of modern Britons reflects many centuries of invasions and migrations from Scandinavia and the European continent. Today Britons are a mixture of Celtic, Roman, Anglo-Saxon, Norse, and Norman influences. English is the predominant language, although Celtic languages such as Welsh and Scottish Gaelic are also spoken. Anglican is the dominant religion in England, while many Scots practice Presbyterianism. A siz-

Places and Possessions of THE UNITED KINGDOM

Entity	Status	Area	Population	Capital/Population
Anguilla (Caribbean island)	Dependent territory	35 mi² (91 km²)	7,000	The Valley, 1,042
Ascension (South Atlantic island)	Dependency of St. Helena	34 mi² (88 km²)	1,300	Georgetown
Bermuda (North Atlantic islands; east of North Carolina)	Dependent territory	21 mi² (54 km²)	60,000	Hamilton, 1,676
British Indian Ocean Territory (Indian Ocean islands)	Dependent territory	23 mi² (60 km²)	None	None
Cayman Islands (Caribbean Sea)	Dependent territory	100 mi² (259 km²)	26,000	George Town, 13,700
Channel Islands (Northwestern Europe)	Dependent territory	75 mi² (194 km²)	138,000	None
Falkland Islands (South Atlantic; east of Argentina)	Dependent territory	4,700 mi² (12,173 km²)	2,200	Stanley, 1,200
Gibraltar (Southwestern Europe; peninsula on Spain's southern coast)	Dependent territory	2.3 mi² (6.0 km²)	33,000	Gibraltar, 33,000
Guernsey (Northwestern European islands)	Bailiwick of Channel Islands	30 mi² (78 km²)	56,000	St. Peter Port, 16,085
Hong Kong (Eastern Asia; islands and mainland area on China's southeastern coast)	Chinese territory under British administration	414 mi² (1,072 km²)	6,009,000	Victoria (Hong Kong), 1,175,860
Isle of Man (Northwestern European island)	Self-governing territory	221 mi² (572 km²)	68,000	Douglas, 20,368
Jersey (Northwestern European island)	Bailiwick of Channel Islands	45 mi² (116 km²)	82,000	St. Helier, 27,083
Montserrat (Caribbean island)	Dependent territory	39 mi² (102 km²)	12,000	Plymouth, 1,568
Orkney Islands (North Atlantic)	Part of Scotland	377 mi² (976 km²)	20,000	Kirkwall, 5,713
Pitcairn (South Pacific islands)	Dependent territory	19 mi² (49 km²)	50	Adamstown, 59
Shetland Islands (North Atlantic)	Part of Scotland	553 mi² (1,433 km²)	22,000	Lerwick, 6,333
South Georgia and the South Sandwich Islands (South Atlantic islands)	Dependent territory	1,450 mi² (3,755 km²)	None	Grytviken Harbour
St. Helena (South Atlantic islands)	Dependent territory	121 mi² (314 km²)	7,700	Jamestown, 1,413
Tristan da Cunha (South Atlantic islands)	Dependency of St. Helena	40 mi² (104 km²)	300	Edinburgh
Turks and Caicos Islands (Caribbean Sea)	Dependent territory	193 mi² (500 km²)	13,000	Grand Turk, 3,146
Virgin Islands, British (Caribbean Sea)	Dependent territory	59 mi² (153 km²)	14,000	Road Town, 2,479

able minority is Roman Catholic. The population is primarily urban and suburban, with a significant percentage living in the southeastern corner of England.

Economy and the Land. A land of limited natural resources, the United Kingdom has relied on trading and, more recently, manufacturing to achieve economic strength. Access to the sea is a traditional economic and political asset. The country maintains a large merchant fleet, which at one time dominated world trade. The industrial revolution developed quickly in Great Britain, and the country continues to be a leading producer of transportation equipment, metal products, and other manufactured goods. Although climate and limited acreage have hindered agricultural development, intensive, mechanized farming methods have allowed the nation to produce half of its food supply. Livestock raising is especially important. Additional contributors to the country's industry are extensive deposits of coal and iron, which make mining important. London is well known as an international financial center. The United Kingdom includes Scotland, England, Wales, Northern Ireland, and several offshore islands. The varied terrain is marked by several mountain ranges, moors, rolling hills, and plains. The climate is tempered by the sea and is subject to frequent changes. Great Britain administers many overseas possessions.

History and Politics. Little is known of the earliest inhabitants of Britain, but evidence such as Stonehenge indicates the existence of a developed culture before the Roman invasion in the 50s B.C. Britain began to trade with the rest of Europe while under Roman rule. The Norman period after A.D. 1066 fostered the establishment of many cultural and political traditions that continue to be reflected in British life. Scotland came under the British Crown in 1603, and in 1707 England and Scotland agreed to unite as Great Britain. Ireland had been conquered by the early seventeenth century, and the 1801 British Act of Union established the United Kingdom of Great Britain and Ireland. Although colonial and economic expansion had taken Great Britain to the Far East, America, Africa, and India, the nation's influence began to diminish at the end of the nineteenth century as the industrial revolution strengthened other nations. World War I significantly weakened the United Kingdom and during the period following World War II, which saw the demise of an empire, many colonies gained independence. The Conservative party has governed the country since 1979. Margaret Thatcher, who headed the party from 1979 to 1990, was replaced by John Major. ■

UNITED STATES

Official name United States of America
PEOPLE
Population 250,800,000. **Density** 68/mi² (26/km²). **Urban** 74%. **Capital** Washington, D.C., 638,432. **Ethnic groups** White 85%, black 12%. **Languages** English, Spanish. **Religions** Baptist and other Protestant 56%, Roman Catholic 28%, Jewish 2%. **Life expectancy** 80 female, 73 male. **Literacy** 91%.
POLITICS
Government Republic. **Parties** Democratic, Republican. **Suffrage** Universal, over 18. **Memberships** NATO, OECD, OAS, UN. **Subdivisions** 50 states, 1 district.
ECONOMY
GDP $3,959,610,000,000 **Per capita** $16,662. **Monetary unit** Dollar. **Trade partners** Exports: Canada, Japan, Mexico. Imports: Japan, Canada, Germany. **Exports** Machinery, manufactures, aircraft and other transportation equipment. **Imports** Machinery, manufactures, transportation equipment, petroleum, food.

Places and Possessions of THE UNITED STATES

Entity	Status	Area	Population	Capital/Population
American Samoa (South Pacific islands)	Unincorporated territory	77 mi² (199 km²)	42,000	Pago Pago, 3,075
Guam (North Pacific island)	Unincorporated territory	209 mi² (541 km²)	144,000	Agana, 896
Johnston Atoll (North Pacific island)	Unincorporated territory	0.5 mi² (1.3 km²)	300	None
Marshall Islands (North Pacific)	Republic in free association with the U.S.	70 mi² (181 km²)	44,000	Majuro (island)
Micronesia, Federated States of (North Pacific islands)	Republic in free association with the U.S.	271 mi² (702 km²)	94,000	Kolonia, 5,549
Midway Islands (North Pacific)	Unincorporated territory	2.0 mi² (5.2 km²)	500	None
Navassa Island (Caribbean Sea)	Unincorporated territory	1.9 mi² (4.9 km²)	None	None
Northern Mariana Islands (North Pacific)	Commonwealth	184 mi² (477 km²)	24,000	Saipan (island)
Pacific Islands, Trust Territory of the (North Pacific)	United Nations trusteeship (U.S. administration)	196 mi² (508 km²)	15,000	None
Palau (Belau) (North Pacific islands)	Part of Trust Territory of the Pacific Islands	196 mi² (508 km²)	15,000	Koror, 6,222
Puerto Rico (Caribbean island)	Commonwealth	3,515 mi² (9,104 km²)	3,604,000	San Juan, 424,600
Virgin Islands of the United States (Caribbean Sea)	Unincorporated territory	133 mi² (344 km²)	117,000	Charlotte Amalie, 11,842
Wake Island (North Pacific)	Unincorporated territory	3.0 mi² (7.8 km²)	300	None

LAND
Description Central North America. **Area** 3,679,245 mi² (9,529,202 km²). **Highest point** Mt. McKinley, 20,320 ft (6,194 m). **Lowest point** Death Valley, California, -282 ft (-86 m).

People. The diverse population of the United States is mostly composed of whites, many descended from eighteenth- and nineteenth-century immigrants; blacks, mainly descended from African slaves; peoples of Spanish and Asian origin; and indigenous Indians, Inuit, and Hawaiians. Religions encompass the world's major faiths; Protestantism, Roman Catholicism, and Judaism predominate. English is the predominant language, though Spanish is spoken by many, and other languages are often found in ethnic enclaves.

Economy and the Land. The United States is an international economic power, and all sectors of the economy are highly developed. Fertile soils produce high crop yields, with considerable land under cultivation. Mineral output includes petroleum and natural gas, coal, copper, lead, and zinc; but high consumption makes the United States dependent on foreign oil. The country is a leading manufacturer, with a well-developed service sector. Mountains, prairies, woodlands, and deserts mark its vast terrain. The climate varies regionally, from mild year-round along the Pacific coast and in the South to temperate in the Northeast and Midwest. In addition to forty-eight contiguous states, the country includes the subarctic state of Alaska and the tropical state of Hawaii, an island group in the Pacific.

History and Politics. Thousands of years ago, Asiatic peoples, ancestors of American Indians, crossed the Bering Strait land bridge and spread across North and South America. Vikings reached North America around A.D. 1000, and Christopher Columbus arrived in 1492. Following early explorations by Portugal and Spain, England established a colony at Jamestown, Virginia, in 1607. Thirteen British colonies waged a successful war of independence against England from 1775 to 1783. United States expansion continued westward throughout the nineteenth century. The issues of black slavery and states' rights led to the American Civil War from 1861 to 1865, a struggle that pitted the North against the South and resulted in the end of slavery. Opportunities for prosperity accompanied the industrial revolution in the late nineteenth century and led to a large influx of immigrants. From 1917 to 1918, the country joined with the Allies in World War I. A severe economic depression began in 1929, and the United States did not really recover until World War II stimulated industry and the economy in general. In 1945, the use of the atomic bomb on Japan ended the war and changed the course of history. The Civil Rights Act of 1964 and the Vietnam War, 1961-75, ushered in an era of great social progress and turmoil in the United States. Technological advances were unparalleled with man's entry into space and the first landing on the moon in 1969. The 1980s saw increasing concern with a deteriorating environment and the nuclear arms race. In January 1991, the United States led a United Nations coalition of military troops to force Iraq out of Kuwait. ■

URUGUAY

Official name Oriental Republic of Uruguay

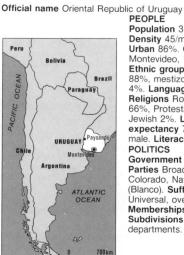

PEOPLE
Population 3,105,000. **Density** 45/mi² (18/km²). **Urban** 86%. **Capital** Montevideo, 1,251,647. **Ethnic groups** White 88%, mestizo 8%, black 4%. **Languages** Spanish. **Religions** Roman Catholic 66%, Protestant 2%, Jewish 2%. **Life expectancy** 75 female, 68 male. **Literacy** 94%.
POLITICS
Government Republic. **Parties** Broad Front, Colorado, National (Blanco). **Suffrage** Universal, over 18. **Memberships** OAS, UN. **Subdivisions** 19 departments.

ECONOMY
GDP $5,054,000,000 **Per capita** $1,725. **Monetary unit** Peso. **Trade partners** Exports: Brazil, U.S., Germany. Imports: Brazil, Argentina, Germany. **Exports** Textiles and other manufactures, meat, grain, wool, leather. **Imports** Industrial chemicals, machinery, petroleum, manufactures, food.
LAND
Description Eastern South America. **Area** 68,500 mi² (177,414 km²). **Highest point** Cerro Catedral, 1,686 ft (514 m). **Lowest point** Sea level.
People. Most Uruguayans are white descendants of nineteenth- and twentieth-century immigrants from Spain, Italy, and other European countries. Mestizos, of Spanish-Indian ancestry, and blacks round out the population. Spanish is the dominant language, and Roman Catholicism is the major religion, with small Protestant and Jewish minorities. Many Uruguayans claim to follow no religion.

Economy and the Land. Uruguay's fertile soil, grassy plains, and temperate climate provide the basis for agriculture and are especially conducive to livestock raising. The country has virtually no mineral resources, and petroleum exploration has been unrewarding. However, refinement of imported fuel is a major industry, and Uruguay has significant hydroelectric potential.

History and Politics. Uruguay's original inhabitants were Indians. In the 1680s, the Portuguese established the first European settlement, followed by a Spanish settlement in the 1720s. By the 1770s, Spain had gained control of the area, but in the 1820s Portugal once again came to power, annexing present-day Uruguay to Brazil. When nationalistic feelings in the early nineteenth century led to an 1828 war by Uruguayan patriots and Argentina against Brazil, the country achieved independence. Political unrest, caused in part by economic depression, resurfaced in the 1970s, leading to military intervention in the government and the jailing of thousands of political prisoners. The country restored its civilian government in 1985. ∎

VANUATU

Official name Republic of Vanuatu
PEOPLE
Population 148,000. **Density** 31/mi² (12/km²). **Urban** 30%. **Capital** Port-Vila, Efate I., 18,905. **Ethnic groups** Ni-Vanuatu 92%, European 2%, other Pacific Islander 2%. **Languages** Bislama, English, French. **Religions** Presbyterian 37%, Anglican 15%, Roman Catholic 15%, other Protestant. **Life expectancy** 72 female, 67 male. **Literacy** 20%.
POLITICS
Government Republic. **Parties** National (Vanua'aku Pati), Union of Moderate Parties, others. **Suffrage** Universal, over 18. **Memberships** CW, UN. **Subdivisions** 11 island councils.
ECONOMY
GDP $103,000,000 **Per capita** $805. **Monetary unit** Vatu. **Trade partners** Exports: Netherlands, Belgium, Japan. Imports: Australia, Japan, New Zealand. **Exports** Copra, beef, wood, cocoa. **Imports** Machinery and transportation equipment, manufactures, food, fuel.
LAND
Description South Pacific islands. **Area** 4,707 mi² (12,190 km²). **Highest point** Mont Tabwémasana, 6,165 ft (1,879 m). **Lowest point** Sea level.
People. The majority of Vanuatuans are Melanesian. Europeans and Polynesians compose minorities. Languages include English and French, the languages of former rulers; and Bislama, a mixture of English and Melanesian. Most Vanuatuans are Christian, although indigenous religions are also practiced.

Economy and the Land. The economy is based on agriculture, and copra is the primary export crop. Fishing is also important, as is the growing tourist business. Narrow coastal plains, mountainous interiors, and a mostly hot, rainy climate characterize the more than eighty islands of Vanuatu.

History and Politics. In 1606 Portuguese explorers encountered indigenous Melanesian inhabitants on islands that now compose Vanuatu. Captain James Cook of Britain charted the islands in 1774 and named them the New Hebrides after the Hebrides islands of Scotland. British and French merchants and missionaries began to settle the islands in the early 1800s. To resolve conflicting interests, Great Britain and France formed a joint

naval commission to oversee the area in 1887 and a condominium government in 1906. Demands for autonomy began in the 1960s, and the New Hebrides became the independent Republic of Vanuatu in 1980. ∎

VATICAN CITY

Official name State of the Vatican City
PEOPLE
Population 800. **Density** 4,000/mi² (2,000/km²). **Urban** 100%. **Capital** Vatican City, 800. **Ethnic groups** Italian, Swiss. **Languages** Italian, Latin. **Religions** Roman Catholic. **Literacy** 100%.
POLITICS
Government Ecclesiastical city-state. **Parties** None. **Suffrage** Roman Catholic cardinals less than 80 years old. **Memberships** None. **Subdivisions** None. **Monetary unit** Lira.
LAND
Description Southern Europe, landlocked (within the city of Rome, Italy). **Area** 0.2 mi² (0.4 km²). **Highest point** 249 ft (76 m). **Lowest point** 62 ft (19 m).
People. The Vatican City, the smallest independent state in the world, is the administrative and spiritual center of the Roman Catholic church and home to the pope, the church's head. The population is composed of administrative and diplomatic workers of more than a dozen nationalities; Italians and Swiss predominate. A military corps known as the Swiss Guard also resides here. Roman Catholicism is the only religion. The official language is Italian, although acts of the Holy See are drawn up in Latin.

Economy and the Land. The Vatican City does not engage in commerce per se; however, it does issue its own coins and postage stamps. In addition, it is the destination of thousands of tourists and pilgrims each year. Lying on a hill west of the Tiber River, the Vatican City is an urban enclave in northwestern Rome, Italy. The Vatican City enjoys a mild climate moderated by the Mediterranean Sea.

History and Politics. For centuries the popes of the Roman Catholic church ruled the Papal States, an area across central Italy, which included Rome. The popes' temporal authority gradually was reduced to the city of Rome, which itself was eventually annexed by the Kingdom of Italy in 1870. Denying these rulings, the pope declared himself a prisoner in the Vatican, a status that lasted fifty-nine years. The Vatican City has been an independent sovereign state since 1929, when Italy signed the Treaty of the Lateran in return for papal dissolution of the Papal States. The pope heads all branches of government, though day-to-day responsibilities are delegated to staff members. ∎

VENEZUELA

Official name Republic of Venezuela
PEOPLE
Population 19,995,000. **Density** 57/mi² (22/km²). **Urban** 91%. **Capital** Caracas, 1,816,901. **Ethnic**

groups Mestizo 67%, white 21%, black 10%, Indian 2%. **Languages** Spanish, indigenous. **Religions** Roman Catholic 96%, Protestant 2%. **Life expectancy** 74 female, 67 male. **Literacy** 84%.
POLITICS
Government Republic. **Parties** Democratic Action, Movement Toward Socialism, Social Christian, others. **Suffrage** Universal, over 18. **Memberships** OAS, OPEC, UN. **Subdivisions** 20 states, 2 territories, 1 dependency, 1 district.
ECONOMY
GDP $49,604,000,000 **Per capita** $3,093. **Monetary unit** Bolivar. **Trade partners** Exports: U.S., Italy, Netherlands. Imports: U.S., Germany, Japan. **Exports** Petroleum, aluminum. **Imports** Machinery, manufactures, chemicals, transportation equipment, food.
LAND
Description Northern South America. **Area** 352,145 mi² (912,050 km²). **Highest point** Pico Bolívar, 16,427 ft (5,007 m). **Lowest point** Sea level.
People. Spanish colonial rule of Venezuela is reflected in its predominantly mestizo population, people of Spanish-Indian blood, and its official language of Spanish. Minorities include Europeans, blacks, and Indians, who generally speak local languages. Nearly all Venezuelans are Roman Catholic, further evidence of former Spanish domination. Protestants and lesser numbers of Jews and Muslims compose small minorities, and traditional religious practices continue among some Indians.

Economy and the Land. Since the expansion of the petroleum industry in the 1920s, Venezuela has experienced rapid economic growth, but unevenly distributed wealth, a high birthrate, and fluctuations in the price of oil have hampered the economy. Partly because of the emphasis on oil production, agriculture has declined; its contribution to the gross national product is minimal, and Venezuela must import much of its food. Manufacturing and hydroelectric power are being developed. The varied Venezuelan landscape is dominated by the Andes Mountains, a coastal zone, high plateaus, and plains, or llanos. The climate is tropical, but temperatures vary with altitude. Most of the country experiences rainy and dry seasons.

History and Politics. The original inhabitants of modern Venezuela included Arawak and Carib Indians. In 1498 Christopher Columbus was the first European to visit Venezuela. The area became a colony of Spain and was briefly under German rule. Independence was achieved in 1821 under the guidance of Simón Bolívar, Venezuela's national hero. Venezuela became a sovereign state in 1830. The nineteenth century saw political instability and revolutionary fervor, followed by a succession of dictators in the twentieth century. Since 1958, Venezuela has tried to achieve a representative form of government and has held a number of democratic elections. The fall in oil prices, for a country heavily dependent upon oil export, has been an economic hardship in recent years. ∎

VIETNAM

Official name Socialist Republic of Vietnam

PEOPLE
Population 67,850,000. **Density** 530/mi[2] (205/km[2]). **Urban** 22%. **Capital** Hanoi, 1,089,000. **Ethnic groups** Kinh 87%, Hao 2%, Tay 2%. **Languages** Vietnamese, French, Chinese, English, Khmer, indigenous. **Religions** Buddhist, Chondoist, Roman Catholic, Animist, Muslim, Confucian. **Life expectancy** 66 female, 62 male. **Literacy** 84%.

POLITICS
Government Socialist republic. **Parties** Communist. **Suffrage** Universal, over 18. **Memberships** UN. **Subdivisions** 37 provinces, 3 municipalities.

ECONOMY
GNP $18,100,000,000 **Per capita** $312. **Monetary unit** Dong. **Trade partners** U.S.S.R., eastern European countries, Japan. **Exports** Agricultural products, handicrafts, coal, minerals. **Imports** Petroleum, steel, railroad equipment, chemicals, pharmaceuticals, cotton.

LAND
Description Southeastern Asia. **Area** 128,066 mi[2] (331,689 km[2]). **Highest point** Phan Si Pang, 10,312 ft (3,143 m). **Lowest point** Sea level.

People. Despite centuries of foreign invasion and domination, the people of Vietnam remain remarkably homogeneous; ethnic Vietnamese compose the majority of the population. Chinese influence is seen in the major religions of Buddhism and Confucianism. The official language is Vietnamese, but a history of foreign intervention is reflected in wide use of French, English, Chinese, and Russian.

Economy and the Land. The Vietnamese economy has struggled to overcome the effects of war and the difficulties inherent in unifying the once-divided country. Agriculture, centered in the fertile southern plains, continues to employ nearly 70 percent of the people. Vietnam intends to expand its war-damaged mining industry, which has been slowed by lack of skilled personnel and a poor transportation network. Vietnam's economic picture is not likely to improve until the country can resolve its political and social problems. The landscape of Vietnam ranges from mountains to plains, and the climate is tropical.

History and Politics. The first Vietnamese lived in what is now northern Vietnam. After centuries of Chinese rule, Vietnam finally became independent in the 1400s, but civil strife continued for nearly two centuries. French missionary activity began in the early seventeenth century, and by 1883 all of present-day Vietnam, Cambodia, and Laos were under French rule. When Germany occupied France during World War II, control of French Indochina passed to the Japanese until their defeat in 1945. The French presence continued until 1954, when Vietnamese Communists led by Ho Chi Minh gained control of North Vietnam. United States aid to South Vietnam began in 1961 and ended, after years of conflict, with a cease-fire in 1973. Communist victory and unification of the country as the Socialist Republic of Vietnam was achieved in 1975. Vietnamese military policy resulted in fighting with China and the occupation of Cambodia until 1989. Political reforms have aimed at improving their impoverished economic status. ■

VIRGIN ISLANDS, BRITISH
See UNITED KINGDOM.

VIRGIN ISLANDS, UNITED STATES See UNITED STATES.

WAKE ISLAND See UNITED STATES.

WALLIS AND FUTUNA See FRANCE.

WESTERN SAHARA

Official name Western Sahara
PEOPLE
Population 200,000. **Density** 1.9/mi[2] (0.8/km[2]). **Urban** 57%. **Capital** El Aaiún, 93,875. **Ethnic groups** Arab, Berber. **Languages** Arabic. **Religions** Sunni Muslim. **Life expectancy** 41 female, 39 male. **Literacy** 20%.

POLITICS
Government Occupied by Morocco. **Memberships** None. **Subdivisions** None. **Monetary unit** Moroccan dirham. **Trade partners** Morocco. **Exports** Phosphates. **Imports** Fuel, food.

LAND
Description Northwestern Africa. **Area** 102,703 mi[2] (266,000 km[2]). **Highest point** 2,640 ft (805 m). **Lowest point** Sea level.

People. Most Western Saharans are nomadic Arabs or Berbers. Because these nomads often cross national borders in their wanderings, the population of Western Sahara is in a constant state of flux. Islam is the principal religion, and Arabic is the dominant language.

Economy and the Land. Most of Western Sahara is desert, with a rocky, barren soil that severely limits agriculture. Mining of phosphate deposits began in 1972, and phosphates are now the primary export. Western Sahara is almost completely arid; rainfall is negligible, except along the coast.

History and Politics. By the fourth century B.C. Phoenicians and Romans had visited the area. Spain explored the region in the sixteenth century and gained control of the region in 1860, but Spanish Sahara was not designated a province of Spain until 1958. When Spanish control ceased in 1976, the area became known as Western Sahara. Mauritania and Morocco subsequently divided the territory, and Morocco gained control of valuable phosphate deposits. Fighting soon broke out between an independence movement, the Polisario Front, and troops from Morocco and Mauritania. In 1979 Mauritania gave up its claim to the area and withdrew. After years of conflict, Morocco and the Polisario Front agreed in 1988 to a cease-fire and a referendum, which offered Western Saharans a choice between independence and integration with Morocco. However, details of the referendum were never agreed upon and negotiations are at a standstill. ■

WESTERN SAMOA

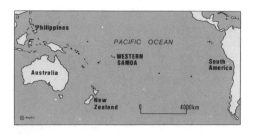

Official name Independent State of Western Samoa
PEOPLE
Population 188,000. **Density** 172/mi[2] (66/km[2]). **Urban** 23%. **Capital** Apia, Upolu I., 33,170. **Ethnic groups** Samoan, mixed European and Polynesian. **Languages** English, Samoan. **Religions** Congregational 50%, Roman Catholic 22%, Methodist 16%, Mormon 8%. **Life expectancy** 69 female, 64 male. **Literacy** 98%.

POLITICS
Government Constitutional monarchy. **Parties** Human Rights Protection, National Development. **Suffrage** Limited adult. **Memberships** CW, UN. **Subdivisions** 11 districts.

ECONOMY
GDP $88,000,000 **Per capita** $550. **Monetary unit** Tala. **Trade partners** Exports: U.S., New Zealand, Australia. Imports: New Zealand, Australia, Japan. **Exports** Coconut oil, fruit and vegetables, cocoa,

aircraft, copra. **Imports** Manufactures, food, petroleum, machinery, transportation equipment.

LAND
Description South Pacific islands. **Area** 1,093 mi[2] (2,831 km[2]). **Highest point** Mt. Silisili, 6,096 ft (1,858 m). **Lowest point** Sea level.

People. Most Western Samoans are of Polynesian descent, and a significant minority are of mixed Samoan and European heritage. Most of the population is Christian and practices a variety of faiths introduced by European missionaries and traders. Samoan and English are the principal languages.

Economy and the Land. The tropical climate of Western Samoa, which is composed of volcanic islands, is suited for agriculture—the country's chief economic support. Bananas, coconuts, and tropical fruits are the most important crops.

History and Politics. Polynesians settled the Samoan islands more than two thousand years ago. Dutch explorers visited the islands in the early 1700s, and English missionaries arrived in 1830. Rivalry between the islands' royal families increased, along with competition among the United Kingdom, the United States, and Germany. In 1900 the United States annexed Eastern Samoa, and Germany obtained Western Samoa. By the end of World War I, New Zealand had gained control of Western Samoa. Growing demand for independence led to United Nations intervention and gradual steps toward self-government. The islands became fully independent in 1962. The nation maintains friendly relations with New Zealand and neighboring Pacific islands. ■

YEMEN

Official name Republic of Yemen
PEOPLE
Population 13,310,000. **Density** 65/mi[2] (25/km[2]). **Urban** 24%. **Capital** Sana, 427,150. **Ethnic groups** Arab, Afro-Arab. **Languages** Arabic. **Religions** Muslim, Christian, Hindu. **Life expectancy** 55 female, 52 male. **Literacy** 16%.

POLITICS
Government Republic. **Parties** None. **Suffrage** Universal, over 18. **Memberships** AL, UN.

ECONOMY
GDP $4,108,000,000 **Per capita** $500. **Monetary unit** Dinar and Riyal. **Trade partners** Exports: Saudi Arabia, Italy, Japan. Imports: Japan, Saudi Arabia, France. **Exports** Machinery, pastry and other food, transportation equipment, manufactures. **Imports** Grain and other food, manufactures, machinery, transportation equipment.

LAND
Description Southwestern Asia. **Area** 205,356 mi[2] (531,869 km[2]). **Highest point** Mt. Nabi Shuayb, 12,008 ft (3,660 m). **Lowest point** Sea level.

People. Most inhabitants of Yemen are Arab, with small minorities of Indians, Pakistanis, and East Africans. Islam is the predominant religion, while Arabic is the language of Yemen. The population includes both Sunni and Shiite Muslims. Small numbers of Christians, Hindus, and Jews also exist. Most of the population lives in the western part of the country.

Economy and the Land. Much of northwestern Yemen has a terrain suited for agriculture, the backbone of the nation's economy. However, ineffective agricultural techniques combined with regional instability often hinder production. Industrial activity is growing slowly, with production based on domestic resources, but exploitation of oil, iron ore, and salt deposits is financially prohibitive at this time. Subsistence farming and nomadic herding characterize the drier, eastern part of the country. Yemen's landscape varies from arid lowlands to fertile, well-cultivated highlands. The climate is temperate in the highlands and hot and dry in the lowlands.

History and Politics. Between 1200 B.C. and A.D. 525, trade empires occupied the area of present-day Yemen, and it was part of the Kingdom of Sheba in the 900s B.C. Christian and Jewish societies thrived before the seventh century, when Islam was introduced. The region's flourishing economy made it a focal point in the development of Islam. The country was divided since the early sixteenth century, when the Ottoman Empire conquered northwestern Yemen. The Turks stayed in power until 1918, when the Turkish military withdrew and gave control to the Zaidis, who established a monarchy. The Imam Badr was overthrown in 1962, when the Yemeni army proclaimed creation of the Yemen Arab Republic. Meanwhile, Aden and the southeastern part of the country were under British domination since 1839, and became a protectorate in the 1930s. By the mid-1960s, Aden had become the focus of Arab nationalists, and in 1967 Britain granted independence to the People's Republic of South Yemen. After a coup by a Marxist faction in 1970, the country's name changed to the People's Democratic Republic of Yemen. During the 1970s, border clashes between the two Yemens were frequent. Relations improved throughout the 1980s, and the two countries merged to form the Republic of Yemen in 1990. ∎

YUGOSLAVIA

Official name Socialist Federal Republic of Yugoslavia
PEOPLE
Population 23,907,000. Density 242/mi² (93/km²). Urban 50%. Capital Belgrade, 1,130,000. Ethnic groups Serbian 36%, Croatian 20%, Bosnian 9%, Slovene 8%, Albanian 8%, Macedonian 6%. Languages Macedonian, Serbo-Croatian, Slovene, Albanian, Hungarian. Religions Eastern Orthodox 50%, Roman Catholic 30%, Muslim 10%, Protestant 1%. Life expectancy 76 female, 70 male. Literacy 91%.
POLITICS
Government Socialist republic. Parties League of Communists, others. Suffrage Universal, over 18; over 16 if employed. Memberships UN. Subdivisions 6 socialist republics, 2 autonomous provinces.
ECONOMY
GDP $44,238,000,000 Per capita $1,917. Monetary unit Dinar. Trade partners Exports: U.S.S.R., Italy, Germany. Imports: Germany, U.S.S.R., Italy. Exports Shoes and other manufactures, machinery, transportation equipment, chemicals. Imports Machinery, chemicals, manufactures, petroleum, crude materials.
LAND
Description Eastern Europe. Area 98,766 mi²

(255,804 km²). Highest point Triglav, 9,396 ft (2,864 m). Lowest point Sea level.

People. The population of Yugoslavia is one of the most diverse in Eastern Europe and includes nearly twenty distinct ethnic groups, in addition to the main Serbian and Croatian groups. Serbo-Croatian, Slovene, and Macedonian are major languages. Religions are also diverse, and often divide along ethnic lines. Most Yugoslavs work in industry, resulting in a steady urban shift since World War II and a corresponding rise in the standard of living.

Economy and the Land. Since 1945, Yugoslavia's economy has made a successful transition from agriculture to industry. Once modeled on that of the Soviet Union, the economy today is somewhat decentralized, based on the theory of workers' self-management. Decisions on production, prices, and income are made to benefit society as a whole, though wealth has tended to concentrate in the highly industrialized north, resulting in increasing social tension. Agriculture also plays an economic part—aided by the moderate climate along the coast of the Adriatic Sea and stronger seasonal variations in the mountainous inland regions.

History and Politics. Yugoslavia has been inhabited for at least one hundred thousand years; its peoples have included Illyrians, Thracians, Greeks, Celts, and Romans. In A.D. 395 the Roman Empire was divided into the West Roman Empire and the Byzantine Empire, with the dividing line through present-day Yugoslavia. People in the western region became Roman Catholic and used the Roman alphabet, while Byzantines adopted the Eastern Orthodox faith and the Cyrillic alphabet. Slavic migrations led to the establishment of independent Slavic states such as Serbia and Croatia, and calls for Slavic unity began in the early 1800s. In 1914 a Slavic patriot assassinated Archduke Ferdinand of Austria-Hungary and triggered World War I. The Kingdom of Serbs, Croats, and Slovenes was formed in 1918. The fighting encouraged King Alexander I to declare himself dictator in 1929 and change the new country's name to Yugoslavia, which was retained after Alexander's assassination in 1934. Germany and the other Axis powers invaded Yugoslavia during World War II and were opposed by a partisan army organized by Josip Broz Tito, who assumed leadership when Yugoslavia became a Communist republic in 1945. Tito's policy of nonalignment caused the Soviet Union to break off diplomatic relations from 1948 to 1955. United States aid from the 1940s to the 1960s encouraged a shift toward Western trade and broadened political and cultural exchanges. Since Tito's death in 1980, the country has been governed by a presidency rotating amongst the republics. In June, 1991, two republics of Yugoslavia, Croatia and Slovenia, declared independence and in September Macedonia did the same. Fierce fighting between the Croatians and the central government continues, and none of the breakaway republics secured international recognition. ∎

ZAIRE

Official name Republic of Zaire
PEOPLE
Population 36,095,000. Density 40/mi² (15/km²). Urban 40%. Capital Kinshasa, 3,000,000. Ethnic groups Kongo, Luba, Mongo, Mangbetu-Azande, others. Languages French, Kikongo, Lingala, Swahili, Tshiluba. Religions Roman Catholic 50%, Protestant

20%, Kimbanguist 10%, Muslim 10%. Life expectancy 56 female, 53 male. Literacy 46%.
POLITICS
Government Republic. Parties Popular Movement of the Revolution, others. Suffrage Universal, over 18. Memberships OAS, UN. Subdivisions 10 regions, 1 independent town.
ECONOMY
GDP $4,588,000,000 Per capita $150. Monetary unit Zaire. Trade partners Exports: Belgium, France, Switzerland. Imports: Belgium, U.S., France. Exports Copper, coffee, diamonds, cobalt, petroleum. Imports Manufactures, food, machinery, transportation equipment, fuel.
LAND
Description Central Africa. Area 905,446 mi² (2,345,095 km²). Highest point Margherita Pk., 16,763 ft (5,109 m). Lowest point Sea level.

People. The diverse population of Zaire is composed of over two hundred African ethnic groups, with Bantu peoples in the majority. Belgian settlers introduced French, but hundreds of indigenous languages are more widely spoken. Much of the population is Christian, another result of former European rule. Many non-Christians practice traditional or syncretic faiths such as Kimbanguism. The majority of Zairians are rural farmers.

Economy and the Land. Zaire is rich in mineral resources, particularly copper, cobalt, diamonds, and petroleum; mining has supplanted agriculture in economic importance and now dominates the economy. Agriculture continues to employ most Zairians, however, and subsistence farming is practiced in nearly every region. Industrial activity—especially petroleum refining and hydroelectric production—is growing. Zaire's terrain is composed of mountains and plateaus. The climate is equatorial, with hot and humid weather in the north and west, and cooler and drier conditions in the south and east.

History and Politics. The earliest inhabitants of modern Zaire were probably Pygmies who settled in the area thousands of years ago. By the A.D. 700s, sophisticated civilizations had developed in what is now southeastern Zaire. In the early 1500s, the Portuguese began the forced emigration of black Africans for slavery. Other Europeans came to the area as the slave trade grew, but the interior remained relatively unexplored until the 1870s. Belgian King Leopold II realized the potential value of the region, and in 1885 his claim was recognized. Belgium took control from Leopold in 1908, renaming the colony the Belgian Congo. Nationalist sentiment grew until rioting broke out in 1959. The country, which was then called the Congo, gained independence in 1960, and a weak government assumed control. Violent civil disorder, provincial secession, and a political assassination characterized the next five years. The country stabilized under the rule of President Mobutu Sese Seko, a former army general. However, widespread charges of corruption have strengthened the cause of rebels based in Angola and forced the government to allow other political parties. ∎

ZAMBIA

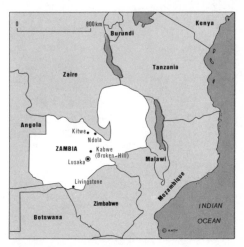

Official name Republic of the Zambia
PEOPLE
Population 8,226,000. Density 28/mi² (11/km²). Urban

56%. **Capital** Lusaka, 535,830. **Ethnic groups** African 99%, European 1%. **Languages** English, Tonga, Lozi, other indigenous. **Religions** Christian 70%, tribal religionist 29%, Muslim and Hindu 1%. **Life expectancy** 57 female, 54 male. **Literacy** 52%.

POLITICS
Government Republic. **Parties** United National Independence. **Suffrage** Universal, over 18. **Memberships** CW, OAU, UN. **Subdivisions** 9 provinces.

ECONOMY
GDP $2,597,000,000 **Per capita** $390. **Monetary unit** Kwacha. **Trade partners** Exports: Japan, Germany, U.K. Imports: South African countries, U.K., U.S.. **Exports** Copper, zinc, and other metals. **Imports** Machinery, textiles and other manufactures, petroleum, chemicals.

LAND
Description Southern Africa, landlocked. **Area** 290,586 mi^2 (752,614 km^2). **Highest point** 7,100 ft (2,164 m). **Lowest point** Along Zambezi River, 1,081 ft (329 m).

People. Virtually all Zambians are black Africans belonging to one of more than seventy Bantu-speaking ethnic groups. Besides the indigenous Bantu languages, many speak English, a reflection of decades of British influence. Although most Zambians are Christian, small minorities are Hindu, Muslim, or hold indigenous beliefs. Many Zambians are subsistence farmers in small villages; however, the mining industry has caused many people to move to urban areas, where wages are rising.

Economy and the Land. The economy is based on copper, Zambia's major export. In an attempt to diversify the economy, the government has emphasized the development of agriculture to help achieve an acceptable balance of trade. Zambia is a subtropical nation marked by high plateaus and great rivers.

History and Politics. European explorers in the nineteenth century discovered an established society of Bantu-speaking inhabitants. In 1888 Cecil Rhodes and the British South Africa Company obtained a mineral-rights concession from local chiefs; and Northern and Southern Rhodesia, now Zambia and Zimbabwe, came under British influence. Northern Rhodesia became a British protectorate in 1924. In 1953 Northern Rhodesia was combined with Southern Rhodesia and Nyasaland, now Malawi, to form a federation, despite African-nationalist opposition to the white-controlled minority government in Southern Rhodesia. The federation was dissolved in 1963, and Northern Rhodesia became the independent Republic of Zambia in 1964. ∎

ZIMBABWE

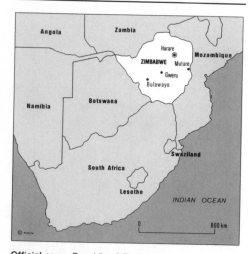

Official name Republic of Zimbabwe
PEOPLE
Population 9,491,000. **Density** 63/mi^2 (24/km^2). **Urban** 28%. **Capital** Harare, 681,000. **Ethnic groups** Shona 71%, Ndebele 16%, white 1%. **Languages** English, ChiShona, SiNdebele. **Religions** Animist, Roman Catholic, Apostolic and other Protestant. **Life expectancy** 63 female, 59 male. **Literacy** 62%.

POLITICS
Government Republic. **Parties** African National Union, Unity Movement. **Suffrage** Universal, over 18. **Memberships** CW, OAU, UN. **Subdivisions** 8 provinces.

ECONOMY
GDP $5,024,000,000 **Per capita** $613. **Monetary unit** Dollar. **Trade partners** Exports: South African countries, U.K., Germany. Imports: South African countries, U.K., U.S.. **Exports** Tobacco, manufactures, gold, iron, cotton. **Imports** Machinery and transportation equipment, manufactures, chemicals, fuel.

LAND
Description Southern Africa, landlocked. **Area** 150,873 mi^2 (390,759 km^2). **Highest point** Inyangani, 8,504 ft (2,592 m). **Lowest point** Confluence of Sabi and Lundi rivers, 530 ft (162 m).

People. The great majority of Zimbabweans are black Africans of Bantu descent, with a small but economically significant minority of white Europeans. Most Zimbabweans are subsistence farmers who live in small villages. The influence of British colonization is seen in the official language, English, and in the influence of Christianity.

Economy and the Land. Zimbabwe's natural mineral resources have played a key role in the country's sustained economic growth. The subtropical climate supports the exportation of many agricultural products and makes large-scale cattle ranching feasible. Though primarily a landlocked country of high plateaus, transportation of goods is facilitated by an excellent system of paved roads and railways.

History and Politics. Zimbabwe was populated by Bantu groups until European exploration in the nineteenth century. British influence began in 1888, when Cecil Rhodes and the British South Africa Company obtained mineral rights to the area from local chiefs. Eventually, the region was divided under British rule as Southern Rhodesia, or present-day Zimbabwe, and Northern Rhodesia, or modern Zambia. In 1953, Southern Rhodesia, Northern Rhodesia, and Nyasaland, now Malawi, formed a federation that ended in discord after ten years; Zambia and Malawi gained their independence, and Southern Rhodesia, which remained under British control, became Rhodesia. In response to British pressure to accept black-majority rule, Rhodesian whites declared independence from the United Kingdom in 1965, which led to economic sanctions imposed by the United Nations. These sanctions and years of antigovernment violence finally forced agreement to the principle of black-majority rule. In 1980 the Zimbabwe African National Union-Patriotic Front won a majority of seats in the House of Representatives, and Rhodesia became independent Zimbabwe. Despite Zimbabwe's move toward stability since independence, some internal unrest continues. ∎